To mark the fiftieth anniversary of the International Court of Justice, a distinguished group of international judges, practitioners and academics has undertaken a major review of its work. The chapters discuss the main areas of substantive law with which the Court has been concerned, and the more significant aspects of its practice and procedure in dealing with cases before it. They discuss the role of the Court in the international legal order and its relationship with the UN's political organs. The thirty-three chapters are presented under five headings: the Court; the sources and evidences of international law; substance of international law; procedural aspects of the Court's work; the Court and the UN. It has been prepared in honour of Sir Robert Jennings, judge and sometime President of the Court.

Fifty years of the
International
Court of Justice

ᆇ

Sir Robert Yewdall Jennings

Fifty years of the International Court of Justice

ભ

Essays in honour of
SIR ROBERT JENNINGS

Edited by
VAUGHAN LOWE
University of Cambridge

and

MALGOSIA FITZMAURICE
Queen Mary and Westfield College
University of London

GROTIUS PUBLICATIONS

CAMBRIDGE
UNIVERSITY PRESS

1996

Published by the Press Syndicate of the University of Cambridge
The Pitt Building, Trumpington Street, Cambridge CB2 1RP
40 West 20th Street, New York, NY 10011–4211, USA
10 Stamford Road, Oakleigh, Melbourne 3166, Australia

First published 1996

Printed in Great Britain at the University Press, Cambridge

A catalogue record for this book is available from the British Library

Library of Congress cataloguing in publication data
Fifty years of the International Court of Justice:
essays in honour of Sir Robert Jennings /
edited by Vaughan Lowe and Malgosia Fitzmaurice.
p.   cm.
Includes index.
ISBN 0 521 55093 9 (hardback)
1. International Court of Justice. I. Jennings, R. Y. (Robert
Yewdall), 1913– . II. Lowe, Vaughan, 1952– . III. Fitzmaurice, M.
JX1971.6.F54 1996
341.5'52 – dc20   95–6516   CIP

ISBN 0 521 55093 9 hardback

1000714763

CONTENTS

৩

Contents

PART III
Substance of international law

PART IV
Procedural aspects of the work of the International Court of Justice

Contents

PART V
The International Court of Justice and
the United Nations

CONTRIBUTORS

❧

Vaughan Lowe fellow of Corpus Christi College, Cambridge

Georges Abi-Saab professor, Institut universitaire des hautes études internationales, Geneva

Philip Allott fellow of Trinity College, Cambridge

Geoffrey Marston fellow of Sidney Sussex College, Cambridge

Maurice Mendelson QC; professor of international law in the University of London, at University College, London

M. Shahabuddeen judge at the International Court of Justice

Sir Ian Sinclair KCMG, QC; barrister at law; member of the Institute of International Law; bencher of the Middle Temple; formerly legal adviser, Foreign and Commonwealth Office

Prosper Weil professeur émérite, Université de droit, d'économie et de sciences sociales de Paris

E. W. Vierdag professor of international law, University of Amsterdam

Francesco Francioni professor of international law, University of Siena

D. W. Bowett CBE, QC, FBA; emeritus Whewell professor of international law in the University of Cambridge; member of the International Law Commission

C. F. Amerasinghe LL D (Cantab); director, Secretariat, World Bank Tribunal; honorary professor of law, University of Colombo, Sri Lanka

Hazel Fox QC; formerly director of the British Institute of International and Comparative Law, London

Harry Post University of Utrecht, Netherlands

Barbara Kwiatkowska professor of international law of the sea and associate director of the Netherlands Institute for the Law of the Sea (NILOS), faculty of law, University of Utrecht, Netherlands

Malgosia Fitzmaurice   senior lecturer, Queen Mary and Westfield College, University of London

Sami Shubber   Lic-en-Dr (Baghdad), postgraduate dip. in law, LLM (London), Ph.D. (Cantab); barrister of Gray's Inn; senior legal officer, WHO, Geneva

Stephen M. Schwebel   judge and vice-president of the International Court of Justice

Antonio Cassese   formerly professor at the European University Institute, Florence; currently president of the International Criminal Tribunal for the Former Yugoslavia, The Hague

John Collier   fellow of Trinity Hall, Cambridge

Christopher Greenwood   fellow of Magdalene College, Cambridge

H. W. A. Thirlway   professor, Institut universitaire des hautes études internationales, Geneva; formerly assistant registrar, International Court of Justice

Shabtai Rosenne   member of the Institute of International Law; honorary member of the American Society of International Law; president, Israel branch of the International Law Association; Arthur Goodhart professor in legal science, University of Cambridge, 1985–6

Sir Arthur Watts   KCMG, QC; barrister at law; formerly legal adviser, Foreign and Commonwealth Office

Gaetano Arangio-Ruiz   professor of international law, University of Rome

E. Lauterpacht   honorary professor of international law and director of the Research Centre for International Law, University of Cambridge

+The late J. M. Ruda   formerly judge and sometime president at the International Court of Justice

Eduardo Valencia-Ospina   registrar of the International Court of Justice

Gillian White   emeritus professor of international law, University of Manchester

Shigeru Oda   judge at the International Court of Justice

Ian Brownlie   QC, DCL, FBA; bencher of Gray's Inn; Chichele professor of public international law, University of Oxford; fellow of All Souls College, Oxford; member of the Institute of International Law

Dame Rosalyn Higgins   QC; judge at the International Court of Justice

James Crawford   Whewell professor of international law, University of Cambridge; member of the International Law Commission

Krzysztof Skubiszewski   president of the Iran–United States Claims Tribunal; formerly minister of foreign affairs, Poland

PREFACE

෯

This volume was prepared for two reasons. First, the essays are offered as tokens of affection and esteem for Sir Robert Jennings by some of his many friends and colleagues; and his recent eightieth birthday and Presidency of the Court provided an appropriate opportunity. We are only sorry that it was not possible to publish a larger volume, to accommodate the many others who would have wished to contribute to this work. Second, the International Court of Justice is approaching its first half-century, and the time seemed ripe for reflection upon its work. The contributors co-operated in preparing what is less of a traditional Festschrift than a set of chapters which together cover the main areas of the Court's work. We are grateful to them for their efforts, and for the willingness with which they accepted the constraints that the co-ordination of the subject matter of their essays necessitated.

ABBREVIATIONS

AJIL	*American Journal of International Law*
ASIL	American Society of International Law
BYbIL	*British Yearbook of International Law*
CLJ	*Cambridge Law Journal*
CMEA	Council for Mutual Economic Assistance
CSC	Continental Shelf Convention
CSCE	Conference on Security and Co-operation in Europe
EC	European Community
ECJ	European Court of Justice
ECOSOC	Economic and Social Council
EEZ	exclusive economic zone
EU	European Union
IAT	International Administrative Tribunal
ICAO	International Civil Aviation Organization
ICC	International Chamber of Commerce
ICCPR	International Covenant on Civil and Political Rights
ICJ	International Court of Justice
ICLQ	*International and Comparative Law Quarterly*
ICSID	International Convention for the Settlement of Investment Disputes
IKBDC	Iraq–Kuwait Boundary Demarcation Commission
ILA	International Law Association
ILC	International Law Commission
ILM	*International Legal Materials*
ILO	International Labour Organization
ILOAT	ILO Administrative Tribunal
ILR	*International Law Reports*
IMCO	International Maritime Consultative Organization
JIL	*Journal of International Law*

LNT	League of Nations Tribunal
LOSC	Law of the Sea Convention
LSE	London School of Economics
NYbIL	*Netherlands Yearbook of International Law*
OAS	Organization of American States
OASAT	OAU Administrative Tribunal
OAU	Organization of African Unity
OJ	*Official Journal of the European Communities*
PCIJ	Permanent Court of International Justice
PRO	Public Record Office (London)
RECIEL	*Review of European Community and International Environmental Law*
Recueil des cours	*Recueil des cours de l'Academie de Droit International*
RGDIP	*Revue général de droit international public*
RIAA	*UN Reports of International Arbitral Awards*
Syr J Int'l L & Comm	*Syracuse Journal of International Law and Commerce*
UNAT	UN Administrative Tribunal
UNCED	UN Conference on Environment and Development
UNCIO	UN Conference on International Organization
UNCITRAL	UN Commission on International Trade Law
UNCLOS	UN Conference on the Law of the Sea
UNTS	UN Treaty Series
VJIL	*Virginia Journal of International Law*
WBAT	World Bank Administrative Tribunal
WHO	World Health Organization
YbIL	*Yearbook of International Law*
YbILC	*Yearbook of the International Law Commission*
ZAOR	*Zeitschrift für ausländisches öffentliches Recht und Völkerrecht*

Sir Robert Yewdall Jennings

Vaughan Lowe

෴

> A lawyer without history or literature is a mechanic, a mere working
> mason; if he possesses some knowledge of these he may venture to call
> himself an architect.

The quotation is from Sir Walter Scott, and is one that Sir Robert Jennings
heard quoted by Arnold McNair, by whom he was taught international law,
and has himself adopted in his writings. Couple with that the observation that
Sir Robert grew up as a Yorkshireman and a non-conformist, that he is quiet,
modest, and likes Mozart, cricket and cats, and for those with a keen eye for
the nuances of the characteristics of the British a fair picture of him begins to
emerge.

The journey that has taken him to the Whewell Chair at Cambridge and to
the presidency of the International Court of Justice is, as one of his favourite
poets put it, a 'migration strange for a stripling of the hills, a northern villager'.[1]
Born in 1913, he has strong Yorkshire roots. His father was the manager of a
small firm, employing half-a-dozen people, which manufactured paper tubes;
and his paternal grandfather was a warehouseman in a mill. His mother was a
weaver at the mill, and her family were butchers. And when his maternal
grandfather, a butcher who was unable to read, went up into the dales to
clinch his business deals, the young Robbie Jennings often went with him in
his pony and trap. Although Robbie was an only child, families in those days
were tightly knit, and he was surrounded by aunts and uncles. The Jennings
family were committed Wesleyan Methodists. His father was a steward, a
position which carried heavy responsibilities for the administration of a
number of chapels in the locality, which Methodism groups together in
'circuits'. His uncles were local preachers who travelled around chapels in

---

[1] Wordsworth, *The Prelude*, Book Third, 34–5.

the circuit conducting services, as did Robbie himself while a student at Cambridge.

Robbie attended the local village school, and won a scholarship to Bradford Grammar School for his secondary education. But he chose not to go. His friends were going to Belle Vue Grammar School, Bradford, and Robbie decided to go there instead. General academic standards at the school were quite reasonable; but one or two of the teachers made a particular impression on him, such as the one he remembers abandoning a geography lesson to tell the boys about the British legal system. None of the school's pupils had ever attempted the admission examinations for Oxford or Cambridge. This did not deter Robbie. Armed with his passionate interests in history and cricket he sat the entrance examination, and was offered a place at Trinity College Oxford. He chose instead, however, to go to Downing College Cambridge, a place offered to him because of the ability he showed as a historian. During his first year money was very tight indeed. He scraped along on his father's savings, but knew that he needed to win an award to enable him to continue. He succeeded. He gained an upper first, as the classification went in those days, and was given a Squire law scholarship and some assistance from his local authority in Yorkshire. Encouraged by both Maitland and McNair, he gained starred first-class honours in both parts of the law tripos, the postgraduate LLB degree, and the Whewell and Cassell scholarships. Downing, too, had given him a scholarship, but it was kept as an 'honorary' scholarship, carrying no money because the college was a poor one, and Robbie was too proud to confess how little money there was from home.

After his years at Cambridge Robbie went abroad for the first time. He set sail on the *Queen Mary* for Harvard, where he was Joseph Hodges Choate fellow in 1936–7. The dean at Harvard echoed the advice McNair had given him at Cambridge, to read widely rather than to narrow his focus. McNair (with admirable good sense) had specifically advised him against staying on to write a Ph.D., and in 1938 Robbie took up his first teaching post, as an assistant lecturer in law at the London School of Economics. There he stayed until he was elected to a fellowship at Jesus College Cambridge in 1939.

During the war Robbie worked in army intelligence. He served in Aldershot and Droitwich and spent some time back in Cambridge on a course for intelligence officers at Trinity College before going to Oxford, where for eighteen months he lived in Jesus College and worked in the Geography Schools on the interpretation of aerial photographs. It was there that he developed a considerable skill, useful in later years, in the reading of maps and naval charts. Major Jennings, as he became, completed his military service on postings to Delhi and to Ceylon.

After the war Robbie resumed his legal career. He had been called to the Bar by Lincoln's Inn in 1943. He served his pupillage in the chambers of a Chancery lawyer at 13 New Court, Lincoln's Inn, in a London still recovering from the Blitz. The building lacked doors and fires, and the barristers often sat in topcoats to keep warm as they worked. Throughout this time he had been lecturing at the LSE on weekday evenings and supervising law students at Jesus College and Downing College Cambridge at weekends. He returned to Jesus College Cambridge full-time as a fellow, teaching a range of law subjects to that unusual and demanding generation of students returned from military service. He made a great contribution to the life of the college, in which he lived as a bachelor, organizing its 'twinning' arrangement with Jesus College Oxford in 1946, and the college high table cricket team in 1948. In 1949 he became a senior tutor – a post that bears much the same relationship to the master of a college as does the prime minister to the monarch – at Jesus, and in that position took overall responsibility for the organization of the academic life of the college until 1955. Robbie was seen to be an accomplished committee man, and was drafted in to serve on many of the key university bodies, including the council of the senate. In 1955 two great events occurred in his life, both of which paved the way for his subsequent career: his marriage to Christine Bennett and his election as Whewell professor of international law at Cambridge, which obliged him to step down as senior tutor.

From 1955 to 1981, Professor Jennings devoted himself to his teaching, both in Cambridge and, from 1959 to 1970, at the Council of Legal Education in London, where he was reader in international law. Despite invitations to take on senior full-time administrative positions in Cambridge and elsewhere, he stayed true to his calling and remained in the Whewell Chair for twenty-six years. He was elected to the Institute of International Law in 1967, and served as its president from 1981 to 1983. Although he had become a Queen's Counsel in 1969, and an honorary bencher of Lincoln's Inn in 1970 (both of which are rare honours for academic lawyers), he did not practice extensively as an international lawyer until relatively late in his academic career: the first case he pleaded before an international tribunal was the *Rio Encuentro* case, followed by the *Beagle Channel* arbitration, which took him on exciting journeys to Tierra del Fuego. During the latter part of his time as Whewell Professor, however, his practice expanded markedly: besides *Rio Encuentro* and *Beagle Channel*, he acted as counsel in the *Franco-British Continental Shelf Delimitation*, and *Dubai–Sharjah Frontier Delimitation* arbitrations, and appeared before the International Court as Counsel in the *Tunisia/Libya Continental Shelf* case. He also acted as a legal consultant to many governments, including those of Argentina, Bangladesh, Brunei, Canada, Jersey, Sharjah,

Sudan and Venezuela, and to the Iranian National Oil Company, as well as to private corporations.

As the university statutes required, he retired from the Whewell Chair in 1981, when he reached the age of sixty-eight. He then began a second career. He took up office as a judge at the International Court and received his knighthood in 1982, and became a member of the Permanent Court of Arbitration and a judge *ad hoc* in the European Court of Human Rights in the same year. He went on to serve as President of the International Court of Justice from 1991 to 1994, a period that saw an unprecedented and unexpected rise in use of the Court by the international community. In that great office, he has done much to champion the Court and to extend and deepen the knowledge of its function and potential. Perhaps his most notable efforts in his judicial capacity have been made in the direction of the United Nations. Sir Robert was the first President of the Court to address the General Assembly; and he held a highly successful series of informal question-and-answer sessions with United Nations legal officers. The work of the Court is reviewed in many of the chapters in this volume. The astonishing rise in the workload of the Court during this period makes the prodigious scholarship that he and his co-editor, Sir Arthur Watts, brought to their magisterial ninth edition of *Oppenheim's International Law*, published in 1992, all the more remarkable.

So much for the historical background. But what of Sir Robert Jennings the lawyer? When a man is elected to what might fairly be described as the highest judicial office on the planet, attention must be focused on the way in which he approaches his task. The chapters in this book examine the work of the International Court of Justice in particular fields of international law, and offer insights into the work of the Court during Sir Robert's membership and presidency of it. Here I want to offer some brief remarks on his general approach to the law in abstract.

It is not surprising that Sir Robert's personal qualities permeate both his judicial and his extra-judicial writings and speeches. Foremost among them is his quiet modesty. He has, he says, been surprised by each of the major steps in his advancement – the elections to the Whewell Chair and to the International Court. This modesty extends into a notably temperate view of the significance of international law in international relations. For example, in the course of his Melland Schill lectures on the rules and principles governing the acquisition of territorial sovereignty, he spoke of the great redistributions of territory that had resulted from the resolutions of peace conferences in which the victor's will held sway. In a passage exemplifying his approach to the role of international law he said:

To interpret these important changes in the balance of power simply in terms of the legal techniques of cession or subjugation is to take a view of the situation that is so narrow and partial as almost to border on the irrelevant; yet this does no more than reflect accurately the minute part that law has been allowed to play in these great historical movements crystallized in the shifts of territorial sovereignty.[2]

It should not be thought that this view is indicative of any lack of faith in international law. As is to be expected of the work of a man who subjects his writing to endless revisions and polishing, the precise formulation is significant. He refers not to the part that the law could or should play, but to the part it has been allowed to play. He does not doubt the transcendent importance of international law, and is firmly committed to what he has called the 'subjection of the totality of international relations . . . to a universal international law',[3] and to a conception of a universal international law which can embrace a world of diversity and of regional legal orders. If a note of idealism is detected in that phrase it would not be altogether a mistake, although it is an idealism that Sir Robert has fused with pragmatism into an alloy of uncommon strength and resilience. The grand view of the potential of international law is, however, unmistakably there.

In his writing there is something close to a sense of amazement at the way in which international law has, during the sixty years of his career in the law, embraced both technological and political changes of a scale that would have been beyond the comprehension of those who crafted the doctrine of international law during the preceding three-and-a-half centuries. Perhaps attracted by the deep mystery of the immaterial regulating the intangible, he sometimes uses the example of the international regulation of radio frequencies as an example of the accommodation of technological change. On the political front he refers to the massive, and as yet unfinished, expansion in the number of independent sovereign states, and the diversity in political and cultural values in international relations that has followed in its wake; and he sees clearly the deeper political implications of legal developments such as the prohibition of the use of force in a system that lacks courts to which states are obliged to have recourse for the definition and enforcement of rights.[4] But significant as the achievements of international law have been, it still has great unfulfilled potential. Sir Robert has remarked in more general terms that 'Where international law, even modern international law, is relatively

---

[2] R. Y. Jennings, *The Acquisition of Territory in International Law* (Manchester, 1963), p. 69.

[3] 'Universal International Law in a Multicultural World', in Martin Bos and Ian Brownlie (eds.), *Liber Amicorum for Lord Wilberforce* (Oxford, 1987), p. 39, at p. 48.

[4] *The Acquisition of Territory in International Law*, esp. p. 69.

undeveloped is in international institutions that are something more than mere instrumentalities whereby sovereign States can associate and work with each other'.⁵ That view, expressed in 1987, reflects the continuation of his belief in the value of the contribution international organizations can make to international relations – a belief which was evident in the active support he gave to local branches of the United Nations Association during his years in Cambridge.

The other element of the alloy is Sir Robert's pragmatism. He has little time for the 'peculiar vice of much of the academic exposition of the subject: the predominance of encapsulated speculative doctrine'.⁶ It is, he has written, 'better to begin the inquiry not from a label but from the actual practice and expectations of States today'.⁷ In particular, following the lead given to him in his early years by McNair, he lays great emphasis on the need to distinguish clearly between *lex lata* and proposals *de lege ferenda*. Before his election to the International Court he wrote: 'It is, I believe, the present laxity and excessive flexibility in the limits of what may plausibly be alleged to be international law, or not to be international law, that is one of the principal reasons for the continued shyness of international litigation among governments.'⁸ Though the confidentiality that screens the drafting of the Court's judgments precludes certainty, one suspects that his adherence to this principle and his determination to preserve the rigour and integrity of international law has been a factor in the startling increase in the popularity of the International Court among governments in recent years.

Even within the limits of *lex lata*, the need for pragmatism shapes his approach to the law. His Separate and Dissenting Opinions in the successive phases of the *Nicaragua* case illustrate the point well, and also illustrate something of his technique as a lawyer.

The attention to detail is immediately apparent. In the *Nicaragua (Jurisdiction)* decision, for instance, Sir Robert engages in a close analysis of the text of article 36 of the Court's Statute, comparing the English and French texts and tracing the emergence of the text through the *travaux préparatoires*.⁹ While he can readily identify in the materials put before the Court the textual subtleties that signal 'a caution to the careful reader',¹⁰ his approach is very far from that

---

⁵ 'Universal International Law in a Multicultural World', at p. 49.
⁶ 'Teachings and Teaching in International Law', in Jerzy Makarczyk (ed.), *Essays in International Law in Honour of Judge Manfred Lachs* (The Hague, 1984), p. 121, at p. 122.
⁷ *Nicaragua (Jurisdiction)*, ICJ Reports, 1984, p. 392, at p. 547.
⁸ *International Law Association, 57th Report* (1976), p. 631.
⁹ ICJ Reports, 1984, p. 392, at pp. 533–9. Cf. *Nicaragua (Merits)*, ICJ Reports, 1986, p. 3, at p. 542.
¹⁰ ICJ Reports, 1984, p. 392, at p. 543.

of the virtuoso detective whose powers of induction from scanty evidence are designed to impress and entertain the reader. Indeed, he frequently measures the progress of his reasoning against the intuitive judgement and common sense of the skilled lawyer: the decision that a particular conclusion is 'startling' often seems to come close to establishing a presumption that it is wrong;[11] and what startles him is that which is contrary to principle.[12] But he is not cavalier in dismissing conclusions that offend against common sense. His views are closely reasoned and carefully justified: he will comb systematically through the available materials and pay particular attention to the propriety of inferring rules of law from raw practice.[13] An attractive compromise will be considered, but rejected if 'the practice of States – certainly the recent practice of States – has already gone beyond it'.[14]

Yet in the end the hand of pragmatism exerts a powerful guiding influence over his judgments. Unlike some of his colleagues on the International Court, Sir Robert never held judicial office in his own country. Nonetheless cases are, for him, not exercises in legal sophistry, but problems to be solved. Underlying his careful scrutiny of state practice is the belief that 'law develops by precedent, and it is that which gives it consistency and predictability'.[15] State practice and expectations are apt to be linked in a single phrase;[16] and the stability of the law and its success as a regulator of international relations rests heavily upon its fulfilment of the legitimate expectations of states. But, as Sir Robert has observed, 'legal precedents like any other must be seen in the light of history and of changing times'.[17] Where precedents support a range of possible solutions, those that are impracticable or inequitable will be rejected.[18] One of the clearest examples of this approach appears in his Dissenting Opinion in the *Nicaragua* case, where Sir Robert did not yield to the temptation, which some have detected at work in the majority opinion in that case, to adopt a political compromise, even though his position as President of the Court put him in a difficult position. He wrote what he believed to be

---

[11] See, e.g., his Separate Opinion in *Nicaragua (Jurisdiction)*, *Ibid.*, p. 392, at p. 544.

[12] *Ibid.*

[13] See, e.g., *Nicaragua (Merits)*, ICJ Reports, 1983, p. 3, at p. 531.

[14] *Nicaragua (Jurisdiction)*, ICJ Reports, 1984, p. 392, at p. 550.

[15] *Ibid.*, p. 392, at p. 547.

[16] *Ibid.*, at p. 553.

[17] *Ibid.*, at p. 547. He is fond of quoting Maitland's statement: 'Nowadays we may see the office of historical research as that of explaining, and therefore lightening, the pressure that the past must exercise upon the present, and the present upon the future. Today we study the day before yesterday, in order that yesterday may not paralyse today, and today may not paralyse tomorrow' (F. W. Maitland, *Collected Papers* (Cambridge, 1911), vol. III, p. 438).

[18] *Nicaragua (Jurisdiction)*, ICJ Reports, 1984, p. 392, at p. 548.

true. He did not accept the Court's view on the nature of the Optional Clause declaration registered in the name of Nicaragua. Nor did he accept that the provision of arms, coupled with logistical or other support, to rebels in a neighbouring state cannot amount to an armed attack. As he observed:

> This looks to me neither realistic nor just in a world where power struggles are in every continent carried on by destabilization, interference in civil strife, comfort, aid and encouragement to rebels, and the like. The original scheme of the United Nations Charter, whereby force would be deployed by the United Nations itself, in accordance with the provisions of Chapter VII of the Charter, has never come into effect. Therefore an essential element in the Charter design is totally missing. In this situation it seems dangerous to define unnecessarily strictly the conditions for lawful self-defence, so as to leave a large area where both a forcible response to force is forbidden, and yet the United Nations employment of force, which was intended to fill that gap, is absent.[19]

That is the Jennings recalled by his friends in Cambridge – a man more concerned to get the job done than to stick rigidly to arcane points of doctrine; a judge more concerned that his judgments should leave the world a better place than that they should contribute to the completion of the symmetry of an abstract juristic scheme.

This brief note on his style would be incomplete without reference to one other characteristic – the deep humanity of his approach, whether it be concerned with the rights of an individual[20] or the rights of an entire people. That is nowhere more clearly evident than in his text on *The Acquisition of Territory in International Law*. He adopts a frankly sceptical, conservative approach to the legal status of the principle of self-determination, distinguishing more clearly than is common among his contemporaries between rules of law and good intentions.[21] But his approach by no means undervalues the interests of the inhabitants of territory. It is, indeed, based firmly on the view that it is the well-being of the inhabitants that is the ultimate objective of the law. Changes in territorial sovereignty are recognized to involve 'a decisive change in the nationality, allegiance and way of life of a population'.[22] The task of the lawyer is 'to fashion a law which will operate in a society where as yet there is no system of compulsory jurisdiction',[23] and it is necessary to guard against the danger of a tribunal, emboldened by the array of legal principles at

---

[19] *Nicaragua (Merits)*, ICJ Reports, 1986, p. 3, at pp. 543–4.

[20] See his Dissenting Opinion in the *Yakimetz* case, ICJ Reports, 1987, p. 18, at pp. 134–58.

[21] *The Acquisition of Territory in International Law*, pp. 78–83. Cf. 'Teaching and Teachings in International Law', p. 121 at p. 128.

[22] *The Acquisition of Territory in International Law*, p. 3.

[23] *Ibid.*, pp. 64–5.

its disposal, from overreaching itself: 'It is not difficult to imagine situations in which the position of an international court, faced with the task of deciding, perhaps over a period of a year or more, on the basis of legal title, the destiny of a vigorous people with a will of its own, might become untenable.'[24] And the bringing of the law into contempt is, in his eyes, one of the cardinal sins.[25]

There is another aspect to this human concern, wrapped up together with his modesty and his profound belief in the value of international law. That is the simplicity and directness of his written and oral style. He once told a colleague in Cambridge that he lectured in such a way that the man on the back row of the lecture theatre who was going to get a lower-second-class degree could understand him – an approach usually, but not invariably, appreciated by his listeners. More concerned to teach than to demonstrate his own cleverness, he lectured in a very personal and friendly style which one of his former students remembers as being more like the confiding of the principles of international law to his students than the ornate delivery adopted by many lecturers. That style persists in both his judicial opinions and his academic writings, and underlines his commitment to the advancement of international law and its communication to the widest possible audience. If the law is once understood, the good sense of compliance with it becomes self-evident.

Modesty, idealism, pragmatism, an impatience with woolly and unproductive thinking, and a practical commitment to the law as an instrument for improving the lives of people: those are the characteristics that strike me as marking the main lines of his character. Others would no doubt choose other characteristics, or put the matter rather differently. His easygoing manner masks an uncompromising commitment to the maintenance of standards, both of intellectual endeavour and of behaviour. And there is an underlying bite in his intellect which can lead to incisive, and occasionally sharp, criticisms of positions and individuals who do not meet his exacting standards. For all that, he has no side. He has a warmth of personality that allows even relatively casual acquaintances to feel comfortable calling him 'Robbie'. The friendships he has developed with colleagues and former pupils throughout the world are quite exceptionally close and warm. But there remains a complex inner preserve within the quietness of the man which it is not easy to know. That private Robbie is the one most at home engrossed in scything the grass or building dry-stone walls around his isolated cottage in the Lake District, and walking with Christine on the fells; who is happiest with his children and grandchildren, his cats and his hi-fi around him; and in whose study at home

---

[24] *Ibid.*, p. 65.   [25] Cf. *ibid.*, p. 54.

Wisden, and Mozart, Bach and Haydn, are more prominent than judicial decisions and the teachings of the most highly qualified publicists of the various nations. That is the Robbie who confessed that he coped with the hectic programme laid on for him and Christine during one official visit abroad, in which they were driven from one reception to another in a limousine, by imagining himself to be a little brown paper parcel being bundled from one group to another. That is the man who, as Wordsworth put it, sees 'with an eye made quiet by the power of harmony, and the deep power of Joy . . . into the life of things'.[26] And the strength and virtue of Sir Robert Jennings the judge is that he is inseparable from Robbie the man.

[26] 'Lines Composed a Few Miles Above Tintern Abbey', vv. 46–8.

LIST OF PUBLICATIONS OF
SIR ROBERT JENNINGS

 су

'The Caroline and McLeod Cases', *AJIL*, 32 (1938), 82–99

'Judicial Legislation in International Law', *Kentucky Law Journal*, 26 (1938), pp. 122–27

'Some International Law Aspects of the Refugee Question', *BYbIL*, 20 (1939), pp. 98–114

'International Civil Aviation and the Law, *BYbIL*, 23 (1945), pp. 191–209

'Open Towns', note in *BYbIL*, 23 (1945), pp. 258–64

'Government in Commission', *BYbIL*, 23 (1946), pp. 358–63

'The Progressive Development of International Law and its Codification', *BYbIL*, 24 (1947), pp. 301–29

'Some Aspects of the International Law of the Air', *Recueil des Cours*, 75, 2 (1949), pp. 5–82

'The Commonwealth and International Law', *BYbIL*, 30 (1953), pp. 320–51

'The International Court's Advisory Opinion on Voting Procedure', *Transactions of the Grotius Society*, 41 (1956)

'Extraterritorial Jurisdiction and the United States Antitrust Laws', *BYbIL*, 31 (1957), pp. 146–75

Chapters on international law in *The Annual Register*, 1957–1965 (inclusive)

'The Progress of International Law', *BYbIL*, 34 (1958), pp. 334–55 (inaugural lecture delivered in Cambridge, 20 January 1958)

'Recent Cases on "Automatic" Reservations to the Optional Clause', *ICLQ*, 7 (1958), pp. 349–66

'International Laws and Colonial Questions' (with H. Lauterpacht), in *Cambridge History of the British Empire* (Cambridge, 1959), vol. III, pp. 667–710

'State Contracts in International Law', *BYbIL*, 37 (1961), pp. 156–82

'The Limits of State Jurisdiction', *Nordisk Tidsskrift*, 32 (1962), pp. 209–29

'Note on the ICJ Advisory Opinion of 20 July 1962, on Certain Expenses of the United Nations', *ICLQ*, 11 (1962), pp. 1169–83

The Acquisition of Territory in International Law (Manchester, 1963)

'International Law', in *Encyclopaedia Britannica* (1963)

'Recent Developments in the International Law Commission: its Relation to Sources of International Law', *ICLQ*, 13 (1964), pp. 385–97

'Nullity and Effectiveness in International Law', in R. Y. Jennings (ed.), *Cambridge Essays in International Law: Essays in Honour of Lord McNair* (London, 1965), pp. 64–87

'Rules Governing Contracts between States and Foreign Nations', in International and Comparative Law Center (Southwestern Legal Foundation, Dallas), *Rights and Duties of Private Investors Abroad* (Albany, NY/San Francisco/New York, 1965), pp. 123–44

'General Course on Principles of International Law', *Recueil des Cours*, 2 (1967), pp. 324–605

'The Commonwealth and State Succession', in Robert R. Wilson (ed.), *International and Comparative Law of the Commonwealth* (Durham, NC, 1968), pp. 27–39

'The Limits of Continental Shelf Jurisdiction: Some Possible Implications of the North Sea Judgment', *ICLQ*, 18 (1969), pp. 819–32

'The United States Draft Policy on the International Seabed Area: Basic Principles', *ICLQ*, 20 (1971), pp. 433–52

'A Changing International Law of the Sea', *CLJ*, 31 (1972), pp. 32–49

'The Proper Reach of Territorial Jurisdiction: A Case Study of Divergent Attitudes', *Georgia Journal of International Law*, 2, 2 (1972), pp. 35–42

'Report on the International Court of Justice', in Max Planck Symposium on Judicial Settlement of Disputes (1974), pp. 35–48

'Arnold McNair', *CLJ*, 23 (1975), pp. 177–81

'Glanville', in P. R. Glazebrook (ed.), *Reshaping the Criminal Law: Essays in Honour of Glanville Williams* (London, 1978), pp. 1–4 (tribute to Professor Glanville Williams)

'Treaties as "Legislation"', in *Jus et Societas: Essays in Tribute to Wolfgang Friedman* (Dordrecht, 1979), pp. 159–68

'Law-Making and Package Deal', in *Mélanges offerts à Paul Reuter. Le droit international: unité et diversité* (Paris, 1981), pp. 347–55

'What is International Law and How do We Tell It When We See It?', *Swiss YbIL*, 37 (1981), pp. 59–88

'The Identification of International Law', in B. Cheng (ed.), *International Law: Teaching and Practice* (London, 1982), pp. 3–9

'Gerald Gray Fitzmaurice', *BYbIL*, 55 (1984), pp. 1–64

'International Law', in R. Bernhardt (ed.), *Encyclopedia of International Law* (Amsterdam, 1984), vol. VII, pp. 278–97

'A New Look at the Place of Adjudication in International Relations Today', in Karl-Heinz Böckstiegel (ed), *Heidelberg Colloquium for Gunther Jaenicke's 70th Birthday* (Cologne/Berlin/Bonn/Munich, 1984), pp. 67–82

'Teaching and Teachings in International Law', in Jerzy Makarczyk (ed.), *Essays in International Law in Honour of Judge Manfred Lachs* (The Hague, 1984), pp. 121–31

'Equity and Equitable Principles', *Swiss YbIL*, 42 (1986), pp. 27–38

'International Court and International Politics', Josephine Onoh Lecture, University of Hull (1986), 16 pp.

'International Force and the International Court of Justice', in A. Cassese (ed.), *The Current Regulation of the Use of Force* (Dordrecht, 1986), pp. 323–35

'The Judicial Enforcement of International Obligations', *ZAOR*, 47 (1987), pp. 3–16

'The Judicial Function and the Rule of Law in International Relations', in P. L. Zanardi et al. (eds.), *Le droit international a l'heure de sa codification. Etudes en l'honneur de Roberto Ago* (Milan, 1987), vol. III, pp. 139–51

'The Place of Jurisdictional Immunity of States in International and Municipal Law' (1987), pp. 3–22 (talk to the European Institute, University of Saarland)

'Universal International Law in a Multicultural World', in Martin Bos and Ian Brownlie (eds.), *Liber Amicorum for the Rt Hon. Lord Wilberforce* (Oxford, 1987)

'Human Rights and Domestic Law Courts', in Franz Matscher and Herbert Petzold (eds.), *Protecting Human Rights: The European Dimension. Studies in Honour of Gerard J. Wiarda* (Cologne, 1988), pp. 295–300

'The Internal Judicial Practice of the International Court of Justice', *BYbIL*, 59 (1988), pp. 31–47

'The Collegiate Responsibility and the Authority of the International Court of Justice', in Y. Dinstein and M. Tabory (eds.), *International Law at a Time of Perplexity: Essays in Honour of Shabtai Rosenne* (Dordrecht, 1989), pp. 344–53

'Customary Law and General Principles of Law as Sources of Space Law', in Karl-Heinz Böckstiegel (ed.), *Environmental Aspects of Activities in Outer Space* (Cologne, 1990), pp. 149–52

'An International Lawyer Takes Stock, *ICLQ*, 39 (1990), pp. 513–29 (F. A. Mann Lecture, 6 December 1989)

'Public International Law Today', in University of Saarland, *Entwicklungslinien in Recht und Wirtschaft* (1990), pp. 111–20

'Chambers of the International Court of Justice and Courts of Arbitration', in *Humanité et droit internationale: Mélanges René-Jean Dupuy* (Paris, 1991), pp. 197–201

'Judicial Reasoning at an International Court', in Georg Rees (ed.), *Vorträge Reden und Berichte aus dem Europa-Institut*, 236 (University of Saarland, 1991), 8 pp.

'Les traités', in M. Bedjaoui (ed.), *Droit international: Bilan et perspectives* (UNESCO, Paris, 1991), vol. I, pp. 143–86; published as 'Treaties', in M. Bedjaoui (ed.), *International Law: Achievements and Prospects* (Dordrecht, 1991), pp. 135–77

'The World Court is Necessarily a Regional Court', *Hague Academy Workshop 1990* (1991), pp. 305–16

'An Expanding Court', in Royal Institute of International Affairs, *The World Today*, 48 (1992), pp. 44–7

Oppenheim's International Law (ed. with Sir Arthur Watts) (Harlow, 1992), vol. I, *Peace*

'The Role of the International Court of Justice in the Development of Environment Protection Law', *Review of European Community and International Environmental Law*, 1 (1992), pp. 240–4 (statement made at the Rio Conference, 1992)

'Reflections on the Term "Dispute"', in Ronald St John Macdonald (ed.), *Essays in Honour of Professor Wang Tieya* (Dordrecht/Boston, 1994), pp. 401–5

'New Problems at the International Court of Justice', in Manuel Rama-Montaldo (ed.), *International Law in an Evolving World: Essays in Honour of Professor Jiménez de Aréchaga* (Montevideo, 1995), pp. 1061–7

TABLE OF CASES BEFORE THE PERMANENT COURT OF INTERNATIONAL JUSTICE AND THE INTERNATIONAL COURT OF JUSTICE

ℰℐ

Notes

Citations are of judgments unless otherwise indicated. Judgments at the merits stage and Advisory Opinions are printed in bold type before all other citations relating to the same phase of the case.

Frequently used short names are indicated in square brackets, italicised, after the full citation.

*indicates a case pending before the ICJ in September 1995.

Extended consideration of a case is indicated by the use of bold type for page references.

Where a citation in a note relates directly to the text of the note itself, the page reference is followed by suffix 'n'.

PART I

The International Court of Justice

❧

1

The International Court as
a world court

Georges Abi-Saab

ço

Having had the privilege of being the pupil of Professor R. Y. Jennings, as he then was, and the beneficiary of his guidance and friendship for over a third of a century, and the even rarer privilege of serving beside him as counsel before the International Court of Justice, then as judge *ad hoc* during his presidency of the Court, I was intrigued by his occasional use of 'World Court' to refer to the ICJ.

Indeed, this reference to the ICJ (and the Permanent Court of International Justice before it) as 'the World Court', which probably goes back to Judge Manley O. Hudson and which is current in legal literature in English, is unknown in other languages such as French, Italian, Spanish or for that matter Arabic. It raises in the mind of the non-common law jurist the following query: in what sense and what ways can the International Court be considered a 'World Court'?

THE INTERNATIONAL COURT AS
A WORLD-WIDE COURT

The first meaning that suggests itself is that it is a court of and for the whole world. As such, it is expected to be universalist in its composition, outlook and vocation, truly representing and at the service of the international community in its entirety, and not dominated by the legal or social culture or special interests of any segment thereof. This in turn would ensure that the Court and its judgments command the confidence of all the nations of the world.

But the 'international community' – construed as the community of independent states constituting the 'civil society' of international law – is itself an evolving phenomenon, which has undergone fundamental change in its composition since the creation of the Court.

At the time of its establishment in 1922 and throughout its two decades of active existence, the PCIJ reflected well the international community of its time. It gathered on its bench a majority of European judges, including nationals of the major European powers (with the notable exception, it is true, of post-revolutionary Russia), in addition to judges from the USA and some Latin-American republics, as well as from China and Japan, which constituted the bulk of non-Western participation in that community (the rest of the world, being dependent, had no standing). This was a relatively coherent community; and the Court faithfully reflected in its stance and its jurisprudence the legal outlook of this Eurocentric community, which was strongly imbued with nineteenth-century positivism.

The situation had changed radically by the time of the reconstitution of the Court as part of the UN Organization, under the new denomination of the International Court of Justice. Indeed, since it started functioning in the late 1940s (a period coinciding with the advent of the cold war), the ICJ has been portrayed, at regular intervals, as being in crisis as a result of the lack or loss of confidence in it by one or the other component of the international community.

At the beginning, during the latter part of the 1940s, and throughout the 1950s, the 'crisis' was presented in terms of 'the decline of the optional clause'[1] and the stagnation of other sources of compulsory jurisdiction of the Court. It was largely explained by the systematically negative attitude of the Soviet Union and its allies towards the Court.

Of course, as members of the UN, these states were automatically parties to the Statute of the Court, 'which forms an integral part of the . . . Charter';[2] and the Soviet Union as a permanent member of the Security Council has continuously had one of its nationals elected to the bench, in addition to another judge from one of the socialist East European countries. But given their absolute concept of sovereignty and their scepticism about the neutrality of men and institutions, the members of the 'socialist bloc', as it then was, adopted a systematic attitude (which has radically changed since) of refusal to submit to the jurisdiction of the Court in general, whether by a unilateral declaration of acceptance of the 'optional clause' system of article 36(2) of the Statute, or via compromissory clauses in treaties or even a compromise after the dispute arises. This led, after the controversy over the *Reservations to the Genocide Convention*,[3] to the relegation of compromissory clauses in law-making treaties prepared under UN auspices to separate protocols.[4]

---

[1] This is the title of a famous article by Sir Humphrey Waldock, *BYbIL*, 32 (1955–6), p. 244
[2] Article 92 of the UN Charter.
[3] Advisory Opinion, ICJ Reports, 1951, p. 15.
[4] It is true that Waldock, followed by a large majority of writers, ascribed the 'decline of the optional clause' also to the explosion of the reservations attached to the declarations of the traditional (Western

From the beginning of the 1960s, with the acceleration of the decoloniz-ation movement and the massive accession of colonial territories to independence, the 'crisis of the Court' was perceived and analysed in terms of the distrust manifested by newly independent states towards the Court. Several explanations were given for this supposed distrust on the part of the new states in the judicial process and their preference for diplomatic methods, for example their lack of familiarity and expertise, as well as the complexity and the lengthy and onerous character of the procedure. But the most recurrent explanation was the underrepresentation of Afro-Asian states on the bench; which was true at that time.

These were, however, subjective explanations, based on transient con-tingencies. Other explanations highlighted more deep-rooted and objective causes, particularly the dissatisfaction of the new states with large parts of classical international law which legitimized their subjugation and reflected the outlook and interests of the limited community from which it ensued and of which they did not partake except as objects of appropriation. Whence their refusal to submit to a procedure of settlement of disputes which is congenitally constrained to the strict application of precisely that law which they contested, until its rules were updated and developed with their participation to make them more universal in their approach and in the values and interests they are called upon to further and protect.[5]

It should be noted, however, that at the beginning this was perceived as a latent or long-term rather than an open crisis – at least until what one cannot help calling 'the disaster of 1966', the second judgment of the Court in the *South West Africa* cases.[6] This decision, the most controversial in the history of the two Courts, was also the only one to have been adopted without a majority, by the casting vote of the President (the Australian Sir Percy Spender). It thrust the Court into an acute crisis, having shattered the confidence of large parts of the world, particularly the Third World, in the Court as it then was. It gave rise to an extended and very critical debate on the role of the Court in the General Assembly, leading to a readjustment in the composition of the bench to make it more representative of the various components of the international community.

and Latin-American) clientele of the Court, some of which went so far as to annihilate all binding effect of the declaration – for example, the US reservation concerning matters falling within their domestic jurisdiction 'as determined by the US', whose questionable legality nourished legal controversy for over a decade.

[5] G. Abi-Saab, 'The Newly Independent States and the Rules of International Law', *Howard Law Review*, 8 (1962), p. 95.

[6] ICJ Reports, 1966, p. 6.

Perhaps the most significant consequence of this crisis was a new self-awareness and change of attitude on the part of the Court itself. It was very distant and reserved in its relations with the UN, states and public opinion in general. Indeed, one of the main criticisms addressed to it was that, in exercising its contentious jurisdiction, it acted as if it were an arbitral tribunal of the nineteenth century and not as an integral part of the UN, attuned to contemporary international law.

But since that crisis, the Court has missed no occasion to emphasize that it belongs to the UN and to put forward the law and principles of the Charter, while endeavouring to be less distant and more accommodating towards states as potential litigants, with a view to attracting them to its forum.

Has the Court gone too far in that direction? In any case, since its judgment on the merits in the *Nicaragua* case,[7] a new 'crisis' has been diagnosed. Earlier it was said that the Third World had no confidence in the Court. But with this judgment, certain voices started to contend that it is now the Western world that no longer has confidence in the Court, where it risks systematically being put into the minority.

Is it true that the Court is too imbued with the UN spirit (and is this really a stigma)? Did it really develop an 'anti-Western bias', thus undermining its credibility within its original constituency?[8]

In fact, the Court was fully aware of the great political risk it was taking by upholding the basic principles of contemporary international law and the Charter in the way it did in its judgment, and which it could not help doing as a court of law. It thus administered – at very high cost – a glaring proof of its objectivity and independence. In consequence, even if the immediate practical effect of that judgment were to have been the political weakening of the Court and a reduction of its volume of business in the short run, it could not but increase its credibility and consolidate its position in the long run.

Fortunately, once the dust settled, even in the short term the pessimistic scenario did not materialize. On the contrary, the Court has never had as many cases simultaneously in its docket, with litigants from all parts of the world, as it has since that judgment, to the point of being overloaded. For, with the passing of the cold war, it became clearer than ever that the Court does not represent and is not at the service of any one segment of the international community, but rather of that community in its entirety.

---

[7] ICJ Reports, 1986, p. 14.

[8] For such contentions see A. Gros, 'La Cour internationale de Justice 1946–1986: les reflexions d'un juge', in Y. Dinstein and M. Tabory (eds.), *International Law at a Time of Perplexity: Essays in Honour of Shabtai Rosenne* (Dordrecht, 1989), p. 289; S. Rosenne, 'The Role of the ICJ in Inter-state Relations Today', *Revue Belge de droit international*, 20 (1987), p. 275.

In the words of Sir Robert Jennings, commenting on the docket of the Court in his first address to the General Assembly as President of the ICJ: 'Glancing at this list of cases, we can say one thing with assurance: this is indeed now a world court, exhibiting in its daily work that quality of universality which is also a feature of this General Assembly'.[9]

THE ICJ AS A JUDICIAL ORGAN OF THE INTERNATIONAL LEGAL ORDER

Another meaning that the term 'World Court' may convey derives from the first: if the Court represents and is designed to serve the international community in its entirety, then its first and foremost role is to uphold the global values of that community rather than to act as a mere mediator between two disputing parties. Technically speaking, this means that the Court is the organ of the legal order of that community and not of the parties to the dispute before it; that it is an instrument put by the international legal order at the disposal of the litigants, without however depending on them in its structural and functional properties or in its judicial policy.

Indeed, the evolution of the Court and its judicial policy since its establishment in 1922 can be summed up in its tendency towards increasing institutionalization in the sense of stabilizing its modes of functioning and decision-making and consolidating its autonomy in this respect *vis-à-vis* the parties, while being put into motion by their *petita* and relying on their consent as the ultimate basis for its jurisdiction.

This is precisely what differentiates the Court from arbitration. It should be recalled that in the nineteenth century (with lingering echoes up to the present), arbitration was currently explained in the literature in terms of the legal institution of 'mandate', and the role of the arbitrators was seen as that of 'mandatories' of the parties, or their agents, acting as a common organ for both of them, whose final act (i.e. the award) was consequently attributable to those parties; in sum, it was a contractual rather than a jurisdictional act, as if the parties had charged their common organ – the arbitral panel – with drawing up and adopting the terms of a settlement in their place.

It is true that such a theory, even if one could consider it not too far-fetched as an explanation of the hesitant beginnings of modern arbitration early in the nineteenth century – e.g. mixed commissions without a third party – is totally unacceptable today. But it is also true that in arbitration the parties are in permanent control over the process from beginning to end.

---

[9] *ICJ Yearbook 1991–1992*, 46, p. 207.

This does not mean that the parties have no influence at all on the international judicial process, but that their influence is much more limited than in arbitration. Thus they have no hand in the composition of the bench, save for the designation of a judge *ad hoc* in the absence of a national judge (by contrast, they have acquired an important role in the composition of *ad hoc* Chambers, as shall be seen below).

As to the procedure itself, on many points the Statute of the ICJ is *jus cogens*. And if it leaves to the parties a certain latitude, this latitude is circumscribed by the institutional aspects of the Court and the parameters or the concept of 'judicial propriety'. Finally, and what is even more important, once the procedure is engaged, a state party can no longer unilaterally block it.

From the outset, the present Court has put even more emphasis on this tendency towards institutionalization and has shown great independence in the articulation of its reasoning and the choice of legal bases of its decisions, relying on the principle *jura novit curia*. For while the judge has to rule on the *petitum*, or the subject matter of the dispute, as defined by the claims of the parties in their submissions, he is not bound by the grounds and arguments advanced by them in support of their claims; nor is he obliged to address all of them (as an arbitrator might feel bound to do), as long as he can provide a complete answer to the *petitum*. This particularly means that the judge is totally free in motivating his decisions, without being reduced to a choice between the legal theses put before him by the parties.

The Court has abundantly used this liberty; paradoxically, however, it has done so mainly for reasons of judicial caution. Thus, in basing its decisions on the merits in cases such as *Nottebohm*[10] and the *Right of Passage over Indian Territory*[11] on grounds other than those put forward (or even envisaged) by the parties, it sought to avoid taking a position on questions that were too controversial or too embarrassing for one of the parties.

Similarly, in procedural law, the Court has gone far in innovation by articulating an extremely complex system of preliminary questions which often have nothing to do with the arguments of the parties. But these bold innovations were used in the 1960s and the early 1970s for 'declinatory' rather than 'affirmative' purposes, to avoid deciding the case on the merits rather than to establish the jurisdiction of the Court to do so in the face of the resistance of one party (namely the *Northern Cameroons* case,[12] the *Nuclear Tests* cases,[13] not to mention the Second Phase of the *South West Africa* cases[14]).

---

[10] ICJ Reports, 1955, p. 4.
[11] ICJ Reports, 1960, p. 6.   [12] ICJ Reports, 1963, p. 15.
[13] ICJ Reports, 1974, pp. 253, 457.   [14] ICJ Reports, 1966, p. 6.

However, as was mentioned earlier, after the 1966 decision in the *South West Africa* cases, the Court endeavoured to move closer to potential litigants and to accommodate them with a view to drawing them to its forum; and that could not be done without affecting its margin of autonomy in their regard, leading to speculation about a tendency towards an 'arbitralization' of the Court.

The most spectacular manifestation of this trend has been the new system of *ad hoc* Chambers, which was introduced in the most recent revision of the Rules in 1978. It was prompted by the *Beagle Channel* case[15] between Chile and Argentina who chose five members of the Court to sit as an arbitral tribunal. By revising its Rules, the Court strove to offer to some extent the same choice to the parties within the Court itself.

Stretching somewhat the meaning of article 26(2) of its Statute (which provides that 'The *number* of judges to constitute such a chamber shall be determined by the Court with the approval of the parties'), article 17(2) of the revised Rules provides: 'When the parties have agreed, the President shall ascertain their views regarding the *composition* of the chamber, and shall report to the Court accordingly', before it elects the members of the chamber (by secret ballot). This enables the Court to accede to the parties' choice while formally preserving its power to constitute the Chamber.

This system of Chambers was subject to two major criticisms. The first is that it reduced the ICJ to another Permanent Court of Arbitration, a mere list of judges or arbitrators from whom the parties pick and choose those they want to sit in their case. This obviously diminishes the institutional character of the Court and the stability and continuity of its composition. And if one goes by the example of the first Chamber thus constituted in the *Gulf of Maine* case,[16] where the parties insisted on having a Chamber composed exclusively of Western judges, it also endangers the universal character of the Court – a pitfall which was avoided, however, in the other three cases hitherto referred to a Chamber.[17]

The other criticism, which flows from the first, highlights the dangers of the increasing heterogeneity in the jurisprudence of the Court which may ensue, thus forgoing one of the major (if not the major) contributions of the Court to international law. This is a danger that is not totally moot, if we compare the reasoning of the Chamber in the *Gulf of Maine* case[18] with

---

[15] 17 *ILM* 634 (1978).

[16] ICJ Reports, 1982, p. 3.

[17] *Frontier Dispute (Burkina Faso/Mali)*, ICJ Reports, 1985, p. 6; *Elettronica Sicula*, ICJ Reports 1987, p. 3; *Land, Island and Maritime Frontier Dispute (El Salvador/Honduras)*, ICJ Reports, 1987, p. 10.

[18] ICJ Reports, 1984, p. 246.

that of the Court in full, in the *Continental Shelf (Libya/Malta)* case[19] a few months later.

These two criticisms draw attention to dangers which, while real, are merely potential, and whose realization depends on the manner and the frequency of use of this procedure (a tonic in small doses, catastrophic if it becomes the rule). With the end of the cold war they seem less likely. Indeed, in spite of the very full docket of the Court, none of the cases before it at present has been referred to a Chamber, and in fact none has been since 1987.[20]

A second indication of the trend towards arbitralization was the consistently negative attitude manifested until recently towards the institution of intervention, i.e. the possibility for a third party to join a case before the Court which might affect its rights or legal interests. This is a well-established institution in all judicial systems and has been included in the Statute of the Court from its inception. But it is unknown in arbitration, whose ambit is totally determined by the parties and is usually confined to them.

It is true that the Court had never admitted intervention on the basis of article 62 of the Statute. But what was new was the tenor of article 81 of the revised Rules, which could imply a new requirement for the admissibility of intervention in addition to the 'interest of a legal nature', namely the existence of a 'jurisdictional title' between the intervenor and the parties to the case. Such a requirement would render intervention totally superfluous as a separate institution, the intervenor being able to reach the same result (and even more) by introducing a new case against the parties and requesting the joinder of the two cases pursuant to article 47.

Since the adoption of this new provision, and until 1990, the Court, while avoiding this 'delicate question', managed systematically to reject requests for intervention, basing itself on diverse arguments which frequently seemed rather contrived. This gave the impression that intervention had fallen into desuetude and that the Court was trying by all possible means, especially in cases introduced by compromis, to protect the parties from the meddling of a third party in their judicial privacy; i.e., an impression of accommodating the parties to the detriment of the institutional and objective character of the Court, and of taking a step further towards arbitralization.

Here again, however, a recent readjustment has taken place, in the judgment of the Chamber of 1990 in the *Land, Island and Maritime Dispute (El Salvador/Honduras)* case,[21] in which for the first time in the history of the two

---

[19] ICJ Reports, 1985, p. 13.
[20] See n. 17 above.   [21] ICJ Reports, 1990, p. 92.

Courts intervention was admitted on the basis of article 62. The Chamber pronounced on the 'delicate question' of the 'jurisdictional title', clearly stating that such a title is not required in this kind of intervention, which finds its title directly in the Statute and derives from the institutional character of the Court, even in cases introduced by compromis.

A third, and even more significant, indication of the trend towards arbitralization could be detected in the decisions of the Court themselves, which revealed a progressive tendency in the 1970s and the 1980s towards transactional justice (particularly in delimitation cases).

This is a reversion to the spirit of arbitration which, given the control of the parties over the whole process and the old contractualist view of the activities of the arbitral organ, seeks above all to settle the dispute by affording minimal satisfaction to both parties, if not making them meet half-way.

Several technical devices have been used by the Court to that end. Prominent among them is the noticeable distending of the logical chain of reasoning between the judicial decision *stricto sensu* (*dispositif*) and the grounds (*motif*) leading to it. The earlier judgments followed a rigorous process of formal logical reasoning: the stated premises inexorably led to the conclusion. By contrast, the style of some of the more recent judgments or Advisory Opinions (e.g. the Advisory Opinion on the *Interpretation of the Agreement between the WHO and Egypt*[22] and the judgment in the *Continental Shelf (Tunisia/Libya)* case[23]) is quite eclectic: a good part of the text blandly restates the contentions of the parties – a technique current in arbitration – or produces alternative lines of reasoning, before the decision suddenly appears without sufficiently revealing the manner by which it was reached. This obviously leaves the Court a greater latitude in choosing among possible solutions.

Another such device is for the Court to reformulate the questions or submissions (e.g. the above-mentioned Advisory Opinion and the judgment in the *Fisheries Jurisdiction* cases).[24] This enables the Court to broach the case from an angle amenable to a transactional solution or to avoid pronouncing itself on certain questions.[25]

Finally, a third device is the flight into equity and equitable principles as an element of applicable law *intra legem*. The resort to equity and equitable

---

[22] ICJ Reports, 1980, p. 73.

[23] ICJ Reports, 1982, p. 18.

[24] ICJ Reports, 1974, pp. 3, 175.

[25] It should be noted that this technique is not totally new, and that it has been used earlier by the Court as well as its predecessor, but in a much more discreet manner. Cf. H. Lauterpacht, *The Development of International Law by the International Court* (2nd edn, London, 1958), p. 206.

principles, without sufficiently defining them or giving them an identifiable objective content, makes it much easier for the Court to reach transactional solutions on a case-by-case basis.

Yet here as well, a rectification of course away from the slippery path of transactional justice is to be found in the judgment on the merits in the *Nicaragua* case.[26] For while 'transactional' in some of its details and qualifications, it was not in its main thrust and total effect. In so doing, at great risk, the Court obviously acted as an organ of international law rather than of the parties, or *a fortiori* of a party, albeit the mightiest.

THE INTERNATIONAL COURT AS A HIGHER COURT ON A WORLD LEVEL

Stating that the ICJ is an organ of the international legal order and not of the parties does not exhaust the matter, however. For it begets another question, namely that of the exact place and role of the Court in this order and in relation to the other adjudicative mechanisms that may exist therein.

This last question arises in the first place in relation to arbitration, which was the only form of adjudicative activity existing in general international law before the establishment of the Court, and which continues to coexist with it. But unlike the situation in municipal law, where arbitration is subject to judicial control and is thus integrated into the judicial system, international arbitration remained outside the Court's orbit. This meant that instead of having an integrated judicial or adjudicative system through which is canalized the judicial function on the international level, we have a scatter of diverse organs through which this function is haphazardly performed.

Professor Georges Scelle tried to correlate them in his draft 'Model Rules on Arbitral Procedure'.[27] His draft purported to shut off all means of evasion once the obligation to arbitrate is undertaken. To that end, it established the jurisdiction of the ICJ *ipso jure* to decide all claims and make up for all the failures to act by parties aiming at preventing the start or the continuation of the arbitration procedure or at contesting the meaning or the validity of ensuing awards. By thus submitting arbitration to the mandatory control of the ICJ, this draft would have established an integrated adjudicative system. But this is precisely the reason why states heavily resisted it, as the international

---

[26] ICJ Reports, 1986, p. 14.

[27] This draft served as a basis for the Model Rules adopted by the International Law Commission, of which the General Assembly merely 'took note' in its resolution 1262 (XIII) of 1958, and which are published in the *ILC Yearbook*, (1958, vol.II), p. 83.

community was not then prepared for such an advanced degree of institutionalization on the international level.

Since the 1950s, however, in parallel with the rapidly growing complexity and intensity of international relations, international law has undergone prodigious developments both in updating its traditional fields and in covering new and more specialized ones. This was accompanied by a proliferation of specialized judicial organs, whether on the universal or the regional level, such as administrative tribunals of international organizations, the new Law of the Sea Tribunal, the European Court of Justice and regional tribunals of human rights, not to mention *ad hoc* ones, such as the International Criminal Tribunals for the Former Yugoslavia and Rwanda.

Such specialized tribunals also exist in municipal law. But the ambit of their specialized jurisdiction is well delimited in relation to the courts of plenary or general jurisdiction, whose jurisdiction remains the rule, the others being the specified exceptions. Moreover frequently, though not systematically, the specialized tribunals are subject to the control of the higher courts of the judicial system.

On the international level, there is no such clear distribution of functions. Indeed, we still have two unrelated, and hence overlapping, modes of exercising general or plenary jurisdiction (albeit on a consensual basis) – the ICJ and arbitration. Though intellectually not wholly satisfying, this situation was tolerable in practice as long as their use remained so sparse that the probability of their collision (conflict of jurisdiction, contradictory decisions, etc.) seemed moot. But with the proliferation of specialized tribunals, which by necessity tread on part of the grounds covered by those tribunals exercising plenary jurisdiction (e.g. the law of the sea), such a danger becomes imminent; so do the threats to the cohesion and unity of international law. This is the more so in view of the fact that almost all of these tribunals are of one (first and last) instance, with no possibility of appeal or cassation making for the unity of interpretation of the law.

It is true that occasionally some vague lineaments of a structure become perceptible. For example, in the inter-war period appeals from the decisions of the Mixed Arbitral Tribunals established pursuant to the Peace Treaties could be lodged with the PCIJ.[28] Similarly, appeals from the judgments of the Administrative Tribunals of the UN and the ILO can be introduced before the ICJ, though via the awkward procedure of requesting an Advisory Opinion. It is to be noted, however, that in both these cases, the possibility of appeal (with the ensuing hierarchical structure) is provided for in the statutes

[28] PCIJ, Series A/B, No. 56 (Order 1933), and No. 63 (Judgment 1933).

of the 'lower' tribunal itself, and does not emanate from general international law or the inherent powers of the ICJ.

In the same vein, arbitral awards can be, as they were twice, attacked before the ICJ.[29] But these were appeals introduced, like any other case, on the basis of a specific jurisdictional title rather than on the basis of the unity and continuity of the adjudicative system.

However, regardless of the legal basis on which they may rest, the multiplication of such appeals in practice does push the situation forwards towards the progressive emergence of an international judicial or adjudicative system, without completely bringing it about.

Indeed, as was so eloquently said by Sir Robert Jennings in his last address to the General Assembly as President of the ICJ: 'There can be only one principal judicial organ of the United Nations, as there is normally only one supreme court of any legally well ordered community.'[30]

THE ICJ AS AN INSTRUMENT OF
WORLD GOVERNANCE

The reference to the Court as 'the principal judicial organ of the United Nations' in the preceding quotation brings out another aspect which goes beyond the Court's position within the international legal order. For if its role therein – as a 'higher' court and the centre-piece around which the exercise of the judicial function tends to crystallize, even in the absence of formal hierarchical structure – has to be extrapolated, this role is expressly designated within the UN, which is the nearest thing in existence to a structure of governance on the international or world level.

As 'the principal judicial organ of the UN', the Court partakes in world governance, notably through its contribution to the peaceful settlement of international disputes, which is the preventive approach to the pursuit of the first UN purpose, the maintenance of peace and security.

This is not the place to evaluate the role of the Court in the settlement of disputes. But the spectacular increase in the volume of business of the Court is witness to its growing contribution thereto. It suffices here, in conclusion, to recall a few insights of Sir Robert Jennings in this regard.

First, the 'new busyness' of the Court can be partly explained by the fact that 'the Court procedure is beginning to be seen as a resort to be employed

---

[29] *Arbitral Award Made by the King of Spain on 23 December 1906*, ICJ Reports, 1960, p. 192; *Arbitral Award of 31 July 1989*, ICJ Reports, 1991, p. 53.
[30] UN Doc. A/48/PV.31 (8 November 1993).

in close relationship with normal diplomatic negotiations' rather than as a 'last resort' when all else has failed, i.e. as an alternative to resort to war; and this 'is after all only to conform to the place that courts enjoy in any developed domestic system of law'.[31]

This growing perception that recourse to the Court 'might usefully be employed at an earlier stage of the dispute' explains why in some recent cases parties have settled their disputes out of court, after (or sometimes before fully) pleading it before the Court.[32] Even in such cases, by defining and refining their positions in legal terms for the purposes of litigation and by better understanding the claims of the adversary, the parties move imperceptibly to a position from which an agreed settlement comes within reach. In the words of Sir Robert: 'Whenever the Court or its procedures can help in this way, the Court is, in an important sense, still productively at work'.[33] This activity of the Court can be said to partake of 'preventive diplomacy' *lato sensu*, by opening the way to a direct settlement of the dispute.

Second, 'preventive diplomacy', as a strategy for the maintenance of peace and security, usually refers more specifically to activities of the political organs of the UN. But the Court as the 'principal judicial organ of the UN' can play a much more active role, in conjunction with these organs, to that end. Criticizing the insufficient use of the Court, the former Secretary-General, Javier Perez de Cuellar, in the introduction to his last annual report, remarks:

> even those disputes which seem entirely political (as the Iraq–Kuwait dispute prior to invasion) have a clearly legal component. If, for any reason, the parties fail to refer the matter to the Court, the process of achieving a fair and objectively commendable settlement and thus defusing an international crisis situation would be facilitated by obtaining the Court's advisory opinion.[34]

Sir Robert, having cited this passage in his first address to the General Assembly as President of the ICJ, adds:

> To have the principal legal organ of the UN more often employed with respect to the legal components of situations with which the UN is concerned would, quite apart from its possible contribution to solving a dispute or a situation, also do immense good for international law. The relevance of international law would thus be brought home to people generally.[35]

---

[31] *Ibid.*

[32] *Passage through the Great Belt (Finland v. Denmark)*, ICJ Reports, 1992, p. 348; *Certain Phosphate Lands in Nauru (Nauru v. Australia)*, ICJ Reports, 1993, p. 322.

[33] 'The Role and Functioning of the Court', *ICJ Yearbook 1992–1993*, 47, pp. 249–53, at p. 251.

[34] UN Doc. A/41/1 (1991), p. 8. This proposal was reiterated by the present Secretary-General in his *Agenda for Peace* (UN Doc. A/47/277 (1992)), para. 38.

[35] 'The Role and Functioning of the Court', *ICJ Yearbook 1991–1992*, 46, pp. 205–12, at p. 210.

Third, if the UN is the nearest thing in existence to a structure of world governance, however vague the resemblance may be, then one way of enhancing its credibility and effectiveness in the eyes of the world is for the UN itself to be seen as subject to the rule of law.

This brings to the fore the question of control of legality within the Organization, and the need for clarifying the exact role and import of the Court as 'the principal judicial organ of the UN', particularly in relation to other organs. In other words, it raises such jurisdictional issues as 'the legal relationship between political and legal appreciation; between the Security Council and the Court; and when and to what extent the Court might or should have powers of judicial review of administrative action, and of political decision'.

With this illustrative enumeration of issues, Sir Robert concludes: 'These are not simple but rather complex questions of basic importance for the legal character of the UN; and it is a gratifying sign of the maturity of the system that they should be dealt with by the ICJ, one way or another'.[36]

---

[36] 'The Role and Functioning of the Court', *ICJ Yearbook 1992–1993*, 47, p. 251.

2

The International Court
and the voice of justice

Philip Allott

ა

COURTS AND JUSTICE

A court of law is theatre, temple and battlefield. A court enacts *social process* as drama, sacrament and contest. Day after day in the court-room the magic of *human self-socializing* is performed publicly, for all to see: the universal made particular, the particular made universal. Day after day in the court-room the triunity of *social self-constituting* is incarnated in unity: the ideal made real in the legal.

Like any other social institution, a court is a transformatory structure-system, transforming social reality in particular ways. Itself the product of the past social reality of a particular society, a court makes a specific contribution to the general social task of forming a given society's future out of that society's past, as it acts in society's continuous present.

A court of law shares with other social institutions also the characteristic that its work of social transformation takes place within a specific form of social reality. A social institution is not merely a systematic structure of action, organizing human work in certain ways; a social institution is a systematic structure within consciousness, organizing the conceiving and perceiving of social reality in characteristic ways.

Since Wittgenstein, it has been convenient to picture these special social realities using the metaphor of the *game*. Religion, natural science, the economy, politics, art – and law – are broad areas of social reality, with necessarily imprecise boundaries, which nevertheless are distinguishable from each other at least in that they use distinct forms of discourse, distinct systems of rationality, distinct teleological programmes, distinct systematic character-istics which determine the making of judgements in the given area – judgements as to the social significance of particular phenomena, judgements as to successful and unsuccessful social performance, including intellectual performance. Each partial social reality, such as law, is its own realm of significance.

The *rules of the games*, so to speak, have common characteristics which flow, in the first place, from substantive overlapping – say, between law and morality (for example, concepts of obligation and responsibility), law and religion (for example, concepts of immanent value and transcendental purpose), natural science and law (for example, concepts of causation and elementary notions of time and space), natural science and social science (for example, concepts of hypothesis and evidence), politics and religion (for example, the phenomena of persuasion and belief, notions of transcendental and instrumental value). Second, partial social realities have common characteristics which flow from the total social reality of which they are partial forms or aspects or perspectives – both the total social reality of a given society and the total process of human socializing in general. And, third, they share characteristics which flow from the common physiological, biological, psychological and linguistic bases of all human action and all human consciousness.

Specific societies generate the specific forms of partial social reality which they find useful or, at least, those forms of partial social reality survive that prove themselves capable of surviving in the social reality of a given society, as it forms itself over time. And this means that a given partial social reality – such as law – forms society as it is formed by society. It participates in producing the social transformations of which it is itself the product. Law helps to make itself as it helps to make society.

It is the most general task of the social institution known as *philosophy* to consider the possible reality of all social realities, the possible game of all social games, the possible rules of all rules of social reality-making.

The partial social reality of *law* is first among equals in the process of social reality-forming. The game that law plays is society's great game.

Law makes all society members into agents of society's self-creating. Law makes all human action into action whose potentiality is the public interest. Law makes all human desire into desire whose object can be the survival and prospering of society.

Law achieves these remarkable feats by treating all human phenomena as capable of having legal significance. Every potential and actual human event is a potential social event and, hence, a potential legal event. There is nothing in society – from the private thoughts of one single human being to the management of a society's total economic activity – that can escape the potentiality of legal reconceiving, that cannot be remade within law's own reality, for law's own purposes.

By reconceiving social phenomena in legal form, society makes its possible futures. As it makes its possible futures, so society makes possible its actual

18

future. Social reality in the future will include social reality as it has been reconceived by law. The law contains a particular set of society's ideas of its possible futures, namely, an idea of what the social reality of that society could be, if that reality were determined in accordance with the law. The law contains an indefinite number of possible social realities, but not an infinite number. The limits of those possibilities are determined by the particular method the law uses to re-form social reality. The particular method of future-choosing that the law uses is the method of *legal relations*. Law is a system of legal relations.

Legal relations are universalizing patterns of interactive human behaviour. Legal relations universalize the infinite particularity of possible human behaviour. When they are applied to actual human behaviour, legal relations particularize society's universal purposes.

Legal relations – rights, powers, freedoms, immunities, duties, liabilities, disabilities – provide a particular form in which the actual interaction of actual human beings can be conceived with a view to bringing about actual social change. As particular human beings will and act in relation to each other, their willed action may take an infinite variety of forms, reflecting the infinite density of social reality at the given time, including all material possibilities and all human desires. But a particular legal relation contains a pattern which establishes a relationship between the willed action of individuals and the interactive behaviour of society in general. By reconceiving human behaviour in the form of a legal relation, society gives itself the possibility of incorporating that behaviour in its future social reality in a form that conforms with the content of the legal relations.

A legal relation is matrix, heuristic and algorithm.

A legal relation is *matrix*, because it abstracts and classifies the infinite particularity of persons, places and events. A person, for the purposes of a legal relation, may be a national, an alien, a parent, a corporation, a minor, a trespasser, a police officer, a judge . . . or a member of any number of other legally significant classes of person. A place, for the purposes of a legal relation, may be a public highway, a private dwelling, a factory, a court . . . or an instance of any number of other legally significant classes of place. An event may be a contract, a sale, a marriage, an assault, a licence, the judgment of a court . . . or an instance of any number of other legally significant classes of event. Legal relations create legal identities.

A legal relation is a *heuristic*, because it simplifies actual reality for computational purposes. Actual reality, as it presents itself in human consciousness, is infinitely complex, uncertain and dynamic. In order to make legal relations operationally effective, as instruments of social transformation, they must exclude much of actual reality. They create an *as if* reality. The law will deal with persons, places and events as if their social interactions were limited to the interactions envisaged by a given legal relation. For the purposes of a given legal relation, the law may exclude any number of aspects of reality which might be significant in another form of social reality – mitigating circumstances in relation to criminal offences, economic inequalities of parties to a contract, wider complexities of all kinds (scientific, technological, economic, sociological, psychological) in the drafting of legislation, extrinsic motivations and human limitations in the exercise of public-realm powers . . . The creation and application of legal relations would be impossible if legal reality had to be wholly coordinate with other social realities, let alone with total social reality. Legal relations create a legal reality.

A legal relation is an *algorithm*, because its function is not merely to re-present social reality but to transform social reality. It is the pattern of a process.

$$\text{situation } A > \text{participants} > \text{legal relation} = \text{situation } B$$

That is to say, the coming together of a relevant situation, relevant participants and a relevant legal relation transforms that situation. It is the matrix aspect of the legal relation that determines the relevant situation and participants. It is the heuristic aspect that determines the relevant content of the situation and the relevant behaviour of the participants. It is the algorithm aspect of the legal relation that determines the way in which the given social situation is altered. Legal relations generate specific social processes.

Through legal relations the law is thus able to inject specific social purpose into specific human behaviour. In this way, the law makes itself a main instrument of the fundamental transformatory process of all human socializing, of the self-constituting of all societies. Through a mechanism that may be called *social exchange*, a natural human power, which is the product of material possibility and human desire, is transformed into a social power when it is used by society to achieve social purposes. As society constructs social reality it reconstructs all such natural powers, establishing social connections between all the natural powers of individuals and subordinate societies. In this way, all human desires and all human purposes and all human energies become available to serve the public interest of society. The reward for the socializing of power is that the power in question becomes socially significant, socially effective. This macro-effect of the socializing of power means, on the one hand, that individual power (say, over land or tools or knowledge or another person) acquires greatly enhanced transformatory energy, and, on the other hand, that society communally is able to achieve total social effects which are exponentially greater than a mere aggregation of individual powers.

The law is the most direct and, perhaps, the most efficient way of social-izing power. A *social* power is a *legal* power when it is the subject of a legal relation. The special effectiveness of the legal version of social exchange flows not only from the characteristic that legal relations are capable of being applied to any and every possible aspect of social reality but also from the inherent and necessary interconnectedness of all legal relations. All legal relations are in systematic interaction with each other, up to and including legal relations about the making, applying and enforcing of legal relations. Every legal right or obligation is an instance of legal rights and obligations in general, and legal rights and obligations in general are instances of law in general.

It is in this sense that we are able to speak of *law* in a society, as a distinct part of social reality, and that we are able to speak of society's *legal constitution*, society constituting itself through law. Law is a self-coherent system of legal relations. The legal constitution is the structure-system of society carried from society's past to its future through law-applying in society's present. Through law society injects its social purposes into the very structure-system of society itself. Through law society is constantly transforming itself in accordance with its purposes, including society's most general purpose, namely, its survival and prospering. Law legalizes and thereby socializes particular human behaviour with a view to human survival and prospering.

As a society constitutes itself through law, and transforms human behaviour in accordance with its conception of its possibilities, society is thus constituting itself ideally, becoming what it imagines that it could be. Law socializes and thereby idealizes human behaviour with a view to human self-surpassing.

Through actual human behaviour in conformity with law, as human beings interact in the real world of actual human action, society constitutes itself *really*, from day to day, transforming actual human lives. The ideal and legal constitutions are actualized in the *real* constituting of the given society, constituting itself actually, in society's continuous present.

Most human interactions occur alegally, that is to say, without explicit reference to relevant legal relations. Most interactions in the family, most low-level economic interactions, most routine professional interactions, most leisure pursuits, take place without regard to the law. It may well be the case that ignoring the law in most situations is a necessary condition of efficient human self-socializing. Just as it is hard to imagine an efficient society in which all personal decisions are taken on the basis of explicitly stated moral premises, so it is hard to suppose that a society, at least a society having high levels of social complexity and energy, could function on the basis that the legal relations relevant to all social interactions should be made explicit.

It might even be the case that the most efficient society is the society in which least attention is paid to the law. The ideal society is the autonomic society, in which law has withered away, and in which the particular, the social and the universal are naturally integrated within the consciousness of each individual human being.

It follows that human action can be action in violation of the law without being action taken *for the purpose of* violating the law; and human action can be action in conformity with the law without being action taken *for the purpose of* conforming to the law. On the other hand, it is also the case that, at least in a modern society, very many social interactions are articulated as specifically legal situations, situations in which the law is invoked to justify an exercise of power in relation to another person, to justify a demand on another person to act in a certain way, to bring about cooperatively a state of affairs contemplated by the law. In such cases, the law is being used as an actual cause of its potential social effects; the law is being used to play its socially transformatory role.

Beyond law-conforming behaviour and law-applying behaviour there is law-enforcing behaviour, that is to say behaviour *for the purpose of* causing law-conforming behaviour. Law-enforcing behaviour can be extra-legal, in so far as it makes use of forms of social power which, in a given society or situation, have not been made the subject of legal relations (self-help, threats, sanctions, inducements, force). Legally based law-enforcing behaviour relies on the interlocking network of legal relations. Secondary and tertiary and *n*th-degree legal relations are explicitly or implicitly invoked, up to and including legal relations of the most general kind, such as fundamental consti-tutional rights, public-realm powers of the legislative, executive and judicial varieties.

Law-enforcing legal relations can be legal relations of any kind (right, power, freedom, immunity, duty, liability, disability). In their matrix effect, they identify the participants in the original and the high-level legal relations, including perhaps a court of competent jurisdiction, particular litigants, a particular accused person. In their heuristic effect, they determine the content of a dispute about law-application (whether it is a dispute about allegedly criminal behaviour, about the exercise of a public-realm power or about the rights of a private individual in relation to another). In the algoristic effect, they determine the way in which the situation in question may be transformed in accordance with all relevant legal relations (including the legal relations that entitle a person to invoke the jurisdiction of a court, or that entitle a court to give judgment or that entitle public officials to give physical effect to the court's judgment).

Thus law enforcement is not in principle different from law conforming and law applying. But law-enforcing legal relations are, as it were, the limiting case of all legal relations. It is the function of all legal relations to bring about law-conforming behaviour; it is the function of law-enforcing legal relations to ensure that other legal relations fulfil that function.

Courts are not a necessary feature of a legal system. Not only law conforming and law applying, but also law enforcing can occur without the intervention of a social institution having the distinctive characteristics of a court. The charismatic power of a tribal chief, an elder, a king, a wise-one, or a priest, the prestige-authority of a royal council or of a committee of social or professional peers, the benign neutrality of a conciliator or mediator, the formalized authority of an arbitrator or arbitrators, specialized tribunals of all kinds – countless forms of law-enforcing institutions have been generated contingently in the many instances of human self-socializing known to us through the course of recorded human history.

No doubt there have been, and there are, courts of many kinds, varying significantly from time to time, from place to place. And there have been, and there are, courts that are travesties of courts. But it seems right to say that there are striking characteristics shared by social institutions that are identified by the word *court* (and by equivalent words in languages other than English) in so many societies, even and perhaps especially in modern (post-1789) societies.

We may usefully imagine the ideal-type (in the spirit of Weberian sociology) of the social phenomenon of the *court*, deconstruct the central-case use (in terms of analytical philosophy) of the word *court*, or reconstruct the idea of reason (to use the Kantian term) which is the idea of a *court*, or identify the idea-object of a *court* (in the spirit of Husserl). At least, as sympathetic semiologists, we may seek to uncover what it is that society, subtly and silently, is saying through the elaborate and eloquent sign-system that is a *court*.

We must note, in the first place, that the court is a self-contained social phenomenon, to an extent that suggests that its isolation is an important part of its social function.

(1) A court is *physically isolated* from the rest of social reality, and even from the rest of legal reality. It is spatially isolated, a closed space, devoted uniquely to its purpose, conveying a strong sense of 'in here' (within 'the law' and within law enforcing), as opposed to 'out there' (the rest of social reality, including law conforming and law applying). It is temporally

isolated. Legal proceedings have a beginning and an end, conveying a strong sense of before-and-after. There are two things: social reality, including the lives of the participants, before and after the court proceedings.

(2) A court is *symbolically distinct* from the rest of social reality, including legal reality, by its elaborate symbolic manifestations. The court-room has distinctive physical attributes, participants behave in distinctive ways, including distinctive ways of dressing, of interacting physically, of communicating orally.

(3) A court is *systematically distinct* from the rest of legal reality, because it actualizes in a particular way the process of social transformation through law. It embodies that process, not through the diffuse dialectic of everyday law conforming and law applying, and not through the symbolically specific processes of legislative law making, but in what is very close to being a physical or material form. Society, law and the human subjects of legal relations seem to be present at last together in the same room, face to face.

In short, some small part of legal reality is temporarily diverted into the court-room and, having been transformed in a particular way in an atmosphere of luxuriant symbolism, is reinserted into the flood of social reality.

The exceptional characteristics of a court are attributable to the fact that it stands guard over several difficult frontiers: the frontier between the individual and society; the frontier between law and the rest of social reality; and the frontier between society and what is beyond society. These three frontiers set the boundaries of human socializing. They are not fixed, but are the subject of endless dialectical tension which determines the development of particular societies through time. And each, in its own way, is haunted by something which it is conventional and convenient to call *justice*.

The *theatrical* aspects of the court phenomenon are an imaginative response to the universalizing function of legal relations.

In the arts in general, but in the theatre (and film) in particular, the power of the imagination, of creator and audience, gives reality to that which is known to be, in a significant sense, unreal. Actors act the personalities of persons who are, but yet are not, persons, participating in events that are, but yet are not, events. The drama, the art-work in general, embodies universality in its unique particularity. We judge this effect by measuring the *beauty* or the *truth* (or some other cognate term) of the work of art.

In the court-room, the universalizing effect of a legal relation (matrix—

heuristic–algorithm) meets the unique particularity of the persons and events that are the subject of the court proceedings. The participants act out their universal roles – judge, jury, accused, litigant, witness – and the *dénouement* of the case (the judgment) is a unique set of coordinates in space–time at which the universal is made utterly particular (judgment for the plaintiff/defendant; the accused is guilty/not guilty), as the utterly particular is made universal (by the application of legal relations which could be applied to all such persons and events). We judge this event by measuring the *justice* (or some cognate term) of the judgment.

The *conflictual* aspects of the court phenomenon are an ironical reflection of the relational character of law. Whether the relationship established by the relevant legal relations is between society and an individual human being or between one human being and another, all the court can do is to adjust the actual situation of the parties, as understood by the court, in accordance with the pattern of the legal relation, as understood by the court.

Legal proceedings accordingly produce winners and losers. More often than not, they produce winners who are surprised by their good fortune, and losers who resent their misfortune. It seems to be the case that those legal proceedings, criminal as well as civil or administrative, that call forth the full systematic capacities of the court system (for example, which exhaust possibilities of appeal) are those cases that could be decided either way and which, in either event, would generate equal measures of surprise and resentment. To an observer, such cases may well seem like trials by ordeal, with the outcome determined by fate or by chance.

This aura of the presence of fate no doubt contributes to the solemnity of the court. There is a sense that the participants have one last chance to alter providence by appropriate prayerful words, through forms of ritual humiliation, through the invoking of what is seen as the majesty of the law, its power and its glory.

But the *ecclesiastical* aspects of the court phenomenon may also be seen as an imaginative response to the fragile authority of the law.

The altar-like *bench*, the vestments of judges and advocates, the numinous symbols of social hierarchy and authority, the hushed and reverent tones, the signs of homage and obeisance – such things may have the incidental effect of overawing the impressionable, the disempowered and the exploited, cloaking with a supernatural aura the power-struggle of society's *real* self-constituting which has generated the relevant legal relations as its restless by-product, and will generate further outcomes as the product of the power-struggle of the court-room.

But it is likely also, and perhaps primarily, that such things are a symbolic expression of anxiety and awe. Anxiety arises from the fact that the law mediates between its two negations – physical force, on the one hand, and human freedom, on the other. Law is the simultaneous negation of force and freedom – a hazardous enterprise. Awe arises from the fact that, in the court-room, the law itself is humbled. Law recognizes an author of its authority. The sub-religious ethos of the court-room reflects a latent recognition that the coherence of social systems derives from a source of coherence that transcends society.

The capacity of human beings to recognize order – the order of the physical universe, of society, of morality, of law, of human personality, of human consciousness – is the capacity to recognize the order of all order. And the order of the order of law is called *justice*. As they witness to the ideal of justice, courts, in everything they do, commit injustice. In all its abstracting of each unique human being from the unique particularity of his or her total physical and social and moral situation, the law does violence to the unique humanity of every human being. The justice of a given society, the social justice embodied in its law, is a shadow, and only a shadow, of the justice of all justice. Social justice negates justice in affirming it. In enforcing the abstract legal relations of a given society, the court offers to justice a sacrifice of some part of the life, the freedom, and the identity of actual human persons. A court is a place of sacrifice.

All the more necessary is it that the court, as powerfully as symbolism permits, conveys to the minds of accused and litigant, but also and especially to the minds of judge and advocate, a permanent warning that there is a justice above and beyond the justice of the law, that the law is always a means and never an end. The voice that is heard in the court-room is the voice of law (*lex loquens*). Its echo is the voice of justice (*ius loquens*).

THE INTERNATIONAL COURT AND JUSTICE

The International Court of Justice was conceived as, and is routinely perceived as, a *court of law*. The United Nations Charter establishes it as *the principal judicial organ of the United Nations*. The Statute of the Court refers to its members as *independent judges* and provides that its function is *to decide in accordance with international law such disputes as are submitted to it*. Decisions of the Court have *binding effect* between the parties to a case.

In addition to receiving the title of *court*, the International Court was given the formal characteristics and the symbolic attributes of a court that have been considered in the first part of this chapter. It is isolated physically, symbolically and systematically from the rest of international legal and social reality; and it reproduces faithfully many elements of the sign-system of the ideal-type court considered above.

However, there are fundamental characteristics of the Court, on the face of its constitutive texts (UN Charter and Statute), which make it necessary to question whether the International Court is a court of law, let alone a court of justice.

(1) *Only states may be parties in cases before the Court.*

(2) *The Court's jurisdiction comprises the cases that are submitted to the Court with the consent of the parties.*

(3) *The General Assembly and Security Council of the UN may request Advisory Opinions from the Court. Other organs of the UN and of UN Specialized Agencies may be authorized to do so by the General Assembly.*

(4) *The Court is directed to apply, in deciding disputes, the miscellany of materials referred to in article 38 of the Statute.*

(5) *The parties to the Statute of the Court are states members of the United Nations (and other states under certain conditions).*

A court epitomizes the *social* reality of the society of which it is an institution. A court epitomizes the *legal* reality whose legal relations it enforces. From the characteristics of a given court we can construct by extrapolation a picture of the legal reality and the social reality it serves. From the characteristics of the International Court that have been noted above, we may discover the nature of the international society of which it is an institution, at least the nature of that society as conceived by those who were responsible for establishing the Court and by those who participate day by day in its functioning.

The international society of which the Court is an institution is apparently a society that is conceived as a society of so-called *states*. This must mean that the social reality of the society is seen as a reality formed from the interaction of such states, and that the legal reality of that society is seen as a reality formed from legal relations among such states.

These inferences at once give rise to a gross problem of theoretical coherence, since a *state* is a conceptual construct, rather than a human being. States are figments of the human imagination, presences *in* consciousness, not *of* consciousness. They have no capacity to will and act in the way that human beings will and act. And yet, as considered above, social and legal reality are forms of consciousness; that is to say, they are an endlessly dynamic flow of potential and actual modifications of the consciousness of actual human beings. Where is the consciousness that is capable of forming an inter-statal social reality? What is the behaviour that is liable to be modified by the existence and application and enforcement of inter-statal legal relations?

The concept of *state* has become so central and so convenient a feature of human self-conceiving that it is now extremely difficult to unthink it, to deconstruct a concept apparently so stable, to identify its specific operational significance within human self-socializing.

The wording of the Court's Statute itself provides a point of departure in this difficult task. *Only states may be parties in cases before the Court.* What is the exclusionary force of the word *only* in Article 34(1)? Presumably it is designed to exclude non-state actors and hence to exclude from the Court's jurisdiction the interactions of non-state actors. If so, then there are two possible corollaries. Either so-called states are deemed to contain within themselves the interaction of all non-state actors, so that inter-statal legal reality (and hence inter-statal social reality) contains those interactions indirectly or virtually; or else the interactions of non-state actors are excluded from inter-statal legal and social reality.

The first corollary (let us call it the *one reality* concept) would mean that the inter-statal social and legal reality is regarded as containing an aggregation of all the total social realities of all the states. The second corollary (let us call it the *two realities* concept) would mean that *inter*-statal social and legal reality is regarded as being distinct from *intra*-statal legal and social realities.

It is a readily observable fact that the second corollary responds to the everyday conceiving of inter-statal society by those persons who participate routinely and professionally in that reality. The *two realities* view is also concordant with international law as it is presently conceived at the fundamental systematic level.

(1) International law relies on no theory of *representation* to condition the participation of a state in the international legal system. It is not necessary to show that a given state has subordinate systems which make it possible for the state to represent inter-statally the total social reality of that state. In particular, international law takes no structural-systematic account of non-statal nations and ethnic groups.

(2) International law recognizes an area of what it calls *domestic jurisdiction*, a concept whose operational significance is precisely to establish a contrast with an area of inter-statal transactions which is the area of international law.

(3) Powerful structural concepts of international law such as *sovereignty*, *sovereign equality*, *political independence* and *non-intervention* are designed to install into the systematic structure of international law the notional and closed conceptual category of the *state*.

(4) International law relies on no theoretical structure establishing a relation-ship between international law and so-called *municipal law* (i.e. the internal legal system of a state). It simply assumes that, from the perspective of international law, international law prevails over municipal law.

(5) Seen from the perspective of the intra–statal social and legal reality of a particular state, inter–statal interactions are conceived as taking place in a systematically different process from intra–statal interactions, namely in what is perceived as a sphere of *foreign policy and diplomacy*, and not within the general constitutional and political systems of the states or their general social and legal realities.

(6) There are countless *extra-statal interactions*, especially economic trans-actions, that seem to fall systematically within neither the inter–statal system nor any particular intra–statal system or systems. Such interactions are routinely treated as anomalous and problematic in relation to the theoretical structures of both the inter–statal and the intra–statal systems.

The concept of *state* as a self-standing, reified, objectified, personified, real entity is an interesting relic of the social and legal reality of medieval Europe. From the twin sources of Roman law and Christian theological metaphysics, the medieval intellectual had an obsessive tendency to treat notional entities, especially social entities, as real entities – the Church of Rome, the papacy, universities, religious orders, towns, manors. Although medieval philosophers themselves eventually deconstructed and exposed this behaviour cogently, not to say passionately (in the so-called *nominalist* critique of so-called *realism*), the practice proved too useful to abandon. As modern societies developed in systematic complexity and in social energy, heroic efforts of conceptualizing and reconceptualizing were called for, and notional real entities were prolifically generated to meet the need.

Metaphysical realism was resurrected in the naturalist fallacy the human sciences have been propagating for the last 160 years, led by the new priest-class in the professionalized universities. The naturalist fallacy treats the works of human consciousness, including social phenomena, as if they were processes of the natural world. The new naturalism has become a new fatalism, suggesting that things human (including states, and war, and global social injustice) are as they are, and will be as they have been.

The concept of *state* found itself in lively conceptual symbiosis with two other notional real entities – *nation* and *society* – and an especially powerful illusion was created. It came to seem, and it still seems to most people, that *state* is analogous to nation or society in being some self-contained and complete social reality. From sometime late in the eighteenth century (and

29

certainly from the time of Hegel onwards), it came to seem that the *state* might and even will act like a human individual, generating behavioural interactions analogous to those of human individuals. And so it came to seem possible that there could be a social reality, and even a legal reality, formed by and of the interactions of states.

The process by which a second social and legal reality, formed from the interaction of *states*, established itself is extremely complex, intellectually and historically. It is a process that has had profound world-historical consequences.

Internally, seen from within a given society, *state* came to refer to a particular aspect of the development of certain societies, namely the systematic separation of a *public realm* from the rest of social and legal reality. This development occurred especially in certain societies in western Europe, as part of the process of rapid social development that increased in momentum from, say, the middle of the fifteenth century, and which would culminate in what have come to be seen as the characteristic social systems of what is called *the modern world* or *modernity*.

Distinct systems within social self-constituting were developed whose function was to act on behalf of society as a whole. A class of society members (whom Hegel would identify as the *universal* class) would play a second role in society, beyond their general role as society members. They would be agents of society's universalizing, using all available methods of social constituting. In particular, legal relations, especially in the form of *legal powers*, would be used abundantly to channel vast quantities of social power into the direct and explicit pursuit of society's public interest.

The concept of *state* is operationally distinct from the concepts of *society* and *nation* but, over time, it managed to assimilate, by association or confusion or conceptual osmosis, something of the content of both those concepts.

What *state* borrowed from *society* was some sense of *social integrity*. *Society* is a generic concept referring to forms of human self-socializing (including families, commercial and industrial corporations, socially constituted nations) which involve the constituting of a structure-system that persists over time in the consciousness of its members (human individuals and subordinate societies), even though its membership may be constantly changing. As considered in the first part of this chapter, the social structure-system creates its own social reality, including the values and purposes embodied in its legal self-constituting, that is to say, in legal relations.

What *state* borrowed from *nation* was some sense of *social subjectivity*. *Nation* is a generic concept referring to a form of human self-identifying which is collective in character, but which profoundly affects the consciousness of its members, becoming an integral part of their personal self-identifying and giving rise to significant and often dynamic effects on their behaviour. Membership of a nation typically, but not exclusively, arises by *birth within* the given social group. A nation (including ethnic and religious groups) may or may not constitute itself as a society and may be present within one or more constituted societies.

The result was that *state* developed simultaneously along two separate but converging tracks. It came to be used as an expression for the *totality* of a society that contained a *public realm* organized in a particular way, that is to say, in which the public interest is the direct responsibility of those having special social powers for that purpose. The *state* as a social totality contained the *state* as distinctive social sub-system.

These developments made possible, but not inevitable, the development of what we have called the second (inter-statal) social and legal reality. What happened was that the internal public realms were externalized to form the inter-statal and legal reality.

A state is simply the public realm of a certain kind of society recognized as such by the public realms of other such societies.

International society came to be the society of the public realms of the participating states. The social subjectivity of the participating states would be expressed by the willing and acting of what came to be called the *governments* of those states (that is to say, the professional controllers of the public realms). All the rest of social and legal reality was, and is, excluded from inter-statal international society, and all other societies and human beings were, and are, not participants in that society. Humanity must see itself in all its immeasurable complexity – billions of human beings, thousands of cultures, countless societies – as an aggregation of states, its future determined by the self-seeking of fewer than two hundred public realms, themselves the fortuitous products of history.

Thus, the established conceptual model of international social reality may be expressed, in summary form, as follows:

(1) international society = inter-statal society = the interaction of states
(2) for the purposes of *(1): state = the reified personified 'state' (RPS) = the public realm externalized (PRE) > represented by the executive branch of government (EBG)*

We may refer to this model of international social reality as the

$$RPS = PRE > EBG \text{ model. (Read > as 'through'.)}$$

Seen from the ideological perspective of the late twentieth century, it might be expected that such an international social reality would have generated a legal reality dominated by two familiar conceptual structures: the rule of law and public law (constitutional law and administrative law). In other words, it might have been expected that the problem of international law would have been seen as a problem directly analogous to the problem of bringing government under law *within* a statally organized society – above all, the problem of preventing the abuse of legal power by public-realm agencies and persons.

Instead, the international legal reality is based on a more ancient model: that of feudal landholding. The fundamental structural concept of international law is the model of relations between neighbouring estate-owners. The relevant substantive legal analogies are property law, contract law and aspects of tort (delict) law. Municipal law of each state is seen as the local law of a particular manor-estate.

The $RPS = PRE > EBG$ model of international social reality took root in western European consciousness in the last quarter of the eighteenth century. The Congress of Vienna may be taken as a grandiose symbolic manifestation of the transition from the old (post-medieval/pre-revolutionary) world to the so-called modern world. The monarchs and their acolytes were beginning to recede as personifications of their nations. Politicians, diplomats and bureaucrats were moving towards centre-stage as the representatives of their 'states'. But, within at least the more economically developed societies, legal reality was responding to the new situation in two striking and closely related ways: social transformation through legislation, and judicial control of the executive branch of government.

The nineteenth century would see the revolutionary social transformation of one European society after another through the process of legislation, that is to say, instant, rationalistic law-making for explicit social purposes. Obviously, new (post-1776/1789) conceptual models of public participation through representation were useful in mobilizing the consent of the mass of the people to such a dramatic increase in the density and authority of legal reality.

In the closely related British and American legal realities, the courts had developed, over the same period, a revolutionary legal concept, which came to be known as the principle of the rule of law. (More strictly, perhaps, we should say that they had brought to the surface of legal consciousness, and then systematized, an ancient principle of English common law). On the continent of Europe, similar developments occurred, establishing the analogous principle of *Rechtsstaat* or *état de droit*.

The principle of the rule of law is that all government is under the law, that even the powers of the executive branch of government (whether or not they are still exercised in the name of the monarch) are subject to the control of systematically independent courts. The rule of law means that the last word on the application and enforcement of every single legal relation, including legal relations involving public authorities, rests with the courts. Or, in other words, when the public interest has been incorporated in a universalizing legal relation, the courts (and not the executive branch of government) will determine finally what is the public interest.

Under the inspiration of Napoleon Bonaparte, who was in this, as in so many other things, the embodiment of the spirit of the age, French legal reality developed in a direction in which Britain and the United States would not follow for a century and more. The idea of administrative law respects the principle of the rule of law, but does so by asserting that legal reality must deal in a quite special way with the extraordinary legal powers of government. There was a sense in which, as a matter of the *real* constitution, if not of the *legal* constitution (which attributed such action to 'the representatives of the people'), executive branches of government were giving legal powers *to themselves* through legislation. It was presciently understood in one continental European legal system after another, and finally in Britain and the United States, that political processes – the day-to-day dialectical struggle of the real constitution in implementation of the legal constitution – might be enough to legitimize the *conferring* of legal powers. Only courts, conceived and perceived as systematic equals of legislature and executive (one facet of the complex principle of the separation of powers) could legitimize the *application and enforcement* of public legal powers.

To insert law-above-power into an international social reality of the *RPS = PRE > EBG* variety is obviously a formidable intellectual challenge. How can superordinate law be applied to what is seen as a co-ordinate society of states? To this day, no satisfactory answer to this question has been found. Indeed, in the period since 1945, the role of international law has declined under the impact of three developments in international social reality which have, as an incidental consequence, left the International Court as a dignified monument of an obsolete social reality.

(1) The theoretical foundations of customary international law have more or less evaporated in a cloud of anomalous confusion.
(2) Since 1945 a formidable new global public realm has been created, a public realm subject neither to the rule of law nor to an international public law.

(3) Since 1945 a new international social reality has been developing, a social reality to which traditional international law and its institutions are largely irrelevant, but which contains extraordinary potentialities for international law and an International Court.

Theoretical foundations

As *intra-statal* legal systems developed ever more complex conceptions of the relationship between society and law, especially in the theories of liberal democracy, and then later of Marxism and socialism, the conceptualization of *inter-statal* international society developed quite separately.

The deplorable article 38 of the Court's Statute (reproducing a provision from the Statute of the Permanent Court) has proved sadly prophetic. The last phrase of 38(1)(d) suggests that paragraph 1 as a whole is intended to identify 'means for the determination of rules of law'. The word 'determination' is ambiguous. What article 38(1) certainly does not do is to state with authority the law-*making* processes of international law, that is to say, the legal relations by which international legal relations are created. What it has turned out to be is an appropriate description of the disorderly and intellectually incoherent ways in which international lawyers and tribunals cobble together what they call the 'rules' of international law.

For some time natural law seemed to provide a way of evading, if not resolving, the problem. In a potent mixture of Platonic idealism, Aristotelian essentialism, Stoic universalism, Christian theocraticism, rationalist apriorism and a Grotian ironic empiricism, the natural-law model managed to generate a law without a legislator, a law above law, a law for all times and places. It seemed to follow that the interaction of states could be, or even must be, seen as subject to such law. Some time in the eighteenth century, the spirit of the age detached itself from the natural-law model – the spirit of a new age of sceptical rationalism, secularism, materialism, Lockeian empiricism and pragmatism. International law half-rescued itself conceptually by taking up two new–old conceptual models – custom and consent. And it thereby doomed itself to intellectual confusion and functional impotence, conditions which have persisted until the present day.

It follows from the nature of legal relations considered in the first part of this chapter that a legal reality must contain systems for the creation of legal relations that are specific and certain. It must be possible for potential participants in legal relations to know in principle how social powers may be transformed into legal relations. If not, then the law cannot have its specific reality-transforming effect. Up until the earlier part of this century, international lawyers convinced themselves (and perhaps governments) that there were two specific and certain processes for the creation of international legal relations – customary international law and treaties (neither of which, however, is mentioned accurately in article 38). In the positivist spirit of the times, these seemed to need little in the way of subtle theoretical justification. They proved themselves in practice.

This benign, if intellectually inadequate, state of affairs was unsettled not only by academic commentators but also by the International Court itself, and its predecessor, the Permanent Court, on those rare occasions when they have found it necessary to express opinions relating to the theoretical foundations of international law. In particular, they have encouraged the idea that customary international law is merely the self-limitation of inherently free legal entities (states), and the idea that *custom* and *consent* are somehow inter-changeable concepts, and even that the subtle idea of *opinio iuris* should be understood as some sort of crude subjective and pragmatic quality-test of rules of international law.

This is not the place to discuss these matters further. Suffice it to say that it is not possible to create a coherent model of a legal system that uses both *custom* and *consent* in unresolved confusion as the basis of non-contractual legal relations. Even in liberal democratic theory, some of whose ideology (including natural freedom and government by consent) was cynically appropriated by international law, the notion of consent does not refer to any particular attitude to particular legal relations on the part of those who are subject to the law. Consent is a word that seeks to express in the most concentrated possible form the participation of the members of a society in, and in the formation of, the social and legal reality of that society. In relation to the legal reality, the only relevant directly voluntarist acts are the choosing by a person to exercise legal power (which always involves a legally significant choice of action) and the choosing to place oneself within a legal relation (by becoming a voter or a parent or a car-driver or whatever it may be). The idea of attaching law-making effect to the subjective attitudes of states (which cannot possibly have such things) or even governments (whose states of mind are unascertainable) is ludicrous.

In a customary-law system (as it is best understood, that is to say, as under-stood in the spirit of Kantian critical philosophy), each participant is a legislator in the sense that the law arises as the universalizing of particular behaviour. A customary-law system is doing implicitly what a legislative-law system does explicitly and institutionally – it universalizes patterns of behaviour (in the form of legal relations) in pursuit of the public interest as determined by the values and purposes of the given society, and as an effect of the justice-seeking of all human self-ordering.

Having now no credible theoretical basis of law-making, international law has been overwhelmed by a flood of incoherences and anomalies: higher international law (human rights, *ius cogens*, *erga omnes* obligations), the relevance of the so-called recognition of states, the category of 'non-recognition', the status of the individual human being, the status of non-statal social groups (nations, peoples, ethnic groups), self-determination, *res communis* (commons, common heritage), *terra nullius*, the status of industrial and commercial corporations in relation to states, the immunity of states from intra-statal jurisdiction, the *erga omnes* legislative effect of treaties and of acts of inter-governmental institutions, *soft law*, the abuse of power by international institutions, the category of 'international crime', self-help, self-defence, so-called countermeasures, intervention (armed or otherwise) in the territory of another state, the categories of 'war' and 'neutrality', transboundary environmental phenomena, inter-generational responsibility.

None of these is a marginal phenomenon which, like adding epicycles to the Ptolemaic system of the universe, can be resolved by one botched compromise after another with traditional international law. They are symptoms of the chronic disintegration of the foundations of international law in its traditional form.

Global public realm

Since 1945 a third social and legal reality has developed, beyond the intra-societal and inter-statal realities. It is a reality that contains a global public realm formed from the activities of intergovernmental organizations. It is a state of states, a many-headed leviathan of leviathans, controlled by a global universal class of public officials in their thousands, spending billions of ECU of money provided by the taxpayers of the world, taking decisions that determine the lives of all human beings everywhere. And it is a public realm virtually unaccountable to the people of the world, politically and legally. It is a development that puts the society of the whole human race into a pre-revolutionary state, posing the sort of challenge that was faced by the post-medieval societies of western Europe.

The systematic progress of the development has been as follows.

intra-societal social reality $->$ *intra-societal public realm* $->$ *internal state[1]* $->$ *externalized public realm* $->$ *inter-statal state[2]* $->$ *inter-statal society* $->$ *global public realm* $->$ *global state[3]* $->$ *global social reality* $->$ *global state[3] internalized (GS³I) in state[1] and state[2].*

We may call this the GS³I model of social reality (read as 'G–S–3–I').

In summary form, we may say that $RPS = PRE > EBG$ has begotten GS³I. The human world is now a GS³I world, in which the internal social reality of statally organized societies is now substantially determined by the activities of a global public realm.

A significant feature of the global super-state is that it treats state-frontiers as permeable. IMF/IBRD treat the internal economies of state societies as matters of global concern. The participants in the UN Security Council now seem to interpret its Chapter VII key-code (*international peace and security*) as covering any global public-order problem anywhere; they seem to believe that the limits of its legal powers are set by their own judgement of expediency. The new World Trade Organization is set to become another great empire of the global public realm, concerning itself with any public-realm matter anywhere that may affect international trade.

The most revealing and poignant instance has been the development of the European Community into the European Union. The EC was established as a public realm shared by the member states. But that public realm was established within a constitutional structure which included other fundamental elements of post-1789 social and legal reality, including forms of political and legal accountability. In particular, the EEC Treaty recognized the principle of the rule of law (article 164) and established a system of administrative law (articles 173 and 175). Above all, the EC contained a Court of Justice which proved to be a strong and creative instrument for the development of the EC's legal reality.

The new EU, on the other hand, has been constructed as a parallel shared public realm in certain ill-defined fields (justice, home affairs, foreign policy, security) which has been placed outside the EC constitutional structure and which is not subject to the jurisdiction of the Court of Justice. In other words, the so-called *intergovernmentalism* of the EU actually means the creation of an external public realm which will exist in a sort of social and legal limbo, part of neither the intra-statal nor the inter-statal constitutional systems, not clearly subject to national law, EC law or international law. It is a brazen act of anachronistic defiance by the executive branches of the governments of the member states, which might have won the approval of a Tudor–Bourbon–Hohenzollern–Romanov–Habsburg monarch.

The global public realm has been created by treaties, and so, at first glance, seems to be a phenomenon of international law. But the torrent of legal texts that establish the intergovernmental systems and which are generated by them are better regarded as legislative in character. They are reminiscent of the society-making legislation that transformed certain rapidly developing societies in the nineteenth century and which has been referred to above.

More precisely, since such global social engineering takes place in what is virtually a political vacuum filled by bureaucratic rationalism, they should be regarded as executive decrees negotiated among the externalized public realms. The global public realm already exhibits the self-absorbed character-istics (familiar from the histories of China, Byzantium, Austria–Hungary, Russia, Prussia and pre-Weimar Germany) of bureaucracies that are not supported by adequate political processes.

It is obvious that traditional international law, with its aura of feudal landholding and its repertory of timorous civil-law analogies, can do next to nothing to establish itself as a power-above-power in relation to such an overwhelmingly dense and dynamic phenomenon. And the International Court, as an inter-manorial feudal court, is not well adapted to take power over the novel legal reality of a new global super-state.

Global social reality

Since 1945, the total social reality of the human world has been changing profoundly. It is this that gives rise to the possibility that the future of humanity will no longer be determined merely as the by-product of the barely socialized interaction of *states*. The survival and prospering of all human beings everywhere will become the ideal, and the everyday purpose, of a true inter-national society of which the global public realm and statally organized societies may continue to be subordinate social systems.

We are now able, at the end of the twentieth century, to identify a *fourth reality*, beyond the inter-statal reality and beyond the reality of the new global public realm.

> *reality*[1] – intra-societal reality;
>
> *reality*[2] – inter-statal reality (the interaction of externalized public realms);
>
> *reality*[3] – the reality of the global public realm (the product of *reality*[2], but taking effect also in *reality*[1]);
>
> *reality*[4] – human reality, the reality of the international society, the society of all societies and of the whole human race.

Needless to say, beyond *reality*[1] there is *reality*[0] (individual consciousness), and beyond *reality*[4] there is *reality*[n] (the physical universe as humanly conceived, and putative non-physical realities thereafter).

We may expect, and we must do what we can to ensure, that the new fourth reality, as the other social realities have done, will generate within itself a new legal reality which will at last be a true international law, and that a reconceived International Court will be at the summit of the new legal system, using the wonderful capacities of a court to mediate between the human universal and the human particular, helping to realize the human ideal through the power of the legal.

The new human social reality contains, first and foremost, the world-wide *economic* reality through which the world is transformed with a view to human survival and prospering. As in statally organized societies, the international economy contains social power that exceeds the social power of the public realm, a power which social reality, including the law, must organize and orientate in the public interest.

Second, the new human reality contains the power of *non-governmental organizations and actors* of all kinds, seeking to contribute to human survival and prospering outside the public realm. They will participate fully in forming the new social reality and they will have appropriate *locus standi* before the institutions of the new legal reality.

And, third, the new human reality contains an *international culture*, the inter-action of human consciousness all over the world, including, as in any society, an unending dialectical struggle to establish the ideals and values and purposes of human society. In particular, it is the place where the idea-complexes of liberal democracy and capitalism will struggle to survive as world-scale phenomena or will undergo new developments in the interaction of countless cultures, religions and systems of value.

Historically, supreme courts have, again and again, proved themselves to be deep wells of unexpected potentiality. Even when they have seemed to be somnolent lackeys of a reactionary ruling class, they have often responded to new social realities sooner and more creatively than other agents of that class. It is as if the peculiar charisma of a court, engendered by all that has been considered in the first part of this chapter, can give to judges the grace to recognize that they have a higher purpose than to serve the current power-holders of the public realm.

There is nothing to prevent the International Court from reconceiving itself as a global supreme court, or from reconceiving the problems of inter-statal society in terms of constitutional and administrative law. There is nothing to prevent the Court from reimagining itself as a source of a new legal reality, of a true international law, which is not merely a system for aggregating the so-called *interests* of so-called *states* in a wasteland of injustice. The true international law is the actualizing in the form of legal relations of the public interest of the true international society, the society of all societies, the society of the whole human race. In the hallowed halls of the International Court of Justice there might be heard the voice of true law echoing at last the world-transforming voice of justice.

3

The London Committee and the Statute of the International Court of Justice

Geoffrey Marston

༄

INTRODUCTION

The history of the evolution of the Statute of the International Court of Justice through the work first of the United Nations Committee of Jurists in Washington in 1944 and thereafter of Commission IV of the United Nations Conference on International Organization in San Francisco in 1945 is well documented.[1] The initiative in 1943–4 of the Informal Inter-Allied Committee on the Future of the Permanent Court of International Justice (hereafter the London Committee) is not so well known. This chapter seeks to describe this initiative and to assess its influence during the preparatory work of the Statute of the International Court of Justice.

THE PERMANENT COURT IN EXILE

On the German invasion of the Netherlands in May 1940, J. G. Guerrero, the President of the Permanent Court of International Justice, J. L. Oliván, its Registrar, and three officials moved from The Hague to Geneva. Of the other judges, those who were able to return to their countries of origin did so, including the judge of British nationality, Vice-President Sir Cecil Hurst. The war had already seriously affected the finances of the League of Nations. Its budget for 1940 imposed salary cuts on the judges, a measure with which the judges had agreed.[2] It was now proposed in the budget for 1941 to reduce still further the allocation for the Court. To this end the report of the League's Supervisory Commission appealed to 'the spirit of understanding' which the

---

[1] See, e.g., *Documents of the United Nations Conference on International Organization, San Francisco, 1945* (UN, New York, 1945–55, 21 vols); hereafter UNCIO), particularly vols XIII and XIV.

[2] *16th Report of the Permanent Court of International Justice*, letter of 17 November 1939 from the President to the Secretary-General (PCIJ, Series E, No. 16, p. 257).

judges had already shown.³ Guerrero and Oliván, having consulted by letter those judges who could be reached, drew up a draft budget for the Court. In an accompanying report dated 11 December 1940,⁴ they stated that the judges consulted had 'unanimously agreed upon the necessity of keeping the Court in existence' and that it was essential to preserve a nucleus consisting of the President, the Registrar and a small number of officials. The report went on: 'In order to achieve this object which they regard as of vital importance, the members of the Court are prepared to make all the necessary sacrifices.' The sacrifices consisted of the suspension of the payment of salaries, although if a judge so wished he could receive 500 Swiss francs a month 'on account'. The President, who had to reside at the seat of the Court throughout the year, was to receive a special allowance together with one-third of his salary, again 'on account'. Furthermore, the services of a considerable proportion of the staff were to be terminated, leaving only the Registrar and five officials.

On 13 December 1940, Guerrero wrote from the Hotel Richemond in Geneva to Hurst, informing him of the steps he had taken, concluding with the words 'provided that I continue to enjoy the confidence of my colleagues, I shall not lack the determination to meet [difficulties] with the single aim of preserving the existence of our institution'.⁵ Hurst replied on 24 December 1940, accepting Guerrero's proposals. He added: 'It seems to me to be important with a view to the ultimate peace settlement that the Court as an institution should remain in being. Whether it can function during the period of hostilities is another matter.'⁶ On the same day, Hurst wrote to Oliván complaining that he had not received any pay since the previous May and that 'it is inconvenient being left without money for so long'.⁷

In order to communicate with the President and the Registrar, Hurst used the secretarial and transmission facilities of his former place of work, the British Foreign Office in London, where he had been legal adviser before his election to the Court in September 1929. Thus Hurst's plight quickly became known to Foreign Office officials and particularly to the current legal adviser, Sir William Malkin. At Malkin's initiative, an approach was made to the Treasury for Hurst to be paid his United Kingdom civil service pension, which had been held in abeyance while he occupied his seat on the Court. The Treasury,

---

³ *Ibid.*, pp. 260–1.
⁴ *Ibid.*, pp. 260–3.
⁵ PRO ref. FO 371/26643 [C381/42/98/1941]. (References to UK archival papers are to records preserved in the Public Record Office (PRO), London. The original departmental file and papers numbers are given in square brackets after the PRO references).
⁶ *Ibid.* [C42/42/98/1941].
⁷ *Ibid.*

however, declared it had no power to make payment while Hurst remained a judge.[8]

On 6 March 1941, a meeting was held in the Foreign Office between Malkin, Hurst, Sir G. Kisch, the British member on the League Supervisory Commission, and Roger Makins (now Lord Sherfield), then a counsellor in the Foreign Office, on the subject of the Court's budget, and particularly the payments to judges, a matter made more acute by the revelation that Guerrero was now claiming the 'handsome salary' of 52,000 Swiss francs. To Malkin there was a wider implication in the possibility that Hurst, in order to get his civil service pension released, might resign from the Court, namely that other judges faced with similar problems might do the same and thus contribute to the Court's disintegration.[9] During the meeting some discussion about the Court's future took place. It was agreed that it was in the general interest that the Court should not be dissolved, thus implying that there should be, in theory at any rate, a cadre of judges available to meet and discharge its function. Hurst added that it might facilitate the future negotiations for the re-establishment of an international court 'if some at all events of the judges of the present Court had disappeared and were not present to claim that they were able to remain on until their successors were appointed'.[10]

MALKIN'S SUGGESTION OF AN INTER-ALLIED COMMITTEE

Malkin continued to give thought to the future of the Permanent Court and on 19 September 1941 he addressed a minute to Sir Alexander Cadogan, the Permanent Under-Secretary of State at the Foreign Office, William Strang, an Assistant Under-Secretary, and Makins, which is worthy of extensive citation.[11] Malkin wrote that he had been considering the future of the Court 'which is a matter which will require to be dealt with in or at any rate very soon after the peace settlement'. He continued:

[8] Treasury to Makins, 27 February 1941 (*ibid*. [C2327/42/98/1941]).
[9] Malkin to Makins, 18 February 1941; Makins to Treasury, 25 February 1941 (*ibid*. [C1696/42/98/1941]).
[10] Malkin's note of the meeting (*ibid*. [C2309/42/98/1941]). A new election of all the members of the Court had been due in September 1939 but had not been held. Consequently, under article 13(3) of the Court's Statute, the judges elected in 1930 and at by-elections thereafter continued to discharge their duties. Hurst consented to 'stand the loss and continue in office, at least for the time being'.
[11] *Ibid*. [C11521/43/98/1941]. The correspondence between Malkin and Hurst, Fischer Williams and Noel Baker was said by Malkin (*ibid*.) to be in an attached file. This file, which would seem to have been a private file of Malkin, was not registered in the Foreign Office official papers and has not been located.

My idea was that it was a question which we and the Allies might be considering with a view to seeing whether agreement could be reached as to the objects to be aimed at. It may be objected that this is somewhat premature in existing circumstances, but on the other hand as time goes on more urgent questions will arise as to which we shall want to discuss our 'peace settlement policy' with the Allies, so there is something to be said for getting on with any questions which can be considered now. I think the Permanent Court is one of these, since the only assumption which it is necessary to make is that the state of the world after the war will be such that some form of international tribunal will be desirable.

By way of a start I prepared the attached questionnaire as an attempt to cover the points which seemed to require discussion. I sent this to Sir C. Hurst for his observations, and have now received them, together with those of Sir J. Fischer Williams and Mr Noel Baker, whom he consulted . . .

The question now arises what, if anything, should be done next. Sir C. Hurst suggests that 'those who are interested in the future of the Court' should prepare 'a draft of a revised edition of the Statute, embodying so much of the changes recommended as H[is] M[ajesty's] G[overnment] are prepared to endorse and to make it the subject of discussion with some or all of the Allied powers'. I do not myself feel that we are ready for this. Apart from ourselves and the three people who have already been consulted, I can think of no one (with the possible exception of Lord Cecil, and there are I believe objections to bringing him into this sort of discussion) whose views would be of value to H.M.G.; I do not know what you feel, but personally I should expect to be in a better position to advise after there had been consultation with the Allies than before, and I do not feel able to make definite recommendations as to the policy of H.M.G. at the present stage.

What I am disposed to suggest therefore, if it is thought that the subject is worth pursuing, is that the Allies should be invited to appoint representatives (not more than one for each country) to constitute a small and I suggest rather informal committee to look into the matter. It would I think be essential that it should be regarded as an expert committee the members of which were not entitled to bind their Governments, so that each Government would be able to approve, modify or reject any recommendations which might emerge. One difficulty is that some at any rate of the Allies might find it difficult to produce anyone who knew anything about the subject, but this situation is likely to continue until their territories are liberated.

Malkin concluded:

It would be necessary to consider whether all the Allies should be invited. The Free French should I think certainly be included, but it may be doubtful whether it is worth while to invite Luxemburg: Ethiopia can no doubt be left out, even if she becomes a full 'Ally' in the near future. The Soviet Government have so far somewhat ostentatiously declined to have anything to do with either the Permanent Court or any form of judicial settlement of international disputes, and this would no doubt be a reason for not inviting them; but on the other hand, if it is thought likely that they will be called upon to play in future a larger part in keeping the world in order, this may be a reason for trying to interest them in this particular form of international activity.

Malkin's questionnaire comprised twenty questions.[12] The first asked whether the Permanent Court should be connected with an international organization, such as the League of Nations, or should be completely independent. Other questions related to the composition, qualifications, nomination, election and independence of its members. Another question asked whether the present system of producing the judgment of the Court was satisfactory, particularly whether the practice of permitting dissenting judgments should be continued. Question 18 read:

> One result of the war may be to produce considerable changes in international life as it has been known for the last century or so. If so, a good deal of international law as found in the books may become obsolete. What steps, if any, are possible and desirable to ensure that the Court recognises this fact?

Question 19 asked:

> Is it or is it not desirable that the Court should become to a much greater extent than at present a law-making body?

THE OVERTURES TO THE UNITED STATES

In response to Malkin's minute, Roger Makins, in a minute dated 21 September 1941,[13] noted that whereas reflection on the future political organization of Europe and the world was apt to be rather barren, the future form of an international tribunal was an exception. He thought that a committee of Allied representatives, including the Soviet Union, should be convened under the chairmanship of Malkin. He added that it would be well to enquire whether the United States would like to be represented.

After Strang and Cadogan had written supporting minutes, the Secretary of State for Foreign Affairs, Anthony Eden, wrote on the file on 9 October 1941:[14] 'Yes, I think better consult US Government first. Will Sir A. Cadogan please speak to Mr H. Johnson.' Cadogan accordingly handed a copy of a memorandum on the subject to Herschel Johnson, chargé d'affaires at the US Embassy in London who, having communicated with the State Department in Washington, in due course transmitted to the Foreign Office the State Department's reply dated 4 November 1941. It read:

---

[12] *Ibid.* [13] *Ibid.* [14] *Ibid.*

Prior to making a definitive decision whether the United States Government will desire to participate in the proposed joint study by the Governments of Great Britain and its Allies of the question which was raised by Sir Alexander Cadogan regarding a future international juridical organization and what form participation should take, the Department of State would appreciate having some indication concerning the extent to which the studies of the Foreign Office have advanced and concerning the considerations which the British Government proposes to employ in determining whether the existing statute of the Permanent Court of International Justice would be adequate for the purpose. The Department would also like to know, since this question opens necessarily for examination the entire problem of international political organization after the war, what reasons the British Government may have in mind for approaching this problem by first studying the question of the future of the Court. Are we correct finally in assuming that the proposed inquiry will be entirely advisory in nature?[15]

The Foreign Office sent a response, drafted by Malkin, to the Embassy stating that as to question 1 the stage had been reached only of formulating the questionnaire; as to question 2 the future of the Court could be studied independently of other questions relating to post-war organization, 'since the only assumption which had to be made was that the future condition of the world would be such that the existence of an international Court would be desirable'; as to question 3 the answer was yes.[16]

No immediate response came from the United States side. On 23 July 1942, however, the US Secretary of State, Cordell Hull, gave a speech to the nation in Washington.[17] In it, he stated that 'it is plain fact that some international agency must be created which can – by force if necessary – keep the peace among the nations in the future'. A little later in his speech, Hull remarked: 'The settlement of disputes by peaceful means, indeed all processes of international cooperation, presuppose respect for law obligations. It is plain that one of the institutions which must be established and given vitality is an international court of justice.' The Hull speech may have been evidence of further activity on the matter within the State Department, for on 21 August 1942 the Counsellor at the US Embassy in London, Freeman Matthews, communicated to the Foreign Office the following message:

---

[15] *Ibid.* [C12412/42/98/1941].

[16] *Ibid.*

[17] Its full text was published in London in *The Times*, 24 July 1942. Hull's speech provided the occasion for a written answer in the House of Commons by Eden in which he stated that His Majesty's Government was 'entirely in favour of the establishment, or re-establishment, after the war of an International Court of Justice' (*Parliamentary Debates*, 5th series, House of Commons, vol. 382, col. 477 (29 July 1944)).

We have now received a brief word from the Department of State. The Department feels that machinery for the orderly and judicial determination of justiciable questions should constitute a part of post-war international organization. It is of the opinion that until the nature of the broader organization may be examined it would seem premature to undertake to express views as to the nature of the dependent question of a judicial organization, the scope of its jurisdiction, or the law to be administered. The Department prefers, therefore, not to comment at this time upon the several questions presented in your memorandum of last March.

I am sorry not to be able to give you a more encouraging answer.[18]

Malkin minuted on 14 September 1942[19] that this response was 'very short-sighted (and somewhat difficult to reconcile with Hull's recent statement)'. He added: 'It seems extremely probable that the question whether an attempt should be made to hold an election for the Court, which will be years over-due at the end of the war, will have to be considered fairly soon after the termination of hostilities, and the position will be even more difficult than it would be anyhow if no previous consideration had been given to the question of the Court by the countries concerned.'

Strang, too, in a letter sent to the British chargé d'affaires in Washington, Sir R. I. Campbell, on 24 September 1942, described the response as 'entirely negative'.[20] Strang gave a history of the relevant events and continued:

In view of this United States attitude we do not feel that we can now proceed to discuss the matter with the remaining Allied Governments. This decision we have only taken very reluctantly since we still think that the problems connected with the Permanent Court can properly be considered in isolation and that it would be wise to give some thought to them before the end of the war. In our view the attitude of the State Department is rather short-sighted and also somewhat difficult to reconcile with Hull's recent statement.

While concluding that there was no advantage in pursuing the subject further in Washington with the State Department or in London with the Embassy before the United States elections in November 1942, Strang asked Campbell whether the question might be discussed with the US Attorney-General, Francis Biddle.[21] On 2 November 1942, Campbell replied[22] that it had been thought within the British Embassy that such an approach might be perceived on the American side as going behind the back of the State Department and

---

[18] PRO ref. FO 371/31000 [C8721/3672/98/1942].

[19] *Ibid.*

[20] *Ibid.*

[21] Strang wrote of Biddle that 'we have reason to believe that he might be interested in the subject and might be willing to re-open the question with the State Department'.

[22] *Ibid.* [C11017/3672/98/1942].

that a better procedure was for the Ambassador to send Hull a memorandum based on Strang's letter, while at the same time expressing the hope that the State Department might be prepared to give further consideration to the matter; this had in fact been done on 21 October 1942 and Hull had expressed 'considerable interest'. The Embassy's strategy bore fruit, for the State Department sent a memorandum dated 16 November 1942 to the British Embassy in Washington which read in material part as follows:

> The Department of State agrees with the views of the Foreign Office that steps should be taken to examine problems connected with the Court; that the question is one which it will be necessary to consider in connection with any peace settlement; and that there would be advantage in reaching in advance an understanding among the associated governments on desired objectives.
>
> The Department is now making a study of the situation but it feels, as previously stated, that since the Court should be so patterned as to conform to the international post-war organization, any consideration of the subject in advance of a formulation of views as to the nature of that organization must necessarily be highly speculative.
>
> While the Department offers no objection to the desire of the Foreign Office to create an informal committee to examine the matter, it feels that it would not be prepared at this stage of its study of the question to participate to advantage in its deliberations. When the Department shall have further explored the subject, it will be glad to inform the British Government and to exchange views with that and other interested governments.[23]

In sending to the Foreign Office the text of the above note, Campbell stated[24] that although it was disappointing that the US was unable to take part in the proposed discussion, the reply was more encouraging than the negative message of 21 August.

THE ESTABLISHMENT AND WORK OF THE LONDON COMMITTEE

Within the Foreign Office it was considered that there was no further major obstacle to the holding of an inter-allied meeting. Accordingly, in January 1943, invitations were sent[25] to the heads of allied governments in London,

23 *Ibid*. [C11754/3672/98/1942].   24 *Ibid*.

25 *Ibid*. Malkin abandoned 'the idea of a committee representing the United Nations' and confined it to 'a certain number of experts who happen to be in London' (Malkin's minute dated 7 January 1943 (PRO ref. FO 371/31000 [C11754/3672/98/1942]). The full list of invitees was Australia, Belgium, Canada, Czechoslovakia, the French National Committee, Greece, India, Luxembourg, the Netherlands, New Zealand, Norway, Poland, South Africa, the Soviet Union and Yugoslavia (see Eden's written answer in *Parliamentary Debates*, 5th Series, House of Commons, vol. 400, col. 1362 (7 June 1944)).

as well as to the French National Committee, the Soviet Union, Canada, Australia, South Africa, New Zealand and India, asking whether each might send an expert to participate in a small and informal committee under the chairmanship of Sir William Malkin to discuss the post-war future of the Permanent Court. The letter of invitation added:

> One particular reason for suggesting that the committee should be of this informal nature is that we have ascertained that the United States Government (who are not of course a party to the Statute of the Court) are not at present prepared to participate in discussions concerning the Permanent Court, although they have made it clear that they see no objection to other governments setting up a committee of this kind.

The Soviet Union, though asked and, on 24 March 1943, reminded, did not reply.[26]

The Committee met in London for the first time on 20 May 1943. Malkin was the chairman and G. G. Fitzmaurice, a Foreign Office legal adviser then on secondment to the Ministry of Economic Warfare, was the secretary. The members signing the report, who acted in their personal capacity and not on behalf of their governments, comprised Kaeckenbeeck (Belgium), Havlicek (Czechoslovakia), Cassin and Gros (French Committee of National Liberation), Stavropoulos (Greece), Schommer (Luxembourg), Star-Busmann (Netherlands), Campbell (New Zealand), Colban (Norway) and Winiarski (Poland). The Canadian member, Johnson, could attend only two meetings and did not sign the report. Yugoslavia, while not appointing a member of the Committee, expressed a wish to be kept informed of its work.

The Committee held nineteen meetings in all and presented its report on 10 February 1944.[27] In the introduction to the report it was stated that the only necessary assumption was that an International Court in some form would be required in future, either the Permanent Court with any necessary modifications to its present Statute or a new Court established by means of a new Statute. The choice of one or the other was 'a question of high policy with which it is not our province to deal'.

The Committee considered that under either hypothesis a new international agreement would be required, if only to revise the method of

---

[26] See Foreign Office letter to British Embassy, Washington, 20 March 1944 (PRO ref. FO 371/39304 [C2712/880/98/1944].

[27] Cmd. 6531; *Supplement to the American Journal of International Law*, 39 (1945), pp. 1–42. The minutes of the meetings, if they were ever recorded and preserved, have not been located. For a critical summary of the report, see Manley O. Hudson, 'The Twenty-third Year of the Permanent Court of International Justice and its Future', *AJIL*, 39 (1945), pp. 1, 2.

election, as there had not been a 'general election' of judges under article 8 of the Statute since 1930 and it was not likely that the organs of the League would be available after the war to fulfil this function.

The Committee then examined the connection of the Court with the contemplated world international organization. It considered that the 'organic connexion'[28] between the League and the Court should not be continued, and that the financing of the Court should not come from such a future organization. The report stated:

> It cannot, we think, be doubted, that the Court has to some extent suffered in the past from its organic connexion with the League, which, whether logically or not, resulted in its prestige being dependent to some extent upon the varying fortunes of the League. Moreover, this organic connexion was doubtless responsible, at any rate in part, for the unwillingness of some States to become parties to the Statute, and for the fact that others severed their connexion with the Court when they withdrew from the League.

The Committee did not mean that there should be no connection between the Court and the organization but rather that 'the Court should be regarded as part of the machinery at the disposal of the Organisation'.

The report went on to stress the Committee's view that the object should be to choose a Court 'composed of the most suitable and competent persons whom the world can produce, from whatever countries they may come' and that therefore there should not be permanent representation of certain countries; furthermore, unlike article 9 of the Statute, no express provision should be made for the representation of the different legal systems. The Committee considered, furthermore, that fifteen was too large a number of judges for the satisfactory working of the Court and suggested a reduction to nine, exclusive of *ad hoc* judges, with a quorum of seven.

After considering the advantages in stability and security of tenure of having judges once elected serving to retiring age, the Committee concluded that the need for new blood supported the retention of the present nine-year tenure. It considered, however, that the system under which the entire Court went out of office every nine years was undesirable and that it should be replaced by a system under which one-third of the judges should go out of office every three years. The Committee rejected the concept of a mandatory age limit as 'it is liable to affect the wrong men'.

---

[28] This was defined in a footnote as follows: 'By organic connexion is meant that the Court was established by one of the articles of the League Covenant, that its judges were elected by the Assembly and Council of the League and that its expenses were a charge on the budget of the League, etc.' (Cmd. 6531, p. 33, fn.).

The Committee considered that the status of *ad hoc* judges – whose frequency of appointment would increase if the number of regular judges were reduced to nine – might be enhanced if each party to the Statute were to nominate one candidate who would then automatically become for the period of nine years a member (though not a judge) of the Court; such a person would be the national judge of his country and would also be available to sit both as a supplementary judge to make up the number of nine when required and as a member of a regional chamber or panel if such a system were introduced.

Turning to the method of nominating candidates, the Committee considered that the system of nomination by national groups in the Permanent Court of Arbitration, as provided in article 4 of the Statute, was unsatisfactory. The report concluded: 'The responsibility for the choice of candidates must, we think, rest upon Governments, and we therefore consider that the only satisfactory method is direct nomination by Governments themselves.' It was upon governments, too, that the Committee wished to place the responsibility for electing the judges from among the corpus of candidates by a system of triennial meetings or alternatively of written ballots sent to an agreed depositary government.

The Committee then examined the jurisdiction of the proposed Court. It recommended that it should be open to all 'civilized States' to become parties to its Statute, whether they were members of the future general international organization or not. The Committee considered that the definition of the competence of the Permanent Court in article 36(1) of the State was objectionably wide and that its competence should be confined to matters that were really 'justiciable'. In the words of the report: 'All possibility should be excluded of its being used to deal with cases which are really political in their nature and require to be dealt with by means of political decision and not by reference to a court of law.'

The Committee was of the definite view that it would be premature to impose compulsory jurisdiction through accession to the Statute alone; it should, however, remain open to states voluntarily to accept compulsory jurisdiction by other means, such as compromissory clauses in treaties and the acceptance – with the right to make certain reservations – of an 'optional clause' in the Statute. The Committee considered that the universalization of the jurisdiction of the Court was more likely to be attained if acceptance of compulsory jurisdiction were made a condition of membership of a future general international organization.

Referring to article 38 of the Statute, the report added:

The wording of this provision is open to criticism and it would not be difficult to make suggestions for improving it; but on the whole the difficulties resulting from it do not seem to be of a sufficiently serious character to necessitate any change. It seems to have worked well in practice, and we consider that any attempt to alter it would cause more difficulties than it would solve.

The Committee next turned to the subject of Advisory Opinions. It considered, not without early doubts on the part of some members who thought that it was anomalous and tended to promote judicial debate of political issues, that this head of jurisdiction should be retained, if only to serve as a method of dealing with constitutional questions arising in a future general international organization. It was thought, furthermore, that the advisory jurisdiction might advantageously be extended to permit references on 'justiciable' matters by other international organizations and even by two or more states acting in concert on an agreed statement of facts, the Court itself serving as the arbiter of whether the request was a proper one for it to consider.

The Committee then dealt with certain questions of procedure, such as the language of the Court and the method of producing judgments. It regarded with general disfavour the possibility of the Court serving as a court of appeal from other tribunals. It restated its recommendation that the finances of the Court should be independent of the contemplated international organization. Turning to the matter of regional chambers to which it devoted considerable attention, the Committee did not wish to make any positive recommendations but set out two alternative proposals should it be considered necessary later for the matter to be dealt with. The first proposal, to which the Committee saw considerable objections, was for three chambers, one at The Hague and two outside Europe, each operating on the basis of a nine-person tribunal staffed by both the 'permanent' judges and the 'national' judges. The alternative proposal, which the Committee thought was 'in the main free from the defects which have been noticed', was that if all the parties to a dispute wished the hearing to be held regionally the Court would be constituted by the 'national' judges, two *juges suppléants* belonging to the region and chosen from among the national judges of the states of that region, and five 'permanent' judges, including the President or Vice-President.

THE REACTION TO THE REPORT OF THE LONDON COMMITTEE

Before the Dumbarton Oaks discussions

The Foreign Office sent a circular, dated March 1944, to British diplomatic missions in the member states of the League of Nations, the Soviet Union and the US asking them to send to the governments concerned copies of the Committee's report. The circular continued:

> You should state that His Majesty's Government understand it to be the view of the Committee that it would be premature, pending consideration of the Report by the governments of the United Nations, to suggest in detail the alterations which would be necessary in the present Statute of the Court if its proposals were to be adopted. The members of the Committee would no doubt be available, if required, to lend their assistance in any eventual redrafting that may be found necessary.
>
> You should state that His Majesty's Government in the United Kingdom will be glad to place themselves at the disposal of the other Governments of the United Nations with a view to facilitating further consideration of the subject, and the ultimate adoption of a general agreed policy on the future of the Permanent Court. With this object His Majesty's Government would be glad to receive as soon as possible, and to communicate to the other United Nations, such observations as other Governments may desire to make on the Report of the Committee.[29]

In fact, only seven governments responded, all approving the report in general terms; the Polish government alone submitted a detailed response.[30]

The official reaction of the United Kingdom government to the report was one of general support, and several of its particular suggestions were incorporated into documents of high policy at this time. In April 1944, the Armistice and Post-War Committee of the War Cabinet considered a number of draft memoranda prepared within the Foreign Office for the purposes of presenting to a conference of heads of Dominion governments and possibly later to inter-allied discussions in Washington. Memorandum A, headed 'The Scope and Nature of the Permanent Organisation', contained the following passage: 'It is assumed that there will be general agreement that a Permanent Court of International Justice will be set up. The proposals of the Informal Inter-Allied Committee which recently reported on this question seem to indicate the general lines that should be followed.'[31]

Having set out the desire to encourage reference of justiciable matters to the International Court of Justice, the document went on to state, under a heading 'An International Court of Justice':

1. The Permanent Court of International Justice should be reconstituted in accordance with a revision of its present Statute;

---

[29] PRO ref. FO 371/39304 [C2712/880/98/1944].
[30] PRO ref. FO 371/50635 [U1733/1169/98/1945].
[31] PRO ref. CAB 66/49 [WP(44)220].

2. The revised Statute should be made a part of the basic instrument of the international organisation.

Memorandum B, headed 'The Pacific Settlement of Disputes', divided disputes between states into 'justiciable' disputes that could be settled by a legal tribunal and those in which 'other considerations are predominant'. In respect of justiciable disputes it went on:

> It would seem that there is likely to be general agreement that justiciable disputes should be generally settled by a Permanent Court of International Justice. The Informal Inter-Allied Committee suggested in its recent report that the Court be open to all States, whether they accept compulsory jurisdiction or not. It would be possible for the International Organisation to make the acceptance of such an obligation a condition of membership, but in such a case it would be necessary to allow States to make certain reservations.
>
> The difference between accepting compulsory jurisdiction with reservations and retaining full freedom of action is likely to have more psychological than practical effect, especially if the World Council can obtain Advisory Opinions from the Court on some point in a dispute, which has been submitted to it.[32]

The memorandum ended with the opinion that justiciable disputes should generally be decided by a Permanent Court of International Justice.

On 17 May 1944, Malkin wrote to the Lord Chancellor, Lord Simon, and to the Attorney-General, Sir Donald Somervell, inviting them to look at the Report. He continued:

> The question of the Court is likely to come up to some extent in the conversations with the Americans and the Russians about the new World Organisation, which are expected to take place some time this summer, and the present intention is that our representatives should be instructed to be guided in general by the recommendations made in that report. Whether this will amount to much in practice may be doubtful, because I do not suppose that the composition and functioning of the Court will be discussed in any detail in those conversations, and on the main question whether the Permanent Court of International Justice should be continued in existence with a revised statute or a new court established, my Committee did not feel competent to make any recommendation. I feel, nevertheless, that before the matter goes further I ought to ask you whether you see any objection to our representatives being instructed on these lines, either for the forthcoming conversations or when the matter comes to be discussed in detail.[33]

Both Simon and Somervell stated that they had no objection.[34]

---

[32] *Ibid.*
[33] PRO ref. FO 371/39305 [C7746/880/98/1944].
[34] *Ibid.*

The two memoranda, unchanged in respect of their observations about an international court and their references to the London Committee report, were approved by the War Cabinet on 4 August 1944 as the basis for the preliminary and exploratory discussions on the official level.[35]

The Dumbarton Oaks discussions

On 24 July 1944, the US government's 'tentative proposals' for a general international organization for the maintenance of peace and security were transmitted to Eden[36] and on 12 August 1944 Eden received a Soviet memorandum on the subject of a future 'International Security Organiz-ation'.[37] Neither document made any reference to the work of the London Committee. Within the Foreign Office a tabular comparison was made between particular provisions in these two documents and those in the UK memoranda. Under the heading 'International Court of Justice', the comparative analysis read:

> The Soviet Government proposes that an international Court of justice should be set up, but there is no indication as to whether it should be constituted on the lines recommended by the recent informal Inter-Allied Committee, as suggested in the British paper; a reconstitution of the existing court as suggested by the Americans; or in some other way.[38]

At the Dumbarton Oaks meetings at which these documents were considered by representatives of the UK, the US and the Soviet Union, and later by China, a legal sub-committee was established chaired by Green Hackworth, the legal adviser to the US State Department. It was perhaps not surprising that it was from the US that on 24 August 1944 the documents circulated for consideration. These consisted of the Statute of the Permanent Court with proposed revisions together with a list of eleven basic questions formulated by the US.[39] Introducing these documents, Hackworth described them as the

---

[35] PRO ref. CAB 65/43 [WM(44) 101st conclusions].

[36] PRO ref. FO 371/40701 [U6572/180/70/1944]. It appears that officials within the State Department had been working as early as 1943 on the draft of a revision of the Permanent Court's Statute (Ruth B. Russell, *A History of the United Nations Charter: The Role of the United States, 1940–1945* (Washington, 1958), pp. 379–82).

[37] PRO ref. FO 371/40705 [U6845/180/70/1944].

[38] *Ibid*. On 23 February 1944 Malkin handed to Jebb a copy of the London Committee report for the purpose of preparation for the Dumbarton Oaks discussions. Jebb minuted: 'Points that struck me as possibly contentious are: (1) The suggestion that judges can stay on till they are 100 if need be. (2) No provision for Russian as a language. (3) The retention of the Optional Clause. (4) Location of the Court in Europe' (PRO ref. FO 371/40686 [U2296/180/70/1944]).

[39] Minutes of the meeting (PRO ref. 371/40710 [U7254/170/70]).

'tentative views' of the American group. Malkin took upon himself the role of defender of the London Committee's work. With reference to the US proposals for the revision of the Statute, he doubted whether it was a function of the present conversations to draw up an amended version of the Statute. He considered that what had to be settled at the present time were two general principles: whether the present court should be continued or whether a new court should be established; and the relation of the court to the general international organization. The informal record of the meeting continued:

> [Malkin] had serious doubt as to the wisdom of going further on account of the limited time now available. He felt that the accomplishment of the principal tasks should not be delayed by a consideration of purely legal questions. He pointed out that a large number of states signatories to the existing statute were not represented in the present Conversations and suggested that it was not necessary for the four major powers to take a lead in matters relating to international judicial organization. The report of the Informal Inter-Allied Committee on the Future of the Permanent Court of International Justice, drawn up at London in February of this year, had been forwarded by the British Government to the governments of all of the United Nations with an invitation to forward their observations upon the recommendations made. The governments of these states might feel that their opinions had not been given sufficient consideration if they were to be confronted at the future conference with an entirely new document.[40]

When the discussion turned to the relationship of the International Court of Justice to the general international organization, Malkin pointed out that there seemed to be agreement among the three groups that the Court should be an organ of the organization. The Inter-Allied Committee report had recommended that 'no organic connection' should be established between the two, at least during their formative period, but it had not been able to take account of the views of the US and the Soviet Union. The record continued: 'Since both governments now appear to be favorable to a close relationship between the two, [Malkin] anticipated that the British Government would experience no difficulty in accepting their point of view.'

That part of the 'Statement of Tentative Proposals' emerging from Dumbarton Oaks dealing with the proposal for an international court of justice made no reference to the London Committee's work.[41]

---

[40] *Ibid.*   [41] Cmd. 6560.

The United Nations Committee of Jurists

The Crimean Conference in February 1945 had suggested that prior to the conference to draw up the general international organization a Committee of Jurists should be established with the task of preparing a draft statute for the International Court of Justice.[42]

Accordingly, draft instructions to the UK delegation to this committee were prepared in the Foreign Office. In circulating them to the Armistice and Post-War Committee of the War Cabinet on 19 March 1945, the Parliamentary Under-Secretary at the Foreign Office, R. K. Law, stated: 'These instructions have been agreed with the Lord Chancellor and the Attorney-General. I think it unnecessary to trouble the Committee for its formal approval of these instructions, but I am circulating them for information.'[43] After stating that the UK representatives should press for the continuance of the Permanent Court rather than the establishment of a new court or, failing this, for the use of the present Statute as the basis of a new Statute, the instructions went on: 'In general, you should be guided by the Report of the Informal Inter-Allied Committee (Cmd. 6531) and should endeavour to secure the acceptance of the recommendations there made, subject to the following observations.' The observations set out in the instructions may be summarized as follows:

(1) As the Dumbarton Oaks proposals, in suggesting the 'organic connexion' of the international court with the new organization, had departed from the recommendations of the Inter-Allied Committee, it was now desirable that the election of judges should be made by the appropriate organs of the organization. The instructions went on: 'On the whole, His Majesty's Government are of opinion that the existing system of elections should be retained, so that the judges would require to be elected both by the General Assembly and the Security Council, since this seems the only means of preventing the voting power of the Latin American countries from playing an undue part in the selection of the judges, especially in the early years of the new Organisation.'

(2) As the government 'attach the greatest importance to a reduction in the existing number of judges', the representative was exhorted to press for a reduction to nine; but if general acceptance could not be reached for this,

---

[42] See Winant (US Ambassador in London) to Eden, 14 March 1945; Eden to Winant, 21 March 1945 (PRO ref. 371/50684 [I1891/12/70/1945]).

[43] PRO ref. CAB 87/69 [APW(45)37].

'in the last resort' the UK government might be prepared to accept a Court of eleven judges with a quorum of seven.

(3) An age limit was to be opposed strongly.

(4) The attitude to regional chambers would depend to a considerable extent on the views expressed by non-European states, particularly the Dominions.

(5) Candidates should be nominated by governments but if there were to be strong support for the continuation of nomination by national groups the representative was given liberty to agree to whichever alternative would command general acceptance.

(6) On the subject of the compulsory jurisdiction of the Court, the UK government stood by the proposals in paragraphs 58–61 of the Inter-Allied Committee report, and if more far-reaching proposals were to be made, the representative should take the view that these ought to be considered by the main conference during its consideration of the pacific settlement of disputes.

(7) Although the UK government had no objection to the proposals in the Inter-Allied Committee report relating to the request for Advisory Opinions, such matters should be left to the main conference.

(8) Likewise, if it should be desired that the finances of the Court should be provided for by the UN, this matter should be left to the main conference.

At the start of the meeting in Washington of the United Nations Committee of Jurists, Fitzmaurice wrote to Malkin expressing the view that there was a 'complete lack of co-ordination between the Governments concerned and their representatives'.[44] He went on to observe that he and his colleague Maurice Bathurst had met representatives of some of the European governments which had contributed members to the London Committee, but only the Netherlands representative appeared to have read the report.

During the first meeting of the Committee of Jurists, held on 9 April 1945, Fitzmaurice, who with Malkin and Bathurst represented the UK, soon made reference to the London Committee report. Having stated that the UK would prefer the continuance in force, with modifications, of the present Statute, he went on:

> The Government of the United Kingdom had considered the question of the juridical organization of such importance that it had sponsored the formation of the informal Inter-Allied Committee on the Future of the Permanent Court of International Justice. This Committee was composed of experts, many of whom

---

[44] PRO ref. FO 371/50695 [U2565/12/70/1945].

were appointed by various European Governments having their headquarters in London. The discussions of this group of experts were in no way binding upon the Governments concerned, although the experts agreed to recommend them to their Governments. The unanimous recommendations reached represented the best views of a group well acquainted with the work of the Court and were therefore deserving of careful consideration. The report of the Inter-Allied Committee would be made available for distribution to the Jurists Committee. The United Kingdom found itself in general agreement with the report, though certain aspects of it might be affected by the conclusions reached at Dumbarton Oaks.[45]

At the second meeting, held on 10 April 1945, the chairman, Hackworth, presented a text for discussion based on the Statute of the Permanent Court with revisions proposed by the US.[46] Thereafter it was this text that provided the basis for discussion. In the course of the discussions, the London Committee report was mentioned only by the United Kingdom representative, Fitzmaurice, on isolated occasions.[47] There was no express mention of the London Committee report in the report of Jules Basdevant, rapporteur of the Committee of Jurists, submitted on 25 April 1945 to the San Francisco Conference.[48] It was not expressly mentioned in the reports of either Nasrat Al-Farsy, rapporteur of Commission IV/1, submitted on 12 June 1945 to Commission IV of the Conference,[49] or C. Parra-Perez, President of Commission IV, submitted to the plenary session on 23 June 1945.[50]

THE INFLUENCE OF THE REPORT OF THE LONDON COMMITTEE

Writing before the start of the San Francisco Conference, Manley Hudson wrote of the London Committee's work: 'The report as a whole is a document of outstanding importance, useful for the problems of the future as well as for those of the present discussions. In the form and in its spirit it leaves little to be desired.'[51] It appears from the above historical account, however, that the work of the London Committee did not have an influence on the

---

[45] UNCIO, vol. XIV, pp. 58–9.

[46] Ibid., pp. 323–47.

[47] E.g. during the seventh meeting on 13 April 1945, Fitzmaurice mentioned paras. 83 and 84 of the London Committee report as representing the view of the UK government on the subject of the presentation of individual Opinions (ibid., pp. 172–3).

[48] Ibid., pp. 821–53.

[49] Ibid., vol. XIII, pp. 381–93.

[50] Ibid., pp. 126–7.

[51] Manley O. Hudson, 'The Twenty-third Year of the Permanent Court of International Justice and its Future', AJIL, 39 (1945), p. 7.

elaboration of the text of the Statute of the International Court of Justice. Only the UK representatives expressly referred to it in the *travaux préparatoires*. Nevertheless, one might usefully see to what extent the report's recommendations were indirectly reflected in the final text of the Statute.

Such a comparison indicates that on the whole the report's suggestions were not followed. It will be recalled that the London Committee recommended that there should not be an 'organic connexion' with any new general international organization. In fact, the new Court was established by a provision in the Charter, its judges are elected by the organs of the UN and its expenses are a charge on the UN budget. The 'organic connexion' has thus been maintained.

The London Committee's suggestion that the judges should be elected by governments from among the corpus of candidates nominated by governments likewise did not find a place in the Statute. Nor did its suggestion, strongly supported by the UK, that the number of judges should be reduced to nine. Nor did its suggestion to make drastic changes to the system of nominating judges *ad hoc*. The London Committee had recommended the abolition of the system by which the election of judges was made simultaneously by the Assembly and Council of the League. A system of dual election, by the General Assembly and the Security Council, was, however, retained in the new Statute. Turning to the jurisdiction of the Court, the Committee's suggestion that two or more states, acting in concert, might be permitted to request an Advisory Opinion, did not appear in the Statute.

In some respects, the London Committee's work found an echo in the Statute. Although the Committee's particular recommendation of regional Chambers was not taken up, the Statute permits Chambers for particular types of case, and for particular cases at the request of the parties, as well as a Chamber of Summary Procedure, and provides in article 28 that all the Chambers may with the consent of the parties sit elsewhere than in The Hague. Its recommendation that one-third of the judges should go out of office every three years finds a reflection in article 13(1) of the Statute. Its suggestion that the constitution of the organization might lay down the conditions on which the members would be bound to have recourse to the Court, and provide measures for ensuring compliance with its decisions has been, as Rosenne wrote, 'haltingly implemented in the Charter'[52] in

---

[52] Shabtai Rosenne, *The Law and Practice of the International Court* (2nd rev. edn, Dordrecht, 1985), p. 62.

article 36(1) which provides that the Court's jurisdiction comprises 'all matters provided for in the Charter of the United Nations'.[53]

Despite its apparent lack of influence, the London Committee's epitaph might appropriately be Rosenne's words:

> It is, indeed, a tribute to the ideals which the very notion of international justice inspires, that at the height of the war this group of men, from eleven different countries, most of them temporarily exiled from their homes, could spare time from their engrossing official and national duties, to consider these problems.[54]

---

[53] Though these words may be otiose; see the Dissenting Opinions in the *Corfu Channel* case (*Preliminary Objections*), ICJ Reports, 1948, p. 32.

[54] Rosenne, *The Law and Practice of the International Court*, p. 28.

PART II

The sources and evidences of international law

෫

4

The International Court of Justice and the sources of international law

Maurice Mendelson

॰

It is a particular pleasure to contribute an essay on the sources of international law to this Festschrift for Sir Robert Jennings in recognition, not only of his distinguished contributions to this topic both as an academic and as a judge, but also of personal acts of kindness.

Every case in the World Court involves the sources of international law in some form, because every case requires an investigation of substantive or adjective rules whose existence and legal effect ultimately depends on their having been created by one of the means recognized as apt for this purpose. Even if one eliminates cases where there was no issue as to the status of the rule, but only as to its content, in the fifty years since the International Court of Justice was established it has had very many occasions to make rulings pertinent to our topic.[1] In the space available here, any review of its contribution is inevitably summary and impressionistic.[2]

The ICJ has not attempted to elaborate a theory of the sources of international law[3] or attempted to catalogue them. This is hardly surprising: its

---

[1] In accordance with objectives of the present volume, this chapter is confined to the ICJ, though there have also been some very interesting decisions on these matters by the PCIJ, such as the *Lotus* case (PCIJ, Series A, No. 10 (1927)). Shortage of space precludes, for the most part, an examination of the Separate and Dissenting Opinions of members of the ICJ.

[2] The present volume is intended to contain a number of other chapters relating to individual sources (or possible sources) of law. This chapter is not based on them; for the most part, I have not seen them before writing it.

[3] A partial exception is the statement in the judgment of the Chamber in the *Gulf of Maine* case (ICJ Reports, 1984, p. 246, at p. 299, para. 111), supporting the inductive approach to customary international law:

A body of detailed rules is not to be looked for in customary international law which in fact comprises a limited set of norms for ensuring the co-existence and vital co-operation of the members of the international community, together with a set of customary rules whose presence in the *opinio juris* of States can be testified by induction based on the analysis of a sufficiently extensive and convincing practice, and not by deduction from preconceived ideas. For a detailed discussion

function is to decide the particular disputes before it, not to elaborate general theories or to decide questions that are not in issue. The need for a list of sources is in any event considerably reduced by the existence of article 38(1) of the Statute, which provides:

> The Court, whose function is to decide in accordance with international law such disputes as are submitted to it, shall apply
>
> (a) international conventions, whether general or particular, establishing rules expressly recognized by the contesting States;
> (b) international custom, as evidence of a general practice accepted as law;
> (c) the general principles of law recognized by civilized nations;
> (d) subject to the provisions of Article 59, judicial decisions and the teachings of the most highly qualified publicists of the various nations, as subsidiary means for the determination of rules of law.

There has been much doctrinal discussion as to whether this constitutes an accurate or exhaustive list of the sources of international law; but what is quite clear is that it authorizes and requires the Court, without more ado, at least to have recourse to the sources specified in paragraph 1.[4] The purpose of this chapter is to consider how the Court has interpreted them, and whether it has had recourse to other sources as well.

Analysis of the Court's approach is complicated by the fact that it quite frequently fails to specify which source it is applying, whether by reference to particular sub-paragraphs of article 38(1) or otherwise. This is seldom the case when the rule in question derives its validity directly from a treaty, because obviously the treaty has to be identified; but in other instances the Court often simply asserts that such-and-such is a 'well-recognized rule [or principle] of international law' or employs some other vague phrase, without identifying whether the rule derives from custom, 'general principles of law recognized by civilized nations', some other source, or a combination of sources.[5]

---

of the concept of 'source' and related matters, see Maurice Mendelson, Appendix to the Second Report of the Rapporteur of the International Law Association's Committee on the Formation of Rules of Customary (General) International Law, in ILA, *Report of the 63rd Conference* (Warsaw, 1988), p. 956.

[4] Strictly, article 38(1) seems by its terms confined to contentious cases, since it refers to 'disputes' and assumes that there are 'contesting States' before the Court, as Jennings has pointed out in his 'General Course on Principles of International Law', *Recueil des cours*, 121 (1967-II), pp. 323, 330. However, in practice, the same sources have been applied in the exercise of the Court's advisory jurisdiction.

[5] Recourse to the individual Opinions and Pleadings may (but does not always) throw light on what the majority meant. If the Court finds that the alleged rule does not exist, it is more likely to explain why.

TREATIES

In a celebrated essay, Sir Gerald Fitzmaurice argued that treaties are not, formally, a source of law at all, but simply a 'source of obligation'.[6] I have argued elsewhere that this distinction is in some respects unhelpful and misleading;[7] but be that as it may, treaties deserve at least some mention here, not least because they are expressly referred to in the very first sub-paragraph of article 38(1) of the Court's Statute.

Through its jurisprudence, the Court has undoubtedly made an important contribution to the elucidation of particular instruments, such as conventions on the law of the sea and on diplomatic relations, as well as the constituent instruments of certain international organizations (notably the UN). This contribution is clearly beyond the scope of the present chapter, for a distinction must be made between substantive treaty law and the law of treaties, the latter being the body of rules governing the validity, interpretation, suspension, termination etc. of international agreements.

But even the Court's contribution to the law of treaties, thus defined, cannot be the subject of a prolonged examination here, for several reasons. First of all, the law of treaties is a very large subject, often dealt with doctrinally as a separate topic from sources. Second, the Court is called upon to apply (explicitly or implicitly) the law of treaties virtually every time it is seised of a case. Even where the substantive rules relied on are said to derive from custom or some other non-conventional source, the Court's jurisdiction is based on treaties or instruments related to treaties (such as the Charter, the Statute, the Rules of Court, declarations under the Optional Clause, special agreements, and the like), whose applicability and meaning it will be called upon to determine. Faced with this huge quantity of material, and bearing in mind also that there is a separate chapter on the law of treaties in this volume, a few brief observations must suffice.

The Court has undoubtedly had an important influence on the law of treaties in some respects. It has, for instance, developed, and in some cases robustly applied, a teleological approach to the interpretation of the constituent instruments of international organizations: see, for instance, the Advisory Opinions on *Reparation for Injuries*,[8] *International Status of South West*

---

[6] 'Some Problems Regarding the Formal Sources of International Law', in *Symbolae Verzijl* (The Hague, 1958), p. 153.

[7] 'Are Treaties Merely a Source of Obligation?', in W. E. Butler (ed.), *Perestroika and International Law* (Dordrecht, 1990), p. 81.

[8] ICJ Reports, 1949, p. 174.

Africa,[9] *Effect of Awards of the UN Administrative Tribunal*,[10] *Certain Expenses of the UN*[11] and *Namibia*[12] (though it has tended to be rather more cautious in other contexts).[13] The *North Sea Continental Shelf* cases ushered in important developments in the concept of the obligation to negotiate an agreement.[14] The Advisory Opinion on *Reservations to the Genocide Convention*[15] played a major part in the development of the law relating to reservations to treaties, and other rulings have also found their way into the Vienna Convention on the Law of Treaties 1969.[16]

Of course, to say that the Court's decisions have played a major part in some areas does not automatically mean that its contributions have been invariably beneficial. For example, the argument could be made (though not necessarily by me) that the *Genocide Convention* decision was a retrograde step, sacrificing the integrity of treaties in a vain quest for universality.[17] Certainly the initial reaction of the International Law Commission, for one, was unfavourable.

It also seems fair to say that the ICJ's role in the development of the law of treaties, especially in the past quarter century, has not been comparable in importance to its contribution to various fields of substantive law – notably maritime delimitation – or to the theory of custom. But this is hardly surprising: the Vienna Convention of 1969 has now occupied most of the field, and even before it was finalized or entered into force the work of the International Law Commission was making itself felt. Even where the Convention is inapplicable as a treaty, *ratione temporis*, *materiae* or *personae*, the Court tends to hold that its provisions reflect customary law, and there has never yet been a case where it has held that it does not do so. A well-drafted code will inevitably reduce the scope for judicial development of the law.

On the other hand, the Court has played an important part in elucidating the relationship between treaties and custom. However, this can be more conveniently dealt with below, in relation to customary law.

---

9 ICJ Reports, 1950, p. 128.　　10 ICJ Reports, 1954, p. 47.

11 ICJ Reports, 1962, p. 151.　　12 ICJ Reports, 1971, p. 16.

13 See e.g. *Interpretation of Peace Treaties (Second Phase)*, ICJ Reports, 1950, p. 221.

14 ICJ Reports, 1969, p. 3, at pp. 46–7, paras. 85–6. But query whether this is part of the law of treaties, as opposed to part of substantive law.

15 ICJ Reports, 1951, p. 15.

16 Compare, for instance, the *Temple* case, ICJ Reports, 1962, p. 6, at p. 26, and the Vienna Convention on the Law of Treaties, art. 48(2).

17 It is interesting to note that, later that year, the Court did for customary law something like what it had just done for treaties: rightly or wrongly, in the *Anglo-Norwegian Fisheries* case (ICJ Reports, 1951, p. 116) it rejected arguments for a (relatively) uniform rule on baselines in favour of a set of rules that not only varied according to individual geographical (and even, to a limited extent, economic) circumstances, but also increased the scope given to particular law by means of concepts such as 'historic claims', acquiescence and persistent dissent.

CUSTOM

Treaties are a relatively straightforward source of law: as they are recorded in writing, there is no doubt about what they say, and if they are properly drafted there is only limited room for argument about what they mean. By contrast, custom is often much less clear. It is by no means always easy to discover what states actually do, and the weight to be given to their acts and the normative conclusions to be drawn from them can be very controversial.[18] One might therefore expect a court to be able to play an important role in elucidating customary rules. In fact, the ICJ's scope for doing so has been somewhat limited by the dependence of its jurisdiction on consent, so that it is a matter of chance whether and in what circumstances it is called upon to declare the law. Nevertheless, when it has had the opportunity, it has played a major part in developing customary rules in a number of fields: maritime delimitation is just one of several that come to mind.

But, as with treaties, we must distinguish between the development and elucidation of, on the one hand, substantive rules of customary law, and, on the other hand, rules about the creation, identification, maintenance, alteration and termination of customary rules. It is only the latter that is within our present remit; and here, the contribution of the Court has been more limited, and not invariably helpful.

The ICJ has no more been prepared to discuss the theoretical basis of customary law than the theory of sources generally. For reasons already indicated, that is hardly surprising or a reason for criticism. But the Court has also made it rather difficult for anyone else to deduce a theory from its pronouncements or to ascertain the precise rules for the formation etc. of custom, due to the rather delphic form in which (if at all) it has tended to express its reasons for concluding that something is or is not a customary rule.[19] It is perhaps unsurprising that where a norm, such as the freedom of the high seas, is generally accepted, the Court tends simply to assert that it is a (well-established) rule (or principle) of customary law (or sometimes, just 'of international law') without more ado: there is no need to 'reinvent the wheel', especially if the point has not been contested by either of the parties. Rather less helpful are those instances where the Court makes an assertion, supported

---

[18] For further discussion, see Maurice Mendelson, 'Practice, Propaganda and Principle in International Law', *Current Legal Problems*, 42 (1989), pp. 1–20.

[19] This is not just an academic problem: practitioners of all sorts need to know what exactly are the rules about how customary international law is formed, modified, etc.

by no – or no adequate – reasoning, that something is or is not (customary) law when the point is not self-evident.[20]

The main topics to be considered here are the Court's treatment of the component elements of general customary law; particular customary law; and treaties as a 'source' of custom.

The component elements of general custom

Following the lead of its predecessor in the *'Lotus'* case,[21] the ICJ has said in terms that a customary rule comprises two elements: state practice (the so-called 'material element') and acceptance as law (the so-called 'subjective element', often rendered by the spurious Latin phrase *opinio juris sive necessitatis*). The *North Sea Continental Shelf* cases[22] and the *Nicaragua* case *(Merits)*[23] are particularly clear instances.[24] In these pronouncements, the Court stated plainly that both criteria have to be satisfied; but in the *Nicaragua* case it seems not to have complied entirely with its own prescription, treating certain General Assembly resolutions, in particular, as evidence of both elements. As will be seen shortly, it is permissible to wonder whether these particular resolutions constituted either state practice or *opinio juris*; but be that as it may, what seems particularly questionable is treating the same resolutions as both state practice and evidence of *opinio juris*. This is not only a form of double counting; taken to its logical extreme it could mean that, if there was no countervailing material, a majority vote[25] in the General Assembly could satisfy all of the requirements for the formation of customary law, and we would thus have a type of 'instant custom', even though the drafters of the UN Charter did not think that they had provided for this kind of law-making, and even though there is little evidence that states generally consider such a source to have evolved. There are other criticisms that may be made of the Court's approach to this question in *Nicaragua*, but it will be more convenient to deal

---

[20] Examples are to be found the *Corfu Channel* case *(Merits)*, ICJ Reports, 1949, p. 4, at p. 22; *Nicaragua* case *(Merits)*, ICJ Reports, 1986, p. 14, at pp. 110–11 and 113–14, paras. 211 and 218.

[21] PCIJ, Series A, No. 10 (1927), esp. at p. 28.

[22] ICJ Reports, 1969, p. 3, at p. 44, para. 77.

[23] ICJ Reports, 1986, p. 14, esp. at pp. 97–8, paras. 183–4.

[24] Other statements along similar lines are to be found in the *Asylum* case, ICJ Reports, 1950, p. 266, at pp. 276–7; *Right of Passage* case *(Merits)*, ICJ Reports, 1960, p. 6, at pp. 39–40; and the *Continental Shelf (Libya/Malta)* case, ICJ Reports, 1985, p. 13, at pp. 29–30, para. 27. But the first two are cases of local and regional custom respectively, where it is strongly arguable that there is a particular need, not only for practice, but for clear evidence of acceptance by the state it is sought to bind; and in the third case, little was made of the point by the Chamber.

[25] Or, at any rate, a majority vote in which the litigants had concurred.

with them under the separate heading of 'Resolutions of international organizations' below.

Expressly or indirectly, the Court has made a number of useful contributions to our understanding of the *material* element of custom. It has sometimes been questioned whether organs of the state other than the executive can create state practice: but legislation and/or national judicial decisions have been taken into account in such cases as *Nottebohm (Second Phase)*,[26] and *Barcelona Traction (Second Phase)*.[27] And in the *Reservations to the Genocide Convention* case[28] the Court was certainly prepared to take into consideration the depositary practice of organs of intergovernmental organizations even if, in the event, it did not regard them as conclusive.[29] Regarding the time factor, although in the past custom has tended to evolve rather slowly, in the *North Sea Continental Shelf* cases it was pointed out that 'even without the passage of any considerable period of time, a very widespread and representative participation . . . might suffice of itself'.[30] What is important, as the Court emphasized in the *Asylum* case, is that there should have been a 'constant and uniform practice', and it was (partly) because, on the facts, the necessary consistency and uniformity had not been shown that the Court refused to recognize the existence of the custom relied on by Colombia.[31] *Nicaragua v. USA (Merits)* added the important qualification that perfect consistency and a rigorous conformity with the alleged rule were not necessary:

> In order to deduce the existence of customary rules, the Court deems it sufficient that the conduct of States should, in general, be consistent with such rules, and that instances of State conduct inconsistent with a given rule should generally have been treated as breaches of that rule, not as indications of the recognition of a new rule. If a State acts in a way prima facie incompatible with a recognized rule, but defends its conduct by appealing to exceptions or justifications contained within the rule itself, then whether or not the State's conduct is in fact justifiable on that basis, the significance of that attitude is to confirm rather than to weaken the rule.[32]

[26] ICJ Reports, 1955, p. 4, at pp. 22–3.
[27] ICJ Reports, 1970, p. 3, at pp. 39–40, para. 69.   [28] ICJ Reports, 1951, p. 15.
[29] There are also several cases concerning the construction of the constituent instruments of an international organization (or an organ thereof), where the practice of the particular body and of other organs and organizations has been taken into account.
[30] ICJ Reports, 1969, p. 3, at p. 42, para. 73.
[31] ICJ Reports, 1950, p. 266, at pp. 276–7. For similar rejections on the ground of lack of uniformity or consistency, see the *Anglo-Norwegian Fisheries* case, ICJ Reports, 1951, p. 116, at p. 131; the *Genocide Convention* case, *ibid.*, p. 15, at p. 25; and (perhaps) the *US Nationals in Morocco* case, ICJ Reports, 1952, p. 176, at p. 200.
[32] ICJ Reports, 1986, p. 14, at p. 98, para. 186. See also the *Anglo-Norwegian Fisheries* case, ICJ Reports, 1951, p. 116, at p. 138: 'Too much importance need not be attached to the few uncertainties, real or apparent, which the United Kingdom Government claims to have discovered in Norwegian practice.'

Regarding the degree of participation required, the *locus classicus* is the finding in the *North Sea Continental Shelf* cases[33] that 'even without the passage of any considerable period of time, a very widespread and representative participation . . . might suffice of itself, provided it included that of States whose interests were specifically affected', even if its application to the facts has been disputed.[34] The formulation is somewhat imprecise, but since circumstances vary so much from case to case, this is understandable.

However, when it comes to the *subjective* element in customary law, the Court's contribution has been less helpful. We have already seen that, in the *North Sea Continental Shelf* and *Nicaragua* cases, it insisted on the need for evidence of *opinio juris*. In the particular circumstances of the former case this insistence was justifiable, because the context was a reliance by the applicants on a number of bilateral treaties for the delimitation of the continental shelf in accordance with the principle of equidistance; as there might be a variety of reasons for delimiting on this basis (including the desire to settle the matter by an obvious form of compromise), the Court was right to insist on the presence of an additional element. At least to some extent this is true also of *Nicaragua* inasmuch as, like the *'Lotus'* case,[35] what was relied upon to establish the existence of a customary rule was abstention: omissions are often equivocal, and in such circumstances it is legitimate to demand something more.[36] But in my (admittedly unorthodox) view, while the concept of *opinio juris* undoubtedly has a role to play, it is not in all cases necessary to establish its separate existence, and if that view is right the unqualified language used by the Court was unfortunate.[37]

Moreover, even if one were to approve the Court's unqualified endorsement of the need for evidence of *opinio juris*, its handling of that concept has not been uniformly helpful. Its pronouncements are somewhat inconsistent on whether the subjective element consists of belief or consent. And, as we shall

---

[33] ICJ Reports, 1969, p. 3, at p. 42, para. 73.

[34] See especially the Dissenting Opinion of Judge Lachs: *ibid.*, p. 219.

[35] PCIJ, Series A, No. 10 (1927), p. 28.

[36] For a fuller discussion, cf. Maurice Mendelson, 'State Acts and Omissions as Explicit or Implicit Claims', in *Le droit international au service de la paix, de la justice, et du développement: Mélanges Michel Virally* (Paris, 1991), p. 373; reproduced (with minor amendments) in ILA, *Report of Cairo Conference* (1992), Annexe to Second Interim Report of the Committee on the Formation of Rules of Customary (General) International Law (in press).

[37] Space does not permit an explanation of the thesis, but this may be a convenient point to note that, in a number of cases, the Court appears to have acknowledged the existence of a customary rule based on state practice, without (at any rate expressly) investigating whether the subjective element was also present: the *Anglo-Norwegian Fisheries* case, ICJ Reports, 1951, p. 116, at p. 128; the *Barcelona Traction* case (*Merits*), ICJ Reports, 1970, p. 3, at p. 42, para. 70; the *Continental Shelf (Libya/Malta)* case, ICJ Reports, 1985, p. 13, at p. 33, para. 34.

see when we come to consider the resolutions of international organizations below, the way in which it treated certain General Assembly resolutions as evidence of *opinio juris* about a customary norm in *Nicaragua v. USA* is open to criticism.

Particular customary law

The Court has made important contributions to the development of the concept of regional or local customary law, and to other forms of particular law, though the random way in which cases reach it has prevented it from doing so in a systematic manner.

In 1950, in the *Asylum* case, it acknowledged the possibility of regional customs existing, though holding on the facts that the existence of an American rule of diplomatic asylum had not been established, at any rate in a way that could be invoked against Peru.[38] What it did not make clear, however, was whether in such a case it is necessary to prove the active participation or acquiescence in the custom of all the states in the region – or at any rate the state it is sought to bind – or whether, rather, the reason why Peru was not bound was because of its persistent dissent. It declined to hold that there was a regional custom among the riparians in the *North Sea Continental Shelf* cases,[39] though the suggestion had been made. In the *Frontier Dispute (Burkina Faso/Mali)*[40] a Chamber of the Court, rather than just holding that *uti possidetis juris* was a principle of Spanish American and, later, of African regional law, went out of its way to find that the principle was one of general application; but in the *Land, Island and Maritime Frontier Dispute*,[41] a differently constituted Chamber treated the principle simply as one applying to former Spanish American colonies, and accepted by the contesting parties, without going into the question of its wider applicability.

The *Right of Passage* case *(Merits)*[42] is a well-known example of a local, bilateral custom established for the benefit of one state in respect of the territory of another. This is only one type of possible local custom, however: the territory of a state (or a part thereof) can be burdened with a particular customary regime for the benefit of several or all other states;[43] conversely, a particular state or states may acquire special rights over part of the earth's

---

[38] ICJ Reports, 1950, p. 266, at pp. 276–8.   [39] ICJ Reports, 1969, p. 3, esp. at p. 37, para. 60.

[40] ICJ Reports, 1986, p. 554, esp. at p. 565, para. 20.

[41] ICJ Reports, 1992, p. 351, esp. at pp. 380–7, paras. 27–42.

[42] ICJ Reports, 1960, p. 6.

[43] CF *US Nationals in Morocco* case, ICJ Reports, 1952, p. 176, at pp. 199–200 (claim not upheld on the facts); *Icelandic Fisheries (Merits)*, ICJ Reports, 1974, p. 3, at pp. 27–31, paras. 61–72.

surface (for instance, a pearl bed within the high seas) in derogation from the general law. This seems to have been a secondary or alternative ground for upholding Norway's straight baseline system in the *Anglo-Norwegian Fisheries* case;[44] but the judgment is not at all clear on the relation between the various strands of reasoning. In the *Libya/Tunisia Continental Shelf* case[45] the Court held that 'historic titles must enjoy respect and be preserved as they have always been by long usage'; but in the particular circumstances it did not find it necessary to do so. However, effect was finally given to this principle, and in resounding form, by a Chamber of the Court in the *Land, Island and Maritime Frontier Dispute*, with regard to the Gulf of Fonseca.[46]

A specific form of particular customary law is said to arise from what might be called the weak form of the 'persistent dissenter rule' whereby, even if opposition does not prevent the formation of a new rule of general law, it will at any rate exempt the dissenting state from the operation of that rule. Certain dicta in the *Asylum* and *Anglo-Norwegian Fisheries* cases[47] lend support to the concept; but the obscure language used by the Court has encouraged doubt and controversy as to the very existence of the rule. This is an important issue, and the uncertainty engendered by these pronouncements is a good illustration of the unsatisfactory results of the Court's tendency to engage in delphic utterances which neither state the majority's view plainly nor pass over the point in silence.[48]

Relation between treaty and custom

While some aspects of the seminal judgment in the *North Sea Continental Shelf* cases[49] have been valuable in helping to elucidate the vexed question of the relation between treaty and custom, other parts of that judgment, and some other decisions, are more questionable.

In its 1969 judgment, the Court rightly concluded the following:

---

[44] ICJ Reports, 1951, p. 116, at pp. 136–9.

[45] ICJ Reports, 1982, p. 18, at p. 73, para. 100.

[46] ICJ Reports, 1992, p. 351, at pp. 586–606, paras. 381–413. One of the ingredients of the Court's reasoning was the absence of protest by other states (esp. at p. 601, para. 405); what it did not make clear was whether this was an essential ingredient – a point also left unresolved by the *Anglo-Norwegian Fisheries* case. But, given that the regime derogates from the general law, it may be speculated that acquiescence is a necessary condition.

[47] ICJ Reports, 1950, p. 266, at p. 278; ICJ Reports, 1951, p. 116, at p. 131, respectively.

[48] The uncertainty flowing from dicta of this type is aggravated if they are *obiter*, as was seemingly the position in the *Asylum* case and arguably so in the *Anglo-Norwegian Fisheries* case.

[49] ICJ Reports, 1969, p. 3.

(1) A multilateral convention might codify existing customary law.

(2) The process of elaborating and concluding a convention might crystallize a customary rule which was previously only emerging.

(3) However, on the facts, neither was true of article 6 of the Geneva Convention on the Continental Shelf 1958. Rather more doubtful, though, was its attempt to bolster this conclusion by referring to the faculty to make reservations to (*inter alia*) article 6. It seemed to think that, normally, such a faculty would be inconsistent with the idea that the rule in question was already obligatory. But it then had some difficulty in explaining why certain other provisions of the Convention, which it did regard as binding under customary law and/or other treaties, were also subject to reservations. Furthermore, it could well be argued that, just because the drafters decide for a variety of possible diplomatic reasons to permit reservations to a treaty, this need not prejudice the issue whether or not the provisions in question reflect customary law.[50]

The Court went on to consider the argument that, even if article 6 did not codify existing, or crystallize emerging, law, a new customary rule requiring delimitation according to the equidistance principle had emerged, partly because of the impact of the Convention itself, and partly because of post-1958 practice along the same lines. Once again, it rightly held that, although this was a theoretical possibility, it could not be assumed to be so, and it was necessary to examine the facts. But in reaching a negative conclusion, the majority relied on arguments, some of which are rather dubious.

(4) In considering whether the impact of the Convention itself had given rise to a new rule of customary international law, the Court thought that the number of ratifications the Geneva Convention had received to date did not satisfy its criterion of 'a very widespread and representative participation . . . provided it included that of States whose interests were specially affected'. This conclusion was hotly disputed by some dissenting judges and some commentators; but it is essentially a question of judgment on the particular facts and need not detain us here.

(5) What is perhaps more troubling is the Court's assumption that, if the number and spread of ratifications had been greater, the Convention would of itself have given rise to a new rule of customary law. Why should a merely conventional obligation have this effect, with the consequence

---

[50] Judge Jennings, in his stimulating article 'What is International Law and How do We Tell It when We See it?', *Annuaire suisse de droit international*, 37 (1981), pp. 59, 87, tellingly notes that reservations were banned under the Law of the Sea Convention precisely because some provisions were *lex ferenda* and part of a 'package deal'.

that even non-parties to the treaty would be bound by the customary rule? The answer seems to be that, in the Court's view, it would do so only if an *opinio juris* had arisen that the rule was now part of customary law. But presumably this *opinio juris* would have had to have arisen after the conclusion of the treaty (because otherwise it would be a question of codifying or crystallizing existing law); and presumably, also, the *opinio juris* of the parties would not itself be conclusive for non-parties, though doubtless persuasive.

(6) In the same part of the judgment, recognizing (rightly) that the short time that had elapsed since the conclusion and entry into force of the Convention was not a determinative consideration, the majority pointed out that an extensive and virtually uniform state practice would suffice, provided it was accompanied by *opinio juris*. But if actual state practice is required (whether during the process of negotiating the Convention or subsequently), then it would seem that the mere fact of ratifying a conventional provision is not enough to transform it into customary law.

(7) Still on the question of whether the very adoption of the Convention had given rise to a new rule of customary law, the Court thought that this could only come about if the provision in question was 'of a fundamentally norm-creating character'. This term did not at the time, and still does not, form part of the normal conceptual apparatus of the international lawyer: what the Court seems to have meant was that a rule that was subject to exceptions and exclusion was not apt to become part of the corpus of general law, and it supported its reasoning by the following, rather dubious, points: (a) the 'equidistance/special circumstances' rule in article 6 was dependent on the states concerned not having reached agreement on the boundary; (b) the equidistance principle did not apply if there were (unspecified) special circumstances; (c) reservations could be made to article 6. It has already been submitted in relation to (3) above, that the point about reservations is of doubtful validity. The same can be said of points (a) and (b): most legal rules are *ius dispositivum*, not *cogens*, and there is nothing particularly unusual about rules being subject to conditions or to exceptions. If all that the Court meant was that it was easier for a clear-cut, unequivocal rule to become accepted as customary law, that might or might not be correct; but even then the right test would be to see what the attitude of states actually was, not to proceed on the basis of unproven assumptions and *a priori* reasoning.

The Court then went on to consider whether state practice since the conclusion of the Geneva Convention had given rise to a new customary rule. Once again, this was a possibility, but not one lightly to be assumed.

Some fifteen delimitations based on equidistance had been carried out, mainly by bilateral agreement but some unilaterally.

(8) To begin with, over half the states concerned were or were shortly to become parties to the Geneva Convention, and as, presumably, they were acting (actually or potentially) in application of the Convention, no inference could be drawn from their conduct about the existence of a customary rule. This is a very important point which, in the present author's view, must be correct as a matter of logic (though query with regard to states that were merely on the point of ratifying); but it has not always been kept sight of in the Court's other judgments.

(9) The Court was able to dispose of the practice of the remaining states, non-parties to the Convention, by pointing out that, not only were they few, but there was no evidence that their willingness to delimit according to the equidistance principle was motivated by a sense of legal obligation. This was another of those cases where (as with many forms of abstention) the conduct is in itself equivocal, and so the Court held (rightly it is submitted) that, in the absence of evidence of *opinio juris*, it could not infer that a customary rule had come into being.

How far have the various principles about the relation between treaty and custom, expressed or adumbrated in the *North Sea* cases, been respected in other decisions of the Court? Earlier, in the *Asylum* case[51] the Court had refused to regard the Montevideo Convention on Political Asylum of 1933 as 'proof of customary law', partly because its content and context suggested that it was not.[52] In the *Nottebohm* case *(Second Phase)*[53] a number of bilateral treaties concluded by the United States, as well as a Pan-American Convention, were fleetingly cited by the Court, among many other things, in support of the doctrine of the 'genuine link' of nationality. But in the *Barcelona Traction* case *(Second Phase)*, decided a year after the *North Sea* cases, the Court – rightly, it is submitted – refused to treat bilateral treaty arrangements regarding

---

[51] ICJ Reports, 1950, p. 266, at pp. 276–8.

[52] The Court also pointed out that only eleven states had ratified the Montevideo Convention of 1933. Given the limited number of Latin-American states who would have been eligible to ratify, this reason, unaccompanied as it is by further explanation, is perhaps a little surprising. The same could be said for the Court's further conclusion that, even if a regional custom of the type contended for did exist, it would not bind Peru, which had repudiated it by refusing to ratify the Montevideo Conventions of 1933 and 1939: by and of itself, a failure to ratify a convention does not necessarily prove anything one way or the other about the customary status of its content, yet the Court did not refer to any explanations by Peru or like material. Cf. the Court's reference to Norway's refusal to adhere to the North Sea Fisheries Convention of 1882 in the *Anglo-Norwegian Fisheries* case (ICJ Reports, 1959, p. 116, at p. 139).

[53] ICJ Reports, 1955, p. 4, at pp. 22–3.

compensation for nationalization of foreign property as evidencing any customary norm: 'Such arrangements are *sui generis* and provide no guide in the present case.'[54] In the *Icelandic Fisheries* case *(Merits)* the Court identified two concepts which had emerged in the wake of the abortive discussions at the 1958 and 1960 Geneva Conferences on the Law of the Sea: that of fishing zones, and that of preferential rights for coastal states. Among other things, it relied on a number of bilateral and multilateral fisheries conventions – not, though, as the foundation of a new rule of customary law, but as evidence of the recognition of preferential rights, the modalities of whose application they were regulating.[55] Given the caveats uttered in the *North Sea Continental Shelf* and *Barcelona Traction* cases about the reliance to be placed on what might be mere compromises, this was perhaps rather bold; but there was other evidence to support the view that there had been a shift in the perceptions of states. By the time the *Libya/Tunisia Continental Shelf* case[56] came to be decided in 1982, the Third UN Conference on the Law of the Sea (UNCLOS III) was well under way and a succession of 'informal negotiating texts' had been produced. Moreover, the parties had invited the Court to take into account, among other things, 'the recent trends admitted at the . . . Conference'. Nevertheless, the Court did not place substantial reliance on the draft treaty in reaching its conclusions. Two years later, when a Chamber came to decide the *Gulf of Maine* case,[57] the 1982 Convention had already been finalized. The Chamber did not rely on it as such, but did accept that the pertinent delimitation provisions reflected the current state of customary law on the subject, in view of the considerable consensus on which they were based. (In any case, they did little more than throw the decision-maker back onto the principles of customary law.) The following year, in the *Libya/Malta Continental Shelf* case,[58] the Court was again prepared to make use of the Convention, even though it was not yet in force and even though there were doubts about how widely it would be ratified. Here, it took into account not only the relevant delimitation formula – which, as already indicated, did not say anything very new – but also the existence of the exclusive economic zone and the 'distance principle' whereby the sea-bed and subsoil beyond the territorial sea, up to 200 nautical miles from the baseline, appertained to the coastal state regardless of whether there was a natural prolongation of the landmass. This was mainly

---

[54] ICJ Reports, 1970, p. 3, at p. 40, para. 61.
[55] ICJ Reports, 1974, p. 3, at pp. 22–6, paras. 51–8.
[56] ICJ Reports, 1982, p. 18.
[57] ICJ Reports, 1984, p. 246, at pp. 294–5, paras. 94–6.
[58] ICJ Reports, 1985, p. 13, at pp. 29–34, paras. 26–34.

because it was clear that a substantial consensus on these points had emerged at UNCLOS III; furthermore, there was a not insignificant amount of state practice along similar lines. Up to 1986, then, the Court was generally quite cautious in its handling of treaties as a possible evidential or material[59] source of customary law.

The treatment of the relationship between treaty and custom in the *Nicaragua* case *(Merits)*[60] has on the whole been much more open to criticism. Although there was a considerable degree of agreement between the parties on the customary law relating to non-intervention and the non-use of force (if not their precise content and application), the Court said that it was obliged to conduct its own investigation into state practice and *opinio juris*, and one of the places it looked was at treaty law.[61] Now, while the judgment in the *North Sea Continental Shelf* cases established that a treaty can be evidence of an existing customary rule or help generate a new one, it also (rightly) stressed that it does not necessarily do so, and the facts have to be carefully examined before that conclusion is reached. In *Nicaragua*, little effort was made to satisfy that requirement; general and regional conventions were cited with virtually no attempt to explain how they were declaratory of, or had given rise to new, customary law. For instance, in order to support its argument that the prior request of the victim of an armed attack was a precondition of resort to collective self-defence under customary law, the Court invoked the Inter-American Treaty of Reciprocal Assistance of 1947, under which a prior request is the condition for the rendering of assistance to the victim of an armed attack. But, as its title suggests, this is a treaty whereby the parties undertook obligations of mutual assistance, which certainly do not exist under customary law. As such, they were entitled to subject that assistance to conditions. This does not prove that the same condition applies when what is in issue is not the obligation to come to the aid of the victim, but the right to do so. Neither did the Court make any effort to explain how these treaty provisions reflected or had been transformed into even regional, let alone universal, customary law.

But the strongest criticisms of the Court's approach to the relationship between treaty and custom in that case concern its treatment of the UN

---

[59] *Pace* Ian Brownlie, *Principles of Public International Law* (4th edn, Oxford, 1990), pp. 1–2, the two concepts are not identical: see Mendelson, Appendix to the ILA *Report of the 63rd Conference*, at pp. 956–8.

[60] ICJ Reports, 1986, p. 14.

[61] *Ibid.*; see esp. pp. 100–7, paras. 189–204. Its treatment of General Assembly resolutions will be considered below.

Charter.[62] This gave rise to strong dissent by (*inter alios*) Judge Jennings. A US reservation to its Optional Clause declaration had been held to preclude consideration of disputes arising under multilateral treaties. The Court therefore concluded that it was not entitled to examine the parties' compliance with the Charter, but only with customary law.[63] In doing so, it had to meet a US objection that the Charter 'subsumed and supervened' any rules of customary law; and so the Court went out of its way to prove that the two bodies of law were different. It pointed out, for instance, that rules like proportionality and necessity pre-dated the Charter and were not expressly referred to in it; and that, if one party terminates or suspends its performance of a treaty obligation by virtue of breach by another party, that does not affect its customary-law obligations.[64] Two main criticisms can be levelled against the Court's approach.

(1) Having established that the Charter and customary law were distinct, the majority repeatedly derived the content of the relevant customary rules mainly from – the Charter. Now, it is of course, perfectly possible that certain of its provisions are merely declaratory of pre-existing customary law; but there is no doubt at all that others are innovations. It was therefore incumbent on the Court, in accordance with principles of the *North Sea* cases which it cited with approval, to demonstrate that the relevant Charter provisions either declared or crystallized existing law or had been accepted by means of subsequent state practice into the corpus of general international law, and to do so, moreover, without relying (at any rate solely) on the practice of member states under the Charter itself, for in that case there was a treaty reason for their conduct. Unfortunately, the Court's examination of these questions was rather perfunctory, and the main sources of corroboration it relied on were General Assembly resolutions (which arguably were really about Charter law, not customary law),[65] or other treaties, which it would be question-begging (without more) to assume were simply declaratory of existing customary law.

(2) It may be conceded that, to some extent, the Charter has not completely

---

[62] Esp. at pp. 92–111, paras. 172–211. *Mutatis mutandis*, similar observations apply to the Charter of the OAS and certain other regional treaties.

[63] Its consideration of the 1956 bilateral Treaty of Friendship, Commerce and Navigation does not concern us here.

[64] It also deployed a number of other, for the most part unpersuasive, arguments: for details, see Maurice Mendelson, 'The *Nicaragua* case and Customary International Law', *Coexistence*, 26 (1989), pp. 85, 86–91 (also published in W. E. Butler (ed.), *The Non-use of Force in International Law* (Dordrecht, 1989), pp. 85, 86–91), among many other critics.

[65] A point reverted to below in the discussion of General Assembly resolutions.

replaced customary law. For example, it is the latter that governs the relations between non-members of the UN, or between them and the members. And if a member withdrew from the Organization, no doubt it would become or continue to be bound by the customary rules. To that extent, the Charter has not 'subsumed and supervened' customary law. But those were not the circumstances obtaining here. Both of the litigants were at all material times parties to the Charter, and there was no dispute between them that that instrument continued to govern their mutual relations. Under international law, treaties normally do supersede customary rules, at least in the sense that they become the source of obligation to rely on; arguably, this is *a fortiori* the case where the Charter is concerned, if one can draw an analogy from article 103 and treat it as a 'supremacy clause' which also applies to custom. Throughout the whole period covered by the dispute, throughout the whole of the litigation, and to this day, it was fundamentally and pre-eminently Charter obligations that the two parties owed each other, whatever the limits on the Court's competence. To say the least, the majority could usefully have gone to greater lengths to explain how and why it was that, between the particular parties in the particular circumstances, customary law had not been subsumed by the Charter, and how, moreover, it could reach conclusions about US compliance with its customary obligations without thereby expressing a forbidden opinion about its compliance with its Charter obligations, especially if the former were to so great an extent expressed in or derived from the latter.

To summarize this discussion of the Court's contribution to the theory of customary law, it might perhaps be respectfully said that in some ways it has helped to clarify some troublesome points, but in others it has added unnecessarily to the confusion.

GENERAL PRINCIPLES OF LAW

As is well known, there is considerable controversy as to the meaning of article 38(1)(c) of the Statute, whereby the Court is to apply 'general principles of law recognized by civilized nations' – a controversy by no means resolved by the drafting history. Leaving aside natural law, which has no real place in a positivist society, the main contenders are: general principles of municipal law; general principles of international law; and general principles of legal systems generally, with particular reference to rules of judicial and arbitral procedure.

The Court has never expressly indicated that it was applying article 38(1)(c) as such, nor has it done anything to resolve the controversy.[66] And although there is quite a debate among legal theorists as to the difference and hierarchical relation between rules and principles, none of this finds any reflection in the utterances of the ICJ, which tends to treat the two terms as synonymous.[67]

In many cases the reference to 'principles' is clearly to principles of international law, examples being non-intervention and the non-use of force, and that delimitation of the continental shelf and similar zones should be effected by agreement where possible.[68] Such principles may be derived either from treaty or from custom. Occasionally (and less frequently than its predecessor) the Court has also referred to principles derived from municipal law, though not expressly identified as such.[69] Instances are the concepts of estoppel, *res judicata*, and the equality of the parties.[70] It is sometimes suggested that the concept of 'equitable principles', which forms part of the law of, for example, delimitation of the continental shelf and exclusive economic zone, is also derived from general principles of municipal law; but in fact it does not come in via article 38(1)(c), but as part of customary and treaty rules which ordain the application of these goals, techniques and principles.

The expectation of many commentators has been that, if an answer to a question could not be found in the principal sources (treaty and custom), recourse would be had to general principles (of municipal law) to fill the gap. But instances of this in the jurisprudence of the Court are relatively rare. Why is this? One reason seems to be that the Court has at its disposal another 'gap-filler' which is nowhere expressly mentioned in article 38(1): the sometimes rather mysterious process that bears the compendious name 'judicial

---

[66] A fleeting reference in *South West Africa (Second Phase)*, ICJ Reports, 1966, p. 6, at p. 47, para. 88, suggests that at least one conception of the Court is that the reference is to general principles of municipal law.

[67] In *US Diplomatic Staff in Tehran*, ICJ Reports, 1980, p. 3, at p. 42, para. 91, the Court referred to the 'principles of the Charter of the United Nations', to the 'fundamental principles enunciated in the Universal Declaration of Human Rights', and to the 'fundamental character . . . of the whole corpus of the international rules of which diplomatic and consular law is comprised'. The term 'principle' tends perhaps to denote a higher level of generality than 'rule' – but not always: cf. the *Gulf of Maine* case, ICJ Reports, 1984, p. 246, at p. 292, para. 89.

[68] Respectively *Nicaragua (Merits)*, ICJ Reports, 1986, at p. 14, at pp. 99–100 and 106–7, paras. 188 and 202; *Gulf of Maine* case, ICJ Reports, 1984, p. 246, at pp. 292–3, para. 90.

[69] It might also be argued that these are general principles of all legal systems, including domestic law and international law. But since, by definition, any such principles must figure in domestic law, and since, moreover, there is the safeguard that principles of domestic law can only be employed by international tribunals if they are suitable for transplantation, it all comes to very much the same thing.

[70] Respectively *Elettronica Sicula (ELSI)*, ICJ Reports, 1989, p. 15, at pp. 43–4, paras. 53–4 (estoppel); *Land, Island and Maritime Frontier Dispute (Application to Intervene)*, ICJ Reports, 1990, p. 92, at p. 118, para. 63 (estoppel); *ibid.*, 1992, pp. 600–1, paras. 402–3 (*res judicata*); *Judgments of the ILO Administrative Tribunal*, ICJ Reports, 1956, p. 77, at pp. 85–6 (equality of parties).

reasoning'. Even if there is no provision of treaty or customary law directly in point, the Court has been adept at drawing logical deductions,[71] reasoning by analogy or rejecting analogies,[72] discovering implied terms,[73] taking a teleological viewpoint,[74] and so on. Consequently, the need to look for other means of filling the gaps is greatly reduced.[75]

JUDICIAL DECISIONS

The direction in article 38(1)(d) of the Statute to apply 'judicial decisions . . . as subsidiary means for the determination of rules of law' is subject to article 59, the effect of which is that there is no doctrine of binding precedent in the ICJ. But precedents, even if they are not controlling, clearly have considerable persuasive force, and the Court regularly cites its own previous decisions, and those of the Permanent Court, in its judgments and Opinions. It has, indeed, never expressly departed from a previous decision of either tribunal. That is not to say, however, that it has followed them rigidly: for instance, the strict rule laid down in the *Eastern Carelia* case has been distinguished in the *Peace Treaties*[76] and later cases; there have been considerable changes of emphasis in succeeding cases on maritime delimitation; and the previously relatively strict approach of the Court to the elements of customary law seems to have been considerably relaxed in the *Nicaragua* case.

When considering the Court's treatment of the decisions of other international, and national, courts and tribunals, it is desirable to distinguish five different situations.

(1) Where it is the decision of the other tribunal that is the issue in the proceedings, or at any rate part of the history of the case: examples involving international tribunals include the various applications for review of decisions of the UN Administrative Tribunal; the *Case Concerning the Arbitral Award of 31 July 1989 (Guinea-Bissau v. Senegal)*;[77]

---

[71] As in the *Genocide Convention* case, ICJ Reports, 1951, p. 15, at p. 26.
[72] As in the *Reparation for Injuries* case, ICJ Reports, 1949, p. 174 at pp. 178–80; and *Barcelona Traction (Second Phase)*, ICJ Reports, 1970, p. 3.
[73] As in the *Reparation for Injuries* case, ICJ Reports, 1949, p. 174.
[74] As in *Certain Expenses of the UN*, ICJ Reports, 1962, p. 151.
[75] H. W. A. Thirlway, 'The Law and Procedure of the International Court of Justice 1960–1989, Part 2', *BYbIL*, 61 (1990), p. 1, at p. 111 suggests another reason: parties before the Court seldom rely on general principles of municipal law. He does not suggest a reason, but a possible one is the prodigious investment in comparative law research and analysis that may be felt necessary if such principles are to be relied on.
[76] Respectively, PCIJ, Series B, No. 5 (1923); and ICJ Reports, 1950, p. 221.
[77] ICJ Reports, 1991, p. 53.

and *Land, Island, and Maritime Frontier Dispute*, where one of the issues was the effect to be given to a decision of the Central American Court of Justice.[78] Similarly, orders of national courts may give rise to international proceedings, as in the *ELSI* case.[79] Nothing more need be said about such cases here: they are not being examined by the court as precedents.

(2) The decisions of municipal courts may be treated as a form of state practice (since the judiciary is a component of the state). This has already been discussed under the rubric of customary law. The decisions of international courts and tribunals are also sometimes discussed in the literature as a form of state practice, but this is very doubtful. These bodies may be instrumentalities of states inasmuch as they have been set up by them and operate only with their consent, but it is only partly true to say that they are making decisions on behalf of the states appearing before them, nor do those decisions necessarily reflect the position of the states concerned.

(3) Decisions of national courts on questions of municipal law may provide suitable analogies for international law, or even form part of the corpus of 'general principles of law recognised by civilized nations'.

(4) Decisions of courts and tribunals may be cited as evidence of the prevailing *opinio juris* on a particular question. Without going here into vexed questions of the meaning of this elusive concept, it seems clear that the Court, like other decision-makers, considers it legitimate to take into account not just the opinions of states, but of other participants in the international legal process, which includes international and even (in appropriate circumstances) national tribunals.

(5) Finally, a decision of another tribunal on a question of international law may be relied on for the persuasiveness of its reasoning and the quality of the research which underlies it.

It is only with categories (4) and (5) that we need concern ourselves here; here the decisions concerned are being treated in some sense as precedents.

There can be little doubt that these decisions have a significant influence on the decisions of the Court. They are frequently cited in the pleadings, and experienced counsel would not do that if they did not think it worthwhile; and Individual Opinions of judges sometimes dwell on these precedents in a way that suggests that they must have been considered in the internal discussions of the Court that preceded the judgment or Advisory Opinion. Nevertheless, the fact remains that the majority decisions of the Court have

---

[78] ICJ Reports, 1992, p. 351, at p. 600, para. 402ff.   [79] ICJ Reports, 1989, p. 15.

only rarely cited a specific decision of another international court or tribunal,[80] and never one of a national tribunal, as authority in this sense, though occasionally they will refer compendiously to the case law of other international, and even national, tribunals.[81] One may speculate about the reasons for this reticence. One was given in the *Barcelona Traction* case *(Second Phase)*:[82] decisions of international tribunals may be conditioned by the terms of the instruments establishing them; and similarly, one might add, decisions of national courts on points of international law may be restricted by rules of national law. Another reason may be that not all international or national courts are of equal standing or equal quality, and it may be felt somewhat invidious to pick and choose among them. Yet another consideration may be that of prestige: even though there are other international courts in existence today, the ICJ is regarded, and presumably regards itself, as the supreme public international law tribunal, and as such would not wish to be seen to rely too heavily on the jurisprudence of other bodies. And finally, of course, the fact that these precedents are in no way binding on the ICJ reduces the need for them to be minutely examined.

Nevertheless, the growing volume and accessibility of this jurisprudence makes it a valuable resource to which the Court seems to be gradually resorting more openly, while the growing quantity of the Court's own case law is likely to result in a more extensive discussion of its own precedents than has hitherto been the case.

Finally, it may be observed that, although the decisions of the Court are not as such binding on other decision-makers (whether third parties or government advisers), and although the absence of true compulsory jurisdiction makes it statistically very improbable that any given international dispute will end up in The Hague, decisions of the Court have in practice a very considerable influence on the view of the law taken by other decision-makers.

TEACHINGS OF PUBLICISTS

The 'teachings of the most highly qualified publicists of the various nations' are listed by article 31(1)(d) of the Statute as the other 'subsidiary means for

---

[80] Exceptions are the references to the *Alabama* award in the *Nottebohm (Preliminary Objection)* case, ICJ Reports, 1953, p. 111, at p. 115 and in the *UN Headquarters Agreement* case, ICJ Reports, 1988, p. 12, at p. 34, para. 57; and to the *Anglo-French Continental Shelf* award in several cases on maritime delimitation, notably the *Gulf of Maine* case, ICJ Reports, 1984, p. 246, at pp. 293, 302–3 and 324, paras. 92, 123 and 187, respectively.

[81] An example is *Nottebohm (Second Phase)*, ICJ Reports, 1955, p. 4, at pp. 22–3.

[82] ICJ Reports, 1970, p. 3, at p. 40, para. 63.

the determination of rules of law'. Here, too, writers are frequently cited in the pleadings, and their mention in the Individual Opinions suggests that their views may well play a part in the deliberations of the Court. Majority decisions, though, rarely refer to the opinions of writers even compendiously;[83] and it has been traditional not to refer to individual writers by name. (The citation of Oppenheim, H. Lauterpacht and Gidel in the recent *Land, Island and Maritime Frontier Dispute* judgment[84] may be a new departure.) The International Law Commission, however, holds a rather special place, being an official UN body. Its opinions have been cited, not only in order to elucidate treaties it has helped to draft,[85] but also as evidence of the general *opinio juris*.[86] In the *Land, Island and Maritime Frontier Dispute* reference was also made to a UN Secretariat study.[87] What is perhaps a little surprising is that majority judgments and opinions have avoided specific reference to the reports and resolutions of the Institut de Droit International or the International Law Association.

Commentators frequently refer to writers as providing evidence of the law. This is one, but not their only, function. Some writers, such as Gidel, do provide useful evidence of state practice etc., which they laboriously assemble. But when it comes to litigation, the Court will naturally prefer to rely if possible on the primary sources they cite rather than the testimony at one remove of their authors. The other useful contribution of the writers is their reasoning. But, once again, even if the Court is persuaded by that reasoning, it can simply adopt it without reference to its source.

The reasons for the Court's reluctance to make more open reference to individuals are easy to guess. For one thing, writers vary considerably in skill, diligence, intellectual honesty, independence and eminence, but it may be thought invidious to distinguish between them. Second, the Court is itself composed of eminent jurists who may be reluctant to treat others as 'authorities'. And the quantity of literature that emanates from the developed world is so much greater than that produced elsewhere that there may possibly be a fear (whether well founded or not) that other viewpoints may not be properly represented in the literature. Finally, a detailed discussion of numerous authors is rather inconsistent with the somewhat 'broad-brush' approach to reasoning that tends to typify the Court's majority opinions.

---

[83] One such case is *Nottebohm (Second Phase)*, ICJ Reports, 1955, p. 4, at pp. 22–3.
[84] ICJ Reports, 1992, p. 351, at p. 593, para. 394.
[85] As in the *North Sea Continental Shelf* cases, ICJ Reports, 1969, p. 3, *passim*.
[86] As in the *Nicaragua (Merits)* case, ICJ Reports, 1986, p. 14, at p. 100, para. 190.
[87] ICJ Reports, 1992, p. 351, at pp. 593–4, para. 394.

UNILATERAL ACTS

Some commentators (especially from civil law jurisdictions) list unilateral acts as a source of international law not mentioned in article 38(1). In reality, it is impossible to generalize about so heterogeneous a category, including as it does declarations, notifications, protests, waivers, recognition, acquiescence, the conferment of nationality, and so on. Many such transactions acquire significance only in the context of some wider transaction – for instance protest in the context of the formation of customary law or in relation to territorial claims, and declarations of acceptance of the Court's 'compulsory jurisdiction' within the context of the treaty obligations embodied in the Statute. They are not 'free standing'. It might perhaps also be pointed out that many of these acts are a source of particular rights and obligations rather than of 'law'.[88]

One type of unilateral act that perhaps requires special notice is the declaration. Certain types of declaration create obligations for a particular state either in relation to particular other states, or even *erga omnes*, the dedication of a canal to international traffic being an example. The regime thus established may be largely indistinguishable from what might be created by treaty, or even by custom. In the *Nuclear Tests* judgment the Court made a very important statement about the binding effect of declarations,[89] which has subsequently formed the core of doctrinal discussion about unilateral acts. Space does not permit further exploration of this multifaceted topic here; suffice it to say that it is perhaps unfortunate that the leading pronouncement in this field should be one whose well-foundedness on the facts and in principle was and remains highly controversial.

RESOLUTIONS OF INTERNATIONAL ORGANIZATIONS

The constitutions of international organizations can endow particular organs, such as the Security Council, with the power to make decisions binding on the members in certain circumstances, and from time to time the Court has had to consider such decisions.[90] Equally, an organ might be given quasi-judicial powers to determine disputes between members, or between the organisation and staff members; such decisions may come up for review by

---

[88] It is fair to point out, however, that I have myself expressed reservations about the value of this distinction when applied to treaties; cf. 'Are Treaties Merely a Source of Obligation?', above, n. 7.

[89] ICJ Reports, 1974, p. 253, at pp. 267–8, paras. 42–6. The judgment in the case brought by New Zealand is identical in this respect.

[90] E.g. in *Certain Expenses of the United Nations*, ICJ Reports, 1962, p. 151.

the Court, or be used by it as precedents in other cases. None of this need concern us here. Instead, mention should be made of the Court's handling of resolutions of the UN General Assembly, in particular, which purport to declare or lay down rules of general law. This is a large and controversial subject, but considerations of space once again preclude an extended treatment.

On the one hand, it is clear that the founders of the UN did not envisage that the Assembly would have the power to legislate. On the other hand, Assembly resolutions plainly both can and do influence the creation of both customary and conventional rules. They can also constitute 'soft law': norms whose binding force is not strictly legal or so-called legal norms whose content is highly discretionary. None of this is particularly problematic. The real questions for us here are: in a world that is in some ways becoming increasingly communal, can Assembly resolutions independently generate law for states,[91] or at any rate those voting for them?; and how persuasive are such resolutions as evidence of existing customary[92] law?

The Court's answer to the first question seems to be negative.[93] Admittedly, in the *US Diplomatic Staff in Tehran* case, its reference to 'fundamental principles enunciated in the Universal Declaration of Human Rights'[94] could be interpreted as attributing a more than merely evidential role to that resolution. But in the *Nicaragua (Merits)* case,[95] where the Court dealt extensively with Assembly resolutions, it plainly did not regard them as an independent source of law. It was only insofar as they could be subsumed under the heading of customary law that it could take them into account.

As a matter of principle, there is no reason why Assembly resolutions should not in appropriate circumstances be treated as evidence of the *opinio juris* of states (or at least those voting in favour), bearing in mind that there is no particular form prescribed by the law for the expression of such beliefs. But whether they do so depends very much on the terms of the resolution and the context. In *Nicaragua*, the Court made great play of a number of resolutions, including in particular resolution 2625 (XXV), the Declaration on Principles of International Law concerning Friendly Relations and Co-operation among

---

[91] We may leave aside 'housekeeping' resolutions and those that, being otherwise within the competence of the organ, may cause legal consequences for states, such as the termination of a mandate.

[92] Assembly resolutions as authoritative interpretations of the Charter are outside the scope of this essay.

[93] However, see the *Namibia* case, ICJ Reports, 1971, p. 16, at p. 31, para. 52.

[94] ICJ Reports, 1980, p. 3, at p. 42, para. 91.

[95] ICJ Reports, 1986, p. 14.

States in accordance with the Charter of the United Nations.[96] This and other resolutions may quite possibly constitute authoritative interpretations of the Charter, but that is not the point: the Court had already held that it was precluded from applying multilateral treaties, including the Charter, and was confined to the position at customary law. The majority were obviously aware of this problem: for instance, they stated that it was (only) with 'all due caution' that these resolutions could be used as evidence of *opinio juris*. But the assertion that these instruments were indeed intended to declare the customary law is, with respect, merely an assertion. There is, in fact, material in the Declaration that could support such a conclusion – but there is also material pointing in the opposite direction. The point is simply that insufficient effort was made to demonstrate the validity of the assertion that a resolution plainly intended to elaborate on the Charter went beyond it, and entered into the realm of custom.[97]

Even if one were to accept these resolutions as evidence of *opinio juris*, that would not be sufficient to create binding law. The Court, as we have already seen, had solemnly declared that there are two elements in customary law: not just *opinio juris*, but also the material element of state practice. But it is hard to see how it complied with its own injunction in *Nicaragua*. True, it did cite a number of treaties; but the appropriateness of doing so has already been questioned above, and in any case they seem to have been invoked more as evidence of *opinio juris* than as the material element.[98] And although it is at any rate arguable that making a statement or casting a vote in the Assembly is a (weak) form of practice, to treat the same action as both practice and *opinio juris* seems, as already pointed out, to be a form of double counting, impermissible not only because of its inconsistency with the Court's identification of two separate elements of customary law, but also because the consequence would be 'instant (customary) law'. This is something that was not intended by the drafters of the Charter, and which, even today, states in general show no sign of welcoming.

At the end of the day, whether and to what extent General Assembly resolutions can play a part in the formation of international law is determined by the attitude of states as a whole: if they will it, there is no obstacle in

---

[96] *Ibid.* at pp. 98–108, paras. 187–205.

[97] The Definition of Aggression annexed to General Assembly resolution 3314 (XXIX) is even more firmly tied to the Charter; and the language quoted by the Court from resolution 78 of the General Assembly of the OAS of 21 April 1972 is in terms confined to members of the Organization and so cannot, without more, be assumed to enunciate an obligation more general than that imposed by the OAS Charter.

[98] The Court was also anxious to stress (perhaps unnecessarily strictly) that the recognition by the parties to the proceedings that something was a rule of customary law did not suffice.

theory or in existing law. In the next half century, the Court will have to show considerable sensitivity to the climate of international opinion; and, no doubt, for a long time to come its members will be divided between 'progressives' and 'conservatives' on this politically very important issue.

CONCLUDING OBSERVATIONS

Accounts of the sources of international law almost invariably begin by setting out article 38(1) of the Statute. This is convenient and understandable if one concentrates on the Court, for it is bound by the Statute and has in fact never found it necessary to stray beyond the confines of article 38(1). But in a more general account of sources, it may give a false perspective. For all its importance and the encouraging increase in its case load, the Court is by no means the sole, or even the main, decision-maker in the system. Government legal officials, for instance, make many more decisions than the Court. They operate under different constraints, and their approach to the sources can and does differ in some respects. For example, they tend to place much greater reliance on judicial decisions and the writings of publicists; and, performing diplomatic as well as purely legal functions, they may be more free to give some effect to General Assembly resolutions than is the Court.[99] So this brief account has not been an appraisal of the sources of international law at large, but simply of the Court's approach to them.

That said, it cannot be denied that, even if it is not the sole or the main decider of legal questions, and even if the absence of compulsory jurisdiction means that international law cannot be defined in terms of what the Court will do, the ICJ remains the most prestigious legal decision-maker within the system, and its pronouncements carry very great weight. Consequently, the light it has thrown on the many conundrums about the sources of international law are the more precious, and its failures to illuminate all the more regrettable.

The Court has made some influential contributions to the development and elucidation of aspects of the law of treaties and of customary law, including the concepts of local and regional law, and – at least initially – the relation between treaty and custom. The *Genocide Convention*, *Asylum*, *Right of Passage* and *North Sea Continental Shelf* cases come particularly to mind. And where it is open to

---

[99] For elaboration of this argument, see Maurice Mendelson, 'Formation of International Law and the Observational Standpoint', Appendix to the First Report of the Rapporteur, Annexe 1 to the First Interim Report of the International Committee on the Formation of Rules of Customary (General) International Law, in ILA, *Report of the 63rd Conference* (Warsaw, 1988), p. 941.

criticism, the problem is usually not so much error as obscurity of language (as in the *Anglo-Norwegian Fisheries* case) and a tendency simply to state conclusions without spelling out the reasoning behind them. It is understandable that the Court may not wish to decide more than it has to;[100] neither should we underestimate the difficulty of getting fifteen or more distinguished judges from different backgrounds to agree. Nevertheless, such failings and omissions as have occurred are regrettable. It is not merely a question of scientific accuracy and completeness. Many of the cases coming before the Court are politically sensitive – perhaps increasingly so; the more cogent the Court's reasoning, and the more demonstrably grounded in a sound theory of sources, the more acceptable its decisions are likely to be to the litigants and the international community at large.

In commemorating the fiftieth anniversary of the Court and celebrating its considerable achievements, it seemed nevertheless appropriate to note some perceived deficiencies in the hope that the next half century (or preferably less) will see them rectified. Nor do such comments seem out of place in a celebration of the career of Sir Robert Jennings: while a strong supporter of the Court as an academic and one of its most distinguished members as a judge and as President, he has not refrained from criticism or dissent where he felt they were called for.

---

[100] Indeed, difficulties can be created if the Court tries to accumulate reasons for its decision, some of which are in fact less convincing than others: see above for a critique of some of the reasoning in the *North Sea Continental Shelf* cases, for instance.

5

Municipal law reasoning in
international law

M. Shahabuddeen

❧

Discussing the well-known municipal law principle directed to the avoidance of absurdity, Blackstone wrote

> As to the effects and consequence the rule is, that where words bear either none, or a very absurd signification, if literally understood, we must a little deviate from the received sense of them. Therefore the Bolognan law, mentioned by Puffendorf, which enacted 'that whosoever drew blood in the streets should be punished with the utmost severity', was held after long debate not to extend to the surgeon, who opened the vein of a person that fell down in the street with a fit.[1]

Whenever a possible absurdity arises in the course of construing an instrument executed at the more exalted level of inter-state relations, it cannot be wrong to suppose that the relevant rule of treaty interpretation owes something to that municipal law principle.[2] The hapless Bologna surgeon no doubt had some little reason to be grateful to it for stepping in to save him from being 'punished with the utmost severity' for an act which, though within the letter of the law, could not seriously be thought to have been within its intent; nor could the result have been the less pleasant for having been reached only 'after long debate'.

Recourse to municipal law in the development of international law, the somewhat delicate theme on which I have been invited to offer a view, is now less uninhibited than during the formative phase of the newer discipline; it is probably true to say that it is frowned upon. To what extent does its influence obey admonitions about its use?

---

[1] Blackstone, *Commentaries*, vol. I (1813 edn), p. 80, cited in Rupert Cross, 'Blackstone v. Bentham', *LQR*, 92 (1976), p. 521. And see Samuel Pufendorf, *De jure naturae et gentium* (trans. of the 1688 edn, Oxford, 1934), vol. II, Book V, chapter XII, section 8, pp. 802–3.

[2] The extent to which treaty law has derived from municipal law is of course well known. See *South West Africa (Preliminary Objections)*, ICJ Reports, 1962, p. 579, Judge *ad hoc* van Wyk, dissenting; and Luigi Ferrari-Bravo, 'International Law and Municipal Law: The Complementarity of Systems', in R. St J. Macdonald and D. M. Johnston (eds.), *The Structure and Process of International Law* (Dordrecht, 1986), p. 716.

The shunning of municipal law

Remarking that there is 'no agreed enumeration of rights and obligations *erga omnes*', the recently issued ninth edition of *Oppenheim* states, in the very first paragraph at p. 5 of volume I, that 'the law in this area is still developing . . . by analogy with the *actio popularis* (or *actio communis*) known to some national legal systems'. So, through analogy, municipal law is still at work in developing international law. That being so, it may be assumed that the learned editors of that authoritative work (including the distinguished subject of this *liber amicorum*) are not without sympathy for the complaint made in 1927 by the youthful Lauterpacht in these words:

> It has become a custom with publicists writing on certain disputed questions of international law to base their argument on the assertion that the opinion with which they happen to disagree is nothing else than a misleading analogy to a conception of private law. It is now generally accepted that the recourse to private law, which was, perhaps, justified in the formative period of international law owing to the then prevalent patrimonial conception of State, has subsequently impeded the growth of international law, and ought to be discouraged. The habit of falling back on private law is looked upon as betraying a regrettable tendency to imitation, as ignoring the special structure of international relations, and as threatening to thwart, by introducing technicalities and intricacies of municipal jurisprudence, every attempt at a fruitful and creative scientific activity in the domain of international law. And even in those rare cases in which an author is forced, by the sheer identity of the legal relations with which he has to deal, to adopt a solution suggested by a general principle of private law, the recourse to analogy is usually accompanied by embarrassed counsels of caution or by apologetic explanations.[3]

The custom of publicists to which Lauterpacht alluded (as alive today as it was in 1927), coupled with possible apprehension of being suspected of harbouring a private law orientation, must have demanded courage for him to ask: 'does this disparagement of private law receive confirmation from the practice of states and from the history of international law?' The answer his inquiry produced drew from McNair this assessment:

> The result of this investigation is to vindicate the practice of resort to rules and conceptions of private law for the purpose of the development of international law, and to give to it the dignity of a scientific basis. The modern detractors of this practice are apt to treat it as being at best an ingenious and empirical expedient for

---

[3] H. Lauterpacht, *Private Law Sources and Analogies of International Law (with special reference to international arbitration)* (London, 1927), Preface, p. vii.

filling up a gap or getting out of an impasse; but I venture to think that the author makes good his claim to establish it on grounds of intrinsic merit and reasonableness.[4]

Lauterpacht's answer emerged out of an investigation of the practice of states and the history of international law. His work was, as he said, 'in a sense, a commentary on Article 38(3) of the Statute' of the Permanent Court of International Justice, relating to general principles of law.[5] The exact role played by municipal law analogies in the working of that provision is not always clear. Speaking of the extension of reasoning that comes about through the use of analogy and through recourse to general principles, Charles De Visscher remarked on a clear tendency 'dans la jurisprudence de la Cour . . . à ne guère expliciter le processus intellectuel de l'extension, à éviter de distinguer systématiquement entre l'analogie et le recours aux principes généraux'.[6] The somewhat shadowy operation of that provision is not, however, the subject of this short chapter. Nor is any question being raised as to the way in which municipal legal systems treat international law, or as to the way in which international law treats any particular system of municipal law. The interest is in the utility of drawing on the processes of municipal law reasoning for the purpose of appreciating a concept or solving a problem in international law which is materially similar to a corresponding concept or problem in municipal law. The limited submission (scarcely original) is that no specific provision of the Statute needs to be cited as authority to enable the Court to benefit from the scientific value of the reasoning of other jurists, wherever situated, always provided that it remains master of its house.

The dangers of recourse to municipal law

There is little need to dwell on the dangers involved in the use of municipal law ideas. Many were noticed, explained and emphasized by Lauterpacht himself: the tendency on the part of many writers to resort to notions peculiar to their own municipal law; the fact that not every relation between states has its counterpart in private law; the fact that solutions may easily be found by making logical deductions from existing rules of international law or by means of analogy to them; and the absence of any universally compulsory judicial tribunal to determine what the law is or of a central authority to enforce it.[7]

---

[4] *Ibid.*, Foreword, p. v.
[5] *Ibid.*, p. viii.
[6] Charles De Visscher, *Problèmes d'interprétation judiciaire en droit international public* (Paris, 1963), p. 39.
[7] Lauterpacht, *Private Law Sources*, pp. 84ff.

There is hardly a book in the field that does not allude to these and other dangers, and rightly so.

As an early example of the problems, one sees Lord Finlay drawing upon municipal practice relating to contracts made on behalf of a company in the course of formation in considering whether Poland was bound by clause 19 of the Armistice Convention of 11 November 1918 and entitled to its benefits, although that instrument had been concluded before it became a state.[8] The Court, relying on basic principles of treaty law, answered in the negative.[9] Speaking of the municipal law concept *pas d'intérêt, pas d'action*, Judge Koretsky later put the matter this way: 'Long ago there were warnings against the danger of an unreserved transference of the principles of civil law and process into international (public) law and into the procedure of international courts. Here the character of relations and rights is of another kind. Here one cannot think in civil law categories.'[10] It would be an act of temerity to brush aside these warnings. Nor is it intended to do so. There might, nevertheless, be value in a study being done (as it were, by updating Lauterpacht) on the possibility that in some cases the dangers are exaggerated; that in others they do not inhere in the essence of the relevant municipal law concept; and that in yet others, even where the latter is distinguishable, the very grounds of distinction can sometimes help to clarify the international-law concept. This chapter, which is not such a study, merely suggests that these questions may be usefully examined, or re-examined. Having done so, it will now pass on to consider a few samples of the relationship between municipal law ideas and international law ideas, using, in the case of the latter, some aspects of the judicial character of the Court, the law it applies, and its rules of procedure and evidence.

The Court

A field of leading importance in the interplay between international and municipal law concepts concerns the sense in which the International Court of Justice may be said to be a court. Everyone knows that the Court is in several respects unlike a municipal court. Is it possible, however, that the distinction is sometimes pressed to the point where doubts are unnecessarily raised in the average legal mind as to whether it is after all a court? Is its title a misnomer? There are several interesting aspects to the problem; I shall allude

---

[8] *Certain German Interests in Polish Upper Silesia (Merits)*, PCIJ, Series A, No. 7 (1926), p. 84.
[9] *Ibid.*, pp. 25–9.
[10] *South West Africa (Second Phase)*, Dissenting Opinion, ICJ Reports, 1966, p. 242.

to one concerning the character of the power exercised by the Court. Is there any sense in which it would be right to call it 'judicial power'?

In some countries the courts are located within a constitutional framework of checks and balances and given power to rule on the legality of actions of other repositories of state power, including the power to strike down legislation. Where courts are not situated within such a constitutional structure, *Marbury v. Madison* type of reasoning is not necessarily imported to vest them with that kind of power.[11] To assume that the International Court of Justice has judicial power in that special sense might well be to beg the question in cases in which the issue may be whether or not the Court can invalidate the acts of other principal organs of the United Nations and, if so, within what limits.[12] Whatever the answer to that question, it cannot flow from a mere assumption that the Court has judicial power in that special sense. A caution on this point is appropriate. But does it extend to justify the view that the Court has no judicial power at all?

Sometimes it is said that the Court has judicial functions but not judicial power.[13] I understand statements of this nature as intended, unexceptionably, to convey not that the Court has no judicial power at all, but that it has no judicial power in the specific sense in which a municipal court is vested with the judicial power of the state to interpose for the settlement of disputes, irrespective of whether the parties accept its authority. Obviously, the Court, not disposing of any kind of *imperium*, lacks judicial power in that sense.[14] It is improbable, however, that a court can exercise judicial functions without enabling judicial power in any sense; a power in exercise of which a judicial body discharges judicial functions is *prima facie* a judicial power. In the case of its advisory jurisdiction, the Court spoke of 'the normal exercise of its judicial powers'.[15] In the case of its contentious jurisdiction, it likewise observed that 'once the Court has been regularly seised, the Court must exercise its powers, as these are defined in the Statute'.[16] More recently Judge Weeramantry, while recognizing that the Court does not have 'the full judicial powers normally

---

[11] (1803 US) 1 Cranch 137; and see René David and Henry P. de Vries, *The French Legal System: An Introduction to Civil Law Systems* (New York, 1958), p. 34, para. 3.

[12] See and consider Manfred Lachs, 'The Decision-making Powers and the Judiciary within the United Nations', in P. Fischer, H. F. Koch and A. Verdross (eds.), *Volkerrecht und Rechtsphilosophie: Internationale Festschrift für Stephan Verosta* (Berlin, 1980), at pp. 397–400.

[13] Luigi Condorelli, 'L'Autorité de la décision des juridictions internationales permanentes', in *La Juridiction internationale permanente*, Colloque de Lyon (1987), p. 309.

[14] See Individual Opinion of Judge Alvarez in *Conditions of Admission of a State to Membership in the United Nations*, ICJ Reports, 1948, p. 68.

[15] *Ibid.*, p. 61.

[16] *Nottebohm (Preliminary Objection)*, ICJ Reports, 1953, p. 122.

associated with a court of superior jurisdiction', obviously considered, *a contrario*, that such power as the Court has is judicial power.[17] These references are understandable; the Court is a standing judicial body established by conventional international law, with jurisdiction to determine issues in accordance with law and, in contentious cases, with 'binding force' on the parties.

It is only necessary to add that the question of execution of decisions is beside the point. Enforcement is distinguishable from adjudication; it is, arguably, an executive responsibility not forming part of the true functions of a municipal court, even though occasionally undertaken by it.[18] More pertinently, as against the government, a municipal court has no army to enforce its decision; compliance is ultimately a function of the government's own sense of legality and legitimacy. The position of the World Court in relation to litigating states is substantially similar.

Thus, it would be incorrect to view the Court as if it were a court exercising judicial power on exactly the same basis as that on which a municipal court does. But that consideration, relating to differences in the basis of the power, is not a convincing reason for suggesting that no analogy exists as to the essential nature of the power itself.

It is, plainly, on the municipal model that one must draw for an appreciation of the inherent but uncatalogued limitations to which the Court referred when, speaking of its judicial function, it said: 'That function is circumscribed by inherent limitations which are none the less imperative because they may be difficult to catalogue, and may not frequently present themselves as a conclusive bar to adjudication in a concrete case'.[19] The municipal model was not far from the mind of the Court when, after examining the Statute of the United Nations Administrative Tribunal, it said that it contained provisions that 'are of an essentially judicial character and conform with the rules generally laid down in statutes or law issued for courts of justice, such as, for instance, in the Statute of the International Court of Justice'.[20] That statement proceeded on the footing that the judicial character of the Court was not different from that of more familiar municipal models.

---

[17] *Application of the Convention on the Prevention and Punishment of the Crime of Genocide (Bosnia and Herzegovina v. Yugoslavia (Serbia and Montenegro)) (Provisional Measures)*, Separate Opinion, ICJ Reports, 1993, p. 387.

[18] See *ibid.*, p. 366, for Henri Rolin's remarks.

[19] *Northern Cameroons*, ICJ Reports, 1963, p. 30.

[20] *Effect of Awards of Compensation made by the United Nations Administrative Tribunal*, ICJ Reports, 1954, p. 52; and see *ibid.*, ICJ Pleadings, pp. 26–7.

The law

Some suggested differences may be more apparent than real. In the *Reservations to the Genocide Convention* case the Court observed that the concept of 'the integrity of the convention', involving 'the proposition that no reservation was valid unless it was accepted by all the contracting parties without exception', was 'directly inspired by the notion of contract'.[21] For the reasons given by the Court, the contract notion was subject to limitations in its application to a convention of the kind being considered by it. It is useful, however, to note that, in not following the 'contractual conception of the absolute integrity of the convention', the Court said: 'This view, however, cannot prevail if, having regard to the character of the convention, its purpose and its mode of adoption, it can be established that the parties intended to derogate from that rule by admitting the faculty to make reservations thereto'.[22] Thus, the essential reason why the municipal concept did not prevail was 'that the parties intended to derogate' from it. This effectively threw the matter back on consent – a consent to derogate – and in turn gave rise to a question as to how real was the suggested deviation from the essence of the municipal contractual norm and the reasoning relating to the latter.[23]

In the *Right of Passage over Indian Territory* case, one question was whether Portugal's declaration accepting the compulsory jurisdiction of the Court took effect in relation to India as from the time of its deposit so as to entitle Portugal to sue three days later and before the Secretary-General had had reasonable time to transmit it to other parties to the Statute, including India, which was not in fact as yet aware of it. Answering in the negative, Vice-President Badawi, dissenting, referred to 'the classical notion of offer and acceptance' underlying municipal contract law.[24] The Court, by contrast, held that Portugal's declaration became effective as at the time of deposit. It considered that the 'contractual relation between the Parties' and 'the consensual bond' between them in respect of compulsory jurisdiction was established by the act of deposit of the declaration.[25] Contractual relationship there was; but, if it is seen as resting solely on the deposit of declarations, the matter does raise the issue presented by India as to how it could be affected by

---

[21] ICJ Reports, 1951, p. 21.

[22] *Ibid.*, p. 24.

[23] Cf. *Barcelona Traction, Light and Power Company Limited (Preliminary Objections)*, Judge Armand-Ugon, Dissenting Opinion, ICJ Reports, 1964, p. 135.

[24] ICJ Reports, 1957, p. 157.

[25] *Ibid.*, p. 146.

another state's declaration of which it did not have reasonable opportunity to become aware. The suggestion of oddity in the operation of the system bears an appearance of departure from the mutuality inhering in the municipal contractual idea. Was there a departure? Not on the following view.

States that have made declarations are parties to the Optional Clause system. But the real 'contractual relation' between them is established when they become parties to the Statute; the declarations are made pursuant to the terms of that already established relationship, and merely trigger it off in a particular field. Portugal's declaration was made pursuant to the contractual bargain so made between itself and India. The legal incidents that it produced flowed from the original bargain. The fact that it took effect as at the time of deposit was due to the circumstance that this was something which the parties accepted in advance by agreeing to the Statute that produced that effect. That represented not a departure from the essence of the municipal contractual idea of offer and acceptance, but only an application of the idea in the particular circumstances of the case: however unbalanced the result might appear to be, that was the true contractual bargain struck by the parties when they both accepted the Statute. Thus, notwithstanding an appearance of departure from the municipal norm, the decision is consistent with the substance of the latter and may without difficulty be explained in terms of its elements.

Procedure and evidence

Even within a national order, there are different courts with different procedures; no lawyer is so innocent as to suppose that the World Court's procedural regime will not exhibit features peculiar to its special character. In case of need, the books vie with each other to counsel him to abandon any baggage. But perhaps not all of it?

Would there, for example, be a handicap in trying to appreciate what exactly is the law on the subject of preliminary objections as it concerns the Court, unless one can contrast it against the corresponding subject in municipal systems where the idea of such objections began? At a time when the Court's own rules did not deal with the subject, was it perhaps the municipal experience in the field that forced its way into the Court's jurisprudence?

Take also the subject of provisional measures. When it is said that the Court cannot, by way of indicating such measures, make what is in effect an interim judgment, may recourse be had to municipal law ideas of such a judgment for the purpose of appreciating the proper reach of the statement? An interim judgment is a phenomenon of municipal law.

Consider too the question of evidence. It is commonplace that the technicalities of municipal rules of evidence have no exact counterpart in proceedings before an international tribunal. In an effort to avoid those technicalities one can, however, risk losing sight of the considerations of substantial justice that they were designed to protect. Is it true, for instance, as may well be the impression, that, in proceedings for an indication of provisional measures, it is impermissible to apply something in the nature of municipal procedures for determining whether, on the evidence, there is a *prima facie* case or other sufficient basis on which the Court may act? Reflection will show that those procedures were intended to prevent possibilities of injustice that inescapably inhere in a system under which a court, although required to consider the circumstances of the case, purports to do so without making any appraisal of the evidential material presented to it in proof of those circumstances, or without having to explain the basis on which it is proceeding if in fact it makes such an appraisal. There seems to be nothing in the procedural regime of the Court sufficiently compelling to constrain it to proceed in so strange and obscure a manner.

Consider also the question whether proceedings between two states may be maintained in the absence, as a party, of a third state which is in possession of relevant evidence. In default of specific guidance in international law, it would seem helpful to draw on municipal law reasoning to the effect that the fact that a person is a necessary witness does not mean that he is a necessary party.[26]

Then take the question of the power to exclude improperly obtained evidence. The position is not identical in all municipal systems, but in places where the tendency to exclude is greatest it appears that the reasoning depends on the view that the state, in criminal matters, should avoid abusing its superior powers of gathering evidence. To some extent, at any rate, that aspect could be a distinguishing factor in international proceedings. Does that mean that the international judge, were he confronted with the question of excluding evidence alleged to have been improperly obtained, would in fact proceed to answer it without considering such municipal legal experience as there is on the point? If, because of the particular aspect referred to, he does not find assistance in municipal systems in which there is power to exclude improperly obtained evidence, he is almost certain to find it in municipal systems in which such evidence is admissible subject to considerations of weight.

---

[26] See *Amon v. Raphael Tuck & Sons, Ltd.* [1956] 1 All ER 273, at pp. 286–7, Devlin J.

Differences may require adaptation, not rejection

Returning now to Judge Sir Arnold McNair, one might recall his classic statement to the following effect:

> What is the duty of an international tribunal when confronted with a new legal institution the object and terminology of which are reminiscent of the rules and institutions of private law? To what extent is it useful or necessary to examine what may at first sight appear to be relevant analogies in private law systems and draw help and inspiration from them? International law has recruited and continues to recruit many of its rules and institutions from private systems of law. Article 38 (1) *(c)* of the Statute of the Court bears witness that this process is still active, and it will be noted that this article authorizes the Court to 'apply . . . *(c)* the general principles of law recognized by civilized nations'. The way in which international law borrows from this source is not by means of importing private law institutions 'lock, stock and barrel', ready-made and fully equipped with a set of rules. It would be difficult to reconcile such a process with the application of 'the general principles of law'. In my opinion, the true view of the duty of international tribunals in this matter is to regard any features or terminology which are reminiscent of the rules and institutions of private law as an indication of policy and principles rather than as directly importing these rules and institutions.[27]

Though warning against borrowing 'lock, stock and barrel' from municipal law, Judge McNair was far from doubting that disciplined recourse to that source could be properly and usefully had. The concept of a mandate in international law is not identical with the concept of a mandate in municipal law. Does the difference altogether exclude useful recourse to the municipal law idea? Referring to the relevant private law principles, he observed: 'These are some of the general principles of private law which throw light upon this new institution, and I am convinced that in its future development the law governing the trust is a source from which much can be derived'.[28] Thus, even apart from the operation of article 38, paragraph 1 *(c)* of the Statute of the Court relating to general principles of law, 'the general principles of private law (may) *throw light* upon' a new institution of international law. The existence of differences between the municipal law concept and the international law concept is not always a bar to recourse to the former

---

[27] *International Status of South West Africa*, ICJ Reports, 1950, p. 148. See also *South West Africa (Second Phase)*, Judge Tanaka, Dissenting Opinion, ICJ Reports, 1966, pp. 294–5, and *Barcelona Traction Light and Power Company Ltd. (Second Phase)*, Judge Fitzmaurice, Separate Opinion, ICJ Reports, 1970, p. 66, n. 4.

[28] *International Status of South West Africa*, ICJ Reports, 1950, p. 149.

for the purpose of understanding the latter; what may be needed is some appropriate allowance to be made in the process of making the recourse. Judge McNair put it this way:

> Any English lawyer who was instructed to prepare the legal instruments required to give effect to the policy of Article 22 [of the Covenant] would inevitably be reminded of, and influenced by, the trust of English and American law, though he would soon realize the need of much adaptation for the purposes of the new international institution.[29]

Correctly handled and rightly understood, differences may call for 'adaptation', not necessarily for outright rejection.

Analogy

Some words may be added on this subject. Admonitions about recourse to private law are normally linked to admonitions about the use of analogy. In the words of Judge Badawi Pasha:

> In international law, recourse to analogy should only be had with reserve and circumspection. Contrary to what is the case in municipal law, and precisely owing to the principle of State sovereignty, the use of analogy has never been a customary technique in international law.[30]

As a scientific method, the value of analogy does not rate high in many areas of inquiry; but, as remarked by Perelman, in many fields, particularly philosophy, it is an essential method of reasoning.[31] The approach is this: a case that is sufficiently similar to another case attracts the application of the rule governing the latter. The method, known to Aristotle as that of reasoning by example, is the 'basic pattern of legal reasoning'.[32] It is, more particularly, the method on which a system of precedents is based; to use the words of Jerome Frank: 'To apply the rule laid down in one case to the facts of another case . . . involves "reasoning by analogy"'.[33] 'The problem for the law', as Levi put it, is: 'When will it be just to treat different cases as though they were the same? A working legal system must therefore be willing to pick out key similarities and to reason from them to the justice of applying a common

---

[29] *Ibid.*, p. 148.
[30] *Reparation for Injuries Suffered in the Service of the United Nations*, Dissenting Opinion, ICJ Reports, 1949, p. 211. And see Vice-President Koo's remarks in *Barcelona Traction, Light and Power Company Ltd.*, Separate Opinion, ICJ Reports, 1964, pp. 56–7.
[31] Ch. Perelman, *Logique juridique, Nouvelle rhétorique* (Paris, 1976), p. 129, para. 68.
[32] Edward H. Levi, *An Introduction to Legal Reasoning* (London/Chicago, 1949). p. 1.
[33] Jerome Frank, *Courts on Trial: Myth and Reality in American Justice* (Princeton, 1950), p. 275.

classification.'[34] As is implied, not every difference suffices to exclude recourse to reasoning by example. 'In subsequent cases', notes Guest, 'the common classification may have to be qualified, or restricted, or extended, to meet the new situations which emerge'.[35] Or, to return to Perelman, the question is: 'Quels sont les traits propres au cas particulier qu'il y a lieu de négliger, parce que accidentals et non représentatifs?'[36]

The problem is complicated where two significantly different frames of reference are involved, as in the case of municipal law and international law. On the other hand, the restraint exerted by that fact is to some extent offset by a consideration referred to by Charles De Visscher thus: 'Dans l'ordre juridique international, où les lacunes du droit obligent le juge à concevoir largement le rôle de l'interprétation, l'analogie, plus que partout ailleurs, doit être envisagée comme un procédé normal du raisonnement juridique.'[37] Hence, granted the differences between the national and the international legal orders, even as between these the application of the method is permissible. It must be used with circumspection; but it is not banned. The Court made use of it in the *Effect of Awards* case, when holding that

> the contention that the General Assembly is inherently incapable of creating a tribunal competent to make decisions binding on itself cannot be accepted. It cannot be justified by analogy to national laws, for it is common practice in national legislatures to create courts with the capacity to render decisions legally binding on the legislatures which brought them into being.[38]

The problem concerns not the admissibility of analogy as a method, or its applicability to municipal law concepts, but the limits within which it may be applied in having recourse to these. When a seemingly similar concept occurs in both municipal law and international law but, as is often the case, with differences, to what extent should the differences mean that the municipal idea is to be jettisoned and the international concept left to be ascertained independently? It seems at least arguable that, even where the international judge asserts that the differences are such as to make the municipal law idea inapplicable, a possible interpretation of what he is actually (if not always) doing is that he is using the substance of the municipal idea, but construing it with modifications, exceptions and adaptations required by the different

---

[34] Levi, *An Introduction to Legal Reasoning*, p. 2.

[35] A. G. Guest, 'Logic in the Law', in A. G. Guest (ed.), *Oxford Essays in Jurisprudence* (Oxford, 1961), p. 191.

[36] Perelman, *Logique juridique*, p. 129, para. 67.

[37] De Visscher, *Problèmes d'interprétation*, p. 39.

[38] *Effect of Awards of Compensation Made by the United Nations Administrative Tribunal*, ICJ Reports, 1954, p. 61.

international context so as to give him the benefit of the general guidance of the idea, as construed with the adjustments so made, in searching for the true rule governing the particular problem before him. Thus, even where the absence of exact analogy bars transposition of the municipal law principle, ascertainment, through careful analysis of municipal law, of the precise reason that prevents transposition may conceivably aid in finding the different rule required for the resolution of the international legal problem. As was remarked by Fitzmaurice: 'In order to ascertain what a thing is, it is sometimes very useful to begin by enquiring what it is not.'[39]

Conclusion

The tendency to approach a concept in international law on the hasty assumption that one is dealing with an equivalent concept in municipal law is to be deprecated. Equally, if less obviously, there is danger in supposing that, because international law is an independent discipline – something on which Anzilotti and others rightly insisted[40] – any dissimilarity in ideas is wider than may really be the case; even where differences exist, they may not be wide enough to preclude useful recourse to the municipal experience for the purpose of appreciating an international law idea. It is possible that, even in cases where the municipal law concept is formally put aside, its influence is not altogether eliminated; in some cases it is exerted *sub silentio*.

Nor should this be surprising. Judge McNair was not singular in noting that 'international law has recruited and continues to recruit many of its rules and institutions from private systems of law'. It would be wrong to overestimate the size of the inheritance or the strength with which it operates beyond the formative period of international law; but it is not right to decry it. Whence Lauterpacht's protest against 'the time-honoured repudiation and disparagement of the analogy to municipal – and, in particular, to private – law'.[41] It is an open question to what extent that repudiation and disparagement is a valid index of the autonomy of international law. It is one thing to warn sagely against the precipitate transposition of municipal law ideas to the international legal plane, and very many indeed are the situations in which they have no useful role; it is another thing to attempt, almost as a matter of ideological faith, to come to grips with international law notions rigidly divorced from a

---

[39] *Reparation for Injuries Suffered in the Service of the United Nations*, ICJ Pleadings, 1949, p. 111.

[40] See Ferrari-Bravo, 'International Law and Municipal Law', at pp. 728–9; and Giorgio Gaja, 'Positivism and Dualism in Dionisio Anzilotti', *European JIL*, 3 (1992), p. 134.

[41] H. Lauterpacht, *The Function of Law in the International Community* (Oxford, 1933), p. 432.

municipal conceptual framework which in many instances influenced their formation. With submission, the view is offered that in more cases than bear the outward marks of recognition, municipal law reasoning, correctly handled, can and does play a part in the thinking out of international legal problems.

6

Estoppel and acquiescence

Sir Ian Sinclair

જ્જી

The concepts of estoppel and acquiescence are difficult to disentangle from other related concepts, such as recognition, admissions and recourse to subsequent conduct in the interpretation of a treaty. As one noted authority states when analysing the relevance of these concepts to the judicial determination of territorial disputes: 'Recognition, acquiescence, admissions constituting a part of the evidence of sovereignty, and estoppel form an inter-related subject-matter, and it is far from easy to establish the points of distinction.'[1] Referring more particularly to the concept of estoppel, the same authority argues:

> A considerable weight of authority supports the view that estoppel is a general principle of international law, resting on principles of good faith and consistency, and shorn of the technical features to be found in municipal law. Without dissenting from this as a general and preliminary proposition, it is necessary to point out that estoppel in municipal law is regarded with great caution, and that the 'principle' has no particular coherence in international law, its incidence and effects not being uniform. Thus before a tribunal the principle may operate to resolve ambiguities and as a principle of equity and justice: here it becomes a part of the evidence and judicial reasoning.[2]

Practitioners in international law, particularly those who have been involved as counsel in long-standing territorial disputes, are aware that arguments founded on notions of estoppel and acquiescence figure prominently in the armoury of weapons at their disposal. Territorial disputes with deep historical roots inevitably require that counsel on both sides have to analyse the detailed and rigorous historical research that will have been undertaken in order to understand the nature and scope of the dispute. The research will in all

---

[1] Ian Brownlie, *Principles of Public International Law* (4th edn, Oxford, 1990), p. 161.
[2] *Ibid.*, p. 641.

probability have uncovered evidence of inconsistency of conduct on the part of one or both states parties to the dispute. That evidence may demonstrate that, on the occasion of some incident in the past, state A will have taken a position *vis-à-vis* state B at variance with the position it is now asserting in proceedings against state B. It may equally demonstrate that state A has entered into international agreements with state B or indeed with other states, the terms of which are incompatible with the position it is now asserting in proceedings against state B. The evidence may also disclose that state B has failed to protest against a previous act of state A challenging the title of state B to a given territory or parcel of territory. Any evidence of inconsistency of conduct of this type is likely to be prayed in aid as providing grounds for a finding by the tribunal of estoppel or acquiescence.

What do we mean by estoppel? In international law, the term 'estoppel' has been used to denote a legal principle which operates so as to preclude a party from denying before a tribunal the truth of a statement of fact made previously by that party to another whereby that other has acted to his detriment or the party making the statement has secured some benefit.[3] A similarly narrow view of the concept of estoppel is taken by Thirlway:

> A claim of estoppel may – and indeed frequently does – relate to the existence, non-existence or deemed existence of a particular state of mind of the respondent State, and in particular its acceptance of, or consent to, a particular matter; but while a claim of acquiescence asserts that the State concerned *did* accept or agree on that point, a claim of estoppel accepts, by implication that the respondent State did *not* accept or agree, but contends that, having misled the applicant State by behaving as though it did agree, it cannot be permitted to deny the conclusion which its conduct suggested.[4]

The definition of estoppel given by Martin, the author of a recently published monograph on the topic, resembles this closely in substance if not in language. Martin states:

> Lorsqu'une Partie, par ses déclarations, ses actes ou ses comportements, a conduit une autre Partie à croire en l'existence d'un certain état de choses sur la foi duquel elle l'a incitée à agir, ou s'abstenir à agir, de telle sorte qu'il en est résulté une modification dans leurs positions relatives (au préjudice de la seconde ou à l'avantage de la première, ou les deux à la fois), la première est empêchée par

---

[3] D. W. Bowett, 'Estoppel before International Tribunals and its relation to Acquiescence', *BYbIL*, 33 (1957), p. 176.

[4] H. W. A. Thirlway, 'The Law and Procedure of the International Court of Justice, 1960–80', *BYbIL*, 60 (1989), p. 29.

l'estoppel d'établir à l'encontre de la seconde un état de choses different de celui qu'elle a anterieurement représenté comme existant.[5]

The Chamber of the Court in the *Gulf of Maine* case stressed the close link between the concepts of estoppel and acquiescence and described the distinction between them in the following terms:

> The Chamber observes that in any case the concepts of acquiescence and estoppel, irrespective of the status accorded to them by international law, both follow from the fundamental principles of good faith and equity. They are, however, based on different legal reasoning since acquiescence is equivalent to tacit recognition manifested by unilateral conduct which the other party may interpret as consent, while estoppel is linked to the idea of preclusion.[6]

It is perhaps the common ancestry of the two concepts in the principles of good faith and equity that merits particular attention. This lends some credence to the notion that estoppel (or a concept analogous to estoppel) constitutes a general principle of law deriving from the maxim *allegans contraria non est audiendus*. Cheng indeed views equitable estoppel as being a general principle of law applicable in the international sphere; and he finds authority for this proposition, not only in arbitral awards such as that in the *Shufeldt* case (US/Guatemala),[7] but also in judgments and Advisory Opinions of the Permanent Court of International Justice.[8] Although he cites in this context the judgment of the Permanent Court in the *Diversion of the River Meuse* case,[9] where a Dutch claim that proposed Belgian works to divert the river were in violation of a bilateral treaty between the Netherlands and Belgium was rejected, there is considerable force in the observation made by another learned commentator that the rejection was based primarily on a finding that the proposed works did not amount to a violation of the treaty, and only secondarily on the consideration that the Netherlands was hardly in a position to object to the Belgian project because it had itself constructed locks

---

[5] A. Martin, L'estoppel en droit international public (Paris, 1979), pp. 259–60. A Chamber of the Court in giving judgment on Nicaragua's application to intervene in the *Case Concerning the Land, Island and Maritime Frontier Dispute (El Salvador/Honduras)* defined estoppel as: 'a statement or representation made by one party to another and reliance upon it by that other party to his detriment or to the advantage of the party making it' (ICJ Reports, 1990, p. 30).

[6] ICJ Reports, 1984, p. 305.

[7] *RIAA* 2, p. 1079, at p. 1094, where the arbitrator expressed the view (although admittedly in an *obiter dictum*) that the US contention of estoppel based on the recognition by the Guatemalan government of the validity of a contract over a period of six years, was 'sound and in keeping with the principles of international law'.

[8] B. Cheng, *General Principles of Law* (London, 1953), pp. 141–9.

[9] PCIJ, Series A/B, No. 70 (1937), p. 25.

comparable to those to which it was now objecting.[10] Cheng also refers to the judgment of the Permanent Court in the *Serbian Loans* case.[11] It will be recalled that, in that case, the Permanent Court refused to accept an argument that France was estopped from claiming, on behalf of the French bondholders, repayment of the loans in gold francs because the bondholders had in previous years accepted part-payment of the loans in paper francs. On this point, the Permanent Court stated:

> When the requirements of the principle of estoppel to establish a loss of right are considered, it is quite clear that no sufficient basis has been shown for applying the principle in this case. There has been no clear and unequivocal representation of the bondholders upon which the debtor State was entitled to rely and has relied. The debtor State has not modified its position.[12]

Here the Court is in effect determining that the conditions for the successful invocation of a plea of estoppel have not been met. But was this truly a case in which estoppel could be invoked? The terms of the loan contracts (providing for the repayment of the loans in gold francs) were clear. All that was in issue was whether those terms had been modified as a result of the subsequent conduct of the parties. Was there a subsequent agreement between the bond-holders and the debtor states or had the bondholders definitively renounced their right to be repaid in gold francs? Over and above the reasons given by the Permanent Court for rejecting the plea of estoppel in this case was the consideration that one of the basic elements of estoppel was not present – namely, that the conduct of the state concerned (France) had not operated as a bar to the establishment of the truth.[13] In this context it is necessary to bear in mind the profound observation about estoppel made by Sir Gerald Fitzmaurice in his Separate Opinion in the *Temple* case: 'Such a plea is essentially a means of excluding a denial that might be *correct* – irrespective of its correctness. It prevents the assertion of what might in fact be true.'[14]

There is another element of estoppel which, as the Permanent Court noted, was not present in the *Serbian Loans* case. That is the element of the 'clear and unequivocal representation'. In order to found an estoppel, the representation must be unambiguous, at least in the sense that it must reasonably support the meaning attributed to it by the party raising the estoppel; and that party must

---

[10] Christian Dominicé, 'A propos du principe de l'estoppel en droit des gens', in *Recueil d'études de droit international en hommage à Paul Guggenheim* (Geneva, 1968), p. 327, at pp. 337–8.

[11] PCIJ, Series A, No. 20 (1929), p. 5.

[12] *Ibid.*, p. 39.

[13] This is, broadly, the analysis made by Dominicé, 'A propos du principe de l'estoppel', at pp. 339–41.

[14] ICJ Reports, 1962, p. 63.

satisfy the tribunal that it understood the statement to have that meaning. The rationale for this requirement is almost certainly that suggested in a recent article on estoppel:

> Clear and unequivocal representation, prejudice or detriment are not simply addenda; they trigger the very justification for specific protection of settled expectations. A rule of principle which would prohibit any modification of conduct, statement or representation vastly overestimates the potentials of law and is not even suitable or desirable in order to promote protection of good faith, reliance and confidence in international relations.[15]

It will be apparent from the foregoing that some of the early case law of the Permanent Court cited as examples of the application of the principle of estoppel in international law may be explicable on other grounds. This is not to say that the basis for the rulings given by the Permanent Court in the *Diversion of the River Meuse* and the *Serbian Loans* cases (in both cases denying pleas of estoppel) does not lie, at least in some measure, in the application of the principle of good faith.

The late Sir Hersch Lauterpacht was reluctant to characterize particular instances of state conduct inconsistent with the attitude previously adopted by the state concerned as giving rise inevitably to an estoppel (at least in the strict sense), although he was quite prepared to attach legal consequences to such inconsistency of conduct:

> It does not much matter whether, in considering the parties to be bound by their own conduct, the Court resorts to the terminology of the doctrine of estoppel or not . . . It is a question of emphasis whether reliance on the conduct of the parties to a treaty subsequent to its conclusion is treated from the point of view of the doctrine of estoppel preventing a party from asserting an interpretation inconsistent with its conduct or whether it is considered as a legitimate factor in the process of interpretation in the sense that subsequent conduct throws light upon the intentions of the parties at the time of the conclusion of the treaty. Both represent, in substance, a general principle of law.[16]

It is when we come to analyse the jurisprudence of the present Court that we begin to discern the true parameters of estoppel and acquiescence. What the Court has done, in a series of judgments since 1950, is to sketch out the circumstances in which a plea of estoppel or acquiescence may be admitted. It has done so in the main by determining the circumstances in which a plea of estoppel or acquiescence will *not* be entertained; but in a few key cases, the

---

[15] R. Bernhardt (ed.), *Encyclopedia of International Law* (Amsterdam, 1984), vol. VII, p. 79.
[16] H. Lauterpacht, *The Development of International Law by the International Court* (rev. edn, London, 1958), p. 170.

Court has upheld pleas based upon conduct of a party inconsistent with its own previously professed position.

The first case in which the two concepts, or variants of them, were considered in depth by the present Court was the *Case Concerning the Arbitral Award made by the King of Spain on 23 December 1906*.[17] In this case, Nicaragua sought to challenge the validity of the 1906 award on several grounds. The first was that the designation in 1904 of the King of Spain as arbitrator in a boundary dispute between Honduras and Nicaragua had not been effected in accordance with the terms of the Gamez–Bonilla Treaty of 1894. The Court gave short shrift to this argument, pointing out that 'no question was at any time raised in the arbitral proceedings before the King with regard either to the validity of his designation as arbitrator or his jurisdiction as such'.[18] A second ground of challenge was based on the argument that the Treaty of 1894 had lapsed before the King of Spain agreed to act as arbitrator. The Court rejected this argument with equal firmness, but went on to add:

> Finally, the Court considers that, having regard to the fact that the designation of the King of Spain as arbitrator was freely agreed to by Nicaragua, that no objection was taken by Nicaragua to the jurisdiction of the King of Spain as arbitrator either on the ground of irregularity in his designation as arbitrator or on the ground that the . . . Treaty had lapsed even before the King of Spain had signified his acceptance of the office of arbitrator, and that Nicaragua fully participated in the arbitral proceedings before the King, it is no longer open to Nicaragua to rely on either of these contentions as furnishing a ground for the nullity of the Award.[19]

Nicaragua also argued that, for a number of reasons, the award made by the King of Spain was invalid. The Court dismissed this argument, essentially on the ground that Nicaragua was precluded from asserting it:

> In the judgement of the Court, Nicaragua, by express declaration and by conduct, recognized the Award as valid and it is no longer open to Nicaragua to go back upon that recognition and to challenge the validity of the Award. Nicaragua's failure to raise any question with regard to the validity of the Award for several years after the full terms of the Award had become known to it further confirms the conclusion at which the Court has arrived.[20]

It will be noted that the Court, in its judgment in this case, carefully avoids making reference to the concept of estoppel as such. The Dissenting Opinion of the judge *ad hoc* appointed by Nicaragua (Urrutia Holguin) may well explain why the Court did not touch upon the notion of estoppel; for Judge

---

[17] ICJ Reports, 1960, p. 192.   [18] *Ibid.*, at p. 207.
[19] *Ibid.*, at p. 209.   [20] *Ibid.*, at pp. 213–14.

ad hoc Urrutia Holguin pointed out that the conditions for invoking a plea of estoppel had not been met, since Honduras had not proved any effective reliance on the conduct of Nicaragua, far less any change of position to its detriment.[21]

The delicate manner in which the Court handles pleas of acquiescence or estoppel is evidenced once again by its judgment in the case of the *Temple of Preah Vihear* between Thailand and Cambodia. The facts, so far as relevant to this issue, were as follows. By a treaty of 1904 between Thailand (then Siam) and France, as the protecting power for Cambodia, it was agreed that the boundary between Siam and Cambodia should follow the watershed between two river basins, the delimitation to be carried out by Mixed Commissions composed of officers appointed by the two states. A Mixed Commission was set up and maps were eventually produced and printed and published by a French firm. The relevant map showed the boundary as leaving the Temple of Preah Vihear to Cambodia. The map had apparently been produced by French officers on the instructions of the Mixed Commission, but the latter had never approved it. It was later established that the line of the watershed ran the other side of the temple, so that, if the mapped boundary-line had followed the watershed, as contemplated by the 1904 treaty, the temple would have been left to Thailand.

France had handed over copies of the maps to Thailand. The Court specifically found that the circumstances in which the maps had been handed over to Thailand 'were such as called for some reaction, within a reasonable period, on the part of the Siamese authorities, if they wished to disagree with the map or had any serious question to raise in regard to it. They did not do so, either then or for many years, and thereby must be held to have acquiesced.'[22] This is a clear finding of acquiescence by silence; there was no estoppel as Cambodia had provided no evidence that it had, in the years following the delivery of the maps, acted on the basis of Thailand's apparent acceptance of the map so as to change its position to its own detriment.

The Court did not, however, rely solely on the conduct of Thailand in the years immediately following the production of the relevant map. The Court relied on a broader concept of preclusion based upon Thailand's conduct over many years:

> Even if there were any doubt as to Siam's acceptance of the map in 1908, and hence of the frontier indicated thereon, the Court would consider, in the light of the subsequent course of events, that Thailand is now precluded by her conduct from asserting that she did not accept it. She has, for fifty years, enjoyed such benefits as

---

[21] *Ibid.*, at pp. 222, 236.   [22] ICJ Reports, 1962, p. 23.

the Treaty of 1904 conferred on her, if only the benefit of a stable frontier . . . It is not now open to Thailand, while continuing to claim and enjoy the benefits of the settlement, to deny that she was even a consenting party to it.[23]

The subsequent case law of the Court shows a marked reluctance on its part to characterize the conduct of a state as giving rise to an estoppel in subsequent proceedings. In the *North Sea Continental Shelf* cases, the Court rejected an argument that the equidistance rule for the delimitation of continental shelves for which provision was made in article 6 of the 1958 General Convention on the Continental Shelf had become binding on the Federal Republic of Germany by virtue of her conduct, notwithstanding that the Federal Republic had not become a party to that convention. In denying this argument, the Court stated:

> It appears to the Court that only the existence of a situation of estoppel could suffice to lend substance to this contention – that is to say if the Federal Republic were now precluded from denying the applicability of the conventional régime, by reason of past conduct, declarations etc., which not only clearly and consistently evinced acceptance of that régime, but also had caused Denmark or the Netherlands, in reliance on such conduct, detrimentally to change position or suffer some prejudice. Of this there is no evidence whatever in the present case.[24]

So also in the *Gulf of Maine* case, the Chamber of the Court firmly rejected Canadian arguments that United States conduct in not reacting to the issue of exploration permits by Canada and in not informing Canada of the issuance of US exploration permits covering part of the disputed area amounted to an estoppel. The Chamber commented: 'While it may be conceded that the United States showed a certain imprudence in maintaining silence after Canada had issued the first permits for exploration on Georges Bank, any attempt to attribute to such silence, a brief silence at that, legal consequences taking the concrete form of an estoppel, seems to be going too far.'[25] As regards US conduct in not informing Canada of the issuance of US exploration permits, the Chamber states that 'the United States attitude towards Canada was unclear and perhaps ambiguous, but not to the point of entitling Canada to invoke the doctrine of estoppel'.[26]

A question that has frequently arisen in recent cases is whether silence by one state in face of a claim made by another state can give rise to an estoppel or can be invoked as evidence of acquiescence in that claim so as to disentitle the affected state from subsequently challenging it. Attention has already been

---

[23] *Ibid.*, at p. 32.   [24] ICJ Reports, 1969, p. 26.
[25] ICJ Reports, 1984, p. 308, para. 140.   [26] *Ibid.*, para. 141.

directed to certain passages in the Court's judgments in the *Arbitral Award made by the King of Spain* case, in the *Temple* case and in the *Gulf of Maine* case, which assess the significance to be attributed to silences on the part of one or other of the states in dispute.[27] The weight to be attached to a failure on the part of a state to react or protest against a claim asserted or action taken by another state has been analysed more fully in other pronouncements by the Court or by individual judges. In the *Temple* case itself, Judge Fitzmaurice, in his Separate Opinion, was prepared to acknowledge that, in certain circum-stances, a silence can amount to acquiescence which can itself operate as a preclusion in subsequent proceedings: 'But acquiescence can operate as a preclusion or estoppel in certain cases, for instance where silence, on an occasion where there was a duty or need to speak or act, implies agreement, or a waiver of rights.'[28]

The period of time in which a silence has been maintained will be an important factor in determining whether that silence can be held to amount to acquiescence. For example, in the *Anglo-Norwegian Fisheries* case, successive United Kingdom governments had failed to protest, over a period of some seventy years, against the application by Norway of a particular system for the delimitation of the outer limits of her territorial sea: 'The notoriety of the facts, the general toleration of the international community, Great Britain's position in the North Sea, her own interest in the question, and her prolonged abstention would in any case warrant Norway's enforcement of her system against the United Kingdom.'[29] With this should be contrasted the Chamber's ruling in the *Gulf of Maine* case that 'a brief silence' by the US in not reacting to the issuance by Canada of exploration permits for the Georges Bank could not be taken as amounting to an estoppel. Although the Chamber in the *Gulf of Maine* case specifically disavowed an intent to draw conclusions from the judgment of the full Court in the *Anglo-Norwegian Fisheries* case, it did draw attention to 'the long duration of the Norwegian practice (70 years)'.[30] It also characterized the Nicaraguan conduct which was at issue in the *Arbitral Award of the King of Spain* case and which justified a finding of acquiescence as being 'conduct that had continued over a very long period'.[31]

In the *Elettronica Sicula (ELSI)* case, the issue was not so much the period of time in which silence had been maintained as the effect of that silence in the particular circumstances. The US argued that Italy was estopped from raising a plea of the non-exhaustion of local remedies as a bar to the admissibility of

---

[27] See the citations referred to in notes 19, 22 and 25 above.
[28] ICJ Reports, 1962, p. 62.   [29] ICJ Reports, 1951, p. 139.
[30] ICJ Reports, 1984, p. 309.   [31] *Ibid*., p. 310.

the claims advanced on behalf of the US companies concerned, since Italy had not raised that plea in the diplomatic exchanges prior to reference of the dispute to the Court. The Court rejected the US argument on the following grounds: 'Although it cannot be excluded that an estoppel could in certain circumstances arise from a silence when something ought to have been said, there are obvious difficulties in constructing an estoppel from a mere failure to mention a matter at a particular point in somewhat desultory diplomatic exchanges.'[32]

The effect of silence was at issue again between Finland and Denmark in the recent *Passage through the Great Belt* case which, it will be recalled, was settled very shortly before the oral proceedings on the merits were due to open in The Hague in mid-September 1992. The written pleadings on the merits, consisting of a Memorial by Finland and a Counter-Memorial by Denmark, will in due course be published by the Court in the Pleadings series, but reference to them has already been made in an excellent survey of the case which has recently been published.[33] Koskenniemi draws attention in this survey to the arguments exchanged in the written pleadings on the issue of acquiescence. Briefly, informal Danish proposals to construct a bridge over the Great Belt (an international strait between two Danish islands, providing the principal navigable waterway for shipping between the Baltic and the North Sea) dated back to the 1930s. But, for various reasons, no clear proposal emerged until 1977, when the Danish Ministry of Foreign Affairs notified foreign missions in Copenhagen by a circular note of 12 May 1977, of plans for the erection of a bridge for road and rail traffic across the Great Belt. The plan so notified was for a high-level bridge across the eastern channel (the navigable channel for large deep-draught ships) and a low-level bridge across the western channel. The Danish parliament had endorsed the erection of such a bridge by virtue of a law of 13 June 1973. The notification gave an assurance that the construction of the section across the eastern channel would, in conformity with international law, allow international shipping between the Kattegat and the Baltic to proceed as in the past; but it then went on to indicate that the vertical clearance for passage under the bridge would be 62 metres.

Finland did not react to this circular note, notwithstanding that one Finnish shipyard had been engaged since 1972 in the construction, for delivery to

---

[32] ICJ Reports, 1989, p. 44.
[33] Martti Koskenniemi, 'L'affaire du passage par le Grand-Belt', *AFDI*, 38 (1992), pp. 905–47. The present writer has at this point to declare an interest, having acted as one of the counsel for Finland in this case.

destinations beyond the Danish straits, of drill ships and oil rigs having a height exceeding 62 metres. Several of such drill ships and oil rigs had in fact passed through the Great Belt during the period between 1972 and 1977. In 1978, the then Danish government suspended work on the bridge project for an indefinite period. The suspension of the project was for economic reasons and the Danish minister concerned expressed the view that work on the project might be resumed in four or five years. It was not however until 1987 that the project for a fixed link across the Great Belt was resurrected. In that year, the Danish parliament enacted a new law of 10 June 1987 on the Construction of a Fixed Link across the Great Belt. The new law repealed the 1973 law and simultaneously made provision for a complex two-stage project comprising:

(a) initially, a rail link for traffic in both directions proceeding across the eastern channel by means of a tunnel and across the western channel by means of a low-level bridge;

(b) subsequently, and as a second stage, the construction of a four-lane motorway proceeding across the eastern channel by means of a high-level bridge with the required navigational clearance *or* in an immersed tunnel, and across the western channel on the same low bridge as the rail link.

It was this revised project that was duly notified to foreign missions in Copenhagen by a second circular note of 30 June 1987. This second circular note confirmed that it had not yet been decided whether the motorway should cross the eastern channel on a high-level bridge or through a tunnel; but it again conveyed an unqualified assurance that, if the bridge solution were selected, the erection of the bridge crossing the eastern channel would, in conformity with international law, allow for the maintenance of free passage for international shipping between the Kattegat and the Baltic Sea as in the past. Finland did not react to this second circular note.

It was not until November 1988 that Danish ministers approved a recommendation made by the main contractor for the project in favour of a high-level motorway bridge across the eastern channel. This decision was not conveyed to foreign diplomatic missions at the time. In the summer of 1989, the Danish authorities decided unilaterally, and without further consultation with user states, that the vertical clearance for the bridge should be 65 metres. It was not until October 1989 that Denmark notified foreign diplomatic missions of these decisions; and, by that time, the Finnish Embassy in Copenhagen had indicated its concern to the Danish Board of Navigation.

These are the bare facts relevant to the argument between the parties on alleged acquiescence by Finland in the project to build a high-level motorway bridge across the eastern channel of the Great Belt. Denmark naturally contended that the failure of Finland to react to the Danish plans for a high-level bridge across the Great Belt (Finland's 'silences') constituted acquiescence in the project so notified; from this perspective, Denmark was anxious to stress the continuity of the project from 1977 to 1989. By way of contrast, Finland stressed four points in reply to the Danish contention:

(1) The initial project of which notice had been given in 1977 had already been abandoned in 1978, within approximately one year from the date of the despatch of the circular note of 1977, so that thereafter there was no reason for Finland to protest against a plan that Denmark itself had already discarded.

(2) The Danish circular notes of 1977 and 1987 had given unqualified assurances about the maintenance of free passage for international shipping through the Great Belt as in the past, and indeed the circular note of 1987 had indicated that the decision between a high-level bridge and immersed tunnel was still entirely open.

(3) Between 1977 and 1987, no less than thirteen Finnish drill ships and oil rigs had passed through the Great Belt without objection having been raised by the Danish authorities.

(4) It was highly questionable as a matter of law whether Denmark was entitled to rely on tacit consent in the form of acquiescence as a basis for unilateral action by way of derogation from the generally recognized right of free passage for international shipping through straits.

As regards point (4), Finland indeed argued that what was needed was the express agreement of the user states and, in this context, cited in support passages from an Anglo-French joint report of 1963 about early proposals to construct a fixed link across the Dover Strait for rail and road use.

In the light of the settlement reached between the parties just before the oral hearings were due to begin, the Court had no opportunity to pronounce on the strength of these opposing arguments. It is therefore difficult to assess what view the Court might have taken. Koskenniemi suggests that, had the Court been disposed to accept in principle that the right of free passage through international straits applied also to special ships such as drill ships and oil rigs, it might nonetheless have called upon Finland to meet the extra costs of technical modifications to the Danish plans which would be necessary to accommodate the right so recognized – and this partly in consequence of Finland's failure to draw its concerns to the attention of Denmark at an earlier stage.[34]

---

[34] Koskenniemi, 'L'affaire du passage', at p. 933.

As we have already seen, the present Court has been noticeably reluctant to regard the conduct of one or other of the two states in dispute as estopping that state from advancing particular claims or positions in subsequent litigation. In the *North Sea Continental Shelf* cases, the Court could find no evidence to sustain a finding of estoppel against the Federal Republic of Germany; in the *Gulf of Maine* case, the Chamber rejected the Canadian estoppel arguments; and, in the *ELSI* case, the Chamber again refused to uphold the US contention that Italy was estopped by her conduct from raising in the proceedings, a plea of non-exhaustion of local remedies. Other examples of this tendency to construe very strictly the requirements of an estoppel can be given. Thus, in the *Military and Paramilitary Activities in and against Nicaragua* case, the US sought to argue *inter alia* that Nicaragua was estopped from invoking as against the US its pre-war acceptance of the jurisdiction of the Permanent Court by reason of the fact that it had consistently represented to the US that it was not bound by the Optional Clause. The Court, however, found that the particular incidents relied on by the US, which it appeared were inconsistent with Nicaragua's general conduct, were not sufficient to 'overturn that conclusion, let alone to support an estoppel'.[35] In the *Barcelona Traction* case *(Second Phase)*,[36] the Court was also confronted with an argument based on the notion of estoppel, since Spain contended, by way of a preliminary objection to the renewed proceedings, that it would not have agreed to the discontinuance of the first set of proceedings instituted by Belgium had it not been given the impression that the discontinuance was final. The Court rejected this argument on the ground that it had not been established that there had been 'misleading Belgian representations' and that, in any event, Spain had not suffered any real detriment; so, again, the estoppel argument was denied.[37]

If the Court has been extremely cautious in upholding arguments founded on an alleged estoppel, it has been more open in admitting the significance of conduct capable of being represented as acquiescence in a particular claim or position asserted by another state. The jurisprudence of the Court demonstrates that silence or lack of protest maintained over a significant period of time may be treated as tacit recognition of, or acquiescence in, a position taken by another state. The absence of reaction by the British government to the Norwegian straight baseline system was treated by the Court in the *Anglo-Norwegian Fisheries* case as a factor rendering that system opposable to the

---

[35] ICJ Reports, 1984, p. 414.

[36] ICJ Reports, 1964, p. 6.

[37] For a fuller analysis of this case, see Dominicé, 'A propos du principe de l'estoppel', at pp. 327–9.

UK.[38] In the *Temple* case, an express finding of acquiescence was based on the failure of Thailand to react within a reasonable period to the maps handed over by France.[39] The Nicaraguan objection to the designation of the King of Spain as arbitrator in the *Arbitral Award made by the King of Spain on 23 December 1906* case was rejected on the ground that Nicaragua had 'freely agreed to' the designation and had taken 'no objection' to his jurisdiction as arbitrator (language appropriate to a finding of acquiescence).[40]

In some instances, a tacit finding of acquiescence may be invoked by the Court to buttress a conclusion reached on other grounds. For example, in the *Minquiers* and *Erechos* cases,[41] the Court appears to have based its decision in favour of Great Britain on the frequent and consistent displays of administrative and judicial authority over these islets by the Jersey authorities, particularly during the nineteenth century. But the Court also relied, at least to some extent, on the ambiguous conduct of France. There was, for example, evidence that, at one point, the French Minister of the Marine had suggested that French fishermen should be prohibited from going to the Erechos, because the UK considered these islets as British; there was also evidence that another French minister had admitted in a letter written in 1819 that the Minquiers were a British possession.[42] Although the French conduct was not held to have amounted to acquiescence as such, it was conduct that evidenced French doubts, and had to be taken into account by the Court in evaluating the comparative strength of the two competing claims to title.

The recent judgment of a Chamber of the Court in the case concerning the *Land, Island and Maritime Frontier Dispute (El Salvador/Honduras)* carries the jurisprudence on acquiescence a bit further. One of the key points argued before the Chamber was whether the *uti possidetis juris* principle was absolute or could be qualified by the operation of such notions as acquiescence or recognition. The Chamber, in an important passage, states:

> If the *uti possidetis juris* position can be qualified by adjudication and by treaty, the question then arises whether it can be qualified in other ways, for example, by acquiescence or recognition. There seems to be no reason in principle why these factors should not operate, where there is sufficient evidence to show that the parties have in effect clearly accepted a variation, or at least an interpretation, of the *uti possidetis juris* position.[43]

---

[38] See text to note 29 above.   [39] See text to note 22 above.

[40] See text to note 19 above. In the same sense, see Thirlway, 'Law and Procedure', at p. 46.

[41] ICJ Reports, 1953, p. 47.

[42] *Ibid.*, p. 71. Cf. Philippe Cahier, 'Le comportement des Etats comme source de droits et d'obligations', in *Recueil d'études de droit international en hommage à Paul Guggenheim*, pp. 246–8.

[43] ICJ Reports, 1992, p. 401, para. 67.

The Chamber applied this view of the matter to its consideration of the course of the first sector of the land boundary:

> The Chamber does not consider that the effect of the application of the principle *uti possidetis juris* in Spanish America was to freeze for all time the provincial boundaries which, with the advent of independence, became the frontiers of the new States. It was obviously open to those States to vary the boundaries between them by agreement; and some forms of activity, or inactivity, might amount to acquiescence in a boundary other than that of 1821.[44]

The Chamber followed up this pronouncement by concluding that the conduct of Honduras from 1881 until 1972 could be regarded as acquiescence in a boundary corresponding to the boundary between the Tepanguuir lands granted to Citala and those of Ocotepeque.[45]

As regards sovereignty over disputed islands in the Gulf of Fonseca, the Chamber followed a broadly similar line:

> The Chamber must . . . proceed . . . to consider the conduct of the parties in the period following independence, as indicative of the then view of what must have been the 1821 position. This may further be supplemented by considerations independent of the *uti possidetis juris* principle, in particular the possible significance of the same conduct, or the conduct of the parties in more recent years, as possibly constituting acquiescence.[46]

In consequence, the Chamber considered that a protest by Honduras made in January 1991, coming after a long history of acts of sovereignty by El Salvador in the island of Meanguera, was made too late to affect the presumption of acquiescence on the part of Honduras. The Chamber continued: 'The conduct of Honduras *vis-à-vis* earlier *effectivités* reveals an admission, recognition, acquiescence or other form of tacit consent to the situation.'[47]

The Court delivered judgment in the case of the *Territorial Dispute (Libyan Arab Jamahiriya/Chad)* as recently as 3 February 1994.[48] It might have been thought that the Court would pronounce on the relative strength of the arguments based on acquiescence which both parties had deployed in the course of the written and oral pleadings. The judgment is, however, largely silent on this aspect of the dispute. The Court found that the boundary between Libya and Chad was defined by the Treaty of Friendship and Good Neighbourliness concluded between France and Libya on 10 August 1955. The Court found support, in subsequent treaties between France and Libya, or between Chad and Libya: 'for the proposition that after 1955, the existence

---

[44] *Ibid.*, p. 408, para. 80.   [45] *Ibid.*   [46] *Ibid.*, p. 563, para. 341.
[47] *Ibid.*, p. 577, para. 364.   [48] ICJ Reports, 1994, p. 6.

of a determined frontier was accepted and acted upon by the parties'.[49] The Court may have attached marginal significance to the consideration that, during the nine-year period between the independence of Libya (at the end of 1951) and the independence of Chad (in 1960), France had submitted annual reports on the territory of what was to become Chad, showing the area of Chad's territory as 1,284,000 square kilometres, which expressly included 538,000 square kilometres for the BET.[50] The Court continued:

> As will be clear from the indications above as to the frontier resulting from the 1955 Treaty . . . , the BET is part of the territory of Chad on the basis of that frontier, but would not be so on the basis of Libya's claim, Libya did not challenge the territorial dimensions of Chad as set out by France.[51]

However, the Court makes no express finding of Libyan acquiescence in the frontier as found by the Court.[52] This is among the many matters that the Court concluded that it need not consider: 'The Court's conclusion that the [1955] Treaty contains an agreed boundary renders it unnecessary to consider the history of the "borderlands" claimed by Libya on the basis of title inherited from the indigenous people, the Senousi Order, the Ottoman Empire and Italy.'[53]

The issue of Libyan (or Chadian) acquiescence is however addressed in the Separate Opinion of Judge Ajibola. Judge Ajibola, after reviewing the conduct

---

[49] *Ibid.*, p. 33, para. 66.
[50] The 'BET' stands for the regions of Borkou, Ennedi and Tibesti, large areas of which were claimed by Libya.
[51] ICJ Reports, 1994, p. 34, para. 68.
[52] On the Court's approach, there was no need to rely on Libya's acquiescence, since the frontier had been conclusively determined by a treaty to which Libya was an original party and Chad a party in succession to France.
[53] ICJ Reports, 1994, p. 36, para. 75. Among the other issues argued by the parties on which the Court felt no need to pronounce were:

(a) the principle of *uti possidetis*;
(b) the applicability of the Declaration adopted by the OAU at Cairo in 1964;
(c) the effectiveness of occupation of relevant areas in the past;
(d) the question whether such occupation was constant, peaceful and acknowledged;
(e) the question whether the 1955 Treaty was declaratory or constitutive;
(f) the concept of *terra nullius*;
(g) the nature of Senoussi, Ottoman or French administration;
(h) the concept of spheres of influence;
(i) the hinterland doctrine;
(j) the inter-temporal law; and
(k) the history of the dispute as argued before the UN and the OAU.

From this brief summary of the matters not addressed by the Court, which is drawn from paras. 75 and 76 of the judgment, it will be apparent that the Court was able to avoid a whole series of difficult issues by adopting a particular interpretation of the 1955 Treaty.

of both parties from 1955 onwards, concludes that: 'the silence or acquiescence of Libya from the date of signing the 1955 Treaty to the present time,
without any protest whatsoever, clearly militates against its claim.'[54] Judge
Ajibola asserts that there were many occasions when Libya could have
protested to Chad or even France (between 1955 and 1960) that the 1955
Treaty was invalid or had failed to create the expected boundary, yet Libya was
silent.

This brief survey of the case law of the present Court on estoppel and
acquiescence sufficiently bears out the point that there is a close link between
these two concepts, and indeed that they must be considered as part of the
wider pattern of state conduct which an international tribunal may find to be
relevant to the determination of an inter-state dispute. The survey, however,
equally demonstrates that the Court will be reluctant to penalize a state unduly
for inconsistency of conduct, and in particular to find that the conduct relied
on has created an estoppel in the strict sense. As part of their litigation
strategy, states involved in cases before the Court, particularly land and
maritime boundary cases, will regularly invoke arguments based on estoppel
or acquiescence, if only because disputes with deep historical roots will almost
certainly reveal instances of conduct by one or the other state at variance with
what it may later profess to be its position. But the Court has shown wisdom
and restraint in requiring in effect that conduct that might arguably amount to
acquiescence must be maintained over a certain period of time. Estoppel and
acquiescence will continue to play a significant part in the decision-making
process of the Court; but the Court will likewise continue to exercise
considerable caution in admitting too decisive a role for either of these
concepts in the final determination of inter-state disputes.

[54] Separate Opinion of Judge Ajibola, para. 110.

7

L'équité dans la jurisprudence de la Cour Internationale de Justice

Un mystère en voie de dissipation?

Prosper Weil

☙

Dans son étude 'Equity and Equitable Principles', Sir Robert Jennings écrivait en 1986:

> Looking at the cases hitherto there appears at first sight to be a jumble of different and disparate elements; but it is believed that they can, now that we have a whole series of judgments and awards, be arranged into a pattern which has some pretensions to simplicity, clarity and even elegance.[1]

Ce qui n'était encore à ce moment-là qu'espoir timidement entrevu est devenu depuis lors quasi-certitude, et c'est en grande partie au dédicataire de ce livre que nous le devons qui, par ses travaux doctrinaux[2] comme par son action au sein, puis à la présidence de la Cour Internationale de Justice, a contribué puissamment à conduire la jurisprudence vers une clarification du contenu et de la place de l'équité en droit international. C'est en hommage à cette chronique d'une évolution suscitée que le présent essai a été écrit.

Nombre de concepts du droit international relèvent davantage de l'évocation poétique que de la précision scientifique. L'équité est de ceux-là. Aussi n'est-il pas étonnant que les juristes – qui, en dépit de leur réputation de rigueur intellectuelle, sont attirés par l'ambiguïté comme les papillons vers la lumière – se soient précipités en cohortes serrées sur cette notion protéiforme, sur cette 'énigme'[3] si difficile à percer.

---

[1] *Annuaire suisse de droit international*, 42 (1986), p. 27 ss., à la p. 38.
[2] Outre l'article précité voir 'The Principles Governing Marine Boundaries', in K. Hailbronner, G. Ress et T. Stein (eds.), *Staat und Völkerrechtsordnung. Festschrift für Karl Doehring* (Berlin, 1989), p. 398 ss.
[3] M. Bedjaoui, 'L'"énigme" des "principes équitables" dans le droit des délimitations maritimes', *Rivista española de derecho internacional*, 18 (1990), p. 267 ss.

L'ambition de la présente étude n'est pas d'apporter une pierre supplémentaire à cet imposant édifice doctrinal. Son objet est plus modeste. Elle laissera de côté les situations, de plus en plus nombreuses, où une règle conventionnelle prévoit qu'un problème sera résolu conformément à l'équité ou à des principes équitables: droit de la mer, droit spatial, droit fluvial, droit des télécommunications, etc.[4] Elle laissera de côté également la place faite à des considérations d'équité par la Cour permanente de Justice internationale et par les tribunaux arbitraux. C'est sur la jurisprudence de la Cour internationale de Justice au cours de son premier demi-siècle d'existence que cet essai portera exclusivement.[5] S'il est vrai que '[t]oute l'histoire du droit international est richement tissée des réflexions diverses sur la question de l'équité',[6] il n'est pas moins vrai que, prenant le relais d'une Cour permanente très réservée à l'égard de l'équité, la Cour internationale a eu recours de plus en plus fréquemment à ce concept, dont elle a entrepris en même temps de préciser la fonction et le contenu.

Sur l'aspect quantitatif il n'est pas nécessaire de s'arrêter longuement. Déclenché par l'arrêt de 1969 relatif aux affaires de la *Mer du Nord*,[7] le mouvement s'est confirmé avec *Barcelona Traction* de 1970.[8] A partir des années 80 il s'est considérablement accéléré: en matière de partage des ressources halieutiques avec *Compétence en matière de pêcheries* de 1974,[9] en matière de délimitation maritime avec *Tunisie/Libye* de 1982,[10] *Golfe du Maine* de 1984,[11] *Libye/Malte* de 1985[12] et *Jan Mayen* de 1993,[13] en matière des frontières terrestres avec *Burkina Faso/Mali* de 1986[14] et *El Salvador/Honduras* de 1992.[15]

Plus important pourtant que cet aspect quantitatif est l'effort entrepris par la Cour pour élaborer une véritable doctrine de l'équité. Certes plusieurs aspects demeurent-ils encore inexplorés. Il en est ainsi, par exemple, du problème des

---

[4] Cf. op. ind. Weeramantry, *Délimitation maritime dans la région située entre le Groenland et Jan Mayen, CIJ Recueil, 1993*, pp. 234–5, par. 75–7, et p. 246, par. 119.

[5] En conséquence, seuls seront cités les arrêts et les opinions jointes à ces derniers, ainsi que les mémoires et plaidoiries afférents à des affaires jugées par la Cour. Aucune jurisprudence arbitrale ne sera citée. Pas davantage ne sera-t-il fait référence à la littérature juridique consacrée au problème de l'équité, à l'exception des travaux doctrinaux de membres de la Cour.

[6] Weeramantry, *CIJ Recueil, 1993*, p. 278, par. 248.

[7] *Plateau continental de la mer du Nord, CIJ Recueil, 1969*, p. 3.

[8] *Barcelona Traction, Light and Power Company Limited, CIJ Recueil, 1970*, p. 3.

[9] *Compétence en matière de pêcheries (Royaume-Uni c. Islande), fond, CIJ Recueil, 1974*, p. 3.

[10] *Plateau continental (Tunisie/Jamahiriya arabe libyenne), CIJ Recueil, 1982*, p. 18.

[11] *Délimitation de la frontière maritime dans la région du golfe du Maine, CIJ Recueil, 1984*, p. 246.

[12] *Plateau continental (Jamahiriya arabe libyenne/Malte), CIJ Recueil, 1985*, p. 13.

[13] *Délimitation maritime dans la région située entre le Groenland et Jan Mayen, CIJ Recueil, 1993*, p. 38.

[14] *Différend frontalier (Burkina Faso/Mali), CIJ Recueil, 1986*, p. 554.

[15] *Différend frontalier terrestre, insulaire et maritime (El Salvador/Honduras), CIJ Recueil, 1992*, p. 35.

rapports entre le droit, la justice et l'équité. De même qu'elle s'est refusée à établir une distinction subtile entre les 'principes' et les 'règles' du droit international,[16] la Cour a eu la sagesse de ne pas s'aventurer dans de savantes dissertations sur la distinction entre droit, justice et équité. La formule souvent citée d'après laquelle 'quel que soit le raisonnement juridique du juge, ses décisions doivent par définition être justes, donc en ce sens équitables',[17] paraît établir une parité absolue entre ces trois concepts. Des arrêts ultérieurs sembleront cependant faire de l'équité et du droit des émanations de la justice, et donc les distinguer de cette dernière.[18] Tous ces *dicta* ne vont toutefois pas au-delà d'un syncrétisme de bon aloi.

Sur le plan juridique lui-même, la Cour ne paraît pas avoir cherché à démêler l'écheveau des diverses composantes de l'équité. 'Principes' équitables, 'procédés' ou 'méthodes' équitables, 'résultat' ou 'solution' équitable: par-delà cette 'terminologie flottante'[19] se profile une certaine réticence de la Cour à déterminer avec précision à quel aspect particulier elle entend attacher l'équité. Sans doute paraît-elle avoir privilégié le résultat sur tout autre aspect: 'c'est le résultat qui importe', a-t-elle déclaré.[20] Les rapports entre 'les quatre aspects de l'équité'[21] – principes procédures, méthodes, résultat – n'en continuent pas moin sà baigner dans un certain clair-obscur.

Ces aspects marginaux mis à part, la Cour s'est lancée dans l'aventure de l'équité avec un indéniable courage intellectuel. Elle l'a fait selon sa méthode habituelle du *trial and error*, par touches successives, suivies de corrections et de retours en arrière. Elle l'a fait, comme cela était sans doute inévitable, en frôlant parfois le précipice. L'évolution n'a pas été linéaire, et les contradictions ne manquent pas, ni d'un arrêt à l'autre, ni à l'intérieur d'un même arrêt. Un discours éclaté était sans doute le prix à payer pour une entreprise aussi risquée. On imagine mal quinze juges – et pas toujours les mêmes d'une affaire à l'autre – partager les mêmes vues sur des problèmes qui touchent aussi profondément à la perception du phénomène juridique, pour ne pas dire à la conscience humaine. C'est dire qu'il n'est possible de rendre compte de cette entreprise de domestication de l'équité qu'en pratiquant certains raccourcis simplificateurs. En dépit de son parcours en dents de scie, l'évolution, pourtant, est certaine.

[16] *Golfe du Maine, CIJ Recueil, 1984*, p. 288, par. 79 ('une expression double pour énoncer la même idée').
[17] *Mer du Nord, CIJ Recueil, 1969*, p. 48, par. 88.
[18] Par ex. *Tunisie/Libye, CIJ Recueil, 1982*, p. 60, par. 71, et *Libye/Malte, CIJ Recueil, 1985*, p. 39, par. 45.
[19] Bedjaoui, 'L'"énigme" des "principes équitables"', p. 374.
[20] *Tunisie/Libye, CIJ Recueil, 1982*, p. 59, par. 70. Cf. *Libye/Malte, CIJ Recueil, 1985*, pp. 38–9, par. 45; *Jan Mayen, CIJ Recueil, 1993*, p. 59, par. 48, et p. 62, par. 54.
[21] Weeramantry, *CIJ Recueil, 1993*, p. 224, par. 42.

Comme l'écrit M. Bedjaoui, après une 'phase d'incertitude, marquée par une jurisprudence mouvante . . . , le concept (d'équité) est enfin apprivoisé'.[22] Plus récemment, le juge Weeramantry a pu écrire de son côté que la jurisprudence de la Cour 'en est maintenant arrivée à un point où elle reflète un *corpus* considérable de principes équitables et où la Cour s'appuie fréquemment sur l'équité pour parvenir à une décision'.[23] Même si à bien des égards l'équité est 'toujours mystérieuse',[24] son mystère commence à se dissiper.

Au cours de ces dernières années, la Cour s'est en effet attelée à une double tâche: d'abord, arracher l'équité à ses racines subjectives pour la faire basculer du côté de la normativité juridique; ensuite, définir les rapports entre cette nouvelle venue dans le monde juridique et le droit international proprement dit. La première opération a été relativement facile à mener à bien: il aura suffi de quelques proclamations rhétoriques pour désubjectiviser l'équité et pour la distinguer de la simple intuition de juste et de l'injuste. C'est une fois l'équité intégrée au monde de la normativité juridique que les difficultés sont surgi. Prise entre le marteau de la subjectivité absolue et l'enclume de la normativité pure et dure, la Cour a dû emprunter une voie étroite, parsemée d'embûches. Si le divorce est aujourd'hui consommé entre l'équité et l'*ex aequo et bono*, l'union de l'équité avec le droit ne l'est pas encore complètement.

LE CARACTÈRE NORMATIF DE L'ÉQUITÉ

La "règle de l'équité"

Comme tout système juridique, le droit international se compose de règles dont l'inspiration et la finalité se trouvent dans les valeurs humaines, morale ou sociales. L'équité constitue donc à coup sûr une source matérielle du droit international. Cela est tout spécialement vrai de certains principes parfois appelés, de manière significative, principes d'équité: *pacta sunt servanda*, bonne foi, abus du droit, obligation de réparer, *rebus sic stantibus*, *exceptio non adimpleti contractus*, etc. Ces principes revêtent une importance d'autant plus grande en droit international que ce dernier est plus pauvre en règles concrètes et doit se contenter, plus que les droits internes, de standards généraux plus ou moins riches en potentialités de concrétisation. Dans un système dont les acteurs sont si peu animés de préoccupations éthiques, la proclamation de

---

[22] 'L'"énigme" des "principes équitables"', p. 369.

[23] *CIJ Recueil, 1993*, p. 238, par. 88.

[24] Bedjaoui, 'L'"énigme" des "principes équitables"', p. 377.

124

principes d'équité est plus nécessaire que partout ailleurs. C'est à propos de ces principes que le juge Hudson écrivait, dans un passage souvent cité de son opinion en l'affaire des *Prises d'eau à la Meuse*:

> Les règles bien connues sous le nom de principes d'équité ont depuis longtemps été considérées comme faisant partie du droit international, et, à ce titre, elles ont souvent été appliquées par les tribunaux internationaux . . . Une démarcation nette entre le droit et l'équité ne doit pas trouver place dans la jurisprudence internationale.[25]

Pas davantage n'a-t-il jamais été contesté que l'équité puisse intervenir dans l'interprétation et l'application des règles du droit international. Entre plusieurs manières possibles de comprendre et d'appliquer une norme juridique, préférence doit être donnée à celle qui apparaît la plus équitable. En pareil cas, l'équité n'est pas une source directement normative de droits ou d'obligations, mais simplement un critère ou une considération qui permet de choisir entre plusieurs manières d'interpréter ou d'appliquer une norme. C'est cette approche – que l'on désigne parfois, on le verra, d'équité *infra legem* – que reflétait déjà la résolution de l'Institut de droit international de 1937 aux termes de laquelle: 'L'équité est normalement inhérente à une saine application du droit, et . . . le juge international est, de par sa fonction même, appelé à en tenir compte dans la mesure compatible avec le respect du droit.'[26] C'est cette approche aussi qui se traduira dans le célèbre *dictum* de *Barcelona Traction* d'après lequel, 'dans le domaine de la protection diplomatique comme dans tous les autres domaines, le droit international exige une application raisonnable', c'est-à-dire une application commandée par des 'raisons d'équité', par des 'considérations d'équité'.[27] C'est la même approche encore qui trouvera expression dans *Tunisie/Libye*, où la Cour rappellera qu' 'en appliquant le droit international positif, un tribunal peut choisir entre plusieurs interprétations possibles celle qui lui paraît la plus conforme aux exigences de la justice dans les circonstances de l'espèce',[28] ainsi que dans *Burkina Faso/Mali*, où la Chambre déclarera qu' 'elle prendra en considération l'équité telle qu'elle s'exprime dans son aspect *infra legem*, c'est-à-dire cette forme d'équité qui constitue une méthode d'interprétation du droit et en est l'une des qualités'.[29]

De l'équité inspiratrice de règles de droit ou 'méthode d'interprétation' de

---

[25] *CPJI, série A/B, n. 70*, p. 76.

[26] *Annuaire de l'Institut dr droit international* (1937), t. 37, pp. 161–2.

[27] *CIJ Recueil, 1970*, p. 48, par. 93.

[28] *CIJ Recueil, 1982*, p. 60, par. 71.

[29] *CIJ Recueil, 1986*, pp. 567–8, par. 28.

la règle de droit à l'équité directement génératrice de droits et d'obligations des Etats il y avait toutefois un pas. C'est ce pas que la Cour a franchi en 1969, dans *Mer du Nord*, à propos de la délimitation du plateau continental, lorsqu'elle a parlé en toutes lettres de 'la règle de l'équité',[30] reconnaissant par là à l'équité, sans équivoque possible, un caractère directement normatif.

Cette reconnaissance implique-t-elle que l'équité constitue désormais une source formelle du droit international? Problème délicat, puisque l'article 38 du Statut de la Cour ne mentionne pas l'équité parmi les sources formelles. Aussi certains auteurs se sont-ils demandés si c'est en tant que règle coutumière ou en tant que principe général de droit que la 'règle de l'équité' est applicable. A ce problème la Cour ne paraît pas avoir attaché d'intérêt. En matière de délimitation maritime, par exemple, elle considère que c'est le droit international coutumier qui impose une délimitation effectuée en application de principes équitables de manière à aboutir à un résultat équitable, tant et si bien qu'en cette matière du moins la 'règle de l'équité' se voit reconnaître le caractère d'une règle coutumière. Ce qui n'a pas empêché la Cour de déclarer ailleurs que 'la notion juridique est un principe général directement applicable en tant que droit',[31] ce qui pourrait donner à penser que c'est en tant que principe général de droit que l'équité est normativement applicable. Règle coutumière ou principe général de droit? Le débat – largement sémantique – demeure ouvert.

Équité et *ex aequo et bono*

Pour conforter la normativité fraîchement reconnue à l'équité, la Cour a immédiatement, et parallèlement, entrepris de proclamer haut et fort que cette équité-là, cette équité juridique, n'a rien à voir avec ce que le commun des mortels entend par le même vocable, à savoir une intuition du juste et de l'injuste éminemment subjective et variable. De là l'insistance mise par la Cour à affirmer que l'"équité en tant que notion juridique'[32] doit être soigneusement distinguée de l'*ex aequo et bono*.

Cette distinction avait déjà été esquissée dans l'avis consultatif de 1956 en l'affaire des *Jugements du tribunal administratif de l'OIT sur requêtes contre l'Unesco*: alors même que le tribunal administratif de l'OIT avait déclaré fixer une indemnité *ex aequo et bono*, expliquait la Cour, il n'avait pas entendu par là 'se départir des principes du droit, mais simplement fixer, conformément à ce que

---

[30] *CIJ Recueil, 1969*, p. 48, par. 88.
[31] *CIJ Recueil, 1982*, p. 60, par. 71.
[32] *CIJ Recueil, 1982*, p. 60, par. 71.

prescrivait la règle de droit, la juste mesure de la réparation, le chiffre raisonnable de celle-ci'.[33]

Mais c'est dans *Mer du Nord*, en 1969, que la Cour, en même temps qu'elle consacrait pour la première fois la 'règle de l'équité', prenait soin d'arracher cette équité nouvellement normative à ses racines métajuridiques: 'il ne s'agit pas d'appliquer l'équité simplement comme une représentation de la justice abstraite . . . Il n'est par conséquent pas question . . . d'une décision *ex aequo et bono*, ce qui ne serait possible que dans les conditions prescrites à l'article 38, paragraphe 2, du Statut de la Cour.'[34] La distinction sera inlassablement répétée par les arrêts ultérieurs.[35]

Bien qu'elle reposât sur une base textuelle indiscutable,[36] la distinction entre l'équité juridique et l'équité *ex aequo et bono* n'en a pas moins été dénoncée comme nominale et rhétorique. En statuant conformément à une soi-disant 'règle d'équité' sans que les Parties lui aient demandé de le faire, la Cour, a-t-on dit, méconnaîtrait sa fonction judiciaire et outrepasserait les pouvoirs qu'elle tient de l'article 38 de son Statut. Le fait est que la jurisprudence a beau situer l'équité du côté de la normativité juridique, c'est plutôt vers l'*ex aequo et bono* qu'elle a donné parfois l'impression de pencher, brouillant ainsi la distinction entre les deux concepts. Comme l'écrivait Sir Robert Jennings, ' . . . what the litigants get is in effect a decision *ex aequo et bono* whether they wanted it nor not. At any rate, the very serious question arises of what exactly is the difference between a decision according to equitable principles and a decision *ex aequo et bono*.'[37]

Pour répondre à cette dernière question, nous disposons de quelques

---

[33] *CIJ Recueil, 1956*, p. 100.

[34] *CIJ Recueil, 1969*, p. 47, par 85 et p. 48, par. 88.

[35] 'Il ne s'agit pas simplement d'arriver à une solution équitable, mais d'arriver à une solution équitable qui repose sur le droit applicable' (*Compétence en matière de pêcheries, CIJ Recueil, 1974*, p. 33, par. 78). 'Il faut distinguer entre l'application de principes équitables et le fait de rendre une décision *ex aequo et bono*, ce que la Cour ne peut faire que si les Parties en sont convenues . . . En pareil cas la Cour n'a plus à appliquer strictement des règles juridiques, le but étant de parvenir à un règlement approprié. La tâche de la Cour est ici toute différente: elle soit appliquer les principes équitables comme partie intégrante du droit international' (*Tunisie/Libye, CIJ Recueil, 1982*, p. 60, par. 71). 'La Chambre est tenue par son statut et requise par les Parties non pas de décider *ex aequo et bono*, mais d'asseoir le résultat à atteindre sur une base de droit' (*Golfe du Maine, CIJ Recueil, 1984*, p. 39, par. 45). 'La justice, dont l'équité est une émanation, n'est pas la justice abstraite, mais la justice selon la règle de droit' (*Libye/Malte, CIJ Recueil, 1985*, p. 39, par. 45). 'Il est clair que la Chambre ne peut, en la présente affaire, statuer *ex aequo et bono*. (Elle n'a) pas reçu des Parties la mission de procéder à un ajustement de leurs intérêts respectifs' (*Burkina Faso/Mali, CIJ Recueil, 1986*, p. 567, par. 28 et p. 633, par. 149). Cf. *El Salvador/Honduras, CIJ Recueil, 1992*, p. 514, par. 262. Voir aussi les opinions individuelles Schwebel, Shahabuddeen et Weeramantry dans *Jan Mayen* (*CIJ Recueil, 1993*, pp. 127–8, 192–3 et 226 ss).

[36] Sur la genèse de l'article 38, voir Weeramantry, *CIJ Recueil, 1993*, p. 229, par. 59.

[37] 'The Principles Governing Marine Boundaries', p. 401.

indications *a contrario*. Si elle était appelée à statuer *ex aequo et bono* – ce qui ne s'est jamais produit – la Cour pourrait 'se départir des principes de droit', se borner à 'arriver à une solution équitable' sans que cette dernière 'repose sur le droit applicable', se contenter de 'parvenir à un règlement approprié' sans 'appliquer strictement des règles juridiques'. 'Si un pouvoir de statuer *ex aequo et bono*, a précisé récemment un membre de la Cour, n'exige pas qu'on s'écarte des principes du droit, se marque distinctive est qu'il permet de le faire.'[38] Statuer *ex aequo et bono* n'exige pas de formation juridique particulière, a observé Sir Robert Jennings; appliquer l'équité juridique en requiert une.[39]

Si la distinction a pu paraître moins tranchée dans la réalité que ce que les *dicta* de la Cour laissent entendre, ce n'est pas seulement parce que la Cour n'a pas toujours réussi à échapper aux pièges du subjectivisme; c'est aussi parce que certains traits sont communs à l'équité *ex aequo et bono* et à l'équité juridique. Ainsi, on vient de le voir, rien n'interdit à un juge chargé de statuer *ex aequo et bono* de faire état de considérations juridiques: même si le droit ne s'impose pas à l'*ex aequo et bono*, il n'y est pas interdit de séjour. Plus important est le phénomène inverse: les solutions intermédiaires consistant à *split the difference*, qui caractérisent l'équité *ex aequo et bono*, ne sont pas incompatibles avec l'équité juridique; et ce n'est pas parce que le juge 'partage la différence' qu'il quitte pour autant le terrain de la 'règle de l'équité' pour se réfugier dans le non-droit de la 'conciliation' ou de la 'justice distributive' – ce à quoi la Cour déclare se refuser.[40] Ainsi, s'agissant de la délimitation du plateau continental, la Cour a envisagé dès 1969 que l'équité juridique peut conduire dans certaines situations à une division égale de l'espace sur lequel les titres des deux Etats se chevauchent.[41] Elle ajoutait toutefois immédiatement que 'l'équité n'implique pas l'égalité';[42] ce qui ne signifie pas qu'elle l'exclue, tant et si bien que la porte est ouverte à une division tantôt par parts égales tantôt par parts inégales, selon les circonstances. C'est dans le droit fil de cette approche que, dans leur opinion conjointe de *Libye/Malte*, les juges Ruda, Bedjaoui et Jiménez de Aréchaga se sont prononcés en faveur d'une solution de partage égal de la zone revendiquée par les parties. Il ne faut pas voir là, soulignent-ils, 'une transaction, que la Cour n'a pas à entreprendre'. 'Un telle division, précisent-ils, incarne parfois l'équité "à l'état pur". C'est le partage égal qui, dans certaines

---

[38] Op. ind. Shahabuddeen, *Jan Mayen*, *CIJ Recueil, 1993*, p. 193.

[39] 'Equity and Equitable Principles', p. 30.

[40] *CIJ Recueil, 1982*, p. 60, par. 71.

[41] *CIJ Recueil, 1969*, p. 36, par. 57; p. 52, par. 99; p. 53, par. 101. Cf. *Golfe du Maine, CIJ Recueil, 1984*, p. 327, par. 195.

[42] *CIJ Recueil, 1969*, p. 49, par. 91.

circonstances spéciales, paraît se recommander de lui-même pour satisfaire pleinement l'équité.'[43] Dans la même optique, la Cour a décidé dans *Jan Mayen* qu'en vue d'assurer aux parties un accès équitable aux ressources halieutiques de la principale zone de pêche située entre les côtes des deux pays la zone de chevauchement des revendications des deux parties devait être divisée en deux parts de superficies égales; les autres secteurs disputés ont, en revanche, été divisés de manière inégale afin de tenir compte de la disparité dans les longueurs côtières.[44]

L'insistance mise par la Cour à distinguer l'équité juridique de l'équité *ex aequo et bono* montre certes que tout risque de confusion n'a pas disparu et que des efforts sont périodiquement nécessaires pour remonter la pente. Elle ne condamne pas le principe même de la distinction.[45]

LES RAPPORTS ENTRE ÉQUITÉ ET DROIT

Une fois érigée en 'notion juridique' et solidement installée dans le monde de la normativité juridique, l'équité allait affronter un défi autrement difficile que celui de sa séparation avec le sentiment intuitif du juste et de l'injuste: celui de ses rapports avec la règle de droit classique.

Ces rapports, il faut le reconnaître, ont été plutôt orageux. Equité et droit n'ont pas toujours fait bon ménage. En simplifiant, on serait tenté de dire que les relations entre l'équité et de droit ont été conçues par la Cour de trois manières différentes: comme des rapports de juxtaposition et d'extranéité, où l'équité se situe à côté du droit; comme des rapports de substitution, où l'équité vient à la place du droit; comme des rapports d'intégration, où l'équité est partie intégrante du droit tout en y occupant une place spécifique. La jurisprudence de la Cour paraît osciller entre une union libre, dans laquelle équité et droit vivent chacun sa vie; un engouement extrême pour l'équité, qui subjugue le droit jusqu'à l'absorber – une attraction fatale, en quelque sorte, du droit pour l'équité; et, enfin, un mariage de raison dominé par des relations apaisées. Si, dans l'ensemble, ces trois conceptions se sont succédé dans le temps, aucune d'elles n'a jamais été exclusive des deux autres, même si, à tel stade de l'évolution ou dans tel arrêt, l'une d'elles peut sembler avoir pris le dessus. A aucun moment la jurisprudence n'a été monolithique; à chaque moment elle a été déchirée. Et si aujourd'hui c'est l'approche synthétique de l'intégration sage qui paraît avoir le vent en poupe, nul ne peut

---

[43] *CIJ Recueil, 1985*, p. 91, par. 38.
[44] *Ibid.*, pp. 80–1, par. 92.
[45] Shahabuddeen, *Jan Mayen, CIJ Recueil, 1993*, p. 194.

être assuré qu'elle poursuivra sa route et moins encore qu'elle arrivera à bon port.

L'équité à côté du droit: des rapports de juxtaposition

Confrontée au problème des relations entre l'équité et le droit, la Cour ne pouvait échapper à la conception classique d'une relation d'extranéité où l'équité se situe en dehors du droit, à côté de lui, selon trois modèles abondamment décrits par les auteurs: une équité *infra* (ou *secundum*) *legem*; une équité *praeter legem*; une équité *contra legem*. De manière assez suprenante, il faudra attendre 1986 pour que la Cour se réfère expressément à cette terminologie:[46] dans *Burkina Faso/Mali*, puis dans *El Salvador/Honduras*, elle écartera l'équité *praeter legem* et l'équité *contra legem* pour prendre en considération l'équité *infra legem*.[47]

Pour traditionnelle qu'elle soit, cette classification tripartite n'a pourtant ni contenu précis ni utilité réelle.

On s'accorde généralement pour voir dans l'équité *infra legem* les considérations qui permettent de choisir entre plusieurs manières d'interpréter ou d'appliquer une règle de droit. Mais alors, comme on l'a vu précédemment, ce n'est plus d'une équité normative qu'il s'agit, mais, plus simplement, de l'équité dans l'interprétation et l'application du droit,[48] ce qui n'est assurément pas la même chose.

On s'accorde également pour définir l'équité *praeter legem* comme le recours à des considérations d'équité en vue de 'combler les lacunes et en quelque sorte les interstices du droit'.[49] Tout comme les principes généraux du droit, l'équité constitue un mécanisme permettant de pallier la pauvreté inhérente du droit international, d'anticiper en quelque sorte l'évolution du droit et d'éviter au juge le *non liquet*. Ainsi, c'est en vue de combler une lacune ou une incertitude du droit en matière de délimitation d'une frontière terrestre que la Cour a fait appel à l'équité dans *Burkina Faso/Mali* et dans *El Salvador/Honduras*, mais dans les deux cas c'est à l'équité *infra legem*, et non pas à l'équité *praeter legem* comme on aurait pu s'y attendre, qu'elle a affirmé recourir.[50]

---

[46] Mention de cette terminologie figure toutefois dans certaines opinions jointes (voir par ex. op. ind. Ammoun, *Mer du Nord, CIJ Recueil, 1969*, p. 132 ss).

[47] *CIJ Recueil, 1986*, p. 567, par. 28 et p. 633, par. 149; *CIJ Recueil, 1992*, p. 514, par. 262. Cf. Weeramantry, *CIJ Recueil, 1993*, p. 231 ss.

[48] Cf. op. ind. Abi-Saab, *Burkina Faso/Mali, CIJ Recueil, 1986*, p. 663, qui évoque des 'considérations d'équité *infra legem* dans l'interprétation et l'application du droit'.

[49] Weeramantry, *CIJ Recueil, 1993*, p. 231, par. 65.

[50] *CIJ Recueil, 1986*, p. 633, par. 150; *CIJ Recueil, 1992*, p. 514, par. 262.

On s'accorde enfin pour voir dans l'équité *contra legem* une solution condamnée par le droit mais dictée par l'équité. Là encore, pourtant, le contenu précis de cette notion est loin d'être clair. S'agit-il de contredire au nom de l'équité une solution dictée par le droit? C'est alors une solution de convenance, qui 'se départit des principes du droit', que l'on envisage – en d'autres termes, une solution *ex aequo et bono*. Lorsque, dans *Burkina Faso/Mali*, la Chambre, après avoir déclaré qu'elle 'ne peut, en la présente affaire, statuer *ex aequo et bono*', ajoute qu''elle doit également écarter en l'espèce tout recours à l'équité *contra legem*,[51] on voit mal où elle situe la différence entre l'équité *contra legem* et l'équité *ex aequo et bono*. S'agit-il, au contraire, lorsqu'on évoque l'équité *contra legem*, de corriger ou d'ajuster une règle générale en vue de tenir compte de la spécificité du cas individuel, ainsi que la Cour l'a fait – sans employer le mot – dans *Barcelona Traction* pour la protection diplomatique[52] et dans *Jan Mayen* pour la délimitation maritime?[53] En ce cas, c'est à une équité intégrée au droit que l'on se réfère, et non pas à une équité contre le droit.

Manifestement, la classification traditionnelle est inadéquate pour rendre compte des nuances de l'équité. Comment, par exemple, situer, au regard de cette classification, l'équité autonome qui se substitue au droit? Ni *infra*, ni *praeter*, ni *contra*: c'est à une conception étrangère aux catégories classiques que l'on a à faire.

L'équité tenant lieu de droit: des rapports de substitution

Succombant aux séductions de l'équité dont elle avait découvert les charmes dans *Mer du Nord*, la Cour a adopté, dans *Tunisie/Libye* et *Golfe du Maine*, une conception des relations entre l'équité et le droit qui exaltait l'équité au point d'en faire pratiquement un substitut du droit. Après avoir écarté, comme 'sans équivalent dans l'évolution du droit international', la conception opposant 'l'équité aux règles du droit positif, dont la rigueur doit être tempérée pour que justice soit rendue', elle proclama dans *Tunisie/Libye* que 'la notion juridique d'équité est un principe général directement applicable en tant que droit'.[54] C'est dans le mot 'directement' que résidait l'essentiel de cette théorie, car l'équité n'a pas pour fonction, dans cette approche, de corriger *a posteriori* l'effet indésirable produit parfois par la règle de droit; elle est la source immédiate et directe de la solution. En ce qui concerne plus spécialement la délimitation maritime, *Golfe du Maine* précisa que le droit international

---

[51] *CIJ Recueil, 1986*, p. 567, par. 28.   [52] *CIJ Recueil, 1970*, p. 48, par. 92–3.
[53] *CIJ Recueil, 1993*, p. 61, par. 51 et p. 64, par. 59.   [54] *CIJ Recueil, 1982*, p. 60, par. 71.

proprement dit ne comporte pas 'un corps de règles détaillées' et qu'il ne faut pas espérer y trouver 'un ensemble déjà tout formé de règles prêtes à être appliquées'.[55] Le droit international, affirma cet arrêt, se réduit en cette matière à une 'norme fondamentale' qui prescrit que tout délimitation doit être effectuée en application de principes équitables en vue d'assurer un résultat équitable.[56]

Il ne s'agit certes pas, la Cour y insiste, d'un retour à l'*ex aequo et bono*, puisque c'est le droit qui prescrit la recherche d'un résultat équitable en application de principes équitables et que c'est sur habilitation et renvoi du droit que l'équité va s'appliquer. Si l'équité demeure donc en principe, dans cette conception, juridiquement normative, sa juridicité n'est toutefois assurée que par un lien ténu, plus rhétorique que réel. Le droit entrouvre en quelque sorte la porte, il apparaît pour un instant de raison – le temps de prévoir le recours à l'équité; après quoi il se retire sur la pointe des pieds, laissant l'équité occuper seule le terrain. La règle de droit n'a plus qu'une fonction unique: celle d' introniser l'équité comme souveraine maîtresse de la matière. L'équité a beau se prévaloir d'un mandat du droit: dès lors que celui-ci ne contient aucune règle régissant la substance de la matière et se borne à laisser le champ libre à l'équité, la norme applicable se ramène en définitive à l'équité, tant et si bien que celle-ci se voit érigée en facteur normatif autonome. L'équité tient lieu de règle, elle se substitue au droit, elle devient un *ersatz* du droit.

La Cour a beau insister sur le fait qu'il 'faut distinguer entre l'application de principes équitables et le fait de rendre une décision *ex aequo et bono*'.[57] Elle a beau affirmer qu''on est . . . fort loin de l'exercice d'un pouvoir discrétion-naire ou de la conciliation' et qu''il ne s'agit pas non plus d'un recours à la justice distributive'.[58] Elle a beau proclamer qu'en appliquant la 'norme fondamentale' du résultat équitable elle entend 'asseoir le résultat à atteindre sur une base de droit'.[59] Il ne faut pas se cacher derrière son ombre: ces belles phrases tiennent davantage de l'autosuggestion ou de l'exorcisme que d'une analyse scientifique. Avec cette conception la normativité juridique de l'équité, même si elle ne disparaît pas complètement, se trouve pratiquement réduite au degré zéro. Une règle de droit dont le seul contenu est de renvoyer à l'équité n'est qu'un trompe-l'oeil, puisque le droit n'apparaît que pour démissionner immédiatement et céder la place à l'équité. Que dirait-on, en droit interne, d'une loi qui se bornerait à prévoir qu'en cas de divorce la garde des enfants et les problèmes patrimoniaux seront résolus en application de

---

[55] *CIJ Recueil, 1984*, p. 290, par. 81 et p. 299, par. 111.
[56] *Ibid.*, pp. 299–300, par. 111–12.   [57] *CIJ Recueil, 1982*, p. 60, par. 71.
[58] *Ibid.*   [59] *CIJ Recueil, 1984*, p. 278, par. 59.

principes équitables en vue d'aboutir à un résultat équitable? Entre l'équité ainsi comprise et l'équité pure de l'*ex aequo et bono* la différence n'a plus l'épaisseur que d'une feuille de soie.

Il en est d'autant plus ainsi que cette conception comportait plusieurs aspects qui concouraient à priver l'équité de toute valeur juridiquement normative autre que verbale: la primauté des faits; la théorie de l'*unicum*, la primauté du résultat; la totale subjectivité de l'équité.

La primauté des faits, tout d'abord:

> Appliquer l'équité, écrit le juge Jiménez de Aréchaga, signifie . . . que le tribunal doit rendre la justice, dans le cas concret dont il est saisi, par une décision conçue en fonction de l'ensemble des faits propres à cette affaire et adaptée à ces faits [*a decision shaped by and adjusted to the relevant 'factual matrix'*] . . . Ce n'est . . . pas par une décision particulière de justice que l'on parvient à l'équité, mais par la justice de chaque décision particulière.[60]

La théorie de l'*unicum* ensuite, selon laquelle, puisque les faits varient d'une espèce à l'autre, aucun critère, aucun principe, aucune méthode ne s'impose dans toutes les affaires. Chaque espèce est *sui generis*, 'chaque litige . . . doit être examiné et résolu en lui-même en fonction des circonstances qui lui sont propres',[61] 'chaque cas concret est finalement différent des autres, . . . il est un *unicum*'.[62]

La primauté du résultat équitable, en troisième lieu, qui justifie le recours à n'importe quel principe et à n'importe quelle méthode: 'C'est le résultat qui importe . . . Tous les principes ne sont pas en soi équitables: c'est l'équité de la solution qui leur confère cette qualité'.[63]

La totale subjectivité de l'équité, enfin: pas de définition *ex ante*, donc prévisible, de ce qu'il faut regarder comme équitable ou comme inéquitable; le juge prendra position dans chaque espèce sans se référer à aucun critère normatif prédéterminé.

En matière de délimitation maritime, cette conception a conduit à la théorie de l'indifférence normative des méthodes applicables et au rejet de l'équidistance comme méthode de premier pas dont les résultats seraient ajustés dans une seconde phase de l'opération de délimitation. Toute méthode ou combinaison de méthodes était juridiquement acceptable dès lors qu'elle

---

[60] *CIJ Recueil, 1982*, p. 106, par. 24–5. Cf. E. Jiménez de Aréchaga, 'The Conception of Equity in Maritime Delimitation", in P. L. Zanardi et al. (eds.), *Le droit international à l'heure de sa codification. Etudes en l'honneur de Roberto Ago* (Milan, 1987), t. II, p. 229 ss., à la page 232.

[61] *CIJ Recueil, 1982*, p. 60, par. 72 et p. 92, par. 132.

[62] *CIJ Recueil, 1984*, p. 290, par. 81.

[63] *CIJ Recueil, 1982*, p. 59, par. 70.

conduisait à une solution que le juge regardait comme équitable. Quant aux principes équitables, ils perdaient tout contenu, car la philosophie de ce qui est équitable et de ce qui ne l'est pas variait d'une affaire à l'autre, d'un juge à l'autre, tant et si bien que la décision de la Cour ne représentait plus l'application de normes préexistantes mais était la résultante de l'addition des subjectivités d'une majorité. C'était la méthode de la non-méthode, le principe du non-principe. Ce n'était peut-être pas de l'*ex aequo et bono*, mais on n'en était pas loin.

L'équité dans le droit: des rapports d'intégration

La théorie de l'équité autonome, factuelle, variable et subjective a soulevé des critiques d'autant plus vives qu'elle constituait un abandon de l'approche que la Cour avait adoptée dans *Mer du Nord* et dans *Barcelona Traction*. Critiques doctrinales, bien sûr, mais aussi résistance de la part de certains membres de la Cour.

Dans *Tunisie/Libye* déjà, le juge Gros s'était élevé contre l'abandon par la Cour de l'équité correctrice au profit d'une équité autonome directement génératrice de la solution et tenant pratiquement lieu de droit. 'L'équité, écrivait-il, n'est pas une sorte de vision indépendante et subjective qui se substitue au droit';[64] en remplaçant le 'contrôle de l'équitable'[65] par une 'solution par l'équité', 'l'arrêt s'est égaré dans le subjectivisme'.[66] Deux ans plus tard, dans *Golfe du Maine*, le juge Gros allait reprendre, en les amplifiant, ses critiques contre la substitution à 'l'équité contrôlée' d'un 'système d'équité érigé en doctrine séparée du droit'. En rendant un arrêt qui 'se résume . . . en quelques mots: le résultat est équitable', la Chambre s'est placée, quoi qu'elle en dise, hors du droit, car 'une équité discrétionnairement découverte n'est pas une forme d'application du droit'. 'A chacun son équité', telle lui semblait être la doctrine nouvelle: 'Je doute, écrivait-il, que la justice internationale résiste à une équité ayant pour mesure l'oeil du juge'.[67] Le juge Oda se déclarait tout aussi insatisfait par une solution directement issue de l'équité et qui 'ne repose sur aucun principe ou aucune règle de droit applicable'.[68] 'On peut s'attendre', écrivait de son côté le juge Schwebel, 'à ce que des différences de jugement se fassent jour quant à l'application de principes équitables qui, parfois, ne

[64] *CIJ Recueil*, *1982*, p. 153, par. 19.
[65] *Ibid.*, p. 151, par. 15.
[66] *Ibid.*, p. 156, par. 24.
[67] *CIJ Recueil*, *1984*, p. 382, par. 37; p. 386, par. 42; p. 388, par. 47.
[68] *CIJ Recueil*, *1982*, p. 269, par. 180.

relèveront peut-être d'aucune conclusion certaine en droit'.[69] Quant au dédicataire de cette étude, il déplorait la 'dangerous metamorphosis' qui risquait de conduire 'straight into pure judicial discretion', et il posait la question ultime: 'Is equity then just the lawyer's name for subjective judicial decision more or less formally applied?'[70]

Dans l'affaire du *Golfe du Maine* l'une des parties avait en vain tenté d'obtenir de la Chambre l'abandon de la théorie de l'équité autonome et le retour à la conception correctrice antérieure. Plaidant pour le Canada, le signataire de ces lignes avait fait valoir que

> La délimitation doit être faite selon une méthode . . . dont la justification ne se trouve pas seulement *ex post* dans le caractère équitable du résultat auquel elle aboutit, mais également *ex ante* dans des considérations juridiques de caractère objectif . . . Le méthode . . . appropriée doit être à la fois enracinée dans des considérations juridiques et aboutir à une solution équitable. Les deux sont nécessaires, mais aucune d'elles n'est suffisante.[71]

Il avait souligné en même temps la nécessité d'un 'ancrage' dans le droit revêtant un caractère suffisant de généralité et de prévisibilité:

> Certes ce n'est jamais la même eau qui coule sous le même pont. Mais de là à contester la légitimité de toute ligne directrice de caractère tant soit peu général, il y a un pas que rien n'autorise . . . à franchir. Par sa nature même la norme juridique doit revêtir un certain degré de généralité, faute de quoi l'une des fonctions fondamentales du droit, celle de la prévisibilité et de la sécurité, ne serait pas remplie.[72]

Ces efforts n'avaient pas abouti. Non seulement la Chambre avait donné un éclat particulier aux théories de la 'norme fondamentale' et de l'*unicum*, mais elle avait dénié tout caractère privilégié à la méthode de l'équidistance et rejeté le principe de l'opération en deux phases préconisé par le Canada.[73]

Il faudra attendre *Libye/Malte* de 1985 pour que, devant la levée de boucliers provoquée par les arrêts antérieurs tant dans la doctrine qu'au sein même de la Cour, celle-ci rectifie le tir. Il était temps. Avec l'équité autonome la Cour

---

[69] *CIJ Recueil, 1984*, p. 357. Cf. op. ind. Mosler, *Libye/Malte*, qui regrettait qu'aient prévalu des 'conceptions non précisées sur la nature de l'équité' (*CIJ Recueil, 1985*, p. 120), et op. conj. Ruda, Bedjaoui et Jiménez de Aréchaga, *Libye/Malte*, qui évoquait la norme fondamentale du résultat équitable, 'qui dit tout et rien à la fois' (*ibid.*, p. 90, par. 37).

[70] 'Equity and Equitable Principles', pp. 30–1.

[71] *CIJ Mémoires, Golfe du Maine*, vol. VI, p. 171.

[72] *Ibid.*, vol. VII, p. 31.

[73] *CIJ Recueil, 1984*, p. 297, par. 107; p. 315, par. 163. Sur l'un des segments, la Chambre a toutefois recouru à une équidistance provisoire de premier pas suivie d'un ajustement au nom de l'équité (p. 333, par. 215, et pp. 334–5, par. 217–18).

avait frôlé le précipice. Après avoir longtemps boudé l'équité, la Cour était allée trop loin dans la direction opposée. L'approche qui a prévalu au début des années 80 en matière de délimitation maritime risquait de déborder sur d'autres chapitres du droit international, et en ce cas c'est le droit international tout entier qui menaçait, de proche en proche, de se dissoudre dans le magma d'une équité insaisissable.

Dans *Libye/Malte*, la Libye avait plaidé l'équité autonome dans toute son ampleur,[74] tandis que Malte avait soutenu qu'il ne saurait y avoir de *diktat* des faits et qu'en conséquence une opération de délimitation maritime doit commencer par une ligne provisoire reposant sur le droit et se poursuivre par un ajustement de cette ligne au cas où celle-ci se révélerait inéquitable. Ainsi se trouvaient satisfaites à la fois, estimait Malte, l'exigence d'un degré suffisant de généralité et de prévisibilité inhérent à toute règle de droit, et l'exigence d'un degré suffisant d'adaptation aux données de l'espèce inhérent à la poursuite d'un résultat équitable. Parallèlement, Malte avait dénoncé les dangers d'une conception indéterminée de l'équité, fût-ce dans la phase d'individualisation de la règle de droit: 'toutes les circonstances ne sont pas pertinentes *en droit*', estimait Malte.[75]

Sur l'opération de délimitation en deux temps la Cour ne fit qu'un demi-pas. Pratiquant une espèce de valse-hésitation, elle commença par rejeter le principe d'une opération commençant nécessairement par la prise en considération d'une ligne d'équidistance, puis elle recourut néanmoins à une telle opération avant de préciser qu'il ne fallait pas inférer de là le caractère obligatoire d'un processus en deux phases.[76]

Sur la jurisdiction des critères d'équité, au contraire, la Cour opéra une véritable revirement. L'application de la justice, 'dont l'équité est une émanation', déclara-t-elle, 'doit être marquée par la cohérence et une certaine prévisibilité'. 'Bien qu'elle s'attache plus particulièrement aux circonstances d'une affaire donnée, (l'équité) envisage aussi, au-delà de cette affaire, des principes d'une application plus générale.' Les 'principes d'équité' ne sont pas seulement un 'moyen de parvenir à un résultat équitable dans une instance particulière'; ils doivent être compris 'comme ayant une validité plus globale et donc exprimable en termes généraux'. Les principes équitables doivent en conséquence être 'exprimés en termes susceptibles d'une application générale'; Ils possèdent un 'caractère normatif'.[77] En définitive, 's'il est vrai que les

---

[74] *CIJ Mémoires, Libye/Malte*, vol. III, p. 98.
[75] *Ibid.*, p. 430.
[76] *CIJ Recueil, 1985*, p. 37, par. 43; pp. 46–7, par. 61–2; p. 56, par. 77.
[77] *Ibid.*, p. 39, par. 45–6.

circonstances de chaque cas . . . diffèrent, seul un ensemble clair de principes équitables peut permettre de leur reconnaître le poids qui convient et d'atteindre l'objectif du résultat équitable prescrit par le droit international général.'[78]

La doctrine ne s'y trompa pas: le retour du balancier était amorcé. Même si la victoire de l'équité correctrice n'était qu'à demi assurée, la juridisation de l'équité venait de faire un pas décisif. Le concept d'équité était 'enfin apprivoisé', puisque, 'en réaction à la jurisprudence de 1982 et 1984', la Cour conférait à l'équité 'une dimension normative, sécuritaire, prévisible et générale dans son application'.[79]

Arrêt de transition, *Libye/Malte* allait-il être confirmé ou infirmé? La réponse viendra huit ans plus tard, en 1993, avec *Jan Mayen*: ce fut une confirmation éclatante à la fois de l'équité correctrice et de l'équité structurée. Sur le premier point, la Cour se prononcera sans réserve, dans le cas de côtes se faisant face, en faveur d'une opération en deux temps commençant par 'la ligne médiane comme une ligne provisoire pouvant ensuite être ajustée ou déplacée pour permettre d'aboutir à un résultat équitable'.[80] Sur le second point, la Cour, au moment d'évoquer la prise en considération et la mise en balance des circonstances de l'espèce, 'rappelle la nécessité, mentionnée dans l'affaire *Libye/Malte*, de "la cohérence et [d']une certaine prévisibilité"',[81] puis s'attache à déterminer, facteur par facteur, dans quelle mesure chacun d'eux est pertinent en droit.

Ainsi se trouve apporté un double cran d'arrêt à la dérive subjective.

En premier lieu, la conception correctrice et individualisante de l'équité l'emporte définitivement. Sans doute la Cour ne l'a-t-elle appliquée jusqu'ici qu'à la délimitation maritime, et encore ne l'a-t-elle appliquée qu'à une délimitation entre côtes se faisant face. Mais il n'y a aucune raison pour que cette conception ne soit pas étendue, lorsque l'occasion s'en présentera, à la délimitation entre côtes adjacentes et, au-delà de la délimitation maritime, à d'autres chapitres du droit international.

A vrai dire, c'est à cette conception correctrice et individualisante de l'équité que la Cour s'était déjà référée dans *Mer du Nord* et dans *Barcelona Traction*. Dans la première affaire, l'équité avait servi à corriger le résultat inéquitable auquel peut parfois conduire la méthode de l'équidistance. Dans la seconde, la Cour s'était demandée si, au cas où 'on ne peut appliquer la règle

---

[78] *Ibid.*, p. 55, par. 76.
[79] Bedjaoui, 'L'"énigme" des "principes équitables"', pp. 377–8.
[80] *CIJ Recueil, 1993*, p. 60, par. 50.
[81] *Ibid.*, p. 64, par. 58.

générale selon laquelle le droit de protection diplomatique d'une société revient à son Etat national, il pouvait être indiqué, pour des raisons d'équité, que la protection des actionnaires . . . soit assurée par leur propre Etat national'.[82] C'est cette conception également qu'avait exposée Sir Gerald Fitzmaurice dans son opinion individuelle en cette dernière affaire.[83] Sur ce point *Libye/Malte* s'analyse donc, dans une certaine mesure, comme un retour aux sources.

La théorie actuelle de l'équité est fondée sur l'idée, sur laquelle Malte s'était appuyée devant la Cour,[84] que la norme juridique, qui est générale par nature et donc susceptible de recevoir application dans un certain nombre de cas, produit dans certaines situations un résultat inéquitable et qu'elle prescrit elle-même qu'en pareil cas son contenu pourra être modulé de manière à éviter un tel résultat. Le droit a en quelque sorte deux fers au feu: une règle générale pour la majorité des cas, pour les situations qui pourraient être qualifiées de normales; une règle de rechange, de caractère individuel, pour certaines situations exceptionnelles, dans lesquelles l'application de la règle générale conduirait à des 'résultats de prime abord extraordinaires, anormaux ou déraisonnables'.[85] En un mot, comme l'a expliqué Sir Robert Jennings, 'the role of equity . . . is to mitigate the effects of the application of the rule of law in particular circumstances in which the strict rule of law would work an injustice'.[86] En conséquence, l'équité n'est pas à côté du droit, et en dehors de lui; elle est dans le droit au même titre que la règle générale à laquelle elle peut, dans certains cas, être appelée à apporter un ajustement, et que, de ce fait, elle complète et épaule. 'Equity is distinguishable from law and yet part of it', écrit Sir Robert Jennings, qui rappelle la célèbre formule de Maitland: 'Equity has not come to destroy the law but to fulfil it.' Equité et droit sont tous deux des composantes du système normatif international, tant et si bien que le mot 'droit' peut être employé de deux manières différentes: soit 'to indicate the whole system of law, which of course includes equity within it', soit dans un sens plus étroit 'in which rules of law are actually contrasted with rules or principles of equity'.[87] Le Droit (avec un grand D), le droit *largo sensu*, c'est le droit proprement dit plus l'équité.

Le droit a besoin de l'équité, et l'équité a besoin du droit. Sir Gerald Fitzmaurice avait déjà observé que 'le droit et l'équité ne peuvent réaliser la justice que si on les laisse se compléter mutuellement'.[88] Rapports

---

[82] *CIJ Recueil, 1970*, p. 48, par. 93.   [83] *Ibid.*, pp. 85–6, par. 36.

[84] Voir *CIJ Mémoires, Libye/Malte*, vol. II, p. 293.

[85] *CIJ Recueil, 1969*, p. 23, par. 24.

[86] 'Equity and Equitable Principles', p. 32.

[87] *Ibid.*, p. 28.   [88] *CIJ Recueil, 1970*, p. 86, par. 36.

d'intégration, et non plus de juxtaposition, et moins encore de substitution: 'not rival but complementary', écrit de son côté Sir Robert Jennings.[89] A la confrontation succède la coopération. Le problème du conflit entre équité et droit devient du même coup un faux problème, car 'l'équité faisant elle-même partie du droit, il n'est pas question que l'équité corrige le droit ni que le droit corrige l'équité'.[90] Parler de la fonction 'correctrice' de l'équité est une commodité de langage qui décrit la réalité d'une manière quelque peu inexacte. Appliquer l'équité ce n'est pas 'corriger' la règle de droit; c'est −en vertu de la règle de droit elle-même − appliquer la règle du cas individuel de préférence à la règle de la situation normale.

L'objectif poursuivi par la coopération intégrée du droit et de l'équité est moins d'assurer positivement une solution équitable que d'éviter négative-ment une solution inéquitable: peut-être est-ce là que se situe la ligne de clivage entre l'équité correctrice et l'équité autonome.[91] 'La justice . . . ', écrit le juge Weeramantry, 'ne se prête pas à une formulation complète, mais l'injustice . . . peut souvent être décelée immédiatement . . . Mettre le sentiment de l'injustice au service de la justice est . . . une démarche qui bénéfice d'une puissante justification philosophique.'[92]

Ainsi conçue, l'équité incline vers l'objectivité. C'est moins le sentiment de la justice morale qui conduira à préférer la règle du cas individuel à celle du cas normal que la constatation objective d'un résultat *prima facie* inapproprié, d'une inéquité manifeste, c'est-à-dire évidente et immédiatement constatable. Dans la mesure où le concept de raisonnable a une coloration plus objective que celui d'équitable, la terminologie de la raison peut paraître plus satisfaisante que celle de l'équité, car c'est en définitive une équité selon la raison plutôt qu'une équité selon le coeur qui est recherchée. La raison est affaire de jugement, l'équité est affaire d'intuition et de sentiment.

Aussi comprend-on que les arrêts aient souvent eu recours indifféremment à l'une et l'autre de ces terminologies, considérées comme interchangeables, tant en matière de délimitation maritime[93] que dans d'autres domaines.[94] Si, dans ses arrêts les plus récents, la Cour semble donner le pas à la terminologie

---

[89] 'Equity and Equitable Principles', p. 28.

[90] Shahabuddeen, *Jan Mayen, CIJ Recueil, 1993*, p. 191.

[91] Jennings, Equity and Equitable Principles', p. 33.

[92] *CIJ Recueil, 1993*, pp. 243–4, par. 105–6.

[93] Voir par ex. *CIJ Recueil, 1969*, p. 23, par. 24; p. 49, par. 90; p. 52, par. 97; *Recueil, 1982*, p. 60, par. 72; *Recueil, 1984*, p. 301, par. 115; p. 328, par. 196; p. 335, par. 220.

[94] Par ex. en matière de fixation d'une indemnité (*CIJ Recueil, 1956*, p. 100); en matière de protection diplomatique (*CIJ Recueil, 1970*, p. 48, par. 93); en matière de répartition des ressources halieutiques (*CIJ Recueil, 1974*, p. 33, par. 78).

de l'équité et de l'équitable sur celle de la raison et du raisonnable,[95] il ne faut sans doute pas conclure de cet infléchissement terminologique que le sentiment et l'intuition l'ont emporté sur la raison. D'abord, parce que la Cour a entrepris d'objectiver le contenu de l'équité, la rapprochant ainsi de la raison. Ensuite, parce que l'équité et la raison exigent l'une comme l'autre qu'il soit tenu compte des circonstances de l'espèce et des intérêts en présence. Equité et raison se situent aujourd'hui sur une même longueur d'ondes.

Pour mettre un terme à la dérive subjective de l'équité, il ne suffisait pas d'écarter l'équité autonome au profit de l'équité correctrice. Encore fallait-il que l'individualisation de la décision ne devienne pas à son tour 'synonyme d'éclectisme ou d'arbitraire'.[96] Car si l'on avait laissé à l'équité un contenu indéterminé, la subjectivité, une fois chassée par la grande porte, serait revenue par la petite porte de l'équité correctrice. Pour conférer la stabilité et la prévisibilité sans lesquelles il ne saurait y avoir de sécurité juridique, la structuration et la juridisation de l'équité individualisante devaient obligatoirement accompagner son intégration au système juridique. Là encore, la Cour est en fait revenue à sa conception initiale: dans *Mer du Nord* la Cour n'avait pas seulement envisagé une équité correctrice et individualisante; elle avait conçu cette dernière, Sir Robert Jennings en a fait l'observation, comme 'a juridical and structured notion', et non pas comme ouvrant la porte à une 'mere judicial discretion'.[97] En faisant appel à une équité individualisante et correctrice le juge ne peut ni faire n'importe quoi ni changer de position d'une affaire à l'autre. Une fois défini par la Cour ce qui est équitable et ce qui ne l'est pas, cette définition gardera sa valeur au-delà du cas d'espèce et s'appliquera dans d'autres affaires. Le pouvoir du juge cesse d'être entièrement discrétionnaire, et ses solutions cessent d'être abandonnées aux variations de sa subjectivité. L'équité est disciplinée.

On sait ainsi d'ores et déjà, à la lumière de *Libye/Malte* et de *Jan Mayen*, que dans une délimitation maritime l'équité commande de tenir compte d'une disparité importante des longueurs respectives des côtes, mais on sait aussi qu'elle n'exige pas que soient attribuées aux parties des superficies d'espaces maritimes en proportion directe avec les rapports de leurs longueurs côtières. On sait que l'équité requiert que soit assuré aux parties un accès équitable aux ressources halieutiques, mais on sait aussi qu'elle ne demande pas que la délimitation soit effectuée en fonction de la population et des facteurs socio-

[95] Ainsi, dans *Jan Mayen*, c'est résultat 'équitable' qui est déclaré constituer le but de toute délimitation maritime, et c'est d'un accès 'équitable' aux ressources halieutiques qu'il est fait état (*CIJ Recueil, 1993*, p. 62, par., 54; p. 72, par. 75; p. 79, par. 92).

[96] Shahabuddeen, *Jan Mayen*, *CIJ Recueil, 1993*, p. 195.

[97] Jennings, "Equity and Equitable Principles', p. 30.

économiques. On sait que la dimension respective des deux territoires n'a pas à être prise en considération dans une appréciation d'équité, mais on sait aussi que les considérations de sécurité et, partant, de distance entre la frontière maritime et la côte, ne doivent pas être négligées. On sait également que l'équité ne commande pas qu'une partie transpose dans ses relations avec une autre une solution particulière qu'elle a adoptée précédement vis-à-vis d'une tierce partie dans un contexte différent, et que le droit international ne prescrit pas, en vue de parvenir à une solution équitable, d'adopter une méthode unique pour la délimitation des espaces maritimes de toutes les côtes d'une même île ou d'un même Etat. Au fil du développement de la jurisprudence, on en saura toujours davantage sur ce qui doit être considéré comme équitable en droit, que ce soit en matière de délimitation maritime ou en n'importe quelle autre matière.

L'avancée effectuée par *Jan Mayen* sur la voie de la juridisation de l'équité n'a pas paru suffisante à tous les membres de la Cour. Pourquoi, se sont demandés certains dans leur opinions jointes à l'arrêt, la Cour trouve-t-elle équitable ceci, et inéquitable cela? Après tout, la solution inverse aurait parfois été tout aussi concevable. Pourquoi, par exemple, est-il équitable d'attribuer une part plus grande des espaces maritimes – une 'prime' en quelque sorte, dit le juge Schwebel – à l'Etat qui possède la côte la plus longue et, corollairement, de 'pénaliser' celui qui possède la côte la plus courte?[98] Pourquoi est-il équitable de partager les ressources halieutiques, et en vertu de quel critère faut-il le faire?[99] L'équité exige-t-elle toujours que l'on partage, est-elle 'synonyme de division de la différence'?[100] Interrogation qui fait écho à la question inverse posée par d'autres juges en d'autres occasions, et à laquelle il a été fait allusion plus haut: le partage de la différence est-il réservé à l'*ex aequo et bono*? ne faut-il pas admettre que dans certains cas c'est là la solution exigée par l'équité juridique? Telle est, effectivement, la solution adoptée par la Cour dans *Jan Mayen*. Mais alors c'est une autre interrogation qui surgit: que faut-il partager, la zone de chevauchement des titres ou la zone de chevauchement des revendications? C'est cette dernière formule que la Cour a adoptée dans *Jan Mayen*, mais cette formule ne risque-t-elle pas, comme le souligne le juge Schwebel, de 'récompenser la revendication maximaliste' et de 'pénaliser la modération'? Peut-on considérer comme juridiquement équitable, demande-t-il, d''encourager les revendications immodérées et (de) décourager les revendications modérées'?[101]

---

[98] Op. ind. Oda et Schwebel, *CIJ Recueil, 1993*, p. 115, par. 92 et p. 127.
[99] Op. ind. Oda et Schwebel, *ibid.*, p. 115, par. 94 et p. 120.
[100] Op. ind. Shabuddeen, *ibid.*, p. 191.   [101] *Ibid.*, pp. 126–7.

Une fois décidé ce qui est équitable et ce qui ne l'est pas, les difficultés ne s'arrêtent pas. Encore faut-il déterminer l'impact de cette décision sur chaque cas d'espèce ainsi que le poids respectif des divers facteurs reconnus comme relevant de l'équité juridique. Or il n'existe de toute évidence aucun 'mécanisme de quantification précise'[102] et, en matière de délimitation maritime, aucun moyen mathématique 'pour tracer une ligne en totale objectivité'.[103] 'Pourquoi exactement ce déplacement (de la ligne médiane)? Pourquoi pas un peu plus, ou un peu moins'?[104] De là, inévitablement, un 'calcul peu transparent' de la 'mesure de l'ajustement' effectué afin de parvenir à un résultat équitable; de là aussi le sentiment que cet ajustement est en définitive mesuré par la Cour 'de façon impressionniste'.[105] L'équité permet des solutions diverses, observent plusieurs juges, et le choix de telle solution ne s'impose pas plus que celui de telle autre. C'est ainsi que, dans *Jan Mayen*, le juge Schwebel déclare se rallier à la solution de la Cour par résignation en quelque sorte, parce que cette solution ne vaut pas moins – même si elle ne vaut pas plus – que bien d'autres: 'si ce qui est équitable, écrit-il, est aussi variable que le temps à La Haye', alors la solution adoptée par la Cour est aussi défendable qu'une autre.[106] Bref, selon ces juges, l'équité n'est à l'heure actuelle pas encore suffisamment disciplinée et structurée pour qu'elle cesse d'être un 'concept juridique indéterminé'[107] qui conduit à faire 'application d'un droit dont les principes demeurent en grande partie indéfinis', offrant ainsi à la Cour 'une exceptionnelle faculté discrétionnaire dans l'exercice de sa fonction judiciaire'.[108]

Il est vrai que trop de séquelles subsistent à l'heure actuelle de la dérive subjectiviste à laquelle la Cour a succombé dans le passé, et l'on peut souhaiter que la Cour s'attache à l'avenir, chaque fois de l'occasion s'en présentera, à resserrer toujours davantage les mailles du filet normatif, à restreindre toujours davantage la marge de discrétion judiciaire, à accroître toujours davantage la prévisibilité de l'équité et, du même coup, le sécurité juridique. Mais il faut voir la réalité en face: même enfermé dans certaines 'limites', le 'pouvoir discrétionnaire que . . . confère (au juge) la nécessité de parvenir à un résultat équitable'[109] ne sera jamais réduit à néant. Même resserrées au maximum, les mailles du filet normatif laisseront toujours subsister un ultime carré de pouvoir d'appréciation. Quels que soient les raffinements que la jurisprudence apportera à la définition des principes équitables, le 'caractère normatif' de ces

---

[102] Op. ind. Weeramantry, *ibid.*, p. 255, par. 157.   [103] Op. ind. Oda, *ibid.*, p. 116, par. 98.
[104] Op. ind. Shahabuddeen, *ibid.*, p. 192.   [105] Op. ind. Schwebel, *ibid.*, p. 126.
[106] *Ibid.*, p. 120. Cf. op. ind. Shahabuddeen, *ibid.*, p. 152.
[107] Op. ind. Shahabuddeen, *ibid.*, p. 152.
[108] Op. ind. Schwebel, *ibid.*, p. 128.   [109] *CIJ Recueil, 1993*, p. 79, par. 90.

derniers ne permettra jamais de déboucher automatiquement sur une solution prédéterminée, et il restera toujours 'un hiatus, regrettable mais sans doute inévitable, entre, d'une part, l'argumentation développée dans une décision judiciaire et, d'autre part, la conclusion concrète' qu'en tire le juge: 'les plus belles dissertations juridiques ne parviendront pas à éliminer une part peut-être irréductible de ce subjectivisme prétorien' qui fait l''honneur' de la mission du juge.[110] Privée de toute indétermination, la fonction judiciaire ne serait qu'esclavage du donné, alors qu'elle est, et doit rester, oeuvre humaine. Dénonçant '[l]e danger d'une conceptualisation excessive des principes équitables', le juge Weeramantry va jusqu'à écrire que 'le jour où l'équité sera complètement capturée dans une définition ou une formule, sa créativité sera épuisée'.[111]

On peut ajouter que la 'règle de l'équité' n'est pas la seule norme juridique marquée par une marge d'indétermination et d'incertitude qui laisse subsister une appréciation plus ou moins discrétionnaire du juge. Il s'agit là, après tout, de l'un de ces standards juridiques que connaissent tous les systèmes de droit, mais qui occupent une place particulièrement grande dans le système international. C'est seulement au fil des espèces que ces standards généraux et abstraits prennent forme et se concrétisent petit à petit, rétrécissant ainsi la marge de discrétion judiciaire et augmentant parallèlement la prévisibilité et la sécurité juridique. Les droits nationaux n'ont rien trouvé de choquant à prévoir la réparation de la souffrance physique, de la douleur morale ou de l'atteinte à la réputation – toutes matières échappant par nature à la quantification et nécessairement laissées à l'appréciation du juge. Ils ne sont pas demandés, à propos de chaque décision judiciaire accordant une indemnité: pourquoi pas plus, pourquoi pas moins? En droit international également, la forme de la réparation et son importance demeurent largement du domaine de la discrétion judiciaire. Ce qui importe, c'est que cette discrétion judiciaire s'exerce 'de manière disciplinée et par rapport à des critères vérifiables'[112] – et c'est cela précisément que la Cour a commencé d'entreprendre. Il n'y a pas, et il n'y aura jamais, 'de réponse unique qui soit "juste" de manière absolue, comme si le jugement consistait à faire "une addition correcte"'; il y a inévitablement, et il y aura toujours, 'une gamme de choix' à l'intérieur de certains 'paramètres prescrits faisant ainsi nécessairement et intrinsèquement partie du processus judiciaire'.[113] Pour citer une dernière fois le dédicataire de

[110] Op. conj. Ruda, Bedjaoui et Jiménez de Aréchaga, *Libye/Malte*, *CIJ Recueil*, *1985*, p. 90. par. 37.
[111] *CIJ Recueil, 1993*, p. 256, par. 159.
[112] Op. ind. Shahabuddeen, *ibid.*, p. 197.
[113] Op. ind. Weeramantry, *ibid.*, p. 252, par. 142.

ce livre: 'No reasonable litigant expects the decision of a court to be predictable; but the range of considerations used for a decision and the procedures for their application should certainly be predictable.'[114]

CONCLUSION

Après avoir hissé l'équité au rang d'une norme juridique, la Cour a failli un moment succomber au chant des sirènes de l'équité quasi discrétionnaire tenant lieu de droit, et réduire le droit à l'application de l'équité. Consciente du risque qu'elle faisait courir au droit international en y introduisant de la sorte une normativité condamnée à la subjectivité, au cas par cas et à l'imprévisibilité, elle a aujourd'hui renversé la vapeur et entrepris une oeuvre de redressement qui tend à accorder à l'équité une place certes importante, mais nettement circonscrite, dans le système normatif international, tout en lui conférant le contenu stable et prévisible requis de toute norme juridique digne de ce nom. On aimerait espérer qu'en amorçant ainsi une percée spectaculaire en vue de l'intégration pacifique de l'équité dans le droit, la Cour s'est engagée sans retour sur la voie royale de la réconciliation de ces frères jumeaux, mais dans le passé trop souvent ennemis, que sont l'équité et le droit.

[114] 'Equity and Equitable Principles', p. 38.

144

8

The International Court of Justice and the law of treaties

E. W. Vierdag

❧

I

The International Court of Justice has made numerous pronouncements on questions related to the law of treaties, and it is not possible to give an account of them within the confines of this chapter. Therefore it seems necessary to look at some of the more important dicta on rules and principles of the law of treaties from the perspective of a particular point of view. The point of view chosen here can succinctly be called: formality and flexibility ('and', not 'versus'). The question to be asked is what weight the Court in its dealing with matters of the law of treaties has attached to requirements of a formal nature, and in what cases it has given full legal effect to acts and did so irrespective of possibly applicable formal requirements. Clearly, the growing diversity among the participants in the international community that make treaties may call for a measure of suppleness; on the other hand, that same development may no less lead to an urgent and fully justified demand that the security of the law be safeguarded.

As said, not all dicta by the Court in the field of treaties can be reviewed, so a selection of what would seem to be the more significant ones had to be made. In the contributions made by the Court to the law of treaties the Advisory Opinion on *Reservations to the Genocide Convention* of 28 May 1951 still stands out. That Opinion will therefore presently serve as the point of departure.

Whenever it seems that the 1969 Vienna Convention on the Law of Treaties contains rules that are relevant in considering the work of the Court, reference will be made to them; one only has to think of the Convention's rules on treaty interpretation (articles 31 to 33 inclusive). As far as can be ascertained the question whether, and if so, to what extent the Vienna Convention must be regarded by virtue of article 38(1)(a) – and perhaps (b) as well – of the Statute as authoritative for the Court when dealing with matters of the law of treaties has hardly, if at all, received attention. Yet for the purposes of the present chapter this question of the relation between on the one hand the Convention, originating from the International Law Commission, an organ of the UN General Assembly, and adopted by the UN Conference in 1969, and on the other hand the Court, the UN's 'principal judicial organ', cannot be disposed of as a side issue. It is questionable whether the Court should investigate in each and every case in how far the Convention establishes 'rules expressly recognized by the contesting States', as article 38 stipulates – apart from the question whether one or some or all of these states are parties to the Convention. Could (parts of) the Convention be binding on the Court in other ways? Whenever the Court has found it appropriate, it has referred to the Convention in its jurisprudence; and this may be an indication that in its view the instrument has – in large part at least – been received in the whole of general international law. This issue cannot be discussed further here; it deserves a separate examination. In what follows the Convention will be taken into account, according to what may safely be presumed to be the Court's view of it.

In the first parts of this chapter reference will be made to the work of the Court as a whole; attention will be chiefly paid, besides the *Genocide* Advisory Opinion, to the *North Sea Continental Shelf* cases and the *Aegean Sea Continental Shelf* case. In part III, which will be devoted to a discussion of the 1984 judgment on jurisdiction and admissibility in the *Nicaragua* case, references will be made to statements by one individual judge as well.

A few words on terminology are useful: it seems proper that a distinction is usually made between 'the law of treaties', on the one hand, and 'treaty law' on the other, the former referring to the rules governing *inter alia* the making, operation and termination of treaties, the latter referring to the contents of a treaty as distinguished from the contents of corresponding rules of customary law. As appears from the title, in what follows the subject is the 'law of treaties'; but it would leave an incomplete impression unless one judgment were at least mentioned here, in which the question of 'treaty law' as distinguished from the corresponding customary law occupies so dominant a place: the judgment in the case concerning *Military and Paramilitary Activities in and against Nicaragua (Merits)* (1986).

II

The Advisory Opinion on *Reservations to the Genocide Convention* is not only important in the development of the rules governing reservations to multilateral conventions; it is of relevance also because it draws our attention to what we now have been accustomed to call – following article 11 of the Vienna Convention – 'means of expressing consent to be bound by a treaty', on which the Opinion contains relevant passages.

As far as the principles regarding the making and the effects of reservations are concerned, the ILC in its draft articles on reservations (articles 16 to 20 inclusive of the 1966 final draft) let itself be guided by the Court's holdings. It did so in spite of the fact that it had earlier observed, commenting on the Opinion in the report on reservations submitted upon its request to the General Assembly in 1951, that the Court's criterion for the admissibility of reservations – 'compatibility with the object and purpose of the convention' – was 'open to objection as a criterion of general application'. This was so because the Commission considered the question of compatibility to be 'too subjective for application to multilateral conventions generally'.[1] But later on in the ILC and thereafter in the UN Conference the compatibility criterion met with very little resistance and was readily adopted. It is important to note that this criterion must guide not only the making of reservations but also the acceptance of and objection to reservations.

One of the cornerstones of the system devised by the Court and elaborated by the ILC was the distinction between acceptance of and objection to reservations by the other contracting states. According to article 17(4)(b) of the final draft, an objection precludes the entry into force of the treaty as between the objecting and reserving states unless a contrary intention is expressed by the objecting state. Regrettably, after heavy lobbying, mainly by the former Soviet Union and a few of its former allies, the UN Conference during its Second Plenary Session adopted, on 29 April 1969, a Soviet amendment according to which the presumption is reversed. The result, which is to be found in article 20(4)(b) of the Convention, is that not much is left of this distinction: whether a reservation is accepted or not, the treaty enters into force between the reserving state and the other contracting states, including those that objected. This is a bizarre situation in law, and an awkward one, only to be redressed by another express act on the part of the objecting state.

With regard to the point of view of formality and flexibility, one is inclined to consider the 1951 Opinion as an expression of the latter: the rigid rule of unanimity in the acceptance of reservations had to yield to rules that are indeed usually referred to as a 'flexible system'. However, it is important to note that the Court seriously questioned the validity of a rule that requires unanimous acceptance of a reservation for the state that formulated it to

---

[1] *YbILC* 2 (1966, vol.II), p. 204.

become a party to a treaty. 'It does not appear . . . that the conception of the absolute integrity of a convention has been transformed into a rule of international law.'[2] Also, there was always the difficulty of assessing silence as tacit consent. So from the point of view of the Court itself, its adoption of this ostensibly flexible approach to the admissibility of reservations would for this reason not necessarily amount to an adoption of genuine flexibility.

The Opinion sanctioned the flexible practice of the Organization of American States, which is mentioned in it, and it has furthered a process leading to a set of liberal rules that is adapted to the diversity among international persons that conclude treaties, noted in the introductory remarks. These rules open the road to treaties for states that without the rules could never reach those treaties.

In order to answer the questions put by the General Assembly the Court had to distinguish neatly between the various phases leading to ratification as a means expressing consent to be bound by a treaty, and their specific legal effects. Of course, the Court's predecessor had on earlier occasions pronounced on the character of such means, e.g. pointing to 'the ordinary rules of international law amongst which is the rule that conventions, save in certain exceptional cases, are binding only by virtue of their ratification'.[3] In the 1951 Opinion, in the answer to the third question put to the Court by the General Assembly, the most widely used means (ratification, preceded by signature) were examined and legal effects of both component acts were indicated, limited of course to reservations. First the position of a state that has signed a treaty subject to ratification, but has not yet ratified, was examined; and next that of a state entitled to sign a treaty or to accede to it but which has not yet performed either of these acts.

The Court elucidated the meaning of 'signatory State'. Of course, signature, if subject to ratification, is not a means of expressing consent to be bound in the sense of article 11 of the Vienna Convention. In that case it does not make the signatory state a party to the treaty. The difference between signature in such a case and signature as a means by itself is reflected in the Convention in the difference between the signature under article 14(1)(c) and the three forms of signature provided for in article 12, namely signature, initialling agreed to establish signature, and signature *ad referendum*. The signature subject to ratification, while not making the signatory state a party, nevertheless constitutes a first step towards participation. In dicta that have lost nothing of their significance, the Court held that it establishes 'a provisional status' in

---

[2] ICJ Reports, 1951, p. 24.   [3] PCIJ, Series A, No. 23 (1929), p. 20.

148

favour of the signatory state. 'This status would justify more favourable treatment being meted out to signatory States . . . than to States which have neither signed nor acceded. As distinct from the latter States, signatory States have taken certain of the steps necessary for the exercise of the right of being a party.'[4] The corollary obligation incurred by signatory states is laid down in article 18 of the Vienna Convention.

The Opinion unequivocally confirmed that ratification is the decisive act by which the state binds itself to a treaty. Of course, there are other means of expressing consent to be bound, some of them spelt out in article 11, although the true significance of that provision presumably lies in the closing words: 'or by any other means if so agreed'. But because the Genocide Convention was open for signature and ratification, and could be acceded to after 1 January 1950,[5] the Court limited itself to these means of expressing consent. The dicta on ratification and accession, as well as the answers given, show that it held firmly to the principle that the performance of the acts agreed upon as means of expressing consent to be bound is essential. In that sense the Opinion can be characterized as true to form.

The holding of the Court on reservations has found its fixed place in the body of international law. At this point a short excursion on a question of substance may be allowed. Other holdings of the Court have also found their way into conventional instruments. Well-known examples of this include its ruling in the *Asylum* case[6] on the qualification of the offence by the state granting diplomatic asylum, later incorporated in the 1954 Caracas Convention on Diplomatic Asylum (article 7); and the requirements with which the drawing of a straight baseline must comply in order to be lawful, enumerated in the judgment in the *Anglo-Norwegian Fisheries* case.[7] The latter were later largely reproduced in article 7 of the 1982 UN Convention on the Law of the Sea.

Two instances in the law of treaties may be put forward in this context, where regrettably the makers of the Vienna Convention did not act likewise. Had they done so, this might, it is respectfully submitted, have resulted in useful provisions.

First, the concept of 'signatory State', as elaborated in the *Genocide* Opinion, is not to be found as such in the Vienna Convention. In article 2(1) one finds definitions of 'negotiating State', 'contracting State' and 'party', the first of these being a state that has taken part in the drawing up and adoption

---

[4] ICJ Reports, 1951, p. 28.   [5] Article XI.
[6] ICJ Reports, 1950, p. 266.   [7] ICJ Reports, 1951, p. 116.

of the text of a treaty – and thus clearly a state that has not as yet acquired a status with respect to that treaty. One instance where this situation produces a somewhat peculiar result may be mentioned here: article 25 on 'Provisional application' provides *inter alia* that a treaty is applied provisionally pending its entry into force if the negotiating states have so agreed. From extensive and rather constant and uniform state practice in the matter it appears clearly, however, that provisional application of treaties is generally agreed upon and performed by states after signature of a treaty, the signature being subject to ratification. (The provisional application is agreed upon with a view to the fact that in many cases constitutional procedures leading to ratification can take quite some time, and that as a result entry into force can be considerably delayed.) It would therefore have been in line with the customary rules if in article 25 reference had been made to agreement among the signatory states, not among negotiating states, which do not as yet have a legal relation with the treaty.

Second, it is important to note that the Opinion contains a dictum that is still of the highest significance in the law of treaties, but as it is rather hidden in it, it has not usually been given the attention it merits. It runs as follows: 'It is . . . a generally recognized principle that a multilateral convention is the result of an agreement freely concluded upon its clauses and that consequently none of the contracting parties is entitled to frustrate or impair, by means of . . . particular agreements, the purpose and *raison d'être* of the convention.'[8] The lasting importance of this dictum lies *inter alia* in the fact that the makers of the Vienna Convention did not include a clear indication of – let alone a rule on – the ranking of treaties, apart from the reference to article 103 of the UN Charter in article 30(1). The matter is left to the drafters of the treaties, but by no means do all treaties contain provisions on their relation to other treaties. Article 30(3), and by reference also article 30(4), more or less automatically give – in cases of silence on this point – precedence to the *lex posterior* over the *lex prior*. However, this leaves open the question how it must be determined what, in international treaty law, is *lex prior* and what is *lex posterior*. There may not be an answer to that question because, as a rule, multilateral treaties have only one date that is common to all negotiating states: the date of the adoption of the text of treaties or the 'opening for signature' of treaties. For after that date the remainder of the procedure of expressing consent to be bound is performed individually by each of these states and therefore will take place at different moments of time. As a result, a single treaty can be *lex prior* with respect to another treaty for one state, but *lex*

---

[8] *Ibid.*, p. 21.

posterior with respect to that treaty for another state. For that reason, and also given the plethora of treaties in almost all fields of international law and the high incidence of potential overlap, not to say conflict, the notion of treaties having a different rank, as acknowledged in the dictum, is surely to be retained in international law as an ordering principle, and to be applied as such whenever appropriate.

From a crucial passage in the 1969 judgment in the *North Sea Continental Shelf* cases[9] it appears again that the Court considers an agreement among the negotiating states, as to the means they shall use for the expression of their consent to be bound by that treaty, to be of the essence. It is illuminating to quote this eloquent passage (in para. 28) in full here:

> In principle, when a number of States, including the one whose conduct is invoked, and those invoking it, have drawn up a convention specifically providing for a particular method by which the intention to become bound by the régime of the convention is to be manifested – namely by the carrying out of certain prescribed formalities (ratification, accession), it is not lightly to be presumed that a State which has not carried out these formalities, though at all times fully able and entitled to do so, has nevertheless somehow become bound in another way. Indeed if it were a question not of obligation but of rights – if, that is to say, a State which, though entitled to do so, had not ratified or acceded, attempted to claim rights under the convention, on the basis of a declared willingness to be bound by it, or of conduct evincing acceptance of the conventional régime, it would simply be told that, not having become a party to that convention it could not claim any rights under it until the professed willingness and acceptance had been manifested in the prescribed form.

The presumption that a state has become bound to rules as laid down in a treaty without being a party to it can be made under article 38 of the Vienna Convention: nothing in the provisions on treaties and third states in articles 34 to 37 precludes a rule set forth in a treaty becoming binding on a third state as a customary rule of international law. But the judgment sets very severe standards for the acceptance of the presumption that this has happened; and rightly so, for if it would be otherwise the security of the law might become seriously impaired.

The Court's position reflected the reverse – but still comparable in spite of wide factual disparities – situation in an earlier case, where one of the parties to a boundary treaty sought to undo the operation of the treaty on the

---

[9] ICJ Reports, 1969, p. 1.

assertion that it had yielded to acts of sovereignty performed by that party contrary to the treaty, claiming that the other party's rights under the treaty were lost through non-assertion and acquiescence.[10] The Court firmly upheld the conventional regime as against purported legal effects of activities that allegedly had set it aside, just as the Court was a decade later to uphold the agreed regime on means of expressing consent in the *Continental Shelf* cases in spite of claims that positions taken by interested states had somehow brought about relevant change.

Yet another judgment confirms the Court's determination not to allow a state to be bound by a rule without a clear basis of obligation, customary or conventional: the judgment of 19 December 1978 in the *Aegean Sea Continental Shelf* case between Greece and Turkey. The former state relied for its argument that the Court had jurisdiction to entertain its application *inter alia* on the joint communiqué, issued in Brussels on 31 May 1975 after a meeting of the Prime Ministers of both countries. The relevant passages of this communiqué, which bears no signatures or initials, are reproduced in the judgment as follows:

> In the course of their meeting the two Prime Ministers had an opportunity to give consideration to the problems which led to the existing situation as regards relations between their countries.
>
> They decided [*ont décidé*] that those problems should be resolved [*doivent être résolus*] peacefully by means of negotiations and as regards the continental shelf of the Aegean Sea by the International Court at The Hague. They defined the general lines on the basis of which the forthcoming meetings of the representatives of the two Governments would take place.
>
> In that connection they decided to bring forward the date of the meeting of experts concerning the question of the continental shelf of the Aegean Sea and that of the experts on the question of air space.[11]

Greece contended that a text such as this may constitute an agreement under international law: 'It is necessary, and it is sufficient for the communiqué to include – in addition to the customary forms, protestations of friendship, recital of major principles and declarations of intent – provisions of a treaty nature.' The Turkish government considered it 'evident that a joint communiqué does not amount to an agreement under international law'.

The Court reacted to these contentions with a very apt response. With a reference to articles 2, 3 and 11 of the Vienna Convention it stated:

[10] *Sovereignty over Frontier Land*, ICJ Reports, 1959, p. 227.
[11] ICJ Reports, 1978, pp. 39–40.

On the question of form, the Court need only observe that it knows of no rule of international law which might preclude a joint communiqué from constituting an international agreement to submit a dispute to arbitration or to judicial settlement . . . Accordingly, whether the . . . Communiqué . . . does or does not constitute such an agreement essentially depends on the nature of the act or transaction to which the Communiqué gives expression; and it does not settle the question simply to refer to the form . . . in which that act of transaction was embodied. On the contrary, in determining what was indeed the nature of the act or transaction embodied in the Brussels Communiqué, the Court must have regard above all to its actual terms and to the particular circumstances in which it was drawn up.

The Court focused on the various diplomatic activities of both states with regard to the resolution of their dispute during the period that immediately preceded the meeting in Brussels, and on the position they took in respect of the question how to engage the Court. It was clear that the Turkish government, especially, had consistently maintained that reference of the dispute to the Court had to be 'on the basis of a joint submission after the conclusion of a special agreement defining the issues to be resolved by the Court'. It was the opinion of the Court that neither the context nor the terms of the Brussels communiqué warrant the conclusion that it was intended to, or did constitute 'an immediate commitment . . . to accept unconditionally the unilateral submission of the present dispute to the Court'.[12] The Court found that it was without jurisdiction to entertain the application by Greece.

It is to be understood that the Court withheld effect from the communiqué solely as an instrument conferring jurisdiction to the Court to entertain the claim, but that its holding did not in any way affect whatever other commitments may be inferred from it for the two governments that issued it. According to its clear terms both governments were under an obligation to negotiate a Special Agreement on the basis of which the dispute concerning the continental shelf of the Aegean Sea could be referred to the Court.

The careful research by the Court into the positions of the governments that issued the communiqué, in order to ascertain their true intentions as expressed in its wording, represents another example of the Court's endeavour to avoid imposing on states obligations that are not firmly rooted in customary law or that do not unequivocally correspond to a state's intention to be bound, whether expressed or implied. Judging from the record so far, there is full justification for the proposition that the Court strictly adheres to formality.

---

[12] *Ibid.*, p. 44.

III

Ever since the establishment of the Permanent Court of International Justice and the International Court of Justice, it has been obvious that great care is always taken to demonstrate the internal consistency of the Court's jurisprudence. Frequent quotations from and references to earlier holdings in judgments manifest the Court's endeavour to maintain consistency, although this practice must in no way be considered to amount to an admission that a principle of *stare decisis* applies. It is hoped that the previous paragraphs sufficiently show some relevant instances of that endeavour.

It must be asked to what extent the judgment in the case concerning *Military and Paramilitary Activities in and against Nicaragua, Jurisdiction of the Court and Admissibility of the Application*[13] fits into this judicial policy, as there are elements in it that may appear to constitute a break with the past. An examination of this matter requires a few words on what this judgment is about.

As Nicaragua filed its application instituting proceedings against the United States, it relied *inter alia* on the Declarations made by the two states under article 36 of the Statute of the Court, the one by the US made in 1946 and the one by Nicaragua made in 1929. On both sides it was open to serious doubt whether the requirement of reciprocity laid down in article 36(2) and expressed by the words 'any other State accepting the same obligation' was met. First of all, the defendant had deposited on 6 April 1984 a notification in which it had stated that its declaration would no longer apply to 'disputes with any Central American State or arising out of or related to events in Central America'. The notification was to have immediate effect, although according to its own terms the 1946 Declaration was valid until six months after notice is given to terminate it.

The Declaration of the applicant was made upon signature by Nicaragua on 24 September 1929 of the Protocol of Signature of the Statute of the Permanent Court of International Justice of 16 December 1920. The Assembly of the League had decided that the Statute of the Court was to be submitted to the members for adoption 'in the form of a protocol duly ratified'. Accordingly, the third paragraph of the Protocol stipulates: 'The present Protocol . . . is subject to ratification. Each Power shall send its ratification to the Secretary-General of the League of Nations; the latter shall notify such ratification to the other signatory Powers. The ratifications shall be deposited in the archives of the Secretariat of the League of Nations.' The

---

[13] 26 November 1984; ICJ Reports, 1984, p. 392.

154

competent Nicaraguan constitutional organs ratified the Protocol in 1935, but no instrument of ratification was ever received by the Secretary-General of the League. After this fact was brought to the attention of the Nicaraguan Minister of Foreign Affairs, in 1942, no action was taken, and no action has been taken subsequently, although Nicaragua was 'at all times fully able and entitled to do so', as the Court had formulated it in 1969 in the *North Sea Continental Shelf* cases. It appears that Nicaragua had never become a party to the 1920 Statute; the question was therefore whether the Nicaraguan Declaration was a valid one, and constituted – by virtue of article 36(5) of the Statute – a valid acceptance of the jurisdiction of the present Court under article 36(2) of the Statute. It is to be noted that the Nicaraguan Declaration does not contain any clause on duration or termination, and also that Nicaragua, when it became a party to the new Statute on 24 October 1945, made no declaration under article 36(2) and (4).

It appears that two notions that are significant in international law are involved in this connection. As far as the American position is concerned, there is the principle of reciprocity in compulsory jurisdiction and its precise scope. And as regards the Nicaraguan position, there is the question of the meaning of expressing consent to be bound. First, a few words must be said about the Court's treatment of the American notification that purported to exclude with immediate effect a category of disputes from the field of application of the 1946 Declaration. And next the Court's dealing with Nicaragua's incomplete adherence to the 1920 Protocol will be looked at.

The US contended that because the Nicaraguan Declaration did not contain a clause on termination upon notice, as the American Declaration did, Nicaragua had not accepted 'the same obligation' in the sense of article 36(2). To have accepted this argument would have meant for the Court a departure from the position that it had maintained at least since the judgment in the *Norwegian Loans* case:[14] reciprocity in the context of compulsory jurisdiction is limited to the conferment of jurisdiction. Its effect is to define the common ground of two declarations, and therefore has to do with the contents of these declarations. 'There the effect of reciprocity ends,' as the Court said in the *Interhandel* case, two years later.[15] So in *Nicaragua* it rejected the American contention in clear terms (paragraph 62): 'The notion of reciprocity is concerned with the scope and substance of the commitments entered into, including reservations, and not with the formal conditions of their creation, duration or extinction.' Interestingly, in spite of this holding the Court

---

[14] ICJ Reports, 1957, p. 9.   [15] ICJ Reports, 1959, p. 23.

nevertheless went on to examine, 'if reciprocity is to be relied on', the effect that reciprocity would have in the particular situation of the American notification. If the US invokes the Nicaraguan Declaration in order to be able to modify its own Declaration with immediate effect, it is necessary for the former Declaration to be terminable with immediate effect.

> But the right of immediate termination of declarations with infinite duration is far from established. It appears from the requirements of good faith that they should be treated, by analogy, according to the law of treaties, which requires a reasonable time for withdrawal from or termination of treaties that contain no provision regarding the duration of their validity. (paragraph 63)

The American notification was dated 6 April 1984; the Nicaraguan application was filed on 9 April. If Nicaragua had tried to terminate its Declaration on 6 April with effect from 9 April, that would, according to the Court, not have amounted to a 'reasonable time'. So the US could not rely on the Nicaraguan Declaration for the immediate effect of its notification, even if reciprocity would have applied.

The cursory reference to the law of treaties 'by analogy' is somewhat surprising: treaties, on the one hand, and declarations under article 36, on the other, do have in common that they are based on consent, but it would seem that the analogy ends there. If it is true that consent with respect to declarations is as essential as it is to treaties – and that is what the Court's dictum implies – it is only fair that the US be kept to its word: the six-month term after notice.

It is on the basis of 'the law of treaties' that the Court introduced the condition of 'reasonable time', and stated that Nicaragua, if it should wish to do so, could not in its turn validly terminate its Declaration on three days' notice, thus implying that Nicaragua could even less do so with immediate effect. It is submitted that here the analogy with the law of treaties has produced a spurious perspective. The condition that in the case of a treaty without a clause on denunciation or withdrawal, there must be a reasonable time before denunciation of or withdrawal from the treaty becomes effective, is clearly intended to protect possible rights or interests of the other party or parties to the treaty. Accordingly, article 56(2) of the Vienna Convention prescribes that the denouncing or withdrawing party shall give not less than twelve months' notice of its intention to denounce a treaty or to withdraw from it. In its commentary the ILC said that it 'considered it essential that any implied right to denounce or withdraw from a treaty should be subject to a reasonable period of notice . . . In formulating a general rule, the Commission considered it desirable to lay down a longer rather than a shorter period in order to give adequate protection to the interests of the other parties to the treaty.'[16] However, no rights or interests of states are likewise possibly affected by the termination (or a partial termination through a modification) of a Declaration without a clause on termination – provided, of course, that the (partial) termination is notified before an application is filed against the state in question. So it is extremely doubtful whether the analogy with rules on treaties drawn by the Court is appropriate; a search for governing principles should rather have been in rules pertaining to unilateral acts. And so one wonders further with respect to what or whom the 'good faith' to which the Court refers is to be observed in a case of (partial) termination of a Declaration. Surely not with respect to the only international entity that is indeed directly affected by the termination: the Court itself.

Up to this point the Nicaraguan Declaration was discussed on the basis that it was a valid one; but the US had argued that because the expression by Nicaragua of its consent to be bound by the 1920 Geneva Protocol of Signature of the Statute of the Permanent Court of International Justice was not effective, the Declaration was never valid. As a result, the reasoning goes, the condition of article 36(5) was not complied with, and therefore the Court had no jurisdiction under article 36(2). As mentioned above (on p. 155), the defect consisted in the failure by Nicaragua to deposit its instrument of ratification of the Protocol of Signature with the Secretary-General of the League of Nations, as prescribed by the Protocol. Some tend to see this matter – erroneously, as will be argued – as a mere technicality that should not stand in the way.

It is submitted that besides holdings by the Court itself, article 16 of the Vienna Convention on *inter alia* the deposit of instruments of ratification is an authoritative rule in the matter.[17] It provides that such instruments 'establish the consent of a State to be bound by a treaty upon: . . . (b) their deposit with the depositary'. In its comment on this provision the ILC observed that 'the existing general rule clearly is that the act of deposit by itself establishes the legal nexus'.[18] By the same token it is the law – and this was the law in 1920 and has been the law ever since 1920 and was still the law in 1984 – that without the act there is no nexus.

---

[16] *YbILC*, (1966, vol. II), p. 251.
[17] At the UN Conference it was adopted by ninety-nine votes to none, with one abstention: Official Records, vol. II, p. 28.
[18] *YbILC*, (1966, vol. II), p. 201.

The Court observed that Nicaragua was not able to prove that it 'accomplished the indispensable step' of depositing its instrument of ratification with the Secretary-General of the League of Nations, even after having been duly informed by the League Secretariat of the consequences of the failure to do so, pointing out that 'le dépôt [of the instrument] est nécessaire pour faire naître effectivement l'obligation'. The Court decided accordingly (paragraph 26) that Nicaragua was not a party to the Protocol and that the Declaration 'had not acquired binding force'; but it then continued, saying 'prior to such effect as Article 36, paragraph 5, of the Statute . . . might produce'.

What, it must be asked, do these words mean? How did the Court finally manage to arrive at its conclusion that Nicaragua had accepted 'the same obligation'?

Article 36(5) was embodied in the Statute in 1945 in order to secure as much as possible the complete transfer of the system of compulsory jurisdiction as it existed under the Permanent Court to the new Court. It prescribes that Declarations made under article 36 with respect to the former Court, 'and which are still in force', shall be deemed to be acceptances of the jurisdiction of the latter for the period they still have to run. The Court engaged in a complex expatiation on 'effects produced' by the provision with regard to Nicaragua's position. It is intended to have a look at what seem to be some of the main considerations.

It had been argued that there is an 'apparent discrepancy' between the English words 'still in force' in article 36(5) and the French text, which says 'pour une durée qui n'est pas encore expirée'. The Court went so far in its acceptance of this contention as to state (paragraph 30) that 'it does not appear possible to reconcile the two versions . . . by considering that both versions refer to binding declarations'. It had been argued on the other side that the French phrase is the equivalent of the English. And indeed, the drafting history of article 36(5) reveals that the French version was in no way intended to introduce any modification in the rule as expressed in the English version. So if one were to raise the question to what 'la durée' refers, the right answer would simply be: 'la durée' means 'la durée de la force obligatoire'. But the Court stated that it must interpret paragraph 5 on the basis of the 'actual terms used, which do not include the word "binding"'.

This is, with all respect, a most peculiar position: surely there had never been any reason at all for the inclusion of the word 'binding' in article 36(5) because the system of compulsory jurisdiction laid down in article 36 is based, as appears from paragraph 2, on a recognition of the jurisdiction of the Court 'without special agreement'. Under article 36 the jurisdiction of the Court has in all cases a consensual basis: paragraph 1 refers to 'treaties and Conventions in force', containing clauses granting jurisdiction in advance; further, there may be a 'special agreement' referring a dispute to the Court; and paragraph 2 refers to declarations by which they recognize the Court's jurisdiction 'without special agreement'. The recognition embodied in a Declaration must therefore legally be equivalent to such an agreement between parties to a dispute, and is therefore as binding as any special agreement between them would be. So to include the word "binding" in paragraph 5 would have produced nothing but a pleonasm.

It is astonishing that the majority of the Court by this reasoning seemed to ignore the fact that the system of compulsory jurisdiction under article 36(2) – if it is to have any legal meaning and effect at all – must by its very nature be based on declarations that are necessarily binding.

If an international judge or arbiter is confronted with two authentic treaty texts that he considers to contain a divergency, there is a generally accepted way to try to solve the problem. As it is phrased in article 33(4) of the Vienna Convention, the meaning shall be adopted 'which best reconciles the texts, having regard to the object and purpose of the treaty'. In the case of paragraph 5 this rule would have meant that the Court should have interpreted paragraph 5 in the light of paragraph 2. In a case conducted in English, the English text to be interpreted ('still in force') being absolutely clear, there is no valid reason whatsoever to have recourse to the *travaux préparatoires*, as also appears from article 32 of the Vienna Convention. Moreover, a proper consultation of the *travaux préparatoires* of article 36(5) of the Statute would have made clear that there is no justification at all to be found there for the Court's position. So it is startling to see how the Court played the French version off against the English one.

The Court said also that if the French text does not imply the duration or expiration of a binding commitment, 'it is necessary for some legal effect to have come into existence. But this effect does not necessarily have to be of a binding nature. A declaration validly made under Article 36 of the Statute of the Permanent Court had a certain validity which could be preserved or destroyed, and it is perfectly possible to read the French text as implying only this validity' (paragraph 30 *in fine*). With due respect, it is submitted that this reasoning does not meet the standards the Court has in the course of its existence set itself by its jurisprudence. What is 'some legal effect'? What is 'a certain validity'? What is it to say that it is 'perfectly possible' to read something in a treaty text? Apparently the reasoning does not correspond to any accepted method of treaty interpretation.

Besides, the Court proclaimed the opinion that the English version of article 36(5) 'in no way expressly excludes a valid declaration of unexpired duration, made by a State not party to the Protocol . . . , and therefore not of a binding character' (paragraph 31 *in fine*). But it must then be seen in what this precisely results. In paragraph 32 the Court first referred to the intention that inspired article 36(5), namely 'to preserve existing acceptances and to avoid that the creation of a new Court should frustrate progress already achieved', as it quoted from a statement made in 1959.[19] 'Progress' means progress towards the adoption of a system of compulsory jurisdiction; as such it is obviously a key term in the Court's deliberations: in this and the next paragraph of the judgment it was used not less than eight times. The Nicaraguan Declaration may not be binding, it is 'in existence', and as such it contributes to that progress. Even though it is not a binding commitment, it is 'by no means negligible'. To wipe out the progress evidenced by it would not square with the concern of the drafters of the Statute in 1945.

The next step is that according to the Court 'the general system of devolution from the old Court to the new . . . lends support to the interpretation whereby Article 36, paragraph 5, even covers declarations that had not previously acquired binding force'. The Court then arrived at the conclusion that taking all this into account, it could apply to Nicaragua what it had stated in the *Aerial Incident* case:[20] signature and ratification of the UN Charter and the Statute (in which article 36(5) appears) effectively give consent to the transfer to the Court of a declaration accepting the jurisdiction of the Permanent Court (para. 35). In the *Aerial Incident* case there was, however, no question of binding or non-binding declarations, or of article 36(5) also covering non-binding declarations, so this judgment affords absolutely no support for the thesis of the Court.

How, somewhere in the process of this judgment, the transformation of an invalid Declaration into a valid one has taken place has so far not become clear.

Presumably because it realized that this is so, the Court went on, in the next paragraph, to adduce supplementary grounds, for which it looked to the 'conduct of States and international organizations'. In that respect, it said, 'particular weight' must be ascribed to the *ICJ Yearbook*, the reports that the Court has submitted since 1968 to the UN General Assembly, and the documentation on multilateral treaties published annually by the Secretary-

---

[19] ICJ Reports, 1959, p. 145.   [20] *Ibid.*, p. 142.

General as depositary. The reason why the Court attached importance to the listing of Nicaragua as one of the states that had accepted the compulsory jurisdiction of the Court, 'even if' some of these publications do contain notes on 'certain facts' concerning Nicaragua's ratification of the 1920 Protocol, appears to be the fact that this state was not mentioned in the list of the states accepting compulsory jurisdiction in the Permanent Court's last report. The listing of Nicaragua in the documents published after the entry into force of the Charter and the Statute – even though invariably accompanied by disclaimers and qualifying notes – makes it difficult for the Court to

> escape the conclusion that the basis of this innovation was to be found in the possibility that a declaration which, though not of binding character, was still valid, and was so for a period that had not yet expired, permitted the application of Article 36, paragraph 5, so long as the State in question, by ratifying the Statute . . . , provided it with the institutional foundation that it had hitherto lacked. From that moment on, Nicaragua would have become 'bound' [*sic*] by its 1929 Declaration, and could, for practical purposes, appropriately be included in the same *Yearbook* list as the States which had been bound even prior to the coming into force of the post-war Statute. (paragraph 37 *in fine*)

The Court noted that no state had ever rejected the mentioning of Nicaragua in the context of article 36(5) in the pertinent publications or challenged the interpretation of this provision appearing from the listing. But with an eye to, e.g., the footnote annually accompanying the listing of Nicaragua in the Court's *Yearbook* (until *Yearbook* No. 38, that is; since then – see page 89 of *Yearbook* No. 39, covering 1984–5 – there has been a new footnote, referring the reader to the judgment discussed here) one wonders what would have been the use and effect of a rejection.

It is difficult to imagine a more vigorous protest against the role attributed by the Court to administrative publications in order to back up its interpretation of article 36(5) than that by Judge Jennings in his Separate Opinion. This part of the Opinion is in effect a very strongly worded dissent. To his mind it is 'wrong in principle' that the Court does not distinguish between administrative and judicial functions.

> To hold, after the exchange of voluminous written pleadings and two rounds of oral proceedings, that the matter was, before all this, virtually settled as a result of the action of the Registrar acting on behalf of the Court in its administrative capacity, and without benefit of judicial argument and procedure, is not free from an element of absurdity.[21]

---

[21] ICJ Reports, 1984, p. 540.

That the Court gave weight to entries in e.g. the *Yearbook*, in spite of unequivocal disclaimers, is 'startling'. The same holds for the Court's mentioning of the reports to the General Assembly: 'it is an astonishing proposition that the result of a full adjudication of a difficult legal question, can be in some way foreclosed by a list in routine reports made by the Court in its administrative capacity.'[22]

IV

It comes as no surprise that the Court has dealt with different treaties in different ways. In each case involving one or more treaties the Court was and is confronted with instruments of widely different character, each of them unique. In the first contentious case ever before the World Court, the SS *Wimbledon* case, decided by the Permanent Court in 1923,[23] the Court had to deal with part XII of the Peace Treaty of Versailles, in particular the section on the Kiel Canal. The Court qualified the provisions of this section as 'self-contained', an intriguing conception repeated, much to the interest of international lawyers, almost sixty years later by the present Court in the *Hostages* case,[24] now referring to the regime of diplomatic law laid down in the 1961 Vienna Convention on Diplomatic Relations. But with all the variety there always was, as a constant factor, the truth to form.

Much attention was paid in the foregoing to the 1984 judgment on jurisdiction in the litigation between Nicaragua and the US, but that judgment contains some most highly controversial dicta by the Court on matters concerning the law of treaties. Some commentators have observed that the pertinent dicta of this judgment have very little significance as a precedent, for they just 'solved' the duplicity of the Nicaraguan position, which was necessarily on its own in the world. The new footnote in the Court's *Yearbooks* since No. 39 (1984–5) bears witness to that. But it is submitted that this comment is beside the point, the point being that the Court abandoned in this judgment generally accepted standards of treaty interpretation (*in casu* incidentally involving the interpretation of a provision of its own Statute).

The point of view of this chapter was: formality and flexibility. Seen from that perspective it is relevant that in this particular case the Court resorted to 'flexibility' through reasoning that deviated in an infelicitous way from a firmly established practice of formality where means of expressing consent to be bound by treaties are concerned.

[22] *Ibid.*   [23] PCIJ, Series A, No. 1 (1923).   [24] ICJ Reports, 1980, p. 40.

It is to be trusted that the Court will be steadfast in its traditional fidelity to form in matters of the law of treaties, thus enhancing the security and stability that the treaty instrument is – ideally – intended to bring about in international relations. Of course, nothing in the above is to be understood as pretending to be a theory of the sources of international law, or as a plea for regarding international law as a closed system. As far as it contains a plea, it is for honouring the forms of the law of treaties that have been agreed upon by the negotiating states.[25]

It is proper that – by way of a postscript – a few remarks be added about two recent judgments of the Court: the judgment of 3 February 1994 in the case between Libya and Chad,[26] and especially the judgment of 1 July 1994 in the case concerning *Maritime Delimitation and Territorial Questions.*[27] This judgment contains dicta that are of the greatest importance for the law of treaties.

The first case concerned a territorial dispute between Libya and Chad. In the judgment of 3 February the Court firmly upheld the validity of a Treaty of Friendship and Good Neighbourliness between France and Libya, concluded in 1955, against a variety of objections on the part of Libya, *inter alia* – interestingly – the contention that Libya lacked at the time of its conclusion 'the experience to engage in difficult negotiations' (see para. 36 of the judgment). The Court decided that the Treaty 'conclusively determines' the dispute (para. 75). (Chad had succeeded France with respect to the Treaty.)

The judgment of 1 July 1994 between Qatar and Bahrain confirms the fidelity of the Court to form, but it demonstrates at the same time that this by no means implies a requirement of a formal or formalistic procedure. In the 1978 judgment in the case of the *Aegean Sea Continental Shelf*, referred to above, the Court showed its readiness carefully to examine the contents of a joint communiqué in order to see whether there were any elements of a binding nature in it regarding the Court's jurisdiction (it found none). The question whether the joint communique as such was to be regarded as an international agreement was not broached.

In the 1994 judgment the Court declared that it would 'first enquire into the nature of the texts upon which Qatar relies before turning to an analysis of the content of those texts'.[28] Naturally, this enquiry 'into the nature of the

---

[25] Article 2(1)(e) *juncto* article 24(4), Vienna Convention.

[26] ICJ Reports, 1994, p. 6.

[27] *Qatar v. Bahrain, Jurisdiction and Admissibility*; ICJ Reports, 1994, p. 112.

[28] *Ibid.*, at p. 120, para. 21.

texts' is important not only for the question of what sort of engagement deserves to be labelled 'treaty' in the sense of article 2(1)(a) of the Vienna Convention, but also, and perhaps even more, for an answer to the question by what acts international persons generate commitments among themselves which they cannot disregard and which they therefore have to comply with in good faith.

In the dispute between Qatar and Bahrain the applicant brought two texts before the Court with respect to its jurisdiction and the admissibility of the claim: exchanges of letters between the King of Saudi Arabia and the Heads of State of Bahrain and Qatar, in December 1987, as well as an agreement concluded on 25 December 1990, consisting of Minutes of consultations among the Ministers of Foreign Affairs of Bahrain, Qatar and Saudi Arabia, and signed by all three of them. In it, the agreement of 1987 was reaffirmed. Both agreements were to the effect that if no other settlement of the dispute could be reached within a certain period of time, the dispute was to be referred to the International Court of Justice. The Court found that

> the Parties agreed that the exchanges of letters of December 1987 constitute an international agreement with binding force in their mutual relations. Bahrain however maintained that the Minutes of 25 December 1990 were no more than a simple record of negotiations . . . ; that accordingly they did not rank as an international agreement and could not, therefore, serve as a basis for the jurisdiction of the Court. The Court observed, in the first place, that international agreements may take a number of forms and be given a diversity of names.

After referring to the definition of 'treaty' in article 2 of the Vienna Convention on the Law of Treaties, the Court went on to refer to the dictum in its judgment in the *Aegean Sea Continental Shelf* case, where it held that 'it knows of no rule of international law which might preclude a joint communiqué from constituting an international agreement to submit a dispute to arbitration or judicial settlement'. And it continued by referring to its dictum that in order to ascertain whether an agreement of that kind has been concluded, 'the Court must have regard above all to its actual terms and to the particular circumstances in which it was drawn up' (paragraphs 22, 23).

After examining the particular circumstances of the drawing up of the 1990 Minutes, the Court held:

> Thus the 1990 Minutes include a reaffirmation of obligations previously entered into . . . Accordingly, and contrary to the contentions of Bahrain, the Minutes are not a simple record of a meeting, . . . they do not merely give an account of discussions and summarize points of agreement and disagreement. They enumerate the commitments to which the Parties have consented. They thus

create rights and obligations in international law for the Parties. They constitute an international agreement. (paragraph 25)

Bahrain maintained that the signatories of the Minutes 'never intended to conclude an agreement of this kind'. The Minister of Foreign Affairs had stated that he had never considered committing his country to a binding agreement. According to the Bahrain constitution treaties concerning the territory of the state can come into effect only after their 'positive enactment as a law'. The Minister had only been prepared to subscribe to a statement recording a political understanding.

The Court's reply to this statement will no doubt turn out to be a most consequential, but probably also a controversial, ruling on the question of the significance of the 'intention of the parties', a concept commonly regarded as crucial in the law of treaties. It is as follows:

> The Court does not find it necessary to consider what might have been the intentions of the Foreign Minister of Bahrain or, for that matter, those of the Foreign Minister of Qatar. The two Ministers signed a text recording commitments accepted by their Governments, some of which were given immediate application. Having signed such a text, the Foreign Minister of Bahrain is not in a position subsequently to say that he intended to subscribe only to a 'statement recording a political understanding', and not to an international agreement. (paragraph 27)

The position of the Court is equally straightforward with respect to other central issues of the law of treaties: registration, compliance with constitutional rules relating to the conclusion of treaties, and, again, intention. Without prejudice to article 102 of the Charter, 'non registration . . . does not have any consequence for the actual validity of the agreement, which remains no less binding upon the parties' (paragraph 29). And in its rejection of Bahrain's contention that its standpoint is confirmed by the fact that Qatar had not followed the procedures required by its own constitution for the conclusion of treaties, the Court held:

> [There is nothing] in the material before the Court which would justify deducing from any disregard by Qatar of its constitutional rules relating to the conclusion of treaties that it did not intend to conclude, and did not consider that it had concluded, an instrument of that kind; nor could any such intention, even if shown to exist, prevail over the actual terms of the instrument in question. (paragraph 29)

These holdings are pronounced by a majority of fifteen judges, one judge dissenting, surprisingly not the judge *ad hoc* chosen by Bahrain. They will soon appear to have a decisive impact on *inter alia* the prevalent practice of drawing up all sorts of informal arrangements between states, governments, ministries, state agencies and the like, the possible legal significance of which is commonly ignored or left ambiguous. It is to be hoped that the Court's dicta will heighten the awareness of the legal consequences that this practice may have.

9

International 'soft law': a contemporary assessment

Francesco Francioni

❧

WHY REVISIT SOFT LAW?

It is a distinct privilege – in the original sense of something 'given' rather than of a personal entitlement – to join such a distinguished company of scholars in paying tribute to Sir Robert Jennings. The sense of genuine pride that this causes me is accompanied, however, by the slight apprehension I feel with regard to the subject of my contribution: soft law.

This for several reasons. The first is the suspicion that the very expression 'soft law' may appear to be an oxymoron, a contradiction between the term 'soft' and the idea of law as a system of binding enforceable rules. This figure of speech could prove to be an unsuitable subject for honouring Sir Robert, since his scholarship and jurisprudence have never lost sight of the funda-mental distinction between legal norms and aspirational goals.[1]

The second reason relates to the lack of a rigorous and generally accepted definition of the term 'soft law', which makes it quite unclear how to define the perimeter of our subject. In legal literature, 'soft law means different things to different people',[2] a relativism that leaves it unclear whether one should apply the concept only to written law or also to unwritten norms,[3] to softness deriving from the formal status of the prescription and/or also to softness relating to the normative content of an otherwise obligatory prescription. Obviously, I cannot within the limits of this chapter examine in detail all the possible components of a general definition. All I can say is that I hope the following analysis will contribute to a more precise definition of the concept. To introduce such analysis, it is sufficient to start simply with a working

---

[1] R. Y. Jennings, 'The Discipline of International Law', McNair Lecture, *International Law Association, 57th Report* (1976), p. 632.

[2] G. Handl, 'A Hard Look at Soft Law', *Proceedings ASIL* (1988), p. 371.

[3] Literature on the subject tends to restrict the analysis to written instruments. For a general overview, see R. R. Baxter, 'International Law in "Her Infinite Variety"', *ICLQ*, 29 (1980), p. 549.

definition of soft law as those international norms, principles and procedures that, by being outside the system of formal sources of article 38, paragraph 1 of the ICJ Statute or by lacking the requisite normative content to create enforceable rights and obligations, are nevertheless capable of producing certain legal effects.

But even within the reassuring boundaries of this definition, a further, and perhaps most important reservation about the subject may linger with the reader. This is the doubt that the debate over the nature and effects of soft law may have consumed all possibilities of clarification and legal analysis. For nearly twenty years, this debate has tried to focus on the costs and benefits of soft law. Some writers have enthusiastically endorsed this normative category, highlighting the need for flexibility and responsiveness to the contemporary need for accommodation between competing interests in a diversified and conflictual world community.[4] Others have warned against normative relativism and the risk of conceptual confusion involved in the attempt to bring within the region of 'law' merely political or aspirational concepts.[5] Others, again, have utterly dismissed the notion of 'soft law' as useless, fashionable, even pathological.[6]

Since the various positions have been so richly articulated already, what is the use of revisiting this subject today? What promises may it hold for new insights and fresh contributions of ideas?

To address these questions, I think we need to orient ourselves in two different directions.

The first concerns the past, and precisely the role of the International Court of Justice in fashioning a concept of soft law and disclosing different nuances of it.

The second direction concerns the future, particularly the prospect of an increasing use of soft law in the context of the transformations the international society is undergoing in this last decade of the century.

THE ICJ ON SOFT LAW

Although the ICJ has never treated the subject of soft law *ex professo*, there is a substantial body of its jurisprudence that tends to spill over the boundary of

---

[4] J. Gold, 'Strengthening the Soft International Law of Exchange Arrangements', *AJIL*, 77 (1983), p. 443; C. Chinkin, in *Proceedings ASIL* (1988), p. 389; C. Schreuer, 'Recommendations and the Traditional Sources of International Law', *German YbIL*, p. 103ff.

[5] P. Weil, 'Towards Relative Normativity in International Law', *AJIL*, 77 (1983), p. 413.

[6] G. Arangio-Ruiz, *The UN Declaration on Friendly Relations and the System of Sources of International Law* (Alphen aan den Rijn, 1979), pp. 29 and 196; Weil, 'Towards Relative Normativity'.

the formal 'sources' of international law as laid out in article 38, paragraph 1 of the Statute. This jurisprudence, as we well know, is mainly concerned with the notion of equity and equitable principles in the area of maritime delimitation, a topic that falls outside the scope of this chapter, in that it forms the specific object of other contributions in this collection. However, even if the aspect of equity is excluded, a limited but significant case law remains, in which the ICJ has made reference to normative concepts, General Assembly resolutions and declarations which, because they are not contemplated by article 38, paragraph 1, may be considered under the general umbrella of soft law.

The first case goes back to the early years of existence of the ICJ. In the 1948 *Corfu Channel* decision the Court was confronted with the United Kingdom's claim that Albania was internationally responsible and under a duty to pay damages for the explosion of mines in Albanian territorial waters, resulting in damage to British ships and loss of life of British personnel on board. The Court found that the obligations incumbent on the Albanian government of notifying the existence of a minefield and of warning the approaching vessels of the imminent danger they were exposed to could not be based on Hague Convention No. VIII, which is applicable in time of war, but on 'certain general and well-recognized principles, namely: *elementary considerations of humanity*, even more exacting in peace than in war'.[7] This pronouncement of the Court is relevant to our discussion for two reasons. First, because it would be difficult to imagine a softer body of law than 'elementary considerations of humanity'; second, because it reveals an explicit recognition that principles of soft law may be drawn from an unwritten source.

In the early period of activity of the Court we may find another precedent, the Advisory Opinion on *Reparations for Injuries Suffered in the Service of the United Nations*, in which the principles of soft law are deduced from the context of the UN Charter. Here the issue was whether the UN could be allowed to exercise diplomatic protection of its agents for injuries suffered in the performance of their duties. In the absence of specific treaty rules or precedent on the matter, the Court relied on the very 'soft' foundation of the general object and purpose of the Charter to assert a broad right of the UN to intervene against the offending state.[8]

The 1951 decision on the *Anglo-Norwegian Fisheries*[9] case is not usually cited in the context of soft law. However, it is submitted that also in this case the Court resorted to soft law principles to weaken the rigidity of existing hard

---

[7] ICJ Reports, 1949, p. 22.   [8] *Ibid.*, p. 174.   [9] ICJ Reports, 1951, pp. 128ff.

law and bend their interpretation to the desired outcome. How else can we interpret the complex formula according to which Norway was allowed to adopt a system of straight baselines? This system was held permissible, in derogation of the rule of the low-water mark, in order to fit 'practical needs', provided that such baselines would not 'depart to any appreciable extent from the general direction of the coast'. This very flexible formula has become part of hard law with the Geneva Convention of 1958 and the UN Convention of 1982. However, in its original 1951 enunciation, it presented all the elements of a soft law prescription, i.e. the absence of its legal expression in a treaty, custom or general principle, the lack of a precise normative content, and the fact that it was left essentially to the unilateral determination of the interested state. It is not surprising, therefore, that its application in subsequent practice has led to abuses and to the generalized phenomenon of 'creeping jurisdiction' over coastal waters.

The 1960s seemed to sweep a conservative wind through the Court, quite inconsistent with the progressive spirit of the time. A rigid positive law approach prevailed in the 1966 *South West Africa* case when the Court discounted the same considerations of humanity, which had been held decisive in the 1949 *Corfu Channel* ruling, because, absent 'a sufficient expression in legal form', such considerations could not be elevated to the dignity of sources of international obligations.[10]

However, this is more an isolated episode than a turning-point in the Court's jurisprudence. In the 1971 Advisory Opinion on *Namibia*, the Court moved two steps further in the process of recognizing legal effects of soft law. First, in dealing with the question whether the General Assembly had the authority to bring to an end the Mandate for South West Africa, it gave an affirmative reply and made the following bold statement with respect to the legal significance of General Assembly resolutions: 'it would not be correct to assume that because the General Assembly is in principle vested with recommendatory powers, it is debarred from adopting in specific cases within the framework of its competence, resolutions which make determinations or have operative design.'[11] Second, the Court declared the conduct of South Africa in practising apartheid to be a violation of international human rights as expressed in the Charter. Given the very vague content of the human rights provision contained in the Charter, and given the absence of relevant human rights treaties binding on South Africa, it is natural to conclude that this decision was heavily influenced by the body of soft human rights law

---

[10] ICJ Reports, 1966, pp. 6ff.   [11] ICJ Reports, 1971, p. 50.

developed by the UN, primarily the 1948 Universal Declaration and subsequent resolutions on self-determination and on the elimination of all forms of racial discrimination.

A few years later, in the 1975 Advisory Opinion on *Western Sahara*, it fully confirmed its disposition to draw legal effects from General Assembly resolutions, acts that *per se* do not possess obligatory force but that in the specific case were deemed to acquire such force by virtue of their being a specification of the general Charter principle on self-determination (article 1, para. 2).[12] Besides this better-known feature, the Court's opinion in *Western Sahara* is remarkable for its very subtle treatment of territorial sovereignty. In trying to determine whether in the pre-colonial period the territory of Western Sahara was *terra nullius* or was subject to some states' sovereignty, the Court adopted a typical soft law technique in giving relevance to the social and political organization of the nomadic inhabitants of the land, thus concluding that it did not constitute *terra nullius*.[13] Similarly, a soft law approach characterized the qualification of the ties existing at the time of colonization between the peoples of Western Sahara on the one hand, and Morocco and Mauritania on the other. Rather than adopt a rigid either/or approach as to the existence of sovereignty ties, the Court recognized that certain 'legal ties' existed which included relations of allegiance to Morocco and rights relating to the land. These ties, however, the Court realistically concluded, were not of such a nature as to prevent the application of the principle of self-determination 'through the free will and genuine expression of the will of the peoples in the Territory'.[14]

Again in the 1970s, the Court had two more opportunities to determine the legal effects of soft law. In the Greek–Turkish dispute over the *Aegean Continental Shelf*, the question arose as to whether an informal joint communique signed by the Foreign Ministers of the two countries and embodying *inter alia* an exchange of views on the subject of referring the dispute to the ICJ could create an obligation to submit the case to the jurisdiction of the Court. Unfortunately, the 1978 judgment did not help to clarify the formal legal significance of such soft engagement, since it turned rather on a question of content which the Court found to disclose a conditional rather than unqualified acceptance of its jurisdiction.[15] The same cautious attitude emerged in the recent interim order of 8 April 1993 on the case concerning the *Application of the Convention on the Prevention and Punish-*

---

[12] ICJ Reports, 1975, pp. 12ff. and esp. paras. 52–6 of the Opinion.
[13] *Ibid.*, paras. 79–83.
[14] *Ibid.*, para. 169   [15] ICJ Reports, 1978, pp. 44ff.

ment of the Crime of Genocide (Bosnia v. Yugoslavia) with regard to a letter written by the defendant to an addressee other than the plaintiff in which the opinion was expressed that disputes not solved by agreement should be submitted to the ICJ.[16] The other precedent is the *Fisheries Jurisdiction* dispute in which, as is well known, Iceland disputed the Court's jurisdiction to determine the legality of its fishing zone *vis à vis* the UK. In asserting its jurisdiction, the Court not only emphasized substantive principles of equity, but – what is more important for our discussion – it recognized that even a soft obligation regarding the parties' duty to negotiate a settlement was in itself a proper object for adjudication.[17]

To complete this brief overview of the Court's case law, a reference may be useful to the 1986 *Nicaragua* case. Here the Court, in considering whether the US had infringed customary international law regarding the prohibition of the use of force, concluded that such prohibition could be established on the strength of the evidence provided by General Assembly resolutions. The Court observed that '*opinio juris* may, though with all due caution, be deduced from, *inter alia*, the attitude of the Parties and the attitude of States toward certain General Assembly resolutions, and particularly resolution 2625 (XXV)'.[18] Granted, in this case the Court was forced to look for alternative sources of prohibition of the use of force, other than article 2(4) of the Charter, because it was prevented from applying multilateral treaties – including the Charter – by the US 'Vandenberg' reservation to their acceptance of the Court's jurisdiction. However, one should not underestimate the novelty of this precedent, since the Court found the acceptance of the resolution determinative of a norm of international law despite ample state practice to the contrary, and despite the absence of any specific indication of *opinio juris* deduced from the concrete individual behaviour of states. To measure the softening of the standard of proof of customary norms achieved with this decision one has only to compare it to the 1969 judgment on the *North Sea Continental Shelf*[19] which was focused much more traditionally on the element of state practice and on *opinio juris* traceable in state behaviour.[20]

What is the overall assessment of this case law? Very briefly, one can identify several positive aspects of the ICJ jurisprudence:

---

[16] ICJ Reports, 1993, paras. 29–32.
[17] ICJ Reports, 1974 (*Merits*), p. 3, para. 75.
[18] ICJ Reports, 1986, p. 14, esp. at paras. 188–94 and 202–9.
[19] ICJ Reports, 1969, pp. 4ff., esp. at paras. 61ff.
[20] See also B. Simma, *Proceedings ASIL* (1988), p. 378.

(1) Without ever articulating it as a distinct category of sources, the Court has nevertheless contributed to furthering the development of the concept of soft law.

(2) This concept has been understood to include unwritten prescriptions such as general considerations of humanity and the dictates of conscience.

(3) More frequently, the Court has applied soft law contained in international documents, notably General Assembly resolutions, whose strength and legal efficacy has been generally deemed to increase whenever the relevant documents reflected general principles of the Charter (self-determination, human rights, use of force).

(4) Reference to soft law instruments has also been understood as a method for facilitating the process of their transformation into hard law, especially via the element of *opinio juris* as witnessed in the *Nicaragua* case.

Despite these positive contributions, this case law may not, in the view of this writer, be interpreted in such a way as to warrant a redefinition of the formal sources of international law as laid down in article 38, paragraph 1 of the ICJ Statute. But this is not a limit of the Court's jurisprudence; it is rather the necessary consequence of the reluctance to give the General Assembly law-making powers or to further reduce the role of state consent in the formation of customary law.

In a different respect, the Court's jurisprudence may appear disappointing. That is in regard to the development of soft international economic law. Despite the perceived risk in the 1970s that soft law would become the 'Trojan horse' of the 'new international economic law', the Court has shown a rather conservative attitude in this field. Notably, in the *Barcelona Traction* case the Court refused to 'soften' the mantle of independent legal personality of a corporation and to resort to notions of equity in order to allow the diplomatic protection by a state whose *locus standi* would be premissed, rather than on the bond nationality, on the ownership of the shares.[21] But even in this respect, the Court's jurisprudence cannot be considered 'rigid' and conservative. On the contrary, it has shown itself to be balanced and far sighted; and it has contributed to the rebuilding of consensus on the minimum standard of protection of foreign investments beyond the radical and schematic solutions advocated in the 1970s by both developing and industrial countries.

[21] ICJ Reports, 1970, p. 3, esp. at paras. 92ff.

SOFT LAW AND COMMON INTERESTS

I come now to the last part of this analysis which concerns the prospect of an increasing role for soft law in the context of the transformations the international society is undergoing in this last part of the century.

These transformations include not only a significant increase in the number of states as a consequence of the successful claim to statehood of many peoples after 1989, but especially the increasing institutionalization of international co-operation to address issues of common concern. Prominent among them are the maintenance of peace and security, the protection of human dignity and the preservation of the earth's environment. Faced with these challenges, the original model of international law, as a system of jurisdictional rules designed to accommodate spheres of sovereign power among states, is quickly becoming inadequate. Governance of issues of global concern requires creative co-operation rather than simple co-ordination among sovereign entities. Likewise, state sovereignty and autonomy cannot be maintained as absolute concepts in a world that is more and more interconnected and dependent on the honest effort of each participant to resolve issues of universal concern. The list of these concerns has been on the international agenda for quite a while and it includes, besides the already-mentioned concerns for peace, the environment and human rights, such more specific issues as nuclear proliferation, drug traffic, control of biotechnologies, preservation of the world cultural heritage, prevention of international terrorism, and punishment of international crimes.

Confronted with these global challenges, some lawyers are tempted simply to retrench behind the traditional scepticism that international law is inherently incapable of dealing with these challenges.[22] Others advocate futuristic forms of world government – such as an international tribunal for the environment, an international criminal court – or, more concretely, they argue for the attribution to the UN and international institutions of the power to make universal international law regardless of the consent to be bound by some recalcitrant states.[23] Both these positions are excessive, in my opinion. The sceptics neglect the capacity that the international community has historically proved to have to overcome the decentralized nature of its law and to agree spontaneously on fundamental principles reflecting the common good. The principles of the freedom of the high seas, self-determination, and the common heritage of mankind regarding resources located in international

---

[22] D. Stone, 'Beyond Rio: Insuring against Global Warming', *AJIL*, 86 (1992), p. 447.
[23] J. Charney, 'Universal International Law', *AJIL* 87 (1993), p. 529.

spaces are all examples of this enduring capacity. At the other end of the spectrum, those who want to encourage the deduction of 'universal' international law from instruments adopted within the UN or other multilateral fora cannot satisfactorily explain how such instruments can acquire a binding force with respect to non-consenting states in view of the absence of independent legislative powers of the UN or similar multilateral fora. Besides, without questioning the intellectual integrity of those who argue in favour of such legislative power, it is difficult not to feel uneasy about the shifting attitude towards the UN with the cyclical recurrence of peaks of confidence corresponding to periods when the preferred camp – be it the major industrial powers or the less-developed countries – has a solid control of the organization, and then sharp drops, sometimes to the point of sheer contempt, in times of less triumphant participation in the life of the Organization.

A more reasonable approach than the above two extremes may be precisely the one based on the use of soft law for the fostering of uniform standards reflecting the general world community interest. There are countless examples today of the use of soft law in this sense. Antarctic Treaty recommendations concerning safety, environmental protection, inspection, and a whole variety of other questions related to the good governance of that continent are formally soft instruments; but they can be treated – and in fact they are treated by most states – as binding regulations once introduced in the respective domestic law systems.[24] Other instruments, such as the 1989 World Charter for Nature, and the 1992 Rio Declaration on Environment and Development, are less susceptible of being transformed into hard regulations, and their role is mainly that of providing a framework of principles, objectives and programmes to orient and legitimize further legislative action. With regard to General Assembly resolutions, they have since the beginning of the UN activities performed the role of forerunners of hard law in many areas of common concern such as human rights, suppression of international crimes, status of international resources, rights of the child and many others. All these manifestations of soft law may pave the way to the adoption of hard law in the form of multilateral treaties with a vocation to universality. This has happened in the field of human rights, with regard to principles governing activities in outer space, with regard to the status of the international sea-bed area, to mention only a few examples. But the formulation of soft law does not only

---

[24] See A. Colella, 'The Legal Nature of Antarctic Recommendations and their Implementation in the Domestic Legal Systems', in F. Francioni (ed.), *International Environmental Law for Antarctica* (Milan, 1992), pp. 203–24; and B. Conforti, 'The Direct Applicability in Domestic Law of Recommendations Adopted under Art. IX of the Antarctic Treaty', in *Ibid.*, pp. 225–32.

work as a preparatory stage for the transition to hard treaty law. Experience shows that both in domestic jurisprudence and in legislation or codification relevant to international law the existence of a body of soft law stimulates a mimetic process to the effect of reproducing the same prescription in an obligatory mode. This happened with the 1987 United States Restatement III, whose section 702 includes 'generally accepted' human rights[25] whose legal status is largely drawn from a background of soft law (at the time the US was not even a party to most of the relevant treaties!) and with the jurisprudence of domestic courts which have on some occasions enforced provisions of the Universal Declaration on Human Rights as customary law.[26]

SOFT ENFORCEMENT

A further consequence of the current emphasis on world community interests, besides the already-indicated development of universal substantive standards, is the tendency to fashion 'soft remedies' and 'soft enforcement procedures'. The characteristic of these new forms is that they tend to replace the traditional adversarial methods of enforcement based on sanctions, international liability and payment of damages. There are several illustrations of them. Some form the logical counterpart of a body of law that is itself predominantly soft. This is the case with those supervision procedures within the UN system that tend to review the state of compliance in the field of non-actionable international human rights such as economic, social and cultural rights for which a special Committee was established in 1987 within ECOSOC. Other enforcement procedures, however, are linked to ordinary hard law, normally treaty law, whose guarantee could be provided by the usual means of enforcement, including sanctions and international responsibility.

In this case, why should one resort to soft means of enforcement? One reason is that states are still showing a great reluctance to accept responsibility at the level of public international law.[27] A soft control mechanism can thus be

---

[25] Section 702 contemplates as breach of customary law of human rights (a) genocide; (b) slavery and slave trade; (c) murder and enforced disappearance of individuals; (d) torture; (e) prolonged arbitrary detention; (f) systematic racial discrimination; and (g) a consistent pattern of gross violations of human rights.

[26] For the Italian case law, see Tar Friuli-Venezia Giulia 23 settembre 1982 in P. Picone and B. Conforti, *La Giurisprudenza italiana di diritto internazionale pubblico, repertorio 1960–1987* (Naples, 1988), p. 245; Trib. minorenni Bari, 4 giugno 1987, *in re Koltsidas*, in *Rivista di diritto internazionale*, 71 (1988), p. 227; Corte Costituzionale, 7 aprile 1988 n. 404, in *Giurisprudenza Costituzionale* 1 (1988), p. 1789.

[27] See B. Conforti, 'Do States Really Accept Responsibility for Environmental Damage', in F. Francioni and T. Scovazzi (eds.), *International Responsibility for Environmental Harm* (London, 1991), pp. 179ff, as well as the in-depth and innovative study by M. Jovane, *La riparazione nella teoria e nella prassi dell'illecito internazionale* (Milan, 1990).

a second-best approach in the absence of an agreed-upon means for enforcing responsibility. Another reason may be the purely cosmetic concern to use less offensive language than the traditional terms of 'violation' and 'breach' in a diplomatic context that postulates the pursuit of common interests through a continuous process of co-operation among participating states. This is the case with most of the environmental law treaties and with the Antarctic Treaty.

But the most important reason for the increasing role of soft implementation procedures is the contemporary widening of the scope of application of the concept of *erga omnes* obligations. These obligations, as recognized by the ICJ in its celebrated dictum of 1970,[28] have made it possible to picture the international community as the title holder of certain collective interests such as human rights and environmental quality. However, this *erga omnes* effect of the obligation, ironically, entails the dilution of the normative intensity of secondary rules on responsibility and reparation which become applicable in the event of a breach. Once we recognize that the breach concerns the international community as a whole, rather than a specific injured state, the system of remedies becomes more precarious, the *locus standi* of claimants debatable, the possibility of multiple overlapping claims a confusing reality. Hence the tendency to remove the haunting spectre of international responsibility from such fields as violations of human rights, damage to global commons, injuries to the cultural heritage of humankind and the like. In these fields we can witness the preference for an approach based on monitoring compliance and implementation. A recent model is provided by the non-compliance procedure established under article 8 of the Montreal Protocol on Substances that Deplete the Ozone Layer.[29] This mechanism includes an Implementation Committee whose main function is to oversee the correct application of the complex programme of gradual phasing-out of prohibited substances; to deal with possible infractions by way of recommendations; and to resolve disputes by facilitating 'amicable solutions' rather than by adversarial means and adjudicatory deliberations. Another model of unquestionable success is the World Heritage Committee established under the UNESCO Convention concerning the Protection of the World Cultural and Natural Heritage, whose annual meetings permit a continuous monitoring of the state of conservation of sites and monuments of universal interest for humankind.[30]

---

[28] *Barcelona Traction, Light and Power Co*, ICJ Reports, 1970, p. 3, paras. 33ff.

[29] Text in 25 *ILM*, 150ff. (1987).

[30] Text in UNESCO, *Conventions and Recommendations of Unesco Concerning the Protection of the Cultural Heritage* (1985), pp. 75ff.

Resort to this type of soft procedures presents the advantage of stimulating a pull towards spontaneous observance of standards set in the common interest. At the same time, it can be an important element in the progressive institutionalization of international co-operation, since the process of continuous verification over compliance can only lead to increased transparency and to the furthering of a fiduciary relationship among participating states.

A final question one may touch upon concerns the relationship between soft means of implementation and the functioning of the ordinary means of redress in general international law. Are soft procedures exclusive of countermeasures, *exceptio non adimpleti* and rules on state responsibility? This question is pertinent in view of the absence in international law of a centralized system of judicial remedies and of the central role that unilateral remedies maintain as an instrument to obtain redress against an alleged wrongful act. In practice this question will arise whenever the soft implementation procedure has failed to satisfy a contracting party which, for instance, objects to an amicable compromise and insists on some form of responsibility; or when a state reiterates the breach or becomes a systematic defaulting state. In these instances it would have little sense to exclude the operation of ordinary countermeasures under customary international law or under the Vienna Convention on the Law of Treaties. Soft law and soft remedies cannot be understood in such a way as to displace and curtail the operation of hard law. Besides, it would be inconsistent with arbitral precedents which recognize the admissibility of unilateral remedies, even with respect to the alleged breach of treaties that encapsulate specific third-party procedure for the settlement of disputes arising from their application or interpretation.[31]

---

[31] *Air Services Agreement Case (France v. United States)*, *RIAA*, 18 (1987), pp. 416ff.

PART III
Substance of international law

ᏮᎾ

10

The Court's role in relation to international organizations

D. W. Bowett

ᏬᎧ

> To have the principal judicial organ of the United Nations more often employed with respect to the legal components of situations with which the United Nations is concerned would, quite apart from its possible contribution to solving a dispute or situation, also do immense good for international law.
> Speech by Sir Robert Yewdall Jennings to the UN General Assembly: UN Doc. A/46/PV.44 at 6–23 (1991)

The integration of the Court into the United Nations system as its 'principal judicial organ' conveys little of what, conceptually, it was designed to achieve. One aim would be that it should be the normal means of settling legal disputes between member states, and this aim finds some reflection in articles 36(3), 93 and 94 of the Charter.[1] A quite different aim would be that it should give legal advice to the UN organs as regards the performance of their functions, with the emphasis being on the needs of those organs for this assistance. A third, and again quite different, aim would be to have the Court act as an organ of judicial review, with the emphasis being on the need of member states to ensure that the UN organs confined themselves to those powers that had been conferred on them by the constituent treaty.

Clearly, article 96 of the Charter, and chapter IV of the Court's Statute, adopt the second concept – the advisory role – and not the third.

THE ADVISORY ROLE OF THE COURT

Some measure of the utility of this role can be found in the frequency of its use. Under the League of Nations, over a period of nineteen years,

---

[1] For fuller discussion of this aspect of the Court's role see chapters 1–3 and 19 of this volume. Major studies on the Court's advisory jurisdiction are K. Keith, *The Extent of the Advisory Jurisdiction of the ICJ* (Leyden, 1971); D. Pratap, *The Advisory Jurisdiction of the ICJ* (Oxford, 1972); M. Pomerance, *The Advisory Jurisdiction of the International Court in the League and UN Eras* (Baltimore, 1973).

twenty-nine requests were received by the Permanent Court, and twenty-seven Opinions were delivered.[2] By comparison, under the UN and over a period of forty-seven years, twenty Opinions have been requested and given.

If one considers, in addition, the fact that the Specialized Agencies now have an independent power to request Opinions,[3] and have a wider range of activities than under the League, and that three of the Opinions arose in the form of a review of judgments of the UN Administrative Tribunal – a type of Opinion not used under the League,[4] the conclusion must be that the UN itself has tended to use the Court less than the League of Nations did. Even more striking is the fact that, under the League, it was the Council that requested the opinions (the League Assembly never did); whereas, under the UN, the Security Council has only once requested an Opinion (the *Namibia* case).[5] Clearly there has been a change of emphasis both in constitutional terms and in attitude. Under article 14 of the Covenant the PCIJ acted as legal adviser to the Council of the League in its handling of disputes, and the Council routinely adopted the Court's advice in its reports on disputes before it. The Security Council has never seen the role of the ICJ in this way, nor has it wanted to see such a role for the Court.

Bearing in mind the composition of the Security Council, this is not surprising. Two of the permanent members – the Soviet Union (now Russia) and China – have never used the Court in any contentious dispute. France, since the *Nuclear Tests*[6] case, has essentially boycotted the Court. And at least since the *Nicaragua*[7] case, the USA has shown some ambivalence towards it. It is scarcely surprising, therefore, that the Security Council has made little use of the Court, either in its advisory capacity or by recommending states to refer their disputes to the Court under article 36(3) of the Charter. The Council's preference for 'political' solutions, without the benefit of the Court's assistance on legal questions,[8] is one of the more regrettable features of the UN's record.

---

[2] One was withdrawn (*Oecumenical Patriarchata*) and one was never actually filed (*Saar Officials*).

[3] Other international organizations associated with the League could utilize the PCIJ, but by submitting their requests via the Council of the League.

[4] If the current burden of cases continues, there must be some question of whether the International Court should continue to discharge this function of reviewing the judgments of Administrative Tribunals. An alternative system of review, or even appeal, could well be devised, perhaps using members drawn from the various Administrative Tribunals – the UN, ILO and World Bank – to form a review panel.

[5] *Legal Consequences for States of the Continued Presence of South Africa in Namibia (South West Africa)* etc., ICJ Reports, 1971, p. 16.

[6] *Nuclear Tests* judgment, ICJ Reports, 1974, p. 253. France has preferred arbitration for disputes such as the *Anglo/French Continental Shelf* case of 1977, the *Rainbow Warrior* case, 1990 and *St Pierre et Miquelon*, 1992.

[7] *Military and Paramilitary Activities in and against Nicaragua (Merits)*, ICJ Reports, 1986, p. 14.

[8] See generally Tae Jin Kahng, *Law, Politics and the Security Council* (The Hague, 1964).

The Security Council's apathy towards the Court cannot be explained away by the suggestion that the Court is unsuitable where the questions are 'political'. Obviously, no one would suggest that a 'political' question be addressed to the Court: the Court's task is to reply to any legal question. But where the Security Council is dealing with complex political issues in which distinct legal questions are at issue[9] then the fact is that the Council has not been inclined to seek the Court's help even on those legal issues. The Court itself has never felt inhibited in giving an Advisory Opinion simply because a legal question has marked political overtones or implications. Summarizing its position based on its jurisprudence, the Court said this in the *WHO Regional Office* case:

> That jurisprudence establishes that if, as in the present case, a question submitted in a request is one that otherwise falls within the normal exercise of its judicial process, the Court has not to deal with the motives which may have inspired the request . . . Indeed, in situations in which political considerations are prominent it may be particularly necessary for an international organisation to obtain an advisory opinion from the Court as to the legal principles applicable with respect to the matter under debate, especially when these may include the interpretation of its constitution.[10]

However, a more serious inhibition might be thought to lie in the *Eastern Carelia* principle,[11] namely the principle that, since the jurisdiction of the Court in contentious cases rests on consent, the Court ought not to give an opinion that is tantamount to deciding an issue in dispute between states where those states have not consented to its jurisdiction. Admittedly, the present Court has tended to limit the effect of this inhibition, at least in cases where the primary purpose of the Opinion is to give guidance to a UN organ. As the Court said in the *Peace Treaties* case:

> The circumstances of the present case are profoundly different from those which were before the Permanent Court of International Justice in the Eastern Carelia case (Advisory Opinion No. 5) where that Court declined to give an Opinion because it found that the question put to it was directly related to the main point

---

9 For illustrations of such questions see E. Lauterpacht, *Aspects of the Administration of International Justice* (Cambridge, 1991), pp. 39–41.

10 Advisory Opinion of 20 December 1980, ICJ Reports, 1980, p. 73, at p. 87. For the principal earlier cases see *Conditions of Admission etc.*, Advisory Opinion of 28 May 1948, ICJ Reports, 1948, p. 61; *Competence of the General Assembly etc.*, Advisory Opinion of 3 March 1950, ICJ Reports, 1950, p. 6; *Certain Expenses of the UN etc.*, Advisory Opinion of 20 July 1962, ICJ Reports, 1962, p. 155.

11 *Status of Eastern Carelia*, Advisory Opinion, PCIJ, Series B, No. 5 (1923). S. Rosenne, *The Law and Practice of the International Court* (Leyden, 1965), vol. II, pp. 709–11 treats this as an illustration of the Court's adherence to an essential principle of the judicial process: *audi alteram partem*.

of a dispute actually pending between two States, so that answering the question would be substantially equivalent to deciding the dispute between the parties, and that at the same time it raised a question of fact which could not be elucidated without hearing both parties . . . In the present case the Court is dealing with a Request for an Opinion, the sole object of which is to enlighten the General Assembly.[12]

But it might be thought that where the Security Council was dealing with an actual, pending dispute between states under Chapter VI of the Charter, the *Eastern Carelia* principle would in practice exclude the Council from using the Court's advisory role.

There are perhaps two answers to this. The first is that the Council has never offered this as the reason for its reluctance to use the Court. The second is that the whole basis of the *Eastern Carelia* principle merits re-examination. The right of a state to be bound by the Court's judgment only where it has consented to the Court's jurisdiction is certainly an important principle, but is it entitled to priority in all cases? Let us suppose a dispute exists in the following circumstances.

(1) The dispute has been characterized by the Security Council as one the continuance of which is likely to endanger international peace and security under Chapter VI of the UN Charter.

(2) The state, or states, involved have declined the Council's recommendation under article 36(3) that they refer their dispute to the Court.

(3) The Council is not itself able to recommend terms of settlement under article 37(2) without guidance from the Court as to the respective legal rights of the parties.

In those circumstances, why should *Eastern Carelia* override? Is the principle of consent so paramount that it must be respected, even though there is an incipient threat to peace, and the Council needs the Court's advice to exercise its powers under article 37(2)? This is a question that merits examination, although clearly such an examination will acquire purpose only when the Security Council is more disposed to use the Court.

---

[12] *Interpretation of the Peace Treaties (First Phase)*, Advisory Opinion of 30 March 1950, ICJ Reports, 1950, p. 72. In the *Namibia (South West Africa)* case, Advisory Opinion of 21 June 1971, ICJ Reports, 1971, the Court rejected South Africa's objection to the propriety of the Opinion based on *Eastern Carelia*, on the ground that, whereas in *Eastern Carelia* the state party to the dispute was not a member of the League, South Africa was a member of the UN and had participated throughout in any 'dispute' over South-West Africa. Moreover, no actual dispute was pending, and the fact that differences existed – common in all requests for an Opinion – was irrelevant. See also the *Western Sahara* case, Advisory Opinion of 16 October 1975, ICJ Reports, 1975, p. 13, at pp. 22–7, where the Court also stressed that, in *Eastern Carelia*, one party was neither a member of the League nor a party to the Court's Statute.

Somewhat paradoxically, the General Assembly may have used the Court overmuch. There are cases in which the dispute has been essentially a political dispute, internal to the Organization, and in which, although there was a 'legal question', the answer to it was fairly obvious or, whatever the answer, it was unlikely to have much effect on the dispute. The early cases on *Conditions for Admission of a State*,[13] or *Competence of the General Assembly*[14] were perhaps of this character. For, in reality, the interpretation of article 4 of the Charter was scarcely the issue: the interpretation was in fact rather obvious. The real difficulty was the political impasse over the admission of new members produced by the East–West rift. And it is difficult to suggest that the Court's Opinion solved the problem. The solution came years later, in 1955, when a political compromise was reached – admitting sixteen new members *en bloc*.

The Expenses case[15] is in the same category. The Court's answer was entirely predictable, and made virtually no difference to the entrenched positions of the opponents of the powers assumed by the General Assembly as regards military peacekeeping. It would seem as though, in such cases, in the essentially political disputes within the UN, one side or the other sees some prospect of advantage in having the Court pronounce in its favour. But this would only be realistic if the dispute really was a dispute over the 'legal question'. If it is not, then the involvement of the Court is unproductive and, since it would be likely to lead to the Opinion being ignored, scarcely apt to enhance the prestige and standing of the Court.

The recent request for an Opinion by WHO[16] on the question whether the use of nuclear weapons by a member state would breach obligations under international law or the WHO constitution may prove to be a further example, for it is difficult to see that this has been regarded by WHO as a genuine 'constitutional' question.

This is not to suggest that the majority of the General Assembly's requests have been of this character. On the contrary, most have raised quite genuine legal questions. But in those few cases where the Court is simply being embroiled in a political dispute, to which it can make very little contribution,

---

[13] Advisory Opinion of 28 May 1948, ICJ Reports, 1948, p. 65.
[14] Advisory Opinion of 30 March 1950, ICJ Reports, 1950, p. 10.
[15] ICJ Reports, 1962, p. 151.
[16] Resolution WHA 46.40, adopted by the 46th World Health Assembly on 14 May 1993. The resolution does not indicate which constitutional provision the Assembly believes may be breached by such use and, indeed, it is hard to find such a provision.

the question then arises whether the Court ought to exercise its discretion to refuse to give an Opinion.

It is clear that the Court is not bound to give an Advisory Opinion, even if the requesting organ or organization is fully *intra vires* in requesting it: the language of article 65 of the Statute is permissive rather than mandatory. As the Court said in the *Interpretation of the Peace Treaties*: 'Article 65 of the Statute is permissive. It gives the Court the power to examine whether the circumstances of the cases are of such a character as should lead it to decline to answer the Request . . . the Court possesses a large amount of discretion in the matter.'[17] The point was reiterated by the Court in its Advisory Opinion on *Reservations to the Genocide Convention*,[18] and again in the *Certain Expenses* case.[19] It would seem that where the Court is satisfied that the question posed is not a 'legal question', or is *ultra vires* the requesting organ (because unrelated to the scope of its activities), the Court is bound to refuse to give an Opinion. The exercise of the Court's discretion arises where the question is more one of propriety than of powers.

This being said, the Court has nevertheless indicated that, as the principal judicial organ of the UN, its opinion on a legal question posed by an organ or Specialized Agency of the UN ought normally to be given when requested.

> But as the Court also said in the same Opinion [that is, *Interpretation of the Peace Treaties*, ICJ Reports, 1950, p. 72] 'the reply of the Court, itself an "organ of the United Nations", represents its participation in the activities of the Organisation, and, in principle, should not be refused' (*ibid.*, p. 71). Still more emphatically, in its Opinion of 23 October 1956, the Court said that only compelling reasons should lead it to refuse to give a requested advisory opinion (*Judgment of the Administrative Tribunal of the ILO upon complaints made against UNESCO*, ICJ Reports, 1956, p. 86).[20]

What is now suggested is that where the Court's analysis of the background to the request leads to the conclusion (a) that the 'legal question' posed is of minimal relevance to the real dispute, and (b) that the Court's opinion is likely to be ignored by those states that take a contrary position, and thus make little contribution to the solution of the dispute, the Court should decline to give an Opinion.

---

[17] Advisory Opinion of 30 March 1950, ICJ Reports, 1950, pp. 71–2.
[18] Advisory Opinion of 28 May 1951, ICJ Reports, 1951, p. 19.
[19] Advisory Opinion of 20 July 1962, ICJ Reports, 1962, p. 155.
[20] *Expenses of the UN*, Advisory Opinion of 20 July 1962, ICJ Reports, 1962, p. 155.

POSSIBILITIES FOR EXPANSION OF THE COURT'S RULE

Various possibilities for expansion of the Court's role have been mooted,[21] and several of these directly concern the Court's role in relation to international organisations.

The *Reparations* case[22] upheld the capacity of the UN to bring, and defend, international claims, and it is commonplace for the UN and other international organisations, in concluding agreements with states, to provide for arbitration of disputes arising from those agreements.[23] Under the 1982 Law of the Sea Convention an agency of the UN – the new Authority – is envisaged as having procedural capacity in disputes with states before the proposed Sea-bed Disputes Chamber of the Law of the Sea Tribunal.[24]

The need for settlement procedures is thus self-evident, and consideration has been given to the possibilities of using the Court to meet this need, either by extending the use of the Advisory Opinion or (a more radical proposal) by giving to the UN, and perhaps the Specialized Agencies, direct standing to sue, or be sued, as a party.

The further extension of the right to request Advisory Opinions

According this right to the Secretary-General

Although this idea has long been mooted, it may have its drawbacks. Certainly the Court's Opinion may be of direct relevance to the work of the Secretary-General – as in the *Reservations* case – but the argument for the grant of the power of request to the Secretary-General presupposes that neither the Security Council nor the General Assembly is prepared to make that request. In such circumstances it would seem highly likely that the Secretary-General lacks the political support, in the matter of making the request, of one or both main political organs. The grant of the power would therefore seem to

---

[21] See H. W. A. Thirlway, 'Advisory Opinions of International Courts', in R. Bernhardt (ed.), *Encyclopedia of Public International Law* (Amsterdam, 1981), vol. I, pp. 4–9. In 1970 the UN General Assembly solicited the view of states regarding the Court's role (Resolution 2723 XXV) and various suggestions are contained in these views: UN Doc. A/8382, agenda item 90, 26th Session (1971), paras. 263–305.

[22] ICJ Reports, 1949, p. 174.

[23] For arbitrations involving other organizations see *Commission of the European Atomic Energy Community v. UK Atomic Energy Authority* (Hambro, Sole Arbitrator, 25 February 1967), 44 *ILR* 409. And, of course, the European Community, represented by the Commission, is regularly involved in litigation before the Court of the European Communities. As for the UN itself, agreements such as headquarters agreements, or status of forces agreements relating to UN peacekeeping forces commonly provide for arbitration and/or claims commissions.

[24] Article 187.

heighten the risk of conflict between the Secretary-General and those main organs, and this may be too high a price to pay for the advantage gained.

According the right to states

The practice whereby states can seek Advisory Opinions is already accepted in the European Communities, the Court having the power to advise on the compatibility of any proposed treaty with a non-member state or international organization with the basic, Community treaties.[25]

The notion that states, parties to the Statute of the Court, might do this has its attractions, for states frequently face questions where they are unsure of the position under international law, and the newer, smaller states in particular may not have the experienced legal advisers in their Foreign Offices who can give the necessary advice with confidence.[26] But there could be drawbacks.

First, such a 'free legal advice' service might prove so attractive that it would greatly increase the Court's workload.[27] Second, the *Eastern Carelia* principle[28] would have to apply. If the question raised with the Court involved an actual, pending dispute with another state, it would be quite wrong for the Court to advise one party without hearing the other party, and receiving its consent.

The greater use of the 'compulsive' or 'binding' Advisory Opinion

The technique of giving to what is *prima facie* a purely Advisory Opinion a binding character, by allowing parties the facility to agree that the Opinion should have that character, in a separate instrument, is well established: its use was anticipated in section 30 of the 1946 UN Convention on Privileges and Immunities of the UN.[29] It is a technique that has been used in several treaties on privileges and immunities, headquarters agreements,[30] and other UN

---

[25] EEC Treaty, article 228(2).

[26] The power could even be vested in the Supreme Courts of member states, faced with a question of international law, when those courts would prefer an independent opinion rather than rely on the state's legal advisers.

[27] Certainly if, as now, the procedure remains broadly similar to that for contentious cases. Thirlway, 'Advisory Opinions', pp. 6–7 suggests the advisory procedure might be simplified and shortened.

[28] Above, text at note 11.

[29] 1 UNTS 15. But note that it has never been used for this purpose. The Advisory Opinion of 15 December 1989 (*Applicability of article XI, section 22 of the Convention on the Privileges and Immunities of the UN*), ICJ Reports, 1989, p. 177 was not based on section 30, because a dispute with Romania existed, and Romania had ratified the Convention with a reservation excluding recourse to the Court under section 30 in such a case. See R. Ago, 'Binding Advisory Opinions of the ICJ', *AJIL* 85 (1991), p. 439 at pp. 445–8.

[30] See Ago, 'Binding Advisory Opinions', p. 439, fn 2.

treaties and, of course, as part of the system under which the Court reviews judgments of Administrative tribunals.[31]

In all such cases the 'binding' character of the Opinion derives not from the Opinion, or the Court's Statute, but from some other instrument – whether it be a treaty, the Statute of an Administrative Tribunal, or the Staff Rules and Regulations.[32] Thus, in theory, the technique could be extended by adopting more instruments incorporating this device.

The wisdom of such an extension is, however, very questionable,[33] for it remains a device, the purpose of which is to alleviate, or compensate for, the lack of direct standing of international organizations before the Court.[34] It is high time that the problem was faced directly, and such standing conferred on international organizations.

The grant of *locus standi* to international organizations in contentious cases

Given that the UN and Specialized Agencies have the right to bring international claims, and do in fact both bring and defend claims, there seems little logic in refusing access to the Court and compelling these organizations to use arbitration as an alternative. The idea that the Court might be unsuitable because, as a UN organ, it would lack impartiality in disputes between a UN organ and a third party is not to be entertained seriously: the Court's independence has been demonstrated beyond question.

It could be left to each organization to specify the scope of the jurisdiction it accepted, by declarations similar to those made by states under the Optional Clause. It might be expected that they would exclude disputes relating to the internal functioning of the organization,[35] concentrating on claims connected with its external functions (the claims against the UN arising out of the Congo

---

[31] Ago's misgivings relate principally to this use, and centre on the interposition of a political body, the UN Committee on Review of Administrative Tribunal Judgments, in a judicial process.

[32] See Rosenne, *The Law and Practice of the International Court*, p. 682; Guillaume Bacot, 'Réflexions sur les clauses qui rendent obligatoires les avis consultatifs de la CPIJ et de la CIJ', *RGDIP*, 84 (1980), p. 1027; Ago, 'Binding Advisory Opinions', pp. 440–2. The views of P. Benvenuti, *L'Accertmento del diritto mediante i pareri consutivi della Corte Internationale di Gustizia* (Milan, 1985), pp. 55ff. go further, in assimilating an Opinion more to a judgment but, as Ago shows (pp. 442–4), this is not the Court's own view.

[33] See Ago's conclusions, 'Binding Advisory Opinions', pp. 449–51.

[34] See Christian Dominicé, 'Le Reglement juridictionnel du contentieux externe des organisations internationales', in *Mélanges Michel Virally, Le Droit International au Service de la Paix, de la Justice et du Développement* (Paris, 1991), pp. 225–38 at p. 234.

[35] Dominicé, 'La Reglement juridictionnel', p. 235. And see, generally, Lauterpacht, *Aspects of the Administration of International Justice*, pp. 60–6.

operations are a good example). Whether the Court is to become an organ of judicial review is a separate question, considered below, which ought not to be decided by too broad an acceptance of jurisdiction.

Moreover, the handling of any new capacity to appear before the Court would require careful consideration.[36] Which organ or organs would initiate an application to the Court? Who would control the actual conduct of litigation: the legal counsel or the organ authorizing the application? Would the UN's commitment to be bound by any judgment require an amendment of article 94? Such questions would require careful study before any organization would be in a position to accept procedural capacity in contentious cases.

The grant of powers of judicial review in relation to decisions of international organizations

The Court may necessarily have to discuss, and decide upon (or opine upon), the validity of resolutions, acts or decisions of the organs of international organizations in the course of giving judgment in a contentious case, or rendering an Advisory Opinion. It is in this context that, in its jurisprudence so far, the Court has given to such organs the benefit of an initial presumption of legality.[37]

But, as the Court itself noted in the *Expenses* case,[38] this is not the same thing as giving to member states a direct right of challenge to the validity of the acts of UN organs.

The current case for providing the Court with a direct power of judicial review rests on three considerations. The first is the quite general proposition that, in most democratic societies, governmental (and sometimes legislative) acts are reviewable by the established courts so as to ensure that they are valid under the constitution. And, if this is generally deemed desirable in a democratic system, the question must be posed: why not in the UN? The second is that, with the termination of the cold war, the political balance implicit in the East–West rivalry has been removed, so that the Security Council can now operate without political or legal controls.[39] And the third is that, where such

---

[36] See D. W. Bowett *AJIL* 86 (1992), pp. 342–3.

[37] E.g. *Certain Expenses of the UN etc.*, Advisory Opinion of 29 July 1962, ICJ Reports, 1962, at p. 168; *Legal Consequences for States etc.*, Advisory Opinion of 21 June 1971, ICJ Reports, 1971, at p. 22; *Case Concerning Questions of Interpretation etc.* (the Lockerbie case), Order of 14 April 1992, ICJ Reports, 1992, p. 3, para. 42.

[38] ICJ Reports, 1962, at p. 168.

[39] M. Bedjaoui, 'Du contrôle de légalité des actes du Conseil de Sécurité', *Nouveaux itinéraires en droit: Hommage à François Rigaux* (Brussels, 1993), at pp. 72–5.

organs are not plenary organs, the states not represented on them need some means to ensure that what is done in their name is constitutional.[40] This concern has been heightened by the Court's recent order in the *Lockerbie* case, in which the Court suggests that a Security Council decision is not only binding, under article 25, but by virtue of article 103 prevails over any other treaty obligation.[41]

It must be conceded that there are few signs that, at present, the members of the Security Council are prepared to contemplate judicial review by the Court: the Western powers would see this as a hindrance and neither Russia nor China display any great confidence in the Court. But in the long-term interests of the UN the idea is worth pursuing.

The objection that this would invite the Court to question the Council's political judgement, or discretion, is not compelling.[42] Most legal systems have a tradition of judicial abstention from 'political questions', and it should not be expected that the Court would attempt to substitute its political judgement for that of the Security Council. Nor would it be right to allow the Court to challenge decisions for mere procedural irregularities,[43] absent a denial of any hearing to a state subsequently condemned to suffer some sanction or penalty: for organs must remain the masters of their own procedures, and remedies for abuse ought to be found in means internal to the Organization. A more substantial criticism is that the Council needs to act speedily, whereas the Court's procedure is long and cumbersome. But in fact the Court has, on

---

[40] But there has been equal concern over the risk that, in a plenary body such as the Assembly, the majority will ride roughshod over the minority and ignore constitutional restraints on the powers of the plenary body: see L. Gross, 'Voting in the Security Council and the PLO', *AJIL* 70 (1976), pp. 470–1; and, less critically, Ebere Osieke, 'The Legal Validity of Ultra Vires Decisions of International Organizations', *AJIL* 77 (1983), p. 239, at pp. 250–1.

[41] Order of 14 April 1992, ICJ Reports, 1992, p. 3, para. 42. With respect, this view seems to be wrong. Article 103 asserts the primacy of Charter treaty obligations. A Council decision ought not to be assimilated to a treaty obligation. It is the Council's task to specify the consequences for states of their Charter obligations, and whereas these obligations may prevail it does not follow that a decision *per se* does. For if the Council were to decide that an obligation existed for a member state which was not warranted by, or implicit in, the pre-existing Charter obligations, that decision could be resisted. The Security Council is not a legislative body. This is the fallacy in the argument of David D. Caron, 'The Legitimacy of the Collective Authority of the Security Council' *AJIL*, 87 (1993), at p. 552.

[42] Although Giorgio Gaja, 'Reflexions sur le rôle du Conseil de Sécurité dans le nouvel ordre mondial' *RGDIP*, 99 (1993), at p. 318 argues for a more precise, and limiting, definition of a threat to the peace under article 39 of the Charter.

[43] But see I. Brownlie in R. StJ. MacDonald (ed.), 'The Decisions of Political Organs of the United Nations and the Rule of Law', *Essays in Honour of Professor Wang Teiya* (Dordrecht, 1993), chap. 6, who at pp. 94–5 argues that decisions should be reviewable for procedural fairness, citing the *Interpretation of the Treaty of Lausanne (Iraq Boundary)*, PCIJ, Series B, No. 12 (1925), pp. 31–2.

occasions, acted quickly,[44] and it is not beyond question that the Court might take further steps to ensure a speedy response.[45]

If these objections can be met, as it is believed they can, a limited number of grounds ought, in principle, to be accepted: decisions that are *ultra vires*, or that deny a state penalized by the Court (or any organ) a right to a hearing, or are manifestly defective – for example, when based upon an error of fact, or an error of law – should in principle be set aside.

There is therefore much to be done in considering how the Court's role could be strengthened in relation to international organizations. The experience of the past half century is barely satisfactory, and the fault lies not with the Court, but rather with the reluctance of states to see its role expanded. To explain this reluctance in terms of a lack of confidence in the Court is wrong. It implies the fault may lie with the Court. Yet, surveying the Court's record, there is little to justify such a lack of confidence. Setting aside the aberration over South West Africa in 1966,[46] the Court's record, objectively assessed, justifies confidence rather than lack of confidence. So a reluctance to expand its role is more probably based on the marked preference by some states to pursue their national policies unfettered by legal restraints. Yet the purposes of the UN embrace the settlement of disputes 'in conformity with the principles of justice and international law'. It may be time to remind member states of that commitment.

---

[44] Bedjaoui, 'Du contrôle de legalité', pp. 102–3 cites the Court's speedy reaction in the *Hostages* case, and the *Burkina-Faso/Mali Frontier Dispute* as examples.

[45] The use of Chambers is not the answer. For purposes of judicial review the Court would need the authority of the full Court.

[46] *South West Africa (Second Phase)*, judgment, ICJ Reports, 1966, at p. 6.

11

Cases of the International Court of Justice relating to employment in international organizations

C. F. Amerasinghe

ℰℐ

There are five Advisory Opinions[1] rendered by the International Court of Justice in cases pertaining to employment relations in international organizations. They were all Opinions requested either by the UN or UNESCO in connection with the operation of the UN Administrative Tribunal (UNAT) and the ILO Administrative Tribunal (ILOAT) respectively. The first Opinion given in 1954 was the result of a general reference by the UN General Assembly and concerned some basic questions regarding the UNAT. The other four were requests for review of decisions given in cases decided by the UNAT and the ILOAT in disputes between staff members and their organizations.

In the *Effect of Awards* case the General Assembly of the UN requested, under its general power to request Opinions, an Opinion on matters of law relating to the work of the General Assembly. The Opinion embodies rulings on some very important issues of law relating to employment relations and also discussed some general questions relating to that relationship.

In international organizations an executive or deliberative organ may initially rule on an employment dispute. There is generally no constitutional provision authorizing such a person or organ to settle the dispute. Nevertheless, such administrative settlement has been the prevailing procedure, in general at least for preliminary purposes, in all international organizations. Thus there can be no serious doubt that the executive or deliberative organs

---

[1] The *Effect of Awards of Compensation made by the UN Administrative Tribunal* case, ICJ Reports, 1954, p. 47 (hereafter the *Effect of Awards* case); the *Judgments of the Administrative Tribunal of the ILO* case, ICJ Reports, 1956, p. 77 (hereafter the *Judgments of the ILOAT* case); the *Application for Review of Judgment No. 158 of the UNAT* case, ICJ Reports, 1973, p. 166 (hereafter the *Judgment No. 158* case); the *Application for Review of Judgment No. 273 of the UNAT* case, ICJ Reports, 1982, p. 325 (hereafter the *Judgment No. 273* case); the *Application for Review of Judgment No. 333 of the UNAT* case, ICJ Reports, 1987, p. 18 (hereafter referred to as the *Judgment No. 333* case).

of the organization are entitled to decide these internal disputes themselves as, indeed, executive organs do in national states. This position was amply supported by the ICJ in its Advisory Opinion in the *Effect of Awards* case, where it stated that:

> In the absence of the establishment of an Administrative Tribunal, the function of resolving disputes between staff and Organization could be discharged by the Secretary General by virtue of the provisions of Articles 97 and 101. Accordingly, in the three years or more preceding the establishment of the Administrative Tribunal, the Secretary General coped with this problem by means of joint administrative machinery, leading to ultimate decision by himself.[2]

Neither article 97 nor article 101 of the Charter expressly authorized the Secretary-General to involve himself in the settlement of disputes between staff and the organization in employment-related matters. It is only by the application of a doctrine of implied powers that such a power can be deduced from these articles. Insofar as the power to settle disputes in employment-related matters was necessary for the Secretary-General to achieve the highest standards of efficiency, competence and integrity, it is functionally related to the requirements of article 101.

It has been suggested that the power of the Secretary-General of the UN or, indeed, the executive head of any international organization, to decide internal disputes relating to employment matters exists irrespective of such express provisions as those cited by the Court.[3] This view is based on the theory that an international organization has certain inherent powers or capacities by virtue of the fact that it has an international personality, albeit of a unique character.[4] Suffice it to say that, particularly since the issue involved concerns jurisdiction over internal organs of an organization, the theory may be an adequate foundation upon which to base the powers of the administrative head or other organ of an international organization to settle internal employment disputes.[5]

As pointed out by the ICJ in the passage quoted above, the Secretary-General of the UN dealt with the settlement of employment disputes by means of joint administrative machinery. Indeed, he continues to do so. In most organizations the administrative head of the institution has set up some

---

[2] ICJ Reports, 1954, p. 47, at p. 61.

[3] Finn Seyersted, 'Settlement of Internal Disputes of Intergovernmental Organizations by Internal and External Courts', *ZAOR*, 24 (1964), p. 1, at pp. 78–9.

[4] See Finn Seyersted, 'United Nations Forces: Some Legal Problems', *BYbIL*, 37 (1961), p. 351, at pp. 453ff. The ICJ has held that international organizations have international personality: *Reparation for Certain Injuries Suffered in the Service of the United Nations*, ICJ Reports, 1949, p. 174 at pp. 178–9.

[5] See Seyersted, 'Settlement of Internal Disputes', at pp. 9–10.

kind of advisory board or committee to examine disputes and advise him before he takes a decision in the process of settling the dispute in question. Thus, in the UN there is a Joint Appeals Board and in the World Bank there is an Appeals Committee to which complainants take their cases and which advise the administration after investigating disputes. These bodies give advisory opinions to the executive organ which takes the decisions.

The ICJ has also ruled on the power of organizations to establish International Administrative Tribunals (IATs). In the view of the ICJ the General Assembly of the UN had the power to establish an Administrative Tribunal. In the *Effect of Awards* case the Court explained the reasons for its conclusion at length and justified it as follows:

> When the Secretariat was organized, a situation arose in which the relations between the staff members and the Organisation were governed by a complex code of law. This code consisted of the Staff Regulations established by the General Assembly, defining the fundamental rights and obligations of the staff, and the Staff Rules, made by the Secretary General in order to implement the Staff Regulations. It was inevitable that there would be disputes between the Organization and staff members as to their rights and duties. The Charter contains no provision which authorizes any of the principal organs of the United Nations to adjudicate upon these disputes and Article 105 secures for the United Nations jurisdictional immunities in national courts. It would, in the opinion of the Court, hardly be consistent with the expressed aim of the Charter to promote freedom and justice for individuals and with the constant preoccupation of the United Nations Organization to promote this aim that it should afford no judicial or arbitral remedy to its own staff for the settlement of any disputes which may arise between it and them.
>
> In these circumstances, the Court finds that the power to establish a tribunal, to do justice as between the Organization and the staff members, was essential to ensure the efficient working of the Secretariat, and to give effect to the paramount consideration of securing the highest standards of efficiency, competence and integrity. Capacity to do this arises by necessary intendment out of the Charter.[6]

The Court based its conclusion clearly on the principle discussed above, namely that the organization must be deemed to have those powers that, though not expressly provided in the constituent instrument, were conferred on it by necessary implication as being essential to the performance of its duties.[7]

It is of importance that the ICJ in the *Effect of Awards* case took the view that the UN had the authority to establish a true judicial organ with independence

---

[6] ICJ Reports, 1949, p. 47 at p. 57.

[7] *Ibid.*, at p. 56, citing the *Reparations for Injuries* case, ICJ Reports, 1949, p. 174, at p. 182.

and the capacity to give binding decisions like any court of a national state. The Administrative Tribunal set up by the UN was not a subordinate organ of the General Assembly of the UN exercising delegated powers. The argument that the Tribunal was subordinate to the General Assembly which could not be bound by its judgments was rejected by the Court.[8] The conclusion reached was that the UN had authority to create a judicial body, namely an Administrative Tribunal, which could decide disputes relating to employment and could bind the organization, including the principal organ of the organization which created it, namely the General Assembly.

It is also of significance that the Court in its Advisory Opinion expressed the view that, though provision could be made by the General Assembly which had established the Tribunal for the review of future judgments of the Administrative Tribunal (which in any case would be binding, until thus reviewed), as it had not been done up to that time,

> the General Assembly itself, in view of its composition and functions, could hardly act as a judicial organ – considering the arguments of the parties, appraising the evidence produced by them, establishing the facts and declaring the law applicable to them – all the more so as one party to the disputes is the United Nations Organization itself.[9]

This confirms the position that the Administrative Tribunal was a judicial organ whose judgments could only be reviewed by another body of a judicial nature, the creation of such organs to settle disputes in the field of employment relations being well within the powers of the organization. The mere fact that the deliberative and legislative organ of the organization created such bodies did not result in the former having control over them as subsidiary organs. They may be 'subsidiary', but not 'subordinate'.

It may be noted that it was not the burden of the ICJ's argument that the provisions of article 101 of the Charter were necessary to give the UN the authority to establish an Administrative Tribunal in the form in which it was established. The Court clearly used the express provisions of that article to buttress its reasoning. More basic was the notion of essentiality for the performance of its duties or functions. In this connection, it is significant that, though the League of Nations and the International Institute of Agriculture did not have provisions in their constitutions like article 101 of the UN Charter, they both established Administrative Tribunals without having their authority to do so ever questioned. In fact in the case of the International

---

[8] See ICJ Reports, 1954, p. 47, at p. 61.   [9] *Ibid.*, at p. 56.

Institute of Agriculture the Italian Court of Cassation, in a case decided two years before the Administrative Tribunal of that organization was established, pointed out that the League of Nations had already set up a Tribunal and that the Institute ought to do likewise, without doubting the competence of either to set up Tribunals.[10]

The jurisdiction of International Administrative Tribunals is exercised against the organization and not against an individual or the head of the organization, as the case may be, although sometimes the claims are nominally filed against the head of the organization, such as the Secretary–General. This principle emerges clearly from the decision of the ICJ in the *Effect of Awards* case. In this case, which concerned the UN, the Court stated:

> If he [the Secretary-General] terminates the contract of service without the assent of the staff member and this action results in a dispute which is referred to the Administrative Tribunal, the parties to this dispute before the Tribunal are the staff member concerned and the United Nations Organisation, represented by the Secretary General, and these parties will become bound by the judgment of the Tribunal.[11]

The judgments of International Administrative Tribunals are final and binding.[12] Indeed, the fact that these decisions are binding makes them judicial in nature. Even if their Statutes do not state that their decisions are binding, by the very nature of IATs and because of the purpose for which they have been set up, their decisions are regarded as binding.[13] In regard to the UNAT, it is significant that the ICJ in the *Effect of Awards* case, in connection with the nature of the UNAT and its decisions, stated:

> This examination of the relevant provisions of the Statute shows that the Tribunal is established, not as an advisory organ or a mere subordinate committee of the General Assembly, but as an independent and truly judicial body pronouncing final judgments without appeal within the limited field of its functions. According to a well-established and generally recognized principle of law, a judgment rendered by such a judicial body is *res judicata* and has binding force between the parties to the dispute.[14]

Later the ICJ stated in the same case that:

---

10 See *International Institute of Agriculture v. Profili*, 5 *ILR*, 413 (1931), Case No. 254.

11 ICJ Reports, 1954, p. 47, at p. 53.

12 See, e.g., the UNAT Statute, article 10.2; the ILOAT Statute, article VI.1; the WBAT Statute, article XI.1.

13 For example, the Statutes of the OECD Appeals Board (article 8(b)), and the Appeals Board of the Council of Europe (article 12.2), merely state that there shall be no appeals from decisions.

14 ICJ Reports, 1954, p. 47, at p. 53.

The parties to this dispute before the Tribunal are the staff member concerned and the United Nations Organization represented by the Secretary General, and these parties will become bound by the judgment of the Tribunal. This judgment is, according to Article 10 of the Tribunal's Statute, final and without appeal. The Statute has provided for no kind of review. As this final judgment has binding force on the United Nations Organization as the juridical person responsible for the proper observance of the contract of service, that Organization becomes legally bound to carry out the judgment and to pay the compensation awarded to the staff member. It follows that the General Assembly, as an organ of the United Nations, must likewise be bound by the judgment.[15]

The ICJ also confirmed that this meant that the UN could not refuse on any ground to execute the judgments of the UNAT.[16] What was said by the ICJ in regard to the UNAT and its judgments is clearly applicable, *mutatis mutandis*, to the judgments of other IATs, as far as the binding and final nature of their decisions is concerned.

Several Tribunals and the ICJ have made the point that employment in most organizations was on the basis of a contract. In the *Effect of Awards* case, the ICJ made statements to the effect that employees of the UN had contracts of service with the UN:

It must therefore be examined who are to be regarded as parties bound by an award of compensation made in favour of a staff member of the United Nations whose *contract of service* has been terminated without his assent.

Such a *contract of service* is concluded between the staff member concerned and the Secretary General in his capacity as the chief administrative officer of the United Nations Organization, acting on behalf of the organization as its representative. When the Secretary General concludes such a *contract of service* with a staff

---

[15] *Ibid.*

[16] 'The General Assembly has not the right on any grounds to refuse to give effect to an award of compensation made by the Administrative Tribunal of the United Nations in favor of a staff member of the United Nations whose contract of service has been terminated without his assent' (*ibid.*, at p. 62). Some Statutes explicitly state, in one way or another, that judgments of Tribunals must be carried out by the organizations: see, e.g., article XII.3 of the WBAT Statute. The view taken by the Assembly of the League of Nations was different from that taken by the ICJ. In adopting the conclusions of a report of a subcommittee of its Second Committee which were based more on 'what was politic and right' rather than on what was in accordance with strict law, the Assembly decided that it was like a sovereign legislature, could retroactively annul judgments of the LNT by legislation and, therefore, was under no obligation to execute the judgments of the LNT. The Assembly of the League of Nations took this decision after the judgments in *Mayras* etc., LNT Judgments Nos. 24 to 36 [1946], cases which were connected with the dissolution of the League of Nations. The episode is dealt with in M. Akehurst, *The Law Governing Employment in International Organizations* (Cambridge, 1967), pp. 210ff. The conclusion of the Assembly of the League of Nations cannot be regarded as reflecting the correct legal position, particularly in the light of the judgment of the ICJ in the *Effect of Awards* case.

member, he engages the legal responsibility of the Organization which is the juridical person on whose behalf he acts.[17]

The ICJ, in the *Effect of Awards* case, referred to the Charter as giving the General Assembly authority to establish the UNAT with power to render judgments which were final and without appeal.[18] However, while this is an indirect admission that the Charter is a source of law in employment relations in the UN, the Court did not pronounce on what the position would be if there was a conflict between the Charter and such sources of law as the Staff Regulations, or on whether the Charter could be applied, if appropriate, where there was a lacuna in such written law.

The ICJ has indicated in the *Effect of Awards* case that an IAT may not award compensation in excess of the maximum specified in its Statute.[19]

Although the power of international organizations to legislate as such in respect of their staff whose employment was initially based on contract, in particular, was not clearly admitted in the early days of the League of Nations,[20] it is now generally conceded that international organizations do have such a power. Not only did the ICJ in the *Effect of Awards* case describe the General Assembly of the UN as 'an authority exercising a power to make regulations' and state that the General Assembly could amend the Staff regulations and make new ones,[21] but many of the states and organizations that submitted Pleadings in the *Effect of Awards* case were of the opinion that the General Assembly of the UN had a legislative power over the staff of the UN, although this power was a limited one.[22]

It is also generally admitted that organizations have in principle the power to change or amend the rules governing the employment relationship with the result that such amendments apply to staff members employed before their adoption. Granted the power to make rules governing the employment relationship, it has been said by the UNAT: 'This power to adopt general provisions implies in principle the right to amend the rules established.'[23] In *de Merode*, the WBAT stated: 'It is a well-established legal principle that the

[17] ICJ Reports, 1954, p. 47, at p. 53 (emphasis added).

[18] *Ibid.*, at p. 57.

[19] *Ibid.*, at p. 54.

[20] See the statement by the Secretary-General of the League of Nations at the time of the institution of the LNT in 1927, where it was said that legislative acts became applicable to staff only by virtue of their contracts of employment: see *Judgments of the ILOAT Case:* Pleadings, Oral Arguments and Documents, International Court of Justice (1956), at p. 91.

[21] ICJ Reports, 1954, p. 47, at p. 61.

[22] See *Effect of Awards Case: Pleadings, Oral Arguments and Documents*, International Court of Justice (1954), pp. 30–2, 103, 106, 110, 113, 258, 307, 309–10, 313, 340, 343–4, 353, 368–9, 372–83.

[23] *Puvrez*, UNAT Judgment No. 82 (1961) (ICAO), JUNAT Nos. 71–86, p. 78 at p. 85.

power to make rules implies in principle the right to amend them. This power flows from the responsibilities of the competent authorities of the Bank.'[24]

The ICJ stated, in reference to the present article 13 of the Statute of the UNAT which was made part of the Staff Regulations, that the General Assembly of the UN had power to amend the Statute of the UNAT by virtue of that article and to provide for means of redress by another organ.[25] Clearly, the ICJ did not import any limitations into the power of amendment given by this article, as it was of the view that the UN could go to the extent of abolishing the UNAT, if it desired so to do.

Perhaps the only way to reconcile the view of the ICJ that the Statute of the UNAT may be amended with the view taken by the OASAT that an open-ended amendment clause is subject to certain limitations[26] is by interpreting the statement of the ICJ made in the *Effect of Awards* case as applying only to the case of the UNAT Statute. It is to be noted that the ICJ did not say explicitly that any amendment to the Statute should not be retroactive or affect the rights of staff members that had already vested but neither did it deny that amendments should not have this effect. Indeed, it is possible for the ICJ in future to say without fear of contradiction that its statement was not intended to permit retroactive amendments or amendments that would affect vested rights, such as those that staff members who had already filed applications with the Tribunal would have. The statement must, however, be taken to mean that the ICJ did not regard the Statute as creating *per se* an acquired right or rights which under any theory of limitations could not be taken away from the staff by amendment.

The other four cases in which Opinions were given by the ICJ were cases referred to it by the General Assembly of the UN or by UNESCO under provisions permitting the ICJ to review decisions of the UNAT and the ILOAT.

The Statute of the UNAT permits reference to the ICJ on the ground that the Tribunal has (i) exceeded its jurisdiction or competence; or (ii) failed to exercise jurisdiction vested in it; or (iii) erred on a question of law relating to the provisions of the UN Charter; or (iv) committed a fundamental error in procedure which has caused a failure of justice. The case must now be referred to the ICJ for an Advisory Opinion by a Committee which examines written applications to it by a member state of the UN, the Secretary-General or the

---

[24] WBAT Reports (1981), Decision No. 1 at p. 15. See also *Effect of Awards* case, ICJ Reports, 1954, p. 47, at p. 61.

[25] *Effect of Awards* case, ICJ Reports, 1954, p. 47, at p. 56.

[26] See *Comolli*, OASAT Judgment No. 17 (1975); *Ryan and Others*, OASAT Judgment No. 35 (1978).

person in respect of whom a judgment has been rendered. The Committee is for all intents and purposes appointed by the General Assembly of the UN. The Statute of the ILOAT permits reference of a judgment of the ILOAT to the ICJ for an Advisory Opinion where the Governing Body of the ILO or the Administrative Branch of the Pension Fund challenges such judgment confirming the jurisdiction of the ILOAT or considers that the judgment is vitiated by a fundamental fault in the procedure followed.

Thus far the review has unsuccessfully been requested in three judgments rendered by the UNAT and one rendered by the ILOAT. In the *Judgment No. 158* case[27] the decision of the UNAT in *Fasla*[28] was questioned on the grounds that (i) the UNAT had not exercised the jurisdiction vested in it; and (ii) there had been a fundamental error of procedure which occasioned a failure of justice. The ICJ found that none of the contentions were proven. In the *Judgment No. 273* case[29] the question related to the effect of a General Assembly resolution pertaining to repatriation grants upon which the UNAT had pronounced in *Mortished*.[30] The ICJ interpreted the question as requiring it to determine whether the UNAT had exceeded its jurisdiction or competence or had erred on a question of law relating to the provisions of the Charter. On both questions the ICJ found in the negative. In the *Judgment No. 333* case[31] the questions related to (i) whether the UNAT had not exercised jurisdiction vested in it; or (ii) whether the UNAT had erred on questions of law relating to provisions of the Charter in *Yakimetz*.[32] The case concerned the failure to extend the employment of the applicant. The ICJ in answering both questions found that the UNAT had acted properly.

The *Judgments of the ILOAT* case[33] concerned the jurisdiction of the ILOAT to determine certain questions which arose in connection with several cases brought against UNESCO relating to the non-renewal of fixed-term contracts. The ICJ held that the ILOAT had acted properly in exercising jurisdiction in regard to all these questions.

As is apparent, the ICJ is not a court of appeal from IATs but exercises limited functions of review. The Court has spent a great deal of time, particularly in the three Opinions relating to cases decided by the UNAT, explaining the nature and limits of its jurisdiction as a court of review, though in no instance has it refused to accept jurisdiction over the issues presented to

---

[27] ICJ Reports, 1973, p. 166.
[28] UNAT Judgment No. 158 (1972), JUNAT Nos. 114–66, p. 355.
[29] ICJ Reports, 1982, p. 325.
[30] UNAT Judgment No. 283 (1981), JUNAT Nos. 230–300, p. 426.
[31] ICJ Reports, 1987, p. 18.
[32] UNAT Judgment No. 333 (1984).   [33] ICJ Reports, 1956, p. 77.

it. Further, in all four cases it found that the IATs had acted properly in terms of the issues raised before it. However, what is important in the Advisory Opinions is not so much the positive conclusions reached on the issues referred to the Court but what the Court had to say in the course of arriving at these conclusions on international administrative law, particularly as applied by these Tribunals. The contribution made by the ICJ lies in this area, while it must be recognized that as the Court has repeatedly said, it does not examine the merits of the cases before the IATs or substitute its judgment on the merits for that of the IATs.

By far the most important case was the *Judgments of the ILOAT* case. There the Court, among other things, asserted categorically that the ILOAT was an international tribunal,[34] although it decided internal disputes of international organizations.

The Court had something to say on the sources of law particularly in relation to statutory provisions. Article II of the ILOAT Statute was in issue. The *Judgments of the ILOAT* case was directly concerned with the competence of the ILOAT in certain cases involving UNESCO. The argument made by the applicant staff members was that they had a right to renewal of their fixed-term contracts, because an administrative memorandum which was complementary to their contracts and the Staff Regulations gave them such a right. On the issue of the Tribunal's jurisdiction the Court formulated the question as whether the ILOAT was entitled to find that there existed before it a complaint sufficient to bring it within the scope of the applicants' 'terms of appointment' or the 'Staff Regulations'.[35] It was held that since the applicants' case rested on the content of an administrative memorandum, the basic argument of the applicants that their terms of appointment had been violated had some serious juridical basis and, therefore the Tribunal had jurisdiction. This was so, even though the actual contracts of employment stated something contrary to what the administrative memorandum provided.

While the main issue before the Court was one of competence, implied in the approach taken by the Court is a pronouncement on the sources of law. Insofar as the Court stated that the reference to the administrative memorandum was a sufficient juridical basis for the argument that the applicants' terms of appointment had been violated, it accepted the administrative memorandum as a source of law, even though, as it happened, it was in contradiction to the explicit provisions of the applicants' contracts of appointment.

---

[34] *Ibid.*, at p. 97.
[35] These are the sources of law referred to in the Statute (article II).

Some conclusions may be drawn from the above inference. First, it is clear that the Court did not take a restrictive view of the sources of law based on the express wording of article II of the Statute of the ILOAT. Administrative memoranda are nowhere mentioned in the provisions of article II, yet the Court regarded them as a source of law. Second, it is not certain whether the Court was interpreting the words of article II to refer to sources of law. In saying that the applicants' reference to the administrative memorandum gave their argument a sufficient juridical basis, because they were advancing a genuine claim that their terms of appointment had been violated, the Court was not necessarily also saying that article II, in addition to dealing with competence, referred to all the sources of law that would be relevant in determining whether there had been a non-observance of the terms of appointment of the applicants. It is perfectly compatible with the Court's view that the resolution of the issue as to whether the terms of appointment of the applicants had not been observed should depend on sources of law to be selected by the Tribunal and should not flow from an interpretation of the words 'terms of appointment' in article II.

The ICJ, it may be noted, also acknowledged in the same case that administrative practice could be a source of the internal law of an organization governing employment relations. It said:

> The fact is that there has developed in this matter a body of practice to the effect that holders of fixed-term contracts . . . have often been treated as entitled to be considered for continued employment . . . in a manner transcending the strict wording of the contract . . . The practice as here surveyed is a relevant factor in the interpretation of the contracts in question. It lends force to the view that there may be circumstances in which the non-renewal of a fixed-term contract provides a legitimate ground for complaint.[36]

The Court recognized that the practice in UNESCO of treating fixed-term contract holders as being entitled to be considered for renewal of their contracts was a source of law, even though it was categorically in contradiction to the provisions both of the contracts themselves and the Staff Regulations which stated that upon expiry the contracts came to an end without prospects of renewal.

The Court recognized that the ILOAT (like other IATs) was a court of limited jurisdiction (*jurisdiction d'attribution*) and not one of general jurisdiction (*jurisdiction de droit commun*).[37]

In *Duberg* the ILOAT had confirmed its jurisdiction to hear complaints

---

[36] *Ibid.*, at p. 91.   [37] *Ibid.*, at p. 97.

brought by officials of UNESCO concerning the validity of decisions not to renew their fixed-term contracts.[38] Staff Rule 104.6 of UNESCO at that time stated that 'a fixed-term appointment shall expire, without notice or indemnity, upon completion of the fixed-term'. The Tribunal interpreted this text as dealing only with the duration of the contract and concluded that it in no way barred the Tribunal from assuming jurisdiction over a complaint requesting that the legality of the positive or negative decision taken by the administrative authority relating to the renewal of such a contract be examined. The ICJ was called upon to pronounce on the question whether the ILOAT had exceeded its jurisdiction in those cases in which the ILOAT had decided that it had jurisdiction. The ICJ held that the ILOAT had not exceeded its jurisdiction in declaring those cases admissible, irrespective of the latter's decision on the merits.[39] The reasoning of the ICJ took into account the fact that UNESCO had issued an administrative memorandum which was law-creating and thereby promised to a certain category of staff members the renewal of their fixed-term contracts subject to their fulfilling certain requirements. On the basis of this memorandum the ICJ held that the claim that the fixed-term contracts should have been renewed was more than a mere allegation and gave rise to a genuine dispute of a legal nature based on a contractual offer and relating to the terms of employment of the staff members. The ICJ also found that the position of a holder of a fixed-term contract who had not had his contract renewed was not the same as that of an applicant for a new appointment in the organization who had no *locus standi* before the Tribunal, and hence the Tribunal did have jurisdiction over such a person.

Agreeing with the ILOAT,[40] the ICJ held that applicants for new appointments who failed to obtain them could not be regarded as staff members.[41] This was so as contrasted with holders of fixed-term contracts who were claiming renewals or conversions and who, the ICJ said, could rightly be considered former staff members who had standing to litigate before the ILOAT. The ICJ, in interpreting the Staff Regulations and Staff Rules of UNESCO, stated[42] that a fixed-term contract was renewable which implied that renewal constituted a further stage of a former contract. Thus, it said, there was established a link between renewal and the original contract and the position on the expiration of his contract of the holder of such a contract was

---

[38] ILOAT Judgment No. 17 (1953) (UNESCO).

[39] ICJ Reports, 1956, p. 77, at p. 95.

[40] *Chen (No. 2)*, ILOAT Judgment No. 347 (1983) (WHO), at p. 3.

[41] ICJ Reports, 1956, p. 77, at p. 92.   [42] *Ibid.*, at p. 93.

not identical with that of an applicant for a new position who had failed to obtain it.

In the same case the Court held[43] that, in order that the ILOAT have competence *ratione materiae*, it is necessary that the complaint should indicate some genuine relationship between the complaint and the provisions invoked but that it is not required that the facts alleged should necessarily lead to the results alleged by the applicants, which is a matter for decision on the merits. On the other hand, it was insufficient that an artificial or remote connection be established between the facts of the claim and the rules alleged to have been infringed.

The Court also subscribed to the view that, because the precise determination of the actual amount of compensation to be awarded cannot be based on any specific rule of law, what international administrative tribunals do is to fix the true measure of compensation and the reasonable figure of such compensation.[44]

While many Statutes of IATs state that judgments should be reasoned,[45] the ICJ made it clear in the *Judgment No. 158* case that it is the essence of judicial decisions that judgments must be reasoned,[46] so that even in the absence of an express requirement, this condition would have to be satisfied. The Court explained what this meant. While stating that failure to give a reasoned judgment could result in an error of procedure, and that a statement of reasons is necessary for the validity of a judgment of an International Administrative Tribunal, it examined the question of what form and degree of reasoning will satisfy that requirement and concluded:

> The applicant appears to assume that, for a judgment to be adequately reasoned, every particular plea has to be discussed and reasons given for upholding or rejecting each one. But neither practice nor principle warrants so rigorous an interpretation of the rule, which appears generally to be understood as simply requiring that a judgment shall be supported by a stated process of reasoning. This statement must indicate in a general way the reasoning upon which the judgment is based; but it need not enter meticulously into every claim and contention on either side. While a judicial organ is obliged to pass upon all the formal submissions made by a party, it is not obliged, in framing its judgment, to develop its reasoning in the form of a detailed examination of each of the various heads of claim submitted. Nor are there any obligatory forms or techniques for drawing up judgments; a tribunal may employ direct or indirect reasoning, and state specific or

---

[43] *Ibid.*, at p. 89.
[44] *Ibid.*, at p. 100.
[45] See, e.g., UNAT Statute article 10.3; WBAT Statute article XII.2; ILOAT Statute article VI.2.
[46] ICJ Reports, 1973, p. 166, at p. 210.

merely implied conclusions, provided that the reasons on which the judgment is based are apparent. The question whether a judgment is so deficient in reasoning as to amount to a denial of the right to a fair hearing and a failure of justice, is therefore one which necessarily has to be appreciated in the light both of the particular case and of the judgment as a whole.[47]

It is of interest that the WBAT in a decision given on an application for review adopted this explanation in full.[48]

The Court in the same case was of the view that a tribunal was under no obligation to investigate or examine *proprio motu* a plea that had not been made, even though the subject matter was within its competence.[49] The Court did not say that the plea, if not made, would be outside the jurisdiction of the Tribunal. Thus, it may or may not examine the plea without committing a procedural error.

The ICJ said of the UNAT's power to award costs: 'Although not expressly empowered by its Statute to award costs, the Tribunal did so in some of its early cases on the basis of what it considered to be an inherent power.'[50] The Court did not disagree with the action taken by the Tribunal, while at the same time noting that the Tribunal had set itself a policy in regard to the award of costs since the early cases and that the UN Secretariat had established a Panel of Counsel in disciplinary and appeal cases who were assigned to assist applicants as part of their official duties without cost to the applicants, which fact had negatively affected the awarding of costs.[51] The Court also stated:

> Account must also be taken of the basic principle regarding the question of costs in contentious proceedings before international tribunals, to the effect that each party shall bear its own in the absence of a specific decision of the tribunal awarding costs . . . An award of costs in derogation of this general principle, and imposing on one of the parties the obligation to reimburse expenses incurred by its adversary, requires not only an express decision, but also a statement of reasons in support. On the other hand, the decision merely to allow the general principle to apply does not necessarily require detailed reasoning, and may even be adopted by implication.[52]

In *Fasla*[53] the applicant had been represented by a member of the UN Panel of Counsel. He had requested payment of $1,000 for exceptional costs in preparing his case. On the merits the Tribunal had awarded him compensation, but in regard to costs rejected his request as unfounded because he had

---

[47] *Ibid.*, at pp. 210–11.
[48] *van Gent*, WBAT Reports (1983, part II), Decision No. 13, at p. 9.
[49] ICJ Reports, 1973, p. 166, at pp. 206–7.
[50] *Ibid.*, at p. 200.
[51] *Ibid.* [52] *Ibid.*, at p. 212.
[53] UNAT Judgment No. 158 (1972), JUNAT Nos. 114–66, p. 355.

had the assistance of a member of the Panel of Counsel. The ICJ, while pointing out that the Tribunal's decision in regard to costs was somewhat laconic and ignored the applicant's argument that he did not claim costs for the assistance of outside counsel but for expenses actually incurred, held that it was clear that the question of costs was very much a matter for the appreciation of the Tribunal and concluded that, since the award of costs was a matter within the Tribunal's discretion, it was incumbent upon the applicant to have demonstrated that the costs were unavoidable, reasonable in amount, and in excess of the normal expenses of litigation before the Tribunal.[54]

The value of the Court's ruling in the *Judgment No. 273* case, which was that the UNAT had not exceeded its jurisdiction nor erred on a question of law relating to the provisions of the Charter in deciding that acquired rights of the applicant in the case before the UNAT had been violated by the application to him of a recent resolution of the General Assembly, is that impliedly the Court sanctioned the application of the doctrine of acquired rights under the Staff Regulations of the UN on the basis that such application was neither an excess of jurisdiction nor a violation of the Charter of the UN. The doctrine, being a part of the internal law of the UN, was held to have been appropriately applied by the UNAT, while the Court was not empowered to decide on the merits whether the doctrine had been properly applied to the facts.

The first matter of importance with which the ICJ dealt in the *Judgment No. 333* case was one relating to the nature of the judgment. In an earlier case the Court had dealt with the question of what requirements a reasoned judgment should meet. In this case the Court addressed the same issue in relation to pleas made in the case. The Court confirmed what it said in the *Judgment No. 273* case and further stated:

> Similarly in the present case, the Judgment of the Tribunal does not state specifically that it was the view of the Tribunal that, while a fixed-term appointment on secondment cannot be renewed or extended without the consent of the seconding Government, there is no automatic bar to the holder of such appointment being given a career appointment on its expiration. Nor does the Tribunal ever specifically reject or uphold the contention that the Secretary-General, because he was convinced that there was such a bar, could not have given 'every reasonable consideration' to the Applicant's application for appointment. If however, it can be established with sufficient certainty that 'the Tribunal addressed its mind' to the matters on which these contentions were based, 'and drew its own conclusions therefrom', then, whatever view be taken of the conclusion reached by the

---

[54] ICJ Reports, 1973, p. 166, at p. 207.

Tribunal on the evidence available, there was no failure to exercise jurisdiction in that respect.[55]

Thus, there is no requirement that every plea be mentioned *eo nomine* in the judgment.

The Court would also appear to have given support to the principle of international administrative law that a discretionary power exercised by the administration of an international organization could be reviewed by an IAT if there had been a misuse of power as a result of its having been exercised with an improper motive.[56] The Court seems in the light of the above principle to have supported the view that all the administration was under an obligation to do under the express internal law of the UN, where an officer on secondment from his government was released after the term of his secondment expired, was to give reasonable consideration to his request to be given an appointment after his secondment terminated.[57]

The Court also pronounced on the impact of articles 100, 101, 8 and 2 of the Charter of the UN in relation to the obligations of the administration *vis-à-vis* staff members. The Court said

> It is clear that the expression 'the paramount consideration' (in French, *la considération dominante*) in Article 101 of the Charter is not synonymous with 'the sole consideration'; it is simply a consideration to which greater weight is normally to be given than to any other. Nor does it mean that 'efficiency, competence and integrity' together constitute a sufficient consideration, in the sense that a high enough standard of each gives rise to an entitlement to appointment. It is also clear, since paragraph 1 of the Article provides that 'The staff shall be appointed by the Secretary-General under regulations established by the General Assembly', that the task of balancing the various considerations, in cases where they incline in different directions, is for the Secretary-General, subject to any general directions which might be given to him by the General Assembly. Resolution 37/126 itself constitutes such a direction, and one which operated in favour of the Applicant as compared with any outside candidate, or one without his record of more than 'five years' continuing good service' . . .
>
> The decision was that of the Secretary-General; and it was not for the Tribunal, nor indeed for the Court, to substitute its own appreciation of the problem for that of the Secretary-General. The Court could only find that the Tribunal had in this respect 'erred on a question of law relating to the provisions of the Charter' if it found that the Tribunal had upheld a decision of the Secretary-General which could not be reconciled with the relevant article of the Charter. That does not appear to the Court to be the case. The decision of the Secretary-General cannot

---

[55] ICJ Reports, 1987, p. 18, at p. 44.
[56] *Ibid.*, at p. 53.   [57] *Ibid.*, at p. 57.

be said to have failed to respect the 'paramount' character of the considerations mentioned in Article 101, paragraph 3, simply because he took into account 'all the circumstances' enumerated in his Answer (paragraph 80 above) in order to give effect to 'the interests of the Organization'.[58]

As for article 8 the Court emphasized that it explicitly prohibited discrimination based on sex and strictly did not incorporate other kinds of discrimination or inequality of treatment.[59] However, the Court did also imply that other kinds of discrimination or inequality of treatment were prohibited, though it did say that it did not have to deal with this issue because there was no evidence of such discrimination.[60]

Finally, the Court recognized that article 2(1) coupled with article 100(2) imposed upon the administration certain obligations of independence from member governments in the taking of decisions relating to the appointment of staff members which, however, the UNAT also had recognized and correctly found had not been flouted in the case.[61]

The powers of review of the ICJ over judgments of the UNAT and ILOAT are limited. However, it has been necessary, as has been seen above, for the Court to examine certain aspects of international administrative law and pronounce on them in the course of exercising this jurisdiction. This function it has performed well. It is significant that it has virtually and by implication supported the actions of the two Tribunals whose judgments it has reviewed.

[58] *Ibid.*, at p. 63.   [59] *Ibid.*, at p. 70.
[60] *Ibid.*, at pp. 70ff.   [61] *Ibid.*, at p. 71.

12

Jurisdiction and immunities

Hazel Fox

A survey of the International Court's treatment of state jurisdiction and immunities cannot but note the infrequency of occasion, due to the consensual nature of its jurisdiction, on which the Court has dealt with these issues. The first section of this chapter examines these lost opportunities. In the cases in which the Court has had such opportunity, there has been no general analysis equal to that to be found in the Permanent Court's judgment in the *Lotus*. A traditional approach to issues of jurisdiction may be construed more by implication than express statement from the Court's judgments. Implicitly, the Court appears to recognize territory and nationality as bases for jurisdiction, and to acknowledge the reciprocal nature of such jurisdiction with a consequent duty not to intervene and the rule of exhaustion of local remedies. However, the International Court as a court administering international law between states is more concerned with the effects on the international law of acts of exercise of jurisdiction than with their effects within the internal legal order of the state exercising jurisdiction. Here, it has explored the consequences of such acts of jurisdiction as a basis for title to territory and a ground for state responsibility. The second and third sections of this chapter will address these topics. A fourth section considers the Court's treatment of limits on state jurisdiction including immunities granted to other states and international organizations. In the fifth section brief mention is made of claims to exercise jurisdiction beyond the traditional bases of territory and nationality.

To venture any remarks on jurisdiction in honour of one who has written so illuminatingly and authoritatively on the subject himself is courting disaster. Quite apart from the magisterial ninth edition of *Oppenheim's International Law*, volume I, *Peace*, which Judge Jennings has edited with Sir Arthur Watts, he has from his earliest writings in the *British Yearbook of International Law* conducted a continuing debate on the scope and limitations of state jurisdiction.

One constant theme in those writings has been the lack of compulsory jurisdiction of the International Court. In the slow process of making effective its status as the primary judicial organ of the United Nations, wielding the judicial competence of the international community, the Court increasingly chafes at the restrictions the consensual basis of its jurisdiction imposes. That consensual jurisdiction derives from a state-oriented structure of international law, and one that places emphasis on the freedom of the state to exercise jurisdiction over territory and people.

It therefore seems relevant before considering the cases on state jurisdiction that have come before the Court to consider the jurisdictional disputes that have not. Two categories of dispute may be distinguished; those not referred to the Court by states, and those, although referred, that never reach determination on the merits.

JURISDICTIONAL ISSUES NOT BROUGHT TO THE COURT

Disputes not referred to the Court

Of the recognized bases of jurisdiction those depending on the link of territoriality and nationality are the most frequently referred to in the Court's judgments, although, as will be seen, more by way of tacit assumption than by explicit analysis or endorsement. Yet, even here, no challenge has been made in court proceedings to the considerable expansion of territorial jurisdiction that has been effected by the adoption of a restrictive rule of state immunity by municipal courts and which has permitted the exercise of territorial jurisdiction over the foreign state in respect of commercial transactions.

The failure to refer disputes to the International Court where state activities have been subjected to municipal court proceedings, such as those relating to the dishonoured Chinese railway bonds in *Jackson v. The Peoples' Republic of China*,[1] is particularly surprising, given that the municipal court proceedings amount to 'an assertion of jurisdiction' where consent or waiver of the subjected state is irrelevant. It seems a paradox, as Judge Jennings himself has noted, that sovereign governments have allowed, largely without protest, this exercise by a single state of jurisdiction, albeit on a reciprocal basis, over areas previously regarded as immune under international law, while they

---

[1] 794 F2d 1490; 25 *ILM* 1466 (1986).

refuse any surrender of jurisdiction to an independent international court, except by explicit consent of both parties.[2]

Another much–debated area of jurisdiction since the Second World War has been the exercise of extra-territorial jurisdiction over acts outside a state's territory in respect of non-nationals having substantial effects within the state's territory, particularly in relation to competition and labour laws, shipping contracts, securities and exchange controls, and export controls. The Permanent Court in the *Lotus* case[3] accepted such a basis for criminal jurisdiction on the part of Turkey over a non–national outside its territory who caused injury to a Turkish national on a ship on the high seas flying the Turkish flag. While the Permanent Court in that case agreed that the territorial principle prohibited a state from 'exercising its power in any form in the territory of another State',[4] it was not prepared to construe the principle as prohibiting the exercise of a state's jurisdiction to persons, property and acts outside its territory or from 'exercising jurisdiction in its own territory in respect of any case which relates to acts which have taken place abroad'.[5] It did not consider that such extra-territorial jurisdiction of a state required special permission, but rather that it depended on the discretion of each state to exercise it as it regarded best and most appropriate, and that resulting concurrent conflicting exercises of jurisdiction by states were to be resolved by international conventions.

Surprisingly, in the light of this broad approach, no case has been referred to the International Court to elucidate a state's exercise of extra-territorial jurisdiction or protective jurisdiction in respect of acts committed outside its territory, particularly where such acts constitute criminal offences directed against the security or other interests of the state. Yet disputes arising from such extra-territorial jurisdiction have been particularly sharp in relation to foreign–owned subsidiary companies or branches and in the requiring of information from foreign firms.

When one turns to jurisdiction based on passive personality or universality the same absence of referral to the Court is to be observed. Only recently in respect of the *Application of the Genocide Convention* case[6] is there to be found any discussion of universal jurisdiction, and then only in the Dissenting Opinions.

A number of explanations are offered for the non-referral of cases to the

---

[2] See R. Y. Jennings, 'The Judicial Enforcement of International Obligations", *ZAOR*, 47 (1987), p. 3, at p. 9.

[3] PCIJ, Series A, No. 10 (1927).   [4] *Ibid.*, p. 18.

[5] *Ibid.*, p. 19.   [6] ICJ Reports, 1993, pp. 3 and 325.

Court.[7] Jennings and Watts offer one explanation: 'The existence of over-lapping jurisdiction is acceptable and convenient; and forbearance by States in the exercise of their jurisdictional powers avoids conflict in all but a small (although important) minority of cases'.[8]

Dr Mann offered another; he pointed out that the consequence of an excess of jurisdiction is nullity; an attempt by one state to exercise control in another state's territory or over its nationals will simply be ignored or treated as invalid in other courts, whether they be international or municipal.[9] Consequently, states acting on that assumption will not trouble to refer the matter to adjudication. The case of *Nottebohm*[10] provides an example of such non-effectiveness on the international level; the grant of nationality by naturalization was valid for municipal law purposes but had no effect in international law as a basis of diplomatic protection since it failed to conform to international law requirements regarding the nationality of the claim.

Of course, the ability to ignore or treat the exercise of jurisdiction as a nullity depends on the lack of effectiveness of the state's exercise; this raises a nice question of when assertion of jurisdiction becomes effective application, and is discussed below in relation to the *UNHQ Agreement* case.[11] Judge Jennings himself has discussed the complexities of legal consequences from an abusive exercise of jurisdiction in his essay on 'Nullity and Effectiveness in International Law'.[12]

A third explanation may be derived from the reception that rulings of the International Court on jurisdictional issues have received. The 1952 Brussels Convention,[13] and article 11 of the 1958 Geneva High Seas Convention,[14] re-enacted in the 1982 Law of the Sea Convention,[15] reversed the Permanent Court's ruling in the *Lotus* case, giving jurisdiction, in the event of criminal proceedings taken as a result of collision on the high seas, to the flag state of the ship on which the accused was present or to the state of his nationality. The 'genuine connection' stipulated in the *Nottebohm* case[16] has been restrictively applied so as not to defeat nationality by birth and consequential diplomatic protection. The non-opposability to the UK of Iceland's

---

[7] See L. C. Damrosch, *The International Court of Justice at the Crossroads* (Dobbs Ferry, NY, 1987), p. xxii.

[8] See *Oppenheim's International Law* (9th edn, Harlow, 1992), at p. 457.

[9] 'The Doctrine of Jurisdiction in International Law', *Recueil des cours*, 111, 1 (1964), p. 1, at p. 12.

[10] ICJ Reports, 1955, p. 4.

[11] ICJ Reports, 1988, p. 3.

[12] See R. Y. Jennings (ed.), *Cambridge Essays in International Law – Essays in Honour of Lord McNair* (London, 1965), p. 64.

[13] 429 UNTS 233.   [14] 450 UNTS 82.

[15] UN Doc. A/CONF 62/122/   [16] ICJ Reports, 1955, p. 4, at p. 23.

jurisdiction over its declared 50-mile exclusive fishery zone, which the Court determined in the *Fisheries Jurisdiction (UK)* case,[17] has been overtaken by the evolving concept of the exclusive economic zone (EEZ). The mandatory resolution 748/92 of the Security Council and article 103 of the UN Charter prevailed over the obligations relating to extradition arising out of the destruction of PanAm Flight 103 in the *Lockerbie* case.[18] These cases may lead states to the perception that for one reason or another rulings of the Court on jurisdictional issues become quickly inapplicable and outmoded. Recent trends in state practice with regard to civil commercial matters appear to have gone beyond any solution the Court might have offered by application of the 'effects' doctrine in territorial jurisdiction. The interpenetration of markets and the global scope of financial transactions – US 3,000 billion dollars worth of transactions electronically effected daily – have encouraged treaty-led harmonization both of substantive law and jurisdictional competences; in the European field the Brussels Convention on Jurisdiction and the Enforcement of Judgments in Civil and Commercial Matters[19] and the Rome Convention on the Law Applicable to Contractual Obligations[20] exemplify regional instruments to harmonize private international law rules relating to jurisdiction. Elsewhere regulation is by reference to cross-border or establishment-based transactions, universal harmonized standards enforced by reciprocal recognition of the power of the home state to regulate banks, securities houses and commercial enterprisers centred in its territory. It would seem that a decision of the International Court here can offer little in what, in a field affected by fast-changing technology, remains a trial-and-error approach to the resolution of jurisdictional conflicts.

Further, in the maritime delimitation cases (such as the *Gulf of Maine*[21] (a Chamber case), *Tunisia/Libya*,[22] *Libya/Malta*[23] and the *Jan Mayen*[24] cases), the techniques employed by the Court of equitable principles and special circumstances have introduced an element of unpredictability into the decisions of the International Court. Faced with this uncertainty, in the majority of disputes relating to the demarcation of the boundaries of states' jurisdiction, the states concerned may prefer to keep control of the outcome by negotiation and agreement.

The lack of referral by states of such jurisdictional issues is thus shown to be itself an example of the continuing wish of states to retain freedom of decision,

---

[17] ICJ Reports, 1974, p. 4.

[18] ICJ Reports 1992, p. 3; for the Order made in the concurrent action against the USA, see *ibid.*, p. 114.

[19] OJ 1978 L304/77, as amended OJ 1989 L285 (extended to relations between EC and EFTA states by the Lugano Convention OJ 1988 L319/9).

[20] OJ 1980 L 266/1.   [21] ICJ Reports 1984, p. 246.   [22] ICJ Reports, 1982, p. 18.

[23] ICJ Reports, 1985, p. 13.   [24] ICJ Reports, 1993, p. 38.

'the wide measure of discretion' to which the Permanent Court referred in the *Lotus* case.[25]

This is not to say that the few cases in which jurisdictional issues have been referred to the Court have not had a major influence on the development of international law. A full examination of the arguments for and against a particular exercise of jurisdiction followed by an authoritative ruling of the Court accelerates this formation of a general consensus as to the principle or rule to be applied. That consensus may not always conform to the ruling of the Court, but it does not mean that it has not served to crystallize the appropriate law.

Disputes referred to the Court but which never reach determination on the merits

Turning to this second class of cases, it is tantalizing to consider the lost opportunities for elucidation of the law on jurisdiction that these cases represent. They can be categorized by type of jurisdictional issue raised and the cause or reason why no determination on the merits was reached.

Summary removal of a case from the general list

These cases concern circumstances in which the applicant – while inviting the state named as respondent to accept the Court's jurisdiction *ad hoc* – itself concedes that there is no subsisting title of jurisdiction and consequently requires no reasoned decision of the Court rendered after full hearing of the parties. The *Aerial Incident* cases,[26] where a territorial sovereign's right to shoot down a military or civil aircraft inadvertently infringing its airspace, and the *Antarctica* cases,[27] concerning claims to Antarctica based on exercise of territorial jurisdiction, were removed from the Court's list in this manner when it became clear that the respondent states were not prepared to accept the Court's jurisdiction.

Lack of jurisdiction

Here, after consideration the Court decides there is no basis of jurisdiction on which to found the case against the respondent state. Despite the initial grant of interim measures, the Court held that lack of jurisdiction prevented it from

---

[25] PCIJ, Series A, No. 10, at p. 19.

[26] *USA v. Czechoslovakia* (removed from list), ICJ Reports, 1956, p. 6; *USA v. USSR* (removed from list), *ibid.*, p. 8; *USA v. USSR*, ICJ Reports, 1959, p. 276.

[27] *UK v. Argentina* (removed from list), ICJ Reports, 1956, p. 12; *UK v. Chile* (removed from list), *ibid.*, p. 15.

deciding whether the concession agreement to the company imposed legal restrictions on Iran's expropriation of the British-owned Anglo-Iranian Oil Company (*Anglo-Iranian Oil Company* case).[28]

Reservation of domestic jurisdiction

In the *Norwegian Loans* case[29] and the *Aegean Sea Continental Shelf* case[30] the Court construed exclusion clauses to acceptance of the Court's jurisdiction as denying it jurisdiction. The state's right to pay alien bondholders in local currency, not gold, or to stop seismic drilling on the continental shelf were consequently not further examined.

Subsequent action by the parties

In *The Trial of Pakistani Prisoners of War* case,[31] Pakistan claimed exclusive jurisdiction under the Genocide Convention over Pakistani nationals held in custody in Indian territory, who had been accused of committing acts of genocide in Pakistani territory. During the hearings Pakistan asked the court to postpone further consideration of its request for interim measures and the Court accordingly decided eight to four, that there was no urgency for such measures, thus avoiding determination both of the need to determine and a ruling on the awkward issue of any *prima facie* basis for the Court's jurisdiction.

In the *Nuclear Tests* case[32] Australia and New Zealand asserted rights to determine what acts should take place in their territories, in particular whether their territories and people be exposed to radiation from artificial sources. France's unilateral statements were construed by the Court as constituting a legal undertaking to cease atmospheric nuclear tests and hence as meeting the objectives of the applicant so that a dispute no longer existed, and the Court dismissed the proceedings.

Referral to another forum

In the *Jurisdiction of the ICAO Council* case[33] India asserted a right to suspend over-flights by reason of a material breach of treaty but was held bound by the compromissory clauses in the treaties regulating such over-flights, their validity being independent of any alleged modification of the treaties in which they were contained. The dispute was accordingly referred back to the ICAO Council for determination.

---

[28] ICJ Reports, 1952, p. 93.   [29] ICJ Reports, 1957, p. 9.
[30] ICJ Reports, 1978, p. 3.   [31] ICJ Reports, 1973, p. 328.
[32] ICJ Reports, 1974, p. 253.   [33] ICJ Reports, 1972, p. 46.

THE COURT'S ASSUMPTION AS TO TERRITORIAL AND PERSONAL JURISDICTION OF STATES

As already indicated, much of the Court's practice relating to state jurisdiction is to be found in assumptions which underlie many of its judgments, even those not specifically addressing issues of state jurisdiction. A profile of state jurisdiction much in accordance with its treatment in standard textbooks can thus be deduced from such assumptions, though clearly Separate and Dissenting Opinions may seek to introduce novel features. Thus in the *Reparations* case[34] the status of the United Nations Organization is contrasted to that of a state 'who possesses the totality of international rights and duties recognized by international law',[35] and the protection afforded to UN agents by the UN distinguished from the diplomatic protection traditionally exercised by the national state, though there are important exceptions to the rule.[36]

In the first *Asylum* case[37] territorial jurisdiction is explained and its primacy stated over any jurisdiction exercisable by a diplomatic mission enjoying immunity. Presence in the territory of the state is identified as the basis to justify the exercise of jurisdiction whether by grant or refusal of extradition: 'In the case of extradition the refugee is within the territory of the State of refuge. A decision with regard to extradition implies only the normal exercise of the territorial sovereignty. The refugee is outside the territory of the State where the offence was committed, and a decision to grant him asylum [by refusal of extradition] in no way derogates from the sovereignty of the State.'[38] The extension of diplomatic asylum to a fugitive from justice of the territorial state, on the other hand, leads to a derogation of sovereignty by reason of the prior presence of the fugitive within its territory. Consequently the competence of the state enjoying diplomatic immunities is treated as exceptional and not one to be unilaterally construed by that state (see further below). This analysis of the Court relating to the right to extradite may have some relevance in the *Lockerbie* cases should they ever reach the merits stage.

Personal jurisdiction based on nationality was assumed as a basis for jurisdiction in the *Nottebohm*[39] and *Barcelona Traction*[40] cases, both cases being concerned with the entitlement of the state to exercise diplomatic protection rather than the nature of its exercise.

---

[34] ICJ Reports, 1949, p. 174.
[35] *Ibid.*, at p. 180.   [36] *Ibid.*, at pp. 181–2.
[37] ICJ Reports, 1950, p. 266.   [38] *Ibid.*, at p. 274.
[39] ICJ Reports, 1955, p. 4.   [40] ICJ Reports, 1970, p. 3.

Apart from the general assumptions made by the Court, its judgments provide interesting insights into the nature and limits of state jurisdiction.

EXERCISE OF JURISDICTION AS AN ACT OF THE STATE

Acts of state which take the form of exercise of jurisdiction are somewhat elusive when one seeks to assess their effect in international law. States themselves are artificial entities and can only act through individuals; conduct of state officials which gives rise to international conflicts covers not only executive acts with direct physical consequences but the more intangible assertion of authority on behalf of the state which these officials make. These regulatory acts of state officials present a particular challenge to international law in that they assert, but do not necessarily bring about physical consequences to conform with such assertion, over an area of control in parallel or at times in conflict with international law. That so much of state jurisdiction amounts to assertion of control rather than physical enforcement explains the tolerance of concurrent competing jurisdictions between states. For international law it raises difficult questions of the nature of an exercise of municipal jurisdiction, the stage at which it produces an effect in international law and, in Judge Oda's words, 'a cardinal problem of maintaining the supremacy of international law in the context of its internal (municipal) application'.[41]

Authority to exercise jurisdiction

Regulatory acts of state officials derive their authority and the form of their exercise of jurisdiction from the internal laws and legal order of the state. There is, therefore, rarely any problem about the attribution of the regulatory act to the state. Unlike other acts of state, their imputability to the state is not in issue; issues of imputability such as arose in the *US Diplomatic and Consular Staff in Tehran* case[42] relating to the Iranian government's responsibility with regard to the two stages of the militants' occupation of the US Embassy and detention of hostages, or the US government's control of the Contras' activities in Nicaragua in the *Military and Paramilitary Activities* case[43] do not

[41] See *Advisory Opinion on the Applicability of the Obligation to Arbitrate under Section 21 of the United Nations Headquarters Agreement*, ICJ Reports, 1988, p. 12; Separate Opinion of Judge Oda, p. 37, at p. 41.

[42] ICJ Reports, 1980, p. 3.

[43] ICJ Reports, 1986, p. 14.

arise. Interestingly enough, however, in both cases consequences of acts of exercise of jurisdiction were included in the applicant state's claims. In the *US Hostages* case the Court held that the failure to exercise regulatory acts rendered Iran in breach in the first stage of its obligation under article 22(2) of the Vienna Convention in Diplomatic Relations 1961[44] to take 'appropriate steps' to protect the premises, staff and archives of the US Mission; in the *Nicaragua/US* case the imposition of an economic embargo by Presidential Order was held to be a breach of the 1956 Treaty of Friendship, Amity and Commerce (FCN Treaty)[45] between the USA and Nicaragua.

Authorization by internal law is not conclusive of a state's authority for purposes of international law. The *prima facie* identification of the organization of a state by its own internal laws cannot override the principle that a state may not invoke its internal law as proof of compliance with international law. Some aspects of international requirements of authority to act on behalf of a state were investigated by the Court in the *Application of the Genocide Convention (First Case)*[46] when indicating provisional measures against Serbia. In that case the Court accepted that UN recognition as a member of the UN entitled Bosnia to be a party to its Statute. The Court also applied, by reference to the *ex officio* powers of a Head of State to represent a state (Vienna Convention on the Law of Treaties,[47] article 7(2)), UN recognition, and not democratic election, as Serbia contended, as the criterion to establish that it was 'seised of the case on the authority of a Head of State [President Izetbegovich], treated as such in the United Nations'.[48] It was unable, however, to use the criterion of UN recognition with regard to Serbia since the Security Council and the General Assembly had declared that Serbia could not continue automatically UN membership of the former Socialist Federal Republic of Yugoslavia (SFRY). Instead, it applied a principle of continuity to give Serbia access to the Court by means of 'a special provision contained in a treaty in force'[49] under article 35(2) of its Statute, relying on Serbia's acceptance of the commitments of the Genocide Convention, its proclamation of itself as 'continuing the State, international legal and political personality of the SFRY' and its undertaking 'strictly [to] abide by all the commitments that the SFRY assumed internationally'.[50] The decision has been criticized as according some degree of recognition to Serbia and

---

[44] 500 UNTS 95.
[45] 367 UNTS 14.   [46] ICJ Reports, 1993, p. 3.
[47] UN Doc. A/CONF 39/27.   [48] ICJ Reports, 1993, p. 3, at p. 11.
[49] *Ibid.*, at p. 14.   [50] *Ibid.*, at p. 15.

preventing the primary organs of the UN speaking with one voice on the status of a state.

Regulatory acts of state jurisdiction as violations of international law

From the above examples it will be seen that a regulatory act of state may constitute a violation of international law, even though the basis of its exercise is recognized by international law. Thus in the *Nicaragua v. USA* case the regulatory act by which the order of President Reagan imposed an economic embargo on Nicaraguan ships in US waters was made on a recognized territorial basis but nonetheless held to be a violation of the 1956 FCN Treaty, as constituting an interference with the freedom of Nicaraguan vessels conferred by article XIX, paragraph 3, 'to come with their cargoes to all ports, places and waters' of the United States.[51] Even where exercise of recognized jurisdiction is alleged to violate international law a persistent pattern of exercise or deliberate sequence of regulatory acts, rather than a single act, is likely to be the substance of the claim.

Regulatory acts as a basis of title to territory

In the group of cases adjudicating title to territory (*Minquiers and Ecrehos*,[52] the *Temple* case[53]) the International Court has had frequent occasion to consider the degree of state participation that regulatory acts of state officials involve. Thus in determining title to territory the Court in the *Minquiers and Ecrehos* case stated: 'Of the manifold acts involved by the UK government, the court attaches particular probative value to the acts which relate to the exercise of jurisdiction and local administration and legislation'.[54] It here adopted the accepted division of jurisdiction into authority to prescribe law, to subject persons and things to adjudication in the courts and to enforce the laws by executive action, and found the UK to have exercised all three in relation to the Ecrehos islands: legislative jurisdiction by virtue of a Treasury warrant including the 'Ecrehou rocks' within the limits of Jersey as a port, adjudicative jurisdiction by the Jersey courts' exercise of criminal jurisdiction over the islands, including inquests on corpses, and executive jurisdiction in the levying of rates on fishermen's huts, registration of contracts of sale of real

---

[51] ICJ Reports, 1986, p. 14, at p. 140. [52] ICJ Reports, 1953, p. 47.
[53] ICJ Reports, 1962, p. 6. [54] ICJ Reports, 1963, p. 47, at p. 65.

property, licensing of fishing boats, establishment of a customs house and taking of a census.[55]

In *Frontier Dispute (Burkina Faso/Mali)*[56] a different use of jurisdictional acts of the territorial sovereign was made, in order to accord by the use of *uti possidetis* pre-eminence to legal title over effective possession as a basis of sovereignty. In this case decrees establishing and abolishing the colony of Upper Volta made by the French Republic and Orders issued by the Governor-General of French West Africa were used as evidence of administrative boundaries and frontiers established by colonial powers and by application of the principle of *uti possidetis* transformed into international frontiers. Similar use of provincial authorities' grants of land was made in the *Land, Island and Maritime Frontier Dispute (El Salvador/Honduras, Nicaragua Intervening)*[57] although the difficulty in applying the principle in controversial situations was there apparent, the Chamber noting '*uti possidetis juris* is essentially a retrospective principle, investing as international boundaries administrative limits intended originally for quite other purposes'.[58]

In the title to territory cases the Court has construed the situation as one of win or lose; the identification of a single sovereign state is a precondition for the exercise of territorial jurisdiction. The *Passage Over Indian Territory* case[59] required 'the reconciling of the requirements of two sovereignties'.[60] Although long and continuous practice was accepted as giving an enforceable right in international law to Portugal, in respect of non-military passage to its enclaves located in the midst of Indian territory, India, as sovereign of the territory over which the passage was exercised, was recognized as having the right to regulate passage for customs, revenue and security reasons.[61]

For the purposes of establishing title, these varying acts of exercise of jurisdiction of themselves were sufficient to support the applicant's case. In claims relating to mistreatment of aliens, the rule of exhaustion of local remedies provides opportunity before any finding of international responsibility for a second exercise of jurisdiction by the respondent state to remedy any deficiencies resulting from the first exercise. Thus in the *Interhandel* case[62] the expropriation of the shares held in a Swiss company as 'enemy property',

---

[55] *Ibid.*, pp. 65–6.

[56] ICJ Reports, 1986, p. 554, at pp. 580–2.

[57] ICJ Reports, 1992, p. 351.

[58] *Ibid.*, at p. 388. The *Western Sahara* case recognized that ties of allegiance and rights relating to land might constitute 'legal ties' but not amount to any tie of territorial sovereignty or foundation for application of the right to self determination: ICJ Reports, 1975, p. 3, at p. 64.

[59] ICJ Reports, 1960, p. 6.   [60] *Ibid.*; see Declaration of Judge Basdevant at pp. 48–9.

[61] *Ibid.*, at p. 40.   [62] ICJ Reports, 1959, p. 6.

by an exercise of jurisdiction vesting them in the US government, was held not to be a denial of justice and thus not a violation of international law unless Switzerland could show that the decision was not subject to review in US courts; as proceedings were still pending, and it was established that they applied to the US government and would take into account international law standards, Switzerland was unable, at the time of the proceedings, to show a final exercise of jurisdiction on the part of US, violative of her international rights. In *ELSI*,[63] a Chamber of the Court had a more difficult task, since at the time of the proceedings local remedies had been exhausted in Italy and it had to decide whether the remedies afforded by Italian law had provided reparation to a standard sufficient to comply with international law.

The Chamber held that the initial requisition of ELSI's assets by the Mayor of Palermo was only one of a number of causes that prevented the possibility of orderly liquidation to which the United States claimed the US holding companies were entitled under the 1948 FCN treaty between the two countries. An assessment of ELSI's solvency as a matter of Italian law was material in determining that by reason of ELSI's financial position being so desperate no feasibility of orderly liquidation had been established.[64]

Timing of actionable effect

The stage at which an exercise of municipal jurisdiction may produce an actionable effect in international law varies according to the international obligation. In *US Diplomatic and Consular Staff in Tehran* the receiving state's duty to protect the visiting state's mission was strict and continuing requiring no precondition for its performance.[65] In the *Corfu Channel* case the state was declared to be under obligation not knowingly to allow its territory to be used contrary to the rights of other states; here, responsibility was conditional solely on the existence of knowledge on the part of state officials, not of any exercise of jurisdiction.[66]

The stage at which an exercise of municipal jurisdiction effects a change in conduct of the person to whom it is addressed came under discussion in the *Applicability of the Obligation to Arbitrate under Section 21 of the UN Headquarters Agreement* (the *UNHQ Agreement* case).[67] Here the US seems to have sought to apply in an international context a principle of US constitutional law of 'ripeness' which in relation to a case or controversy affects the standing of an

---

[63] ICJ Reports, 1989, p. 15.
[64] *Ibid.*, at p. 61.   [65] ICJ Reports, 1980, p. 3, at p. 31.
[66] ICJ Reports, 1949, p. 4, at p. 22.   [67] ICJ Reports, 1988, p. 12.

applicant to challenge the constitutional validity of an act of the government.[68] The US contended that neither the signing into law of the Anti-terrorism Act, nor its entry into force, nor the Attorney-General's decision to apply it, nor his resort to court proceedings to close the PLO Mission, constituted a dispute relating to UN rights under the HQ Agreement, since the case was still pending before an American court, and until the decision of the court, the US would not take other action to close the PLO Observer Mission in New York.[69] In effect, the US argued that it accepted that closure would be contrary to US international obligations but that the timing of such closure was still being evaluated within the government; consequently until the constitutional validity of the Anti-terrorism Act had been finally determined by a US court of law there was no issue between the US and UN constituting an arbitrable dispute under section 21 of the UNHQ Agreement. The Court held in its Advisory Opinion that there was an arbitrable dispute; to hold otherwise would subject the arbitration procedure under section 21 of the HQ Agreement to exhaustion of local remedies which was against the letter and spirit of the Agreement.[70] It would also permit, in disregard of the principle that international law prevails over municipal law, the US to plead its municipal law as a defence to its international law failure to have recourse to arbitration as required by the HQ Agreement. For the purposes of the US obligation under the HQ Agreement the US measures were held by the court to constitute effective application so as to give rise to a dispute as to 'the interpretation or application' of that Agreement, even though in US domestic law the Act might only be regarded as having effective application when the PLO Mission was in fact closed. In his Separate Opinion Judge Oda stressed that 'the difference between the United Nations and the United States was thus not the issue whether the *forced closure* of the office would or would

---

[68] Powell J concurring in the Supreme Court's decision in *Goldwater v. Carter* 444 US 996 (1979); 62 L Ed 2 428 explained the doctrine:

> This Court has recognized that an issue should not be decided if it is not ripe for judicial review (*Buckley v. Valeo* 424 US 1) *par curiam*. Prudential considerations persuade me that a dispute between Congress and the President is not ready for judicial review unless and until each branch has taken action asserting its constitutional authority. Differences between the President and Congress are commonplace under our system. The differences should and almost do turn on political rather than legal considerations. The judicial branch should not decide issues affecting the allocation of power between the President and Congress until the political branches reach a constitutional impasse. Otherwise we would encourage small groups of even individual Members of Congress to seek judicial review of issues before the normal political process has the opportunity to resolve the conflict.

[69] ICJ Reports, 1988, p. 12, at p. 29.
[70] *Ibid.*, at p. 29.

not violate the Head Quarters Agreement [both parties agreed it would], but rather the issue as to what course of action within the US domestic legal structure would be tantamount to the *forced closure* of the PLO's New York office, in which both parties would see a violation of the Agreement'.[71] Judge Schwebel elaborated: 'When a party actually alleges, if not in form then in substance, only a failure to apply the treaty, and makes clear that there is no dispute over its interpretation, is there, for purposes of dispute settlement, a dispute over the treaty's interpretation? I have my doubts.'[72] But Judge Shahabuddeen considered that even if the dispute related solely to application and bearing in mind the dispute settlement clause covered both interpretation and application, 'a present threat of interference' by closure opposed by the UN Secretary-General constituted a sufficient dispute as to current violation of the Agreement to trigger the arbitration procedure under section 21.[73]

LIMITS TO STATE JURISDICTION

Despite the relatively few cases where it has given a decision relating to state jurisdiction on the merits, the International Court has developed in its practice a number of principles and methods by which to bring manifestations of jurisdiction on the part of states within the framework of international law.

The duty of non-intervention

First, it has given effect to the principle of non-intervention which is a corollary of the right of every state to conduct its affairs without outside interference. That principle prohibits coercive intervention whether by direct use of force or in indirect form of support for subversive or terrorist activities in external or internal affairs of other states. The *Nicaragua v. USA* case *(Merits)*[74] investigated fully the scope of this duty of non-intervention with regard to direct and indirect use of force and the right of the attacked state or of a third state to respond to such intervention by forcible intervention on its own part. It is not proposed here to examine the scope of that decision which essentially relates to abnormal situations of armed conflict between states.

For the purposes of this chapter the focus is on forms of intervention that prevent the exercise of territorial jurisdiction in peacetime by a state over its territory.

In the *Corfu Channel* case, after mines had struck two ships causing loss of

---

[71] *Ibid.*, at p. 39.   [72] *Ibid.*, at p. 51.
[73] *Ibid.*, at p. 61.   [74] ICJ Reports, 1986, p. 14.

life, Operation Retail, a minesweeping of the channel, was conducted by British authorities for the purpose of securing possession of evidence in the territory of another state in order to submit it to an international tribunal and thus to facilitate its task of adjudicating international responsibility. The Court held Operation Retail to be intervention and an impermissible form of self-help.[75] In similar vein, in the *US Diplomatic and Consular Staff in Tehran* case the Court condemned the US abortive attempt to free the hostages by incursion into Iran's territory as action 'of a kind calculated to undermine respect for the judicial process in international relations'.[76] As with the British smarting from lost ships and personnel in the *Corfu Channel* case, so the US had ample provocation for the detention of their nationals held hostage in its Embassy for over five months. But as the Court pointed out, the right to self-help was of particular concern when it occurred at a time when the Court was itself in the course of preparing the judgment on which US had sought its adjudication, and when the parties were subject to a Court Order not to aggravate the tension between the two countries.

Limits within the territory of the territorial state

In situations where international law accords rights to another state within the sovereign state's territory, the exercise of the latter's territorial jurisdiction is subject to obligations even within its own territory. The question of the right of a people to the natural resources of a territory as a limitation on the exercise of international jurisdiction has been alluded to in the *Nauru* case,[77] and may be an issue in the *East Timor* case. In *Nauru (Preliminary Objections)*[78] the court allowed Nauru's claim for rehabilitation of phosphate lands worked out before its independence in 1967 to proceed against Australia alone, even though she was only one of the three administering states under the Trusteeship Agreement. The court held the administering authority itself to have no

---

[75] ICJ Reports, 1949, p. 4, at p. 35.

[76] ICJ Reports, 1980, p. 3, at p. 43. The abduction of a Mexican national by US enforcement agents sanctioned in *United States v. Alvarez-Machain* 112 S. Ct 2188 (1992) would appear to be another impermissible form of intervention on which the Sixth Committee of the General Assembly is considering requesting an Advisory Opinion from the Court in respect of the rule prohibiting extra-territorial exercise of criminal jurisdiction, particularly through the use of unilateral measures of coercion such as abduction UN Doc. A/C. 6/48/SR. 37 (1993); Virginia Morris and M.-Christiane Bourloyannis-Vrailis, 'Current Developments', *AJIL*, 87 (1993), p. 322; *AJIL*, 88 (1994), pp. 357–8.

[77] The case was removed from the list following a settlement between the parties: see ICJ Reports, 1993, p. 322.

[78] ICJ Reports, 1992, p. 240.

international legal personality distinct from the three administering states; any responsibility for rehabilitation, therefore, rested with the three states of whom Australia 'played a very special role' in the administration of the territory.[79] Judge Shahabuddeen in his Separate Opinion identified that special element as 'the full powers of legislation, administration and jurisdiction' conferred on Australia over the territory of Nauru by the Trusteeship Agreement.[80] While the issue was for determination at the Merits stage, it was implicit, he said, in Nauru's case that the exercise of such full powers was subject to the obligation not to allow the destruction of the homeland of the Nauruan people by the failure to regulate the phosphate industry or to ensure the rehabilitation of its worked-out areas.[81]

In dismissing the second Australian objection, the Court held that there had been no waiver by the Nauruan local authorities, prior to independence, of their claim relating to rehabilitation, but noted that in so deciding it had not considered it necessary 'to consider whether any waiver by the Nauruan authorities prior to accession to independence is opposable to the Republic of Nauru'.[82] From this cryptic aside, it might be possible to conjecture that entitlement to exercise present territorial jurisdiction over a particular area of territory gives no right to exhaust natural resources so as to devastate the land for future generations of the population or subsequent successors to the exercise of territorial jurisdiction. However, the context was the construction of a Trusteeship Agreement and a present duty on the administering state to have regard to the interests of the future population of the territory does not, even if the ICJ's remark provides any foundation for such a legal proposition, necessarily support the extension of such an obligation to a state exercising full territorial jurisdiction over a non-colonial people.

A restriction on use of the territory of the territorial sovereign entitled to exercise jurisdiction also was declared in the *Corfu Channel* case where a state was declared to be under an obligation not to allow knowingly its territory to be used for acts contrary to the rights of other states.[83] The exclusive control the territorial state enjoys in its territory was also held to permit a state, when victim of such an act, a more liberal recourse to inferences of fact and circumstantial evidence to establish knowledge of the illegality on the part of the territorial state.[84] Similarly, where a state admits aliens to its territory the rule of exhaustion of local remedies provides some restriction on the unrestrained exercise of jurisdiction. The rule defeats a plea of exclusive

---

[79] *Ibid.*, at p. 258.   [80] *Ibid.*, at p. 279.
[81] *Ibid.*, at p. 282.   [82] *Ibid.*, at p. 247.
[83] ICJ Reports, 1949, p. 4, at p. 22.   [84] *Ibid.*, at p. 18.

domestic jurisdiction and, as already referred to in the *Interhandel*[85] and *ELSI*[86] cases, enables the International Court to monitor that the remedies are effective and not manifestly futile.

Immunities

The grant of privileges and immunities by the territorial state to another state or to an international organization is a further type of limitation on a state's territorial jurisdiction and one that, as regards diplomatic and consular immunities, the Court in the *US Hostages* case was prepared to base, not solely on the bilateral and multilateral treaties in force between Iran and United States, but on 'obligations under the whole corpus of international rules of which diplomatic law is comprised, rules the fundamental character of which the Court must here again strongly affirm'.[87]

In *The Applicability of Article 1, Section 22 of the Convention on the Privileges and Immunities of United Nations* (the *Mazilu* case)[88] the Court gave a liberal construction of the UN Convention, in response to a request, under article 96(2) of the UN Charter, of the Economic and Social Council, of the meaning of 'experts on mission', construing them as applying to persons entrusted by UN with missions, not being officials of the Organization, whether or not it was necessary to travel on the mission. In the absence of any reservation by Romania concerning the applicability of article VI to its nationals (as made by Mexico and US), it held that Romania was obliged under the Convention to respect such status of an expert even though he was a Romanian national.

Accordingly, the Court held Mr Mazilu, a Romanian national, as Special Rapporteur of the Subcommission on Discrimination and Protection of Minorities, entitled to the protected status of 'expert on mission' so long as his UN mandate continued, even though he had not left Romania, had not undertaken to do so, might not currently be fit to do so, and wished to travel to Geneva rather than New York.

In construing the scope of these immunities the court has consistently maintained that they are not open to unilateral determination either by the receiving state or the visiting state or an organization that has its headquarters or a regional office in the territory. Thus in the *Asylum* case[89] the Court held that the state wishing to shelter fugitives from the justice of the municipal

---

[85] ICJ Reports, 1959, p. 6.
[86] ICJ Reports, 1989, p. 15.   [87] ICJ Reports, 1980, p. 3, at p. 42.
[88] ICJ Reports, 1989, p. 177.   [89] ICJ Reports, 1950, p. 266.

courts of the receiving state had no unilateral competence to determine whether or not they were political refugees. In the *Interpretation of the Agreement between WHO and Egypt*[90] the Court commented:

> In the World Health Assembly and in some of the written and oral statements before the Court there seems to have been a disposition to regard international organisations as possessing some form of absolute power to determine and, if need be, change the location of the sites of their headquarters and regional offices. But States for their part possess a sovereign power of decision with respect to their acceptance of the headquarters or regional office of an organisation within their territories; and an organisation's power of decision is no more absolute in this aspect than is that of a State.

The Court accordingly held that 'by the mutual understandings reached between Egypt and the Organisation from 1949 to 1951 . . . a contractual local régime was created' which entailed mutual obligations of co-operation and good faith and the duty of WHO to consult Egypt before it decided whether and how to transfer its regional office in Alexandria.[91]

Following through this approach, the Court in the *US Hostages* case[92] rejected the assertion in letters of Iran of December 1979 and March 1980 to the Court (Iran did not appear) that the criminal activities and twenty-five years of continual interference by the US in the internal affairs of Iran justified the latter's withdrawal of diplomatic immunity. It treated the grant of diplomatic and consular immunities as giving rise to a self-contained regime, operative in case of abuse and entirely efficacious: 'Diplomatic law itself provides the necessary means of defence against, and sanction for, illicit activities by members of diplomatic and consular missions.'[93]

Although admittedly the justification for intrusion into the Mission advanced by the Iranian government was political, far-fetched and indicating no particular urgency for the extreme measures that were in fact taken, the Court's ruling seems to settle conclusively the debate, not resolved in the *travaux préparatoires* of the Vienna Convention on Diplomatic Relations, whether a receiving state might disregard the inviolability of the Mission and its diplomats where the latter is alleged to commit a material breach of the Vienna Convention on Treaties, article 62, by flagrant disregard of local laws and intervention in internal affairs. The Court's ruling, however, does not really address the problem present in incidents such as the St James's Square incident[94] where a receiving state claims a right of self-defence in the face of

---

[90] ICJ Reports, 1980, p. 72, at p. 89.   [91] *Ibid*., at pp. 92–4.
[92] ICJ Reports, 1980, p. 3.   [93] *Ibid*., at p. 38.
[94] House of Commons Foreign Affairs Committee, 1st Report 1984–5 *HC* 127.

immediate physical danger presented by the conduct of the Mission; in that case the shooting into a public square from a window of the Libyan People's Bureau.

Primacy of treaty

A more general restriction on the exercise of territorial jurisdiction, which treaty-based grant of immunity to a state or international organization illustrates, is the primacy accorded to treaty by the Court. Wherever the existence of a territorial jurisdiction appears in treaty form the Court relies on the treaty, wherever possible, to introduce an international dimension into the dispute and construes the freedom of the state to exercise jurisdiction by reference to qualifications in the treaty. The Permanent Court in the *Lotus* case rejected the French contention that for a territorial state to exercise jurisdiction over a foreign national required specific authorization, from treaty or other rule of international law, but accepted that the consequent 'wide measure of discretion' enjoyed by a state was 'limited in certain cases by prohibitive rules' and 'should not overlap the limits which international law places upon its jurisdiction.'[95] Subsequent practice of both the Permanent and International Court has dwelt more on these limits than the wide discretion. The Court has developed a clear jurisprudence beginning with the *US Nationals in Morocco* case[96] that with regard to a matter not in principle regulated by international law, the right of a state to use its discretion may nevertheless come to be regulated by international law. The question of whether a matter is solely within a state's domestic jurisdiction is an essentially relative question and depends on the stage of development of international relations.

In the *US Nationals in Morocco* the Court construed the General Act of Algeciras of 1906 as applying a principle of 'economic liberty without any inequality' to Morocco's relations with all third states, thus preventing any preference to be accorded to France as the Protecting State.[97] Similarly the US, by virtue of the most favoured-nation clause, was entitled to consular jurisdiction enjoyed by other states under treaties with Morocco, but was equally subject to revision and reduction of that consular jurisdiction effected by subsequent treaties.[98] The decision in the *Jurisdiction of the ICAO Council*[99] already referred to also illustrates this respect for treaty commitment; while

---

[95] PCIJ, Series A, No. 10 (1927), at p. 19.
[96] ICJ Reports, 1952, p. 176.   [97] *Ibid.*, at pp. 181–6.
[98] *Ibid.*, at pp. 199–201.   [99] ICJ Reports, 1972, p. 46.

material breach of treaty might justify suspension of over-flights by India it did not permit a refusal to apply the compromissory clause in the violated treaties. India was not free to determine unilaterally whether or not to allow over-flights.

Interestingly, the Court in the *Libyan/Chad Territorial Dispute*[100] also accorded primacy to the 1955 Treaty as constituting a determination of a permanent frontier, and consequently refused to consider evidence of exercise of sovereignty to indicate which of the two states enjoyed effective control of the disputed frontier territory.

On occasion, however, the terms in which the treaty under consideration is drafted may prevent the Court from according primacy to the treaty. Thus in *Guardianship of Infants* case[101] the applicant state, Sweden, relied on a treaty, the 1902 Hague Convention Relating to Guardianship of Infants, as qualifying the exercise of jurisdiction by the territorial state. In that case the Court construed the 1902 Convention restrictively and as not prohibiting the application to a foreign infant residing abroad of the law of the forum including protective upbringing on matters other than guardianship.[102] It thereby avoided an opportunity to clarify whether, and if so on what occasion, a mandatory requirement of *ordre public* might prevent the application of a treaty provision.

Critics of the case have argued that it gave insufficient weight to the primacy of treaties. The jurisdictional issue itself was resolved in the Hague Convention on the Protection of Infants of 1961 which applied the law of the child's habitual residence to all forms of protection of minors. It is there expressly provided that while respect is to be accorded to *ex lege* custody or guardianship based on the law of the child's nationality, such law may be disregarded if it is manifestly contrary to public policy of the applicable law.

Another more recent example is to be found in the *Lockerbie* case.[103] The UK, as the state where the act was committed, sought extradition from Libya of two of its nationals alleged to have caused the destruction of PanAm Flight 103: Libya, as the state of nationality of the alleged offenders, and of the territory where they were present, refused the request for extradition. There was thus a conflict of jurisdiction between the territorial state and the state of nationality, that state also having custody of the alleged offenders. Libya, however, initiated proceedings before the International Court in reliance on

---

[100] ICJ Reports, 1994, p. 6.
[101] ICJ Reports, 1958, p. 55.
[102] *Ibid.*, at p. 71.
[103] ICJ Reports, 1992, p. 3. Libya also brought similar proceedings against the USA.

its rights under the 1971 Montreal Convention for the Suppression of Hijacking of Aircraft. In particular it asserted that article 7 resolved the conflict by authorizing a choice of courses to the state having custody, and that the UK as a treaty party was required to assist it in the performance of the course it had adopted, namely prosecution in its own courts. It therefore sought interim measures from the Court to enjoin the UK from any coercive action to obtain extradition.

By including in that coercive action 'any initiative of the UN in the Security Council'[104] Libya introduced into the proceedings the constitutional relationship between the International Court and the Security Council. While the recommendatory nature of the Security Council's resolution 713 under Chapter VI of the Charter requesting Libya's co-operation might not have pre-empted the taking of interim measures by the Court, the adoption of resolution 748 under Chapter VII was mandatory and dispositive. The Court said: 'Whatever the situation previous to the adoption of resolution [748] the rights claimed by Libya under the Montreal Convention cannot now be regarded as appropriate for protection by the indication of provisional measures.'[105]

The issue of competing jurisdictions was therefore not addressed by the Court and, if the sanctions against Libya remain in force, may not even be addressed at the merits stage. Two divergent analyses of territorial jurisdiction were, however, displayed in the Concurring and Dissenting Opinions. On the one hand, the request for extradition and the refusal to extradite were treated as arising under general international law. Judge Oda, who concurred in the Court's refusal to grant the interim measures sought by Libya, was prepared to find no *prima facie* basis of jurisdiction under the compulsory dispute settlement clause of the Montreal Convention for the violation of Libya's sovereign rights by the UK's alleged coercive reinforcement of its request for extradition. That Convention, in his view, merely conferred concurrent and competing jurisdiction on different states in respect of unlawful acts against the safety of aircraft.[106]

A similar approach is to be found in the joint declaration of Judges Evensen, Tarassov, Guillaume and Aguilar Mawdsley which states: 'In article 8 the Convention makes extradition easier [than under general international law where the requested state is never under obligation to carry it out] but

---

[104] Verbatim Record CR92/2 p. 76 (trans. from French); see Fiona Beveridge, 'The Lockerbie Affair', *ICLQ*, 41 (1992), p. 907, at p. 917.

[105] ICJ Reports, 1992, p. 15.

[106] *Ibid.*, pp. 18–19.

without creating any obligation in that regard. Thus the Montreal Convention . . . did not prohibit Libya from refusing to extradite the accused to the UK.'[107]

The alternative position resolving the conflict of jurisdictions by application of a primacy of treaty principle was elaborated by Judge Bedjaoui in his Dissenting Opinion. He was prepared to construe a treaty obligation as giving rise to an accompanying right not to be hindered (être entravé) in its fulfilment. Article 7 of the Montreal Convention gave Libya an option between two obligations, to extradite or to prosecute; it had chosen the latter and consequently, additional to any rights it might enjoy under general international law, this gave rise to a treaty right to call on the UK not to hinder Libya's compliance therewith.[108]

The true centre of gravity of this dispute probably does not lie in these conflicting positions on jurisdiction. The UK has always contended that the Security Council action concerned state responsibility for terrorist activities and enjoyed primacy over any exercise of state jurisdiction.

NEW DEVELOPMENTS IN THE JURISDICTIONAL FIELD

In this final section we turn to consider whether the Court has given its support for any new developments in the field of jurisdiction. In the *Lockerbie* case at the merits stage it may yet have to address the question of hierarchy or ranking of jurisdictions, to determine whether the competence of the Security Council is subject to restrictions based on general international law and the jurisdictional right of a state not to extradite its nationals.

Pressure is also building up in the international system for the use of jurisdiction by states as a method to further common interests of the international community, the protection of human rights, suppression of offences against mankind such as war crimes, torture and drug dealing, and the protection of the environment.

The ILC in article 19(1) of its Draft Articles on State Responsibility identified a category of international crimes in respect of internationally wrongful acts which result from breach by a state of an international

---

[107] *Ibid*., at pp. 24–5.

[108] *Ibid*., at p. 39. The dispute reveals a conflicting interpretation of the *aut dedere, aut punire* clause; does it entitle the states parties to the treaty to exercise universal jurisdiction or merely empower the state refusing extradition to prosecute the offence? Further, in the case itself, the primary jurisdiction, based on the place where the crime was committed, treats the acts, though extra-territorial, as capable of constituting an offence under Scots law; whereas it is not clear whether the secondary jurisdiction, the Libyan law of nationality, recognizes such an extra-territorial basis for the offence.

obligation enacted for the protection of fundamental interests of the international community, and instanced aggression, serious breaches of safeguards
relating to rights of self-determination, the human being and the human
environment as coming within that category.[109] The Second Rapporteur in
article 5(2)(e) of part II of the Draft Articles on State Responsibility has
widened the concept of an 'injured State' to include 'if the right infringed by
the act of a State arises from a multilateral treaty or from a rule of customary
international law, any other State party to the multilateral treaty or bound by
the relevant rule of customary law, if it is established that . . . the right has been
created or is established for the protection of human rights and fundamental
freedoms'.[110] The US Third Restatement of the Foreign Relations Law goes
a stage further and asserts that universal jurisdiction in international law exists
not only over piracy, slave trade, and war crimes (uncontroversial), but also
over genocide, attacks on or hijacking of aircraft and perhaps certain acts of
terrorism'.[111]

These developments would seek to expand the relationship between
entitlement to exercise municipal jurisdiction and to enforce international law.
It would seem that the Court has made a clear connection, and is supported
by general doctrine in doing so, between territorial jurisdiction and the
entitlement on the international level to resort to diplomatic or legal measures
for the infringement of territorial jurisdiction, to treaty and unilateral
statement to vary its extent, and to the use of proportionate forcible measures
to preserve its exercise. It has shown itself less certain in developing such a
relationship based on nationality jurisdiction. In the *Nottebohm*[112] case, the
grant of nationality by naturalization was held not automatically to entitle a
state to exercise diplomatic protection against the state of nationality by birth,
unless the propositions had a 'genuine connection' with the naturalizing state;
and in the *Barcelona Traction*[113] case the state of the nationality of the majority
shareholders was held not entitled to exercise diplomatic protection in respect
of loss arising out of the compulsory receivership of a company, so long as the
state of registration of the company was legally in a position to exercise
diplomatic protection. Earlier, the Court had rejected any enlargement of

---

[109] *YbILC*, (1976, vol. II part 2), pp. 95–122.
[110] For text as provisionally adopted by the Commission see *YbILC*, (1986, vol. II part 2), p. 38.
[111] *Restatement of the Law – The Foreign Relations Law of the United States* (St Paul, MN, 1987), vol. I,
para. 404, at p. 254.
[112] ICJ Reports, 1955, p. 4.
[113] ICJ Reports, 1970, p. 3; but note Judge Jessup's Separate Opinion stating at p. 166: 'There is a trend in
the direction of extending the jurisdictional power of the State to deal with foreign enterprises which
have contact with the State's territorial domain.'

universal jurisdiction so as to permit states to pursue international remedies for common interests of the international community. In its judgment of 18 July 1966 in the *South West Africa* cases by a narrow margin – the President's casting vote – the Court refused: 'The equivalent of an "*actio popularis*" or right resident in any member of a community to take legal action in vindication of a public interest . . . a right of this kind . . . is not known in international law as it stands at present.'[114]

This negative approach was however qualified in the *Barcelona Traction* case by the much-quoted paragraph:

> An essential distinction should be drawn between the obligations of a State towards the international community as a whole, and those arising *vis à vis* another State in the field of diplomatic protection. By their very nature the former are a concern of all States. In view of the importance of the rights involved, all States can be held to have a legal interest in their protection; they are obligations *erga omnes*.[115]

Although the Court identified obligations concerning the basic rights of the human person as included in these obligations *erga omnes* it did not in that judgment, nor elsewhere, state whether it thereby recognized all states to have the right of recourse to international courts to protect those interests. By stating 'not a mere interest affected, but solely a right infringed involves responsibility' it appeared to qualify the earlier paragraph. Surely further clarification from the Court is required before the obligations *erga omnes* can be construed to mean, as does Rapporteur Ago, that 'every State even if it is not immediately and directly affected by the breach, should be considered justified in invoking the responsibility of the State committing the internationally wrongful act'.[116]

It is also to be noted that, in the *Barcelona Traction* case, the judgment later declares in orthodox fashion that on the universal case level (unlike the regional European Convention on Human Rights machinery), human-rights violations depend on treaty and 'do not confer on States the capacity to protect the victims of infringements of such rights irrespective of their nationality'.[117]

The question is an important one, not least because expectations have been encouraged by the ratification of international and regional human rights treaties, CERDS, CEDAW, the Conventions on the Rights of the Child, Genocide, and Torture, which the accompanying treaty machinery for

---

[114] *South West Africa* case *(Second Phase)*, ICJ Reports, 1966, p. 6, at p. 47.

[115] ICJ Reports, 1970, p. 3, at p. 32.

[116] Fifth Report of R. Ago, *YbILC*, 2, 1 (1976), at p. 29.

[117] ICJ Reports, 1970, p. 3, at p. 47.

enforcement does not fulfil. A state may, therefore, come under popular pressure to respond to these expectations and to do so by taking legal action either by international measures or by proceedings within its own jurisdiction. May it expand the basis for exercise of criminal jurisdiction over those who violate human rights or its civil jurisdiction to give reparation to the victim, though the state has no connection based on territoriality, nationality or custody of the offender? May it bring proceedings in the International Court against a state that fails to enforce respect for human rights in its own jurisdiction, or widen the exception to state immunity so as to permit proceedings against a defaulting state in its municipal courts? Would resort to these measures constitute intervention in the domestic jurisdiction of the other state?

Important as these questions are, they have rarely been referred to the Court. Only in a recent case has there been some reference.

In the *Application of the Genocide Convention* case[118] the Court indicated interim measures against Serbia which required it to ensure that military, paramilitary or irregular armed units or persons subject to its control, direction or influence did not commit acts of genocide against the Muslim population of Bosnia–Herzegovina. The limitation to acts of genocide arose by reason that the Court had found its *prima facie* jurisdiction limited to obligations covered by the Genocide Convention, and the Court construed those obligations to impose restrictions on Serbia's conduct beyond its own territory.

Ad hoc judge Kreca challenged this construction of the Genocide Convention as a treaty of universal repression, arguing that the Convention firmly opted for a territorial principle of the obligation of prevention and 'the only action relating to crimes committed outside the territory of the Contracting Party is by organs of the United Nations within the scope of the general competence'.[119] He considered that the Court's order that Serbia should control units in another state's territory would constitute a violation of the prohibition of intervention.[120]

Judge Tarassov, in his Dissenting Opinion to the first request for provisional measures[121] had considered the Order of the Court that Serbia should ensure that any units which might be under its control should not commit or assist in any way any genocidal act against any group in Bosnia to be very close to a prejudgement of Serbia's action with regard to one element (the Muslim) of the Bosnian population and further to appear to extend a state's responsibility

---

[118] ICJ Reports, 1993, p. 325.   [119] *Ibid.*, at p. 464.
[120] *Ibid.*   [121] ICJ Reports, 1993, p. 3, at p. 26.

'when the persons who are accused of such acts are not its citizens and not within its territorial jurisdiction'.[122] In his Dissent in the Further Request for Provisional Measures[123] he asserted that primary responsibility for acts of genocide lay with the government of Bosnia–Herzegovina 'for acts committed on its territory by its own citizens irrespective of whether they are Moslems, Serbs or Croats officials or private individuals'.[124] He disapproved of any suggestion 'that ethnic homogeneity of a given State's population could be taken to imply that State's responsibility for the actions of the same ethnic group living in another State and committed on the territory of the latter'.[125]

To sum up the theme of this chapter: lost opportunities to develop the law, the preference of states for a trial-and-error approach to its formation outside the ICJ, the Court's own tendency to restrict, rather than expand, by reference to international law principles a state's jurisdiction – these are the lasting impressions left by the Court's cases. Only by giving compulsory jurisdiction to the Court itself will it be put in a position to develop a coherent doctrine on jurisdiction and immunities.

---

[122] *Ibid.*, at p. 27.   [123] *Ibid.*, p. 325, at p. 449.
[124] *Ibid.*, at p. 450.   [125] *Ibid.*, at p. 449.

13

Adjudication as a mode of acquisition of territory?

Some observations on the Iraq–Kuwait boundary demarcation in light of the jurisprudence of the International Court of Justice

Harry Post

ॐ

INTRODUCTION

In its resolution 687 of 8 April 1991 which presented to Iraq the bill for its invasion of Kuwait and for Operation Desert Storm, the Security Council among many other things demanded that Iraq (and Kuwait) respect the inviolability of their mutual international boundary. In the same resolution, the Security Council considered this boundary to have been recognized by both neighbouring states in 'Minutes' agreed upon in 1963. However, notwithstanding this agreement on the delimitation of the boundary, the Council also noted that the boundary was still in need of demarcation. In paragraph 3 of the resolution, the Secretary-General was called upon to assist Iraq and Kuwait in this matter and, in the same paragraph, received some instructions on how to proceed. On 2 May 1991, he reported to establish the Iraq–Kuwait Boundary Demarcation Commission.

The following pages analyse international jurisprudence, notably of the International Court of Justice and of the IKBDC, in support of the thesis that has long been advanced in international legal doctrine, that adjudication on territorial title is a sixth traditional mode of acquisition of territory in international law?[1] 'Traditional', because, apart from cession, conquest, occupation,

---

[1] On these territorial modes, see Robert Y. Jennings, *The Acquisition of Territory in International Law* (Manchester, 1963), pp. 6ff; although conceived in the early 1960s, this small book is still most relevant and even indispensable for all serious studies of territorial disputes and territorial adjudication. See also Sir Robert Jennings and Sir Arthur Watts (eds.), *Oppenheim's International Law* (9th edn, Harlow, 1992), pp. 679ff; or Ian Brownlie, *Principles of Public International Law* (4th edn, Oxford, 1990), pp. 131ff.

accretion and prescription, adjudication, too, was known in Roman law as a mode of acquiring dominion over property. However, it was the only one of these Roman law modes not adopted in international law.[2] Often, but not always, international lawyers have dismissed this claim to prominence of adjudication on the ground of the declaratory, instead of constitutive, effect of judicial decisions on territorial disputes.

Examination of the relevant judgments of the ICJ (and of its predecessor), however, indicates that constitutive elements in decisions on territorial disputes have not always been absent, as suggested. Notably in two of the Court's more recent decisions, constitutive effects seemed to be hidden under a formal cover of considerations of equity.

Even more prominently, the Iraq–Kuwait boundary demarcation might have brought the issue of the possible constitutive effect of adjudication on territorial title to the fore. After all, the United Nations Security Council has put the matter of the determination of the Iraq–Kuwait boundary and the demarcation task of the IKBDC in the context of its binding resolutions.

An analysis of the IKBDC and its important work is, in my view, also of interest for a better understanding of a more general matter which, on the one hand, surpasses the issue of acquisition of territory but, on the other hand, has an important direct impact on the role of adjudication on territorial rights in general, and on the role of the International Court of Justice and arbitral tribunals in that respect, in particular; the IKBDC may have put the burning issue of whether there are limits to the power of the UN Security Council into a somewhat different perspective than has been so far presumed. Apparently, in the area of territorial dispute, the explicit consent of the parties concerned to territorial dispositions, is (still) indispensable.

However, it is not the objective of this chapter to provide an all-encompassing and detailed legal analysis of the important work of the IKBDC.[3] Although it fully warrants such a study, any undertaking of this sort would effectively prevent consideration of the state of the law in respect to the main thesis. In short, the Iraq–Kuwait boundary demarcation is reviewed here (pp. 249–60) in order, primarily, to present a tentative analysis to provide a basis for some theoretical reflections on the state of adjudication as a mode of

---

[2] The appropriateness of these traditional modes has been severely criticized by international lawyers, and on good grounds, most of which are concurred with by this author, although that criticism has to and can be left aside here (see, notably, Jennings, *The Acquisition of Territory*, p. 7; or Brownlie, *Principles of Public International Law*, pp. 131–2).

[3] See, for a much more extensive study, M. H. Mendelsohn and S. C. Hulton, 'The Iraq–Kuwait Boundary', in *BYbIL*, 65 (1994), pp. 135ff.

acquisition and, second, to make some observations on the issue of a possible limit to the power of the UN Security Council in territorial matters. In the opening section, the former topic is introduced by a brief excursion into some rather 'classic' texts. Subsequently, the jurisprudence of the ICJ on territorial disputes is analysed. In the concluding section, remarks on the powers of the Security Council regarding territorial dispositions are followed by some suggestions on the state of adjudication as a mode of acquisition of territory in international law.

ADJUDICATION ON TERRITORIAL TITLE

Judicial adjudication

In 1927, writing on modes of acquisition of territory, Hersch Lauterpacht was probably still justified when he said: 'Adjudication [as a mode of acquisition] is, so far, unknown to international law.'[4] The primary reason was that, at the time, decisions of international tribunals were generally seen as declaratory of existing rights and not as constitutive of new rights. This rather straightforward opinion on the powers, or rather lack of powers, of international judicial bodies in respect to the establishment of territorial rights may come as something of a surprise in view of the abundance of decisions by arbitration tribunals on such rights that had already been taken at the time Lauterpacht was writing.[5] However, as will be seen on pp. 239–43, his assessment of the state of the law in this respect is generally confirmed by other academic authorities. However, an important preliminary question to be answered in this respect is what precisely is meant by a declaratory or a constitutive effect.

Quasi-judicial adjudication

To some extent, Lauterpacht qualified his own statement when he referred to adjudication as a 'quasi-judicial' process leading to similar decisions on the allocation of territory, but taken by a body other than a judicial body. If this is the case, the decision may still be declaratory, e.g., if the decision has not been more than an affirmation of existing territorial rights subsumed in

---

4 Hersch Lauterpacht, *Private Law Sources and Analogies of International Law* (Harlow, 1927; repr. London, 1970), p. 107, note 3.

5 See, for an impressive review, A. L. W. Munkman, 'Adjudication and Adjustment – international judicial decision and the settlement of territorial and boundary disputes', *BYbIL*, 46 (1972–3), pp. 1ff (here, adjudication is broadly taken as including arbitration).

an award of an arbitral tribunal or the World Court.[6] In the first place he mentions three cases that 'were more than declaratory of existing rights'. In two of them, the Council of the League of Nations took far-reaching decisions.[7] Previously, in 1913, in the matter of the status of Skutari (now Albania), the 'Concert of European Powers' did something comparable.

In the same vein, he has noted that articles 10 (the indirect prohibition of conquest) and 19 (on the League's powers of revision of treaties) of the Covenant of the League of Nations suggest also that international law might adopt adjudication, this 'last' of the Roman law modes of acquiring dominion.[8]

Writing at the same period as Sir Hersch Lauterpacht, and being one of the few other authors to say anything on the subject, Karl Strupp embraced Lauterpacht's 'double' approach to adjudication when he described it as follows: 'Il y a *adjudication* si des territoires sont attribués par une communauté d'Etats (Congrès de Vienne, Congrès de Berlin, Société des Nations) ou par une sentence d'une Cour de Justice internationale ou d'un Corps international (1913, v. Scutari).'[9]

Professor Verzijl argues that adjudication is an independent mode by which territory can be acquired only when an adjudicating authority 'is entitled or especially empowered to allocate [territory] to a State to which it does not appertain'.[10] In order for a state legitimately to acquire a territorial title on the basis of adjudication, a further condition, of course, is that

---

[6] The League's Council decisions on the territory of Memel and on the Vilayet of Mosul (see note 7 below) were both preceded by Advisory Opinions of the PCIJ. Apart from the World Courts and arbitration tribunals, Ian Brownlie includes under adjudication by a judicial organ bodies 'acting judicially in respect of the issue of title including, for example, the Council of the League of Nations': *Principles of Public International Law*, p. 137, note 69.

[7] The Council's decisions on the award of Memel to Lithuania (League of Nations Doc. C 159, M. 39, 1924, VII), and regarding the Vilayet of Mosul to Iraq (G. Fr. de Martens, *Nouveau Recueil Général*, 3e série, vol. XXI, pp. 689–91). Although, in the latter case, the Council decision states that the frontier between Turkey and Iraq *shall* be fixed, it also stipulates, in para. 2, a condition which says that the British Government first has to submit a new treaty with Iraq before the decision shall be declared definitive (*ibid.*, p. 691).

[8] Besides occupation, cession, conquest (or subjugation), prescription and accretion (see, e.g., Jennings and Watts (eds.), *Oppenheim's International Law*, pp. 679–718).

[9] K. Strupp, *Eléments du droit international public universel, Européen et Américain* (2nd edn, Paris, 1930), p. 156. See also, more elaborated, in K. Strupp/Hans-Jürgen Schlochauer (eds.), *Wörterbuch des Völkerrecht* (Berlin, 1960), vol. II, p. 621.

[10] J. H. W. Verzijl, *International Law in Historical Perspective, State Territory* (Leyden, 1970), part III, p. 378. This position corresponds to that of Lauterpacht who, on the basis of an analogy with Roman law, argues: 'The *adjudicatio* had a constitutive effect. It transferred to a party the right of ownership which it had not before' (Lauterpacht, *Private Law Sources*, p. 107).

the authority also makes use of its power of allocation to this constitutive effect.[11]

Writing forty years later than his distinguished British colleague, Verzijl is somewhat more positive about the possibility of constitutive effects of adjudication on a territorial dispute, although he also seems to think primarily about adjudication by quasi-judicial bodies. He mentions two main cases where such adjudications can and have taken place: decisions on the dismemberment of an insufficiently coherent state, and decisions on the allocation of territory of a state forced to renounce that territory (usually as a consequence of a lost war). He adds that in both types of case decisions will usually be taken by a political rather than a judicial body.

In Verzijl's view such adjudication on territory has occurred quite frequently. He refers, *inter alia*, to the 1913 'reshuffle of the Balkan States' and to the territorial decisions following both world wars, as well as to the 1920 Arbitral Award determining the frontier between Estonia and Latvia, and the 1925 resolution of the Council of the League of Nations adjudicating Mosul to Iraq.[12]

In his discussion of the subject, Verzijl notes some features of constitutive adjudication which seem still worth taking into account. He points to an element of arbitrariness in adjudications on the disintegrated parts in cases of dismemberment, due to the absence of relevant positive rules of general international law. This leads, in particular, to the possibility of a choice between various criteria which can be applied, such as the ethnic composition of the population (in Verzijl's view probably the principal criterion), economic coherence, religious factors, the need for defence, etc.[13]

Due to this lack of positive rules of international law in such cases, the relationship between constitutive adjudication and a decision *ex aequo et bono* is also touched upon.[14] As is well known, in the case of the World Courts, article 38(2) of their Statutes allows such a decision 'if the parties agree

---

[11] Verzijl points to several disputes 'which linger in the crepuscular middle zone between adjudication proper and a declaration of law'. Notably, he refers to territorial dispute solution by way of weighing the relative strengths of the claims of parties, and cases that are in fact 'free' adjudications, although they are phrased as declaratory of an existing legal situation (see Verzijl, *International Law in Historical Perspective*, pp. 378–9; the latter 'grey' zone will concern us again: see pp. 260–3 below).

[12] *Ibid.*, p. 380, also for references. Paul Guggenheim also refers to this latter case, and accepts that 'L'adjudication d'un territoire à un Etat par un organe judiciaire ou administratif sur la base d'un traité international constitue également une form de l'extension légale du territoire' (*Traité du Droit International Public* (Geneva, 1953), vol. I, p. 442, note 2).

[13] Verzijl, *International Law in Historical Perspective*, p. 380.

[14] *Ibid.*, p. 379. See also Knut Ipsen, *Menzel's Völkerrecht* (3rd edn, Munich, 1990), p. 277.

thereto', which, as yet, has never occurred.[15] Although of course usually less authoritatively stated, in the case of arbitral tribunals, the same condition of authorization by the parties seems to hold.[16] Whether there is somewhat more freedom for arbitral tribunals than for the World Courts to interpret a Special Agreement to allow a decision *ex aequo et bono* is debatable, but the possibility cannot be excluded.[17]

The freedom of a non-judicial adjudication body to assume such 'constitutive' powers (e.g., in light of the general purpose of the decision asked) is likely, of course, to be broader. Professor Brownlie's argument under this heading is illustrative: 'If a political organ like the Security Council does not decide the issue judicially and in accordance with the law, it is simply exercising a power of disposition which may be derived from the Charter (this is a difficult question) or from a treaty specially conferring such power.'[18] In respect to a 'quasi-judicial' adjudication, and in particular in modern international law in the case of the Security Council, an important matter seems to be the form of the agreement with the party (or parties) whose territory is disposed of. Does there need to be an *ad hoc* agreement between – or with – those parties if the Security Council wants to assume the power to adjudicate, perhaps constitutively, on its or their territory by way of a mandatory decision (or, for that matter, to assume the power to decide *ex aequo et bono*)? Or can the agreement also validly be supposed to have been given on the basis of a more general mandate adhered to previously, as might have been done by 'accepting' a general resolution of the Security Council, such as resolution 687, or simply by becoming a party to the UN Charter? An *ad hoc* agreement of the parties expressing their consent to such a disposition is, in probably all cases, politically more attractive. However, if the Security Council so decides under Chapter VII, is such an agreement, or the acceptance by the parties concerned of a mandatory resolution to that extent, (also) necessary under

---

[15] In the *Free Zones* case, the question whether the PCIJ had power to decide 'disregarding rights recognized by it and taking into account considerations of pure expediency only' led to a negative answer by the smallest majority, primarily due to the lack of an explicit provision to that extent in the Special Agreement (PCIJ, Series A, No. 24 (1930), p. 10; similarly, the ICJ in its *Burkina Faso v. Mali* case, in ICJ Reports, 1986, at pp. 567–8). See further Jennings and Watts (eds.), *Oppenheim's International Law*, pp. 43–4.

[16] As the Tribunal argued in the (1956) *Ottoman Empire Lighthouses Claims* (*RIAA*, 12, at pp. 187–8).

[17] The majority view of the Arbitral Tribunal in the *Rann of Kutch* case (*Indo-Pakistan Western Boundary (Rann of Kutch)* case between India and Pakistan; 7 *ILM* 692 (1968)) on the allocation of certain parcels of land to Pakistan seems, e.g., very difficult indeed to justify on the basis of equity *infra legem* (see also pp. 245–9 below).

[18] Brownlie, *Principles of Public International Law*, p. 137, note 69. See also Jost Delbrück and Rüdiger Wolfrum, *Dahm's Völkerrecht* (2nd edn, Berlin, 1989), vol. I.1, p. 378.

international law?[19] In respect to a part of the decision by the Iraq–Kuwait Boundary Demarcation Commission, as will be seen on pp. 249–63 below, such questions appeared to be of some relevance.

The International Court of Justice and constitutive effect

There is not much reason to think that in its first three cases on territorial disputes,[20] the International Court of Justice has done anything other than declaring the relevant state of the law (which, anyhow, was already complicated enough). In both the 1953 *Minquiers and Ecrehos* case and the 1959 *Frontier Land* case, the ICJ was asked to assess the law and declare on the title of the territory under dispute. In its 1953 decision, the Court was asked to decide whether Great Britain or France had sovereignty over the two groups of islets and rocks in question. It was not asked to concern itself with old or perhaps new boundaries, which its decision on the title might imply.[21]

The *Frontier Land* case seemed more directly to concern the course of the frontier between the two neighbouring countries. However, in effect the Court was asked to adjudge and declare that the sovereignty over two 'plots' of land belonged either to Belgium or The Netherlands. These plots were defined in an exact and invariable way.[22]

The *Temple of Preah Vihear* case, unlike the two preceding cases not based on a Special Agreement but on an application by Cambodia, perhaps left somewhat more leeway. The Court was asked to determine territorial sovereignty over the region of the temple and its precincts. In order to do so the Court had to consider the work of a Mixed Commission of Delimitation set up under a French–Thai treaty of 13 February 1904. Cambodia's position

---

[19] See Delbrück and Wolfrum, *Dahm's Völkerrecht*, p. 378. The authors of this text believe in principle that the Security Council indeed has such powers under the Charter, but at the time of writing are not very optimistic as to the possibility of their use. They even conclude that the principle of adjudication on territorial sovereignty in the constitutive sense 'kommt . . . wohl eher historische Bedeutung zu' (*ibid.*). Mendelson and Hulton, 'The Iraq–Kuwait Boundary', p. 147 are more (perhaps somewhat overly) positive on the Security Council's powers in this regard.

[20] Although the Arbitral Award at issue concerned a territorial dispute, the ICJ case concerning *The Arbitral Award made by the King of Spain on 23 December 1906* (ICJ Reports, 1960, pp. 192ff) itself did not, and is therefore not included among the Court's cases on territorial disputes. The *Right of Passage over Indian Territory (Merits)* case (*ibid.*, pp. 6ff) is not included either. Here, the Court's cases on issues of maritime delimitation, a related but also fundamentally different matter, will not be examined (see, e.g., on these differences Prosper Weil, *The Law of Maritime Delimitation – Reflections* (Cambridge, 1989), pp. 91–5).

[21] ICJ Reports, 1953, pp. 47ff. The parties themselves, in article I of their Special Agreement, had excluded the possibility that the groups could have the status of *res nullius* or that of *condominium*.

[22] ICJ Reports, 1959, pp. 214ff.

as to the sovereignty over the temple area was primarily based on the frontier traced on a map which, although not produced by the Commission, was drawn as a result of the latter's activities. The Court, however, agreed with Thailand that this map was not binding on the parties.

The frontier according to article I of the 1904 treaty should follow the watershed line. Thailand admitted that some discretion in determining this watershed line was allowed to avoid anomalies, but a departure from the 'true' watershed line to include the temple area in Cambodian territory would far exceed such discretion.

Unfortunately, in view of the topic of this study, the Court avoided discussing the possible scope of discretion in drawing a watershed line (by the Mixed Commission or any other body). In its decision it gave an – affirmative – answer to a rather different question: whether or not the parties had adopted the map just mentioned, and the frontier line indicated on it, as representing the outcome of the work on delimitation of the frontier in the region of Preah Vihear, thereby conferring on it a binding character. The Court's decision therefore involved, primarily, an assessment of whether or not particular acts by the parties, notably by Thailand, should be interpreted as consent to the map and the frontier indicated on it.

Something quite similar happened in the most recent of the Court's decisions, its 1994 judgment in the *Territorial Dispute* case between Libya and Chad. Here, the Court concluded on the basis of a careful analysis of the relevant behaviour of both parties that 'the contracting parties wished, by the 1955 [Treaty of Friendship and Good Neighbourliness], and particularly by its Article 3, to define their common frontier'.[23] A difference with the *Temple* case, however, is that this conclusion did not immediately lead to a precise frontier line. Article 3 referred to an annexe I listing a number of international instruments. On the basis of this list the Court now had to conclude a frontier line between the parties. Due to the nature of some of these instruments this still proved to be a rather complicated matter, but not one that was impossible to solve on the basis of the rules of international law.[24] The Court's judgment can be seen as quite successful in the sense of declaring the existing course of the boundary even without recourse to considerations of equity, as it needed to do rather extensively in the other two more recent cases on land territory.

---

[23] Judgment of 3 February 1994 in the case concerning the *Territorial Dispute* between the Libyan Arab Jamahiriya and the Republic of Chad, not yet published, para. 57. In the Court's opinion this 1955 Treaty 'completely' determined the boundary (*ibid.*, para. 76).

[24] See for the eastern part of the boundary (east of the meridian 16 degrees east) *ibid.*, paras. 59 and 60, and for the (smaller) western part of the boundary (west of 16 degrees east) *ibid.*, para. 63.

In view of the subject matter here under examination, the *Frontier Dispute* case between Burkina Faso and Mali is of particular interest. Here (a Chamber of) the ICJ for the first time was really asked to decide what the line of the frontier between the two contesting parties in the disputed area was. In order to do so, the Court saw fit to explain how it saw certain limits to its powers. On the one hand, the judgment makes clear that a decision *ex aequo et bono* is not allowed here. The parties did not agree thereto, and the Chamber did not undertake to see whether in a territorial dispute of this nature it perhaps had any customary powers nevertheless allowing such a decision.[25] On the other hand, both parties to the case agreed that equity *infra legem* could be resorted to, although Burkina Faso expressed as its worries 'that it was far from clear what the practical implications would be in this case. It emphasized that in the field of territorial boundary delimitation there is no equivalent to the concept of "equitable principles" as frequently referred to by the law applicable in the delimitation of maritime areas.'[26]

The Chamber explained that it understood by equity *infra legem* 'that form of equity which constitutes a method of interpretation of the law in force, and is one of its attributes',[27] and repeated the dictum from its decisions in the *Fisheries Jurisdiction* cases: 'It is not a matter of finding simply an equitable solution, but an equitable solution derived from the applicable law.'[28]

Probably, the Chamber did not really solve Burkina Faso's legal uncertainty when it ended its deliberations on this matter by asserting that to know how equity will be applied in practice 'will emerge from its application throughout this Judgment of the principles and rules which it finds to be applicable'.[29]

Generally speaking, the Chamber's equitable 'adjustments' of its application of the law can be considered as forming part of the normal application of the specific rules of law on drawing a boundary. They therefore concern equity *infra legem*, and can be said to be part of the Chamber's attempt to declare the state of the law regarding the course of the frontier.

In one case, however, where a frontier pool was divided into two equal halves, although fair or wise enough, it seems problematic still to provide sufficient justification in those terms. Here, although the 'form' may still

---

[25] This seems highly unlikely (see, e.g., on the customary powers of this sort of arbitral tribunal, the *Ottoman Empire Lighthouses* case, *RIAA*, 12, at pp. 187–8).

[26] *Case Concerning the Frontier Dispute*, ICJ Reports, 1986, p. 567. In general, on equity, see e.g., R. Y. Jennings, 'Equity and Equitable Principles', *Annuaire suisse de droit international*, 42 (1986), pp. 27ff; or Daniel Bardonnet 'Equité et frontières terrestres', in *Mélanges offerts à Paul Reuter* (Paris, 1981), pp. 35ff (as said, before, here the different but also related matter of maritime delimitation will be left aside).

[27] ICJ Reports, 1986, pp. 567–8.

[28] ICJ Reports, 1974, pp. 33 and 202.

[29] ICJ Reports, 1986, p. 568.

be equity *infra legem*, materially this qualification is more difficult to give. Apparently, the Chamber applied equitable criteria of quite a different nature. In effect the judgement says so:

> If the competent authorities had endorsed the agreement of 15 January 1965, it would have been unnecessary for the purpose of the present case to ascertain whether that agreement was of a *declaratory or modifying character* in relation to the 1932 boundaries. But this did not happen, and the Chamber has received no mandate from the Parties to substitute its own free choice of an appropriate frontier for theirs.[30]

The Chamber did not see it as justified to 'resort to the concept of equity in order to modify an established frontier'. Furthermore, it could not take account of the important 1965 agreement between the parties, because they had not endorsed it. However, after recalling that the Chamber was actually asked to draw a precise line, it considered that 'the circumstances in which that agreement was concluded' could be taken into account. The Chamber apparently considered that its power to resort to equity *infra legem* would allow it to do so. It continued then to divide the pool of Soum into two equal halves ('in the absence of any precise indication in the texts of the position of the frontier line').[31]

At this point it seems appropriate to recall Sir Robert Jennings's argument from his 1963 book: 'In the case where an arbitration is given power to determine frontiers, the decision may itself, perhaps, be a true mode of acquisition of territorial sovereignty.'[32] For the determination of the precise line the frontier should follow, the modes of acquisition do not help very much. To this avail specific rules have developed which provide some aid to a commission authorized to draw the frontier in detail. Probably, most of these specific practical rules cannot be said to be rules of customary law (i.e., which bind states when they have not concluded any boundary treaty or other agreement). Only the thalweg rule may be a serious candidate.[33] Although the

---

[30] *Ibid.*, pp. 632–3 (emphasis added). See, e.g., Gino Naldi, 'The case concerning the Frontier Dispute (Burkina Faso/Republic of Mali): *uti possidetis* in an African Perspective', *ICLQ*, 36 (1987), p. 895.

[31] ICJ Reports, 1986, p. 533. The Chamber added: 'Although "Equity does not necessarily imply equality" (*North Sea Continental Shelf*, ICJ Reports, 1969, p. 49), where there are no special circumstances the latter is generally the best expression of the former.'

[32] Jennings, *The Acquisition of Territory in International Law*, p. 13. In a footnote (*ibid.*) he adds: 'Hence, the inclusion by some authorities of "adjudication" as a mode of acquisition of territorial sovereignty.'

[33] Even in the case of the thalweg rule, probably the best candidate for customary status, the large practice and unclear *opinio juris* of states regarding boundary rivers is nevertheless certainly not uniform. That other rules of boundary demarcation would be customary is still much less clear (e.g., the mid-channel rule in the case of a non-navigable boundary river or a canal, or the watershed rule for a boundary mountain ridge). In Professor Brownlie's view these rules are 'presumptions and principles of equity

actual process of drawing a boundary, as well as the relevant rules, differ then entirely from determining territorial sovereignty on the basis of a mode of acquisition, nevertheless the former concerns territorial title, in Jennings's terms, 'in the fullest sense of the word'.[34]

In the case of a sheer technical process of demarcating a boundary already laid down in fairly clear terms or even in considerable detail, this process or the division of territory resulting from it is not likely to cause major legal (or other) problems between the neighbouring states. However, when the 'delimitation' is broad and general, or even vague, or if 'normal' legal evidence is lacking, as on this particular part of the boundary in the *Frontier Dispute* case, the Tribunal can no longer be said to be 'only' demarcating the boundary. In its specific application of equity *infra legem* the Chamber can be said to have produced a constitutive effect, instead of 'only' declaring what the state of the law is.

In this respect, the decision in this case is reminiscent of the prevailing opinion of the Chairman in the *Rann of Kutch* arbitration where he stated 'It would be inequitable to recognise these inlets as foreign territory. It would be conducive to friction and conflict. The paramount consideration of promoting peace and stability in this region compels the recognition and confirmation that this territory, which is wholly surrounded by Pakistan territory, also be regarded as such.'[35]

In its 1992 decision in the *Land, Island and Maritime Frontier Dispute*, another Chamber of the Court referred back to the position regarding the application of equity *infra legem* in the *Frontier Dispute* decision, and emphasized that only if no evidence could be found for the course of the boundary is equity *infra legem* applied. In this case 'evidence' has a rather wide meaning. The Chamber, in its search for the *uti possidetis* line, takes, e.g., a variety of local topographical factors into account which it presumes are of a sort that 'have been a factor in boundary-making everywhere'.[36] Within its wide powers regarding evidence to be used, it is allowed to do so.[37]

---

rather than mandatory rules' (*Principles of Public International Law*, pp. 124–5). These rules are, indeed, not mandatory rules (in the sense of *ius cogens*), but some may be 'normal' binding rules (see Harry Post, 'Border Conflicts between Iran and Iraq: Review and Legal Reflections'; in Ige F. Dekker and Harry H. G. Post, *The Gulf War of 1980–1989* (Dordrecht/Boston/London, 1992), p. 26).

[34] He continues: 'It is *par excellence* the type of case where a decision who has the better right of neighbouring claimants is a decision of title *erga omnes* (*The Acquisition of Territory in International Law*, p. 13).

[35] 7 *ILM* 692 (1968).

[36] *Case Concerning the Land, Island and Maritime Frontier Dispute*, between El Salvador and Honduras, Nicaragua intervening: ICJ Reports, 1992, p. 351, at p. 390.

[37] According to article 5 of the Special Agreement between the parties, the Chamber is explicitly allowed, 'where pertinent', to apply the provisions of the (1980) General Treaty of Peace between Honduras

Only in drawing the boundary in the fourth, and longest, of the disputed sectors of the land boundary, was the Chamber obliged explicitly to have recourse to equity *infra legem*. At this point, the Chamber cites the arguments, just presented, from the *Frontier Dispute* case for the justification of the division of the frontier pool of Soum.[38] As in the latter case, and basically for the same reason, this Chamber, too, may be said at this point not to have declared the law, but to have produced a constitutive effect.

In the jurisprudence of the old World Court on frontier demarcations, Professor Schwarzenberger has reported a comparable effect to that in these two ICJ cases. However, in these PCIJ cases, no reference to (any form of) equity was made. He observes that peacemakers often exercised quasi-legislative functions and that this element is not entirely lacking in the decisions of their subordinate organs, frontier commissions and arbitral tribunals either, when they have the task of 'filling in the details of the sketch'. He then adds: 'Whether or not their awards have a declaratory character in form, in substance they necessarily entail a strong constitutive element.'[39] Schwarzenberger continues by convincingly showing that the PCIJ has consistently interpreted the powers of these 'subordinate' international bodies in such a way as 'to promote the object for the achievement of which they had been established: the creation of definite and complete frontiers'.[40] There is reason then to believe that the ICJ interprets its own powers in such cases in a comparable way. At least in its two recent decisions concerning boundary demarcation the Court has not been afraid to include constitutive elements in order successfully to accomplish the drawing of a precise frontier line.

In its jurisprudence on disputes on land territory, the ICJ so far has not gone much further than including relatively modest constitutive elements in the judgments. At first sight, it seems that the Iraq–Kuwait Boundary Demarcation Commission has produced more substantive constitutive effects in its decision.

and El Salvador. Notably, its article 26 appeared of interest. This article allowed a wide variety of evidence and arguments to be taken into account for the delimitation of the boundary (see *ibid.*, p. 391).

[38] 'In endeavouring to do so, however, it encounters a difficulty: neither side has offered any evidence whatever as to the line of the *uti possidetis juris* in this region' (*ibid.*, p. 513, and p. 514 for the citation of the *Frontier Dispute* case).

[39] Georg Schwarzenberger, *International Law* (3rd edn, London, 1957), vol. I, p. 311.

[40] *Ibid.*; as examples, Schwarzenberger refers to the Court's Advisory Opinions in the *Jaworzina Boundary* case (1923) between Czechoslovakia and Poland (PCIJ, Series B, No. 8), in the *Monastery of Saint-Naoum* (1924), between Albania and Yugoslavia (PCIJ, Series B, No. 9) and, in particular, to the Court's Opinion in the *Mosul Boundary* case (1925) between Great Britain and Turkey (PCIJ, Series B, No. 12).

THE DEMARCATION OF THE BOUNDARY
BETWEEN IRAQ AND KUWAIT

Resolution 687 as the legal basis of the demarcation

Apart from many other important matters regarding the aftermath of Operation Desert Storm, Security Council resolution 687 of 3 April 1991 addresses the demarcation of the boundary between Iraq and Kuwait. It is presumed that this boundary had already been delimited, i.e., in the 'Agreed Minutes Between the State of Kuwait and the Republic of Iraq Regarding the Restoration of Friendly Relations, Recognition and Related Matters' of 4 October 1963.[41] In paragraph 2 of the resolution, thus acting under Chapter VII of the UN Charter, the Security Council '*demands* that Iraq and Kuwait respect the inviolability of the international boundary and the allocation of islands' set out in this document.[42] Furthermore, in paragraph 3, the Council '*calls upon* the Secretary-General to lend his assistance to make arrangements with Iraq and Kuwait to demarcate the boundary between Iraq and Kuwait' and, finally, in paragraph 4 of this section A on the international boundary, the Security Council '*decides* to guarantee the inviolability of the above-mentioned international boundary and to take as appropriate all necessary measures to that end in accordance with the Charter of the United Nations'.[43]

In a letter dated 4 April 1991, the government of Kuwait expressed its intention 'scrupulously to comply' with the provisions of the resolution.[44] Iraq also gave notice of its acceptance of resolution 687 but after a score of objections, including some against the provisions on the demarcation of the boundary. In a letter of 6 April 1991, its Permanent Representative to the UN says that notwithstanding the resolution's reaffirmation in its preamble that Iraq is an independent and sovereign state, a good number of its provisions impair that sovereignty. As an example, the letter mentions that where 'the question of boundaries is concerned, the Security Council has determined

---

[41] In the preamble to the resolution, the Security Council notes that by signing the 'Agreed Minutes' both states recognized 'formally the boundary between Iraq and Kuwait and the allocation of islands' and that, furthermore, Iraq thus 'recognized the independence and complete sovereignty of the State of Kuwait within its borders' as specified and accepted in an exchange of letters between Iraq and the ruler of Kuwait in 1932.

[42] In the preamble to the resolution, the signing by Iraq and Kuwait of these 'Agreed Minutes' has already been noted, 'thereby recognizing formally the boundary between Iraq and Kuwait and the allocation of islands'.

[43] At least at face value this 'guarantee' is without precedent for the Security Council; it was repeated in resolution 833, adopted in 1993.

[44] UN Doc. S/22457.

in advance the boundary between Iraq and Kuwait'[45] and adds: 'And yet it is well known, from the juridical and practical standpoint, that in international relations boundary issues must be the subject of an agreement between States, since this is the only basis capable of guaranteeing the stability of frontiers.'[46]

In this respect, Iraq also points to resolution 660 of 2 August 1990 (adopted immediately after the Iraqi invasion), which calls upon Iraq and Kuwait to resolve their differences through negotiation, and submits that 'the question of the boundary is well-known to be one of the main differences'. Now, in Iraq's view, the Council has deprived it of 'its right to establish its territorial rights in accordance with the principles of international law'.[47]

Furthermore, the letter emphasizes that the 1963 'Agreed Minutes', mentioned in paragraph 3 of the resolution, has 'not yet been subjected to the constitutional procedures required for ratification of the Agreed Minutes by the legislative branch and the President of Iraq, thus leaving the question of the boundary pending and unresolved'.[48] Following all these and other objections, the letter is nevertheless concluded with: 'it has no choice but to accept this resolution'.[49]

In a further reaction, later that month, the Iraqi Minister of Foreign Affairs repeated and elaborated on his government's point of view. He repeated the general argument that regarding the question of the boundary the Security Council had imposed a specific position, 'whereas the custom in law and practice in international relations is that boundary questions are left to an agreement between states, because this is the sole basis that can guarantee the principle of the stability of boundaries'.[50] However, like the reaction to resolution 687, and again after many other objections, this letter also concludes

---

[45] UN Doc. S/22456. This viewpoint has been repeated in later documents, i.e., in UN Doc. S/22558, Annexe II.

[46] UN Doc. S/22456 (6 April 1991). Although the substance of the argument may be called legal (an agreement between states is needed), the argument tabled seems more political in nature.

[47] See, similarly, the arguments of the representative of Iraq in the debate preceding the adoption of resolution 687 (UN Doc. S/PV.2981 (3 April 1991), p. 32).

[48] UN Doc. S/22456. The argument is repeated in a letter to the Secretary-General dated 23 April 1991 (UN Doc. S/22558, Annexe II).

[49] UN Doc. S/22456. During the Security Council's debates on draft resolution 687, the representative of Iraq 'reserved its right to demand its legitimate territorial rights in accordance with international law' (UN Doc. S/PV.2981).

[50] UN Doc. S/22558, p. 5. Similarly, as in its letter of 6 April, there is also reference to Security Council resolution 660, which called on Kuwait and Iraq to resolve their differences through negotiations. Moreover, Iraq points to some specific issues on the evidentiary value of certain documents which may be referred to for the demarcation referred to in paragraph 3 of resolution 687 (see also pp. 260–3 below).

by stating that, despite all its objections, Iraq will co-operate: 'We do this because the circumstances forcing our acceptance persist.'

The Secretary-General, Mr Perez de Cuellar, in a letter dated 30 April 1991,[51] responding to the Iraqi objections, seemed to agree with Iraq's more general argument that in a case such as this consent of the parties is needed. He did not address the legal merits of Iraq's more specific objection that the 1963 'Agreed Minutes' did not bind Iraq.

In his letter, the Secretary-General reacted, *inter alia*, to the Iraqi comment that the Security Council has no competence to impose a demarcation, because 'in international law, a boundary demarcation between two states can be carried out only by agreement between the parties'. Mr Perez de Cuellar did not deny Iraq's suggestion of such a limitation to the competence of the Security Council. He emphasized that resolution 687, binding on the parties by virtue of Chapter VII of the Charter, in its paragraph 2, referred to the 1963 'Agreed Minutes' for its demand 'to respect the inviolability of their international boundary and the allocation of islands', and that, in paragraph 3, the Council called upon him to lend his 'assistance to make arrangements with Iraq and Kuwait to demarcate the boundary between Iraq and Kuwait'. He then recalled that Iraq had 'formally notified its acceptance of the provisions of that resolution',[52] and concluded: 'Therefore, the element of agreement as far as Iraq is concerned, is provided by your Government's official notifications of acceptance.' As Kuwait's consent had also been expressed, he submitted that 'the necessary element of consent has been provided by the two parties'.

The Secretary-General's viewpoint then seems to be that, indeed, a boundary demarcation between two states can only be carried out validly if the parties concerned have expressed their consent thereto. Moreover, apparently, a Security Council resolution adopted under Chapter VII, despite its mandatory character, does not suffice here.

The Secretary-General did not directly address Iraq's more specific objection to the 1963 'Agreed Minutes', i.e., that the question of its boundary with Kuwait was still pending and unresolved due to certain Iraqi constitutional procedures which were not fulfilled.

---

[51] UN Doc. S/22558, pp. 8 and 9. The other Iraqi comments addressed by the Secretary-General touch less upon the core of the subject matter of this essay, although some, like the matter of the use of proper maps or other 'appropriate material', may do upon more detailed analysis (see pp. 260–3 below).

[52] In its letter of 6 April – see p. 250. In the letter of 23 April Iraq reconfirmed its acceptance of para. 3. The Secretary-General did not address the (unlikely) possibility that Iraq's agreement might have been obtained by duress and, if so, whether that would vitiate its consent (see Mendelson and Hulton, 'The Iraq–Kuwait Boundary', pp. 149–50).

If this more specific Iraqi viewpoint were correct, the Security Council may be said in resolution 687 to have made a (binding) decision on the Iraq–Kuwait international boundary with (much) more than only a declaratory effect. However, this would, of course, only be the case if the 'Agreed Minutes' were, indeed, not binding on Iraq, and this may be said to be rather unlikely on the basis of the arguments submitted. In effect, Iraq argued at this point that the 'Agreed Minutes' still needed ratification in order to express its consent to be bound. However, the text of the 'Agreed Minutes' does not provide that consent to be bound needs to be expressed by ratification.[53] In such a case, due signature is generally assumed to be an adequate expression of consent to be bound.[54] Iraq did not invoke the invalidity of the 'Agreed Minutes' on the basis of a provision of its internal law; almost on the contrary. Iraq seems to have argued that the constitutional requirements could still be fulfilled: 'the "Agreed Minutes" . . . have not *yet* been subjected to the constitutional procedures.'[55]

The Iraq–Kuwait Boundary Demarcation Commission

Procedure and powers

On 2 May 1991, within a month of the adoption of resolution 687 as its paragraph 3 called for the Secretary-General had taken action and reported back to the Security Council. 'After consultations with the governments of Iraq and Kuwait', he established the 'United Nations Iraq–Kuwait Boundary Demarcation Commission'. The Commission was composed of three independent experts nominated by the Secretary-General, consisting of Mr Mochtar Kusuma-Atmadja of Indonesia, who served as Chairman, and two representatives, one of Kuwait and one of Iraq. On 20 November 1992 Mr Kusuma-Atmadja, for personal reasons, resigned as Chairman, and Mr Nicolas Valticos of Greece was appointed as his successor.

---

[53] See 485 UNTS 7063; articles 12 to 14 of the Vienna Convention on the Law of Treaties are relevant to determine whether Iraq and Kuwait have indeed adequately expressed their consent to be bound to the 'Agreed Minutes'. In their substance, these articles are generally assumed to express long-standing customary international law.

[54] As Professor Brownlie says: 'Where the treaty is not subject to ratification . . . signature . . . establishes consent to be bound' (Brownlie, *Principles of Public International Law*, p. 606).

[55] UN Doc. S/22558, Annexe II (emphasis added). Iraq might have referred to the still somewhat controversial rules on invalidity on the ground of provisions of internal law (see Brownlie, *Principles of Public International Law*, pp. 610–11). See, for convincing general criticism of the Iraqi arguments, M. H. Mendelson and S. C. Hulton, 'La Revendication par l'Iraq de la Souveraineté sur Koweït', *Annuaire français de droit international* (1990), 36, p. 195, at pp. 217–21.

The Commission established its own rules of procedure, which included a provision that 'the relevant provisions of the report of the Secretary-General (S/22558) would constitute the terms of reference of the Commission'.[56] According to the rules of procedure (and the provisions of the Secretary-General's report) the decisions of the Commission regarding the demarcation of the boundary are final and, it may be presumed, binding upon Iraq and Kuwait.[57] The rules further said that the quorum would be met by the presence of at least three of the five members, including the Chairman and at least one of the representatives (of Iraq and Kuwait). The decisions would be taken by majority voting.

Kuwait reacted favourably to the Secretary-General's report in which the IKBDC and its terms were set out (which then was not yet made public), and conveyed its readiness to co-operate in implementing those terms.[58]

Iraq's reaction was quite different. In a letter dated 23 April 1991, as was mentioned above, its Minister of Foreign Affairs repeated most of the objections regarding the demarcation of the boundary. Furthermore, Iraq objected also to procedural aspects of the Secretary-General's arrangement, such as majority voting, could not see any justification for bearing half of the costs of the demarcation process (or any costs whatsoever), because it considered the thrust of the Secretary-General's proposals as a 'virtual "act of capitulation"', and questioned the legal ground for using a specific map as part of the material to be used for the demarcation.[59] However, Mr Ahmed Hussein ended his letter by stating that the Iraqi government was prepared to 'consult with you concerning the comments contained in this letter' and 'will cooperate with you and will nominate a representative of our government to participate in the Demarcation Commission, even if you take no account of the views and comments we have expressed above. We do this because the circumstances forcing our acceptance persist.'[60]

In his reaction, the Secretary-General saw no reason in Iraq's more fundamental objections (see above pp. 250–1) nor its procedural objections

---

[56] UN Doc. S/25811, p. 10. The rules of procedure have been stated in IKBDC's 'interim report' which has not yet been published (IKBDC/Rep.2, as mentioned in UN Doc. S/25811, p. 42).

[57] In UN Doc. S/22558, the Secretary-General said: 'The coordinates established by the Commission will constitute the final demarcation of the international boundary between Iraq and Kuwait in accordance with the Agreed Minutes of 4 October 1963' (see also the Final Report (UN Doc. S/25811), para. 12, at p. 10).

[58] Letter, dated 19 April 1991 (as Annexe I to UN Doc. S/22558).

[59] This map had already been mentioned in paragraph 3 of resolution 687, as part of the 'appropriate material' on which the demarcation of the boundary was supposed to draw.

[60] UN Doc. S/22558, Annexe II.

to delay the establishment of the 'Iraq–Kuwait Boundary Demarcation Commission', which was done on 2 May 1991.[61]

The 'delimitation formula'

The first article of the 1963 'Agreed Minutes' provides that 'The Republic of Iraq recognized the independence and complete sovereignty of the State of Kuwait with its boundaries as specified in the letter of the Prime Minister of Iraq dated 21.7.1932 and which was accepted by the ruler of Kuwait in his letter dated 10.8.1932.'[62] The 1932 exchange of letters here referred to contains the following description of the existing frontier between the two countries:

> From the intersection of the Wadi-el-Audja with the Batin and thence northwards along the Batin to a point just south of the latitude of Safwan, thence eastwards passing south of Safwan Wells, Jebel Sanam and Um Qasr leaving them to Iraq and so on to the junction of the Khor Zobeir with the Khor Abdulla. The islands of Warbah, Bubiyan, Maskan (or Mashjan), Failakah, Auhah, Kubbar, Qaru and Umm-el-Maradim appertain to Kuwait.[63]

This description is referred to in the IKBDC reports as the 'delimitation formula for the demarcation of the Iraq–Kuwait boundary by the Commission'.[64] The IKBDC has divided the boundary into western, northern and eastern sections in accordance with this formula, which proved to be problematic in the case of the eastern section.

The IKBDC decisions

Two years after the establishment of the Commission, the current Secretary-General of the UN, Mr Boutros-Ghali, in a letter dated 21 May 1993, released the Final Report of the Commission to the Security Council.[65] During these two years, the IKBDC produced several documents and (interim) reports of which, in particular, the detailed 'Further Report' of 28 July 1992, on the western and northern sections, also reporting the precise final decisions on

---

[61] Among certain other matters, the letter also addressed the Iraqi concerns about the meaning of the selection of the 'appropriate material relevant to the demarcation of the boundary', including its objections to the so-called 'United Kingdom map' and, somewhat indirectly, the Iraqi objection to majority voting.

[62] 485 UNTS 7063.

[63] See UN Doc. S/25811 (21 May 1993) (the IKBDC 'Final Report'), para. 10, at p. 9 (repr. 94 *ILR* 1); cf. E. Lauterpacht, C. J. Greenwood, M. Weller and D. Bethlehem (eds.), *The Kuwait Crisis: Basic Documents* (Cambridge, 1991), p. 49. For at least some idea of the geographical locations, see fig. 1.

[64] UN Doc. S/25811, para. 11, at p. 9.

[65] UN Doc. S/25811 (21 May 1993).

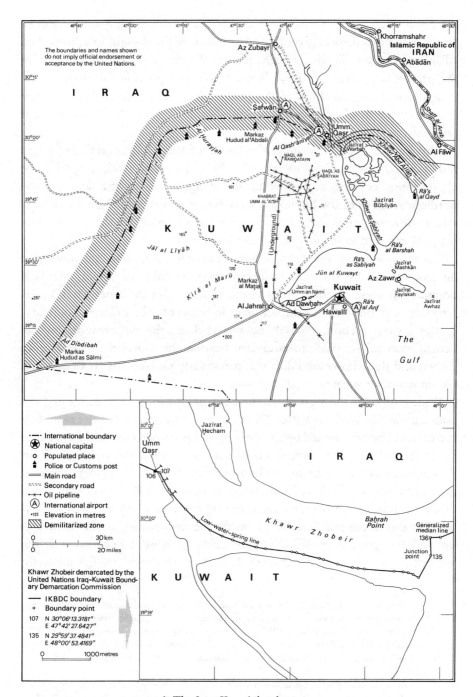

1 The Iraq–Kuwait border area

these sections, caused extensive reaction of the parties, notably on the part of Iraq.[66] The Final Report gives the demarcation of the eastern, or Khowr Abd Allah section but, further, largely repeats the findings and conclusions of the previous reports. The Final Report does not provide the detailed and comprehensive explanations of the Further Report, which makes the latter useful in terms of a better understanding of some of the IKBDC's most salient decisions.

This Further Report includes the results of the Commission's important fifth session, held in New York from 8 to 16 April 1992. Notably, the Commission concerned itself with the demarcation of the western and northern sections of the boundary. In doing so it was guided by the delimitation formula just described, and could further draw on the 'appropriate material' referred to in paragraph 3 of resolution 687.

On the one hand, this Further Report contains a number of substantive decisions taken by the Commission during its fifth session on the land boundary in these northern and western sections. On the other hand, it also refers to the Commission's further plans in respect to the offshore boundary, in the eastern section. As will be seen below, the embarcation on the demarcation of the offshore boundary beyond the junction of the Khowr Zobeir and the Khowr Abdullah was particularly problematic in view of the Commission's mandate.

With respect to the western section, the delimitation formula located the boundary in the Wadi Al Batin. The Commission decided that the boundary there should be determined by the thalweg and proceeded to define its course. In its Report the Commission noted that since 1936 the only significant development along the boundary between the Wadi Al Batin and Safwan is the establishment of oil-well complexes at Ratga and Rumaila. The Commission's independent experts asked the representatives of Iraq and Kuwait whether this development was relevant for the demarcation of the boundary, but did not receive evidence of any effects.[67] Kuwait concurred in the affirmative vote leaving the thalweg boundary unaffected by the oil wells;

---

[66] This 'Further Report' (see Marc Weller, *Iraq and Kuwait: The Hostilities and their Aftermath* (Cambridge, 1993), p. 456) is pursuant to para. 6 – asking for regular rapportage – of the Secretary-General's report of 2 May 1991 which founded the IKBDC (UN Doc. S/22558). On its previous work, the IKBDC reported in an 'Interim Report' (IKBDC/Rep.2 of 31 October 1991). The Annexe to the 'Final Report' of the IKBDC (in UN Doc. S/25811) contains a 'list of documents and reports of the Commission'.

[67] Weller, *Iraq and Kuwait*, p. 466, at para. 125. A UN press release of 27 July 1992 says: 'It should be noted that the oil wells in the fields between Safwan and the Batin exploited in the past by Iraq fell already in Kuwait according to the boundary shown on the British map referred to in Security Council resolution 687 (1991)' (IK/114, p. 455).

Iraq did not vote. No really substantive comments by either party were reported.[68]

The northern section caused more problems. According to the delimitation formula, this segment runs from the northern end of Wadi Al Batin, from 'a point just south of the latitude of Safwan; thence eastwards passing south of Safwan wells, Jebel Sanam and Umm Qasr leaving them to Iraq'. The precise location of the 'point just south of the latitude of Safwan', the turning-point for the course of the boundary further to the east, appeared to require painstaking historical and factual research into 'draft conventions and agreements, notes and official documents'. The reason for this research was the unclear location of a 'noticeboard' which from 1923 to 1939 had marked the boundary at a point south of Safwan. The position of this noticeboard was known to both Kuwait and Iraq at the time of the 1932 exchange of letters 'and was known by both over the subsequent seven years as the international boundary'.[69] The position of the noticeboard appeared not to have been measured. Reconstructing its location proved to be rather cumbersome and led in the end to an approximation of the location in 1932. Summarizing and reviewing the many paragraphs of the Further Report on this matter would lead to too much detail in light of the scope of this chapter.[70]

In Iraq's view the decisions on this point 'flatly contradicted' the delimitation formula, which referred to 'south of the latitude of Safwan' only for determining the terminal point at the Batin.[71] Iraq's representative did not participate in the voting on the location of this point, the Chairman abstained and the other three members voted in favour.[72]

The precise location of the point 'south of the latitude of Safwan' was particularly important, because the intersection of its latitude and the thalweg of Wadi Al Batin determined the end of the western section and the starting-point of the northern section of the boundary. Moreover, it was quite imaginable that this latitude would also be used to determine the location of

---

[68] Weller, *Iraq and Kuwait*, p. 479, paras. 266 and 267, on the voting. The representative of Iraq referred to decisions adopted during earlier sessions of the IKBDC, which at the time it had qualified as adopted hastily. However, no specification is provided. In addition, the representative submits that the 'thalweg' criterion has not been strictly followed (*ibid.*, p. 470, paras. 177–8).

[69] UN Doc. S/25811 (the 'Final Report'), para. 71, at p. 20.

[70] See 'Further Report', pp. 462–4, paras. 74–94 (Weller, *Iraq and Kuwait*, p. 456); see UN Doc. S/25811 ('Final Report'), pp. 20–1, paras. 70–5 for a simplified version.

[71] Weller, *Iraq and Kuwait*, p. 471, para. 180. The paragraph ends: 'The decision of the Commission had created a point at Safwan not mentioned in the delimitation formula.' It is difficult to see what the (legal) gist of the Iraqi criticism is here, or of the other objections presented in paras. 181–7.

[72] *Ibid.*, p. 479, para. 268 on the vote and pp. 461–4, paras. 74–92 on the technical grounds. The experts can be said here to have made extensive use of the 'appropriate material', as allowed in para. 4 of the Secretary-General's Report (see p. 253 above).

the point south of Umm Qasr, the end-point of the northern and the starting-point of the eastern sections.[73] However, finally, the Commission decided to locate this point in accordance with a 1936 United Kingdom map, corresponding here to another UK map, specifically referred to in paragraph 3 of Security Council resolution 687 as 'appropriate material' to be drawn on. This decision meant that a delicate matter had been solved because it implied 'leaving the Umm Qasr port complex and Umm Qasr village within Iraqi territory'.[74]

The eastern section of the boundary leads eastwards from the shore of the Khowr Zhobeir at Umm Qasr. The Commission decided that in this segment the boundary was to follow the low-water-springs line up to the junction of the thalwegs of the Khowr Zhobeir and the Khowr Abd Allah.[75] While the representative of Iraq again did not participate in the vote on this part of the boundary, the other members voted in favour, and the representative of Kuwait voted against. The Kuwaiti vote was because 'he considered that the question of the offshore section had not been adequately discussed', but it is fairly obvious from the discussions that he had a line in mind running closer to the middle of the Khowr Zhobeir.[76]

In order to determine the location of the junction of the two Khowrs in 1932, the experts again examined the available maps. The Commission discovered that an inadequate 1917 map was often used, and had influenced other charts and maps. The result of the distortions produced by the older maps had led to an inappropriate location of the intersection of the Khowrs, which was now adapted according to newly available maps.[77]

Further demarcation of the boundary all through the Khowr Abd Allah brought up the fundamental question of whether the Commission's mandate extended that far. The delimitation formula did not seem to provide much help here, because the description of the frontier ended with ' . . . and so on

---

[73] See, e.g., the Final Report, p. 13, para. 33.

[74] Final Report, p. 23, para. 81; and the Further Report, in Weller, *Iraq and Kuwait*, p. 479, para. 269. The representative of Kuwait noted that he had wanted a point at Umm Qasr further to the north (*ibid.*, at p. 475, para. 226), but nevertheless concurred in the affirmative vote.

[75] *Ibid.*, p. 480, para. 275. It is not entirely clear from the Report what the grounds are for the representative of Kuwait voting against the decision that the boundary line from the point south of Umm Qasr should be the low-water line up to the location directly opposite the junction of the Khowrs.

[76] *Ibid.*, p. 480, para. 276.

[77] *Ibid.*, pp. 469–70, paras. 161–74. The Kuwaiti representative came close to objecting at this point. He recalled that the Commission's independent experts had first located the point south of Umm Qasr on the basis of the point at Safwan and the intersection of the Khowrs, and then argued that it 'would not be satisfactory for the Commission to set aside the evidence it had carefully developed. However, the representative of Kuwait assured that he stood ready to work for broad agreement on the Commission's work.'

to the junction of the Khowr Zobeir with the Khowr Abdullah'. In other words, the description ended precisely where the question about the Commission's further mandate had arisen. The Commission, nevertheless, according to the Final Report, felt that the additional sentence of the delimitation formula mentioning the islands of Warbah, Bubiyan, etc. as appertaining to Kuwait, together with other historical evidence, gave sufficient grounds to proceed with the demarcation of the Khowr Abd Allah section.[78] It decided that 'the existing boundary to be demarcated was the median line, it being understood that navigational access should be possible for both States to the various parts of their respective territory bordering the demarcated boundary'.[79] On 27 May 1993 the Security Council, acting under Chapter VII of the Charter, adopted resolution 833 in which it reaffirmed that the decisions of the IKBDC regarding the demarcation of the boundary were final, and '*demands* that Iraq and Kuwait in accordance with international law and relevant Security Council resolutions respect the inviolability of the international boundary, as demarcated by the Commission, and the right to navigational access'.

Kuwait's general reaction was favourable to the Report, albeit with some qualifications, the most important one concerning the demarcation of the boundary in the Khowr Zhobeir just mentioned.[80] In a letter to the Secretary-General, it said 'that it will honour and be bound by Security Council resolution 833 (1993)'.[81]

---

[78] The IKBDC was supported in its decision by para. 3 of resolution 773 of 26 August 1992 (which, however, was not based on Chapter VII of the Charter). According to the 'Further Report', the additional historical (and other) evidence was presented, in particular in a working paper introduced by the Kuwaiti representative (in *ibid.*, pp. 477–8, paras. 252–6). In considering this evidence the Commission also took into account that the map referred to in para. 3 of resolution 687 confirmed the existence of a boundary through the Khowr Abd Allah (*ibid.*, p. 478, para. 256). The Commission, moreover, seems also to refer to certain conclusions regarding the state of the law of the sea at the time of the conclusion of the 1958 Geneva Conventions (*ibid.*, p. 478, para. 261).

[79] UN Doc. S/25811 (the Final Report), p. 24, para. 90. See the detailed argument in Mendelson and Hulton, 'The Iraq–Kuwait Boundary', pp. 178–86. With regard to the navigational access of both states, the Commission, after consideration of a note prepared by the Office of Legal Affairs of the UN Secretariat, adopted a statement which was included in the Final Report (UN Doc. S/25811, p. 27, para. 97). In this statement, the Commission noted that the 1982 United Nations Convention on the Law of the Sea (UNCLOS), ratified by both Iraq and Kuwait, provided such a right of navigation and access, which in the Commission's view in this case 'implies a non-suspendible right of navigation for both States' (see also Mendelson and Hulton, 'The Iraq–Kuwait Boundary', pp. 186–90).

[80] In a general review of what had been achieved, the Kuwaiti representative pointed out that Kuwait had wanted a point at Safwan which would be located (slightly) to the north of the point the Commission had chosen, and also at Umm Qasr would have wanted a point to the north of the point actually defined by the Commission. Hence, it was certainly not true that 'all Kuwait had wanted Kuwait had got', as the Iraqi representative had suggested (Weller, *Iraq and Kuwait*, p. 472, para. 195; see on the Kuwaiti statement, p. 475, para. 226).

[81] UN Doc. S/25963.

The representative of Iraq explained his position of non-participation in the voting on the demarcation of most of the boundary. The main reason for this behaviour was that he considered that the decisions had been adopted too hastily. Moreover, the Iraqi representative objected to the way in which the point south of Safwan had been determined, in particular the way maps were used (and which ones), and to the very limited role of (Iraqi) occupancy in border areas. Finally, the Iraqi representative voiced his doubts as to the equity of the decisions taken.[82]

It took Iraq a long time to express its acceptance of the findings of the IKBDC. It did not react favourably to resolution 833 (nor to resolution 949). However, very recently, in a letter dated 12 November 1994, it communicated to the President of the Security Council

> Iraq's irrevocable and unqualified recognition of the sovereignty, territorial integrity and political independence of the State of Kuwait, and of the international boundary between the Republic of Iraq and the State of Kuwait as demarcated by the United Nations Iraq–Kuwait Boundary Demarcation Commission, and confirm Iraq's respect for the inviolability of that boundary, in accordance with Security Council resolution 833 (1993).[83]

CONCLUDING REMARKS

A limit to the power of the Security Council?

On several occasions, in particular when the demarcation process of the Iraq–Kuwait international boundary was initiated, the government of Iraq has made clear that it believed that boundary issues could only be solved subject to agreement between the states concerned. In its view, this was not only so because such an agreement was the only real basis for guaranteeing the stability of boundaries, but also because international law so demands.

The Secretary-General of the UN in principle seemed to share this point of view. In response to Iraqi objections that such agreement was lacking, he

---

[82] As appears from the Final Report (pp. 11 and 12, para. 21), at the sessions held between 23 May 1991 (the first) and 16 April 1992 (the fifth), all members participated. The Iraqi representative did not attend the subsequent sessions, held between 15 July 1992 and 20 May 1993. Earlier, he had not taken part in a vote on the location of the boundary in the western sector, but did vote (against) in another vote on that part of the boundary; see Weller, *Iraq and Kuwait*, pp. 470–3, paras. 175–208.

[83] As stated in Revolutionary Command Council Decision No. 200 of 10 November 1994, signed by its President, Mr Saddam-Hussein, and the declaration of the Iraqi National Assembly, of the same date. See UN Doc. S/1994/1288, enclosing copies of these documents.

responded by pointing to the acceptance by both Kuwait and Iraq of the arrangements set out in resolution 687 and his own Report on its paragraph 3. Therefore, he submitted that 'the necessary element of consent has been provided by the two parties'.

It cannot be entirely excluded that the binding character itself of the legal foundation to the whole demarcation, (binding) resolution 687 and, later, resolution 833 or a mandatory resolution with still stronger language, under international law, would have sufficed as an expression of this 'necessary element of consent'. However, the continuous emphasis also later on in the process, on the necessity of acceptance of the boundary as demarcated by the IKBDC, seems to make this unlikely.

Adjudication as a mode of acquisition in modern international law

Another objection submitted by Iraq leads right to the issue of the possible constitutive effect of adjudication. Iraq has argued that contrary to the starting-point of resolution 687, in its view, the question of the Iraq–Kuwait boundary is still pending and unresolved because it has not (yet) been subjected to the constitutional procedures required in Iraq for ratification. If Iraq were justified in its view, the Security Council would not be involved in demarcation (which both the Council and the Secretary-General never failed to stress) but, instead, in a process of delimitation. In that case, it might be fair to argue that the process which, after all leads to a final and binding decision, in fact had a constitutive effect. However, it does not look very likely that on closer analysis the Iraqi argument would be justifiable under international law. In view of the explicit acceptance by Kuwait and Iraq of the arrangements, the Secretary-General did not need to address this particular Iraqi objection.

Through the demarcation process the IKBDC was not reallocating territory between Kuwait and Iraq. This has been stated frequently, both in the Security Council resolutions and by the Secretary-General. However, a critical note may be appended here: it is not always obvious that the Commission was 'simply carrying out the technical task necessary to demarcate for the first time the precise coordinates of the boundary set out in the "Agreed Minutes"', as resolution 833 stated.

The choice of the low-water-springs line as the demarcation in the Khowr Zhobeir is not to be deduced from the so-called delimitation formula, but nevertheless seems still legally justifiable, that is, if the Commission is followed in its not too narrow interpretation of 'drawing on appropriate material'. The Commission is allowed by paragraph 3 of resolution 687 to draw on such material. However, the map explicitly mentioned in the same paragraph as an example draws a different line.[84]

The most debatable part of the demarcation seems to have taken place in the Khowr Abd Allah, in the easternmost section of the boundary. Here, the relationship to the delimitation formula is very remote indeed. The Commission draws on additional evidence mainly provided by Kuwait and, partially, on an assessment of the state of the law of the sea in the mid-1950s. The position that its decision leads to demarcation of the boundary in the Khowr Abd Allah, instead of to its delimitation, seems difficult to defend.

However, this is not to argue the invalidity under international law of the Commission's decisions which have been sanctioned by the Security Council and, moreover were accepted by Iraq and Kuwait. Seen in terms of international law, the Commission's decisions do illustrate the often-difficult distinction between 'technical' demarcation and drawing a new boundary or even reallocating territory.[85]

What is of relevance here, too, is that if it is justified to label part of the Commission's demarcation of the Iraq–Kuwait boundary as, in fact, delimitation or drawing of a new boundary, the Commission in its final (and binding) decision has produced a constitutive effect. In view of the introduction in the first section of this chapter of such a constitutive effect as the condition for qualifying adjudication as a 'mode of acquisition of territory in international law', part of the IKBDC decisions can then be said to provide support for the point of view that, within international law, indeed, such a way of acquiring territory is perfectly possible.

Such a conclusion fits in well with the review of the jurisprudence of the ICJ on territorial disputes. Some of the more recent decisions of Chambers of the Court on the course of frontiers, although reasonable and wise enough, seem difficult to justify as an application of equity *infra legem* and therefore as declaratory of existing law. Moreover, the inclusion of constitutive elements by the Court and, more substantively by the IKBDC, corresponds with observations made on older jurisprudence, in particular, if it is taken to include quasi-judicial adjudication.

In this respect Security Council resolution 833 would also provide an example. By sanctioning in this resolution the decisions of the IKBDC just

---

[84] It may be added as a critical remark that, in its decisions, the Commission tends to draw somewhat more than is common practice in territorial adjudication on the maps. In view of the state of international law in this regard, this may be debatable.

[85] See, e.g., Gerard Tanja's comments and study on this difficult distinction, in his 'Comments'; in Dekker and Post (eds.), *The Gulf War*, pp. 44–8; also Mendelson and Hulton, 'The Iraq–Kuwait Boundary', pp. 144–5.

mentioned, the Security Council has produced the same constitutive effect. The Security Council's quasi-judicial adjudication on a territorial issue would thus also provide support for the thesis respectfully submitted that adjudication is a mode of acquisition of territory. In that regard, it must be noted that, in particular, in cases where parties are more or less forced to enter a process of demarcation, at least one of them is likely to dispute the exact course of the international boundary or whether there was a boundary at a specific time. In this demarcation both Iraq (although perhaps not very convincingly) and Kuwait did in fact argue so. In such circumstances the parties challenge the starting-point of the process, i.e. that only 'technical' demarcation is at stake. If they are justified, the (quasi-) judicial body takes a decision with constitutive effect, is involved in acquisition (and loss) of territorial title and might need all its power and authority legally and politically to get away with it.

14

Equitable maritime boundary delimitation

As exemplified in the work of the World Court during the Presidency of Sir Robert Yewdall Jennings

Barbara Kwiatkowska

ↄↄ

> International law can never be a panacea, for law is only one aspect of the immensely complex as well as immensely urgent problem that faces our civilization today. But international law is, if only one aspect, nevertheless an essential aspect.
>
> R. Y. Jennings, 'The Progress of International Law', *BYbIL*, 34 (1958), p. 334, at p. 355

INTRODUCTORY REMARKS

It is an honour to have a place in this tribute to Judge Sir Robert Yewdall Jennings, who is by nature as much scholar as practitioner, and whose outstanding professionalism has been of continuing guidance in my attempts to grasp the essence of equitable maritime boundary delimitation and other issues of international law.

The international law of the sea has taken an important part in Sir Robert's approach to the development of international law and its role in a modern multicultural world, which involves the inescapable evolution of that law towards universality in terms of, as he put it, not uniformity but rather 'richness of variety and diversity'.[1] As he remarked, the law of the sea has always been 'a specially significant part of the entire international law system'.[2]

The great economic and political importance of traditional law of the

---

[1] R. Y. Jennings, 'Universal International Law in a Multicultural World', in *International Law and The Grotian Heritage* (The Hague, 1985), p. 187, at p. 197; R. Y. Jennings, 'Universal International Law in a Multicultural World', in M. Bos and I. Brownlie (eds.), *Liber Amicorum for the Rt Hon. Lord Wilberforce* (Oxford, 1987), p. 39, at p. 50. Cf. M. Bedjaoui, 'General Introduction', in M. Bedjaoui (ed.), *International Law: Achievements and Prospects* (Paris, 1991), pp. 1–18.

[2] R. Y. Jennings, 'An International Lawyer Takes Stock, *ICLQ*, 39 (1990), p. 513, at p. 519.

sea, as emphasized by the then Professor Jennings in 1963,[3] found adequate reflection in his excellent General Course delivered at The Hague Academy in 1967[4] and in a major article on the continental shelf published in 1969.[5] During the negotiations on the new law of the sea at the Third United Nations Conference on the Law of the Sea (UNCLOS III), Sir Robert stressed the need to reassess the whole process of international law-making in view of this, as he put it, 'remarkable experiment in law-making' in which the new states of the Third World had, for the first time, been able to play a full part.[6] The (in many respects unprecedented) negotiations of UNCLOS III that had led to the new 1982 UN Law of the Sea Convention (LOSC) inspired Sir Robert to anticipate, in his lecture in tribute to Lord Arnold McNair and in other writings, that a new way of making and developing general international law within the multilateral treaty-making process would evolve.[7]

Although not a member of the ICJ at the time of delivery of the precedential *North Sea Continental Shelf* judgment, the then Professor Jennings had already importantly contributed to the development of the law of equitable maritime delimitation through his works referred to above.[8] These were followed by his direct involvement as a counsel for Tunisia in the *Tunisia/ Libya Continental Shelf* case, which was the first case to consider the new legal regime of the oceans as codified and progressively developed in what was then the draft of the LOSC.[9] During the subsequent *Libya/Malta Continental Shelf*

[3] R. Y. Jennings, 'Recent Developments in the International Law Commission: Its Relation to the Sources of International Law', *ICLQ*, 13 (1964), p. 385, at p. 389. The text of this article is the substance of a speech delivered by Sir Robert in Edinburgh on 14 December 1963. Cf. R. Y. Jennings, 'The Limits of State Jurisdiction', *Nordisk Tidsskrift for International Ret*, 32 (1962), p. 209, at pp. 223–4.

[4] R. Y. Jennings, 'General Course on Principles of International Law', *Recueil des cours*, 121, 2 (1967), p. 325, at pp. 386–408.

[5] R. Y. Jennings, 'The limits of Continental Shelf Jurisdiction: Some Possible Implications of the North Sea Case Judgment', *ICLQ*, 18 (1969), pp. 819–32.

[6] Jennings, in 'Universal International Law', in *International Law and The Grotian Heritage*, at p. 196, and also pp. 192–3.

[7] R. Y. Jennings, 'The Discipline of International Law' (lecture in tribute to Arnold McNair), in *Report of the 57th Conference of the International Law Association (ILA), Held at Madrid, 30 August–4 September 1976* (London, 1978), pp. 622–32; R. Y. Jennings, 'Gerald Gray Fitzmaurice', *BYbIL*, 55 (1984), p. 1, at pp. 28–9; Jennings, 'Universal International Law', in Bos and Brownlie (eds.), *Liber Amicorum*, at pp. 49–50; Jennings, 'An International Lawyer Takes Stock', at pp. 518–19; R. Y. Jennings, 'Treaties', in M. Bedjaoui (ed.), *International Law: Achievements and Prospects* (Paris, 1991), at pp. 135, 148; H. W. A. Thirlway (Principal Legal Secretary, ICJ Registry), 'The Law and Procedure of the International Court of Justice 1960–1989, Part Two', *BYbIL*, 61 (1990), p. 1, at pp. 86–102, esp. pp. 100–2. Cf. R. Y. Jennings, 'The Progressive Development of International Law and Its Codification', *BYbIL*, 24 (1947), p. 301, at pp. 303–7.

[8] Esp. in notes 4 and 5 above, and 'The Discipline of International Law', in note 7 above.

[9] Argument of Professor Jennings, Counsel for the Government of Tunisia, in the *Case Concerning the Continental Shelf (Tunisia/Libyan Arab Jamahirya)*, ICJ Pleadings, Oral Arguments, Documents, No. 492, vol. IV, pp. 403–26; Reply by Professor Jennings, *ibid.*, No. 493, vol. V, pp. 260–79 and pp. 345–8.

case, Sir Robert Jennings, by then a judge on the Court, dissented from the 1984 judgment on the *Application by Italy for Permission to Intervene*[10] and voted in favour of the majority 1985 judgment on the merits of that case.[11] As the *Libya/Malta* case marked an important stage in the application of equity to maritime boundary delimitation, Sir Robert subsequently published in 1986[12] and 1989[13] two brilliant essays reflecting on the complexity of the issues involved in this process. He used as a frame of reference the *Libya/Malta* judgment and also the preceding 1969 *North Sea*, 1982 *Tunisia/Libya* and 1984 *Delimitation of the Maritime Boundary in the Gulf of Maine Area* judgments. Maritime boundary delimitation found also a prominent reflection in that work of unequalled excellence, the ninth edition of *Oppenheim's International Law*, published in 1992 under the joint editorship of Sir Robert Jennings and Sir Arthur Watts.[14]

In view of Sir Robert's particular interest in equitable maritime delimitation as part of the law of the sea and of general international law, and given the existence of comprehensive analyses of the Court's judgments and several arbitral awards undertaken elsewhere,[15] it appeared appropriate to focus in this contribution on those judgments that were delivered by the World Court under the Presidency of Sir Robert Jennings,[16] as coupled with the Vice-

---

[10] ICJ Reports, 1984, p. 3, at pp. 28–9, decided by eleven votes to five (including Judge Sir Robert Jennings), and Dissenting Opinion of Sir Robert Jennings, *ibid.*, pp. 148–60.

[11] ICJ Reports, 1985, p. 13, at p. 57, decided by fourteen votes (including Judge Sir Robert Jennings) to three.

[12] R. Y. Jennings, 'Equity and Equitable Principles', *Annuaire suisse de droit international*, 42 (1986), pp. 27–38.

[13] R. Y. Jennings, 'The Principles Governing Marine Boundaries', in K. Hailbronner, G. Ress and T. Stein (eds.), *Staat und Völkerrechtsordnung, Festschrift für Karl Doehring* (Berlin, 1989), pp. 398–407.

[14] R. Y. Jennings and A. Watts (eds.), *Oppenheim's International Law* (Harlow, 1992), vol. I, parts 2 to 4, pp. 613–14, 776–82 and 805–7.

[15] P. Weil, *The Law of Maritime Delimitation – Reflections* (Cambridge, 1989); *International Boundary Cases: The Continental Shelf*, with a preface by E. Lauterpacht (Cambridge, 1992), vols. I and II; E. D. Brown, *Sea-bed Energy and Minerals: The International Legal Regime* (Dordrecht, 1992), vol. I; J. I. Charney and L. M. Alexander (eds.), *International Maritime Boundaries* (Dordrecht, 1993), vols. I and II; H. W. A. Thirlway, 'The Law and Practice of the International Court of Justice 1960–1989, Part Five' (including, by way of exception, the 1993 *Denmark v. Norway Maritime Boundary in the Area Between Greenland and Jan Mayen* judgment), *BYbIL*, 64 (1993), pp. 1–54.

[16] Sir Robert Jennings has been member of the Court since 6 February 1982 and he was the Court's President during the triennium February 1991–February 1994. His second nine-year term of office expires on 5 February 2000. See *ICJ Yearbook 1990–1991*, 45 (The Hague, 1991), pp. 8–9, and *ICJ Yearbook 1991–1992*, 46 (The Hague, 1992), pp. 8–9 and 19 (Sir Robert's biography). On the election of Sir Robert as judge, see S. Rosenne, 'The Election of Five Members of the International Court of Justice in 1981', *AJIL*, 76 (1982), pp. 364–70; and S. Rosenne, *The World Court: What It Is and How It Works* (4th rev. edn, Dordrecht, 1989), pp. 64–6. See also *AJIL*, 85 (1991), p. 384, noting that given the growing role of the Court, the elections of Sir Robert as President and of Judge Oda as Vice-President 'are a significant tribute to, and responsibility for, two outstanding scholars of international law'.

Presidency of Judge Shigeru Oda[17] and the Registrarship of Dr Eduardo Valencia-Ospina.[18] These judgments include those rendered in the *Guinea-Bissau v. Senegal Arbitral Award* of 31 July 1989, the *El Salvador/Honduras Land, Island and Maritime Frontier Dispute* (decided by a Chamber of the Court), and the *Denmark v. Norway Maritime Boundary in the Area between Greenland and Jan Mayen* cases. In contrast to the *Denmark v. Norway* case, neither of the first two cases directly involved maritime boundary delimitation. However, the settlements reached in both the *1989 Arbitral Award* and the *El Salvador/Honduras* cases include certain elements of major importance from the viewpoint of future delimitations. The new *Guinea-Bissau v. Senegal Maritime Delimitation* case is presently pending before the Court, whereas the *Qatar v. Bahrain Maritime Delimitation and Territorial Questions* case still awaits the Court's decision on the issues of the jurisdiction of the Court and the admissibility of Qatar's claim, with oral pleadings in the latter case having taken place on 28 February–11 March 1994.

Apart from their importance to actual and prospective maritime boundary delimitations, the three cases decided under the Presidency of Sir Robert Jennings discussed below share the major characteristic of promoting stability in the law. Significantly, one will find in the writings of Sir Robert particular importance attached to how the Court 'endeavours not only to dispose of a case submitted to it, but also to do so in a manner which reflects the Court's position and authority as the principal judicial organ of the United Nations, and as a body which represents in its membership "the main forms of civilization" and "the principal legal systems" of the world; as indeed it is supposed to do by article 9 of its Statute'.[19] Accordingly, Sir Robert has devoted special

---

[17] Judge Oda has been a member of the Court since 1976 and was the Court's Vice-President during the triennium February 1991–February 1994. His third nine-year term of office expires on 5 February 2003. On Judge Oda's re-election for a third term, see the 1993 UN General Assembly decision 48/308 on election of five members of the ICJ.

[18] Dr Valencia-Ospina, who was previously the Court's Deputy-Registrar (1984–7) and before that had served for twenty years in the Office of Legal Affairs of the UN Secretariat, was elected as the Court's Registrar on 19 February 1987. His second seven-year term of office expires on 19 February 2001. See *AJIL*, 81 (1987), p. 762; ICJ Communique No. 94/6 of 16 February 1994.

[19] R. Y. Jennings, 'Chambers of the International Court of Justice and Courts of Arbitration', in *Humanité et droit international, Mélanges René-Jean Dupuy* (Paris, 1991), pp. 197, 197–8. Cf. R. Y. Jennings, 'The Internal Judicial Practice of the International Court of Justice', *BYbIL*, 59 (1988), pp. 31–47; R. Y. Jennings, 'The Collegiate Responsibility and Authority of the International Court of Justice', in Y. Dinstein and M. Tabory (eds.), *International Law at a Time of Perplexity: Essays in Honour of Shabtai Rosenne* (Dordrecht, 1989), pp. 343–53; R. Y. Jennings, 'Reflections on the Term "Dispute"', in R. St J. Macdonald (ed.), *Essays in Honour of Professor Wang Tieya* (Dordrecht, 1993), pp. 401–5; statements by the President Sir Robert Jennings to the UN General Assembly: on 8 November 1991, in *ICJ Yearbook 1991–1992*, 46 (The Hague, 1992), at pp. 205–12, and on 21 October 1992, UN Doc. A/47/PV.43, 6–16 (1992), quoted by P. H. F. Bekker (ICJ Registry staff member), 'International Legal

---

attention to the decisions of the Court and other judicial bodies as a source of international law. In his statement on The Role of the ICJ in the Development of International Environmental Protection Law delivered in 1992 at the United Nations Conference on Environment and Development, he remarked:

> A glance at, for example, the now near 90 volumes of the *International Law Reports* demonstrates very clearly the extent to which judicial decisions are now an important source of international law. Moreover, a glance at virtually any report of a decision by the International Court of Justice itself, will show the extent to which the decision is indebted to the 'jurisprudence' of previous decisions. In this way, principles and rules of law are gradually developed and elaborated by the very process of interpreting and applying them to the specific and often unforeseen factual situations that arise in actual disputes brought before the Court.[20]

This, in his view, does not mean that the Court can 'make' new law in the sense that a legislature can make law, but the difference between making and determining law remains 'one of degree rather than of kind'.[21]

Aid in Practice: The ICJ Trust Fund', *AJIL*, 87 (1993), pp. 659, n. 10, 661, and 666, n. 48; and S. Rosenne, the President of the International Court of Justice, chap. 22 below, in this volume.

    On the judicial work of the Court during the biennium 1991–2 when, under the Presidency of Sir Robert Jennings, 'the Court had a longer case list than at any previous stage in its history', see P. H. F. Bekker, 'Letter to the Editor in Chief', *AJIL*, 87 (1993), pp. 429–32. It seems also significant that, under Presidency of Sir Robert, the Court discontinued four cases within two years. See *Nicaragua v. USA Military and Paramilitary Activities in and against Nicaragua*, Order of 26 September 1991, ICJ Reports, 1991, p. 47; *Nicaragua v. Honduras Border and Transborder Armed Actions*, Order of 27 May 1992, ICJ Reports, 1992, p. 222; *Finland v. Denmark Passage through the Great Belt*, Order of 10 September 1992, ICJ Reports, 1992, p. 348; and *Nauru v. Australia, Certain Phosphate Lands in Nauru*, Order of 13 September 1993, ICJ Reports, 1993, p. 322. Cf. emphasis in the 1992 statement by Sir Robert to the General Assembly on how the Court procedures and diplomatic negotiations can in practice 'be employed complementarily and not necessarily on a basis of mutual exclusivity': UN Doc. A/47/PV.43, at pp. 8–11; Bekker, 'International Legal Aid', at p. 661, n. 10. For an excellent overall account of the judicial practice of the Court and its prospects, see M. Bedjaoui, 'Mythes et réalités d'une reliance du règlement judiciaire des différences internationaux', in Y. Daudet (ed.), *Actualités des conflits internationaux* (Paris, 1993), pp. 125–46.

[20] For the text of the statement, which was read on behalf of the Court's President by Registrar Valencia-Ospina, see *ICJ Yearbook 1991–1992*, 46 (The Hague, 1992), pp. 212–18, at p. 214. The statement was also reproduced as R. Y. Jennings, 'Need for Environmental Court', *Environmental Policy and Law*, 22 (1992), p. 312, at pp. 312–13. Cf. R. Y. Jennings, 'The Progress of International Law', *BYbIL*, 34 (1958), p. 334, at pp. 339–40; Jennings, 'An International Lawyer Takes Stock', at pp. 519–20 and n. 4, at pp. 340–5; Jennings and Watts (eds.), *Oppenheim's International Law*, Introduction and Part 1, at pp. 41–2; R. Y. Jennings, 'Commentary' in *Implementation of the Law of the Sea Convention Through International Institutions* (Honolulu, 1990), p. 653, at p. 655 and comment by Ambassador S. Rosenne and response to him by Sir Robert, *Ibid.*, at pp. 660–1; Thirlway, 'The Law and Procedure of the ICJ, Part Two', at pp. 127–33.

[21] Jennings, 'General Course on Principles of International Law', p. 341. Cf. Jennings, 'The Discipline of International Law', p. 624. Cf. also Sir Gerald Fitzmaurice, 'Judicial Innovation – Its Uses and Its Perils – As Exemplified in Some of the Work of the International Court of Justice During Lord

THE 1989 *GUINEA-BISSAU V. SENEGAL* ARBITRAL AWARD CASE

The two decisions rendered by the Court in 1990 and 1991 in the *Guinea-Bissau v. Senegal 1989 Arbitral Award* case concerned the procedural questions of provisional measures and the validity of an Arbitral Award, respectively.[22] With respect to the former decision, Judge Sir Robert Jennings voted with the majority in favour of the Court's dismissal, in its Order of 2 March 1990, of Guinea-Bissau's request for the indication of provisional measures.[23] And in the *1989 Arbitral Award* judgment delivered by the Court on 12 November 1991 under the Presidency of Sir Robert, all three submissions made by Guinea-Bissau were rejected.[24] The submission that the 1989 *Guinea-Bissau/Senegal* Award was inexistent was rejected unanimously, while the submission that the Award was absolutely null and void was rejected by eleven votes (including that of President Jennings) to four.[25] The third submission of Guinea-Bissau, namely that Senegal was not justified in seeking to require it to apply the Award, was rejected by twelve votes (including that of President Jennings) to three,[26] with the Court finding that the 1989 Award was valid and

McNair's Period of Office', in R. Y. Jennings (ed.), *Cambridge Essays in International Law: Essays in Honour of Lord McNair* (London, 1965), pp. 24, 24–5; Jennings 'Gerald Gray Fitzmaurice', pp. 30–45 and 61.

[22] The 1989 *Guinea-Bissau/Senegal Award* was adopted by the votes of President of the Arbitration Tribunal Barberis and Arbitrator Gros, over the negative vote of Arbitrator Bedjaoui. Previously, in the 1960 *Honduras v. Nicaragua Arbitral Award Made by the King of Spain on 23 December 1906* judgment (ICJ Reports 1960, p. 192), the Court upheld (by thirteen votes to one) the validity of the 1906 Award.

[23] ICJ Reports, 1990, pp. 64, 70, decided by fourteen votes to one. In favour: President Ruda, Vice-President Mbaye, and Judges Lachs, Elias, Oda, Ago, Schwebel, Sir Robert Jennings, Ni, Evensen, Tarassov, Guillaume, Shahabuddeen and Pathak; against: Judge *ad hoc* Thierry (designated by Guinea-Bissau) (Registrar Valencia-Ospina). The Court also declined to indicate provisional measures in its Order of 29 July 1991 in the *Finland v. Denmark Passage through the Great Belt* case, decided unanimously by President Sir Robert Jennings, Vice-President Oda, Judges Lachs, Ago, Schwebel, Bedjaoui, Ni, Evensen, Tarassov, Guillaume, Shahabuddeen, Aguilar Mawdsley, Weeramantry and Ranjeva, and Judges *ad hoc* Fischer (designated by Denmark) and Broms (designated by Finland) (Registrar Valencia-Ospina), ICJ Reports, 1991, pp. 12, 20–1.

[24] ICJ Reports, 1991, pp. 53, 75–6. The Court was composed of President Sir Robert Jennings, Vice-President Oda, Judges Ago, Schwebel, Ni, Evensen, Tarassov, Guillaume, Shahabuddeen, Aguilar Mawdsley, Weeramantry and Ranjeva, and Judges *ad hoc* Thierry (designated by Guinea-Bissau) and Mbaye (designated by Senegal) (Registrar Valencia-Ospina). Cf. J. P. Quéneudec, 'L'Affaire de la sentence arbitrale du 31 juillet 1989 devant la CIJ (Guinée-Bissau c. Senegal)', *Annuaire français de droit international*, 37 (1991), pp. 419–32. Cf. also R. Y. Jennings, 'Nullity and Effectiveness in International Law', in Jennings (ed.), *Cambridge Essays in International Law*, pp. 65–87; see also n. 20 above and main accompanying text; and remarks on the *1989 Arbitral Award* case by H. W. A. Thirlway, chap. 21 below in this volume.

[25] Four votes against by Judges Aguilar Mawdsley, Weeramantry and Ranjega, and by Judge *ad hoc* Thierry.

[26] Three votes against by Judges Aguilar Mawdsley and Weeramantry, and by Judge *ad hoc* Thierry.

binding for both states, which each had the obligation to apply it. Shortly before the Court delivered the *1989 Arbitral Award* judgment, Guinea–Bissau filed in the ICJ Registry, on 12 March 1991, its application instituting proceedings in the new *Guinea-Bissau v. Senegal Maritime Delimitation* case. The Court was requested to adjudge:

> What should be, on the basis of the international law of the sea and of all the relevant elements of the case, including the future decision of the Court in the case concerning the arbitral '*award*' of 31 July 1989, the line (to be drawn on a map) delimiting all the maritime territories appertaining respectively to Guinea–Bissau and Senegal (§ 14).

The *1989 Arbitral Award* judgment is of direct relevance to future delimitation in that it reaffirms the findings of the 1989 Award concerning the validity of the 1960 Franco–Portuguese Agreement with respect to delimitation of the territorial sea, contiguous zone and the continental shelf between Senegal and Guinea–Bissau (at the time of the Agreement's conclusion, between an autonomous state of the *communauté* and the Portuguese Province of Guinea).[27] In accordance with the 1960 Agreement, these three spaces are delimited by the straight (loxodromic) line drawn at 240° from the point of intersection of the prolongation of the land frontier and the low-water line of the two states, represented for that purpose by the Cape Roxo lighthouse. This single boundary line delimits the continental shelf 'over the whole extent of that maritime space as defined at present', but it does not apply to the delimitation of the 200-mile exclusive economic zone (EEZ), which did not exist at the time of adoption of the 1960 Agreement.[28] Having regard to Guinea–Bissau's 1991 application in the new case referred to above, and the long and difficult arbitral procedure between the two states (negotiations

---

[27] Note that in the *Libya/Chad Territorial Dispute* case neither party questioned the validity of the 1955 Franco (Equatorial Africa)/Libyan Treaty of Friendship and Good Neighbourliness. But Libya contended that the Court, when interpreting the Treaty, should take into account the fact that at the time of the Treaty's conclusion, Libya 'lacked the experience to engage in difficult negotiations with a Power enjoying the benefit of long international experience'. However, the Court found that the (land) boundary between the two parties is defined by the 1955 Treaty. See *Libya/Chad* judgment of 3 February 1994, paras. 36ff and 77, decided by sixteen votes to one, ICJ Reports, 1994, pp. 6, 20 and 40. In favour: President Sir Robert Jennings, Vice-President Oda, and Judges Ago, Schwebel, Bedjaoui, Ni, Evensen, Tarassov, Guillaume, Shahabuddeen, Aguilar Mawdsley, Weeramantry, Ranjeva, Ajibola and Herczegh, and Judge *ad hoc* Abi-Saab (designated by Chad); against: Judge *ad hoc* Sette-Camara (designated by Libya) (Registrar Valencia-Ospina). On the unanimous *Burkina Faso/Mali Frontier Dispute* judgment of 22 December 1986 (delivered by the Chamber under the Presidency of Judge Bedjaoui, ICJ Reports, 1986, pp. 554–651), which also involved the colonial (land) boundary, see M. Leigh, 'Judicial Decisions', *AJIL*, 81 (1987), pp. 411–14.

[28] ICJ Reports, 1991, pp. 59–60 (quoting paras. 80, 85 and 88 of the 1989 Award).

began in 1977), as well as to proceedings before the Court in the *1989 Arbitral Award* case, the 1991 judgment considered it highly desirable that the unsettled elements of the dispute, that is, the EEZ delimitation between Guinea-Bissau and Senegal, should be resolved as soon as possible.

Because of the existence of the 240° line delimiting the continental shelf, the future Guinea-Bissau–Senegal delimitation will be essentially different from that in the *Gulf of Maine* case. In the latter case, which for the first time involved the determination of a single boundary, there did not exist (as in the *Denmark v. Norway* case discussed below) any line delimiting the continental shelf. In the Guinea-Bissau–Senegal delimitation, the two states could, as Vice-President Shigeru Oda pointed out in his Separate Opinion appended to the 1991 judgment, either choose an EEZ line varying from the existing continental shelf line, thus producing two coexisting lines, or else opt for a single line delimiting both maritime spaces, which line Judge Oda favoured.[29]

If the two states preferred to opt for a single boundary line, they would still face a further choice. In particular, they could determine their EEZ boundary to be identical to the existing 240° line for the continental shelf. This would accord with the practice relating to virtually all existing continental shelf delimitations, which have evolved formally or informally into single boundaries also dividing the 200-mile zones. Nevertheless, Guinea-Bissau and Senegal could alternatively subject the existing continental shelf line to alteration or adjustment to the new line to be agreed for the EEZ, so as to produce a single boundary for both these maritime spaces that would differ from the 240° line. This solution could not be excluded in view of Guinea-Bissau's communique of 14 November 1991. In particular, while declaring (as did Senegal in its corresponding statement) its willingness to abide by the Court's 1991 *1989 Arbitral Award* judgment, Guinea-Bissau emphasized that 'the door is still open for solving the question of *the entire* maritime territories of the two states'.[30]

At a meeting convened by President Sir Robert Jennings with the representatives of Guinea-Bissau and Senegal on 28 February 1992, the two

[29] *Ibid.*, pp. 90–1.
[30] Note Verbale from Guinea-Bissau (emphasis added), in *UN Law of the Sea Bulletin*, 20 (1992), p. 52; and Note Verbale from Senegal, *ibid.*, p. 53. Cf. remarks of K. Highet, Counsel of Guinea-Bissau (which advocated a line between 270° and 264° for the EEZ delimitation) that a fragmentary award (confirming the 240° line favoured by Senegal as the only continental shelf boundary that would ignore the Bijagos Archipelago) is worse than none at all. In the absence of that award Guinea-Bissau would, in Highet's opinion, be free to achieve an overall equitable solution (ICJ, *Guinea-Bissau v. Senegal*, Verbatim Record of Pleadings, CR 91/3, 80).

parties requested that no time-limit be fixed for the initial pleadings in the new *Maritime Delimitation* case, pending the outcome of their negotiations on that matter.[31] Those negotiations were to continue for six months, after which, if they had not been successful, a further meeting would be held with the President. Having received no indications from the parties as to the state of their negotiations, President Jennings convened a further meeting with the Agents on 6 October 1992. The Court agreed to a joint request made by the two states that a further period of three months, with a possible further extension of three months, be allowed for continuation of the negotiations, and expressed satisfaction at the efforts being made by the parties to resolve their dispute by negotiation, in the spirit of the recommendation made in the 1991 judgment.

THE *EL SALVADOR/HONDURAS LAND, ISLAND AND MARITIME FRONTIER DISPUTE* CASE

The *El Salvador/Honduras Land, Island and Maritime Frontier Dispute* case was settled by a Chamber which, according to the unanimous Court's Constitution of Chamber Order of 8 May 1987[32] and Composition of Chamber Order of 13 December 1989,[33] comprised of Judge Sette-Camara as the Chamber's President, Judges Oda and Sir Robert Jennings (the Vice-President and the President of the Court respectively) and two Judges *ad hoc* – Valticos (designated by El Salvador) and initially Virally (designated by Honduras), replaced after his death by Torres Bernárdez. The Chamber ultimately decided that the 1986 El Salvador–Honduras Special Agreement did not confer upon it jurisdiction to effect any delimitation of maritime areas whether within or outside the Gulf of Fonseca.[34] Nevertheless, the unprecedented decision taken by the Chamber in its 1990 judgment permitting Nicaragua to intervene and various elements of the 1992 judgment on the Merits, are of major importance in the context of maritime boundary delimitation.

---

[31] ICJ Communique No. 92/24 of 9 October 1992.

[32] ICJ Reports, 1987, pp. 10–13, decided unanimously by President Nagendra Singh, Vice-President Mbaye and Judges Lachs, Ruda, Oda, Ago, Sette-Camara, Schwebel, Sir Robert Jennings, Bedjaoui, Ni, Evensen and Tarassov (Registrar Valencia-Ospina).

[33] ICJ Reports, 1989, pp. 162–3, decided unanimously by President Ruda and Judges Elias, Oda, Ago, Schwebel, Sir Robert Jennings, Bedjaoui, Ni, Evensen, Tarassov, Guillaume, Shahabuddeen and Pathak (Registrar Valencia-Ospina).

[34] ICJ Reports, 1992, pp. 251, 582–6 and 617 (para. 432(2) decided by four votes (including that of President Jennings) to one (of Judge *ad hoc* Torres Bernárdez) (Registrar Valencia-Ospina).

THIRD-STATE INTERVENTION

In its unanimous judgment of 13 September 1990 on the *Application by Nicaragua for Permission to Intervene* the Chamber, for the first time in the history of the ICJ and its predecessor, the Permanent Court of International Justice, granted Nicaragua permission to intervene as a non–party under article 62 of the ICJ Statute.[35] Keeping in mind that the selection of the Chamber's members (taking account of the wishes of the parties) was made before the question of intervention was raised in the case,[36] it should be recalled that from among the Chamber's members, President Sette-Camara and Judges Oda and Sir Robert Jennings had dissented to the 1984 *Libya/Malta* judgment on the *Application by Italy for Permission to Intervene*,[37] whereas Judge Oda had appended his Separate Opinion to the unanimous 1981 *Tunisia/Libya* judgment on the *Application by Malta for Permission to Intervene*.[38] Although in both Libyan cases the requests for permission to intervene (opposed by each of the respective principal parties) were not granted, those two cases might be regarded as having opened up a new perspective for international litigation. In particular, the requests of the two would-be interveners, Malta and Italy, had the effect of reducing considerably the areas of the congested and politically sensitive central Mediterranean Sea

[35] ICJ Reports, 1990, pp. 92, 137 (Registrar Valencia-Ospina). See also the Court's Order on the *Application for Permission to Intervene* of 28 February 1990, decided by twelve votes to three. In favour: President Ruda, Vice-President Mbaye and Judges Lachs, Oda, Ago, Schwebel, Sir Robert Jennings, Bedjaoui, Ni, Evensen, Guillaume and Pathak; against: Judges Elias, Tarassov and Shahabuddeen (Registrar Valencia-Ospina), ICJ Reports, 1990, pp. 3–6. Cf. S. Rosenne, *Intervention in the International Court of Justice* (Dordrecht, 1993), at pp. 148–55; and for discussion of the Dissenting Opinion of Judge Shahabuddeen, see E. Lauterpacht, *Aspects of the Administration of International Justice* (Cambridge, 1991), pp. 90–8; and Thirlway, chap. 20 below, this volume.

[36] Cf. Diplomatic Note circulated by the Permanent Mission of Nicaragua to other Missions accredited to the United Nations emphasizing that Nicaragua (which in its 1989 application sought intervention before the full Court) did not participate in the selection or composition of the Chamber nor did it have a judge *ad hoc*. (Unofficial translation of the Diplomatic Note was obtained in January 1993 through the kindness of Ambassador C. Argüello, Embassy of Nicaragua, The Hague.) Cf. also J. J. Quintana, 'Letter to the Editor in Chief', *AJIL*, 86 (1992), pp. 542, 545; Rosenne, *Intervention in the International Court of Justice*, pp. 122–4.

[37] See n. 10 above and Dissenting Opinions of Vice-President Sette-Camara and Judge Oda, ICJ Reports, 1984, pp. 71–89 and 90–114. See also reply by Professor Jennings, ICJ Pleadings, Oral Arguments, Documents, No. 493, vol. V, pp. 272–4. Cf. Brown, *Sea-bed Energy and Minerals*, pp. 264–5; *International Boundary Cases*, pp. 1361–4; argument of P. Weil, Counsel of El Salvador, ICJ, *El Salvador/ Honduras*, Verbatim Record of Pleadings, C 4/CR 90/3, p. 49; argument of I. Brownlie, Counsel of Nicaragua, ICJ, *El Salvador/Honduras: Nicaragua Intervening*, Verbatim Record of Pleadings, C 4/CR 91/43, pp. 67–8; argument of I. Brownlie, Counsel of Norway, ICJ, *Denmark v. Norway*, Verbatim Record of Pleadings, CR 93/7, p. 24.

[38] ICJ Reports, 1981, pp. 23–34.

which the Court found came within its jurisdiction in these cases. It might therefore be argued that, in spite of the Court's decision dismissing the application to intervene, the would-be interveners had to an important extent achieved their objectives.[39]

In his Separate Opinion, which is the only one appended to the 1990 *El Salvador/Honduras* judgment, Judge Oda concurred with the Chamber's judgment permitting Nicaragua to intervene, but criticized the scope of this intervention limited (in accordance with Honduras's contention)[40] to the legal regime of the waters within the Gulf of Fonseca. The limitation excluded from the intervention the questions of delimitation within the Gulf and of the legal situation of the maritime spaces (including their prospective delimitation) outside the Gulf.[41] However, the Chamber's position would appear to be justifiable in view of the aim of Honduras to confine the relevant area for the purposes of a hypothetical delimitation with El Salvador to the western sectors within and outside the Gulf of Fonseca. A clear confinement to these sectors, limited by perpendicular lines drawn from the mid-point on the closing line of the Gulf back inside the Gulf to reach the Honduran coast on the one hand, and out to the 200-mile limit on the other hand, would not prejudice any future delimitation which Nicaragua might seek either within or outside the Gulf.[42]

In his Declaration appended to the 1992 judgment on the merits, Judge Oda reaffirmed the views expressed in his previous Opinions and disputed the Chamber's findings as to the lack of any binding effect of the 1992 judgment on the intervening state.[43] Although not a party to the case, Nicaragua will, according to Judge Oda, be bound by the judgment insofar as it relates to the legal regime of maritime spaces of the Gulf of Fonseca. Judge *ad hoc* Torrez Bernárdez, in his Separate Opinion, concurred with the view of Vice-President Oda with respect to the effects of the 1992 judgment, other than that of *res judicata* (article 59 of the Statute) on a non-party state intervening

---

[39] Cf. Rosenne, *The World Court*, p. 212; Dissenting Opinion of Judge Schwebel, ICJ Reports, 1985, pp. 172, 183–4, and 177–8.

[40] ICJ Reports, 1992, p. 120, para. 69; argument of D. W. Bowett, Counsel of Honduras, ICJ, *El Salvador/Honduras*, Verbatim Record of Pleadings, C 4/CR 90/4, pp. 27–53, and C 4/CR 90/5, pp. 53–9.

[41] ICJ Reports, 1990, pp. 138–44.

[42] *Ibid.*, p. 123; ICJ, *El Salvador/Honduras*, Memoire du Gouvernement de la Republique du Honduras, vol. II, 1 June 1988, map C.5 (within the Gulf), p. 704, and map C.6 (outside the Gulf), p. 720; Bowett, ICJ, *El Salvador Honduras*, Verbatim Record of Pleadings, CR 90/4, and in ICJ, *El Salvador/Honduras: Nicaragua Intervening*, Verbatim Record of Pleadings, C 4/CR 91/44, pp. 11–14.

[43] ICJ Reports, 1992, pp. 619–20.

under article 62.[44] In his major work on intervention in the World Court, Ambassador Rosenne stressed that:

> Regardless of the tenor of Article 59 of the Statute (in its English version at least), surely a judgment stating what the law is as regards a – any – territorial dispute is valid *erga omnes*. Consequently, for this reason alone (and there are others) the negative statement that the judgment is not *res judicata* for Nicaragua does not appear to give a complete picture of the position in law.[45]

In Rosenne's view, instead of involving itself in the different question of the effect of the *res judicata* and article 59, the Chamber should rather have taken Nicaragua's initial statement at its face value, as a unilateral undertaking to abide by the terms of the judgment, and it should have embodied that statement in an appropriate form in the operative clause of the judgment.

Notwithstanding the limited scope of the permission to intervene granted to Nicaragua, the *El Salvador/Honduras* case marked a significant stage in the development of a third state's right to intervene in maritime boundary delimitation cases, which had commenced with the unanimous rejection by the Court of Malta's request to such effect in 1981, been followed by the majority rejection of Italy's right to intervene in 1984, and culminated in the unanimous acceptance by the Chamber of Nicaragua's (limited) intervention in 1990. This remarkable acceptance can, to a significant extent, be ascribed to the influence of the three advocates of a more liberal approach to intervention under article 62 of the Statute, namely Judges Sette-Camara, Oda and Sir Robert Jennings who, as was already mentioned, formed part of the Chamber in the Nicaraguan application case and who all filed Separate and Dissenting Opinions in the two negative Libyan decisions.[46]

An opinion has been expressed that in the 1990 *El Salvador/Honduras* judgment the Chamber dealt with the question of jurisdiction in 'a manner that appears to differ from the way in which the full Court dealt with comparable problems in the past', which could be perceived as a possible precursor of a relaxation of consent in the practice of the ICJ.[47] However, the

---

[44] *Ibid.*, pp. 629, 730–1. Cf. main text accompanying n. 67 below.

[45] Rosenne, *Intervention in the International Court of Justice*, p. 155.

[46] Cf. R. St J. Macdonald and V. Hughes, 'Intervention before the International Court of Justice', *African Journal of International and Comparative Law*, 5 (1993), pp. 1, 31–2.

[47] Lauterpacht, *Aspects of the Administration of International Justice*, pp. 26–30. Cf. Argument of E. Lauterpacht, Advocate of El Salvador, ICJ, *El Salvador/Honduras*, Verbatim Record of Pleadings, C 4/CR 90/3, pp. 80–4. But see J. G. Merrills, *International Dispute Settlement* (Cambridge, 1991), p. 129, maintaining that as far as the composition of Chambers is concerned, 'practice does not suggest an undue narrowness of outlook, and this is confirmed if we consider the other matters of concern, the quality and authority of the decisions'.

view that the Chamber reversed the previous decisions of the full Court, and the anticipation that the Court (in a markedly different composition) might, in turn, reject in future the Chamber's judgment as a precedent, appears somewhat to underestimate the fact that the 1990 judgment is in entire conformity with the previous decisions of the Court and could be regarded as but a gloss on their effect.

In particular in its 1990 judgment, in accordance with the principle of judicial consistency, the Chamber fully accepted that the lack of a jurisdictional link between the state that seeks to intervene and the parties to the case is a fundamental stumbling block to a would-be intervener.[48] But since Nicaragua obviously had an effective legal interest in the case as required by article 62 of the ICJ Statute, the Chamber allowed intervention without the intervening state having the status of a party to the dispute, thus holding that where there is no jurisdictional link a third state cannot be a party, even though it might intervene. Not being a party makes a material difference and precludes application of article 59 of the Statute and the respective provisions of the Rules of the Court.[49] A significant element of the Chamber's decision thus lies in the distinction between an intervening party and a mere intervener, which does permit some kind of useful intervention while allowing full logical effect to the lack of any jurisdictional link.

One could, therefore, agree with Macdonald and Hughes that the Nicaragua decision is a significant achievement that could work to augment the Court's clientele rather than adversely to affect the future of the Court. States in a position to believe that they have interests of a legal nature that may be affected by particular decisions of the ICJ, and that have heretofore considered applying for permission to intervene, but have not done so because they believed that their efforts would fail, may in future decide to proceed with their applications.[50] According to Ambassador Rosenne: 'There would appear to be unsuspected potentialities in this form of judicial proceeding, recently increased by the introduction of the concept of non-party intervention, the full implications of which may not yet be fully visible.'[51]

---

[48] ICJ Reports, 1990, pp. 131–6.

[49] When Nicaragua declared its intention to be bound by the Chamber's Judgment (ICJ Reports, 1990, p. 109, para. 38), it probably did not contemplate the possibility of being allowed to intervene as a non-party. If Nicaragua meant only that article 59 would presumably apply, its Declaration has no meaning or effect which would be against the rules of interpretation. See also ICJ Reports, 1992, pp. 609–10, paras. 422 and 424.

[50] Macdonald and Hughes, 'Intervention before the International Court of Justice, p. 33.

[51] Rosenne, *Intervention in the International Court of Justice*, pp. 200 and 188–90.

SOME ISSUES OF SUBSTANCE

In the complex 1992 *El Salvador/Honduras, Nicaragua Intervening* judgment on the Merits of 11 September 1992, which is the most voluminous decision rendered in the history of the Court, five issues relating to the El Salvador–Honduras land frontier and two issues concerning the legal situation of the islands in the area were decided unanimously by all five members of the Chamber.[52] The lack of jurisdiction to delimit the maritime areas referred to above,[53] the legal situation of the maritime spaces within and outside the Gulf of Fonseca,[54] and the remaining four issues of substance[55] were decided by a majority vote of four (including President Sir Robert Jennings) to one.

In view of the notorious lack of any 'agreed and codified general rules' for pluri-state historic bays,[56] and in a situation where the Chamber was neither a court of appeal from the Central American Court nor was charged with determining whether by reason of error the 1971 *El Salvador v. Nicaragua* judgment of the latter Court was invalid, the Chamber confirmed and developed this judgment as 'a relevant precedent decision of a competent court and as, in the words of Article 38 of the Court's Statute, "a subsidiary means for the determination of rules of law".'[57] The 1917 judgment ascribed to the pluri-state Gulf of Fonseca the nature of a historic bay with the character of a closed sea subject to a condominium of the three states, except for an internal 3-mile belt of territorial waters and the waters delimited in 1900 between Honduras and Nicaragua. The historical factors, including the fact that the waters concerned were waters of a single state (Spain and thereafter the Federal Republic of Central America) bay during the greater part of their history, were found by the three states, and other (e.g., the USA) states concerned, as well as by many commentators, to be decisive for the

---

[52] ICJ Reports, 1992, pp. 610–13 (paras. 425–7) and pp. 614–15 (paras. 429–30), relating to the first, second, third, fifth and sixth sectors of the common land frontier, and p. 616 (para. 431(3) and (4)), deciding that the islands of El Tigre and Meanguera are parts of the territory of Honduras and El Salvador, respectively.

[53] See n. 34 above.

[54] ICJ Reports, 1992, pp. 616–17, para. 432(1) and (3). One vote against was in both decisions of Vice-President Oda.

[55] *Ibid.*, pp. 613–14, para. 428, relating to the fourth sector of land frontier (one vote against having been of Judge *ad hoc* Valticos), and 615–16, para. 431(1), (2) and (5), relating to the islands (one vote against having been in all three decisions of Judge Torres Bernárdez).

[56] *Ibid.*, p. 589.

[57] *Ibid.*, p. 601. On the 1917 judgment, see M. O. Hudson, *The Permanent Court of International Justice 1920–1942, A Treatise* (New York, 1943), pp. 60–2.

recognition of the Gulf of Fonseca as a historic bay of a special character.[58] As the Chamber asserted:

> What matters . . . is not what is 'always' true, but what was the position in this particular case, in which the maritime area in question had long been historic waters under a single State's sovereignty, apparently without any demarcated administrative limits, and was in 1821 jointly acquired by the three successor States by reason of succession. That seems to be the essence of the decision of the Central American Court for this confined maritime area which so intimately concerns all three coastal States. Certainly there is no reason why a joint sovereignty should not exist over maritime territory.[59]

At the same time, as condominia can cease to exist given the necessary agreement, the Chamber decided that the joint entitlement of all three states of the Gulf will apply unless and until a delimitation (including an agreement on navigational questions) of the relevant maritime area is effected.[60]

As regards the legal situation of the waters outside the Gulf, after it had decided that outside the closing line of the Gulf there can be a further belt of territorial sea, in the sense of the modern law of the sea, of up to 12 miles, the Chamber took the position that the closing line of the Gulf constituted the baseline of the territorial sea.[61] With respect to the closely related question of whether the line between Punta Cosigüina and Punta Ampala was (as contended by Honduras) or was not (as contended by El Salvador) also a baseline, the Chamber decided that the territorial sea, EEZ and continental shelf of El Salvador and Nicaragua were also to be measured outwards from a section of the closing line extending 3 miles along that line from Punta Ampala (in El Salvador) and 3 miles from Punta Cosigüina (in Nicaragua), respectively. But entitlement to those three maritime spaces seaward of the central position

---

[58] Cf. references in ICJ Reports, 1992, pp. 588–94, including to the successive editions of the leading work, *Oppenheim's International Law*, and those found in the ninth edition thereof, ed. Jennings and Watts, pp. 626–33; I. Brownlie, *Principles of Public International Law* (Oxford, 1990), pp. 167–8; remarks by J. I. Charney, in *Contemporary International Law Issues: Opportunities at a Time of Momentous Change*, 1993 Joint ASIL–NVIR Conference (Dordrecht, 1994), pp. 443, 450. Cf. also the importance ascribed to historical factors, including historic bays, in the Memorial of Tunisia, in the case concerning the *Continental Shelf*, ICJ Pleadings, Oral Arguments, Documents, No. 489, vol. I, pp. 30, 73–7; Memorial of Libya, *ibid.*, pp. 454, 502–6; argument of Professor Jennings, pp. 419–21; Reply by Professor Jennings, ICJ Pleadings, Oral Arguments, Documents, No. 492, vol. IV, pp. 277–8; ICJ Reports, 1982, pp. 18, 71–7.

[59] ICJ Reports, 1992, p. 600; also pp. 597–8. In his Dissenting Opinion, Judge Oda maintained that, instead, the waters of the Gulf constitute wholly the sum of the distinct 12-mile territorial seas of each of the three riparian states: *ibid.*, pp. 732, 757–9. Cf. also Judge Oda's Dissenting Opinion to the 1982 *Tunisia/Libya* judgment, ICJ Reports, 1982, pp. 157, 209–11.

[60] ICJ Reports, 1992, pp. 603–5 and 617 (para. 432(1) in f.).

[61] *Ibid.*, pp. 606–7 and 617, para. 432(3).

of the closing line appertains, according to the 1992 judgment, to El Salvador, Honduras and Nicaragua. This decision reflects the Chamber's view that 'since the legal situation on the landward side of the closing line is one of joint sovereignty, it follows that all three of the joint sovereigns must have entitlement outside the closing line to territorial sea, continental shelf and exclusive economic zone'.[62]

Vice-President Oda in his Dissenting Opinion objected to the Chamber's finding that, since a condominium prevails up to the closing line, Honduras is entitled to extend its maritime spaces in the Pacific. He argued to the contrary that Honduras was locked between El Salvador and Nicaragua within the Gulf itself and was, consequently, not entitled to make any claim outside the Gulf.[63] However, this hypothesis contradicted Honduras's objection to it being entirely blocked off from any claim beyond the Gulf's closing line. Instead, according to Honduras, the division of this line (treating its Honduran portion as a national coast) should be proportionate to the length (of some 45 miles) of the Honduran coast, and Honduran maritime areas should be adjusted by varying the angle of the boundary seawards, so as to reflect the difference in the length of the coasts of El Salvador and Honduras.[64]

In view of all the circumstances of the *El Salvador/Honduras, Nicaragua Intervening* case, a future delimitation of the waters within the Gulf, whether directly between the three states concerned or through a third-party settlement, appears unlikely. Hence, if the status of the Gulf, as determined by the 1992 judgment, is to be preserved, the three states may choose to base themselves on this judgment in a prospective delimitation of the waters outside the Gulf.[65] This is confirmed by statements made by the parties to the dispute that they will comply with the Chamber's judgment.[66]

For its part, Nicaragua, referring in its Diplomatic Note to the Chamber's decision that the 1992 judgment is not *res judicata* for Nicaragua, declared that

---

[62] *Ibid.*, p. 608.

[63] *Ibid.*, pp. 759–61.

[64] Cf. main text accompanying n. 42 above; argument of D. W. Bowett, Counsel of Honduras, ICJ, *El Salvador/Honduras: Nicaragua Intervening*, Verbatim Record of Pleadings, C 4/CR 91/45; final statements and submissions of Ambassador Valladares Soto, Agent of Honduras, *ibid.*, C 4/CR 91/50, pp. 10–16.

[65] For one application of the Chamber's decision provided by Professor J. R. V. Prescott of the University of Melbourne, Australia, that would be similar to the result of the 1992 *Canada/France (St Pierre and Miquelon) Maritime Area Delimitation Decision* (see note 87 below), see B. Kwiatkowska, 'Judge Shigeru Oda's Opinions in Law-of-the-sea Cases: Equitable Maritime Boundary Delimitation', *German Yearbook of International Law*, 36 (1993), pp. 225–94.

[66] Joint communique of the Presidents of Honduras and El Salvador of 29 September 1992, quoted and reaffirmed on behalf of both states by Mr Castañeda Cornejo of El Salvador in his statement in the UN General Assembly on 21 October 1992: UN Doc. A/47/PV.43, pp. 17, 21–5.

this judgment 'has not altered nor can it alter Nicaragua's rights in the Gulf of Fonseca or in the maritime spaces in the Pacific Ocean'.[67] At the same time, Nicaragua reiterated 'its willingness to reach bilateral or multilateral agreements with its neighbours, in order to resolve any differences that might arise, and also its willingness to submit any disputes that can not be settled by diplomacy to any of the other peaceful means of resolution provided for in the treaties to which it is a Party'. If the states concerned decide to proceed with the delimitation of their respective maritime spaces, any such delimitation would in any event, as the Chamber indicated, have to be 'effected by agreement on the basis of international law'.[68]

THE *DENMARK V. NORWAY MARITIME BOUNDARY IN THE AREA BETWEEN GREENLAND AND JAN MAYEN* CASE

The judgment delivered by the Court, under the Presidency of Judge Sir Robert Jennings, on 14 June 1993 in the *Denmark v. Norway Maritime Boundary in the Area between Greenland and Jan Mayen* case is a significant contribution to the law of equitable maritime boundary delimitation. The almost unanimous judgment, decided by fourteen votes to one[69] – for the first time since the 1985 *Libya/Malta* judgment – directly involved a maritime delimitation settlement. Previously, as Judge Weeramantry observed, it was no cause for surprise that the flexible principles of equity superimposed upon so fluid a subject as the new law of the sea should have failed to produce a greater predictability of legal results.[70] By contrast, the *Denmark v. Norway* judgment, in response to the need for 'consistency and a degree of predictability' stressed by the *Libya/Malta* judgment,[71] marks the notable development achieved in the context of already crystallized principles and rules of international law of the sea.

Significantly, Sir Robert Jennings, while emphasizing that 'the process

---

[67] For Nicaragua's Diplomatic Note, see n. 36 above; ICJ Reports, 1992, p. 610. Cf. C. Argüello, 'Comments', in *Contemporary International Law Issues: Opportunities at a Time of Momentous Change*, 1992 ASIL–NVIR Conference (Dordrecht, 1994), p. 449; see also main text accompanying notes 43 to 45 above.

[68] ICJ Reports, 1992, pp. 608–9 and 617 (para. 432(3) in f.).

[69] Fourteen votes in favour by President Sir Robert Jennings, Vice-President Oda and Judges Ago, Schwebel, Bedjaoui, Ni, Evensen, Tarassov, Guillaume, Shahabuddeen, Aguilar Mawdsley, Weeramantry, Ranjeva and Ajibola; one vote against by Judge *ad hoc* Fischer (designated by Denmark) (Registrar Valencia-Ospina), ICJ Reports, 1993, pp. 38, 82.

[70] Separate Opinion of Judge Weeramantry, *ibid.*, pp. 211, 257, para. 162.

[71] *Ibid.*, p. 64 (para. 58 in f.)

of delimitation involved *both* law and equity',[72] and that 'law and equity working together should serve the ends of justice by introducing flexibility, adaptability, and even limitations upon the application and meaning of legal rules,'[73] has been a strong advocate of such consistency and predictability. In his opinion: 'A structured and predictable system of equitable procedures is an essential framework for the only kind of equity that a Court of law that has not been given competence to decide *ex aequo et bono*, may properly contemplate.'[74] And while reflecting on the place of policy in international law, Sir Robert remarked that 'the very purpose of law is to provide limits to discretions and to powers of decisions; and it is important not to forget that policy includes legal policy, i.e., the need to see that the system works, that as far as possible it is clear, that it is as far as possible predictable, and so on'.[75]

The 1993 *Denmark v. Norway* judgment testifies to an increased degree of predictability through, to start with, the Court's adherence to the two-stage decision-making process of applying equity to maritime boundary delimitation. Contrary to what is sometimes maintained,[76] the precedent to this effect was not set by the *Libya/Malta* judgment, which merely clarified the process that was already apparent from the Court's reasoning in previous cases. At the first stage of this process, as the Court put it: 'The choice of the criterion and the method which it is to employ in the first place to arrive at a provisional result should be made in a manner *consistent with the concepts underlying the attribution of legal title.'*[77] Once such 'provisional delimitation by using

---

[72] Jennings, 'Equity and Equitable Principles', at p. 36. Cf. his remarks on the distinction between a decision according to equity as required by the law and a decision *ex aequo et bono, ibid.*, pp. 29–30; Jennings, 'General Course on Principles of International Law', pp. 343–4. Cf. also H. W. A. Thirlway, 'The Law and Procedure of the International Court of Justice 1960–1989, Part One', *BYbIL*, 60 (1989), pp. 1, 50–1.

[73] Jennings, 'The Principles Governing Marine Boundaries', at pp. 400–1; quoted by P. Weil, Advocate of Norway, ICJ, *Denmark v. Norway*, Verbatim Record of Pleadings, CR 93/8 (transl.), pp. 2, 64. Cf. Weil, chap. 7 above, in this volume.

[74] Jennings, 'Equity and Equitable Principles', p. 38; quoted by B. Kwiatkowska, 'Equitable Maritime Boundary Delimitation – A Legal Perspective', *International Journal of Marine and Coastal Law*, 3 (1988), pp. 287, 289, and E. Jimenez de Aréchaga, Counsel of Denmark, ICJ, *Denmark v. Norway*, Verbatim Record of Pleadings, CR 93/2, pp. 60, 76. Cf. notes 20 and 21 above; and remarks on dependence of the legitimacy of a rule on its degree of determinacy by T. Franck, 'Legitimacy in the International System', *AJIL*, 82 (1988), pp. 705, 725.

[75] R. Y. Jennings, 'The Proper Reach of Territorial Jurisdiction: A Case Study of Divergent Attitudes', *Georgia Journal of International and Comparative Law*, 2 (1972 Suppl. 2, with introductory statement by Professor R. Higgins), pp. 35, 35–6. Cf. Jennings, 'General Course on Principles of International Law', pp. 430–2; and Jennings, 'Gerald Gray Fitzmaurice', pp. 14–22, emphasizing that: 'Thus, it was Fitzmaurice's preoccupation to defend the juridical integrity of international law, as a complete and consistent system impartially applied, and, as far as may be, reasonably certain and predictable' (p. 22).

[76] See, e.g., Separate Opinion of Judge Shahabuddeen, ICJ Reports, 1993, pp. 130, 192.

[77] ICJ Reports, 1985, pp. 46–7, para. 61 (emphasis added).

a criterion and method both of which are clearly destined to play an important role in producing the final result' has been completed, the Court turns to the second stage. This stage involves examination of the provisional solution 'in the light of the requirements derived from other criteria, which may call for a correction of this initial result'.[78] At the same time, the predictability of the process under consideration does not require the Court to classify and/or to enumerate exhaustively the relevant circumstances involved in the two stages. What is important, instead, is a clarification added by the *Libya/Malta* judgment and reaffirmed by the *Denmark v. Norway* judgment to the dictum in the *North Sea* decision that 'there is no legal limit to the considerations which States may take account of'.[79] In particular, for a court, although there is assuredly no closed list of considerations, only those considerations that are pertinent to the respective maritime spaces as they have developed within the law, and to the application of equity to their delimitation, will qualify for inclusion.

PROVISIONAL DELIMITATION

An increased degree of predictability is also revealed in the Court's reliance on the equidistant (median) line as a provisional boundary between the opposite maritime areas of Eastern Greenland and the island of Jan Mayen. The use of this method at this stage was derived by the Court from the two strands of the applicable law: article 6 of the 1958 UN Continental Shelf Convention (CSC), which the Court had for the first time occasion to apply to the continental shelf delimitation; and the customary law generated by the LOSC which is applicable to the delimitation of the 200-mile fishery zone.[80] In this context, the Court drew a number of masterly observations and conclusions.

The most significant submission by the Court is perhaps the one inspired by the 1977 *United Kingdom/France Continental Shelf* decision that an equidistance/special circumstances rule under article 6 of the CSC 'produces much the same result' as an equitable principles/relevant circumstances rule under customary law in the case of opposite coasts, whether in the case of a delimitation of continental shelf, of fishery zone, or of an all-purpose single

---

[78] *Ibid.*, p. 46, para. 60.

[79] ICJ Reports, 1993, p. 63. Cf. Jennings, 'Commentary', *Implementation of the Law of the Sea*, p. 654; Weil, *The Law of Maritime Delimitation*, pp. 103–14.

[80] ICJ Reports, 1993, pp. 58–64 and sketch-map No. 1, *ibid.*, p. 45, showing a provisional equidistant line AD.

boundary.[81] Although different in origin and in name, the 'special circumstances' and the 'relevant circumstances' thus lend themselves to assimilation as they (like the two rules) reflect differences of approach and terminology rather than of substance.

The Court further explained that the delimitation of the fishery zone is determined by the customary law governing the EEZ delimitation,[82] and that the identical provision of articles 74(1) and 83(1) of the LOSC governing delimitation of the 200-mile EEZ and the continental shelf, respectively, 'reflects the requirements of customary law'.[83] By so doing the Court in its judgment has thus established an appreciable uniformity in the effects of treaty and customary law governing maritime delimitation. This is especially important in that the entry into force of the LOSC on 16 November 1994 for only some sixty-one states (with the UN member states amounting to 184 as of July 1993) will not prevent the applicability to future disputes of both treaty law, whether old (CSC) or new (LOSC), and customary law.

Uniformity, in terms of having recourse to an equidistant line provisionally drawn as a first stage in the delimitation process, is, in the case of a 200-mile zone and (inner) continental shelf not exceeding this limit, implied also by the new customary regimes and the parallelism of those spaces generated by the LOSC. Whereas the *Denmark v. Norway* judgment does not specifically consider the effect of 200-mile distance as the new outer limit of the continental shelf for maritime delimitation,[84] the judgment is significant in confirming the findings of the *Libya/Malta* judgment that the continental shelf and EEZ 'are linked together in modern law', and the result is 'that greater importance must be attributed to elements, such as distance from the coast,

---

[81] *Ibid.*, pp. 62–3 (para. 56). Cf. *ibid.*, p. 58, para. 46. Cf. Jennings, 'General Course on Principles of International Law', p. 401, and 'The Principle Governing Marine Boundaries', pp. 399–400; Jennings and Watts, *Oppenheim's International Law*, pp. 776–7 and 780.

[82] ICJ Reports, 1993, p. 59, para. 47. This results from the fact that in the light of the LOSC and extensive legislative and treaty practice of states, a 200-mile fishery zone is but partial implementation (with respect to fisheries) of the legal regime of an EEZ.

[83] *Ibid.*, p. 59, para. 48. Cf. Separate Opinions of Judge Schwebel, *ibid.*, pp. 118, 127, and Judge Ajibola, *ibid.*, pp. 280, 287. Cf. also argument of Professor Jennings, ICJ Pleadings, Oral Arguments, Documents, vol. IV, p. 404, who, while considering whether at that time the draft of this provision leaned more towards equity or towards equidistance, stressed: 'The provision now embodied in the draft treaty cannot be said to have settled that issue with complete clarity; but it does make it clear beyond any possible doubt that, whatever the method employed, the solution of the problem must be in accordance with equity.'

[84] Nor was such effect specifically pleaded by Norway in the way it was pleaded by Malta in *Libya/Malta* case. See Weil, ICJ, *Denmark v. Norway*. Verbatim Record of Pleadings, CR 93/8, pp. 2–66, CR 93/9 (transl.), pp. 2–36, and CR 93/11 (transl.), pp. 41, 46; P. Weil, Counsel of Malta, ICJ, *Libya/Malta*, Verbatim Record of Pleadings, CR 84/25, pp. 5–79, CR 84/26, pp. 5–36, and CR 85/7, pp. 5, 32–60. Cf. Weil, *The Law of Delimitation*, pp. 38–45.

which are common to both concepts'.[85] Accordingly, the principle of the 200-mile distance, which governs the attribution of legal title to both the EEZ/fishery zone and the inner continental shelf (to the exclusion of natural prolongation), suggests the use of the equitable method of the equidistant (median) line.[86] This result had been admirably anticipated by Judge Sir Robert Jennings as follows:

> Perhaps the answer will turn out to be that since, with the coming of the Exclusive Economic Zone, the principle of distance from the shore has in effect replaced natural prolongation, the wheel has come full circle. For distance must surely lead back to equidistance as the basic boundary line, to be modified of course by equity where its application produced, for one identifiable particular circumstance or another, an inequitable result.[87]

As the distance between Greenland and Jan Mayen is only some 250 miles, each coast generated potential title to not only an EEZ/fishery zone, but also to a continental shelf up to, as the Court expressly stated, a limit recognized by customary law, i.e. in principle up to 200 miles from its baselines.[88] In addition, and most importantly, the Court ascertained that:

> In respect of the continental shelf boundary in the present case, even if it were appropriate to apply, not Article 6 of the 1958 Convention, but *customary law concerning the continental shelf as developed in the decided cases*, it is in accord with precedents to begin with the median line as a provisional line and then to ask whether 'special circumstances' require any adjustment or shifting of that line.[89]

Although, unlike the *Gulf of Maine* case, there was no joint request of Denmark and Norway for a single maritime boundary, in neither case did the

---

[85] ICJ Reports, 1993, p. 59, para. 46. Cf. Charney, in *Contemporary International Law Issues*; Jennings and Watts (eds.), *Oppenheim's International Law*, p. 781.

[86] It would, therefore, be difficult to agree with Separate Opinion of Judge Ajibola, ICJ Reports, 1993, p. 289, in whose view it was not appropriate to rely on the *Denmark v. Norway* case on the applicability of the principle of distance to the continental shelf as determined in the *Libya/Malta* case.

[87] Jennings, 'The Principles Governing Marine Boundaries', p. 408, also pp. 406–7. Cf. argument of Professor Jennings, ICJ Pleadings, Oral Arguments, Documents, No. 492, vol. IV, p. 421, arguing that 'if the 200-miles distance limit were of a determinative influence, it would follow logically that the principle of equidistance is governing . . . '. Cf. also Kwiatkowska, 'Judge Shigeru Oda's Opinions'; Weil, *The Law of Maritime Delimitation*, pp. 201–3; Dissenting Opinion of Arbitrator Weil, para. 37, to the 1992 *Canada/France (St Pierre and Miquelon)* decision, adopted by three votes, by the President of the Court of Arbitration, Jiménez de Aréchaga, and Arbitrators Schachter and Arangio-Ruiz, to two votes, by Arbitrators Weil and Gotlieb (Registrar Paolillo; Expert Cdr Beazley), in 31 *ILM* 1197, 1213 (1992).

[88] ICJ Reports, 1993, p. 69, para. 70.

[89] *Ibid.*, p. 61, para. 51 (emphasis added).

continental shelf boundary yet exist.[90] Denmark asked for a single dual-purpose boundary and Norway for the drawing of two coinciding boundary lines which would remain conceptually different. While admitting that Norway's request amounted in practical terms to a single boundary, the Court agreed that the difference stemmed from the location of the two coinciding lines, which derived from the CSC and customary law, respectively. As a result, unlike the *Gulf of Maine* case where the CSC could not apply to determination of a single (continental shelf and EEZ) line, the Court found the CSC applicable to the delimitation of the continental shelf between Greenland and Jan Mayen.

VERIFICATION/ADJUSTMENT OF A PROVISIONAL LINE

At the second stage of its decision-making process, when applying equity to maritime boundary delimitation, the Court considered all circumstances, including the geographical context of the dispute, proportionality *ex ante*, and economic and other factors relevant to the delimitation of the respective maritime spaces between Greenland and Jan Mayen. Consequently the Court found that neither the equidistant line as provisionally drawn by it and claimed by Norway, or the 200-mile line as claimed by Denmark, should be adopted as the boundary,[91] and it adjusted its provisional line so as to attribute a larger area of maritime space to Denmark than would the equidistant (median) line.[92] For the purpose of defining the final line, the Court divided the area of overlapping claims into Zones 1, 2 and 3 shown on a map annexed to the 1993 judgment.[93] The southern limit of this area, in particular of Zone 1, constitutes the 200-mile line of Iceland established as a result of its preceding delimitation with Jan Mayen.[94] Whereas in view of the duality of the applicable law referred to above, the boundary line is construed by the judgment as two delimitation lines of identical location,[95] all the following, including the operative, paragraphs of the judgment use a singular form in defining this boundary.[96]

---

[90] *Ibid.*, pp. 56–8. Contrary to the contention of Norway, the Court did not find the 1965 Norway/Denmark Agreement applicable to the continental shelf delimitation between Greenland and Jan Mayen: *ibid.*, pp. 48–56. Cf. main text accompanying note 29 above; Jennings and Watts (eds.), *Oppenheim's International Law*, pp. 805–7.

[91] ICJ Reports, 1993, pp. 69–70, para. 71.   [92] *Ibid.*, p. 77, para. 87.

[93] *Ibid.*, pp. 79–81, paras. 91–4, including sketch–map No. 2.

[94] *Ibid.*, p. 68, para. 67 and the line BCD on sketch–maps No. 1 and No. 2. Cf. below, note 116.

[95] ICJ Reports, 1993, p. 79, para. 90.

[96] Cf. note 90 above; Separate Opinions of Judges Shahabuddeen and Ajibola, ICJ Reports, 1993, pp. 197–202 and 286–9, respectively.

With the consideration of the geographical context, the Court stressed the importance of the relationship between, on the one hand, overlapping claims of the two parties to maritime areas situated less than 400 miles apart and, on the other hand, their overlapping entitlements to those areas.[97] The 1993 judgment was, however, criticized by the Separate Opinion of Vice-President Oda for relying mainly on the area of overlapping claims, which included the claim of Denmark to the 200-mile line coinciding with Greenland's maximum entitlement,[98] and the modest claim of Norway to the equidistant line involving an area much smaller than Jan Mayen's maximum entitlement.[99] Similarly, Judge Schwebel, in his Separate Opinion, pointed out that the Court appeared to reward Denmark's maximalist claim or to penalize Norway's moderation through attributing almost three-quarters of the total area of overlapping entitlements to Denmark and a bit more than one-quarter to Norway.[100] The Court thus awarded Greenland a bonus for the length of its coast or penalized Jan Mayen for the shortness of its coast which, according to Judge Schwebel, and likewise Judge Oda, may encourage immoderate and discourage moderate claims in future.

However, in view of Denmark's claim coinciding with its maximum entitlement and Norway's claim coinciding with the Court's provisional boundary line, as well as all the other circumstances of the case, the Court's reasoning can be regarded as justifiable and leading to an equitable result. Prominent among those circumstances was the pronounced disparity between the lengths of the coastal fronts of Greenland (504.3 or 524 km) and Jan Mayen (54.8 or 57.8 km), resulting in a ratio between 1:9.2 and 1:9.1.[101] Thus, contrary to Norway's contention that proportionality in the form of a factor based on the ratio of the lengths of the respective coasts is not an independent principle of delimitation, but rather an *a posteriori* test of the equitableness of a result arrived at by other means,[102] the Court had recourse to proportionality *ex ante* in the former meaning indicated above.

The Court reaffirmed the *prima facie* equitable character of equidistance in delimitation between opposite coasts which are nearly parallel and the important role this method has played in the practice of states; but the Court

---

[97] ICJ Reports, 1993, p. 64 and sketch-map No. 1.

[98] This was perceived by the Advocate of Norway, Weil, in ICJ, *Denmark v. Norway*, Verbatim Record of Pleadings, CR 93/8, p. 34, as a request for 'non-delimitation'.

[99] ICJ Reports, 1993, p. 101, paras. 45–6 and p. 116, para. 97.

[100] *Ibid.*, pp. 126–7. Cf. note 117 below; J. I. Charney, 'Maritime Delimitation in the Area between Greenland and Jan Mayen', *AJIL*, 88 (1994), pp. 105, 109.

[101] ICJ Reports, 1993, p. 64, para. 61.

[102] *Ibid.*, p. 66, para. 63. Cf. Weil, in ICJ, *Denmark v. Norway*, Verbatim Record of Pleadings, CR 93/9, pp. 2–23.

also remarked that the Greenland–Jan Mayen delimitation exemplifies situations 'in which the relationship between the length of the relevant coasts and the maritime areas generated by them by application of the equidistance method, is so disproportionate that it has been found necessary to take this circumstance into account in order to ensure an equitable solution'.[103] As Judge Shahabuddeen indicated in his Separate Opinion, the employment of equidistance between the short island coast of Jan Mayen and the long mainland coast of East Greenland would lead to generation by each kilometre of Jan Mayen's coast of a maritime zone six times as great as that generated by a kilometre of Greenland's coast.[104] Given this discrepancy amounting to a ratio of 6:1 in favour of the short coast, 'insistence that "legal equality" is nevertheless satisfied because the distance between the coasts is still equally divided by the median line becomes' – in Judge Shahabuddeen's view – 'too remote from common understanding to satisfy the kind of practical equality that it should be the aim of equity to achieve in international relations'.[105]

Believing that the law does not require a delimitation based on an endeavour to share out an area of overlap on the basis of comparative figures for the length of the coastal fronts and the areas generated by them, the Court found it necessary to shift its provisional equidistance in such a way as to effect a delimitation closer to the coast of Jan Mayen. Thereby, the Court confirmed the view expressed in the *Libya/Malta* judgment that to take account of the disparity in coastal lengths does not mean a direct mathematical application of the relationship between the length of the coastal fronts concerned.[106] Having regard to the disparity in coastal lengths, a delimitation according to the 200-mile line claimed by Denmark might, in the Court's opinion, from a mathematical perspective seem more equitable than that effected on the basis of the median line. But this result would run wholly counter to the rights of Jan Mayen (potentially entitled to a 200-mile limit) as well as to the demands of equity.[107] Significantly, while commenting on this pronouncement, Hugh Thirlway observes: 'The Court appears here to be stating a general rule, that where maximum claims, which States could make over open sea areas, conflict with those of other States, some compromise, involving reduction of

[103] ICJ Reports, 1993, p. 67, para. 65, also para. 64. Cf. Jennings, 'The Principles Governing Marine Boundaries', p. 408, n. 25.

[104] ICJ Reports, 1993, p. 183.

[105] *Ibid.*, pp. 186–7, and 185, figure No. 10: schematic illustration of influence of coastlines on median line construction.

[106] *Ibid.*, p. 69, para. 69. Cf. D. W. Bowett, Advocate of Denmark, ICJ, *Denmark v. Norway*, Verbatim Record of Pleadings, CR 93/4, pp. 9, 17, and CR 93/10, pp. 48, 52–5.

[107] ICJ Reports, 1993, p. 69, para. 70, p. 77, para. 87, and main text accompanying n. 88 above.

both claims, is always required, whatever the other circumstances; in other words that it can never in any circumstances be equitable for the one claim to prevail over the other.'[108]

Ultimately, the factor of the marked disparity in coastal lengths was decisive in determining the course of the boundary in Zones 2 and 3 of the area of overlapping claims referred to above. These two zones, unlike Zone 1, were not subject to an equal division because, according to the 1993 judgment, such a division of the whole area would give too great a weight to the coastal lengths' disparity.[109] In his Declaration, Judge Aguilar Mawdsley, while concurring with the Court's reasoning, was of the opinion that given the importance attached to this factor in the judgment, Greenland should have received a larger proportion of the disputed area.[110] It would have been logical, in Judge Aguilar's view, at least to make an equal distribution of all the three zones.

As regards other relevant circumstances, the Court gave due consideration to fisheries, the environmental factor of the presence of drift ice, sea-bed resources, security, population and socio-economic factors, and the conduct of the parties.[111] Ultimately, however, it was only the fisheries factor that influenced the shift eastwards of the Court's provisional equidistance and the division of Zone 1 into two parts of equal area so as to ensure an equitable access of the parties to the migratory stock of capeline in this zone.[112] The decision on this matter is preceded by reference in the 1993 judgment to the principle established by the 1984 *Gulf of Maine* judgment that factors such as fishing, navigation, security or sea-bed resources can only be taken into account if their disregard is 'likely to entail catastrophic repercussions for the livelihood and economic well-being of the population of the countries concerned'.[113] In the light of the pronouncements on the inapplicability of such catastrophic repercussions in the *Gulf of Maine* and *Libya/Malta* cases as well as the *Guinea/Guinea-Bissau Maritime Boundary* and *Canada/France Maritime Areas Delimitation* arbitrations, the *Denmark v. Norway* judgment is significant in relying apparently for the first time on this exception in the process of determining a maritime boundary.[114]

---

[108] Thirlway, 'The Law and Practice of the International Court of Justice, Part Five', pp. 39–40. Cf. *ibid.*, p. 17.

[109] ICJ Reports, 1993, p. 81, para. 92.

[110] *Ibid.*, p. 86.

[111] *Ibid.*, pp. 70–7.

[112] *Ibid.*, p. 72, para. 76 and p. 79, paras. 90–2. Cf. note 123 below.

[113] *Ibid.*, p. 71, para. 75.

[114] Cf. Separate Opinion of Judge Schwebel, *ibid.*, p. 120; Bowett, in ICJ, *Denmark v. Norway*, Verbatim Record of Pleadings, CF 93/4, pp. 28–9.

The 1993 judgment reaffirmed the irrelevance of socio-economic factors (other than resource-related factors) to equitable maritime delimitation,[115] and declined to accept Denmark's contention with respect to the relevance of the recommendation of the Conciliation Commission in the 1981 *Iceland/Norway (Jan Mayen) Continental Shelf* case, and the related conduct of states recognizing a full EEZ of 200 miles for Iceland (giving it a considerable area beyond the equidistant line) to the disadvantage of Jan Mayen.[116] Nevertheless, one could feel tempted to share the view expressed by Judge Schwebel who, while questioning, in his Separate Opinion, the equity of the Court's solution, remarked:

> Yet it may be said in defence of the approach of Denmark, if not of the Court, that, however extreme Denmark's claim appears in legal terms, in political terms it is perfectly understandable. Once Norway had extended to Iceland a 200-mile zone in relation to Jan Mayen, naturally Denmark sought no less on behalf of Greenland.[117]

It could be added that in the *Iceland/Norway* case the Conciliation Commission, comprising three outstanding jurists actively involved in UNCLOS III (Ambassadors Richardson, Evensen[118] and Andersen), rejected the contention of Iceland that Jan Mayen qualified as a rock under article 121(3) of the LOSC. Instead – without invoking any detailed arguments – the Commission asserted that 'Jan Mayen as an island is in principle entitled to its own territorial sea, contiguous zone, exclusive economic zone and continental shelf'.[119] This precedential recognition of Jan Mayen's island status could be viewed as part of a compromise in this case involving a full 200-mile EEZ for Iceland in relation to Jan Mayen. The Jan Mayen Conciliation Commission thereby created, however, a suitable climate for the possible extension of the already vague test of capacity to 'sustain human habitation or economic life of their own' under article 121(3), to navigational and resource uses in areas around the potential rocks. Most importantly, as some twenty-five meteorologists inhabiting Jan Mayen are dependent on the outside world for almost everything, the Jan Mayen Commission pointed to the conclusion that the above test of article 121(3) does not necessarily exclude islands obtaining external support for a population that is not necessarily permanent.

---

[115] ICJ Reports, 1993, p. 74, para. 80.

[116] *Ibid.*, pp. 75–7, paras. 82–6. See also the 1981 'Report and Recommendations of the Conciliation Commission on the Continental Shelf Area between Iceland and Jan Mayen', 20 *ILM* 797–842 (1981).

[117] ICJ Reports, 1993, p. 127. Cf. Dissenting Opinion of Judge *ad hoc* Fischer, *ibid.*, pp. 304, 311, para. 16; Bowett, in ICJ, *Denmark v. Norway*, Verbatim Record of Pleadings, pp. 19–24.

[118] Cf. note 123 below.

[119] 'Report and Recommendations', pp. 803–4.

In the *Denmark v. Norway* case, neither the parties nor the Court questioned the legal status of Jan Mayen as an island or its entitlement to maritime spaces under article 121(1)–(2) of the LOSC, which reflect existing customary law. However, Jan Mayen's potential rock status under the controversial article 121(3) has underlined the maximalist claim of Denmark, which expressly invoked the wording of this provision.[120] Such a status of Jan Mayen could also be regarded as underlying Norway's moderate claim and as being an unstated factor in the Court's decision-making process. As Judge Schwebel remarked in his Separate Opinion: 'The singular characteristics of Jan Mayen Island may leave room for argument about whether it meets the standards of Article 121.'[121] Significantly, the Court refrained from specific consideration of Denmark's arguments regarding the size and special character of Jan Mayen's population and the absence of locally based fishing; instead, it declined to weigh these circumstances on the ground of the inapplicability of socio-economic factors to equitable maritime delimitation.[122] Thereby, and by taking account of Norwegian fishing (carried out by vessels based on the mainland, not on Jan Mayen) in the process of equal division of Zone 1,[123] the 1993 judgment of the Court indirectly confirmed the liberal interpretation of the rocks principle initiated by the Jan Mayen Conciliation Commission referred to above.

CONCLUSION

The judgments delivered by the World Court under the Presidency of Sir Robert Jennings in the recent *Guinea-Bissau v. Senegal*, *El Salvador/Honduras: Nicaragua Intervening* and *Denmark v. Norway* cases form, as was shown above, a remarkable contribution to an increased stability in the law and judicial consistency of which Sir Robert has been a notable advocate for over two decades. The Court (and its Chamber) has supported such consistency with respect not only to its own previous decisions, but also to those of other tribunals, including the 1989 *Guinea-Bissau v. Senegal* Arbitral Award and the 1917 *El Salvador v. Nicaragua* judgment of the Central American Court,

---

[120] ICJ Reports, 1993, p. 65, para. 60. Cf. Dissenting Opinion of Judge *ad hoc* Fischer, *ibid.*, pp. 309–14. Cf. also T. Lehmann, Agent of Denmark, ICJ, *Denmark v. Norway*, Verbatim Record of Pleadings, CR 93/10, pp. 8, 21–2; F. Lynge, Counsel of Denmark, *ibid.*, pp. 69, 71–2; and reply thereto by Weil, in ICJ, *Denmark v. Norway*, Verbatim Record of Pleadings, CR 93/11, p. 43.

[121] ICJ Reports, 1993, p. 126.

[122] *Ibid.*, p. 46, para. 15 and pp. 73–4, paras. 79–80.

[123] Cf. emphasis on the island status of Jan Mayen and on the equity of the Court's boundary in the Declaration of Judge Evensen, *ibid.*, pp. 84–5; and main text accompanying note 50 above.

respectively. While in conformity with the principle of judicial consistency, the 1990 *El Salvador/Honduras* judgment, through an unprecedented decision permitting Nicaragua to intervene as a non-party under article 62 of the ICJ Statute, marked a significant stage in the development of third-state rights to intervene in maritime boundary delimitation.

The elegantly drafted *Denmark v. Norway* judgment forms a landmark in the development of the jurisprudence of the World Court on equitable maritime boundary delimitation. In his well-balanced Dissenting Opinion to the preceding 1992 decision of the Court of Arbitration in the *Canada/France (St Pierre and Miquelon)* case, Prosper Weil wondered whether that decision did not in some respects jeopardize the development of the law of maritime delimitation, which had been significantly developed through the 1985 *Libya/Malta* judgment towards a more secure and predictable legal foundation.[124] Weil feared that the 1992 decision reverted to an autonomous – or as Sir Robert Jennings put it, 'free-range'[125] – form of equity as a substitute for law, a form which Weil hoped had been definitively abandoned. The 1993 *Denmark v. Norway* judgment put an end to such uncertainties by strengthening the findings of the *Libya/Malta* judgment and by marking a notable progress in the accommodation of the operation of equity with the now crystallized principles and rules of the new law of the sea.

Through confirmation of the two-stage decision-making process of the Court, which is always 'long, slow and delicate'[126] ('LSD'), and through its masterly findings regarding the issues of substance, the *Denmark v. Norway* judgment fulfilled Sir Robert's anticipation as to the degree of predictability required from equity operating within the law, or within the 'jurist's law' – as Sir Gerald Fitzmaurice would have put it.[127] This results from the Court's pronouncements on the uniformity of the effects of treaty and customary law governing maritime boundary delimitation (including the use of equidistance in the first stage of provisional delimitation between opposite states), as well as on the single boundary line, proportionality, the resource factors and other substantive issues discussed above.

The Court's well-reasoned analysis in the context of the new oceans regime increased the legitimacy of the judgment and added to the prestige of the Court. It has also steered the approach of the Court to applying equity to

---

[124] 1992 Dissenting Opinion of P. Weil, paras. 1 and 28, 1992 *Canada/France (St Pierre and Miquelon)* decision, pp. 1197, 1207–8.

[125] Jennings, 'The Principles Governing Marine Boundaries', p. 407.

[126] K. Highet, Advocate of Norway, ICJ, *Denmark v. Norway*, Verbatim Record of Pleadings, CR 93/9, pp. 47, 59.

[127] Cf. main text accompanying ns 74 and 75 above; and Jennings, 'Gerald Gray Fitzmaurice', p. 21.

maritime boundary delimitation on 'a middle course between being over-conservative and ultra-progressive' which Sir Gerald regarded as an essential condition of a successful operation of the Hague Court.[128] As Judge Ajibola, in his Separate Opinion, remarked:

> The judicial process, like the law, is dynamic. It will continue to develop and be improved upon. The use of equitable principles in this field is definitely on course and equity is not floundering in uncharted seas. There will always be room for fine-tuning, but there is no doubt that the international customary law of maritime boundary delimitation, now solidly based on equitable principles, has come to stay.[129]

As both old (CSC) and new (LOSC) treaty law was rightly found by the 1993 judgment to have the same effect as the existing customary law, this uniformity will significantly facilitate the equitable maritime delimitation settlements between parties and non-parties to the respective treaties. The 'LSD' process of maritime boundary delimitation, whether through third-party settlements or those directly between states (including the prospective Guinea-Bissau–Senegal and El Salvador–Honduras–Nicaragua delimitations), will undoubtedly continue to benefit from the significant guidance found in the *Denmark v. Norway* judgment.

---

[128] Fitzmaurice, 'Judicial Innovation', p. 26, quoted by Jennings, 'Gerald Gray Fitzmaurice', p. 36.
[129] ICJ Reports, 1993, p. 298.

15

Environmental protection and the International Court of Justice

Malgosia Fitzmaurice

☙

INTRODUCTION

To me has fallen the task of contribution to the book in honour of Sir Robert Jennings on the subject of the International Court of Justice and the environment. It has to be said at the outset that, compared to other subjects in this volume, mine has been perhaps, at least until recently, rather less evident in the records of the Court. However, the last two decades have witnessed an enormous increase in international political awareness of the importance of preservation of the environment; and this has been reflected in the growing body of international environmental law. A number of possible bases for the development of general international law principles have been referred to in cases, but as yet no clear general rules have emerged within customary law defining the responsibility of states in relation to the preservation of the environment or to the causing of environmental harm to other states. Perhaps because of this, the reflection in the development of international law of the political importance of environmental issues has lain largely in the field of international conferences, leading to the publication of draft conventions and declarations, and in the conclusion of bilateral and multilateral conventions between states. In terms of general principles, one may cite as having been of particular importance the United Nations Conference on the Human Environment, which was convened in Stockholm in 1972 and which resulted in the Stockholm Declaration, as well as the work of the International Law Commission in relation to environmental matters and the widespread discussion it has provoked. Because of this, a proper consideration of the subject of this chapter requires one to look as much at the potential of the ICJ for future development of the law as at its past treatment of it.

The importance of environmental protection was foreseen by Judge Jennings as early as 1967 in his splendid and comprehensive Hague Academy

Lectures in the chapter on 'State Responsibility'.[1] He then saw environmental protection as an urgent problem, warning, for instance, against the dangers of dumping nuclear waste in the sea, and of the wholesale use of detergents, pesticides and fungicides. Judge Jennings commented as well on certain so-called 'experiments' in space and their sometimes disastrous effects. He stated rightly that 'a governing principle ought to be that nothing of man's environment should be subject to the risk of large-scale change until the natural phenomena which might be changed or obscured, have been studied, and their nature and functions established with reasonable certainty'.[2] His interest in the environment has persisted. Thus, in a more recent publication, we find continued reference to questions originally raised in his Hague Lectures, such as: what are the legal consequences of the attempt to ensure protection of the environment as a matter of common interest; whether a claim for damage to the environment is itself distinct from any economic loss; and the question who, in case of damage to the environment itself, may present such a claim.[3]

In terms of substantive issues, it may be said, though with a considerable degree of simplification, that there have been three major underlying issues in the discussions relating to the development of environmental law over the last two decades. One has been the question of the development of a general concept of delictual liability of states in relation to transboundary pollution; the second has been the question of the development of a liability of states *erga omnes*, or of an international criminal liability, in relation to the protection of the environment; and the third has been the question of the existence of a human right in relation to the quality of the environment. At the same time, there has been much discussion of institutional aspects of the development of environmental law, and in particular of the question of the possible creation of a separate international body for environmental matters, one of which, at least in the eyes of some of its proponents, might act in a number of capacities, of which the judicial capacity is one. The place and role of the ICJ is an important consideration in relation to all of these issues.

With regard to the substantive issues, there is no doubt that the ICJ has contributed to the progressive development of international law in other fields. Several judgments, and in particular Advisory Opinions,[4] have

---

[1] *Recueil des cours*, 2 (Leyden, 1969), p. 512.

[2] *Ibid.*, p. 513.

[3] R. Y. Jennings and A. D. Watts (eds.), *Oppenheim's International Law* (9th edn, Harlow, 1992), vol. I, *Peace*, Introduction and Part I, p. 415.

[4] See in particular a very illuminating article of Judge R. Ago on certain Advisory Opinions which are rendered binding on the basis of the statutes of certain international organizations and international

constituted hallmarks in the shaping of international law. As Judge Jennings has pointed out: 'The importance of judicial precedent in the development – indeed one may say making– of international law has long been far greater than might be surmised from the place given to it in Article 38 of the Court's Statute as a "subsidiary means for the ascertainment of the law".' Especially this is true in the development of customary law.[5] In support of this, it may suffice to mention only the *Reparation for Injuries* case[6] or the *Genocide* case,[7] the first of which influenced the development of the law of international organizations, and the second of which was a milestone in the theory of reservations to treaties. Likewise, all the cases concerning the delimitation of maritime areas contributed in the greatest degree to the development of the law of the sea; and one must also mention the *Anglo-Norwegian Fisheries* case,[8] which influenced the ways in which international customary law is being developed by defining the institution of the persistent objector. There is every reason to expect that the role of the ICJ in shaping environmental law will be as great as it has been in any other field of international law.

In relation to the institutional issue, the ICJ has responded to the growing importance attached by the international community to environmental issues by the creation of a Chamber for Environmental Matters. When announcing the creation of this Chamber, the ICJ referred expressly to two cases then before it 'with important implications for international law on matters relating to the environment' (*Certain Phosphate Lands in Nauru (Nauru v. Australia)* and *Gabcikovo-Nagymaros Project (Hungary/Slovakia)*). One of these cases (the *Nauru* case) has been settled, and the other, though still before the full Court, may well not, on full analysis of the substantive issues, prove suitable for hearing by the special Chamber. Both of them, however, merit some detailed consideration as illustrating the numerous ways in which issues relating to the environment are increasingly likely to arise in cases before the Court. Since the announcement of the creation of the special Chamber, a further matter has come before the Court in the form of a request by the WHO for an Advisory Opinion of the Court on an issue directly bearing upon the legal duties of states in relation to the preservation of the environment.

---

conventions: R. Ago, '"Binding" Advisory Opinions of The International Court of Justice', *AJIL*, 85 (1991), pp. 439–51.

[5] Sir Robert Jennings, 'Chambers of the International Court of Justice and the Court of Arbitration', *Humanité et droit international, Mélanges René-Jean Dupuy* (Paris, 1991), p. 200.

[6] *Reparations for Injuries Suffered with the Service of the United Nations* case, ICJ Reports, 1949, p. 174.

[7] *Reservations to Genocide Convention* case, ICJ Reports, 1951, p. 15.

[8] *Anglo-Norwegian Fisheries* case, ICJ Reports, 1951, p. 131.

TREATMENT OF ENVIRONMENTAL ISSUES IN THE JURISPRUDENCE OF THE COURT

The ICJ case generally accepted as having developed a founding principle in relation to the liability of states causing environmental damage is the *Corfu Channel* case in which the Court said that it was the obligation of every state not knowingly to allow its territory to be used for acts contrary to the rights of other states.[9] This principle had first been formulated in the famous *Trail Smelter* arbitration, where it was stated that 'no state has the right to use or permit the use of its territory in such a manner as to cause injury by fumes in or to the territory of another'.[10] However, the manner and extent of the application of this principle to environmental law is somewhat unclear and the Court, in the *Corfu Channel* case itself, did not specify the exact contents of the rights concerned.[11] The Court has not, subsequently, been called upon to elaborate or clarify this principle in any case. Notwithstanding this, the principle has had enormous influence, not least in constituting one of the foundations of the Stockholm Declaration and of the work of the ILC, as well as being one of the concepts that lies behind the conclusion of a number of multilateral conventions during the last two decades.

Since the decision in the *Corfu Channel* case, there has only really been one case before the ICJ in which the principle in the *Corfu Channel* case might have been further developed by the Court (though in the end the case was not decided on the merits). This was the *Nuclear Tests* case (*Australia v. France*).[12] In this case, Australia and New Zealand claimed that France's nuclear tests in the Pacific caused nuclear fall-out infringing their sovereignty in a manner contrary to international law and resulting in environmental damage. The pleadings in the case rely heavily on the damage done to the environment by nuclear tests. In the Australian submission, it was expressly stated that nuclear tests not only adversely affect human beings and animals, but also contaminate the environment. It was alleged by the Australian government that the main radioactive contamination of the environment by a nuclear explosion is caused by radioactive fall-out deposited on the surface of the earth, including direct contamination of soil, of the water of oceans, lakes, rivers and reservoirs, and of vegetation. It was claimed as well that nuclear fall-out affects the

---

[9] ICJ Reports, 1949, p. 22.
[10] 'Trail Smelter Arbitral Tribunal: Decision (1941)' *AJIL*, 35 (1941), p. 684, at p. 716.
[11] P. Birnie and A. E. Boyle, *International Law and Environment* (Oxford, 1992), p. 90.
[12] ICJ Reports, 1974, p. 253.

atmosphere, thus changing meteorological conditions. The French nuclear explosions resulted in tropospheric fall-out on states and territories in the Southern Hemisphere and on the oceans of that Hemisphere. Australia submitted that the radioactive 'cloud' of debris in the troposphere might make several transits around the globe before being depleted by radioactive decay and deposit.[13]

The application of the New Zealand government emphasized, similarly, the dangers of radiation to people and animals. The dangers of malignant diseases and of the effects of radiation on migratory species were also stressed. It was pointed out expressly that the nuclear tests conducted by France were causing, *inter alia*, continued pollution of the territories of New Zealand, the Cook Islands, Niue and the Tokelau Islands, as well as of their territorial sea and airspace.[14]

Interim measures requested by the governments of Australia and New Zealand were backed by similar reasoning; and it was interesting, from the point of view of environmental protection, that, on 22 June 1973, the Court issued, as an interim measure under article 41 of the Statute, an order indicating that the French government should avoid nuclear tests causing the deposit of radioactive fall-out in Australian territory.[15]

Two points, however, must be raised. The main argument put forward by Australia was based on the assumption that the deposit of radioactive fall-out on the territory of Australia, and its dispersion in Australia's airspace, without Australia's consent, constituted a violation of Australian sovereignty over its territory, impaired Australia's independent right to determine what acts would take place within its territory and exposed its people to radiation from artificial sources. Australia also stressed that the interference with ships and aircraft on the high seas and in the superadjacent airspace, and the pollution of the high seas by radioactive fall-out, constituted infringements of the freedom of the high seas.[16] Thus, Australia's main argument was based on alleged infringement of sovereignty rather than on environmental damage. On the other hand, one may legitimately stress the Australian argument that 'effects of the French nuclear tests upon the resources of the sea or the conditions of the

---

[13] *Nuclear Test* cases (*Australia v. France*), ICJ Pleadings, Oral Arguments, Documents Application, vol. I, pp. 9–10 (hereafter Pleadings, vol. I).

[14] *Nuclear Test* cases (*New Zealand v. France*), ICJ Pleadings, Oral Arguments, Documents Application, vol. II, pp. 6–7 (hereafter Pleadings, vol. II).

[15] ICJ Reports, 1973, p. 135. Notwithstanding the Order of the Court, in the months of July and August 1973 and June to September 1974 France carried out further tests which resulted in fall-out recorded in Australian territory.

[16] *Ibid.*, p. 103.

environment can never be undone and would be irremediable by any payment of damages'.[17]

The oral pleadings in support of the request for interim measures are very illuminating. Mr Ellicott, Counsel for Australia, stressed the environmental issue quite forcefully. He cited principle 21 of the Stockholm Declaration as pertinent in this case, undoubtedly representing a thoroughly modern approach to environmental protection. He assumed that the obligation contained in principle 21 is absolute and without qualification. He remarked on the emerging rule of customary international law that prohibits states from engaging in conduct 'tending towards pollution and the creation of hazard to human health and the environment and in particular a rule prohibiting the conduct of atmospheric nuclear tests'.[18] He pointed out that the Stockholm Declaration reflects the changing standards of environmental protection adopted by the international community. He further referred to the *Corfu Channel* case as representing the clearest judicial acknowledgement of the inviolability of territorial sovereignty and also alleged that France had breached the duty of good neighbourliness and, according to rules of state responsibility, had violated the sovereignty of Australia by conducting an activity (nuclear tests) involving a risk which caused a dangerous level of fall-out on Australian territory.[19]

In the New Zealand request for interim protection measures, we find a whole chapter concerning the consequences of the tests on the environment. The argument emphasized that the French nuclear tests would contaminate the local, regional and global environment and their resources. To keep the South Pacific, at the time a relatively clean region, free from contamination was of the utmost importance to the countries and territories located in the region, where the resources of the sea were the main element of subsistence for the people and the basis of the economy.

The New Zealand government stressed that in recent years the international community had concluded a number of conventions and declarations dealing with the problems of pollution and use of the environment, notably the Conference on Human Environment and the principles enshrined in the Stockholm Declaration which resulted from it.[20] Arguments presented orally during hearing of the request for interim measures also stressed contamination by nuclear fall-out of the human environment and the resulting violation of New Zealand territorial sovereignty.[21]

---

[17] *Ibid.*, p. 104.
[18] Mr Ellicott, Pleadings, vol. I, at p. 185.   [19] Pleadings, vol. I, p. 187
[20] Pleadings, vol. II, pp. 56–7.   [21] Submission of Mr Finlay, *Ibid.*, p. 100.

The judgment of the Court did not deal with the merits of the case, and consequently the opportunity to develop or clarify the then current state of the law concerning liability for environmental damage, and in particular the *Corfu Channel* case principle, either as a matter of delictual liability *vis-à-vis* another state, or on the *erga omnes* principle, did not arise. Some of the environmental issues raised in the pleadings and oral arguments are, however, referred to in Separate Opinions, from which it may be seen that, had the opportunity arisen, there would have been some division of opinion among the judges. Thus Judge Petrén, in his Separate Opinion, posed the question whether there existed a norm of customary international law whereby states are prohibited from causing the deposit of radioactive fall-out on the territory of other states through atmospheric tests.[22] Judge Petrén, having analysed the existing practice of states, in fact came to the conclusion that such a rule did not exist.[23] He saw the attempt at prohibition of atmospheric nuclear tests rather as a political than a legal act, outside the framework of international law as it existed in 1974. On the other hand, the Dissenting Opinion of Judge de Castro reflected a different view. He invoked as a basic principle of international environmental law the principle *sic utere tuo ut alienum non laedas*. He also referred to the above-mentioned judgment in the *Corfu Channel* case and the arbitral award in the *Trail Smelter* case. Thus Judge de Castro as early as 1974 did admit to the possibility of the existence of a rule of international customary law that would prohibit the emission of noxious fumes from neighbouring properties, thus implying that the deposit of radioactive fall-out on the territory of another state is by analogy illegal.[24] He further allowed, in his Dissenting Opinion, the assumption that principle 21 of the Stockholm Declaration, prohibiting transboundary pollution, has probably emerged as a norm of international customary law.

Since the time of the *Nuclear Tests* case, there has been considerable development in state practice through the conclusion of bilateral and multilateral treaties in the environmental field. Furthermore, the ILC, in the work it has carried out on its drafts on State Responsibility and on International Liability for Injurious Consequences of Acts not Prohibited by International Law, has also contributed to the development of thinking in the area of states' obligations towards other states in relation to the environment. The current position, however, is one of some confusion. In the first place, there is still no

---

[22] ICJ Reports, 1974, p. 253; Separate Opinion, Judge Petrén, p. 304.

[23] He writes: 'The example given by China when it exploded a very powerful bomb in the atmosphere is sufficient to demolish the contention that there exists at present a rule of customary international law prohibiting atmospheric nuclear tests': *ibid*., p. 306.

[24] *Ibid*. (Dissenting Opinion, de Castro, pp. 388–9).

definitive view on whether state practice in this field has yet achieved the status of a norm of international law. In the second place, it has to be said that the distinction the ILC sought to make between 'state responsibility' for wrongful conduct and 'international liability' for non-wrongful conduct, and the considerable body of discussion it has provoked, has not served to clarify the situation. It may well be thought that, as one learned author has put it, what is now needed is 'in effect a globalisation of environmental obligations comparable to what has been achieved for the marine environment by the Law of the Sea Convention and related treaties';[25] and, as Judge Jennings recently, and perhaps pointedly, said in his Statement to the UNCED, it is 'a principal task of the ICJ to decide, applying well-established rules and criteria, whether the provisions of multilateral treaties have or have not developed from merely contractual rules into rules of general customary international law'.[26]

In some more recent cases, e.g. concerning delimitation of maritime boundaries, some environmental matters have been raised concerning other, less general, issues; but to these too, the Court has not devoted a great deal of consideration in its judgments. In this connection, one may mention the *Gulf of Maine* case (1984), in which the Chamber rejected, *inter alia*, the ecological argument of the United States favouring the existence of a natural boundary. The United States also put forward an alternative argument that the North-east Channel formed a recognizable limit in the marine environment; but the Chamber did not find such arguments convincing, and stated that the fixing of natural boundaries in such a fluctuating environment as the waters of the ocean is hardly feasible. The Chamber did not go so far as to deny that a delimitation line could follow a discernible natural boundary; but it stated that, in the case under consideration, there were no geological, geomorphological, ecological or other factors sufficiently important, evident or conclusive to represent a single, incontrovertible natural boundary.[27]

Some consideration of quite different environmental matters occurred in the *Case Concerning Maritime Delimitation in the Area between Greenland and Jan Mayen (Denmark v. Norway)* (1993).[28] In that case, the Court had to consider

---

[25] Alan E. Boyle, 'State Responsibility and International Liability for Injurious Consequences of Acts Not Prohibited by International Law: A Necessary Distinction?', *ICLQ*, 39, 1 (1990), p. 1, at p. 23.

[26] Sir Robert Jennings, 'Need for Environmental Court?', *Environmental Policy and Law*, 22/5/6 (1992), pp. 312–14, at p. 313 (this is the text of a statement made by Sir Robert to the UNCED, entitled 'The Role of the ICJ in the Development of International Environment Protection Law') (also reprinted in *RECIEL*, 1 (1992), pp. 240–4).

[27] Barbara Kwiatkowska, 'Economic and Environmental Considerations', in J. Charney and L. M. Alexander (eds.), *International Maritime Boundaries* (Dordrecht, Boston, London, 1993), vol. I, p. 75, at pp. 102–3.

[28] Judgment 14 June 1993, ICJ Reports, 1993, pp. 72–3.

the presence of ice in the waters in this region. The question was raised as to the effect on access to marine resources of the presence of drift ice, perennial ice being a possible hindrance to access to the resources of the region – constituting a special geographical feature. In that case the Court satisfied itself that while 'the ice constitutes a considerable restriction of access to the waters, it does not materially affect access to migratory fishery resources in the southern part of the area of overlapping claims'.[29]

A last instance of relevant jurisprudence in earlier cases may be found in the influence of the *Barcelona Traction* case on the International Law Commission Draft on State Responsibility in article 19 on criminal liability of states.[30] Article 19(3) defines international crimes. One such crime, as enshrined in article 19(3)(d) is 'a serious breach of an international obligation of essential importance for the safeguarding and preservation of the human environment, such as those prohibiting massive pollution of the atmosphere or the seas'. In its commentary the ILC condemned conduct gravely endangering the preservation and conservation of the human environment; and expressly stated that states can be criminally liable for such conduct.[31] The ILC was influenced in its draft by the concept of obligations *erga omnes* as developed by the ICJ in the *Barcelona Traction* case.[32] This chapter is not the proper place to elaborate on this subject; but it is pertinent to emphasize the influence that the ICJ had on the treatment by the ILC of wrongdoing against the environment. According to the ILC, crimes against the environment belong to the category of obligations, responsibility for breach of which 'is engaged not only in regard to the state which was the direct victim of the breach; it is also engaged in regard to all other members of the international community, so that, in the event of breach of these obligations, every state must be considered justified in evoking – preferably through judicial channels – the responsibility of the State committing the internationally wrongful act'.[33]

It may be accepted that, in its capacity as a tribunal to hear contentious issues between states, the ICJ may not be the appropriate forum for the decision of disputes relating directly to the liability of states to the environment itself.[34]

---

[29] *Ibid.*, p. 73.

[30] See M. Spinedi and B. Simmie (eds.), *UN Codification of State Responsibility* (New York/London/Rome, 1987); for arguments in depth on the matter see Geoff Gilbert, 'The Criminal Responsibility of States', *ICLQ*, 39 (1990), p. 345, at pp. 354–5.

[31] *YbILC*, (1976, vol. II, part 2), pp. 109, 119.

[32] *Barcelona Traction, Light and Power Co.* case, ICJ Reports, 1970, pp. 33–4.

[33] *YbILC*, (1976, vol. II, part 2), p. 99.

[34] See e.g. Jennings and Watts (eds.), *Oppenheim's International Law*, p. 415. See also Jennings, 'Need for Environmental Court?', p. 512.

But it can be foreseen that the ICJ, in the course of a contentious case between states, would have an influence on the development of thinking on the obligations of states to the world at large. Furthermore, as Judge Jennings has stated, the ICJ has 'also an advisory jurisdiction the very purpose of which is not the settlement of a particular dispute but an authoritative statement of the law in answer to the requests from certain qualified bodies'.[35] In this capacity, it is to be anticipated that, with growing awareness of the importance of this form of obligation, the ICJ will become active in further development of the law. Indeed, the first instance of this may have arrived in the form of the recent request for an Advisory Opinion by the WHO.

INSTITUTIONAL DEVELOPMENTS IN RELATION TO ENVIRONMENTAL LAW

The ICJ or a special environmental body?

Recently, one of the most controversial, and most frequently discussed, questions in international law has been whether or not a special international body should be set up dedicated to dealing with the issues and problems relating to the protection of the environment. With a certain degree of simplification, it may be said that there are two schools of thought concerning this question, the first of which is against the establishment of any new body, favouring rather the adaption of existing judicial institutions to perform the growing tasks relating to the environment, and the second of which favours the creation of a special new international body for this purpose. The first of these views is represented by Judge Jennings himself, while the other may be seen in the views of Judge Amadeo Postiglione.[36]

Sir Robert Jennings starts from a recognition that environmental matters are in principle matters of a global character and that, therefore, general principles of international law are applicable to them, notwithstanding the specialized nature of the extremely complicated system involved in environmental protection, which includes, *inter alia*, problems of transfer of technology, of international finance and of poverty. Indeed, the issues raised in environmental law are clearly part of general international law, insofar as they concern such topics as the law of treaties and the nature of international customary law; and, in fact, the link between environmental law and general international law, the

---

[35] Jennings, 'Need for Environmental Court?', p. 313.
[36] *Ibid.*; Amadeo Postiglione, 'An International Court for Environment?', *EPL*, 23/2 (1993), pp. 73–8.

fact of its being, indeed, 'part and parcel' of general international law, bestows on environmental law additional authority and binding force.[37]

According to Judge Jennings, the ICJ, because of its dual role (settlement of disputes and development and elaboration of international law) is particularly well suited to deal with all the aspects of international law, including environmental law, and to establish new general principles pertinent to environmental law. In this respect, the capacity of the ICJ to formulate rules of international environmental law through the giving of Advisory Opinions, which constitute an authoritative statement of law, is of particular importance. Another important feature of the ICJ noted by Judge Jennings in this context is the growing importance of article 94 of the UN Charter, giving increased effectiveness to the Security Council, now at least partly freed from the crippling effects of 'veto', in relation to enforcement of the Court's judgments.[38] Finally, the composition of the Court, with judges representing the different civilizations and legal systems of the world, both those of the developed and those of the developing worlds, and its proven ability, despite this, to produce nearly unanimous decisions, renders the ICJ very suitable to be a centre for the decision of environmental matters, with respect to which 'there are great differences between the interests and the points of view of the developed and the developing nations'.[39] Sir Robert Jennings foresaw the possibility of creating special environmental chambers (permanent or *ad hoc*); and his vision became a reality a year later in 1993.

Judge Postiglione is a proponent of the opposite view, namely that it is necessary to establish a special international court of environment within the United Nations framework. He puts forward several reasons in support of this idea. His main reasoning is based on the concept of the existence of an individual human right to the environment, including in particular the right of access to environmental information, the right to participate in administrative and judicial proceedings and the right of access to the courts. He argues in favour of strengthening the effectiveness of international law in relation to the rights of individual parties.

---

[37] Jennings, 'Need for Environmental Court?', p. 313.
[38] Article 94 reads as follows:

> Each member of the United Nations undertakes to comply with the decision of the International Court of Justice in any case to which it is a party.
>
> If any party to a case fails to perform the obligations incumbent upon it under a judgment rendered by the Court, the other party may have recourse to the security council, which may, if it deems necessary, make recommendations or decide upon measures to be taken to give effect to the judgment.

[39] Jennings, 'Need for Environmental Court?', p. 314.

Judge Postiglione sees the role of such a new body as being not merely repressive, but also preventive and declaratory.[40] The justification for the move of jurisdiction from national courts to an international body lies in the way in which, in the sphere of the environment, individual conflicts spread onto the international plane. He further envisages that the new court could also perform advisory, investigative, conciliatory and educational tasks. It would in some respects be similar in character to the European Court of Human Rights in Strasbourg; and, since it would settle disputes to which individuals were parties, it would be different from the ICJ.

He states that at present every state has the right to decide whether it will or will not submit a case to arbitration or to the ICJ. This he assesses as 'a very serious objective obstacle [which] conditions the enforcement of international environmental law'.[41] He sees the ICJ as an organ working substantially within the framework of arbitration, which cannot take action in areas outside the jurisdiction given to it by states.

While there are of course some arguments in favour of the creation of a special court for the environment, these would really be at their strongest in relation to the protection of the rights of an individual to a decent environment. But this concept of a human right to a decent environment is itself very controversial.[42] Many learned authors deny even the existence of such a right. The nature of such a right is itself very vague; its formulation on a national level in the constitutions of various countries is rather imprecise; and the question of how these rights can be enforced remains problematical. The same problems exist, but to an even stronger degree, on the international plane. Indeed, there seems to be a gradual departure from the concept of the existence of a human right to a decent environment in international practice.

---

[40] Postiglione, 'An International Court for Environment?', p. 74.

[41] Ibid., p. 76.

[42] It is outside the scope of this chapter to list all the publications on human rights and the environment. Suffice it to say that the whole concept has been the subject of strong criticism by such prominent lawyers as, for instance, G. Handl. He puts forward several arguments against the concept, e.g. that environmental protection will not benefit from being promoted to a human right since no state will accept this and it will divert attention from more important causes. Further, special features of the environment make it difficult for it to be the subject of an inalienable right. The catalogue of arguments against environmental protection as a human right is indeed vast, though there are, of course counter-arguments. The conclusion may be drawn, however, that the concept of environmental protection as a human right is neither clear cut nor non-controversial. See G. Handl, 'Human Rights, Protection of the Environment: A Mildly "Revisionist" View', in A. Cancado Trinidade (ed.), *Human Rights, Sustainable Development and the Environment* (San José, 1992), pp. 117–41; D. Shelton, 'Human Rights, Environmental Rights, and the Rights to Environment', *Stanford Journal of International Law*, 28 (1991), pp. 103–38; D. Shelton, 'What Happened In Rio to Human Rights?', *Yearbook of International Environmental Law*, 75 (1992).

The Rio Declaration and Agenda 21, in general, are illustrative of this point since they contain very few references to human rights in general.

The approach that emphasizes procedural rights in relation to the environment, i.e. the right to participate in decision-making concerning the environment, is far more acceptable. In fact, the interests of the individual concerning the environment are probably best protected on the basis of private-law solutions. Among these we can include the principles of non-discrimination and of a right to equal access, coupled with the 'polluter pays principle' championed by the OECD[43] and the conventions based on civil liability, which partially exclude the responsibility of states, such as the 1969 Brussels Convention on Civil Liability for Oil Pollution Damage. There remain many disadvantages even in relation to private-law remedies; but these nevertheless still provide the more successful formula for a private individual claiming rights in relation to the environment.[44]

The creation by the ICJ of a Special Environmental Chamber

In 1992, Judge Jennings had referred to the possibility that the ICJ might still exercise its capacity to form a special Chamber in relation to the environment,[45] and such a possibility was also envisaged as early as 1990 by Judge Guillaume;[46] and in 1993 the Court did indeed respond to the growing importance of the environment by constituting the special Chamber of the Court for Environmental Matters under the provisions of article 26(1) to the Court's Statute. This may well be regarded as the most important development in the ICJ concerning the environment, rendering it fully prepared to deal with all kinds of environmental matters which may come before it.

The background to the creation of this Chamber, in terms of the Court's capacity to create Chambers, may be briefly summarized.[47] Of the three types

---

[43] Recommendation c(4) 233, 14 November 1974; Recommendation c(72) 128, 26 May 1972.

[44] For a critical view see Alan E. Boyle, 'Making the Polluter Pay? Alternatives to State Responsibility in the Allocation of Transboundary Costs', in F. Francioni and T. Scovazzi (eds.), *International Responsibility for Environmental Harm* (London, 1991), pp. 363–81.

[45] Jennings, 'Need for Environmental Court?', note 26, p. 314.

[46] G. Guillaume, *Internal Subdivisions of International Tribunals*, Twelfth Congress of the International Academy of Comparative Law, Montreal (19–24 August 1990), p. 21.

[47] For detailed discussion of the Chambers of the ICJ, see in particular: S. Schwebel, 'Ad Hoc Chambers of the International Court of Justice', *American Journal of International Law*, 81 (1987), p. 831; S. Oda, 'Further Thoughts on the Chambers Procedure of the International Court of Justice', *American Journal of International Law*, 82 (1987), p. 556; S. Toope, 'Pragmatic Compromise or More Transition: The Use of Chamber Procedures in International Adjudication', *VJIL*, 31, (1990), p. 53; A. Zimmermann, 'Ad Hoc Chambers of the International Court of Justice', *Dickinson Journal of International Law*, 8 (1989); R. Ostrihansky, 'Chambers of the International Court of Justice', *International and Comparative Law*

of Chamber provided for by the Statute of the Court, the first, namely the Chamber for summary procedure which is elected annually under article 29 'with a view to the speedy dispatch of business', has been little discussed. Indeed, as Sir Robert Jennings has pointed out, 'speedy dispatch . . . would not appear to be what governments ardently desire, for in practice the Chamber for summary procedure never convenes'.[48] Second, article 26(1) of the Court's Statute provides for the creation of specialized Chambers composed of three or more judges, as the Court may determine, for dealing with particular categories of case. The Statute itself refers, by way of example, to two particular categories of case with respect to which such Chambers might be set up, namely labour cases and cases relating to transit and communication. But no special Chamber in either of these categories has been constituted;[49] nor was any case ever referred to the special Chambers for these categories of case provided for under the Statute of the Permanent Court of International Justice. Thus, the Chamber for Environmental Matters is the first to be set up under article 26(1). Under the revised rules of the Court of 14 April 1978, the Court appoints the members of a so-called 'special' Chamber, and determines the extent of its jurisdiction; and judges electing the members should have regard to any special knowledge, expertise and previous experience of the members of the court (article 16(2) of the 1978 Rules).[50] The third category of Chamber is that provided for under article 26(2) of the Court's Statute, namely, the *ad hoc* Chamber for dealing with a particular case. With regard to this third category of Chamber, paragraph 2 of article 26(2) states that the number of judges to constitute a Chamber shall be determined by the Court with the approval of the parties. Articles 17 and 18 of the 1978 Rules further state that the President of the Court has to ascertain the views of the parties regarding the composition of the Chamber and to report to the Court accordingly (article 17(2) of the 1978 Rules). The Court then elects the members of the Chamber by secret ballot and the Chamber elects its own President from among its members (article 18 of the 1978 Rules). It is important to emphasize in this respect that, though the Court would appear in practice to have followed the wishes of the parties in electing the

Quarterly, 37 (1988), p. 31; Sir R. Jennings, 'The Collegiate Responsibility and Authority of the International Court of Justice', in Y. Dinstein and M. Tabory (eds.), *International Law at a Time of Perplexity* (Dordrecht, 1989), p. 333; Jennings, 'Chambers of the International Court of Justice', p. 197.

48 Jennings, 'Chambers of the International Court of Justice', p. 198.
49 Toope, 'Pragmatic Compromise or More Transition?', p. 58.
50 Ostrihansky, 'Chambers of the International Court of Justice', p. 41.

members of *ad hoc* Chambers, it is in no way bound under the Rules to do so.[51]

It has been in respect of the third category, the *ad hoc* Chambers, that there has been most discussion; and, in fact, their creation has generated a considerable degree of controversy. Since this chapter does not primarily deal with the issue of Chambers of the ICJ as such, there is a limit to the extent of the study of this controversy which is appropriate here. However, some of the advantages ascribed to *ad hoc* Chambers of the ICJ, over their rival type of forum, the international arbitral tribunal, are not entirely without relevance in relation to the merits of the ICJ over a special international body to decide on environmental issues, so we may briefly consider them.

The main criticism of *ad hoc* Chambers of the ICJ is that the degree of influence given to the parties to select the judges who will be members of such a Chamber likens the procedure of the ICJ to an arbitration and thus weakens the authority of the Court. Additionally, some authors argue that the authoritative value of the decisions rendered by a Chamber is diminished, as compared to the decisions taken by the whole Court, even taking into account the fact that theoretically the Court is not bound by the principle of *stare decisis*.[52] However, it remains the fact that the Chamber and its members continue to derive their authority from the Court, one of the principal organs of the UN, and not from the parties; and this is the fundamental difference between the procedures before an *ad hoc* Chamber and an arbitration panel.

Judge Jennings, who is a staunch supporter of *ad hoc* Chambers as against international arbitral tribunals, presents a further very convincing argument as to why they are different from arbitration tribunals. First, *ad hoc* Chambers of the ICJ remain very much a vital part of the Court, keeping the Court informed of the progress of proceedings before it; they may, in the course of their work, refer matters to the full Court for consideration, for instance in relation to replacement of a member of a Chamber who has died or resigned (article 18 of the Rules of the Court); and, most importantly, their members remain full members of the Court and continue to be occupied with the work of the Court as such, as well as with the work of the Chamber. Second, Judge Jennings emphasizes that it is the ICJ that shapes the development of international law more than do arbitration proceedings, especially in view of the Court's capacity to give Advisory Opinions, a unique legal tool available to the Court.

[51] Jennings, 'Chambers of the International Court of Justice', p. 197; Ostrihansky, 'Chambers of the International Court of Justice', pp. 41–6.

[52] On controversies see e.g. Schwebel, 'Ad Hoc Chambers', p. 831; and Oda, 'Further Thoughts', p. 556.

So far, there has been little or no discussion of the background to, and prospects following, the setting up of the Chamber for Environmental Matters. But some indication of the Court's thinking emerges from the communique announcing the constitution of the Chamber and it is, therefore, worth looking at this in detail. The communique first refers to the general jurisdiction of the Court under article 36, paragraph 1 of the Court's Statutes, and then goes on to note that 'at present, out of eleven cases in its docket, the full Court is seised of two cases, namely those concerning *Certain Phosphate Lands in Nauru (Nauru v. Australia)* and the *Gabcikovo-Nagymaros Project (Hungary/Slovakia)* with important implications for international law on matters relating to the environment'. Having then quoted the provisions of article 26(2) of the Court's Statute under which the Chamber was constituted, the communique continues as follows:

> In the past the Court has considered the question of the possible formation of a chamber to deal with environmental matters. On those occasions it took the view that it was not yet necessary to set up a standing special chamber, emphasising that it was able to respond rapidly to requests for the constitution of a so-called 'ad hoc' Chamber (pursuant to Article 26, paragraph 2 of the Statute) which could deal also with any environmental case.
>
> In view of the developments in the field of environmental law and protection which have taken place in the last few years, and considering that it should be prepared to the fullest possible extent to deal with any environmental case falling within its jurisdiction, the Court has now deemed it appropriate to establish a seven-member Chamber for Environmental Matters.

The first members of the Chamber appointed by the Court consist of the following judges: Schwebel, Bedjaoui, Evensen, Shahabuddeen, Weeramantry, Ranjeva and Herczegh.

By its decision to set up a special Chamber of this sort, the Court emphasized the necessity for the establishment of a permanent forum which would deal with environment in a better way than would be the case were it left to the parties to request the creation of an *ad hoc* chamber (on the basis of article 26, paragraph 2).[53]

RECENT AND CURRENT CASES BEFORE THE COURT

We may now turn to consideration of cases that have very recently been, or are now pending, before the Court, and involve environmental factors. The first two are those cases expressly referred to in the announcement of the ICJ

[53] Communique of the International Court of Justice, 19 July 1993.

of its formation of the Environmental Chamber. Though both cases do indeed raise important issues having environmental aspects and merit consideration as examples of the numerous ways in which, in the light of modern thinking, environmental issues may be expected to arise in future cases, it may be doubted whether, had it proceeded to the merits, the *Nauru* case would have been, or whether the *Gabcikovo–Nagymaros* will be, considered suitable for allocation to the Environmental Chamber.

The *Nauru* case was discontinued by an Order of the Court dated 13 September 1993, following a settlement between the parties.[54] Strong environmental elements, however, were already visible at the preliminary stage of proceedings. It concerned a claim by Nauru relating to damage to its environment resulting from phosphate-mining activities carried out while its territory was administered by Australia, first under the League of Nations Mandate system, and later under the UN Trusteeship system.

The decisive issues in the case might well, in the end, have been those relating to the obligations of Australia resulting from its particular capacities under the Trusteeship Agreement. But one line of argument, at least, has been seen as possibly founding a straightforward claim by Nauru for environmental damage caused by the activities of another state, Australia.[55] Thus, it was said (before it was known that the case would be settled) that, in relation to its claim to damages for environmental damage, 'Nauru is in a position to forward a novel claim of transnational environmental damage that transcends traditional doctrines of recovery based on injury to private property interests'.[56] Other issues included: the question of whether states may be liable, in respect of environmental damage, for the damage itself, or rather for failure to rehabilitate the land affected by that damage; the issue of whether reparation would be due from Australia, if found responsible, for the whole or only part of the damage Nauru alleged it suffered (with respect to which Judge Oda, while dissenting at a preliminary stage, pointed out that he was 'not denying the importance of the preservation of an environment from any damage that may be caused by the development or exploitation of resources, particularly in the developing regions of the world').[57]

The agreement between Australia and the Republic of Nauru for the

---

[54] *Ibid*.

[55] Antony Anghie, '"The Heart of My Home": Colonialism, Environmental Damage, and the Nauru Case', *Harvard International Law Journal*, 34 (1992), p. 445 at p. 483.

[56] *Ibid*., at p. 480.

[57] On the jurisdictional (and, indeed, a number of other) issues having environmental aspects, which arose in this case see Philippe Sands, 'Reports from International Courts and Tribunals', *Yearbook of International Environmental Law* (1992), pp. 495–7.

settlement of the case in the ICJ specifies that Australia is to assist Nauru in its post-phosphate future and will pay to Nauru a case settlement of 107 million Australian dollars, some of it over a twenty-year period under a 'Rehabilitation and Cooperation Agreement'. This may be said to emphasize that part of Nauru's claim relating to Australia's alleged liability for its failure to rehabilitate the land after the damage caused by phosphate mining. Further, joint undertakings of Nauru and Australia were elaborated in a Joint Declaration of Principles Guiding Relations between Australia and the Republic of Nauru. Overall, the settlement embodies a quite broad agreement on the basis of which several rights are bestowed mutually by both parties. Trade between the two countries will be at least on most-favoured-nation terms and as free of both tariff and other restrictive regulations of commerce as may be consistent with both countries' domestic requirements and international commitments. Australia offered free and unrestricted access into the Australian market for all Nauru products (except sugar) on a non-reciprocal basis (article 10). Australian currency can be used by Nauru as its own transactions currency (article 14). The countries also promote co-operation in fisheries and environmental protection (articles 18 and 20).[58]

The second case referred to above is the case of the Gabcikovo–Nagymaros Project (Hungary/Slovakia) between the Slovak Republic and Hungary concerning the Treaty of 1977 on the construction and operation of the Gabcikovo–Nagymaros system of locks and the termination of the project by Hungary.[59] This treaty provided for the construction of the Gabcikovo–Nagymaros system of locks as a joint investment in order to create a single and indivisible operational system of works (article 1). The operation of the treaty was to be supervised by the governments of the contracting parties through appointed delegates. The treaty is silent on the question of its termination. Following from this, the Slovak Republic alleges that unilateral denunciation of the treaty by Hungary was illegal from the point of view of international law.

Article 2 of the Special Agreement for the Submission to the ICJ of the Differences between the Republic of Hungary and the Slovak Republic concerning the Gabcikovo–Nagymaros Project sets out the following questions for submission to the Court:

(a) Whether the Republic of Hungary was entitled to supersede and subsequently abandon in 1989 the works on the Nagymaros Project and on the part of

---

[58] *ILM*, 32 (1993), pp. 1474–9.
[59] *ILM*, 32 (1993), p. 1247. See also C. Cepelka, 'The Dispute over the Gabcikovo-Nagymaros Systems of Locks is Drawing to a Close', *Polish Yearbook of International Law*, 20 (1993), pp. 63–75.

the Gabcikovo Project for which the treaty attributed responsibility to the Republic of Hungary;

(b) Whether the Czech and Slovak Federal Republic was entitled to proceed, in November 1991, to the 'provisional solution' and to put in operation from October 1992 this system, described in the Report of the Working Group of Independent Experts of the Commission of the European Community, the Republic of Hungary and Czech and Slovak Federal Republic dated 23 November 1992 (damming up of the Danube at river kilometre 1851.7 on Czechoslovak territory and resulting consequences on water and navigation course);

(c) What are the legal effects of the notification, on 19 May 1992, of the termination of the treaty by the Republic of Hungary?[60]

The questions concern general aspects of international law; but study of the Hungarian case reveals that it invokes numerous arguments based on environmental considerations which give an interesting insight into ways in which environmental issues may be expected to come before the Court in the present climate.

Hungary denounced the treaty on environmental grounds, stressing in particular the hydrological and hydraulic changes and the pollution of water that would be caused by the erection of Gabcikovo dam. Hungary alleges that the intended works would have impaired the quality of drinking-water due to severe damage to the filtering system; and, further, that fundamental changes might have occurred in the Dunakiliti reservoir, which would have led to permanent viral and bacterial contamination. Another point emphasized is the alleged possible effect on the growth of plants due to the flow of nutrients and the diminished air ventilation. It is claimed that, in the Dunakiliti reservoir, if the dam were to have been erected, the flow speed and the quality of light penetrating the water would have been seriously impaired, which coupled with over-nutrification would have caused uncontrollable growth of algae, i.e. eutrophication. Moreover, it is alleged that the soil humidity of the inundation areas along the abandoned river-bed of the Danube would have decreased, which would have caused sinking of surface water and the spread of arborescent vegetation over the dry river-bed.[61]

These ecological aspects, however, constitute only a background to the case. The main issues of international law that are involved lie in the fields of treaty law, the most important being the issue of unilateral termination of a treaty which does not contain any relevant provisions to this effect. Some guidance concerning this issue will be found in Part V of the Vienna Convention on the Law of Treaties (1969) (Invalidity, Termination and

---

[60] *Ibid.*, p. 1295.   [61] *Ibid.*, pp. 1279–82.

Suspension of Treaties). Even here, however, Hungary invokes some environmental issues in its argument.

These include, *inter alia*, invoking the principle '*ad impossibilia nemo tenatur*' (one cannot be obliged to perform the impossible) and the principle of fundamental change of circumstances as contained in article 62 of the Vienna Convention. Special importance is attached to paragraph 1(a) of this article which states that a fundamental change of circumstances which has occurred with regard to those circumstances existing at the time of the conclusion of a treaty and which was not foreseen by the parties may be invoked if '(a) the existence of those circumstances constituted an essential basis of the consent of the parties to be bound by the treaty'. One alleged change of circumstances arose because, while the 1977 Treaty emphasized that the construction of the barrage system would strengthen the socialist integration of the member states of the Council for Mutual Economic Assistance (CMEA), that objective had, of course, ceased to be possible with the demise of the CMEA. But another change of circumstances alleged is that environmental issues have gained in importance generally and that the situation that existed in 1977 no longer reflects the degree of care with which ecology is treated at present. Thus, the terms of the 1977 Treaty do not correspond with the requirements of today.

Hungary also invoked the unilateral breach of treaty (article 60(1) and (3) of the Vienna Convention) by the Slovak Republic, alleging that it did not fulfil its duties as prescribed by the 1977 treaty in respect of the protection of nature and of water quality and that, as a consequence of this unilateral breach, Hungary was entitled unilaterally to terminate the treaty. In particular, Hungary relied on the adoption by the Slovak Republic of a so-called 'provisional solution' (not provided for by the treaty) to divert the Danube on Czechoslovak territory, as having constituted a material breach. According to Hungary the 'provisional solution' also violates other norms of international law apart from treaty law, thus justifying application of counter-measures by Hungary.

Hungary relied as well on article 33(1) of the ILC Draft on State Responsibility which enumerates the grounds precluding wrongfulness in termination of a treaty. This article precludes wrongfulness on the grounds of the existence of a state of necessity invoked by a state as justifying its act, provided that:

(a) 'the act was the only means of safeguarding an essential interest of the State against a grave and imminent peril'; and
(b) 'the act did not seriously impair an essential interest of the State towards which the obligation existed'.

The International Law Commission has stated that such a state of necessity may exist in the case of a threat to vital ecological interests; and the Hungarian government does allege that grave and imminent peril would have been caused by the planned barrage system. Hungary further enumerated other norms of customary and treaty law (considered to be *jus cogens* by Hungary) which allegedly were breached by the Slovak Republic, such as breach of sovereignty and territorial integrity including Hungarian frontiers, the rules concerning the use of shared resources in particular international watercourses (equitable utilization) and the prohibition on causing transboundary harm. Hungary also claimed violation of the provisions of the 1976 bilateral treaty between these two countries which regulates water management of the boundary rivers. It also claimed that the 'provisional solution' is contradictory to the spirit of the Belgrade Convention on the Danube of 1948; and cited as well a number of other treaties such as the Paris Treaty of 1947 concerning the demarcation of Hungarian borders and the 1950 bilateral treaty on borders. Finally, Hungary relied on the general development of international law, which gives priority to environmental matters over economic gain.

Unfortunately, the arguments of the Slovak Republic are not yet available, though it may be noted that the 'provisional solution' (alleged by Hungary to be a material breach of the 1977 treaty) was, according to the Slovak Republic, adopted as a counter-measure to the Hungarian suspension of the construction and in order to fulfil the terms of the 1977 treaty.[62]

This short survey of issues arising in this case is in no way intended to provide an appraisal of the strength of any of the legal arguments. It only presents the views of one of the parties. It reflects, however, on the type of problems encountered in this dispute and the way in which environmental factors are woven into many of the arguments of Hungary. Notwithstanding this, it does appear that the crux of the case lies in the issues of general international law, in particular in the proper interpretation of the terms of the Treaty, a conclusion which seems to be confirmed by the terms of the Special Agreement for the Submission to the ICJ which is quoted above. Thus, notwithstanding the strong environmental background to the case, it does not seem to be one that, in the end, would merit being assigned to the new Environmental Chamber rather than proceeding before the full Court.

The last environmental matter now before the Court is likely to prove to be the one of the greatest importance in terms of the future role of the ICJ in the field of environmental law. This is the request for an Advisory Opinion

---

[62] *Ibid.*, pp. 1282–9.

made to the Court in 1993 by the World Health Organization (WHO) on the following question: 'In view of the health and environmental effects, would the use of nuclear weapons by a state in war or other armed conflict be a breach of its obligation under international law including the WHO Constitution?' The letter from the Director General of the WHO transmitting the request was received by the Registry of Court on 3 September 1993; and the Court, by an Order of 13 September 1993, fixed 10 June 1994 as the time-limit within which written statements relating to the question must be submitted to the Court by the WHO and by those of the member states who are entitled to appear before the Court.

CONCLUSIONS

The potential role of the ICJ in the modern approach to the environment was stressed during UNCED in Rio.[63] The ICJ was specifically mentioned as an organ the United Nations prescribed to solve the disputes on sustainable development between states. This exactly conforms to the statement made by Sir Robert Jennings to the UNCED. He emphasized the pivotal role of the ICJ in the development of general international law and in environmental law and in relation to the sanctioning and enforcement of law. Although not excluding the possibility of the establishment of a special Chamber, he, however, rather emphasized the role of the full Court, due to its techniques and procedures, as the most suitable place to reconcile the interests of developing and developed states, thus rendering it particularly eligible for environmental disputes.[64]

The possibilities in this direction, as well as the potential strength of the ICJ arising from its capacity to give authoritative Advisory Opinions (a factor much emphasized by Judge Jennings) are well illustrated in the request for an Advisory Opinion by the WHO referred to above, though it is too early for any detailed comments on it. However, it is apparent that this request reflects the contemporary interest, generally, in military activities and environmental matters which are prominently in sight (and were so, in particular, during the Iraqi conflict). It would seem that the Court is here presented with an opportunity to give some degree of guidance on the application of general international law principles in the environmental field, in particular in the obligations owed by states with respect to the environment to the international community as a whole.

There is still no case before the Court that inevitably invites clarification or

---

[63] A/Conf. 151/26 (vol. III), 14 August 1992.   [64] Jennings, 'Need for Environmental Court?'

development of the law relating to the obligations of states with respect to the environment owed to other states individually; but it may be anticipated that the combination of the considerable need for such clarification, to which reference has been made above, with the suitability of the ICJ to provide it, and with the awareness of the ICJ of the current importance of environmental matters evidenced by their formation of the Environmental Chamber, may well soon bear fruit.

16

The contribution of the International Court of Justice to air law

Sami Shubber

ℰℐℴ

The International Court of Justice has not had, as yet, an appropriate opportunity to contribute in a major way to the development of air law; it has, however, had the chance to deal with some aspects of air law in some of the cases submitted to it. The following are the cases that refer to some elements of air law: the *Aerial Incident*, 1955 (*Israel v. Bulgaria*),[1] the *Appeal Relating to the Jurisdiction of the ICAO Council*, 1972 (*India v. Pakistan*),[2] *Military and Paramilitary Activities in and against Nicaragua*, 1986 (*Nicaragua v. USA (Merits)*);[3] the *Aerial Incident*, 1988 (*Iran v. USA*);[4] and the two cases over the *Lockerbie Incident*, 1992 (*Libya v. UK*)[5] and (*Libya v. US*).[6]

There were other cases involving military aircraft, but the ICJ was unable to deal with them for lack of jurisdiction, e.g. *Treatment in Hungary of Aircraft and Crew of USA*, 1954 (*USA v. Hungarian People's Republic*). The Court ordered that the case be removed from the list because of lack of jurisdiction.[7]

THE *AERIAL INCIDENT*, 1955

This was a case of the shooting down of an El Al aircraft, on a scheduled flight from Vienna to Tel Aviv, by Bulgaria, over Bulgarian territory. The incident resulted in the death of the seven crew members and fifty-one passengers of varying nationalities. Israel made an application to the ICJ invoking the Bulgarian declaration of acceptance of the jurisdiction of the Permanent Court of International Justice of 1921. Bulgaria lodged preliminary objections to the jurisdiction of the ICJ on the ground that its declaration of 1921 was no longer in force in consequence of the dissolution of the PCIJ in 1946 (article

---

[1] ICJ Reports, 1959, p. 127.
[2] ICJ Reports, 1972, p. 46.   [3] ICJ Reports, 1986, p. 14.
[4] ICJ Reports, 1989, p. 132.   [5] ICJ Reports, 1992, p. 3.
[6] *Ibid.*, p. 114.   [7] ICJ Reports, 1954, p. 101.

36, paragraph 5 of the ICJ Statute). The ICJ accepted that Bulgaria's acceptance of the jurisdiction of the PCIJ had long lapsed at the time when Bulgaria obtained admission to the UN in 1955. Therefore the ICJ lacked jurisdiction to deal with the case.

Although the ICJ was unable to deal with the merits of the case, a great deal of air law is to be found in the written pleadings and oral hearings of Israel before the Court. The first and principal request of Israel to the ICJ was to adjudge and declare that Bulgaria was 'responsible under international law for the destruction of the Israel aircraft . . . on 27 July 1955, and for the loss of life and property and all other damage that resulted therefrom'.[8] Then the question of the applicable law was raised, because at that time Bulgaria was not a party to the Chicago Convention on Civil Aviation of 1944. Israel argued

> that the Chicago Convention and its Annexes are . . . to the extent that they restate the general law, employed to illustrate the appropriate rules of international law and as a means for the determination of the international standards to be observed in matters concerning international civil aviation and especially in matters concerning the physical safety of civil aircraft and their occupants.[9]

The question of use of force by the territorial state against an intruding civil aircraft was also raised by Israel, considering the Bulgarian opening of fire against the Israeli aircraft as 'a violation of international law', and that the 'degree of violence used was quite out of proportion to any possible threat to Bulgaria' which that aircraft might have presented.[10] Israel said that the basis for its 'contention is the rule that when measures of force are employed to protect territorial sovereignty, whether on land, on sea or in the air, their employment is subject to the duty to take into consideration the elementary obligations of humanity, and not to use a degree of force in excess of what is commensurate with the reality and the gravity of the threat (if any)'.[11] Israel said that it was seeking from the ICJ 'a clear decision on this basic issue [the destruction of its civil aircraft] which goes to the *root of the whole of the contemporary law of the air* and the security of air travel'.[12]

Israel recognized the right of Bulgaria, the territorial state, to take steps to protect its sovereignty if a violation of its airspace had occurred, provided they would not offend against the principle of elementary obligations of humanity, and not use excessive force. It said: 'This is fully recognized in the general principles of international law governing the territorial airspace and is reflected in [the Chicago Convention]. Article 1 of that Convention postulates the rule,

---

[8] ICJ Reports, 1959, Pleadings, Oral Arguments, Documents, p. 83, para. 58.
[9] *Ibid.*, pp. 83 and 84, and para. 59.   [10] *Ibid.*, p. 84, para. 60.
[11] *Ibid.*, para. 61.   [12] *Ibid.*, p. 85, para. 63 (emphasis added).

which underlies the whole of the modern international public law of the air, that every State has complete and exclusive sovereignty over the airspace above its territory.'[13] Therefore, Israel recognized that if Bulgarian airspace was violated, then Bulgaria was entitled to take appropriate action, such as subjecting the aircraft to examination after landing, and if damage were caused, to seek an appropriate claim for satisfaction or reparation.[14]

The ICJ could have determined the limits of the action of the state whose sovereignty had been violated by the intruding aircraft, had it had jurisdiction to deal with that case, as well as the whole issue of aerial intrusion of civil aircraft in the airspace of a state. Moreover, the ICJ could have considered the question of what rights are conferred, and what obligations are imposed, by international law of the air on a state acting in such circumstances to protect its sovereignty.

The question of the applicability or otherwise of private air-law conventions was also raised in the *Aerial Incident* case, that is to say whether the Warsaw Convention for the Unification of Certain Rules Relating to International Carriage by Air of 1929 would apply to Bulgaria's liability to compensate for the loss of life and damage to property resulting from the destruction of the Israeli aircraft. Israel contended that Bulgaria could not benefit from the Warsaw Convention for the compensation of the victims of the shooting down of its aircraft, because

> this Convention governs the relations between an air carrier and its passengers or cargo owners, and basically it establishes a limitation of the liability of the carrier . . . The Convention is not concerned with the financial liability of any person, including a State not a party to the contract of carriage . . . It does not limit the liability of a State which is under the duty of paying compensation because that State's failure to observe the requirements of customary international law has placed it under the duty, according to international law, of paying compensation.[15]

THE *AERIAL INCIDENT*, 1988

On 3 July 1988, US armed forces in the Gulf shot down an Iranian civil aircraft, which resulted in the death of 290 passengers and crew on board. The Islamic Republic of Iran instituted proceedings before the ICJ against the US, in respect of a dispute concerning the interpretation and application of the

[13] *Ibid.*, p. 86, para. 65.
[14] *Ibid.*, p. 87, para. 67.
[15] *Ibid.*, p. 105, para. 100. For a lucid treatment of the liability of the air carrier under the Warsaw Convention, see B. Cheng's articles in *The Law Society's Gazette*, 60 and 61 (June 1963–May 1964).

Chicago Convention on International Civil Aviation of 1944 and the Montreal Convention for the Suppression of Unlawful Acts against the Safety of Civil Aviation of 1971, which arose from the destruction of that aircraft, and the killing of its passengers and crew.[16] When the Court comes to consider the case, questions of air law, perhaps, similar to those raised in the *Aerial Incident*, 1955, might be raised. Moreover, Iran has invoked the Montreal Convention, as Libya did in its application to the ICJ for provisional measures, in 1992.[17] Therefore, the Court would probably have an excellent opportunity to make a significant contribution to the development of air law in providing authoritative answers to such questions, whether under general public international law of the air or the Montreal Convention. Of course this is assuming that the Court has jurisdiction to deal with the case.

THE APPEAL RELATING TO THE JURISDICTION OF THE ICAO COUNCIL, 1972

This was an application by India constituting an appeal against the decision of the Council of the International Civil Aviation Organization on a complaint brought before the Council by Pakistan. In that complaint Pakistan claimed that India, by refusing to allow over-flight of her territory by Pakistan civil aircraft, was in breach of the Chicago Convention on Civil Aviation of 1944 and the International Air Services Transit Agreement of 1944. India claimed that the decision of the ICAO Council assuming jurisdiction in respect of Pakistan's claim was 'illegal, null and void, or erroneous', because the Council had no jurisdiction to handle the matter, as the Chicago Convention and the Transit Agreement had been terminated or suspended as between India and Pakistan.

Article 84 of the Chicago Convention reads as follows:

Settlement of Disputes
If any disagreement between two or more contracting States relating to the interpretation or application of this Convention and its Annexes cannot be settled by negotiation, it shall, on the application of any State concerned in the disagreement, be decided by the Council. No member of the Council shall vote in the consideration by the Council of any dispute to which it is a party. Any contracting State may, subject to Article 85, appeal from the decision of the Council to an *ad hoc* arbitral tribunal agreed upon with the other parties to the dispute or to the

---

[16] ICJ Reports, 1989, p. 132. Article 1 of the Montreal Convention describes the offences covered by the Convention, which include destruction of civil aircraft.
[17] For details, see below, p. 322.

Permanent Court of International Justice. Any such appeal shall be notified to the Council within sixty days of receipt of notification of the decision of the Council.

Further, section 2 of article II of the Transit Agreement reads as follows:

If any disagreement between two or more contracting States relating to the interpretation or application of this Agreement cannot be settled by negotiation, the provisions of Chapter XVIII of the above-mentioned Convention – [this chapter contains article 84 above] – shall be applicable in the same manner as provided therein with reference to any disagreement relating to the interpretation or application of the above-mentioned Convention.

Pakistan objected to India's appeal on the following grounds: the relevant jurisdictional clauses in article 84 of the Chicago Convention and section 2 of article II of the Transit Agreement only allow an appeal to the ICJ from a decision of the ICAO Council on the merits of the dispute referred to it, and not from a decision concerning the Council's jurisdiction to entertain the reference.[18] Further, since India contends that the Chicago Convention and the Transit Agreement are not in force at all (or at any rate in operation) between the parties, India cannot invoke their jurisdictional clauses for the purposes of appealing to the ICJ, and that the ICJ lacks jurisdiction under its own Statute, because, in the case of disputes referred to it under treaties or conventions, article 36, paragraph 1, of the Statute requires these to be 'treaties and conventions in force', and India denies that the treaties and conventions concerned are in force.[19]

But the Court rejected these objections and held that the ICAO Council's decision assuming jurisdiction in respect of Pakistan's complaint was appealable.[20] It also said that this was the first time any matter of appeal has come to it.[21]

In holding that it had jurisdiction to entertain the appeal and that the ICAO Council was competent to entertain Pakistan's complaint, the ICJ has helped to provide certainty in the law. Moreover, it has ensured that its appellant jurisdiction constitutes a safeguard for the interests of member states of the ICAO and its Council that the functioning of that body and application of the Chicago Convention and Transit Agreement are working satisfactorily. Indeed, the Court itself recognized so much when it said:

The case is presented to the Court in the guise of an ordinary dispute between States (and such a dispute underlies it). Yet in the proceedings before the Court, it is the act of a third entity – the Council of ICAO – which one of the Parties is

---

[18] See ICJ Reports, 1972, p. 52, para. 14.   [19] See *ibid*., pp. 52–3.
[20] *Ibid*., p. 60, para. 24.   [21] *Ibid*., para. 26.

impugning and the other defending. In that aspect of the matter, the appeal to the Court contemplated by the Chicago Convention and the Transit Agreement must be regarded as an element of the general regime established in respect of ICAO. In thus providing for judicial recourse by way of appeal to the Court against decisions of the Council concerning interpretation and application – a type of recourse already figuring in earlier conventions in the sphere of communications – the Chicago Treaties gave member States, and through them the Council, the possibility of ensuring a certain measure of supervision by the Court over those decisions. To this extent, these Treaties enlist the support of the Court for the good functioning of the Organization, and therefore the first reassurance for the Council lies in the knowledge that means exist for determining whether a decision as to its own competence is in conformity or not with the provisions of the treaties governing its action. If nothing in the text requires a different conclusion, an appeal against a decision of the Council as to its own jurisdiction must therefore be receivable since, from the standpoint of the supervision by the Court of the validity of the Council's acts, there is no ground for distinguishing between supervision as to jurisdiction, and supervision as to merits.[22]

The ICJ confirmed the judicial function of the ICAO Council under article 84 of the Chicago Convention. Commenting on the differing views of India and Pakistan with respect to articles 89 and 95[23] of the Chicago Convention, the ICJ held:

The Court must obviously refrain from pronouncing on the validity or otherwise of the opposing views of the Parties as to the object and correct interpretation of Articles 89 and 95 . . . But this opposition cannot but be indicative of a direct conflict of views as to the meaning of these Articles, or in other words of a 'disagreement . . . relating to the interpretation and application of [the Chicago] Convention' – and if there is even one provision – and especially a provision of the importance of Article 89 – as to which this is so, then the Council is vested with jurisdiction.[24]

MILITARY AND PARAMILITARY ACTIVITIES IN AND AGAINST NICARAGUA (MERITS), 1986

This was a case brought by Nicaragua against the US, claiming, *inter alia*, that the US, in breach of its obligations under general and customary international

---

[22] *Ibid.*, pp. 60–1.

[23] Article 89 of the Chicago Convention deals with war and emergency conditions, and provides that the Convention does not affect the freedom of action of any contracting state affected by such situations; whereas article 95 of the Convention deals with the denunciation of the Convention and procedure required therefor.

[24] ICJ Reports, 1972, p. 69, para. 43.

law had violated Nicaraguan sovereignty by armed attacks against it by air and by aerial trespass into its airspace. Nicaragua's complaint about the violation of its airspace referred to over-flights by aircraft at high altitude for intelligence reconnaissance purposes, or aircraft used for supplying the Contras in the field and aircraft producing 'sonic booms'. While this case is, essentially, related to a dispute about the use of force by the US in and against Nicaragua, the existence or otherwise of the right of self-defence and intervention, some aspects of it, as we have seen above, relate to air law. And the ICJ had no hesitation in dealing with them. The Court concluded that the high-altitude reconnaissance flights and the low-altitude flights causing 'sonic booms', which took place between 7 and 11 November 1984, were imputable to the US, and constituted a violation of Nicaraguan airspace. The US action was in breach of its obligation under customary international law not to violate the sovereignty of another state.[25] These rulings by the ICJ constitute a judicial determination, at the highest level, that reconnaissance activities using high-altitude aircraft is unlawful under international law. This might have been known before, but it has now received the stamp of authority from the ICJ. Moreover, 'sonic booms', caused by low-flying aircraft, are not usually used by states as a protest in international relations. The ICJ has now characterized them as unlawful activities, which engage the state responsibility of the actor under international law.

THE *LOCKERBIE INCIDENT*, 1992

These cases were instituted by Libya against the UK and US, claiming that the UK and the US were in breach of several provisions of the Montreal Convention for the Suppression of Unlawful Acts against the Safety of Civil Aviation of 1971. The facts of the *Lockerbie Incident* are as follows: on 21 December 1988, a US civil aircraft (PanAm Flight 103) exploded over Lockerbie in Scotland, resulting in the death of 220 persons. The investigations carried out by the UK and US authorities led to the accusation of two Libyan nationals. Charges were brought against the two Libyans by the Lord Advocate of Scotland, and a Grand Jury of the US District Court for the District of Columbia, in connection with the destruction of PanAm Flight 103. Further, the US and the UK issued on 27 November 1991 a joint declaration asking, *inter alia*, that Libya surrender for trial those charged with the crime. Libya refused to do so and made an application to the ICJ against the UK and the US on 3 March 1992, alleging that the UK and US had

---

[25] See ICJ Reports, 1986, p. 53, para. 91.

breached article 5, paragraphs 2 and 3, article 7, article 8, paragraph 2 and article 11 of the Montreal Convention.[26] Libya also requested the Court to indicate provisional measures to preserve its rights, in conformity with article 41 of the Statute of the ICJ. Libya further alleged that the UK and the US were actively seeking to by-pass the provisions of the Montreal Convention by threatening various actions against Libya in order to compel it to surrender its two accused nationals.[27]

The *Lockerbie Incident* was also referred to the Security Council which took measures not involving the use of armed force against Libya (resolutions 731 (1992) of 21 January 1992 and resolution 748 (1992) of 31 March 1992) under Chapter VII of the UN Charter.[28]

The UN Charter confers on the Security Council 'primary responsibility for the maintenance of international peace and security', and in carrying out this responsibility the Council acts on behalf of the UN members (article 24 of the Charter). Furthermore, under article 25 of the Charter, 'the Members of the United Nations agree to accept and carry out the decisions of the Security Council in accordance with the present Charter'.

It is to be noted that the Security Council resolution of 31 March 1992 was under Chapter VII of the Charter, therefore it is binding on all members of the UN, in accordance with article 25 of the Charter. And that decision was adopted three days after the close of the hearing of the Libyan request for provisional measures under article 41 of the Statute of the ICJ.

Thus, during the oral hearings before the Court the large question of relationship between the ICJ and the Security Council was raised by both Libya, the UK and the USA. Counsel for Libya argued that Libya filed its application for provisional measures before the ICJ 'in order to submit to it the legal aspects of the question which were neglected by the Security Council and should have been the object of the recommendation contained in article 36, paragraph 3 of the Charter, under which "legal disputes should as a general rule be referred by the Parties to the International Court of Justice"'.[29] He also said that recourse to the Security Council does not rule out

---

[26] See ICJ Reports, 1992, p. 4, para. 4; and p. 115, para. 4.

[27] *Ibid.*, p. 7, para. 9; and p. 118, para. 9.

[28] A third resolution was adopted by the Security Council on 11 November 1993 (resolution 883 (1993)). In that resolution, the Security Council determined that Libya's 'continued failure to respond fully and effectively to the requests and decisions in resolutions 731 (1992) and 748 (1992), constitute a threat to international peace and security'. The Council, acting under Chapter VII of the Charter, then decided on measures not involving the use of force against Libya, in order to secure Libya's compliance with its decisions. See sixth preambular paragraph and operative paragraph 2 of the resolution. Those measures fall within the orbit of article 41 of the Charter.

[29] See ICJ, Oral Hearings, CR 92/2 (26 March 1992, Corrigendum CR 92/2 translation), p. 56.

simultaneous or subsequent recourse to the ICJ.[30] He went on: 'Article 36, paragraph 3, already shows that parallel powers may perfectly well and quite normally exist between the Council and the Court. While the Council would deal with the political aspects, it should be possible to submit disputes of a legal nature to the Court.'[31]

Counsel for the UK argued that 'the United Kingdom believes that Libya is attempting to secure, by the route of interim measures, the delegitimising of the Security Council's proper interest in the matter. The Security Council is fully entitled to concern itself with issues of terrorism and the measures needed to address acts of terrorism . . . The International Court of Justice is not in any general sense an appeal tribunal available to Member States who have not been able to make their views prevail in the Security Council.' She went on to say: 'Although the Security Council is not mentioned in terms, the Applicant's unmistakable intention in seeking these measures is to interfere with the exercise by the Security Council of its Charter functions.'[32]

Counsel for the USA argued that 'in fact, Applicant incites the Court into two conflicts with the Security Council. Most starkly, it would have the Court enjoin a member of the Council from participating fully in its work when the Council is actively considering taking action under Chapter VII of the United Nations Charter.'[33] He went on to say: 'Libya's request to the Court for provisional measures . . . if granted, it could do damage to the functioning of the UN Charter's system for the maintenance of international peace and security'.[34]

In its comments on the issue the Court said:

> Whatever the situation previous to the adoption of [Security Council resolution 748 (1992)], the rights claimed by Libya under the Montreal Convention cannot now be regarded as appropriate for protection by the indication of provisional measures. Whereas . . . an indication of the measures requested by Libya would be likely to impair the rights which appear prima facie to be enjoyed by the United Kingdom by virtue of Security Council resolution 748 (1992).[35]

However, the Court declined to deal with the question of relationship between itself and the Security Council, saying that it 'is not called upon to determine any of the other questions raised in the present proceedings'.[36]

---

[30] *Ibid.*, p. 57.

[31] *Ibid.*, p. 58.   [32] See *Ibid.*, CR 92/3, pp. 69 and 70.

[33] *Ibid.*, CR 92/4 (27 March 1992), p. 71.   [34] *Ibid.*, p. 76.

[35] See ICJ Reports, 1992, p. 15, paras. 40–1; the ICJ held the same with respect to the US; see *ibid.*, p. 127, paras. 44–5.

[36] *Ibid.*, p. 15, para. 43, and p. 127, para. 46.

However, in previous cases the ICJ did pronounce on this question. For example, in the case of *Military and Paramilitary Activities in and against Nicaragua*, the Court said: 'The [Security] Council has functions of a political nature assigned to it, whereas the Court exercises purely judicial functions. Both organs can therefore perform their separate but complementary functions with respect to the same events.'[37] The Court went on to say: 'It must also be remembered that, as the *Corfu Channel* case . . . shows, the Court has never shied away from a case brought before it merely because it had political implications or because it involved serious elements of the use of force.' The Court then cited a passage from its judgment in the *Corfu Channel* case and said: 'What is also significant is that the Security Council itself in that case had "undoubtedly intended that the whole dispute should be decided by the Court".'[38]

Finally, the ICJ declined to indicate provisional measures under article 41 of its Statute, because the circumstances of the case were not such as to require the exercise of its power under that provision.[39] But the merits phase is pending before the Court.

It would not be an exaggeration to state that this is probably the first proper occasion for the ICJ to make a significant contribution to air law. It will be the first time the ICJ will examine a whole air-law convention, namely, the Montreal Convention, and not only a limited aspect of it, as has been the case with respect to the Chicago Convention in the case of the Appeal relating to the Jurisdiction of the ICAO Council.

The ICJ will, no doubt, interpret a number of provisions mentioned by the parties during the oral hearings, especially those relating to the right of the parties to exercise jurisdiction over the crime under the Montreal Convention, the lack of any rule in the Convention on the issue of priority or exclusivity of jurisdiction,[40] as well as the controversial issue of extradition. There is also the question whether the principle provided for in the Montreal Convention, namely, try or extradite, applies to suspects who are officers of the government which claims the right to try them rather than extradite them.[41] It may be worthwhile mentioning that any interpretations and pronouncements, as may

---

[37] See ICJ Reports, 1984, p. 435, para. 95.

[38] *Ibid.*, para. 96.

[39] ICJ Reports, 1992, p. 15, para. 43, and p. 127, para. 46.

[40] The question of absence of a rule on priority of jurisdiction was raised by this writer *vis-à-vis* The Hague Convention for the Suppression of Unlawful Seizure of Aircraft of 1970, which was used as a model for the Montreal Convention. See S. Shubber, 'Aircraft Hijacking under The Hague Convention 1970 – A New Regime?', *ICLQ*, 22 (1973), pp. 715ff.

[41] See the question posed by Judge Schwebel during the hearing of the Libyan application for provisional measures, n. 29 above, 28 March 1992, p. 48, paragraph 1.

eventually be advanced by the ICJ in this case, will apply to similar provisions in other conventions in air law and in the area of suppression of terrorism. To give but an example: the Montreal Convention contains provisions on extradition identical to those contained in The Hague Convention for the Suppression of Unlawful Seizure of Aircraft of 1970. They were also used as a basis for the extradition arrangements under the Convention Against the Taking of Hostages of 1979.[42] Therefore the Court's ruling in this case would apply to similar disputes which may arise under those other Conventions. The ICJ may also consider it appropriate to comment on the relationship between the obligations under the Montreal Convention and the UN Charter, especially with respect to measures taken under Chapter VII of the Charter. The Court briefly dealt with this point in the request for the indication of provisional measures.[43]

It might be appropriate to conclude by stating that the contributions to this book are made in the honour of Sir Robert Jennings, who was the first international lawyer after the Second World War to make a significant contribution to the development of air law, as a scholar,[44] a Judge and President of the International Court of Justice.

---

[42] On this Convention, see S. Shubber, 'The International Convention against the taking of Hostages', *BYbIL*, 51 (1981), pp. 205ff.

[43] See ICJ Reports, 1992, p. 15, para. 39, p. 126, para. 42.

[44] See Sir Robert Jennings, 'International Civil Aviation and the Law', *BYbIL* (1945), p. 191; and his 'Some Aspects of the International Law of the Air', *Recueil des Cours*, 75 (1949), p. 513.

17

The treatment of human rights and of aliens in the International Court of Justice

Stephen M. Schwebel

ↂ

IN THE PERMANENT COURT OF INTERNATIONAL JUSTICE

Problems of the treatment of aliens and of human rights loomed large in the Permanent Court of International Justice. In the sphere of human rights, the Court's seminal Advisory Opinion on *Jurisdiction of the Court of Danzig*[1] early established that the very object of an international agreement may be the adoption of some definite rules creating individual rights and obligations – which in 1928 was, in Lauterpacht's words, 'in effect a revolutionary pronouncement'.[2] Earlier, in 1923, in its Opinion on *Nationality Decrees issued in Tunis and Morocco*, the Court had held that the question of whether a certain matter is or is not solely within the jurisdiction of a state 'is an essentially relative question; it depends upon the development of international relations'.[3] Accordingly, as Professors McDougal, Lasswell and Chen put it: 'The choice between "international concern" and "domestic jurisdiction" was thus made to depend not only upon fact, but upon changing fact, permitting

---

This survey of the treatment of human rights and of aliens in the International Court of Justice gives inadequate sense of the contributions of Judge Sir Robert Jennings in these and all other spheres of the work of the Court. The quality of those contributions is publicly demonstrated in his Separate and Dissenting Opinions. It inheres as well in the judgments and Advisory Opinions of the Court and its Chambers issued since his election in 1982, not only because he has played his full part in the Court's deliberations but because he has repeatedly been a member of the drafting committee that prepared the text of the draft judgment for the Court's consideration. In his services as a judge of the Court Judge Jennings was surpassed only by himself, in the years in which he served as President of the Court (1991–4). Having had the privileges of being a student of Professor R. Y. Jennings at Cambridge University (1950–1) and of being his colleague since 1982, it is a particular pleasure to contribute this chapter to a collection published in celebration of his eightieth year, in which his intellect remains as keen as it was in his fortieth and his character is a comfort to all who know him.

[1] *Jurisdiction of the Court of Danzig*, PCIJ, Series B, No. 15, pp. 17–18.
[2] Sir Hersch Lauterpacht, *The Development of International Law by the International Court* (London, 1958), p. 174.
[3] *Nationality Decrees Issued in Tunis and Morocco*, PCIJ, Series B, No. 4, p. 24.

a continuing readjustment of inclusive and exclusive competences as conditions might require.'[4] In its Advisory Opinion in the same year on *German Settlers in Poland*, the Court interpreted 'civil rights' as embracing property rights, and it debarred discrimination in fact even if discrimination in form is absent.[5] In its Advisory Opinion in *Minority Schools in Albania*, the Court enjoined measures that would have compelled a minority 'to renounce that which constitutes the very essence of its being as a minority'[6] and – in a fundamental holding which anticipates what today is denominated as 'affirmative action' – concluded: 'Equality in law precludes discrimination of any kind; whereas equality in fact may involve the necessity of different treatment in order to attain a result which establishes an equilibrium between different situations.'[7] In its Advisory Opinion on the *Consistency of Certain Danzig Legislative Decrees with the Constitution of the Free City*, the Court debarred application of criminal law by analogy: 'It must be possible for the individual to know, beforehand, whether his acts are lawful or liable to punishment.'[8]

In matters of treatment of aliens, the Court was even more fully engaged. In its judgment on jurisdiction in the *Mavrommatis Palestine Concessions* case, the Court set out the classic international law of diplomatic protection, the

> elementary principle of international law that a state is entitled to protect its subjects, when injured by acts contrary to international law committed by another State . . . By taking up the case of one of its subjects and by resorting to diplomatic action or international judicial proceedings on his behalf, a State is in reality asserting its own rights – its right to ensure, in the person of its subjects, respect for the rules of international law.[9]

A variety of questions of the treatment of aliens was dealt with in a succession of judgments and Advisory Opinions, including: *Acquisition of Polish Nationality*;[10] *German Settlers in Poland*;[11] *Exchange of Greek and Turkish Populations*;[12] *Certain German Interests in Polish Upper Silesia*;[13] *Factory at*

---

[4] Myres S. McDougal, Harold D. Lasswell and Lu-Chu Chen, *Human Rights and World Public Order* (New Haven/London, 1980), p. 211.

[5] *German Settlers in Poland*, PCIJ, Series B, No. 6, p. 24.

[6] *Minority Schools in Albania*, PCIJ, Series A/B, No. 64, p. 17.

[7] *Ibid.*, p. 19.

[8] *Consistency of Certain Danzig Legislative Decrees with the Constitution of the Free City*, PCIJ, Series A/B, No. 65, p. 57.

[9] *The Mavrommatis Palestine Concessions*, PCIJ, Series A, No. 2, p. 12.

[10] *Acquisition of Polish nationality*, PCIJ, Series B, No. 7.

[11] *German Settlers in Poland*, PCIJ Series B, No. 6.

[12] *Exchange of Greek and Turkish Populations*, PCIJ, Series B, No. 10.

[13] *Certain German Interests in Polish Upper Silesia*, PCIJ, Series A, No. 7.

Chorzów;[14] *The Lotus;*[15] *Rights of Minorities in Upper Silesia;*[16] *Jurisdiction of the Courts of Danzig;*[17] *Serbian and Brazilian Loans* cases;[18] the *Greco-Bulgarian 'Communities'* case;[19] *Treatment of Polish Nationals and Other Persons of Polish Origin or Speech in the Danzig Territory;*[20] the *Oscar Chinn* case;[21] *Pajzs, Csáky and Esterházy* case;[22] *Lighthouses* case[23] and *Lighthouses in Crete and Samos;*[24] the *Borchgrave* case;[25] *Phosphates in Morocco;*[26] *Panevezys–Saldutiskis Railway* case;[27] and *Société Commerciale de Belgique.*[28] Some of these judgments, such as that in the *Chorzów Factory* case, were and remain of fundamental importance in the development of the law of state responsibility in respect of the treatment of aliens and their property.

IN THE INTERNATIONAL COURT OF JUSTICE

The International Court of Justice, in its nearly fifty years of activity, has not had occasion to deal with questions of the treatment of aliens as often and as significantly as did the Permanent Court of International Justice in its eighteen years of activity. What might have been its most consequential judgments in the field did not reach judgment on the merits: the *Anglo-Iranian Oil Company* case, *Certain Norwegian Loans, Interhandel, Barcelona Traction* and *Certain Phosphate Lands in Nauru.* But the ICJ has had an important involvement in the development of a modern law of international human rights, and a substantial involvement in aspects of the treatment of aliens. This chapter will principally consider the contributions of the Court in the sphere of human rights, and will refer as well to its related treatment of problems of aliens.

[14] *Factory at Chorzów*, PCIJ, Series A, No. 17.
[15] *'Lotus'*, PCIJ, Series A, No. 10.
[16] *Rights of Minorities in Upper Silesia*, PCIJ, Series A, No. 15.
[17] *Jurisdiction of the Courts in Danzig*, PCIJ, Series B, No. 15.
[18] *Serbian and Brazilian Loans* cases, PCIJ, Series A, Nos. 20 and 21.
[19] *Greco-Bulgarian 'Communities'*, PCIJ, Series B, No. 17.
[20] *Treatment of Polish Nationals and Other Persons of Polish Origin or Speech in the Danzig Territory*, PCIJ, Series A/B, No. 44.
[21] *Oscar Chinn* case, PCIJ, Series A/B, No. 63.
[22] *Pajzs, Csáky and Esterházy* case, PCIJ, Series A/B, No. 63.
[23] *Lighthouses* case, PCIJ, Series A/B, No. 62.
[24] *Lighthouses in Crete and Samos*, PCIJ, Series A/B, No. 71.
[25] *Borchgrave* case, PCIJ, Series A/B, No. 72.
[26] *Phosphates in Morocco*, PCIJ, Series A/B, No. 74.
[27] *Panevezys–Saldutiskis Railway* case, PCIJ, Series A/B, No. 76.
[28] *Société Commerciale de Belgique*, PCIJ, Series A/B, No. 78.

Human rights

Corfu Channel *case*

In its first contentious case, the *Corfu Channel* case, the Court held that Albania had an obligation under international law to notify international shipping of the existence of a minefield in Albanian territorial waters, an obligation which derived from 'certain general and well-recognized principles, namely, elementary considerations of humanity, even more exacting in peace than in war'[29] as well as other principles such as the freedom of maritime communication and the obligation of a state not knowingly to allow its territory to be used for acts contrary to the rights of other states. The Court, as will be shown, has had cause to return to the 'elementary considerations of humanity, even more exacting in peace than in war.' The relation of such considerations to the substance and application of human rights requires no elaboration.

Reservations to the Genocide Convention

One of the Court's early Advisory Opinions concerned the making of reservations to treaties, an opinion which had a determinative influence on the provisions on reservations to treaties of the subsequent Vienna Convention on the Law of Treaties. In the course of its Opinion, the Court declared:

> The solution of these problems must be found in the special characteristics of the Genocide Convention. The origins and character of that Convention, the objects pursued by the General Assembly and the contracting parties, the relations which exist between the provisions of the Convention, *inter se*, and between those provisions and these objects, furnish elements of interpretation of the will of the General Assembly and the parties. The origins of the Convention show that it was the intention of the United Nations to condemn and punish genocide as 'a crime under international law' involving a denial of the right of existence of entire human groups, a denial which shocks the conscience of mankind and results in great losses to humanity, and which is contrary to moral law and to the spirit and aims of the United Nations (resolution 96(I) of the General Assembly, December 11th, 1946). The first consequence arising from this conception is that the principles underlying the Convention are principles which are recognized by civilized nations as binding on States, even without any conventional obligation. A second consequence is the universal character both of the condemnation of genocide and of the cooperation required 'in order to liberate mankind from such an odious scourge' (Preamble to the Convention). The Genocide Convention was therefore intended by the General Assembly and by the contracting parties to be definitely universal in scope.

---

[29] *Corfu Channel* case, ICJ Reports, 1949, pp. 4, 22.

It was in fact approved on December 9th, 1948, by a resolution which was unanimously adopted by fifty-six States.

The objects of such a convention must also be considered. The Convention was manifestly adopted for a purely humanitarian and civilizing purpose. It is indeed difficult to imagine a convention that might have this dual character to a greater degree, since its object on the one hand is to safeguard the very existence of certain human groups and on the other to confirm and endorse the most elementary principles of morality. In such a convention the contracting States do not have any interests of their own; they merely have, one and all, a common interest, namely, the accomplishment of those high purposes which are the *raison d'être* of the convention. Consequently, in a convention of this type one cannot speak of individual advantages or disadvantages to States, or of the maintenance of a perfect contractual balance between rights and duties. The high ideals which inspired the Convention provide, by virtue of the common will of the parties, the foundation and measure of all its provisions.[30]

The Court thus recognized that genocide is supremely unlawful under international law, customary as well as conventional, and foreshadowed its later holdings on international obligations *erga omnes*. As will be shown, the Court has had reason to return to its early analysis of the significance of the Genocide Convention.

International Status of South West Africa

In its Advisory Opinion on the *International Status of South West Africa*,[31] the ICJ carried further the conclusion referred to above of the PCIJ in *Jurisdiction of the Courts of Danzig*, by holding that, as a result of resolutions adopted by the Council of the League of Nations in 1923, the inhabitants of the mandated territories acquired the international right of petition, a right maintained by article 80, paragraph 1 of the United Nations Charter, which safeguards 'not only the rights of States, but also the rights of the peoples of mandated territories'.[32] Thus as in the *Courts of Danzig* Opinion, individuals are treated by the Court as invested by an international instrument with an international right, in this case with a procedural right protective of certain fundamental human rights (such as freedom from slavery and forced labour).

Reparation for Injuries *case*

In its Advisory Opinion on *Reparation for Injuries Suffered in the Service of the United Nations*, the Court held that 'the subjects of law in any legal system are

---

[30] Reservations to the Convention on the Prevention and Punishment of the Crime of Genocide, ICJ Reports, 1951, pp. 15, 23.

[31] *International Status of South West Africa*, ICJ Reports, 1950, p. 128.   [32] *Ibid.*, pp. 136, 137.

not necessarily identical in their nature or in the extent of their rights'[33] and concluded that the UN possessed a large measure of international personality, including the right to bring an international claim — a holding which reinforced the principle that international rights do not belong only to states.

Asylum *case*

In the *Asylum* case between Colombia and Peru, to which Colombia's grant of diplomatic asylum to Sr Haya de la Torre gave rise, the Court concluded that regular prosecution by judicial authorities, even if such prosecution relates to revolutionary activities, does not constitute an 'urgent case' within the terms of the Havana Convention, for 'in principle . . . asylum cannot be opposed to the operation of justice'. But the Court significantly qualified this holding by stating that:

> An exception to this rule can occur only if, in the guise of justice, arbitrary action is substituted for the rule of law. Such would be the case if the administration of justice were corrupted by measures clearly prompted by political aims. Asylum protects the political offender against any measures of a manifestly extra-legal character which a government might take against its political opponents.[34]

Peace Treaties *case*

In its advisory proceedings concerning the *Interpretation of Peace Treaties with Bulgaria, Hungary and Romania*, the General Assembly put questions to the Court concerning the obligations of those states to implement dispute settlement procedures of the Peace Treaties. The disputes turned on allegations of failure of the three states to

> take all measures necessary to secure to all persons under [their] jurisdiction, without distinction as to race, sex, language or religion, the enjoyment of human rights and fundamental freedoms, including freedom of expression, of press and publications, of religious worship, of political opinion and of public meeting.[35]

It was contended that the request for an Advisory Opinion was an act *ultra vires* the General Assembly because, in dealing with the question of the observance of human rights and fundamental freedoms in these three states, the Assembly was 'interfering' or 'intervening' in matters essentially within the domestic

---

[33] *Reparation for Injuries Suffered in the Service of the United Nations*, ICJ Reports, 1949, pp. 174, 178.

[34] *Asylum* case, ICJ Reports, 1950, pp. 266, 284.

[35] *Interpretation of Peace Treaties*, ICJ Reports, 1950, pp. 65, 73.

jurisdiction of states. This alleged incompetence of the Assembly was deduced from the terms of article 2, paragraph 7 of the UN Charter.[36]

The Court held this argument to be based on a misunderstanding. The Court itself was not called upon to deal with the charges of the violation of the human rights provisions of the Peace Treaties but only the procedure for dispute settlement under the Treaties. It held that the interpretation of the terms of a treaty for this purpose could not be considered a question essentially within the domestic jurisdiction of a state. 'It is a question of international law which, by its very nature, lies within the competence of the Court.'[37] The Court held that these considerations sufficed also to dispose of the argument based on article 2, paragraph 7.

The UN Charter, hardly less a treaty than the Peace Treaties, proclaims the purpose of achievement of international co-operation in 'promoting and encouraging respect for human rights and for fundamental freedoms for all without distinction as to race, sex, language or religion' (article 1, paragraph 3). It provides, in article 55, that the UN shall promote universal respect for and observance of human rights and fundamental freedoms for all, without distinction as to race, sex, language or religion, and further provides, in article 56, that the members of the UN pledge to take joint and separate action in co-operation with the Organization to achieve these purposes. It appears to follow (see the reference above to *Nationality Decrees Issued in Tunis and Morocco*) that any question of the breach of these treaty obligations – if they be obligations – equally would not be matters essentially within the domestic jurisdiction of a state. The importance of that conclusion to the contemporary international law of human rights is fundamental in view of the fact, discussed below, that the Court was later to hold that these Charter provisions do give rise to international obligations.

South West Africa *cases*

There has been repeated involvement of the Court with the governance of, and the promotion of the independence of, South West Africa – today the independent state of Namibia. One such involvement is referred to above. Another was the *South West Africa* cases brought by Ethiopia and Liberia against South Africa, alleging, among other things, that the practice of

---

[36] Article 2, paragraph 7 of the UN Charter provides: 'Nothing contained in the present Charter shall authorize the United Nations to intervene in matters which are essentially within the domestic jurisdiction of any State, or shall require the Members to submit such matters to settlement under the present Charter; but this principle shall not prejudice the application of enforcement measures under Chapter VII.'

[37] ICJ Reports, 1950, pp. 70–1.

apartheid in South West Africa constituted a violation of South Africa's mandatory obligation to promote to the utmost the well-being of the inhabitants of the territory. South Africa lodged a number of preliminary objections to the standing of Ethiopia and Liberia and the jurisdiction of the Court. The Court, by a vote of eight to seven, held in 1962 that it had jurisdiction to adjudicate upon the merits of the dispute.[38] But four years later, it held, by the casting vote of the President, that the applicants had not established any legal right or interest appertaining to them in the subject matter of the dispute.[39] The Court held that the argument of Ethiopia and Liberia

> amounts to a plea that the Court should allow the equivalent of an 'actio popularis', or right resident in any member of a community to take legal action in vindication of a public interest. But although a right of this kind may be known to certain municipal systems of law, it is not known to international law as it stands at present: nor is the Court able to regard it as imported by the 'general principles of law' referred to in Article 38, paragraph 1 (c), of its Statute.[40]

Accordingly the Court never reached the merits, which had given rise to exceptionally extended and detailed argument over human-rights issues posed by the practice of an overt and acute form of racial discrimination.

Continued Presence of South Africa in Namibia

The Court's 1966 judgment in the *South West Africa* cases was widely and trenchantly criticized, not least in the United Nations General Assembly, which proceeded to find that 'South Africa has failed to fulfil its obligations . . . to ensure the moral and material well-being and security of the indigenous inhabitants of South West Africa and has, in fact, disavowed the Mandate'. The General Assembly accordingly decided that the Mandate conferred upon South Africa to administer the territory 'is therefore terminated' and 'that South Africa has no other right to administer the Territory'.[41]

In 1970, the Security Council requested an Advisory Opinion of the Court on the legal consequences for states of the continued presence of South Africa in Namibia despite a Security Council resolution holding, as a consequence of General Assembly resolution 2145 (XXI), that presence to be illegal. The Court found that 'the continued presence of South Africa in Namibia being illegal, South Africa is under obligation to withdraw its administration from

---

[38] *South West Africa* cases, ICJ Reports, 1962, p. 319.
[39] *South West Africa* cases, ICJ Reports, 1966, pp. 6, 51.
[40] *Ibid.*, p. 47.
[41] General Assembly resolution 2145 XXI.

Namibia immediately and thus to put an end to the occupation of the Territory'.[42] The Court held that the General Assembly had acted within the framework of its competence in terminating the Mandate. Among the several objections to the validity of General Assembly resolution 2145 (XXI) which South Africa maintained before the Court was its claim that the resolution's holding that South Africa had failed to fulfil its obligations in respect of the administration of the mandated territory required detailed factual investigation, which had not been made. The Court responded:

128. . . . the Government of South Africa expressed the desire to supply the Court with further factual information concerning the purposes and objectives of South Africa's policy of separate development or *apartheid*, contending that to establish a breach of South Africa's substantive international obligations under the Mandate it would be necessary to prove that a particular exercise of South Africa's legislative or administrative powers was not directed in good faith towards the purpose of promoting to the utmost the well-being and progress of the inhabitants. It is claimed by the Government of South Africa that no act or omission on its part would constitute a violation of its international obligations unless it is shown that such act or omission was actuated by a motive, or directed towards a purpose other than one to promote the interests of the inhabitants of the Territory.

129. The Government of South Africa having made this request, the Court finds that no factual evidence is needed for the purpose of determining whether the policy of apartheid as applied by South Africa in Namibia is in conformity with the international obligations assumed by South Africa under the Charter of the United Nations. In order to determine whether the laws and decrees applied by South Africa in Namibia, which are a matter of public record, constitute a violation of the purposes and principles of the Charter of the United Nations, the question of intent or governmental direction is not relevant; nor is it necessary to investigate or determine the effects of those measures upon the welfare of the inhabitants.

130. It is undisputed, and is amply supported by documents annexed to South Africa's written statement in these proceedings, that the official governmental policy pursued by South Africa in Namibia is to achieve a complete physical separation of races and ethnic groups in separate areas within the Territory. The application of this policy has required, as has been conceded by South Africa, restrictive measures of control officially adopted and enforced in the Territory by the coercive power of the former Mandatory. These measures establish limitations, exclusions or restrictions for the members of the indigenous population groups in respect of their participation in certain types of activities, fields of study or of training, labor or employment and also submit them to restrictions or exclusions of residence and movement in large parts of the Territory.

131. Under the Charter of the United Nations, the former Mandatory had

---

[42] *Legal Consequences for States of the Continued Presence of South Africa in Namibia (South West Africa) notwithstanding Security Council Resolution 276*, ICJ Reports, 1971, pp. 16, 58.

pledged itself to observe and respect, in a territory having an international status, human rights and fundamental freedoms for all without distinction as to race. To establish instead, and to enforce, distinctions, exclusions, restrictions and limitations exclusively based on grounds of race, color, descent or national or ethnic origin which constitute a denial of fundamental human rights is a flagrant violation of the purposes and principles of the Charter.[43]

These holdings are of fundamental importance to the contemporary character of international law governing human rights. As Egon Schwelb put it:

When the Court speaks of 'conformity with the international obligations assumed . . . under the Charter', of 'a violation of the purposes and principles of the Charter', of the pledge to observe and respect human rights and fundamental freedoms for all, when it finds that certain actions 'constitute a denial of fundamental human rights' and classifies them as 'a flagrant violation of the purposes and principles of the Charter', it leaves no doubt that, in its view, the Charter does impose on Members of the United Nations legal obligations in the human rights field.[44]

It is true that the Court specified that South Africa had pledged itself to observe and respect, 'in a territory having an international status', human rights and fundamental freedoms for all without distinction as to race. But that clause imports an aggravating, not a necessary, circumstance. Schwelb was right to maintain, in commenting upon this passage, that 'what is a flagrant violation of the purposes and principles of the Charter when committed in Namibia, is also such a violation when committed in South Africa proper or, for that matter, in any sovereign Member State.'[45]

Barcelona Traction

In 1970 the Court rendered its judgment in the second phase of the proceedings in the case concerning *The Barcelona Traction, Light and Power Company, Limited*. In the course of holding the applicant's claims inadmissible, the Court made a distinction

between the obligations of a State towards the international community as a whole, and those arising vis-à-vis another State in the field of diplomatic protection. By their very nature the former are the concern of all States. In view of the importance of the rights involved, all States can be held to have a legal interest in their protection; they are obligations *erga omnes*.

---

[43] *Ibid.*, pp. 56–7.

[44] Egon Schwelb, 'The International Court of Justice and the Human Rights Clauses of the Charter', *American Journal of International Law*, 66 (1972), pp. 337, 348.

[45] *Ibid.*, p. 349.

34. Such obligations derive, for example, in contemporary international law, from the outlawing of acts of aggression, and of genocide, as also from the principles and rules concerning the basic rights of the human person, including protection from slavery and racial discrimination. Some of the corresponding rights of protection have entered into the body of general international law (*Reservations to the Convention on the Prevention and Punishment of the Crime of Genocide . . .*); others are conferred by international instruments of a universal or quasi-universal character.[46]

This is another holding of paramount importance for international law concerning human rights. By it, the Court has found that the rules concerning the basic rights of the human person are the concern of all states; that obligations flowing from these rights run *erga omnes*, that is, towards all states. Thus it follows that, when one state protests that another is violating the basic human rights of the latter's own citizens, the former state is not intervening in the latter's internal affairs; it rather is seeking to vindicate international obligations which run towards it as well as all other states.

At the same time, in *Barcelona Traction*, the Court held that 'obligations the performance of which is the subject of diplomatic protection are not of the same category' as obligations *erga omnes*. 'It cannot be held, when one such obligation in particular is in question, in a specific case, that all States have a legal interest in its observance.'[47] The Court found that Belgium lacked standing to maintain a claim against Spain before the Court, on the ground that, while Belgians might be the principal shareholders of Barcelona Traction, that company was of Canadian nationality. Professors McDougal, Lasswell and Chen accordingly conclude: 'In contemporary international law it is thus apparent that the individual human being is almost completely dependent upon a state of nationality for securing a hearing upon the merits upon injuries done to him by other States.'[48]

Nottebohm *case*

The issue in the *Nottebohm* case was whether Liechtenstein could exercise diplomatic protection *vis-à-vis* Guatemala on behalf of Nottebohm, who had been granted, under the law of Liechtenstein, its nationality shortly after the

---

[46] *Barcelona Traction, Light and Power Company, Limited*, ICJ Reports, 1970, pp. 3, 32.
[47] *Ibid.*
[48] Myres S. McDougal, Harold D. Lasswell, Lu-Chu Chen, *Human Rights and World Public Order* (New Haven/London, 1980), p. 878. See to this effect *Panevezys–Saldutiskis Railway*, PCIJ, Series A/B, No. 76, p. 16. However, in the *Reparations* case, the Court observed that 'there are cases in which protection may be exercised by a State on behalf of persons not having its nationality' (ICJ Reports, 1949, p. 818).

outbreak of the Second World War. Nottebohm, a German national, had been a resident of Guatemala since 1905 and continued to reside there after the grant of Liechtenstein nationality. The Court held that, in view of the absence of bonds of attachment between Nottebohm and Liechtenstein, the latter was not entitled to extend its protection to Nottebohm *vis-à-vis* Guatemala and that, accordingly, its claim was inadmissible.[49] While this decision was widely criticized,[50] the 'genuine link' concept that it embodied has been sustained. The principle may have the result that no state is in a position to maintain a claim on behalf of an individual, a result which may foreclose the realization of that individual's human rights. Nevertheless, the law of international claims has traditionally been replete with limitations on the exercise of diplomatic protection which may have precisely such a result. But the question arises, if fundamental human rights do complement obligations that exist *erga omnes*, and if those rights indeed are of fundamental importance, should their pursuance on the international plane be so limited by the traditional rules of diplomatic protection?

Western Sahara

In the course of rendering its Advisory Opinion on the *Western Sahara*, the Court spoke of 'the right of that population [of the Western Sahara] to self-determination'[51] in terms that demonstrate its conviction that peoples have the right 'to determine their future political status by their own freely expressed will'.[52] It supported the application 'of the principle of self-determination through the free and genuine expression of the will of the peoples of the Territory'.[53]

Hostages *case*

In the case concerning *United States Diplomatic and Consular Staff in Tehran*, the Court, in holding unlawful the detention of the hostages, occupation of the Embassy of the United States and rifling of the Embassy archives, also held that:

> Wrongfully to deprive human beings of their freedom and to subject them to physical constraint in conditions of hardship is in itself manifestly incompatible with

---

[49] *Nottebohm* case, ICJ Reports, 1955, pp. 4, 26.

[50] See McDougal et al., *Human Rights and World Public Order*, p. 872 and the sources there cited. However, in the view of the writer of this chapter, the Court's judgment in *Nottebohm* was, on the particular facts of the case, well founded.

[51] *Western Sahara*, ICJ Reports, 1975, pp. 12, 36.

[52] *Ibid.*

[53] *Ibid.*, p. 68.

the principles of the Charter of the United Nations, as well as with the fundamental principles enunciated in the Universal Declaration of Human Rights.[54]

Subsequent grave and prolonged international incidents of hostage-taking were to show the continuing relevance of that holding to the contemporary world.

Military and Paramilitary Activities in and against Nicaragua

In the case of *Military and Paramilitary Activities in and against Nicaragua*, the Court made several holdings of interest – and controversy – in the sphere of human rights. In respect of mine-laying in Nicaraguan waters by United States agencies without US notice to international shipping, the Court, citing the above quotation from the *Corfu Channel* case, held that 'a breach of the principles of humanitarian law'[55] had been committed. It also concluded that the US did not exercise operational control over the Contras and thus could not be held responsible for violations of the law of war which might have been committed by the Contras.

The Court did consider the lawfulness of the production and dissemination by US officials of a war manual which had been provided to the Contras. In so doing, the Court held that the Geneva Conventions of 1949, in their common article 3, define rules that reflect 'elementary considerations of humanity' which are applicable as customary international law.[56] Doubt was expressed at the time by Judges Jennings and Ago,[57] and there has been question raised since, about whether the Court was correct in holding that the rules set out in the common article 3 of the Geneva Conventions have the status of customary international law,[58] a conclusion for which the Court supplied scant support. The Court held that the US was bound to, and had failed to, ensure respect for these rules, in their character as rules of

---

[54] *United States Diplomatic and Consular Staff in Tehran*, ICJ Reports, 1980, pp. 3,42; see quotation from *Corfu Channel* case on p. 330 above.

[55] *Military and Paramilitary Activities in and against Nicaragua*, ICJ Reports, 1986, pp. 14, 112.

[56] *Ibid.*, pp. 113–14.

[57] *Ibid.*, Dissenting Opinion of Judge Jennings, p. 537, and Separate Opinion of Judge Ago, p. 184.

[58] See Theodor Meron, *Human Rights and Humanitarian Norms as Customary Law* (Oxford, 1989), pp. 7–36; and Rosemary Abi-Saab, 'The "General Principles" of Humanitarian Law According to the International Court of Justice', *International Review of the Red Cross*, 256 (1987), p. 367. In earlier cases, the Court required for the establishment of a custom proof 'that the rule invoked . . . is in accordance with a constant and uniform usage practised by the States in question, and that this usage is the expression of a right . . . This follows from Article 38 of the Statute of the Court, which refers to international custom "as evidence of a general practice accepted as law"': *Asylum* case, ICJ Reports, 1950, pp. 276–7, and case concerning *Rights of Nationals of the United States of America in Morocco*, ICJ Reports, 1952, p. 200.

customary international law – rules that provide for humane treatment without any adverse distinction founded on race, colour, religion, sex, birth or wealth or other similar criteria, and that prohibit in respect of persons taking no part in hostilities violence to life and person, taking of hostages, humiliating and degrading treatment and arbitrary sentencing and execution. The Court held that the production and dissemination of a manual advocating some acts incompatible with these standards to have encouraged the commission by the Contras of acts contrary to general principles of humanitarian law.

As one justification of its activities towards Nicaragua, the US had publicly maintained (though it did not plead this position before the Court) that Nicaragua, upon the assumption of power by its revolutionary government, had undertaken commitments to the Organization of American States and its members to respect human rights, and in particular to hold free elections, which commitments it had failed to observe. The Court held that, even in the absence of such commitments, Nicaragua could not with impunity violate human rights. But it continued: 'However, where human rights are protected by international conventions, that protection takes the form of such arrangements for monitoring or ensuring respect for human rights as are provided for in the conventions themselves.'[59] The implication was that the US was not entitled to take other measures to uphold human rights in Nicaragua (and not being party to the conventions in question, it could not invoke them) – a position which may not be wholly consistent with the *erga omnes* character of human-rights obligations elsewhere affirmed by the Court. This holding has been strongly attacked as evidencing a regressive approach by the Court to questions of standing in the maintenance of human rights akin to the approach taken in the *South West Africa* cases.[60] It has been argued that the logic of the position taken by the Court in the *Nicaragua* case is: if a government abuses human rights, but is nevertheless a party to a human rights convention, other states are confined to seeking redress by the means provided by that convention, however limited in scope is the convention, however few the parties to it, and however inadequate those means may be. The Court's holding that, in law, Nicaragua had assumed only a political, not a legal, obligation through its assurances to the OAS, and that those assurances ran only to the Organization and not to its members, have also been criticized as factually and legally

---

[59] ICJ Reports, 1986, p. 134.
[60] Fernando R. Tesón, 'Le Peuple, C'Est Moi! The World Court and Human Rights', *American Journal of International Law*, 81 (1987), p. 173.

erroneous, inconsistent with the Court's jurisprudence, and conceptually regressive.[61]

The Court also held that 'while the United States might form its own appraisal of the situation as to respect for human rights in Nicaragua, the use of force could not be the appropriate method to monitor or ensure such respect'.[62] The Court concluded that the protection of human rights cannot be compatible with the mining of ports, the destruction of oil installations and support for the Contras. It therefore held that any argument derived from the protection of human rights in Nicaragua could not afford a legal justification for the conduct of the US: a holding, which, however, did not of itself exclude that the conduct was justified by considerations of collective self-defence. Whether the Court's extraordinary holdings of fact and law respecting issues of collective self-defence are persuasive poses issues beyond the scope of this chapter.

ELSI *case*

The case concerning *Elettronica Sicula SpA (ELSI)*[63] is the most recent illustration in the Court of a state taking up the claim of its national and espousing it in an area of human rights, i.e., property rights (albeit rights of a corporation, whose shares, however, are ultimately owned by human beings). In that case, the Court found no violation of such rights as established by treaty, and it also found to be absent a claimed arbitrary act, which it defined as an act contrary not to 'a rule of law' but 'to the rule of law'.[64]

Lockerbie *cases*

The underlying charges of fact at issue in the *Lockerbie* cases entail a startling violation of human rights, namely, the cold-blooded murder of hundreds of innocents who had the ill fortune to be passengers on PanAm Flight 103, or residents of the Scottish town of Lockerbie, when the aircraft was destroyed by a bomb.[65] But the questions dealt with in Libya's request for provisional measures in those cases did not directly engage that gross violation of human rights. It remains to be seen what issues will arise at the stage of the merits.

---

[61] *Ibid*. See also the Separate Opinion of Judge Ago, ICJ Reports, 1986, pp. 186–7, and my Dissent, *ibid.*, pp. 274, 382–5, 398–402.

[62] ICJ Reports, 1986, p. 134.

[63] *Elettronica Sicula SpA (ELSI)*, ICJ Reports, 1989, p. 15.

[64] *Ibid.*, p. 76.

[65] *Questions of Interpretation and Application of the 1971 Montreal Convention arising from the Aerial Incident at Lockerbie*, ICJ Reports, 1992, pp. 3, 144.

Genocide in Bosnia

Profound problems of human rights were directly at issue in the case concerning *Application of the Convention on the Prevention and Punishment of the Crime of Genocide*. Not dissimilar questions were posed by aspects of the 1973 case of *Trial of Pakistani Prisoners of War*, but in that case provisional measures were not ordered and the case was settled.[66] In the Bosnian case, the court issued two Orders in response to successive requests by Bosnia–Herzegovina for the indication of provisional measures.

In its Order of 8 April 1993, the Court, in treating allegations by Bosnia of promotion and commission of acts of genocide, and of unlawful armed attacks and multiple other violations of the sovereignty, territorial integrity and political independence of Bosnia by Yugoslavia (Serbia and Montenegro), found that the Genocide Convention appeared to offer a basis of jurisdiction to the extent the dispute related to acts of genocide. It observed that Yugoslavia for its part called for the imposition of provisional measures relating to war crimes and acts of genocide allegedly committed against Serbs living in Bosnia, and again held that its jurisdiction was confined to the Genocide Convention.[67] The Court concluded that, in the circumstances, 'there is grave risk of acts of genocide being committed', and 'whether or not such acts in the past may be legally imputable' to Yugoslavia or Bosnia–Herzegovina, they 'are under a clear obligation to do all in their power to prevent the commission of any such acts in the future'.[68]

The Court declared that

> The crime of genocide 'shocks the conscience of mankind, results in great losses to humanity . . . and is contrary to moral law and to the spirit and aims of the United Nations', in the words of General Assembly resolution 96 (I) of 11 December 1946 on 'the Crime of Genocide', which the Court recalled in its Advisory Opinion on Reservations on the Convention on Genocide.[69]

The Court indicated:

> A. (1) . . .
> The Government of the Federal Republic of Yugoslavia (Serbia and Montenegro) should immediately, in pursuance of its undertaking in the Convention on the Prevention and Punishment of the Crime of Genocide of

---

[66] *Trial of Pakistani Prisoners of War*, ICJ Reports, 1973, pp. 328, 344, 347.

[67] *Application of the Convention on the Prevention and Punishment of the Crime of Genocide*, ICJ Reports, 1993, pp. 2, 30.

[68] *Ibid.*, p. 22.

[69] *Ibid.*, p. 23.

9 December 1948, take all measures within its power to prevent commission of the crime of genocide;

(2) . . .

The Government of the Federal Republic of Yugoslavia (Serbia and Montenegro) should in particular ensure that any military, paramilitary or irregular armed units which may be directed or supported by it, as well as any organizations and persons which may be subject to its control, direction or influence, do not commit any acts of genocide, of conspiracy to commit genocide, of direct and public incitement to commit genocide, or of complicity in genocide, whether directed against the Muslim population of Bosnia and Herzegovina or against any other national, ethnical, racial or religious group;

B. . . .

The Government of the Federal Republic of Yugoslavia (Serbia and Montenegro) and the Government of the Republic of Bosnia and Herzegovina should not take any action and should ensure that no action is taken which may aggravate or extend the existing dispute over the prevention or punishment of the crime of genocide, or render it more difficult of solution.[70]

Bosnia-Herzegovina returned to the Court some three months later seeking additional interim measures of protection. Only some of those measures turned on charges of continued genocide, whereas measures sought by Yugoslavia did.[71] In response, the Court, stating that its jurisdiction was confined to the Genocide Convention and only embraced measures to be taken by the parties, but not by third states or other entities, recalled the holdings of its previous Order. It held that:

Whereas, since the Order of 8 April 1993 was made, and despite that Order, and despite many resolutions of the Security Council of the United Nations, great suffering and loss of life has been sustained by the population of Bosnia–Herzegovina in circumstances which shock the conscience of mankind and flagrantly conflict with moral law and the spirit and aims of the United Nations;

Whereas, since the order of 8 April 1993 was made, the grave risk which the Court then apprehended of action being taken which may aggravate or extend the existing dispute over the prevention and punishment of the crime of genocide, or render it more difficult of solution, has been deepened by the persistence of conflicts on the territory of Bosnia–Herzegovina and the commission of heinous acts in the course of those conflicts;

Whereas the Security Council of the United Nations in resolution 819 (1993) of 16 April 1993 took note of the Court's Order of 8 April 1993 in which the Court indicated that the Federal Republic of Yugoslavia (Serbia and Montenegro) should take all measures within its power to prevent the commission of the crime of genocide, and whereas the Security Council in that resolution reaffirmed its

---

[70] *Ibid.*, p. 24.   [71] *Ibid.*, pp. 325, 332–3, 334.

condemnation of all violations of international humanitarian law, in particular the practice of 'ethnic cleansing';

Whereas the Court, while taking into account *inter alia*, the replies of the two Parties to a question put to them at the hearings as to what steps had been taken by them 'to ensure compliance with the Court's Order of 8 April 1993', is not satisfied that all that might have been done has been done to prevent commission of the crime of genocide in the territory of Bosnia–Herzegovina, and to ensure that no action is taken which may aggravate or extend the existing dispute or render it more difficult of solution;

Whereas as the Court has previously found,

'When the Court finds that the situation requires that measures of this kind should be taken, it is incumbent on each party to take the Court's indication seriously into account . . . '

whereas this is particularly so in such a situation as now exists in Bosnia– Herzegovina where no reparation could efface the results of conduct which the Court may rule to have been contrary to international law;

Whereas the present perilous situation demands, not an indication of provisional measures additional to those indicated by the Court's Order of 8 April 1993 . . . but immediate and effective implementation of those measures.[72]

It then reaffirmed the provisional measures earlier ordered, 'which should be immediately and effectively implemented'.[73]

The merits of the case are pending.

Aliens

Limitations of space permit no more than reference to salient cases of the International Court of Justice bearing upon the treatment of aliens and their interests. Some cases already discussed in their human rights aspects also involve the treatment of aliens, e.g., the *Reparations* case, the *Asylum* and *Haya de la Torre* cases, *United States Diplomatic and Consular Staff in Tehran*, and *Military and Paramilitary Activities in and against Nicaragua*. In addition, the following cases may be noted.

Anglo–Iranian Oil Co. *case*

In the *Anglo-Iranian Oil Company* case, the United Kingdom, exercising its right of diplomatic protection of the company, requested a number of provisional measures. Iran maintained that the dispute over its treatment

---

[72] *Ibid.*, pp. 348–9.

[73] Case concerning *Application of the Convention on the Prevention and Punishment of the Crime of Genocide (Bosnia and Herzegovina v. Yugoslavia (Serbia and Montenegro)*, Order of 13 September 1993, pp. 27, 28.

of Anglo-Iranian pertained to the exercise of its sovereign rights and 'was exclusively within the national jurisdiction' of Iran.[74] The Court, noting that the dispute concerned the alleged violation of international law by the breach of the company's concession agreement and by a denial of justice which would follow from Iran's refusal to accept arbitration in accordance with that agreement, held that 'it cannot be accepted *a priori* that a claim based on such a complaint falls completely outside the scope of international jurisdiction'.[75] It indicated substantial provisional measures which, however, Iran frustrated. Thereafter, the Court considered whether it had jurisdiction to adjudicate the merits of the dispute, a question which essentially turned on interpretation of the scope of the adherence of Iran and the UK to the Court's compulsory jurisdiction under the Optional Clause of the Statute of the Court. The Court held that the Iranian declaration was limited to disputes relating to the application of treaties or conventions accepted by Iran after the ratification of the declaration; and the treaties on which the UK relied antedated that declaration. The UK additionally argued that the concession contract of 1933 between the Iranian government and the company had a double character, also giving rise to a treaty relationship between the UK and Iran because it was concluded pursuant to the good offices of the Council of the League of Nations. The Court rejected that argument, observing that the UK enjoyed no privity of contract under the concession agreement; it did not regulate in any way relations between the two governments.[76] On the facts, that conclusion was compelling, but it has no implications for the responsibility of states in respect of rights that aliens enjoy under contracts and concessions with those states.

Interhandel *case*

In the *Interhandel* case, the Court sustained a preliminary objection by the United States to the admissibility of Switzerland's application, on the ground of failure to exhaust local remedies. In so doing, it held:

> The rule that local remedies must be exhausted before international proceedings may be instituted is a well-established rule of customary international law; the rule has been generally observed in cases in which a State has adopted the cause of its national whose rights are claimed to have been disregarded in another State in violation of international law. Before resort may be had to an international court in such a situation, it has been considered necessary that the State where the

---

[74] *Anglo-Iranian Oil Co.* case, ICJ Reports, 1951, pp. 89, 92.
[75] *Ibid.*, p. 93.
[76] *Anglo-Iranian Oil Company* case, ICJ Reports, 1952, pp. 93, 111–13.

violation occurred should have an opportunity to redress it by its own means, within the framework of its own domestic legal system. *A fortiori* the rule must be observed when domestic proceedings are pending, as in the case of Interhandel, and when the two actions, that of the Swiss company in the United States courts and that of the Swiss Government in this Court, in its principal Submission, are designed to obtain the same result: the restitution of the assets of Interhandel vested in the United States.[77]

Barcelona Traction

Aspects of this exceptionally controverted and controversial case and judgment have been quoted above. It contains many more elements of interest to the situation of aliens, despite the failure of the Court to adjudge the merits of the dispute. Thus the Court stated in respect of the nature of diplomatic protection:

78. The Court would here observe that, within the limits prescribed by international law, a State may exercise diplomatic protection by whatever means and to whatever extent it thinks fit, for it is its own right that the State is asserting. Should the natural or legal persons on whose behalf it is acting consider that their rights are not adequately protected, they have no remedy in international law. All they can do is to resort to municipal law, if means are available, with a view to furthering their cause or obtaining redress. The municipal legislator may lay upon the State an obligation to protect its citizens abroad, and may also confer upon the national a right to demand the performance of that obligation, and clothe the right with the corresponding sanctions. However, all these questions remain within the province of municipal law and do not affect the position internationally.

79. The State must be viewed as the sole judge to decide whether its protection will be granted, to what extent it is granted, and when it will cease. It retains in this respect a discretionary power the exercise of which may be determined by considerations of a political or other nature, unrelated to the particular case. Since the claim of the State is not identical with that of the individual or corporate person whose cause is espoused, the State enjoys complete freedom of action. Whatever the reasons for any change of attitude, the fact cannot in itself constitute a justification for the exercise of diplomatic protection by another government, unless there is some independent and otherwise valid ground for that.

80. This cannot be regarded as amounting to a situation where a violation of law remains without remedy: in short, a legal vacuum. There is no obligation upon the possessors of rights to exercise them. Sometimes no remedy is sought, though rights are infringed. To equate this with the creation of a vacuum would be to equate a right with an obligation.[78]

---

[77] *Interhandel* case, ICJ Reports, 1959, pp. 6, 27.
[78] *Barcelona Traction, Light and Power Company, Limited*, ICJ Reports, 1970, pp. 3, 44–5.

In support of its dispositive ruling that Belgium lacked standing to maintain suit on behalf of Belgian shareholders of a Canadian company – and in endeavouring to meet the charge that Barcelona Traction and its shareholders were the victims of a massive denial of justice – the Court observed:

> 90. Thus, in the present state of the law, the protection of shareholders requires that recourse be had to treaty stipulations or special agreements directly concluded between the private investor and the State in which the investment is placed. States ever more frequently provide for such protection, in both bilateral and multilateral relations, either by means of special instruments or within the framework of wider economic arrangements. Indeed, whether in the form of multilateral or bilateral treaties between States, or in that of agreements between States and companies, there has since the Second World War been considerable development in the protection of foreign investments. The instruments in question contain provisions as to jurisdiction and procedure in case of disputes concerning the treatment of investing companies by the States in which they invest capital. Sometimes companies are themselves vested with a direct right to defend their interests against States through prescribed procedures. No such instrument is in force between the Parties to the present case.
>
> 91. With regard more particularly to human rights, to which reference has already been made in paragraph 34 of this Judgment, it should be noted that these also include protection against denial of justice. However, on the universal level, the instruments which embody human rights do not confer on States the capacity to protect the victims of infringements of such rights irrespective of their nationality. It is therefore still on the regional level that a solution to this problem has had to be sought; thus, within the Council of Europe, of which Spain is not a member, the problem of admissibility encountered by the claim in the present case has been resolved by the European Convention on Human Rights, which entitled each State which is a party to the Convention to lodge a complaint against any other contracting State for violation of the Convention, irrespective of the nationality of the victim.[79]

The consistency of this holding with the logic of its position, set out in paragraphs 33 and 34 of the judgment quoted earlier, that basic human rights give rise to international obligations *erga omnes*, may be questioned. Presumably the Court's answer would be that the rights sought to be protected diplomatically are not basic human rights: as it stated in paragraph 35 of the judgment, 'obligations the performance of which is the subject of diplomatic protection are not of the same category' as 'obligations *erga omnes*'. But is this necessarily true? It may be that, in some cases, diplomatic protection is extended in instances of violation of fundamental human rights; in other cases,

[79] *Ibid.*, p. 47.

not. A supplementary answer of the Court may be that, even if there is a violation of an obligation *erga omnes*, it does not follow that any state to which that obligation runs has the capacity to maintain a claim in respect of it; there may be rights without remedies (so paragraph 91 imports). That too is not a wholly convincing – and certainly not a progressive – position.

The Court, apparently sensitive to the charge that its judgment was at odds with the equities of the case, further stated:

> 96. The Court considers that the adoption of the theory of diplomatic protection of shareholders as such, by opening the door to competing diplomatic claims, could create an atmosphere of confusion and insecurity in international economic relations. The danger would be all the greater inasmuch as the shares of companies whose activity is international are widely scattered and frequently change hands. It might perhaps be claimed that, if the right of protection belonging to the national States of the shareholders were considered as only secondary to that of the national State of the company, there would be less danger of difficulties of the kind contemplated. However, the Court must state that the essence of a secondary right is that it only comes into existence at the time when the original right ceases to exist. As the right of protection vested in the national State of the company cannot be regarded as extinguished because it is not exercised, it is not possible to accept the proposition that in case of its non-exercise the national States of the share-holders have a right of protection secondary to that of the national State of the company . . .
>
> 97. The situations in which foreign shareholders in a company wish to have recourse to diplomatic protection by their own national State may vary. It may happen that the national State of the company simply refuses to grant it its diplomatic protection, or that it begins to exercise it (as in the present case) but does not pursue its action to the end. It may also happen that the national State of the company and the State which has committed a violation of international law with regard to the company arrive at a settlement of the matter, by agreeing on compensation for the company, but that the foreign shareholders find the compensation insufficient. Now, as a matter of principle, it would be difficult to draw a distinction between these three cases so far as the protection of foreign shareholders by their national State is concerned, since in each case they may have suffered real damage. Furthermore, the national State of the company is perfectly free to decide how far it is appropriate for it to protect the company, and is not bound to make public the reasons for its decision. To reconcile this discretionary power of the company's national State with a right of protection falling to the shareholders' national State would be particularly difficult when the former State has concluded, with the State which has contravened international law with regard to the company, an agreement granting the company compensation which the foreign shareholders find inadequate. If, after such a settlement, the national State of the foreign shareholders could in its turn put forward a claim based on the same facts, this would be likely to introduce into the

negotiation of this kind of agreement a lack of security which would be contrary to the stability which it is the object of international law to establish in international relations.

98. . . .

99. It should also be observed that the promoters of a company whose operations will be international must take into account the fact that States have, with regard to their nationals, a discretionary power to grant diplomatic protection or to refuse it. When establishing a company in a foreign country, its promoters are normally impelled by particular considerations; it is often a question of tax or other advantages offered by the host State. It does not seem to be in any way inequitable that the advantages thus obtained should be balanced by the risks arising from the fact that the protection of the company and hence of its shareholders is thus entrusted to a State other than the national State of the shareholders.[80]

ELSI *case*

The case of *Elettronica Sicula SpA (ELSI)* turned on whether the requisition by Sicilian authorities of an electronics factory in Sicily of an Italian company whose shares were wholly owned by two American corporations constituted a violation of terms of a Treaty of Friendship, Commerce and Navigation in force between the United States of America and Italy. The Treaty assured American investors of the right to manage and control their investments in Italy. The essential claim of the US was that the requisition, which had been held to be unlawful by an Italian court, interfered with management and control by preventing the orderly liquidation of the assets of ELSI and by precipitating ELSI's bankruptcy. The Chamber of the Court (of which Judge Sir Robert Jennings was a member) held against the US. The Chamber appeared to accept, if only implicitly, that the requisition deprived the American owners of their Treaty entitlement to 'control and manage' ELSI, but it found that nevertheless the Treaty had not been violated. This, in the majority's view, was because, by the time of the requisition, rights of management and control no longer existed either because the feasibility of an orderly liquidation of ELSI's assets by ELSI at the time in question had not been sufficiently established or because ELSI's state of insolvency by then had given rise to an obligation under Italian law on the part of ELSI to have petitioned for its bankruptcy.[81]

The case was resolved essentially on factual grounds – whether persuasively is open to question. Learned commentary has been critical – in the opinion

---

[80] *Ibid.*, pp. 49–50.
[81] *Elettronica Sicula SpA (ELSI)*, ICJ Reports, 1979, pp. 48ff.

of this dissenter,[82] rightly critical.[83] The implications of the judgment for international law are limited but not altogether supportive of the efficacy of treaties protective of foreign investment. The judgment's classic definition of what is arbitrary has been noted above.[84] The judgment is also noteworthy in its acceptance of the position that the rule of exhaustion of local remedies requires no more than exhaustion of 'all reasonable' local remedies.[85]

[82] *Ibid.*
[83] See F. A. Mann, 'Foreign Investment in the International Court of Justice: The ELSI Case', *American Journal of International Law*, 86 (1992), pp. 92–102; and Ignaz Seidl-Hohenveldern, 'ELSI and Badger, The Two Raytheon Cases', *Rivista di Diritto Internazionale Privato e Processuale*, 26 (1990), pp. 261–76.
[84] ICJ Reports, 1979, p. 76.
[85] *Ibid.*, pp. 42–4, 94.

18

The International Court of Justice and the right of peoples to self-determination

Antonio Cassese

℘

1. No one can deny that self-determination has been one of the most important driving forces in the new international community. It has set in motion a restructuring and redefinition of the world community's basic 'rules of the game'. At the same time, its ideological and political origins render self-determination a multifaceted but extremely ambiguous concept: a concept that is, at one and the same time, both boldly radical (in that it promotes democratic self-government, and free access of peoples to the role of inter-national actors) and deeply subversive and disruptive (in that it undermines territorial integrity and may lead to the fragmentation of the international community into a myriad of national or ethnic entities, all poised to fight one another). Self-determination is also significant jurisprudentially. For one thing, its study enables us to inquire into the underlying tensions and contradictions of international relations as well as the interplay of law and politics on the world scene. For another, self-determination belongs to an area where states' interests and views are so conflicting that states are unable to agree upon definite and specific standards of behaviour and must therefore be content with the loose formulation of very general guidelines or principles. Indeed, this is an area where it is easier for states to proclaim principles than distil hard-and-fast rules: principles, being general, woolly and multifaceted, lend themselves to various and even contradictory applications; in addition, they are suscep-tible to being manipulated and used for conflicting purposes. On the other hand, principles have great normative potential and dynamic force: among other things, one can deduce from them specific rules, to the extent that these rules are not at variance with state practice.[1]

Although, as I have just pointed out, this is an extremely controversial and confused area of international law, and the views and attitudes of states as well

---

[1] For an insightful treatment of the principles of international law, see M. Virally, 'Panorama du droit international contemporain', *Recueil des cours*, 183 (1983, V), pp. 174–5.

as United Nations practice are fairly contradictory, the contention can be made that self-determination is now firmly entrenched in the corpus of inter-national customary law in at least three areas: as an anti-colonial principle, as a ban on foreign military occupation, and as a standard requiring full access to government for racial groups.[2] Clearly, in the first two cases we are confronted with the external dimension of self-determination, whereas in the third case international law provides for internal self-determination. In addition, the contention can be made that a general rule is now gradually emerging to the effect that peoples of sovereign states are entitled to internal self-determination, i.e. democratic government.

2. So far the ICJ has only dealt with self-determination in its anti-colonial dimension. Of course, this is not because of a choice made by the Court, but merely because the cases brought before it only involved questions relating to colonial countries. It is only natural that over the past years the Court should be exclusively seized with this category of issues. For one thing, in the 1960s and 1970s the aftermath of colonialism was still a matter of, at least legal, controversy and it was hoped that some outstanding disputes that states had been unable to settle at the political level could find their solution on a legal plane. For another, issues relating to foreign military occupation (think of the Arab territories occupied by Israel following the 1967 armed conflict, or the occupation of Afghanistan by the Soviet Union in 1980) were so heavily loaded at the political level that any judicial settlement was utterly unthink-able. By the same token, states avoided taking up another dimension of self-determination at the judicial level, that is internal self-determination *qua* right of the whole population of a sovereign state to free and unhindered access to government without any discrimination based on race. There were at least two states in which this right to self-determination was being breached: Southern Rhodesia and South Africa. In both cases states and the relevant bodies of the United Nations ultimately chose a political course of action: they passed resolutions proclaiming general principles (I am referring in particular to the 1970 Declaration on Friendly Relations) and, what is more important, they recommended economic and other sanctions against those states.

Thus, historical and political circumstances led the Court to deal with only the most 'classical' or 'traditional' dimension of self-determination: anti-colonialism. However, even in this area which, among other things, is characterized by less rudimentary international legal regulation, the Court had

---

[2] For a detailed analysis of the status of current international law, I refer to my book on *Self-determination of Peoples – A Legal Reappraisal* (Cambridge, 1995), pp. 37–162.

the opportunity to clarify important matters, spell out loose principles, and set out notions that were previously hidden in the interstices of the existing body of international resolutions and other manifestations of so-called soft law.

Three cases stand out: the *Namibia* case (Advisory Opinion handed down on 21 June 1971), the *Western Sahara* case (Advisory Opinion of 16 October 1975) and the *Frontier Dispute* (judgment delivered on 22 December 1986). I shall briefly focus on the relevant sections of these three pronouncements, with a view to emphasizing the most significant points of the contribution made by the Court.

3. In the Advisory Opinion on *Namibia* the question put to the Court was about 'the legal consequences for States of the continued presence of South Africa in Namibia, notwithstanding Security Council resolution 276 (1970)', i.e. the resolution declaring South African control over Namibia illegal. For the purpose of answering this question, the Court had among other things to delve into the question of the origin and functioning of the C mandate conferred on the Republic of South Africa following the First World War. In this regard the Court made four important points that warrant emphasis.

First of all, after noting that even under the League of Nations system the mandatory powers were to pursue the interests of the inhabitants of the territories under their control,[3] the Court went on to enunciate an exceedingly important legal principle of intertemporal law, whereby old legal institutions ought not to be viewed statically, i.e. within the context surrounding their birth, but must be interpreted and viewed in the light of the legal principles prevailing at the time when legal issues arose concerning them.[4] The Court applied this principle to the Mandate over Namibia and pointed out the following:

> In the domain to which the present proceedings relate, the last fifty years, as indicated above, have brought important developments. These developments leave little doubt that the ultimate objective of the sacred trust was the self-determination and independence of the peoples concerned. In this domain, as elsewhere, the *corpus juris gentium* has been considerably enriched, and this the Court, if it has faithfully to discharge its functions, may not ignore.[5]

---

[3] In this connection the Court quoted (p. 29, para. 46) its Advisory Opinion of 1950 on the *International Status of South West Africa*, where it had stated that 'the Mandate was created, in the interest of the inhabitants of the territory, and of humanity in general, as an international institution with an international object – a sacred trust of civilisation' (ICJ Reports, 1950, p. 132).

[4] 'An international instrument has to be interpreted and applied within the framework of the entire legal system prevailing at the time of the interpretation' (ICJ Reports, 1971, p. 31, para. 53).

[5] *Ibid.*, pp. 31–2, para. 53.

The Court thus rightly emphasized that the principle of self-determination, which in the aftermath of the First World War had not yet acquired a foothold in the international community, became from 1945 an overarching principle of the international community; hence, it must of necessity apply to pre-existing legal institutions as well. In other words, self-determination, besides applying to current and future international relations, also constitutes a funda-mental standard of behaviour which, in a way, projects itself into the past.

A second point in the Advisory Opinion needs to be stressed. In speaking of the legal developments subsequent to the establishment of the mandated territories under the League of Nations system, the Court stated that these

> developments, as enshrined in the Charter of the United Nations, made the principle of self-determination applicable to all of them [i.e. the non-self-governing territories] . . . A further important stage in this development was the Declaration on the Granting of Independence to Colonial Countries and Peoples (General Assembly resolution 1514 (XV) of 14 December 1960) which embraces all peoples and all territories which 'have not yet attained independence'.[6]

Interestingly, by this statement the Court clarified and endorsed a legal development that had occurred between 1945 and 1950. In 1945 the UN Charter had envisaged external self-determination only for territories falling within the international trusteeship system, and not for other non-self-governing territories.[7] However, the evolution of both international practice and of the prevailing views of states, which culminated in the 1960 Declaration, made it clear that the right to external self-determination belonged to all dependent territories. The Court authoritatively confirmed this legal evolution by endorsement with its formal seal.

The Opinion deserves comment in a third respect. The Court had the opportunity to mention article 80, paragraph 1 of the UN Charter, which among other things refers to 'the rights of peoples' of non-self-governing territories.[8] In commenting on this provision, the Court underscored the

---

[6] *Ibid.*, p. 31, para. 52.

[7] Article 76 *b* of the Charter provides that one of the 'basic objectives' of the trusteeship system is to promote the progressive development of the inhabitants of the trust territories 'towards *self-government or independence* as may be appropriate to the particular circumstances of each territory and its peoples and the freely expressed wishes of the peoples concerned'. By contrast, article 73, concerning non-self-governing territories, provides in para. *b* that members of the UN that have or assume responsibilities for the administration of such territories must, among other things 'develop *self-government*' (emphasis added).

[8] This provision reads as follows:

> Except as may be agreed upon in individual trusteeship agreements, made under Articles 77, 79 and 81, placing each territory under the trusteeship system, and until such agreements have been concluded, nothing in this Chapter shall be construed in or of itself to alter in any manner rights

importance of the reference to the rights of 'peoples' of those territories. It pointed out the following:

> A striking feature of this provision is the stipulation in favour of the preservation of the rights of 'any peoples', thus clearly including the inhabitants of the mandated territories and, in particular, their indigenous populations. These rights were thus confirmed to have an existence independent of that of the League of Nations.[9]

It would thus seem that the Court did not share the view of those commentators who maintain that, in legal terms proper, it is inaccurate to speak of 'rights' accruing to peoples, for under current international law legal rights and obligations are respectively conferred or imposed exclusively on states.[10] Arguably, by emphasizing the 'rights' of dependent peoples, the Court took the view that in international law peoples as such can become holders of rights and obligations. One may add that, although the Court did not specify the rights conferred on peoples, it could be inferred that they should at least include 'the right to self-determination' (probably in its 'external' dimension – that is, the right to independent status or to association or integration with an existing state).[11]

There is a fourth point in the Court's Opinion which should not be passed over in silence. The government of South Africa had contended before the Court that it had promoted to the utmost the well-being and progress of the inhabitants of Namibia, and that in particular South Africa's policy of separate development, or apartheid, did not constitute a breach of its international obligations. The Court consequently dwelt, if only briefly, on the matter and found that apartheid constituted 'a denial or fundamental human rights' and hence 'a flagrant violation of the purposes and principles of the

---

whatsoever of any States or any peoples or the terms of existing international instruments to which Members of the United Nations may respectively be parties.

[9] ICJ Reports, 1971, p. 33, para. 59.

[10] It suffices to mention here one of the most authoritative of such commentators, namely G. Arangio-Ruiz, 'The Normative Role of the General Assembly of the United Nations and the Declaration of Principles of Friendly Relations', *Recueil des cours*, 137 (1972, 3), pp. 561–71.

[11] It should, however, be mentioned that the Court in passing adverted to some 'rights' of dependent peoples. Thus, for instance, it held that South Africa, by illegally occupying Namibia, incurred international responsibility and also remained 'accountable for any violations of its international obligations, or of the rights of the people of Namibia' (ICJ Reports, 1971, p. 54, para. 118). The Court also held that 'as to the general consequences resulting from the illegal presence of South Africa in Namibia, all States should bear in mind that the injured entity is a people which must look to the international community for assistance in its progress towards the goals for which the sacred trust was instituted' (*ibid.*, p. 56, para. 127).

Charter'.[12] It is thus apparent that the Court looked upon apartheid only as a gross breach of individual human rights, and not as a violation of the right of the whole population to internal self-determination. In this connection it should be recalled that in 1970 the General Assembly had proclaimed in the 'Declaration on Friendly Relations' that the failure by a sovereign state to grant to a racial group the right to take part freely in government amounted to a breach of the right to (internal) self-determination.

The conclusion is thus warranted that in 1971 the Court, while it enhanced the right of colonial peoples to external self-determination, did not lay sufficient emphasis on the internal dimension of the principle.

4. Now let us turn to the Advisory Opinion on *Western Sahara*, where the Court had the opportunity to dwell at greater length on the issue of self-determination of dependent peoples.

It is well known that the General Assembly had asked the Court to address the following two questions: (1) Was Western Sahara at the time of colonization by Spain a territory belonging to no one (*terra nullius*)? (2) If not, what were the legal ties between this territory and the Kingdom of Morocco and the Mauritanian entity? Plainly, neither of these two questions directly related to self-determination, i.e. to the problem of how the population of Western Sahara could exercise its right to freely decide on its international and internal status. However, it should be noted that the General Assembly had asked the Court for an Opinion so as to be in a position to decide on the choice of a policy designed to accelerate the decolonization process in Western Sahara. Indeed, the states directly concerned (Spain, Morocco, Mauritania and Algeria), while putting different views before the Court, all referred to self-determination. Spain argued that the questions put to the Court were irrelevant, because the General Assembly had already stated that the question was to be viewed within the context of decolonization and had also pronounced on the method of decolonization (namely by consultation with the population concerned through a referendum to be conducted by Spain as the administering power, under United Nations auspices). Morocco countered instead that the two questions were relevant, because the General Assembly was free to choose between two options (self-determination or reintegration of the territory with Morocco as the mother country from which

---

[12] *Ibid.*, p. 57, para. 131. Although article 1 of the UN Charter includes among the purposes of the UN the promotion of respect for the self-determination of peoples, the emphasis placed by the Court on human rights (another goal of the Organization laid down in article 1) leaves room for believing that the Court intended to refer to human rights exclusively.

it had been detached in the process of colonization). Mauritania also argued that the two questions were relevant: the General Assembly was to choose between self-determination and respect for national unity and territorial integrity. In the case at issue it ought to give priority to territorial integrity, since Western Sahara was a territory created by a colonizing power to the detriment of a country to which it belonged. Algeria, like Morocco and Mauritania, argued that the Court should comply with the request made by the General Assembly but, unlike Morocco and Mauritania, suggested that the Court should exclusively base itself on self-determination as the fundamental principle governing decolonization.

Faced with this wide range of views, the Court stated that, although the question of self-determination was not the subject of the questions put to it, it was bound to deal with it. According to the Court at least two grounds supported this view. First, 'in the exercise of its functions [the Court] is necessarily called upon to take into account existing rules of international law which are directly connected with the terms of the request [for an Advisory Opinion] and indispensable for the proper interpretation and understanding of its Opinion'.[13] Second, the Court had to appraise the correctness or otherwise of Spain's objections that the two questions put to the Court were irrelevant. To this end, the Court found it necessary 'to recall briefly the basic principles governing the decolonization policy of the General Assembly, the general lines of previous General Assembly resolutions on the question of Western Sahara, and the preparatory work and context of resolution 3292 (XXIX)'. The Court thus set out to delve into the principle of self-determination.

Whether or not the reasons offered by the Court for its examination of self-determination are plausible, unquestionably it was most fortunate that the Court should pronounce on the matter, thereby casting light on a complex and intricate area of new international law.

5. The views expressed by the Court are exceedingly important in at least four respects. First, the Court took up the statement made in the Opinion on *Namibia* to the effect that by the 1970s the principle of self-determination was applicable to all dependent peoples, and that therefore all of them were entitled to opt for independence, if they so wished.[14] Thus the Court added weight to its previous pronouncement on the matter. The authoritative nature of such pronouncements irrefutably establishes that the granting of such a right to all non–self-governing territories has become part of

---

[13] ICJ Reports, 1975, p. 30, para. 52.   [14] *Ibid.*, p. 31, para. 54.

customary international law. Clearly, in this process of formation of a general rule on the matter, the Court's contribution has been of the utmost importance.

Second, and most importantly, the Court brought to the forefront the very essence of the principle of self-determination: 'the need to pay regard to the freely expressed will of peoples'.[15] This ruling has a twofold importance: it is important with regard to the specific context of colonial self-determination; it is also significant as regards the general concept of self-determination. From the point of view of colonial self-determination, the Court made an important contribution by clarifying the status of international law concerning the implementation of the right to self-determination belonging to dependent peoples. Indeed, prior to the Court's Opinion it was not clear whether the free and genuine expression of the will of dependent populations was always needed. In particular, it was not clear whether such expression of will – required when the dependent people was offered the choice between free association and integration with an independent state – could be dispensed with when the 'dominating' power decided to grant a colonial people political independence. Neither the text of the relevant General Assembly resolutions,[16] nor the practice of colonial states and the UN were conclusive of the matter:[17] such practice, which seemed to support the view that the

---

[15] *Ibid.*, p. 33, para. 59; see also p. 32, para. 55 in f.

[16] General Assembly resolution 1514 (XV), adopted on 14 December 1960, and containing the Declaration on the Granting of Independence to Colonial Countries and Peoples, lays down in operative paragraph 5 that 'immediate steps shall be taken, in Trust and Non-Self-Governing Territories or all other territories which have not yet attained independence, to transfer all powers to the peoples of those territories, without any conditions or reservations, *in accordance with their freely expressed will and desire*, without any distinction as to race, creed or colour, in order to enable them to enjoy complete independence and freedom' (emphasis added). This resolution would thus seem always to require a free expression of popular will. However, resolution 1541 (XV), adopted on 15 December 1960 and outlining the principles that should guide members in determining whether or not an obligation exists to transmit the information called for under article 7 (*e*) of the Charter, takes a different view. After providing in principle VI that a dependent territory can be said to have reached a full measure of self-government in three instances (emergence as a sovereign independent state, free association with an independent state and integration with an independent state), principles VII and IX of the resolution required the free expression of the wishes of the population concerned only for the cases of association or integration with an independent state, and not for the case of accession of colonial peoples to political independence.

[17] See in particular A. Rigo Sureda, *The Evolution of the Right of Self-determination: A Study of the United Nations Practice* (Leyden, 1973); J. F. Engers, 'From Sacred Trust to Self-determination', *Netherlands International Law Review*, 24 (1977), pp. 85ff; J. Crawford, *The Creation of States in International Law* (Oxford, 1979), pp. 89ff; M. Pomerance, *Self-determination in Law and Practice* (The Hague, 1982), pp. 9ff; J. Charpentier, 'Autodétermination et décolonisation', in *Mélanges C. Chaumont* (Paris, 1984), pp. 117ff; M. Shaw, *Title to Territory in Africa* (Oxford, 1986), pp. 92ff; T. M. Franck, *The Power of Legitimacy among Nations* (New York/Oxford, 1990), pp. 160ff.

peoples concerned were always to be consulted, did not clearly show whether referendums or plebiscites were held pursuant to a legal obligation incumbent upon the state concerned, or simply for the sake of being seen to follow UN practice. The Court definitively settled the matter by prescribing a free and genuine expression of the will of the population concerned in any instance of exercise of self-determination by a colonial people, subject to two exceptions. These apply when one is not faced with a 'people' proper and when 'special circumstances' make a plebiscite or referendum unnecessary. However, the Court unfortunately left these exceptions undefined.

The aforementioned dictum of the Court is also important outside the colonial dimension, in that it enunciates the essential nucleus of self-determination, whatever the context within which the concept is applied. Indeed, although in its Opinion the Court only dealt with colonial self-determination, there is room for believing that its pronouncement was intended to have a much broader purport, so much so that it can also be easily applied to a non-colonial context whenever the question of self-determination is at stake. Arguably, one of the areas where the Court's dictum could apply is that of transfer of territorial sovereignty by one state to another by bilateral agreement. It can be contended that in the case of such transfer, the states involved are duty bound to ascertain the wishes of the population concerned by means of a referendum or plebiscite, or by any other appropriate means capable of ensuring a free and genuine expression of will.[18]

Third, the Court adroitly placed the two questions put to it by the General Assembly within the general framework of self-determination. After pointing out, in rather loose terms, that these two questions 'must be considered in the whole context of the decolonization process',[19] the Court moved on to specifics. It stated:

> The right of self-determination leaves the General Assembly a measure of discretion with respect to the forms and procedures by which that right is to be realized . . . As to the future action of the General Assembly, various possibilities exist, for instance with regard to consultations between the interested States, and the procedures and guarantees required for ensuring a free and genuine expression of the will of the people.[20]

---

[18] A contrary view, to the effect that in case of cession no obligation to consult the population concerned exists, is held by such authorities as L. Oppenheim – H. Lauterpacht (ed.), *Oppenheim's International Law* (8th edn, London, 1955), vol. I, pp. 551–2 and I. Brownlie, *Principles of International Law* (4th edn, Oxford, 1993), p. 170. It would seem that R. Y. Jennings, *The Acquisition of Territory in International Law* (Manchester, 1963), p. 78 shares this view.

[19] ICJ Reports, 1975, p. 36, para. 71.

[20] *Ibid.*, p. 36, para. 71, and p. 37, para. 72.

One should not underestimate the importance of this statement, in spite of its expression in such terse terms. The Court clearly implied that, whenever self-determination is at issue, the states concerned should be consulted, at least to the extent that such consultations may facilitate the implementation of self-determination and do not tend to negate or pre-empt the expression of popular will. The Court also laid down the concept that there may be various procedures acceptable for the expression of popular will (referendums, popular consultations, etc.), provided that they enable the population to manifest its choice in a 'free and genuine' way. The Court also pointed out that there ought to be guarantees ensuring that this will is 'free and genuine'. As is plainly evident, notwithstanding the concise drafting of the ruling, it formulated legal standards of sweeping import.

The Court's Opinion is also important in a fourth respect. In pronouncing upon the question of whether or not Western Sahara was *terra nullius* at the time of colonization by Spain, the Court attached importance both to the existence in Western Sahara of indigenous populations and to the conclusion, by such populations, of agreements with the colonizing power, Spain. The Court concluded its analysis with the proposition that the territory was not *terra nullius*. One might be led to believe that the Court thus simply took a stand between the two schools of thought that fought a wrangled battle at the beginning of this century in the legal literature. The first espoused the view that the so-called colonial protectorates which applied between a colonial power and the indigenous population were international treaties proper.[21] As a consequence, the legal title of the colonial power could not be classified as original by virtue of conquest or occupation, but was derivative from the agreement establishing the protectorate. The second school of thought argued that colonial protectorates were merely legal fictions designed to camouflage the reality of colonial conquest – which constituted the sole and veritable title to territorial sovereignty over dependent peoples.[22] However, I suggest that the Court's view was not put forward for academic purposes or, at any rate, has weight going beyond its theoretical value. Arguably the Court, although certainly aware of the political and legal reality of colonial protectorates – a reality so aptly emphasized by such authorities as Westlake[23] and Brierly[24] –

---

[21] See for instance D. Anzilotti, *Corso di diritto internazionale* (1928; 4th edn, Padua, 1955), vol. I, pp. 117–18.

[22] See for instance Oppenheim and Lauterpacht, *International Law*, vol. I, p. 196.

[23] J. Westlake, *International Law* (2nd edn, Cambridge, 1910–12), vol. I, p. 120.

[24] J. L. Brierly, *The Law of Nations* (5th edn, Oxford, 1955), pp. 158–9:

> In the latter half of the nineteenth century the appetites of the colonizing states of Europe for new territory in Africa outran their powers of digestion, and they introduced forms of staking out their

aimed at enhancing, even retrospectively, the role and importance of indigenous peoples. In other terms, the Court once again projected into the past the significance of self-determination and the underlying notion that peoples are not mere pawns in the hands of sovereign states, but conglomerates of individuals whose wishes and aspirations must be taken into account and given legal force as much as possible.

It should be added that the Court's dictum may also apply to present or future relations. Indeed, although the Court dwelt on the question whether Western Sahara was *terra nullius* at the time of Spanish colonization, one may legitimately infer consequences from the Court's reasoning which apply to other situations as well. One of these inferences is as follows. Whenever there are territories inhabited by indigenous populations that are collectively organized (although not in such a manner as to constitute a state proper) and the state wielding sovereign authority over such territories decides to withdraw, it does not follow that the territories automatically become *terra nullius*, and hence open to appropriation by any state. Even if the indigenous populations may not come to be regarded as organized in the form of a state, they must be enabled freely to express their will as to the international status of the territory, i.e. whether they wish to associate or integrate into an existing sovereign state, or acquire some sort of international status gradually leading to independent statehood.

6. The Court returned to the question of colonial self-determination in the *Frontier Dispute* case. On this occasion it tackled the issue of the relationship between the right of colonial peoples to self-determination and observance of the general rule of international law imposing respect for the territorial boundaries of colonial countries at the moment when independence is achieved (*uti possidetis juris*). The Court held that there was only an 'apparent contradiction' between *uti possidetis* and self-determination of peoples:

> At first sight this principle [*uti possidetis*] conflicts outright with another one, the right of peoples to self-determination. In fact, however, the maintenance of the territorial status quo in Africa is often seen as the wisest course, to preserve what has been achieved by peoples who have struggled for their independence, and to avoid a disruption which would deprive the continent of the gains achieved by

claims in territories where for one reason or another they were for the time being unable or unwilling to make an effective occupation. One such device was the invention of 'colonial protectorates', the word 'protectorate' here describing a relation between a state and a native community not sufficiently civilized to be regarded as a state, and not, as heretofore, a relation of dependence between two states . . . it is probably correct to say that the distinction between one of these protectorates and a colony is one of constitutional, rather than international, law.

much sacrifice. The essential requirement of stability in order to survive, to develop and gradually to consolidate their independence in all fields, has induced African States judiciously to consent to the respecting of colonial frontiers, and to take account of it in the interpretation of the principle of self-determination of peoples.[25]

This statement is open to objection. The contention can be made that it confuses the legal plane (where, it is suggested, self-determination and *uti possidetis* cannot but be on a collision course) with the political level, where instead reasons of expediency may make it advisable to compress self-determination for the purpose of allowing for peaceful change. From a strictly legal viewpoint, it is evident that *uti possidetis*, in that it is designed to 'freeze the territorial title' and 'to stop the clock' at the time of a colonial country becoming independent or at the time of the secession of a region from a unitary state (or of a member state from a federated state), is in sharp contrast with the principle of self-determination. This is because the population living on or around the borders of the newly independent state might have preferred to choose a different sovereign or even opt for independent status or some sort of autonomy. We are here confronted with an area in which historical and political considerations have been regarded by states as of such paramount importance as to make it necessary to set aside the right of peoples to self-determination: in this area self-determination has been 'trumped' by overriding political requirements.

The Court wrongly held that the two legal principles are not in conflict and are indeed reconcilable. The truth of the matter is that they are not; they can 'coexist' only if self-determination makes way for the political need to respect existing boundaries.

7. As I pointed out at the outset, self-determination is a highly politically charged area, where conflicting ideological and political values are at stake and the interests of states are not easily reconcilable. In this, as in similar areas such as that of international regulation of the use of force, one cannot expect from judicial pronouncements a decisive contribution to the clarification, crystallization or evolution of the most controversial legal rules. To be sure, this conclusion is not motivated by any unwillingness of the International Court of Justice to make a contribution on the matter. The fact is that sovereign states naturally shy away from resort to judicial procedures when it comes to the settlement of politically and ideologically delicate questions.

[25] ICJ Reports, 1986, p. 567, para. 25. The reference to the 'apparent contradiction' is in para. 26.

Nevertheless, it is apparent from the above survey that at least in one of the areas of self-determination – that of decolonization – the Court has indeed had the occasion to clarify the status of law and also to give an authoritative impulse to the further precision and evolution of international legal rules concerning the external self-determination of colonial peoples. In addition, the Court has sharply pinpointed the essence of the general concept of self-determination, thereby shedding light on other ramifications and applications of this principle.

It is to be hoped that the *East Timor* case, currently pending before the Court, will offer this institution the opportunity to pronounce on other aspects of the principle, and possibly also to contribute to the further precision or even crystallization of general rules in this matter. Areas that would need judicial clarification include: the relationship between the general principle on self-determination and the various specific rules of a customary nature spelling out the principle; the force of *jus cogens* accruing to the principle; the ramifications and implications of the right to external self-determination of peoples subjected to military occupation; the extent to which the general rule on self-determination as an entitlement to democratic government (see above, p. 352) is crystallizing.[26]

Hopefully, sooner or later the Court will have the opportunity to cast light on at least some of these extremely difficult and controversial questions.

---

[26] After the completion of this chapter, on 30 June 1995 the ICJ handed down its judgment on the *East Timor* case. It found that it could not adjudicate upon the dispute between Portugal and Australia because its ruling would have implied a determination of Indonesia's rights and obligations, a determination that was not legally permissible without the consent of Indonesia (this state had not accepted the Court's jurisdiction). However, the Court stated, in passing, that, in its view, 'Portugal's assertion that the right of peoples to self-determination, as it evolved from the Charter and from United Nations practice, has an *erga omnes* character, is irreproachable. The principle of self-determination of peoples has been recognized by the United Nations Charter and in the jurisprudence of the Court (see *Legal Consequences for States of the Continued Presence of South Africa in Namibia (South West Africa) Notwithstanding Security Council Resolution 276 (1970)* ICJ Reports 1971, pp. 31–2, paras. 52–3; *Western Sahara* ICJ Reports 1975, pp. 31–3, paras. 54–9); it is one of the essential principles of contemporary international law' (ICJ, *Case Concerning East Timor*, para. 29). The Court also took note that 'for the two parties, the Territory of East Timor remains a non-self-governing territory and its people has the right to self-determination' (*ibid.*, paras. 37 and 31).

   Also in some of the Separate and Dissenting Opinions annexed to the judgment mention is made of the principle of self-determination. See, in particular, the Separate Opinion of Judge Oda (paras. 18–19), and more extensively, the Dissenting Opinions of Judge Weeramantry (pp. 42–60) and Judge *ad hoc* Skubiszewski (paras. 134–55).

19

The International Court of Justice and the peaceful settlement of disputes

J. G. Collier

❧

It may seem rather odd for anyone to be writing a chapter on the subject of the International Court of Justice and the pacific settlement of international disputes, since the pacific settlement of disputes is the function of the Court, like any other court. However, a discussion entitled thus need not be without point; there have been many attempts to assess the contribution of the Court to the settlement of disputes. But this kind of approach suffers from several shortcomings. It can lead to one simply cataloguing the disputes that have come before it, saying whether the Court's judgment or opinion did settle or assist in settling those disputes. Or it may consist also in a consideration of the importance of the disputes in question from the point of view of world peace, or of the development of international law.

Sometimes this kind of enterprise leads to conclusions such as that the Court has settled relatively few disputes, or that the disputes it has been called upon to settle have been on the whole relatively trivial when set against the background of the state of the world. These conclusions are then used to assert that the Court has too little to do and that it should be given more work.

Apart from enquiries as to the development of international law by the Court such as Sir Hersch Lauterpacht's seminal study, *The Development of International Law by the International Court of Justice*, and Fitzmaurice's analyses of the law and procedure of the ICJ in successive volumes of the *British Yearbook of International Law*, now happily and eruditely taken up by Thirlway, it is not clear to the present writer that the types of investigation just referred to are necessarily the particular province of lawyers. Also, some of the conclusions alluded to above seem rather curious. For instance, it may at first glance seem that the Court has relatively little to do, but this is usually observed by way of comparing it with municipal tribunals or such international tribunals as the European Court of Justice. This situation, of course, is not surprising, since the Court has less than two hundred possible litigants, whereas the ECJ, for example, has millions. Furthermore, some of the proposals to remedy this allegedly dire state of affairs seem quite bizarre. For example, the suggestion that the Court should be given the power to hear references on points of international law by domestic courts, which is based on the power possessed by the ECJ under Article 177 of the Treaty of Rome, bristles with every kind of practical difficulty and rests on quite hopelessly false analogies and comparisons between the two courts and their functions.

Therefore, it is instead intended to put forward a few modest observations on the place of the Court in the traditional scheme of international dispute-settlement procedures, and to ask whether in recent years the Court has, consciously or subconsciously, slightly shifted its own view of its functions in the context of that scheme.

Almost all studies of the law of international dispute settlement are organized in basically the same way, in that the different methods of dispute settlement are discussed in the same order. If we take the *United Nations Handbook on the Peaceful Settlement of Disputes between States*, published in 1992, the order of treatment is: (a) negotiations and consultations; (b) inquiry (or fact-finding); (c) good offices; (d) mediation; (e) conciliation; (f) arbitration; and (g) judicial settlement. (The rest of the book discusses resort to regional agencies and procedures under the Charter and such as are envisaged in other international instruments.) Except that mediation is dealt with before inquiry and that good offices is subsumed under mediation, the same order is observed by Professor Merrills in his *International Dispute Settlement*.[1] This is quite understandable and simply reflects the wording of article 33(1) of the Charter which, it will be recalled, states that 'the parties to any dispute, the continuance of which is likely to endanger the maintenance of international peace and security shall, first of all, seek a solution by negotiation, enquiry, mediation, conciliation, arbitration, judicial settlement . . . '.

This is echoed by the Declaration on Principles of International Law concerning Friendly Relations and Co-operation among States (resolution 2625 (xxv), Annexe) and the Manila Declaration on the Peaceful Settlement of Disputes (resolution 37/10, Annexe), for example. (The lists contained in these three instruments do not contain good offices, though the Manila Declaration mentions good offices elsewhere.)

Several pretty obvious considerations dictate this order of dealing with the methods. First, it more or less reflects the relative frequency with which they are employed. More than ninety-nine per cent of international disputes must be settled in the end by negotiation, although writers on international law do not usually emphasize this, just as writers on the law of contract usually omit

---

[1] (2nd edn, Cambridge, 1991).

to mention that a similar proportion of contractual obligations is discharged by performance. Second, it reflects the degree to which third parties are involved. Third, it reflects the progressively more formal character of the several methods. Fourth, it reflects their degree of institutionalization. Last, it reflects the degree to which international law is applied to the settlement of disputes.

Here are two other suggestions. First, the traditional list seems also, to international lawyers, to be arranged in a hierarchical manner, with negotiation at the bottom and judicial settlement at the top of the tree. International lawyers tend also to believe that the list is arranged in order of importance or significance, judicial settlement being much the most important. The belief in this hierarchy and this relative significance is perfectly natural and understandable from the point of view of international lawyers, because to them a judgment of a court (and the higher the court the better) is, along with a treaty, or in municipal law a statute, more significant than any other source of law or obligation. This is certainly true of lawyers from common-law countries and, as far as international law goes, is probably only little less true of those from non-common-law regions. Further, article 38(1) enjoins the Court, in exercising its function to determine such disputes as are submitted to it, to do so in accordance with international law (unless the parties agree to the Court deciding *ex aequo et bono*). So what the Court decides *is* international law. All the other methods may lead to a settlement on the basis of other rules or principles, as is the case with arbitration, where the parties can lay down the rules to be applied, or indeed to a settlement not based on any law at all, one which results from inquiry or fact-finding being an obvious example of this.

The second suggestion is that, although resort to different methods of settlement may be cumulative, in that several may be resorted to at one time or another to try to settle a single dispute, or alternative, in that, for example, arbitration or judicial settlement may be resorted to, but not both of them in the same dispute, all these methods also tend to be thought of as quite distinct and carried out by quite different bodies or functionaries. Judicial settlement is carried out by a court of judges and not by a panel of arbitrators. Mediation and conciliation are carried out by mediators and conciliators and not by arbitrators or by courts and judges. This is clear and assumed to be true. However, one may ask whether this is really quite so clear and whether it is entirely true? Has the Court itself always observed these distinctions, and has it never undertaken tasks that tradition and orthodoxy allot to other tribunals or bodies concerned with the pacific settlement of disputes?

At this stage, it is perhaps relevant to rehearse typical definitions or descriptions of methods of settlement of disputes, excluding negotiation and fact-finding. 'Mediation' and 'good offices' are terms that are used indifferently. The Hague Conventions of 1899 and 1907 do not differentiate between them and often 'good offices', as we have seen, does not get a separate mention. The Pact of Bogotá of 1948, however, attempts to differentiate between them. 'Mediation' may be taken to denote the participation of a third state or states, a disinterested individual or an organ of the United Nations, with the disputing states in an attempt to reconcile their claims and to advance proposals aimed at a compromise solution. The distinction between mediation and good offices is sometimes taken to be that in the former the mediator takes active steps of his or its own, while good offices consist of action taken by the third party to bring the contending states together to negotiate, without that third party actively participating in discussion of the dispute.

Conciliation is a method of settling a dispute that generally combines the characteristics of inquiry or fact-finding and mediation. The dispute may be referred to a person or commission whose task is to make an impartial elucidation of the facts and to put forward proposals for a settlement, which do not have the binding character of an award.

Arbitration can only be described in general terms, for the actual structures of particular arbitration proceedings may differ considerably. The important point, however, is to try to distinguish arbitration from judicial settlement. At the grave risk of over-simplification, it is thought that the distinctions are as follows. The arbitration agreement may well permit of settlement on extra-legal principles. (This is theoretically true of judicial settlement since article 38(2) of its Statute permits the Court to decide the case *ex aequo et bono* if the parties agree, but since this has never been done and is unlikely to happen it can be ignored and it can be assumed that the Court will apply legal principles.) The agreement may, as has been mentioned, lay down the rules by which the Tribunal is to govern the parties' conduct. The Arbitral Tribunal consists of persons selected by the parties; this is only true of the Court to the extent of appointment by the parties of *ad hoc* judges and their parties' role in the formation of chambers (the latter will be discussed further). A Tribunal is usually created to deal with a particular dispute or class of disputes (this is true of Tribunals created under the auspices of the Permanent Court of Arbitration), whereas the Court has a permanent membership and can deal with any kinds of disputes involving international law. An arbitration is usually held in private and the award is unpublished if the parties so desire (this is perhaps the main advantage of arbitration over litigation in the municipal sphere). The Court must (Statute, article 46) generally – that is, unless the Court itself decides or unless the parties demand that the public be not admitted – hold its hearings in public; and all its judgments and Opinions are published.

The disputing parties may find some or all of these characteristics of arbitration render it preferable to having their dispute settled by the Court. On the other hand, considerations of expense may well tilt their thoughts towards judicial settlement. Whichever means is chosen the parties will have to pay the very large number of counsel, advocates and so on whose assistance appears to be necessary nowadays to present their cases: but arbitration means they will have to find the additional funds to pay the arbitrator or arbitrators and the registrar and other officials of the Tribunal. These costs of a case before the Court are spread among the world's taxpayers and do not fall only on those of the contending states.

It is here submitted that over the last quarter of a century the Court has to a perceptible extent assimilated the exercise of its functions to some of the other methods of settlement of disputes and in so doing has almost abdicated its special function of judicial settlement in substance, though not in form, in favour of one or more of the other methods of settlement.

As regards assimilation to arbitration, this phenomenon has been remarked upon before now. It has come about mainly through resort to the device of forming a Chamber to hear a particular case, pursuant to article 26 of the Statute. This facility had never been resorted to until the *Gulf of Maine* case.[2] It has been used several times since then, in the *Burkina Faso/Mali Frontier Dispute* case,[3] the *Elettronica Sicula* case,[4] and the *El Salvador/Honduras Land, Island and Maritime Frontier* case.[5] It was the first of these that produced a difficult problem which the Court settled, though not to the satisfaction of all the members of the Court. It will be remembered that article 36(2) provides that the number of judges to constitute a Chamber is to be decided by the Court with the approval of the parties, but the contending states, the US and Canada, agreed between themselves not only on the number of judges there should be but who those judges were to be. Significantly, they also agreed that if the Court did not appoint their selected judges, they would instead submit the case to an Arbitral Tribunal composed of those five members. (The precedent for this was the *Beagle Channel* Arbitration,[6] where Chile and Argentina agreed on one ex-member and four sitting members of the Court to compose the Arbitration Tribunal). The Court 'balloted' to select those five judges. Two of the members of the Court disagreed with this way of

---

[2] ICJ Reports, 1984, p. 246.
[3] ICJ Reports, 1986, p. 554.   [4] ICJ Reports, 1987, p. 4.
[5] ICJ Reports, 1993, p. 3.   [6] 17 *ILM* 634 (1978).

proceeding, saying that the Court had allowed itself to be dictated to and in effect had not done the selecting itself.

It will also be recalled that article 17 (2) of the Rules of Court requires the President to ascertain the views of the parties regarding the composition of the chamber. In his celebrated and vigorous Dissent from the judgment in earlier proceedings in the *Land, Island and Maritime Frontier* case,[7] Judge Shahabuddeen argued that if this authorizes consultation regarding anything other than the number of judges to be selected this provision may be *pro tanto ultra vires*.

Judge Shahabuddeen's dissent was from the Court's judgment in that case upon Nicaragua's application to the Court to be allowed to intervene pursuant to article 62 of the Statute. The Court held that this application must be made to the Chamber and not to the Court itself, since once the Chamber is constituted it *is* the Court, not an agent of or subject to control by the Court.

It is impossible not to have some sympathy for the Court in these cases; in the *Gulf of Maine* case, it was placed in a very invidious position by the parties. On the other hand, it is not easy to disagree with the views expressed by Judge Shahabuddeen, though perhaps he was being less worldly-wise than the Court. Nevertheless, whether one agrees with the Court or not, one thing that these decisions suggest is that the separation between arbitration and judicial settlement was reduced to vanishing point. Provided that parties agree on the membership of the tribunal or court, do not object to publicity and are content that their dispute should be settled by the application of public international law as conceived of by the tribunal or court, there is no juridical distinction between settlement by means of arbitration and settlement by the Court through a Chamber thereof. The only difference is that the parties will find arbitration more expensive. This is, no doubt, why the first preference of the US and Canada in the *Gulf of Maine* case was for judicial settlement over arbitration.

But perhaps less clearly perceived has been an approximation of judicial settlement to the less formal methods of settlement, especially mediation and conciliation. It is submitted that there are some indications that the Court, in some cases abetted by the parties, has departed to some extent from what used, at any rate, to be regarded as its function – that is, the actual settlement of disputes in the sense of deciding the substance of what is the real dispute between the parties.

Article 38 of the Statute states that the function of the Court 'is to decide such disputes as are submitted to it'. It clearly fulfils this function in a case

---

[7] ICJ Reports, 1990, p. 3.

concerning the ownership of certain territory, if it decides that the territory belongs to Utopia rather than Ruritania, or in a case concerning a dispute concerning treaty interpretation if it decides that it means x, as contended by Utopia, rather than y, as argued by Ruritania. (Decisions on preliminary objections to the Court's jurisdiction or concerning the admissibility of a claim are, of course, not decisions on the substance of the dispute, but these are not in point here, for if the Court decides that it has no jurisdiction or that the claim is inadmissible it merely means that it cannot hear the case, or cannot hear it now; that is to say, that judicial settlement is not, or is not at present, available as a means of settling the dispute.)

However, in a number of cases, notably those concerned with maritime delimitation, the Court has not been called upon to settle the dispute by deciding it one way or the other and so (hopefully) putting an end to it in the manner alluded to. Rather, it has been asked to give the parties guidance as to the principles and rules they, not the Court, should apply, in settling their dispute by negotiation leading to agreement. This happened in the *North Sea Continental Shelf* cases[8] where the Court held that the delimitation of the parties' continental shelf areas should be in accordance with equitable principles but did not itself delimit the parties' shares. It must be admitted that the wording of article 6(2) of the Continental Shelf Convention of 1958 almost invited this consequence. In the *Tunisia/Libya Continental Shelf* case,[9] those two states agreed to ask the Court to lay down the principles and rules applicable to the determination of their continental shelf boundary; the Court itself was not asked to determine it. It did not determine it, but complied with the parties' request.

It can, of course, be argued that in *Tunisia/Libya* the Court did decide a dispute between the parties, in that it settled their dispute as to what the relevant principles and rules were, and it may all depend on what is meant by a dispute. There is always the possibility that the parties 'dress up' the case to make it appear that they are putting a dispute before the Court just as, for example in requesting an Advisory Opinion, an organ of the UN can effectively prevent the Court refusing to give an Advisory Opinion on the ground that the question is political rather than legal, by framing it in such legalistic terms as to obscure what the basic arguments are, as happened notably in the *Certain Expenses of the United Nations* Advisory Opinion.[10] But in these maritime delimitation cases, the disputing states did not even dress the application up, and it looks as if they asked the Court for an Advisory

---

[8] ICJ Reports, 1969, p. 3.
[9] ICJ Reports, 1982, p. 18.   [10] ICJ Reports, 1962, p. 151.

Opinion. An Advisory Opinion was really what the Court gave, in spite of its competence to do this being confined to responses to requests from international organizations only. Whether this analysis is acceptable or not, what surely is true is that the Court was acting, as between the states, as a kind of conciliator.

And what are we to make of the Court's latest 'judgment', if it can really be called that, of July 1994 in the case concerning maritime delimitation and territorial questions between *Qatar and Bahrain: Jurisdiction and Admissibility*?[11] Qatar unilaterally referred to the Court the question of the title to certain territories which had been in dispute between it and Bahrain, but not that of title to other territories which had been in dispute. In other words, its claim concerned only part of the dispute between the two states, not all of the dispute. Bahrain's riposte was, put simply, that arrangements between the two states concerning the reference of the dispute to the Court were not legally binding and if they were binding, they covered the whole of the dispute, not merely part of it.

The Court made five holdings, the first four of which were:

(a) that the arrangements were international agreements creating rights and obligations for the parties;

(b) by their terms of those agreements the parties had undertaken to submit to the Court the whole of the dispute between them;

(c) the Court decided 'to afford the parties the opportunity to submit to the Court the whole of the dispute, and

(d) fixed 30 November 1994 as the time limit within which the parties are jointly or separately to take action to this end.

This is a rather peculiar series of decisions. One question that immediately springs to mind on reading (c) and (d) is: will the Court refuse to hear the case if, for example, the parties were jointly to refer the whole dispute to it only on 1 December? Would the Court really decline to accept the case? Surely not.[12]

More to the point for present purposes, as Judge Schwebel points out in his succinct but cogent Separate Opinion, the Court did not, in the *dispositif*, really decide any dispute, either the substantial territorial dispute or the dispute over jurisdiction or admissibility. As he observed, the judgment 'lacks the essential quality of a judgment of this Court; it does not adjudge the principal issue before it'. Decisions (a) and (b) are merely 'preliminary decisions which put the Court in a position to pass upon the submissions of the parties

---

[11] ICJ Reports, 1994, p. 112.

[12] This chapter was written some time before 30 November.

which the Court then fails to do at any rate as yet'. Quite so; it is as if, in an English Court W were to petition for divorce from H on the ground that the marriage has irretrievably broken down and H were to deny this and argue also that no divorce should be granted since he and W were not validly married, and the Court were to hold that H and W were validly married but neither grant nor refuse the divorce. In the present case, the Court can scarcely be said to have fully discharged its judicial function.

Moreover, decisions (c) and (d) are of interest for another reason. Though the Court never explicitly said so, it obviously regarded itself as incompetent to entertain or decide the case at that stage. Therefore those decisions amount to an offer by the Court to the parties of its own services in order to settle their dispute if they wish to use them. This seems to be an abdication by the Court of its proper judicial function and a taking up instead of a function close to that of a conciliator. Whether, having regard to the terms of its own Statute, it is, so to speak, *intra vires* for the Court to do this is open to considerable doubt.

However, these remarks are not designed to criticize the Court since what it appears to have done in the cases discussed herein may well be quite harmless. They are solely put forward in order to suggest that the different methods of pacific settlement of disputes may be more intermingled than is usually supposed and that, if this is so, it is to a large extent the International Court of Justice that has brought this situation about.

20

The International Court of Justice and the use of force

Christopher Greenwood

ళ

Shortly after his election to the International Court, Judge Jennings gave a lecture on the subject of the International Court of Justice and the use of force[1] in which he argued that the International Court could play an important role in the settlement of disputes involving the use of force and in the development of that area of international law but rejected as utopian the idea that the Court could control, or even abolish, war by ruling on all conflicts between states. 'Only where there is an issue of a justiciable nature, and a recognizable cause or causes of action' could the Court make a determination.[2] Moreover, Judge Jennings cautioned that even where those requirements were met, the function of the Court should not be seen in isolation but rather as part of the machinery of the United Nations, recognizing that some aspects of a situation involving the use of force might be better dealt with by other parts of that machinery.

At the time that lecture was delivered the only cases in which the Court had been directly confronted with issues of the use of force were the *Corfu Channel*[3] and *Iranian Hostages*[4] cases, although a number of other cases involving the use of force had been commenced but had not proceeded to trial on the merits,[5] while in other cases the Court had made passing comments regarding the law on the use of force, such as its remark in the *Fisheries Jurisdiction* case that 'under contemporary international law an agreement

---

[1] The lecture was subsequently published under the title 'International Force and the International Court of Justice', in A. Cassese (ed.), *The Current Legal Regulation of the Use of Force* (Dordrecht, 1986), pp. 322–5.

[2] *Ibid.*, p. 334.

[3] ICJ Reports, 1949, p. 4.

[4] ICJ Reports, 1980, p. 3.

[5] See, e.g., the *Cases Concerning the Trial of Pakistani Prisoners of War*, ICJ Reports, 1973, pp. 328 and 347, and the applications in the various *Aerial Incident* cases in the 1950s.

concluded under the threat or use of force is void'.[6] Since then, however, the Court has given judgment on the merits in the *Case Concerning Military and Paramilitary Activities in and against Nicaragua*[7] and has indicated provisional measures of protection in the case concerning *Application of the Convention on the Prevention and Punishment of the Crime of Genocide*,[8] in both of which issues concerning the use of force were at the heart of the disputes before the Court. In *Burkina Faso/Mali*[9] a Chamber of the Court, and in *Libyan Arab Jamahiriya/ Chad*[10] the full Court, has given judgment in a territorial dispute which had recently led to hostilities and in which the submission of the case to the Court played an important part in bringing hostilities to an end. Moreover, the Court's docket at the end of 1994 included several cases – the *Genocide* case, the cases between Iran and the United States concerning the *Aerial Incident of 3 July 1988*[11] and the *Oil Platforms*, and requests by the World Health Organization and the United Nations General Assembly for Advisory Opinions regarding the legality of the use of nuclear weapons – which raised issues concerning the use of force, as well as a number of cases in which the use of force formed part of the background. The publication of this Festschrift is therefore an appropriate occasion on which to re-examine some of the issues raised by Judge Jennings in his lecture and to carry out a brief audit of the Court's jurisprudence on the use of force.

THE QUESTION OF JUSTICIABILITY

As Judge Jennings pointed out in his lecture, there are two different ways in which the Court may be faced with a case involving the use of force. It may be asked to rule upon an issue, or group of issues, which do not themselves turn upon the legality or illegality of the use of force but where the use or threat of force 'is incidental to a claim under some other head of State responsibility'. That was the position, for example, in the *Iranian Hostages* case, where the United States claim was based upon violations of diplomatic law but those violations had taken such an extreme and violent form that they amounted to a use of force on the part of Iran. Alternatively, the whole essence

---

[6] ICJ Reports, 1973, p. 3 at p. 14. The Court presumably meant that the *illegal* use of force had this effect, since a treaty imposed on a defeated aggressor state following a successful exercise of the right of self-defence is not generally regarded as vitiated by duress; see R. Y. Jennings and A. D. Watts (eds.), *Oppenheim's International Law* (9th edn., London, 1992), vol. I, pp. 1291–2.

[7] ICJ Reports, 1986, p. 3.   [8] ICJ Reports, 1993, p. 325.

[9] ICJ Reports, 1986, p. 554.   [10] ICJ Reports, 1994, p. 3.

[11] At the time of going to press, the hearing in this case had been postponed *sine die* and it was expected that the parties would agree an out-of-court settlement.

of the claim before the Court may be that the use or threat of force is a violation of international law and thus of the claimant state's rights. The *Nicaragua* case clearly falls into this category. In each category of case, the issues submitted for the decision of the Court must be justiciable.

It has sometimes been argued that issues involving the use of force are inherently non-justiciable. The most extreme form of this argument is that even cases in the first category described in the preceding paragraph are not suitable for adjudication, because they cannot be detached from a broader context involving the use of armed force. In the *Iranian Hostages* case Iran argued that the question before the Court, which concerned the seizure and detention of the US diplomatic personnel 'represented only a marginal and secondary aspect of an overall problem' which could not be isolated from the background of what Iran alleged was twenty-five years of unlawful intervention by the US in the internal affairs of Iran. The Court, however, emphatically rejected this argument. A legal dispute, the Court held, would always exist within a wider political framework but the fact that that framework included aspects, however important, that were non-justiciable was no reason for the Court to decline jurisdiction in respect of those issues that could be reduced to a legal dispute. In other words, an issue that, in the ordinary course of events, would be justiciable is not rendered non-justiciable merely because of the political setting in which it arises.

The second category of case, however, raises more difficult questions, especially where the Court is asked to rule on the legality not of some past use of force but of the use of force in a continuing armed conflict. It was argued by the US in the *Nicaragua* case that it is beyond the judicial function to deal with a continuing armed conflict, since both the determination of the facts and the implementation of the judgment would pose insuperable problems.[12]

The Court, however, rejected this argument. It began by reaffirming that the use of force was a matter subject to international law and thus raised a legal question capable of objective determination by a judicial tribunal (a principle which had earlier been asserted by the International Military Tribunals at Nuremberg and Tokyo and which was not, as such, questioned by the US). Unsurprisingly, the judgment makes no concession to the theory expounded by Dean Acheson at the time of the Cuban Missile Crisis that 'law simply does not deal with such questions of ultimate power – power that comes close to the sources of sovereignty'.[13] Whether or not a particular instance of the use

---

[12] See the US submissions on admissibility in the *Nicaragua* case (*Jurisdiction Phase*), ICJ Reports, 1984, p. 392, at pp. 431–8.
[13] *Proceedings of the American Society of International Law* (1963), p. 14.

of force was lawful was thus a justiciable question and it did not cease to be so merely because the conflict in which it occurred was still in progress. Difficulties over determination of the facts and the implementation of a judgment were not unique to cases in which there was a continuing conflict and those difficulties could not preclude the Court from ruling upon the application of rules of international law to the facts as eventually ascertained.

The approach taken by the Court in the *Nicaragua* and *Iranian Hostages* cases is reflected in the attitudes of the Court and the parties in the most recent case of this kind to come before the Court, the *Genocide* case between Bosnia–Herzegovina and the Federal Republic of Yugoslavia (Serbia and Montenegro). There it seemed to have been taken for granted, at least in the provisional measures stage, that the fact that the case raised issues going to the heart of the conduct of ongoing hostilities did not preclude the Court from dealing with it, both the claimant and respondent requesting the indication of provisional measures.

It should also be noted that in the *Nicaragua* case the Court rejected another non-justiciability argument based on notions of the separation of powers, namely that the use of force in a continuing conflict raised questions of international peace and security which the Charter of the United Nations allotted to the Security Council and thus impliedly removed from the purview of the Court. In *Nicaragua*, as in *Iranian Hostages*, the Court took the view that the Security Council's primary responsibility for the maintenance of international peace and security did not exclude all performance of the judicial function. In neither case, however, was the Court invited to take an adverse view of an instance of the Council's exercise of its powers to deal with a threat to international peace and security. The Court seems to have seen its role as separate from, but complementary to, that of the Council. Whether the Court would regard itself as having the competence to give a ruling that conflicted with a resolution adopted by the Security Council for the restoration of peace and security is a different matter. By the end of 1994 it had twice refused to give such a ruling at the provisional measures stage of a case. In the *Aerial Incident at Lockerbie*[14] it declined to question the validity of a Security Council resolution adopted under Chapter VII. In the *Genocide* case it refused a Bosnian request for the indication of provisional measures which would in effect have opposed the application to Bosnia of an arms embargo imposed by the Council in resolution 713 (1991). It remains to be seen how the Court will approach on the merits a case in which it is asked to give a ruling inconsistent

---

[14] *Libya v. United Kingdom* and *Libya v. United States*, ICJ Reports, 1992, pp. 3 and 113.

with the measures taken by the Council for the restoration of international peace and security.

The Court has thus taken a fairly broad view of its ability to adjudicate upon cases involving the use of force. That does not in any way run counter to the requirement so clearly stated by Judge Jennings that the Court can deal only with disputes that are justiciable and involve a recognized cause of action. The Court's view has been that provided this requirement is met, the fact that the dispute raises questions about the legality of the use of force and that it arises in the context of a continuing armed conflict does not preclude the Court from ruling upon it. Nevertheless, the result is that the dispute which can be the subject of a ruling by the Court will often consist of an issue, or set of issues, considerably narrower than the overall dispute of which it is a part. This tendency is accentuated where the jurisdiction of the Court is based on a provision that confers jurisdiction only in respect of disputes regarding the interpretation or application of a particular convention, for in such cases the jurisdiction thus conferred may not extend even to all of the justiciable disputes that the claimant state may wish to bring before the Court. Thus, if the sole basis for jurisdiction in the *Genocide* case is article IX of the Genocide Convention,[15] the Court will have jurisdiction in respect of allegations of atrocities falling within the definition of article I of the Convention committed in the conflict in Bosnia but not in respect of allegations of resort to force in violation of the Charter or of actions falling short of genocide but contravening the laws of armed conflict.

Nor does the approach the Court has taken in any way invalidate Judge Jennings's comment that the Court's role has to be seen in the context of the United Nations machinery as a whole. While it is submitted that the Court was right to hold in *Nicaragua* that disputes involving the continuing use of force were not entrusted exclusively to the Security Council, it remains the case that the Council will often be far better placed than the Court to deal with such disputes and to secure an end to hostilities. The increased activism of the Council since 1990, together with the growth in the number of cases submitted to the Court, means that great care will have to be shown in dealing with those cases in which both bodies become involved. Similarly, while the Court rightly rejected the argument that the difficulty of establishing the facts and ensuring compliance with the Court's judgments should not preclude the Court from exercising jurisdiction in respect of a dispute arising

---

[15] In its decision on the second request for provisional measures, The court held that this provision was the only basis for jurisdiction which had so far been *prima facie* established; ICJ Reports, 1993, p. 325, at p. 342.

out of an ongoing armed conflict, that does not mean that those difficulties do not exist. The continuing dispute over the evidence in the *Nicaragua* case[16] and the wholesale disregard of the provisional measures indicated by the Court in the *Genocide* case bear witness to the scale of those problems. Even if these problems should not deter the Court from dealing with a case involving an ongoing armed conflict, it would be wrong not to recognize that the Court is likely to be less effective here than in cases such as *Burkina Faso/Mali* or *Chad/Libya* where it is asked to resolve an underlying dispute as part of a peace settlement.

THE COURT AND THE SUBSTANTIVE LAW ON THE USE OF FORCE

This is not the place to undertake a full survey of the Court's contribution to the development of this area of international law. All that can be attempted is a discussion of some of the salient features of its jurisprudence.

Ever since 1945 scholars have debated the extent of the prohibition on the use or threat of force contained in article 2(4) of the United Nations Charter. Is it a comprehensive prohibition, which forbids any threat or use of force by one state against another except those specifically sanctioned by other rules of international law (principally, and perhaps exclusively) those permitting action in self-defence or under the authority of the Security Council? Or does article 2(4) leave some instances in which force may be used or threatened without ever falling foul of its prohibition, even though it is not possible to point to any rule of international law that might justify such action. Supporters of the latter school, which takes a restrictive view of article 2(4), have argued, *inter alia*, that an armed incursion into the territory of another state for purposes of asserting a right (though not falling within the limits of the right of self-defence) or upholding what they describe as 'community values' falls wholly outside the scope of the prohibition in article 2(4). If accepted, their argument would mean that the system of rules regarding the use of force constituted by articles 2(4) (the general rule) and 51 and 39–42 (the exceptions) is incomplete and that there is an ill-defined area within which force may be used without being covered by the general rule and thus without needing to be justified by reference to one of the exceptions to that rule.

In the two cases in which it has had to consider the scope of the modern prohibition on the use of force, the *Corfu Channel* and *Nicaragua* cases, the

---

16 See S. Schwebel, *Justice in International Law* (Cambridge, 1994), p. 142.

Court has tended towards the broad, rather than the restrictive, interpretation of article 2(4).[17] Thus, in considering the legality of Operation Retail, in which British warships swept Albanian waters for mines, the Court was faced with a British argument that this incursion into Albanian waters was lawful because it did not threaten the territorial integrity of Albania and was designed to gather evidence for use in the proceedings before the Court. Although the Court did not refer to article 2(4) of the Charter it was unequivocal in its rejection of the British argument as 'the manifestation of a policy of force, such as has, in the past, given rise to most serious abuses and such as cannot, whatever be the present defects of international organization, find a place in international law'.[18] This well-known passage is clearly based on a broad interpretation of the prohibition of the use of force. Moreover, the reference to the 'present defects of international organization' is particularly important because it amounts to a rejection of the argument that the prohibition on the use of force was conditional on the proper functioning of the collective security mechanism in the Charter. The *Nicaragua* judgment takes a similar approach, the Court assuming that the prohibition on the use of force was a broad one and that a state using force would have to point to a specific principle of international law which would justify its action rather than being able to take advantage of a gap in the scope of that prohibition.[19]

By far the most important and controversial aspect of the Court's jurisprudence on the use of force is the ruling of the majority in *Nicaragua* on the subject of the right of self-defence. Three points require particular attention. First, the Court was clear that the right of self-defence existed only in the event of an armed attack.[20] The Court thus rejected the theory that the right of self-defence can justify an armed response to threats to a state arising from something other than an armed attack. Although this approach has been criticized,[21] it is submitted that it accords both with the prevailing state practice since 1945 and with the text of article 51 of the Charter, since it would have been strange if the draftsman had made express reference to the right of self-defence existing in the event of an armed attack, the

---

[17] In *Nicaragua* the Court was, of course, applying customary law rather than article 2(4) but it is clear that the majority judgment assumed that the two were identical on this point.

[18] ICJ Reports, 1949, p. 3, at p. 35.

[19] See ICJ Reports, 1986, at pp. 100–2.

[20] *Ibid.*, at p. 103.

[21] See, e.g., the Dissenting Opinion of Judge Schwebel, *ibid.*, at pp. 347–8. For an exposition of the view that the right of self-defence extends to cases where there is no armed attack, actual or threatened, see D. W. Bowett, *Self-Defence in International Law* (Manchester, 1959), pp. 192–3.

obvious instance of self-defence, yet said nothing about the possibility of self-defence in other, less obvious cases. The fact that article 51 merely preserves and does not create the right of self-defence does not alter this conclusion.

It is more difficult to agree with the second aspect of the majority's ruling on self-defence, namely its highly restrictive approach to what constitutes an armed attack. This issue arose in the context of the US argument that Nicaragua had committed an armed attack against El Salvador and Honduras by its activities in support of rebel movements in those two countries. The allegation thus related to what might be termed 'indirect aggression' and was made in support of a contention that US support for rebels operating in Nicaragua was a legitimate measure of collective self-defence. The Court rejected many of the allegations against Nicaragua but still found that there had been limited Nicaraguan support for the rebels in El Salvador, and that Nicaragua was responsible for certain cross-border incursions into Honduras and Costa Rica.[22] The Court's findings of fact in this respect have been criticized as not going far enough.[23] However, even if one approaches this part of the judgment on the basis that the facts were as found by the majority, the decision that the conduct was imputable to Nicaragua did not amount to an armed attack and the reasons given for that decision are difficult to support.

This part of the judgment is based on the thesis that not every use of armed force, even if it is contrary to article 2(4) of the Charter, is of sufficient gravity to amount to an armed attack. As the judgment puts it, it is necessary 'to distinguish the most grave forms of the use of force (those constituting an armed attack) from other less grave forms'.[24] The majority continued:

> The Court sees no reason to deny that, in customary law, the prohibition of armed attacks may apply to the sending by a State of armed bands to the territory of another State, if such an operation, because of its scale and effects, would have been classified as an armed attack rather than as a mere frontier incident had it been carried out by regular armed forces.[25]

The mere act of supplying arms and equipment to a rebel movement in another state, it was held, necessarily fell below the threshold of an armed attack.

The majority cited no authority of any kind in support of the distinction it drew between armed attacks and other, 'less grave' uses of force. That distinction, it is submitted, has no basis in state practice or logic and is wholly

---

[22] ICJ Reports, 1986, p. 3, at pp. 86–7. [23] See Schwebel, *Justice in International Law*, p. 142.
[24] ICJ Reports, 1986, p. 3, at p. 101. [25] *Ibid.*, at p. 103.

unjustified. It is entirely unclear where the borderline between an armed attack by regular troops and a 'mere frontier incident' should lie and there is nothing in the practice of states between 1945 and 1986 to suggest that any such line had hitherto been regarded as important. Yet, according to the reasoning of the majority, the question whether a small-scale armed incursion across a frontier has crossed that line will be of critical importance in determining whether or not the victim state has a right to resort to force in self-defence. If there is ample scope for argument about whether an incursion or a cross-frontier bombardment by regular forces has crossed that line, the assessment of irregular military operations will be even more difficult.

Quite apart from the difficulty of determining when the line between less grave forms of force and armed attack has been crossed, it must also be asked why a state that is the victim of one of the lesser forms of force should not resist such force (which the Court accepted was unlawful) by itself resorting to military means. Is a state really debarred from using force against even a small patrol which has violently forced its way across a border and is threatening life and property even on a small scale? There is not the slightest indication that states have regarded themselves as subject to such a limitation, nor does the majority judgment advance any argument as to why such a limitation should exist. Of course one can sympathize with the Court's evident desire to ensure that a minor use of force does not lead to a wholly excessive response. Any exercise of the right of self-defence is, however, subject to the principle of proportionality. Insistence on compliance with that principle is a more effective and realistic way of seeking to prevent an excessive military response than the creation of an artificial distinction between different degrees of the use of force.

Admittedly, the majority conceded that a state that was the victim of an illegal use of force falling short of an armed attack would have the right to take 'counter-measures' – a right which it treated as distinct from the right of self-defence.[26] Moreover, it did not rule out the possibility that such counter-measures might themselves include the use of force. If that is the case, however, then the Court has recognized the existence of a new justification for the use of force outside the comparatively well-defined limits of the right of self-defence. So far as a response by the victim state itself is concerned, it is difficult to see that any useful purpose is served by drawing a distinction between self-defence and forcible counter-measures.

It is only when one turns, finally, to the majority's approach to the right of collective self-defence that the significance of such a distinction becomes

---

[26] *Ibid.*, at p. 110.

apparent. The Court, rightly it is submitted, insisted that the right to use force in collective self-defence could only exist if a state had been the victim of an armed attack and thus had itself the right to use force by way of individual self-defence. The decision thus knocks on the head the wholly illogical, but far from uncommon, notion that a group of states, no one of which has a right to take military action by itself, somehow acquires a right to use force by way of self-defence because they are acting collectively. The decision that the right of a third state to use force by way of collective self-defence was dependent on its having received a request for help from the state that was the victim of the armed attack has attracted more controversy and represented something of an innovation. This aspect of the decision is welcome inasmuch as it affirms that the right of collective self-defence does not entitle a third state to act as an unsought and possibly unwelcome champion. It is also noticeable that those states that went to the assistance of Kuwait, following the Iraqi invasion of 1990, were careful to produce evidence, in the form of letters from the Kuwait government-in-exile, requesting their help.[27] Nevertheless, insistence that the victim state make such a formal and public request for assistance is likely to be unrealistic where one is dealing with covert attacks upon that state, the response to which must itself often be kept secret.[28]

The majority, however, went on to hold that neither the right of collective self-defence nor the right to take counter-measures justifies a third state in intervening against a state that has perpetrated a use of force falling short of an armed attack. If, therefore, state A is responsible for such a lesser use of force against state B, it has committed an unlawful act to which B may respond by taking counter-measures (though not by exercise of the right of self-defence since there has been no armed attack). It is possible that those counter-measures may themselves include the use of force, but if they do, then that force must be entirely the work of state B's own armed forces; state C would not be entitled to intervene militarily even if requested to do so by state B and even though its intervention was confined to a proportionate response to the initial wrongdoing by state A. If, therefore, state B is too weak to take military action itself, it is deprived of the possibility of obtaining assistance from elsewhere against a use of force which is admitted to be unlawful. The majority judgment offers no justification for this result and it is difficult to see that one exists.

Before leaving the question of the Court's contribution to the substantive law, a brief mention should be made of its rulings on questions concerning the

---

[27] See E. Lauterpacht et al., *The Kuwait Crisis: Basic Documents* (Cambridge, 1991), vol. I, p. 245.
[28] See the Dissenting Opinion of Judge Jennings, ICJ Reports, 1986, at p. 545.

jus in bello. In both the *Corfu Channel* and *Nicaragua* cases the Court was confronted with mine-laying in a situation falling short of a formal state of war. In each case the Court ruled that the act of laying naval mines without notification was illegal. The Court did not, however, rely upon Hague Convention No. VIII of 1907, which is said to apply only in time of war, but upon 'certain general and well recognized principles, namely elementary considerations of humanity, even more exacting in peace than in war'.[29] In the *Nicaragua* case, however, it was open to argument that Nicaragua was involved in an international armed conflict to which the 1949 Geneva Conventions applied. Indeed, it could have been argued that Hague Convention No. VIII, though it refers only to war, should today be regarded as applicable to any international armed conflict even if that conflict is not characterized as a war in the formal sense. Nicaragua, however, made no argument to this effect and the US did not take part in the proceedings on the merits. It is scarcely surprising, therefore, that in respect of the mine-laying the Court confined itself to following its earlier decision in *Corfu Channel*.

Similarly, in considering the allegations of international humanitarian law in the Nicaraguan conflict, the Court avoided making a determination about whether that conflict possessed an international or an internal character. Instead, the Court held that the rules contained in common article 3 of the Geneva Conventions,[30] which lays down a basic code of obligations to be followed 'in the case of armed conflict not of an international character occurring in the territory of one of the High Contracting Parties', constituted a 'minimum yardstick' which applied, in addition to the more detailed rules in the Conventions, to international armed conflicts.[31] While this approach is understandable and conduct falling below the standards in article 3 can never be justified, there is a danger that the emphasis on the 'minimum yardstick' may serve to divert attention in future conflicts from violations of the detailed rules contained elsewhere in the Conventions.[32]

One of the most interesting issues the Court has had to consider in relation to the conduct of armed conflict is that of responsibility. In the *Nicaragua* case, the Court, by fourteen votes to one, held the US in violation of its obligations because a CIA official had published and disseminated among the Contra rebel groups a manual on psychological aspects of guerrilla warfare, parts of

---

[29] ICJ Reports, 1949, p. 22, and 1986, p. 112.
[30] Nicaragua, although accusing the US of violations of humanitarian law, did not rely on the Geneva Conventions as such.
[31] ICJ Reports, 1986, at p. 114.
[32] For discussion of this aspect of the case, see T. Meron, *Human Rights and Humanitarian Norms as Customary Law* (Oxford, 1989), pp. 25–37.

which were held to encourage violations of common article 3 of the Geneva Conventions.[33] The basis for this decision that a state acts unlawfully if its officials encourage others to violate humanitarian law was said to be the provisions of article 1 of the Geneva Conventions, which requires states both to respect and to 'ensure respect' for the Conventions in all circumstances, a provision which the Court treated as declaratory of customary international law. The Court, however, rejected a Nicaraguan argument that the US incurred responsibility for all violations of humanitarian law committed by the Contras. This question of state responsibility for violations committed by members of armed bands is likely to be particularly important in future proceedings in the *Genocide* case, where the Federal Republic of Yugoslavia has emphatically denied that it is responsible for the acts of the Bosnian Serb forces.

CONCLUSION

Part of Judge Jennings's thesis in his lecture was that the International Court could play a particularly influential role in resolving disputes to which the use of force was incidental. Two cases decided since then have confirmed this view. In *Burkina Faso/Mali*[34] a boundary dispute was referred to a Chamber of the Court by special agreement between the parties. Subsequently, a border conflict erupted between them. The fighting was brought to an end by a ceasefire agreement concluded under the auspices of the Organization for African Unity and others, but both states took the view that the indication by the Court of provisional measures of protection would help to strengthen that ceasefire. The Chamber indicated such measures and subsequently gave judgment on the boundary dispute. Both states have complied with that judgment, which was given twelve months after the fighting between them took place. Similarly, in *Libyan Arab Jamahiriya/Chad*[35] the parties concluded a special agreement referring to the Court a dispute over territory which had been the subject of an armed conflict of several years' duration. The submission to the Court was an essential part of the peace agreement by which the conflict had been concluded. The Court held on 3 February 1994 that the entire disputed area was part of the Republic of Chad. At that time Libyan forces were in occupation of a large part of the disputed area. An agreement for Libyan withdrawal was concluded under the auspices of the UN, which provided a small monitoring force and Libyan withdrawal was completed,

33 ICJ Reports, 1986, at pp. 129–30.
34 ICJ Reports, 1986, p. 554.   35 ICJ Reports, 1994, p. 3.

on schedule, by the end of May 1994.[36] In both cases the Court played an important role in putting a stop to the use of force by providing a peaceful and effective method for the settlement of the underlying disputes.

Although neither judgment makes any comment on the use of force as such, these two decisions illustrate the circumstances in which the Court is most likely to be able to exercise a substantial influence in respect of the use of force. Cases in which the Court is asked to rule on the widest issues of the use of force itself, as Judge Jennings recognized, almost inevitably pose greater problems, as the continuing controversy regarding the *Nicaragua* judgment and the disregard of the provisional measures the Court indicated in the *Genocide* case illustrate. Nevertheless, even in the latter group of cases the role of the Court should not be underestimated. As Judge Jennings put it:

> Any government engaged in, or contemplating, the use or threat of force, is by that very fact embarked upon a course where international law is of great importance. Such matters as the 1949 Geneva Conventions, the position of third States and their nationals, especially if the force extends to sea, the position of prisoners, the rules of combat, the Red Cross, and so on: all these become of daily inescapable relevance to the actual development of force. In such a position, a judgment of the International Court on even a part of the matter, must of itself, and quite apart from any question of enforcement, be of great significance to all parties.[37]

---

[36] See Security Council resolution 926 (1994) and UN Doc. S/1994/672. Earlier documents appear at *ILM* 33 (1994), p. 785.

[37] 'International Force', see n. 1 above, at p. 334.

PART IV

Procedural aspects of the work of the International Court of Justice

✌

21

Procedural law and the International Court of Justice

H. W. A. Thirlway

ໜ

Procedure, by definition, is no more than a way of getting somewhere; and in the sphere of international judicial action, the destination (the decision) is usually of more interest to jurists than the anfractuosities of the route (the procedural incidents). The law governing international judicial procedure has not been a subject of wide general interest. No English lawyer, recalling Maitland's dictum as to the sepulchral domination of the 'forms of action', will need telling that procedure can sometimes affect or govern substance; yet there is no fully developed general theory of international procedural law, defining its sources, for example. It may be supposed that in principle the enumeration in article 38 of the ICJ Statute is broadly valid for international procedural law as part of international law; but is that sufficient? There is also room for further study of the question whether that law can be reduced to, or deduced from, certain broad principles; or whether, even if the practical law is derived empirically, and by analogy from municipal systems, such principles can be identified as underlying it and inspiring its development.[1]

There is little discussion on the level of such principles to be found in the decisions of the International Court, though some Separate or Dissenting Opinions contain interesting material of this kind. One reason may be that so much of the Court's procedure is codified, in the Statute and Rules of Court; and as a result many procedural problems, perhaps the majority, resolve themselves into questions of interpretation of the Statute, and are thus governed by the law of interpretation of treaties.

There has, however, been consideration of substantial procedural problems in the Court's work in recent years, but this has taken place in certain well-

---

[1] For an interesting study of the matter from the viewpoint of a specialist in civil procedure looking at international procedures 'from outside', as it were, see François Terré, 'Théorie générale de la procédure et droit international public', *Revue de droit suisse*, 93 (1974), p. 41, who took the view that the dominating principle is the adversary principle (*principe de contradiction*).

defined areas: jurisdiction (a procedural problem, if one of a special kind); intervention under articles 62 and 63 of the Statute; provisional measures; and cases of non-appearance, governed by article 53 of the Statute.[2] Since the present publication deals with these subjects elsewhere, it would be superfluous to attempt even a sketch of those issues here; the present chapter will therefore lay its emphasis elsewhere. Two aspects of procedural law will be examined.

First, it is to be observed that a procedural problem raising questions of interpretation of the Statute can arise not only in the context of a case, contentious or advisory, before the Court, but also when the Court exercises its power under article 30 of the Statute to 'frame rules for carrying out its functions' and, in particular, 'rules of procedure'. Such a power, conferred by treaty, must be exercised within the limits by which it is defined in the treaty; and must not be exercised in contradiction with other provisions of the treaty. Some of the Rules adopted at the time of the complete revision of 1978 raise interesting questions in this respect, and will be examined in the first part of this chapter.

Second, procedural law at the international level cannot be limited to the law applied to the International Court to the proceedings conducted before it. Cases have also arisen in which the Court has had occasion to deal in a decision with questions of procedural law in relation to the work or the decisions of other international bodies discharging a judicial or quasi-judicial role. The applicable rules and principles must be the same, even if the applicable texts are different. The second part of this chapter will be devoted to cases of this kind.

I

One of the major changes introduced into the Court's practice by the 1978 revision of the Rules concerned the Chambers, and was intended to breathe new life into that institution. In this the revision may be said to have succeeded;[3] in the present context, however, only two aspects of it will be referred to.

---

[2] A further important procedural decision was the refusal, in the case of *Military and Paramilitary Activities in and against Nicaragua*, of a hearing to El Salvador on its request to intervene: see ICJ Reports, 1984, p. 215, and the subsequent courageous recognition by Judge Lachs that the decision was an error: ICJ Reports, 1986, pp. 170–1.

[3] The changes have already attracted an immense amount of doctrinal comment: see for example the list cited by Judge Shahabuddeen in ICJ Reports, 1990, p. 21, fn. 1; and the chapter by Dr Valencia-Ospina, in this volume.

The first aspect is that of the formation of a Chamber to deal with a particular case. The Statute of the Court (article 26, paragraph 2) provides that the Court may at any time form such a Chamber, and continues: 'The number of judges to constitute such a Chamber shall be determined by the Court with the approval of the parties.' The intention was thus that the parties (jointly) should have complete control of the size of the Chamber; but were they to have any say in its composition, i.e., in the choice of the judges to form the Chamber?

The 1946 Rules give no hint of this. The 1978 Rules do not give a specific answer on the point; but article 17, paragraph 2 provides that, when there is a request for the formation of a Chamber of this type, and the parties have agreed on this, 'the President shall ascertain their views *regarding the composition of the Chamber*, and shall report to the Court accordingly'. In practice, it has become recognized that the parties may indicate to the Court, under the heading of 'composition', the names of the judges whom they would like to see as members of the Chamber; and while the Court retains the freedom to elect whom it likes, effect will normally be given to the parties' wishes, if only because the parties are free to withdraw the case if not satisfied.[4] Given, however, that the Statute provides only for influence by the parties on the number of judges to constitute the Chamber, is this rule and the corresponding practice legally justified?[5]

The other change in the Rules relating to Chambers here to be considered relates to the continued composition of a Chamber formed for a specific case. Article 13, paragraph 3 of the Statute provides, with regard to the periodic re-election of judges, that:

> The Members of the Court shall continue to discharge their duties until their places have been filled. Though replaced, they shall finish any cases which they may have begun.

The new article 17, paragraph 4 of the Rules introduced in 1978 reads: 'Members of the Chamber formed under this Article who have been replaced, in accordance with Article 13 of the Statute following the expiration of their terms of office, shall continue to sit in all phases of the case, whatever the stage

---

[4] That this was in fact the intention of the Court in making the change was stated by President Jiménez de Aréchaga in an article in the *American Journal of International Law*. 'The Amendments to the Rules of Procedure of the International Court of Justice', *AJIL*, 67 (1973), p. 1.

[5] The controversy as it stood in 1989 was fully described by Judge Stephen M. Schwebel, 'Chambers of the International Court of Justice Formed for Particular Cases', in Y. Dinstein and M. Tabory (eds.), *International Law at a Time of Perplexity: Essays in Honour of Shabtai Rosenne* (Dordrecht, 1989), p. 739.

it has then reached.' This is to be contrasted with article 33:

> Except as provided in Article 7 of these Rules, Members of the Court who have been replaced, in accordance with Article 13, paragraph 3, of the Statute following the expiration of their terms of office, shall discharge the duty imposed upon them by that paragraph by continuing to sit until the completion of any phase of a case in respect of which the Court convenes for the oral proceedings prior to the date of such replacement.

The result of this is that two distinct interpretations are placed on a single article of the Statute. The practical advantages of the distinction are clear: the traditional interpretation (article 33) limits to the minimum necessary prolongation of judges' terms of office, while the Chamber interpretation (article 17) is essential if the membership of a Chamber is taken to be regulated *intuitu personae* by the choice of the parties. There is no doubt that either interpretation is legally tenable; but can they both be legally tenable?[6] It is surely of the essence of treaty interpretation that a text is deemed to have one meaning, not several possible meanings of equal status.[7]

In 1990, doubt was cast on the constitutional propriety of these developments, from an unexpected quarter. A Chamber had been formed in 1987 to deal with the case concerning the *Land, Island and Maritime Frontier Dispute* between El Salvador and Honduras, and it was no secret that the Court had, in forming it, taken account of the wishes of the parties as to its composition, conveyed through the President. Furthermore, one of the judges elected to the Chamber had unexpectedly failed to be re-elected to the Court at the triennial election held to take effect from 6 February 1988, and therefore continued to sit as a member (and indeed President) of the Chamber by virtue of article 17, paragraph 4 of the Rules. In November 1989 Nicaragua applied to the Court for permission to intervene in the case under article 62 of the Statute, and the question arose whether that application should be dealt with by the Court or the Chamber. By an Order of 28 February 1990, the Court decided that it was for the Chamber to decide on the application. One of the judges voting against that decision, Judge Shahabuddeen, appended a lengthy Dissenting Opinion in which he explained his reasons for considering 'that the existing procedural arrangements for forming *ad hoc* chambers are not valid'.[8]

Judge Shahabuddeen's view, in summary, was that

---

6 Cf. *ibid.*, p. 754.

7 But compare the Court's decision in the case concerning the *Arbitral Award of 31 July 1991*, p. 53, discussed below, pp. 397–9.

8 ICJ Reports, 1990, p. 18.

the Chamber has been constituted not in accordance with the Statute, but in accordance with an unauthorized arrangement under which the Court has been essaying to transform itself into the Permanent Court of Arbitration, or something akin to it. This represents a major flaw which the Court, as the avowed guardian of its own judicial integrity, cannot correctly overlook.[9]

His reasons for this view – stated in great detail and with characteristic lucidity in his Dissenting Opinion – were essentially based on the two revisions of the Rules just discussed. First, he held that it was not justifiable to give the parties the power to choose the membership of a Chamber. Second, on the question of continued membership of the Chamber, he observed:

> Now, if the Rules under consideration [i.e. articles 17(4) and 33] are valid, the entire oral proceedings of a case before an *ad hoc* chamber may take place before persons none of whom held the office of a Member of the Court at any time during that hearing. So, once again, is this the kind of chamber that the framers of the Statute had in mind when they accepted in Article 27 that 'a judgment given by any of the chambers provided for in Articles 26 and 29 shall be considered as rendered by the Court'?[10]

He recognized realistically that 'the existing practice may well continue unabated. My views may make no difference. It was nevertheless my duty to state them.'[11] No further request for the formation of a Chamber has since been received, so that Judge Shahabuddeen's views have not been tested; but since he was alone in his view in 1990 (the three other dissenting judges based their votes on different grounds), it can in any event be assumed with reasonable confidence that the new practice is here to stay.

For the reasons explained above, the interesting part of Judge Shahabuddeen's opinion for present purposes is not his arguments that the new practice is in conflict with the Statute – though he makes an extremely convincing case for that view – but his observations on the limits of the rule-making power. His conclusion surely admits of no contradiction:

> To sum up, the field of operation of the rule-making power of the Court, as defined by Article 30 of the Statute, is wide but not unlimited. The Court, it may be said, has a certain autonomy in the exercise of its rule-making competence; but autonomy is not omnipotence, and that competence is not unbounded. Rules of Court could only be made in exercise of powers granted by the Statute, whether expressly or impliedly.[12]

---

[9] *Ibid.*, p. 55.   [10] *Ibid.*, p. 52.
[11] *Ibid.*, p. 55.   [12] *Ibid.*, p. 47.

It can hardly be supposed that the majority of the Court disagreed with this statement of principle. The Order of the Court, to which Judge Shahabuddeen's Opinion was appended, contains no comment on the point raised by him. It would hardly have been appropriate for it to do so, since it was not so much the decision taken in that Order that he was attacking, but the way in which the Chamber was constituted – and indeed the decision to adopt the amended Rules in 1972 – though his practical conclusion was that the decision in the Order should have gone the other way.

The successive decisions of the Court in this field can hardly be taken as asserting a power simply to disregard the Statute; they must be interpreted as implying an interpretation of that instrument on the basis of 'whatever is not forbidden is permitted'. This is also suggested by another change effected in the 1978 revision of the Rules. Ever since the creation of the Permanent Court, it had been established that a judgment (and an Advisory Opinion) must state the majority by which it was adopted, and that any judge who chose to do so could state his position in a Separate or Dissenting Opinion; but that otherwise the way in which each judge voted remained shrouded in secrecy. Article 95, paragraph 1 of the 1978 Rules however now provides that 'the judgment . . . shall contain . . . the number and *names* of the judges consti- tuting the majority', and there is similar provision in article 107 for Advisory Opinions. Since abstention is not permitted on a judicial decision, the members of the minority are therefore unveiled, and in practice judgments state their names also.

The records of the 1978 revision of the Rules not having been made public, it is unknown whether this change was resisted, or was unanimously regarded as appropriate. In view of its far-reaching effect on the character of the Court, some doubt may be felt as to the propriety of the change, which was also effected *sponte sua* by the Court, without consultation of the states parties to the Statute.[13]

One further change introduced into the Rules in 1978 merits comment. There was at one time a practice of using the procedures of the Court for political ends by instituting what were known colloquially as 'phoney cases'. The applicant state would file an application against a state that had not accepted the jurisdiction of the Court, and invite it to accept such jurisdiction purely for the purposes of the case. The result was that all members of the United Nations were informed, through the circulation by the Registry of the text of the application pursuant to article 40 of the Statute, of the

---

[13] The Court did in fact receive numerous comments from governments and international lawyers during the course of its revision work. None of the published material includes any suggestion for this change.

contention of the applicant state in relation to the dispute; and at the same time that state appeared publicly as virtuous, as being ready to submit to judicial settlement, and confident of the strength of its case. The respondent was almost invariably an Eastern-bloc state, disinclined for reasons of political principle to make use of the Court. When it declined to participate (as the applicant was perfectly aware it would), it inevitably appeared to lack confidence in its case, the nature of which it had no opportunity to explain to UN members in response to the application.

In 1978, although no cases of this kind had been brought for nearly twenty years,[14] the Court appears to have decided to take the opportunity of putting an end to the practice. A new paragraph in article 38 provides as follows:

> 5. When the applicant State proposes to found the jurisdiction of the Court upon a consent thereto yet to be given or manifested by the State against which such application is made, the application shall be transmitted to that State. It shall not however be entered in the General List, nor any action be taken in the proceedings, unless and until the State against which such application is made consents to the Court's jurisdiction for the purposes of the case.

The intention of the text – to do away with any advantages derived from filing a 'phoney case' – is clear, and may be taken to have been achieved. While, as already noted, applications of this kind had, by 1978, dropped out of fashion, two have recently been filed.[15] In the first case, after the procedure laid down in article 38, paragraph 5 of the Rules had been followed, the parties concluded a special agreement for settlement by the Court of, if not precisely the dispute set out in the abortive application, a dispute relating essentially to the same subject.[16] The other case is, at the time of writing, still in limbo pending a reaction from the numerous states named as respondents.

There must, however, remain a doubt whether it is within the power of the Court to modify the procedures laid down in the Statute; provided an application complies with the requirements of the Statute, article 40 requires that it be given appropriate circulation. The Statute, however, says nothing about any indication, at the stage of the filing of an application, of the

---

[14] The cases in which this occurred were *Treatment in Hungary of Aircraft and Crew of the United States of America* (1954 – two cases); *Aerial Incident of 10 March 1953* (1956); *Antarctica* (1956 – two cases); *Aerial Incident of 4 September 1954* (1958); and *Aerial Incident of 7 November 1954* (1959).

[15] Application by Hungary against Czechoslovakia concerning alleged diversion of the Danube, ICJ Press Communiqué No. 92/25 of 26 October 1992; Application of Yugoslavia against the member states of NATO, ICJ Press Communiqué No. 94/11 of 21 March 1994.

[16] *Case Concerning the Gabčíkovo–Nagymaros Project*, Special Agreement notified to the Court on 2 July 1993.

jurisdictional title relied on; and even article 38 of the Rules only requires, in paragraph 2, that 'the application shall specify *as far as possible* the legal grounds upon which the jurisdiction of the Court is said to be based'. The intention of the Court thus seems to have been to recognize that an application not referring to an existing title of jurisdiction can validly be filed, and thus is in conformity with article 40 of the Statute; yet to apply to it a special procedure which, however justified in practice, is not in harmony with that article. As in the case of judges continuing in office under article 13 of the Statute, the interpretation of the Statute in the Rules seems to contain an internal inconsistency.

If this is so, is there any practical conclusion to be drawn? Judge Shahabuddeen was unsuccessful in 1990 in having the Court reconsider its revisions of 1978; and the situation of the Court renders academic the question whether international procedural law contains any sanctions for procedural irregularities. Academic or not, however, that question remains; and some hint of the Court's attitude to it may emerge from its treatment of questions of the procedural law applied by other bodies.

II

It is particularly the manner in which the Court in its decisions has treated questions of procedural law arising before other judicial or quasi-judicial bodies that prompts the question: does procedural law matter? More specifically, what, if any, are the legal consequences if it is found that a decision has been arrived at through a procedure that does not meet the standards of a proper judicial process – should the decision be invalidated? And subsidiarily, should the answer to this question be at all affected by the fact (if it is a fact) that the decision improperly arrived at was nevertheless a correct decision?

The Court may be seised of problems relating to the decision of another judicial or quasi-judicial body in a number of ways; and in some contexts, if it is suggested that the proceedings before that body involved breaches of procedural law, the preliminary question arises to what extent the Court can take cognizance of such allegations, if to uphold them would involve substituting the Court's own view of the requirements of procedural law for that of the body concerned. In the case concerning the *Arbitral Award of the King of Spain*, it was suggested that the two national arbitrators had not complied with the procedural requirements of the treaty establishing the arbitration, in the steps they took prior to designating the King of Spain as arbitrator. The Court's ruling was that

In the opinion of the Court it was within the power of the arbitrators to interpret and apply the articles in question in order to discharge their function of organising the arbitral tribunal. Whether they had in fact exhausted the membership of the Diplomatic Corps accredited to Guatemala and failed to reach agreement on the election of any other foreign or Central American public figure or whether they had considered such steps as optional and unlikely to lead to a fruitful result, the fact remains that after agreeing that the relevant articles of the Treaty had been complied with they agreed to proceed to the designation of the King of Spain as arbitrator. The Court, therefore, concludes that the requirements of the relevant articles of the Gámez–Bonilla Treaty *as interpreted by the two national arbitrators* had already been complied with when, at the meeting of 2 October 1904, it was agreed by common consent that the King of Spain should be designated as arbitrator and that he should be requested on behalf of both Governments to undertake the task.[17]

So far, therefore, as a procedural question involves the interpretation of the compromis, the Court appears to have regarded the arbitrators' decision on the matter as final. It refused to consider *de novo* what were the procedural requirements of the Treaty and whether they had been respected; i.e., it declined to substitute its own view, as to the correctness of the procedure followed, for that of the arbitrators.

However, the judgment continues with an examination of the conduct of the parties in the course of the arbitration: 'No question was at any time raised in the arbitral proceedings before the King with regard either to the validity of his designation as arbitrator or his jurisdiction as such.'[18] Thus the Court seems to have thought that the interpretation by the arbitrators, subsequently accepted by the parties, was unassailable; which leaves open the question of the validity of such interpretation if unconfirmed by the parties' conduct.

In the more recent case concerning the *Arbitral Award of 31 July 1989*, the Arbitration Tribunal had been acting under a compromis which defined two legal questions, and required the Tribunal to reply to the second question 'in the event of a negative answer to the first question'. The answer which the arbitrators arrived at to the first question was partly affirmative, and thus could equally be said to be partly negative; but they decided that they were 'not called upon to reply to the second question'. One party contended before the Court that the award was null and void, because the Tribunal should have replied to the second question; in other words that the procedural (and jurisdictional) decision that no answer was required to the second question was wrong. The case therefore raised very directly the question of the conclusiveness of a procedural decision of an arbitral body. It was also a

---

[17] ICJ Reports, 1960, p. 206 (emphasis added).　　[18] *Ibid.*, p. 207.

question as to the value of a decision on jurisdiction, and thus an aspect of a problem that is fundamental to international arbitration.

If two states have accepted in advance the solution to a dispute to be indicated by an arbitrator, neither of them can reject that solution on the ground that it is wrong in law. Each party accepts the risk that the arbitrator may accept the thesis of the other party, or even come up with a thesis of his own. But can an award be rejected on the ground that, whether or not the decision itself is sound, it was taken on a question going beyond that which the parties had agreed to submit for arbitration, or reached by a procedure that did not respect the procedural rights of a party? The first case raises the more acute difficulty: if *extra compromissum arbiter nihil facere potest*, what validity can a decision have on a point the arbitrator was not asked to decide? Yet if this is a ground for unilateral rejection of an award, how is the stability of arbitral decisions to be preserved? Similar considerations apply to procedural matters: a state may reasonably argue that it agreed in advance to accept a decision arrived at after a proper judicial procedure; a disregard of principles of procedural law would mean that the decision arrived at would not be a 'judicial' decision of the kind covered by the arbitral submission, and thus a nullity.

In the case of the *Arbitral Award of 31 July 1989*, the Court unfortunately did not tackle the issue of principle: it dealt with the matter by a side wind, by concentrating on the question of the nature of the proceedings brought before it. Referring to the argument of Guinea-Bissau that the Tribunal was wrong to conclude that it was not required to answer the second question, the Court said:

> Guinea-Bissau is in fact criticizing the interpretation in the Award of the provisions of the Arbitration Agreement which determine the Tribunal's jurisdiction, and proposing another interpretation. However, the Court does not have to enquire whether or not the Arbitration Agreement could, with regard to the Tribunal's competence, be interpreted in a number of ways, and if so to consider which would have been preferable. By proceeding in that way the Court would be treating the request as an appeal and not as a *recours en nullité*. The Court could not act in that way in the present case. It has simply to ascertain whether by rendering the disputed Award the Tribunal acted in manifest breach of the competence conferred on it by the Arbitration Agreement, either by deciding in excess of, or by failing to exercise, its jurisdiction.[19]

From a pragmatic viewpoint, this approach is defensible as steering a middle course between the conflicting requirements of the need for stability of arbitral decisions and of the *extra compromissum* rule. It is, however, difficult to justify as a matter of legal theory. The distinction between appeal and *recours en nullité* did mean, as the Court noted earlier in its judgment, that the Court was not asked to say, in the words of the *King of Spain* case, 'whether the arbitrator's decision was right or wrong'.[20] This, however, referred to the decision of the Arbitration Tribunal on the substantive question put to it, not questions of jurisdiction or procedure. Furthermore, it did not mean that, on the substantive question, the Court was asked to say whether the Tribunal had acted 'in manifest breach' of the legal principles and rules it had purported to apply.

The essential issue was whether the parties had agreed that matters of jurisdiction and procedure should be determined conclusively by the Tribunal. If so, the Court would have to treat those decisions as equally exempt from review, along with the decision on the substance. If not, the Court could review the Tribunal's decisions thereon and, if necessary, substitute its own view. The distinction between 'appeal' and '*recours en nullité*' is artificial at the international level; what matters is: what are the questions that the Tribunal, for its part, and subsequently the Court, has been given jurisdiction, by the agreement of the parties, to determine, and on what legal basis?

Nor is an arbitral award automatically and inevitably unappealable. Whether the matter be regarded as one of implementation of a treaty commitment, or as the effect of the principle of *res judicata*, it seems clear that the answer given by an arbitrator to the legal question (on the merits) put to him thenceforth constitutes the law for the parties to the arbitration. Accordingly, if one of the parties to the arbitration subsequently seises the Court, on the basis of Optional-Clause declarations, or a widely drawn clause in a treaty of judicial settlement, the decision of the Court can only be to endorse the conclusion of the arbitrator. But that does not prevent the parties, if they so wish, from asking the Court to determine the question whether the arbitrator's decision was wrong. This would require specific agreement, not so much as a matter of jurisdiction, but to enable the Court to determine a question that would, in the absence of the specific consent of the parties, be hypothetical: i.e., the nature of their obligations, not as defined by the arbitrator, but as they stood independently of his decision.[21]

---

[20] ICJ Reports, 1991, p. 62, para. 25.

[21] Cf. the problem of the interim judgment between the United Kingdom and Iceland in the *Fisheries Jurisdiction* case: ICJ Reports, 1974, pp. 18–20, paras. 37–41, and the Dissenting Opinion of Judge Petrén, *ibid.*, pp. 155–60.

In 1971–2, the Court was seised of what was avowedly an appeal – the *Appeal relating to the Jurisdiction of the ICAO Council,* brought by Pakistan against India. The case involved alleged procedural irregularities by the ICAO Council in arriving at the decision the subject of the appeal. The Court's decision in this respect was as follows:

> The Court however does not deem it necessary or even appropriate to go into this matter, particularly as the alleged irregularities do not prejudice in any fundamental way the requirements of a just procedure. The Court's task in the present proceedings is to give a ruling as to whether the Council has jurisdiction in the case. This is an objective question of law, the answer to which cannot depend on what occurred before the Council. Since the Court holds that the Council did and does have jurisdiction, then, if there were in fact procedural irregularities, the position would be that the Council would have reached the right conclusion in the wrong way. Nevertheless it would have reached the right conclusion. If, on the other hand, the court had held that there was and is no jurisdiction, then, even in the absence of any irregularities, the Council's decision to assume it would have stood reversed.[22]

Judge Morozov, who voted against the judgment,[23] challenged the soundness of this approach which he equated with 'the end justifies the means'; it was also dissented from by Judge Jiménez de Aréchaga, who voted in favour.[24] It is to be noted that the Court's attitude is justified primarily by the possibility of substituting its own (by definition, correct) view on the substance for that of the body from which the appeal is brought; it is only this possibility that justifies treating the proceedings that led up to the original decision as without importance. If the Court is seised solely of a *recours en nullité*, on the authority of the case of the *Arbitral Award of 31 July 1989*, it is not required to determine, and therefore presumably unable to say, whether the first jurisdiction did or did not arrive at the correct conclusion. It would therefore seem that in such circumstances the Court would have to determine whether or not there had been a procedural error, and if it found there had, to draw the appropriate consequences. Furthermore, the idea that all that matters is the correctness of the substantive decision raises a delicate problem of the relationship between procedural justice – the due respect of the principles of procedural law – and the essential justice – a correct decision on the merits of the case – which is the proper end of any judicial process.

In 1982, this problem arose in what was for the Court itself a totally different procedural context: that of a request for an Advisory Opinion under

---

[22] ICJ Reports, 1972, pp. 69–70, para. 45.
[23] *Ibid.,* pp. 158–9.   [24] *Ibid.,* pp. 153–4.

the procedure for review of decisions of the United Nations Administrative Tribunal (*Application for Review of Judgment No. 273 of the United Nations Administrative Tribunal,* usually known as the *Mortished* case). The Tribunal had given a decision in favour of the applicant Mr Mortished; the Committee on Applications for Review of Administrative Tribunal Judgments had asked the Court for an Advisory Opinion on the validity of that decision. In the course of the proceedings of the Committee, which, as the Court found, was discharging quasi-judicial functions, a whole series of grave irregularities had occurred, a number of which had operated to the detriment of Mr Mortished. It was therefore argued that the Court should decline to give an Advisory Opinion at all, a view explicitly accepted by one member of the Court.[25] The result would have been that the UNAT judgment in Mr Mortished's favour would stand. The Court, however, considered, for reasons to be examined in a moment, that it should give the Opinion requested;[26] and found, by a majority, that the criticisms addressed to the Tribunal's judgment were not well founded.

The Court in its decision did in fact go so far as to state that 'the irregularities which feature throughout the proceedings in the present case could well be regarded as "compelling reasons" for a refusal by the Court to entertain the request'.[27] Nevertheless, it held that there was no risk of the Court's judicial role being 'endangered or discredited'; and observed that 'in the present case such refusal would leave in suspense a very serious allegation against the Administrative Tribunal, that it had in effect challenged the authority of the General Assembly'.[28] The Court in fact exonerated the Tribunal; but if it had not – if it had found that the Tribunal *had* 'challenged the authority of the General Assembly' – would this reasoning have been appropriate? Which would have been preferable: for such an allegation to have been left in suspense, or to have been found justified? Like Judge Morozov in 1972, one has the feeling that the end is being permitted to justify the means, that the question whether procedural irregularities should be sanctioned is being determined by considerations that are, or ought to be, legally irrelevant.

In principle, the two questions, that of the validity of the Tribunal's judgment, and that of the irregularities subsequently submitted by the

---

[25] Judge El-Khani, ICJ Reports, 1982, pp. 447ff.

[26] It dealt with the point purely from the point of view of its recognized discretion to give or refuse an Advisory Opinion; it did not discuss the question whether (as Judge Ruda held: ICJ Reports, 1982, p. 376) one at least of the irregularities was such that the Court *could not* act on the request. Logically, this point precedes the question of the exercise of the Court's discretion.

[27] ICJ Reports, 1982, p. 347, para. 45.

[28] *Ibid.*

Committee, and their possible consequences, were wholly unconnected. But was it in fact possible to keep them so? The Court did not, in the public proceedings, take the question of the irregularities first, as a preliminary issue; whether it did so in its internal deliberations will never be known. In any event, at the time when the decision on the question of the irregularities came to be taken, members of the Court would have known that the decision on the merits questions (the correctness of the Tribunal's judgment) was going to be in Mr Mortished's favour. Had it been known that the decision on the merits was going to go the other way, it would have been reasonable for judges to have more doubts on the justice of the overall outcome: to disregard the procedural injustices done to Mr Mortished might have been felt to be justifiable if to do so enabled the Court to find in his favour on the merits, but a dubious course if it would result in his being deprived by such means of the fruits of his victory before the Tribunal.

If procedural irregularities were to be sanctioned, what would procedural justice require? Here a distinction is necessary. What the Court described as 'one of the most important irregularities in the procedure'[29] related to the composition of the Committee, and resulted from an error by a particular state representative who should have acted as Chairman of the Committee; the error appears to have neither disadvantaged nor favoured either of the parties, which did not comment on it. To speak of sanctions for the error as to the Committee's composition would therefore be inappropriate; the question was simply whether the decision of the Committee would have to be regarded as void because the Committee was not properly constituted.[30] The problem of procedural justice arises when a party has acted in breach of procedural principles; and in the *Mortished* case further irregularities were related to the application to the Committee by the US, and the conduct of its representative in the Committee; in other words, the actions of a 'quasi-party' to the 'quasi-judicial' process before the Committee.

A simple criterion would be that an advantage gained by incorrect procedural means should be nullified, or conferred equally on the other side. If a pleading were filed a month late, there can be little doubt that the Court would, as a condition of accepting it, give the other party an extra month for its counter-pleading. Unfortunately in many cases, including that of *Mortished*, matters are not so simple. In the first place, the only sanction available to the Court was to refuse to give the Advisory Opinion; but against whom would this sanction operate? The US was extremely anxious to have an opinion given

[29] *Ibid.*, p. 342, para. 38.
[30] As was the view of Judge Ruda; see note 16 above.

that would invalidate the Tribunal's decision; but it could not be assumed *a priori* that that would be the outcome. Nevertheless, a refusal to give an opinion could be regarded as effectively a sanction on the conduct of the US.

But had the decision to request the Opinion been obtained as a result of the procedural irregularities, in the sense that had they not taken place, would the Committee have taken a negative decision? In view of the majorities obtained on the Committee's decisions, this is by no means evident. An alternative approach, applicable in particular to the exclusion of Mr Mortished's counsel from the Committee's discussions, is to say that since that counsel was improperly deprived of the chance of convincing the Committee that it should reject the US application, it must be assumed that if he had had the chance, he would have been successful. The consequence would be a refusal to give the Advisory Opinion.

It would have been difficult to apply to the proceedings of the Review Committee in the *Mortished* case the approach adopted in the *ICAO Appeal* case. It is essential to the latter approach that it be possible – and appropriate – to say *ex post facto* whether a decision arrived at by dubious procedural means was or was not, nevertheless, a correct decision. The role of the Committee, quasi-judicial as it was, was limited to deciding 'whether or not there is a substantial basis for the application' whereby the Committee was asked to request an Advisory Opinion. Even if the Court eventually decided, as in fact it did in the *Mortished* case, that the Tribunal's judgment was unimpeachable, this would not necessarily mean that there had been no substantial basis for the application; still less that the Committee had been wrong to decide, on the material evidence available to it, that there was such a basis. More important, the Court was not called upon, as it was in the *ICAO Appeal* case, to decide whether the Committee's decision had or had not been correct; and could hardly be expected to go into that question simply in order to determine whether or not account should be taken of procedural irregularities.

On the other hand, the Court in the *Mortished* case was also concerned with a procedural irregularity, or alleged irregularity, occurring during the proceedings of the Administrative Tribunal itself: although the Statute of the Tribunal provided that 'Only three [members of the Tribunal] shall sit in any particular case', the case was heard and determined by a Tribunal of four members. The Court noted that 'it might be suggested that this was irregular, and that if the irregularity were found to be such as to vitiate the decision of the Tribunal, further examination of the question put to the Court would be unnecessary'.[31] This was again an irregularity for which neither of the parties

31 ICJ Reports, 1982, p. 340, para. 33.

before the Tribunal had any responsibility; nor, technically, did the parties before the Committee.[32] The Court made some rather inconclusive observations as to the circumstances in which the President of the Tribunal might, under its Rules, designate a member of the Tribunal to serve as an alternate, and the practice in this respect, before concluding:

> At all events, the Court has not been asked to consider whether the Tribunal might have 'committed a fundamental error in procedure which has occasioned a failure of justice' as contemplated by Article 11, paragraph 1, of the Tribunal's Statute, nor does the matter appear on the face of it to disclose any failure of justice. Accordingly, further consideration of the point does not seem to be called for.[33]

This view was presumably justified by the fact that the dissenting vote of the additional, or alternate, member of the Tribunal had not had any practical effect, since the three regular members were unanimous.

Had the Court adopted the approach employed in the *ICAO Appeal* case, it would have reserved the question of the composition of the Tribunal; and, having found that the Tribunal's judgment was unimpeachable, concluded that there was no point in considering the alleged irregularity. The Court's actual course of action is to be preferred, both because of the dubious legitimacy of the *ICAO Appeal* approach, and because the question was one of the composition of the Tribunal and hence of the possible nullity of its judgment.

It would seem not unfair to conclude from this brief survey that the attitude of the International Court to procedural questions has been perhaps a rather too whole-hearted embracing of the philosophy of the Permanent Court as to questions of form:

> The Court, whose jurisdiction is international, is not bound to attach to matters of form the same degree of importance which they might possess in municipal law.[34]

> The Court cannot allow itself to be hampered by a mere defect of form.[35]

---

[32] As Judge El-Khani noted: 'The alternate [member] . . . by some strange coincidence possessed the nationality of the State which later was to call for the review of Judgment No. 273' (ICJ Reports, 1982, p. 449). The member of the Court possessing that nationality, who dissented from the Court's Opinion, made no comment in his own lengthy opinion on the procedural irregularities.

[33] *Ibid.*, pp. 341–2, para. 35. Judge El-Khani, on the other hand, held that the Review Committee, which could of course have asked the Court to rule on the question of 'fundamental error in procedure', had been at fault in 'failing to consider this aspect of the matter', and that this was an additional ground for a refusal by the Court to give an Advisory Opinion (*ibid.*, p. 449).

[34] *Mavrommatis Palestine Concessions*, PCIJ, Series A, No. 2, p. 34.

[35] *Polish Upper Silesia*, PCIJ, Series A, No. 6, p. 14.

In resolving questions of procedure in the Rules of Court, it has permitted itself a good deal of latitude in exercising the rule-making power conferred by the Statute. In assessing the extent to which other judicial or quasi-judicial bodies have respected the procedural requirements laid upon them, it has had to take account of the way in which the decision of such body has come to be in issue before it (itself a procedural question); but has apparently tended to concentrate its attention on the outcome rather than the procedure. So, far from procedure affecting substance, it is rather substance that has eclipsed procedure. The *ICAO Appeal* case contains an express declaration that if the result is regarded as right, the commission of procedural sins in arriving at it will be pardoned. The sins in that case were perhaps venial; but it is to be hoped that, if and when necessary, the Court will be ready to recognize the possibility of a mortal sin of procedure, justifying the application of appropriate sanctions. What those should be remain to be worked out.

22

The President of the International Court of Justice

Shabtai Rosenne

ᚓᚓ

Like all collegiate organs, the International Court of Justice is headed by a President. In current practice, there are two patterns for the presidency of collegiate international organs. In most 'large' organs composed of states, such as the General Assembly of the United Nations or a major plenipotentiary conference, the President is normally a member of a delegation from which, however, the Rules of Procedure will exclude him. In 'small' bodies, including for this purpose the Security Council (composed of the representatives of states) or the International Law Commission (composed of individuals), the presiding officer is chosen according to the stipulations of the constituent instrument (including the Rules of Procedure), but remains a full member of his delegation or a full participant in the body to which he belongs, retaining his right to vote. In those circumstances, it is customary for the presiding officer to speak last: voting is usually, in this type of organ (but not in the International Court), conducted instantaneously, and today frequently through electronic means. The President of the International Court belongs to this second category.

Article 21 of the Statute requires the Court to elect its President and Vice-President for three years; they may be re-elected. A contemporary interpretation for this three-year term explains:

> It was felt that, given the immense prestige of the position of president of the court, the power which he might exercise and the influence which he might bring to bear upon his colleagues, it was inadvisable to elect him for the full term of his office, that is, nine years. One year, on the contrary, seemed too short, inasmuch as the president is to reside at the seat of the court. A period of three years was adopted as a compromise, as an inducement to merit continuance in office at the expiration

It gives me great pleasure to acknowledge here the kindness, encouragement and friendship that I have enjoyed from Sir Robert Jennings over a long period.

of his term, and of a further term, inasmuch as it is expressly provided that the president and vice-president may be reelected.[1]

Since 1945, this three-year term of office of the President and Vice-President coincides with the recurrent election of one-third of the members of the Court every third year.

Article 22 requires the President (and the Registrar) to reside at the seat of the Court (The Hague). The President presides at all meetings of the Court, directs its work and supervises its administration (Rules of Court, article 12). By article 13, paragraph 3 of the Rules, he has to take the measures necessary to ensure the continuous exercise of the functions of the Presidency at the seat of the Court. In case of his absence he may, so far as is compatible with the Statute and Rules, arrange for the Vice-President or, failing him, the next senior judge, to exercise these functions.[2] Article 20 of the Rules gives him the power in case of urgency to convene the Court at any time.

By article 3, paragraph 5 of the Rules, while holding their offices the President and Vice-President take precedence before all other members of the Court. When that term of office ends, each resumes his place among the members of the Court according to the general rule of precedence.[3] If the President decides to resign from the Court, his decision is to be communicated to the Court (article 5, paragraph 2).[4] Article 6 deals with the powers of the President to apply article 18 of the Statute, concerning the dismissal of a member of the Court. His powers and duties in relation to the Registrar and staff are set out in articles 22 to 29 of the Rules.

Apart from the standard literature on the Court, there is remarkably little writing devoted exclusively to the status and role of the President.[5] A brief

---

[1] J. B. Scott, *The Project of a Permanent Court of International Justice and Resolutions of the Advisory Committee of Jurists: Report and Commentary* (Washington, 1920), p. 78. Over the years the practice has developed of rotating the Presidency among the principal legal systems represented on the Court.

[2] As an illustration, note the order of Vice-President Oda fixing new time-limits in the case concerning the *Application of the Convention on the Prevention and Punishment of the Crime of Genocide*, ICJ Reports, 1993, p. 470.

[3] Under the Rules of 1926 (article 2), the retiring President, whatever his seniority under the general rules, took his seat to the right of the President and the retiring Vice-President to his left. This was abolished in article 2 of the Rules of 1931.

[4] Article 13, para. 4 deals with the resignation of the Presidency. See S. Torres-Benárdez, 'Resignations at the World Court', in Y. Dinstein and M. Tabory (eds.), *International Law at a Time of Perplexity: Essays in Honour of Shabtai Rosenne* (Dordrecht, 1989), p. 953.

[5] On the President of the Permanent Court of International Justice, see R. A. Lienau, *Stellung und Befugnisse des Präsidenten des Ständigen Internationalen Gerichtshofes* (Kiel, 1938). For a comparison between the President of that Court and the President of the Council of the League of Nations, see D. Avramoff, *Le Président du Conseil de la Société des Nations* (Bordeaux, 1932), p. 110. On the President of the present International Court of Justice, see C. Sirat, 'Le Président de la Cour internationale de Justice', *RGDIP*,

discussion on the powers of the President when the Court is not sitting took place early during the Preliminary Session of the Permanent Court in 1922. That was before there had been any experience, and before the Court had adopted any of the Rules of Court. The Court decided to treat each particular case as it arose during the drafting of the Rules. It also adopted a decision of principle to the effect that it could confer on the President the right to take interlocutory decisions.[6]

The Permanent Court established the basic rule that it elects its President by secret ballot. That, the normal rule of international organizations unless the President is chosen by acclamation, now appears in article 11, paragraph 2 of the Rules. A majority of the members of the Court composing it at the time, that is 50 per cent plus one, or eight votes if the full complement of members exists then, is required for the election of the President, a positive requirement introduced in 1978.[7] The previous Rules required a majority of the members of the Court present.[8] The reasons for this change, which enhances the general standing of a President elected under these conditions, have not been made public. The election should take place on or as near as possible after 6 February of each three-year cadence of the Court following the triennial election of one-third of the members of the Court (Rules, article 10). The term of office begins on 6 February or on the date of the election if later, and

---

62 (1958), p. 193; P. C. Spender, 'The Office of President of the International Court of Justice', *The Australian Year Book of International Law*, 1 (1965), p. 9; M. Zafrulla Khan, 'The Appointment of Arbitrators by the President of the International Court of Justice', *Comunicazioni e Studi: Il Processo Internazionale, Studi in onore de Gaetano Morelli*, 14 (1975), p. 1021. Bibliographical information kindly supplied by the Registry of the Court.

6 PCIJ, Series D, No. 2, p. 28.

7 The Advisory Committee of Jurists of 1920 rejected a proposal that the President should be elected by absolute majority: *Procès-verbaux of the Proceedings of the Committee* (1920), p. 459. The Secretariat of the League of Nations advised the Permanent Court that it was free to adopt any method for the election of the President and Vice-President, and thought that election by simple majority would seem to be in conformity with the intentions of the framers of the original Statute: PCIJ, Series D, No. 2 (1922), p. 242. And see article 3 of the draft rules of the Court prepared by the Secretariat: *Ibid.*, p. 253. The Permanent Court in its Preliminary Session, after a brief discussion at the sixth meeting, decided that the election should take place by secret ballot and by an absolute majority of the judges present: Rules of 1922/1936/1946/1972, article 9. The change to the present wording was made in article 11 of the Rules of 1978. See also S. Rosenne, *Procedure in the International Court* (The Hague/London, 1983), p. 35.

8 The only other case requiring an absolute majority of the members of the Court is article 18 of the Rules, on the election of Chambers under articles 26 or 29 of the Statute, and the election of the Registrar and Deputy Registrar under articles 22 and 23 of the Rules. By article 18 of the Statute, the unanimous opinion of the other members of the Court is required for the dismissal of a member on the ground that he has ceased to fulfil the required conditions (there has been no instance of this). By article 29 the Registrar and Deputy Registrar can be removed from office on the opinion of two-thirds of the members of the Court.

ends when the new President is elected. If a vacancy in the presidency occurs before the expiration of the current term, the Court is to decide whether to fill it for the remainder of the term (Rules, article 14).[9]

The President operates in two distinct capacities. He is President of the Court, namely the fifteen elected members of that body designated in the Charter as the principal judicial organ of the United Nations. He is also President of the Bench whenever he sits for a particular case, unless disqualified to act as President, or to sit as a judge, under specific provisions of the Statute and Rules. In those circumstances article 13, paragraph 2 of the Rules provides that when he is precluded by a provision of the Statute or of the Rules either from sitting or from presiding in a particular case, 'he shall continue to exercise the functions of the presidency for all purposes save in respect of that case'.[10]

However, the Statute and the Rules do not clearly distinguish between these two functions. In two instances a single formal rule is applicable to both capacities. By article 13 of the Rules, if the President is unable to exercise the functions of the Presidency, the Vice-President or failing him the senior judge shall exercise them. By article 55 of the statute, all questions shall be decided by a majority of the judges present, and in case of an equality of votes, the President shall have a casting vote (*voix prépondérante*).

As President of the Court, he has general powers and responsibilities in directing the work of the Court as a whole. The President and Vice-President are *ex officio* members of the Court's Budgetary and Administrative Committee. Alongside the administrative duties, which can be demanding, he also has burdensome responsibilities in his representative capacity, both towards the different international organizations and above all the General Assembly, and in relation to the host state and generally. He is the official host of the Court when Dutch and foreign dignitaries visit it. In the order of diplomatic precedence at The Hague, he takes precedence over the Dean of the Diplomatic Corps. In his absence, the Vice-President takes his

---

[9] On this, the terms of office as President and as a member of the Court of Sir Humphrey Waldock were due to come to an end on 6 February 1982. After Sir Humphrey's death on 15 August 1981, the Security Council considered that as the vacancy would be filled through the regular election to be held in the General Assembly of 1981, no purpose would be served by invoking the procedures for filling the occasional vacancy: UN Doc. A/36/451-S/14645, General Assembly, Official Records, 36th Session, Annexes, agenda item 15, p. 4. And see *United Nations Juridical Yearbook* (1981), p. 145. The Vice-President thereupon became Acting President, and no action was taken by the Court to fill the office of President: *ICJ Yearbook 1981–1982*, p. 8.

[10] On the distinction between the Court and the Bench, see the letter of 18 March 1983 from the Registrar to the agent of Canada: *Gulf of Maine* case, Pleadings, VII, p. 297 (doc. 23).

place before the Dean. Although most correspondence with the Court is conducted through the Registrar, following article 26, paragraph 1(*a*) of the Rules, in exceptional instances the President himself will conduct the correspondence.

Under the Instructions for the Registry the financial administration of the Court is the primary responsibility of the Registrar. He is accountable in the first instance to the Court in these matters, but if the Court is not sitting, the supervisory functions are delegated to the President.[11] Under the same instructions, the President has to approve the agenda of administrative questions for the Court (article 6). Every member of the Staff must make a declaration before the President under article 25 of the Rules of Court and article 40 of the Instructions for the Registry.[12] By article 23, paragraph 3 of the Rules of Court of 1946, the Instructions for the Registry were to be drawn up by the Registrar and approved by the President. The Rules of 1978 (article 28), however, now require the approval of the Court. The reasons for this curtailment of the powers of the President in what is a purely administrative matter have not been made public.

Although the Registrar issues the press communiques, where necessary he will consult with the President before issue. Similarly, the naming of a case can be a delicate matter. Whenever the parties have not themselves suggested the name of the case, consultation with the President will be needed.[13]

Previous commentators have noted the discrepancy between the English and French versions of the Statute regarding the President's casting vote. They

[11] Instructions for the Registry, articles 26 to 38: *ICJ Yearbook 1946–1947*, p. 82; S. Rosenne, *Documents on the International Court of Justice* (Dordrecht, 1991), p. 453. Here it may be noted that the meaning of the expression 'when the Court is not sitting' has changed over the years. In 1922 it was envisaged that the Court would meet in judicial sessions, of which there could be more than one in a year. This was changed in the Rules of 1936, when, in article 25, a system of judicial vacations was introduced in lieu of sessions. This was retained in the Rules of 1946. The whole system has been reorganized in article 20 of the current Rules, essential elements of which are that all members of the Court and judges *ad hoc* are expected to attend all meetings of the Court in cases in which they are participating, that the system of judicial vacations and periods and conditions of leave for members of the Court are fixed by the Court 'having regard . . . to the state of its General List and to the requirement of its current work', and that in cases of urgency the President may convene the Court at any time. With the increased workload of the Court, the Court is today virtually in permanent session subject to normal vacations. The ease of modern communications also alters the conception of 'session'.

[12] In the current Staff Regulations (Annexe VI), provision is made for an appeal by a staff member from an administrative decision of the Registrar to the Judge for Staff Appeals within specified time-limits. The filing of such an appeal does not have the effect of suspending action on the administrative decision 'unless the President, in consultation with the judge for staff appeals, directs otherwise'.

[13] For a discussion of a communiqué issued on the authority of the President alone, see the Separate Opinion of Judge Oda and the Dissenting Opinion of Judge Schwebel in the *Military and Paramilitary Activities in and against Nicaragua (Declaration of Intervention)* case, ICJ Reports, 1984, pp. 215, 221, 232, respectively. For an illustration of the naming of a case, compare the original name *Case concerning the*

have also pointed out that the English conception is the one followed by the Court. This means that if there is an equality of votes, the President casts a second vote. As far as concerns general administrative matters, there is no real need for a casting vote: the motion put simply has not received a majority and is therefore not adopted or is rejected. Here the casting vote may be a complicating factor. The practice of the Permanent Court was mixed. On occasion the President left matters as they were, the proposal not being adopted. In other circumstances he voted a second time, sometimes to maintain the status quo and sometimes to change it. There was no clear-cut practice that the President's second vote had to be the same as his first vote.[14] Nothing is known of the practice of the present Court in administrative matters.

In judicial matters, a casting vote is essential to create a 'decision'.

The more important functions of the President are those that he exercises as a member of the Bench (the expression here including also the Acting President under conditions described later). If he is unable to preside, the Vice-President assumes this position. If neither can preside, the senior judge present must assume this function. That person is designated Acting President. By article 45 of the Statute the hearing shall be under the control of the President. Minutes of the hearings are to be signed by the President and the Registrar (article 47). The President and the Registrar sign every judgment, Advisory Opinion and Order (article 58). This is for purposes of authentication, and commits neither of the signatories to the contents. That is all! In particular, the Statute does not mention the delegation of the Court's powers to the President. As mentioned, the Permanent Court very early assumed this power, and no objection has ever been taken to it.

As for the Rules of Court, there have been many changes since the initial Rules of 1922. This chapter will concentrate on the current Rules, those of 1978.

By article 9, paragraph 2, if the Court decides to appoint assessors to sit with it, the President has to take steps to obtain all the information relevant to their choice. There is as yet no practice on this.

Articles 32 to 37 deal with the composition of the Court for a particular case (the Bench). They contain several provisions regarding the presidency of a

Guardianship of an Infant (Order of the President, ICJ Reports, 1957, p. 102) with the name given to the case by the Court after pleading, *Case Concerning the Application of the Convention of 1902 Governing the Guardianship of Infants*, ICJ Reports, 1958, p. 55.

[14] For information regarding the casting vote of the President in the Permanent Court, see PCIJ, Series E, No. 3 (1927), p. 216, No. 6 (1930), p. 299, No. 7 (1931), p. 299, No. 9 (1933), p. 174, No. 10 (1934), p. 163, No. 11 (1935), p. 150, No. 12 (1936), p. 197, No. 13 (1937), p. 153, No. 14 (1938), p. 159, No. 15 (1939), p. 198. No similar information has been published by the present Court.

Bench. After article 12, noted above, the primary norm is in article 32, paragraph 1. If the President of the Court is a national of one of the parties in a case, he shall not exercise the functions of the Presidency in respect of that case. The same rule applies to the Vice-President or the senior judge when called upon to act as President. In 1992, President Sir Robert Jennings correctly extended this rule to the second of 'paired' cases being partly heard in common under article 47 of the Rules. Before the hearings were opened in the provisional measures phase of the two cases concerning the *Interpretation and Application of the 1971 Montreal Convention arising from the Aerial Incident at Lockerbie* cases (*Libya v. United Kingdom*; *Libya v. United States of America*), Sir Robert decided that it would be inappropriate as well as inconvenient for all concerned if he were to preside, as in theory he supposed he might, in the case against the United States. In both cases, therefore, the Vice-President acted as President.[15] In addition, the other general disqualifications are applicable to the President who will recuse himself if necessary.[16]

Article 31 requires the President to ascertain the view of the parties regarding questions of procedure. For this purpose he may 'summon' the agents to meet him as soon as possible after their appointment, and subsequently whenever necessary. The failure of an agent to appear before the President when so summoned may bring into operation article 53 of the

---

[15] *ICJ Yearbook 1991–1992*, p. 198. The rule is applied strictly. Sir Robert was President in the *Certain Phosphate Lands in Nauru (Preliminary Objections)* case, notwithstanding that one of the preliminary objections was that the UK ought to have been named as a respondent. No objection appears to have been taken to this. ICJ Reports, 1992, p. 240. The present Court has encountered 'paired' cases in two forms. One is where a single applicant brings identical or interlinked cases against two respondents. These include: *Treatment in Hungary of Aircraft and Crew of United States of America* (*US v. Hungary. US v. USSR*), ICJ Reports, 1954, pp. 99, 103; the *Antarctica* cases (*UK v. Argentina*; *UK v. Chile*), ICJ Reports, 1956, pp. 12, 15; *Border and Transborder Armed Actions* (*Nicaragua v. Costa Rica*; *Nicaragua v. Honduras*), ICJ Reports, 1987, p. 182, ICJ Reports, 1988, p. 69; *Questions of Interpretation and Application of the 1971 Montreal Convention Arising out of the Aerial Incident at Lockerbie* (*Libya v. UK*; *Libya v. USA*), ICJ Reports, 1992, pp. 3, 114. The second is where two (or more) applicants bring virtually identical cases against a single respondent. These include the *Aerial Incident of 27 July 1955* cases (*Israel v. Bulgaria*; *UK v. Bulgaria*; *USA v. Bulgaria*), ICJ Reports, 1959, pp. 127, 276, ICJ Reports, 1960, p. 146; *Fisheries Jurisdiction* cases (*Federal Republic of Germany v. Iceland*; *UK v. Iceland*), ICJ Reports, 1972, pp. 12, 30, ICJ Reports, 1973, pp. 3, 49, and 302, 313, ICJ Reports, 1974, pp. 3, 175; *Nuclear Tests* cases (*Australia v. France*; *New Zealand v. France*), ICJ Reports, 1974, pp. 253, 457. These have to be distinguished from 'joined' cases leading to a single decision. Article 47, introduced into the Rules in 1978, deals with both types of case. The 'paired' cases can pose delicate problems for the Court and for its President, especially as regards the composition of the Bench.

[16] Thus, President Sir Zafrulla Khan recused himself when the Court considered an objection by South Africa to his presence on the Bench in connection with the Advisory Opinion on *Legal Consequences of the Continued Presence of South Africa in Namibia (South West Africa) Notwithstanding Security Council Resolution 276 (1970)*, Order No. 1, ICJ Reports, 1971, p. 3. Afterwards he resumed his functions as President (p. 6).

Statute, concerning the non-appearance of a party. This is not an invariable rule, and the matter depends on all the circumstances.[17]

By article 32, paragraph 2, the member of the Court who is presiding in a case on the date on which the Court convenes for the oral proceedings shall continue to preside until completion of the current phase of the case, despite the election meanwhile of a new President or Vice-President. That is one of the provisions of the Rules to perpetuate the notion that, for the purposes of the composition of the Court, each phase of a case is separate from earlier or later phases, and may therefore be heard by a different Bench. This is a change from the practice of the Permanent Court, and is open to criticism.[18] Article 34 sets out how the President is to control the application of articles 17 and 24 of the Statute. Those provisions concern the disqualification of a judge from sitting in a particular case, and are designed to avoid conflicts of interest. Article 35 of the Rules deals with the judge *ad hoc* in application of article 31 of the Statute. It gives the President powers concerning the time-limits within which notifications or observations by one or other party have to be made. This is a general power, not limited to when the Court is not sitting, as are most of the delegated powers of the President.

Article 37 delegates to the President, when the Court is not sitting, the power to fix the time-limit within which a party may choose a new judge *ad hoc* if this becomes necessary. By article 44, the President, when the Court is not sitting, may exercise the powers of the Court to make orders regarding the number and order of filing Pleadings, and their time-limits. The President sometimes exercises this power even when the Court is sitting, for instance when it is deliberating on a case and the time-limits to be fixed are not controversial.[19] The President's powers in this respect are, however, specifically 'without prejudice to any subsequent decision of the Court'. That reservation does not confer any right of appeal from these interlocutory

---

[17] Cf. the *Nottebohm* case, ICJ Reports, 1952, p. 10; ICJ Reports, 1953, pp. 8, 111. Effect will always be given to an agreement concerning procedure reached through the application of article 31: *Maritime Delimitation and Territorial Questions between Qatar and Bahrain* case, ICJ Reports, 1991, pp. 50, 51.

[18] In the *Free Zones* case, the Permanent Court decided in 1930 that if the case should come before it again, it should continue to deal with it in the same composition; and that the duties of President were also to continue to be exercised by the judge who had presided over the Court during the previous phases, and whose term of office was to expire on 31 December 1930: PCIJ, Series E, No. 8, p. 246 (1932). In the *Corfu Channel* case, the President in the preliminary objection phase (Guerrero), who was also President at the commencement of the hearings on the merits, continued as Acting President also in the compensation phase several months later, despite the fact that his term of office as President came to an end before the merits phase was concluded: ICJ Reports, 1948, p. 15; ICJ Reports, 1949, pp. 4, 244.

[19] Thus the President made Orders regarding time-limits in the *East Timor* and the *Oil Platforms* cases during the Court's deliberating on another case: ICJ Reports, 1993, pp. 32, 35.

decisions of the President. In this respect the present Court, it is understood, follows the practice established by the Permanent Court in application of article 48 of the Statute (concerning the general conduct of a case). The Permanent Court has reported as follows:

> It was understood (February 18th, 1922) that the Court's right to make orders differing from those already made by the President would not involve a right on the part of the Parties to appeal to the Court against the orders of the President.
>
> During the revision of the Rules at the ordinary session in 1926, an amendment to Rule 33 [of the Rules of 1922] providing that there was no right of appeal for the Parties against a decision of the President, was proposed. This amendment was not adopted, as it was held that it was unnecessary, because the President was simply exercising powers delegated to him by the Court, and consequently there could be no appeal against his decisions.[20]

By article 52, paragraph 1, the President may authorize the correction of 'any slip or error' in any document already filed, if the other party does not consent. By article 52, paragraph 1, the President, if the Court is not sitting, may, after ascertaining the views of the parties, decide to make the written pleadings available to any state entitled to appear before the Court that has asked for them – something that could be important in cases of contemplated intervention. The decision to make the pleadings public, however, rests with the Court itself.

Article 54 empowers the President, if the Court is not sitting, to fix the date for the opening of the oral proceedings, or their postponement. This was once a matter of routine, since in principle cases were heard in the order in which they became ready for hearing. The Rules of 1978 abolish that provision, replacing it by article 54. This substitutes for the formal criterion the idea of 'special circumstances, including the urgency of a particular case' as a factor to decide the date of the hearing in a particular case. That places increased responsibility on the President.

Article 61, paragraph 3 gives every judge the right to put questions to the parties and to ask for explanations. Before exercising that right, the judge should make his intention known to the President, 'who is made responsible by Article 45 of the Statute for the control of the hearing'. There is little known practice about this. In 1937 a member of the Court asked one of the agents to produce two documents. No difficulty was made regarding one of

---

[20] PCIJ, Series E, No. 3, 210 (1927). For the discussions of this question in the Permanent Court, see PCIJ, Series D, No. 2, p. 66 (1922); No. 2, Addendum, p. 68 (1926). In the Rules of 1922, 1926 and 1931 this reservation was worded 'subject to any subsequent decision of the Court'. In 1936 (article 37, paragraph 5), the present wording was adopted, and has remained unchanged.

those documents: as for the other, the agent objected on the ground that it was confidential. The Permanent Court continues:

> It was held that, while the Court should always insist on the production of any document under Article 49 of the Statute, it was preferable in this case not to do so; accordingly, the President at the next hearing announced that he considered the production in question unnecessary and asked the agent concerned not to produce it.[21]

In article 63 the Court has delegated to the President, if it is not sitting, the power, at the request of a party or *proprio motu*, to take the necessary steps for the examination of witnesses otherwise than before the Court itself. Although witnesses have been called in several cases before the present Court or one of its Chambers, there has been no need yet to apply that provision. Article 65 lays down that the examination of witnesses and experts shall be under the control of the President, who, together with the other judges, may himself also put questions to them. A curious incident involving this Rule occurred in the *Elettronica Sicula SpA (ELSI)* case (before a Chamber). The judgment dryly records this in the following passage:

> Mr X [listed as an adviser to the US delegation] addressed the Court for the United States; since he had occasion to refer to matters of fact within his knowledge as a lawyer acting for the Raytheon Company, the President of the Chamber acceded to a request by the Agent of Italy that Mr X be treated *pro tanto* as a witness. Mr X, who informed the Chamber that both Raytheon Company and Mr X himself waived any relevant privilege, was cross-examined.[22]

Article 86, paragraph 3 deals with the application of article 34, paragraph 3 of the Statute, a new provision inserted in 1945. By that, whenever the construction of the constituent instrument of a public international organization or of an international convention adopted thereunder is in question in a case before the Court, the Registrar shall so notify the organization concerned and shall communicate to it copies of all the written proceedings. Article 69, paragraph 3 of the Rules provides that in the circumstances contemplated by article 34, paragraph 3 of the Statute, the Registrar, on the instructions of the Court, or of the President if the Court is not sitting, shall proceed as described in that paragraph. Paragraph 3 continues:

---

[21] PCIJ, Series E, No. 12, p. 151. The view of the present Court regarding article 49 of the Statute is different. It will take note of a refusal of a party to produce a document. *Corfu Channel* case, ICJ Reports, 1949, pp. 4, 32.

[22] ICJ Reports, 1989, pp. 15, 19. The proceedings themselves were more dramatic. See the Pleadings in that case, vol. III at pp. 301, 313.

The Court, or the President if the Court is not sitting, may, as from the date on which the Registrar has communicated copies of the written proceedings and after consulting the chief administrative officer of the public international organization concerned, fix a time-limit within which the organization may submit to the Court its observations in writing.

This is a new power delegated to the President. It comes within the scope of the principle that there is no appeal from the President's decision on this type of question. Instances have occurred that show that this too places new responsibilities on the President.

Articles 74 to 78 are the procedural code for provisional measures of protection, amplifying the bare norm enunciated in article 41 of the Statute. This code grants extensive powers to the President, with corresponding responsibility. When a request for the indication of provisional measures is filed, if the Court is not in session the President has to convene it 'forthwith' for deciding the request 'as a matter of urgency'. The Court, or the President if the Court is not sitting, shall fix a date for the hearing affording the parties an opportunity of being represented at it. Particularly important is article 74, paragraph 4, relating exclusively to the President: 'Pending the meeting of the Court, the President may call upon the parties to act in such a way as will enable any order the Court may make on the request for provisional measures to have its appropriate effect.' This has produced several decisions by the President. In the *Anglo-Iranian Oil Co. (Interim Measures)* case, the President (Basdevant) exercised that power and sent an appropriate message to the respondent government which, however, rejected the President's appeal.[23] In the *United States Diplomatic and Consular Staff in Tehran (Provisional Measures)* case, the President (Sir Humphrey Waldock) exercised that power. He called to the attention of both parties the fact that the matter was *sub judice* before the Court and the need to act in such a way as would enable any order the Court might make to have its appropriate effect.[24] In the *Military and Paramilitary Activities in and against Nicaragua* case, six weeks after the order indicating provisional measures the applicant applied for a further indication of provisional measures. The President (Elias) brought this directly to the attention of the Court without arranging for any hearing. The Court decided that the request should await the outcome of the proceedings on jurisdiction and admissibility then in progress.[25] In the two cases concerning the *Interpretation and Application of the 1971 Montreal Convention arising from the*

[23] ICJ Reports, 1950, pp. 89, 91; Pleadings, p. 707(doc. 20).
[24] ICJ Reports, 1979, pp. 7, 10, para. 6; Pleadings, p. 405 (doc. 6).
[25] This is recorded in the judgment on the merits: ICJ Reports, 1986, pp. 14, 144, para. 287.

Aerial Incident at Lockerbie the Acting President (Oda) fixed the date for the hearings having regard to the wishes of the parties. He refused to exercise his powers under paragraph 4. He said that after the most careful consideration of all the circumstances then known to him, he had come to the conclusion that it would not be appropriate for him to exercise what he termed 'the discretionary power' conferred on the President by article 74, paragraph 4 of the Rules.[26] In the *Application of the Convention on the Prevention and Punishment of the Crime of Genocide (Further Provisional Measures)* case, the President (Sir Robert) acceded to a request by the respondent to fix a date for the hearing that would enable it adequately to prepare its response. He rejected appeals by the applicant to reconsider that date and also an amended request by the applicant 'for an immediate Order without hearing pursuant to Article 75, paragraph 1' of the Rules. The reason for this was that the President followed an earlier decision of the Court on the first request for an indication of provisional measures, to the effect that the Court did not consider that the question arose of the exercise of its powers under article 75, paragraph 1 of the Rules of Court. On the other hand, he exercised his power under article 74, paragraph 4, and addressed an appropriate call to both parties, stressing that the earlier order still applied.[27] These instances are sufficient illustration of the delicate nature of this power given to the President.

Articles 81 to 86 supply a code of procedure for intervention. In addition, a new article 43 requires the Court to consider what directions are to be given to the Registrar who, by article 63 of the Statute, has to notify third states whenever the construction of a treaty to which they are parties is in question. In the conception of the Statute that duty of the Registrar is administrative, and he would usually consult with the President in case of need. It is not clear why the Rules do not vest this power in the President when the Court is not sitting. The failure to delegate this power may become a source of difficulty in practice. By article 83, paragraph 1, the President has a delegated power, when the Court is not sitting, to fix a time-limit within which the parties may submit their observations on an application for permission to intervene under article 62 of the Statute or a declaration of intervention under article 63. He has a similar delegated power under article 85 to fix time-limits for a

---

[26] ICJ Reports, 1992, pp. 3, 8, 9. paras. 16, 17; pp. 114, 120, paras. 17, 18.

[27] ICJ Reports, 1993, pp. 325, 333, 334, paras. 8, 9, 13. In the previous Order the Court had fixed a very short time-limit for the hearing and refused a request by the respondent for an extension. *Ibid.*, pp. 3, 9, para. 7. In that Order the Court recalled that under article 75, paragraph 2, it had the power to indicate provisional measures that are in whole or in part other than those requested, or that ought to be taken or complied with by the party which had itself made the request, and proceeded so to act: *Ibid.*, p. 22, para. 46.

written statement by a state applying to intervene under article 62, and for observations on that written statement by the parties. Article 86 vests a similar delegated power in the President in connection with an admitted intervention under article 63. Article 65, paragraph 2 of the 1946 Rules (and its predecessor) gave the President power, if the Court was not sitting, to fix time-limits within which if the intervention was not opposed the intervener could file a memorial on the merits. This was 'without prejudice to the decision of the Court on whether the application should be granted'. The 1978 Rules drop this. Here too there is no public explanation of the reasons for this curtailment of the President's powers.[28]

Under articles 88 and 89, relating to discontinuance, the President has power to make the necessary Orders when the Court is not sitting. Usually these Orders are a matter of routine, but on occasion control has to be exercised over them. An example is the Order of discontinuance in the *United States Diplomatic and Consular Staff in Tehran* case. Here the President (Sir Humphrey Waldock) refused to accept a discontinuance purportedly subject to a right to reinstate the case. He ordered the discontinuance only after he had been assured that it was unconditional.[29]

Above all, it is in connection with the deliberations of the Bench that the President is placed in the most powerful, most responsible, and most sensitive position. The Statute simply provides that after the hearing the Court shall withdraw to consider the decision. The deliberations take place in private and remain secret (article 54). All questions shall be decided by a majority of the judges present, the President having a casting vote if necessary (article 55). The Rules (articles 94 to 97) carry this a little further, but they are purely formal. The method of deliberation on judicial decisions is now set out in the Resolution on the Court's Judicial Practice adopted on 17 April 1976.[30]

The President (of the Bench) is responsible for the organization of the deliberation. After an appropriate period for the judges to study the case, the first deliberation is held. On this occasion the President outlines the issues that he thinks will require discussion and decision by the Court, any judge having the right to comment and draw attention to any other issues that arise. The resolution (paragraph 4(ii)) also invites the judges to indicate their preliminary impressions regarding any issue or question. At this stage, the

---

[28] See S. Rosenne, *Intervention in the International Court of Justice* (Dordrecht, 1994), chap. 4.

[29] ICJ Reports, 1981, p. 45. For criticism of this Order, see G. Wagon, 'Discontinuance of International Proceedings: The Hostages Case', *American Journal of International Law*, 76 (1982), p. 717.

[30] Acts and Documents concerning the Organization of the Court, No. 5, *Charter of the United Nations, Statute and Rules of Court and Other Documents* (1989), p. 164 (French), p. 165 (English); Rosenne, *Documents on the International Court of Justice*, p. 441.

President will call on the judges in the order in which they signify their desire to speak.

After this, each judge prepares his note expressing his views on the various questions. These notes are circulated to the other judges. A further deliberation then takes place where, as a rule, the President calls on the judges in inverse order of seniority. On the request of any judge, the President shall ask the Court to decide whether a vote shall be taken on any question.

At this point the Court chooses a drafting committee by secret ballot and by an absolute majority of votes of the judges present. The drafting committee should consist of two judges whose views as expressed in the previous deliberations 'have most closely and effectively reflected the opinion of the majority of the Court as it then exists'. The President is *ex officio* a member of the drafting committee unless he does not share the majority opinion as it then appears. In that event the Vice-President or, if he also does not share the majority opinion, a third member elected by the Court, takes his place. However, if the President is not a member of the drafting committee, the draft is to be discussed with him before it is submitted to the Court. The President may also propose amendments. If the drafting committee does not adopt them it shall nevertheless submit the President's proposals to the Court together with its own draft.

The preliminary draft of the decision is circulated and the judges may submit amendments. After consideration by the drafting committee, the revised draft decision is submitted to the Court for first reading. The judges then circulate their individual opinions and the drafting committee prepares the text for the second reading.

At the second reading the President is to enquire whether any judge wishes to submit further amendments. At a suitable interval after the second reading, the President calls upon the judges to give their final vote on the decision or conclusion concerned, in inverse order of seniority. In this vote, no abstentions are permitted. It is at this point that the President's casting vote becomes decisive. Moreover, since he is the last to vote, he knows before he votes whether he will create a situation requiring or enabling him to use his casting vote. In the history of the two Courts, only two decisions have been made by the casting vote of the President. One was the *Lotus* case in the Permanent Court, and the other the judgment in the Second Phase of the *South West Africa* case in the present Court.[31] In neither case is it possible

---

[31] PCIJ, Series A, No. 10 (1927); ICJ Reports, 1966, p. 6. It is curious that in both instances the effects of the decision reached by the casting vote of the President had to be changed by the international community. The effect of the decision in the *Lotus* case was changed in the process of the codification

to know what was the motion that caused the tie in the first place; it is accordingly not possible to know how the President used his casting vote.

As for the voting, the President may propose, and the Court is to decide, whether through illness or other reason deemed adequate by the President a judge may record his final vote otherwise than in person at the meeting of the Court.

In 1978 the Court's Rules Committee, then preparing the revised Rules of 1978, adopted a decision about Separate and Dissenting Opinions, and Declarations. It decided that the President in his capacity as such and as part of his function to direct the work of the Court as a 'special case' could append a Declaration not falling within the normal function of such Declarations. This power has been used once, by President Lachs in an interlocutory decision on the composition of the Court, reserving the right of the judges to express their opinion on that matter at a later stage.[32]

There is no doubt that the role of the President in the deliberations calls for the highest qualities of diplomatic skill coupled with deep knowledge not only of the case itself, but of its broader context. The experience in the two cases decided by the President's casting vote suggests that he should take into account the likely reaction of the international community to a decision reached through the casting vote.

Articles 15 to 18 concern the composition of the Chambers of the Court, and articles 90 to 93 govern the procedure in the Chambers. Regarding the composition, both the President and the Vice-President shall be members of the Chamber of Summary Procedure formed annually under article 29 of the Statute (article 15, paragraph 1 of the Rules).

For an *ad hoc* Chamber to deal with a particular case formed by virtue of article 26, paragraph 2 of the Statute, article 17 of the Rules imposes two separate duties on the President. If only one party requests the formation of such a Chamber, he has to ascertain that the other party agrees. When the parties have agreed, he now has to 'ascertain their views regarding the composition' of the Chamber. The experience of the formation of the Chamber in the *Gulf of Maine* case shows that this can be a delicate matter. In

---

of the law of the sea; that in the *SouthWest Africa* cases was repudiated by the General Assembly in its resolution 2145 (XXI), 27 October 1966. In effect that was confirmed by the Court, in a changed composition, in its Advisory Opinion on the *Legal Consequences for States of the Continued Presence of South Africa in Namibia (SouthWest Africa) Notwithstanding Security Council Resolution 276 (1970)*, ICJ Reports, 1971, p. 16. It is understood that the process of deliberation is simplified in the case of Orders of the Court, including Orders for the indication of provisional measures.

[32] *Western Sahara* case, ICJ Reports, 1975, pp. 6, 9. For that decision of the Rules Committee, see *ICJ Yearbook 1978–1979*, p. 217.

the first place, the Rules contain an apparent divergence from the Statute, replacing the word 'number' by 'composition'. This gives the parties greater control over the formation of such a Chamber. In the *Gulf of Maine* case there was a question of the compatibility of the special agreement (ratification of which had encountered difficulties in the United States Senate) with the Statute and Rules of Court. This had been a matter for negotiation between the parties and informally with the then President (Sir Humphrey Waldock), but he died before the matter could be completed. Through the Acting President (Elias) further negotiations took place. The Court then decided to form the Chamber and to elect its members as requested by the parties a few days before the end of a triennial period of membership of the Court, well after the election of the replacements.[33] It is believed that there have been other Chamber cases in which there were difficulties over the composition of the Chamber.

Article 18 governs the election of the members of all Chambers. Article 18, paragraph 2 provides that if a Chamber when formed includes the President or Vice-President of the Court, the President or Vice-President shall preside over the Chamber. In other cases, the Chamber elects its own President. He continues to preside while he remains a member of the Chamber, even if his term of office as a member of the Court ends. The operative words here are 'when formed'. Thus, the *ad hoc* Chamber for the *ELSI* case as originally formed included the then President of the Court (Nagendra Singh). On his death the Court reconstituted the Chamber and the next President of the Court (Ruda) was elected and became President of the Chamber.[34] On the other hand, two members of the Court who were members of the Chamber formed to decide the *Land, Island and Maritime Frontier Dispute* case were, while the case was pending, elected President and Vice-President of the Court. They continued as members of the Chamber, but their precedence among its members was re-ordered. Furthermore, the term of office of the member of the Court who had been elected President of the Chamber (Sette-Camara) ended while the proceedings were still in progress. He remained President of the Chamber until the judgment was rendered.[35]

The Court first made use of its power to form a Chamber under article 26, paragraph 1 of the Statute, a standing Chamber to deal with a particular

---

[33] ICJ Reports, 1982, p. 3. More on this by S. M. Schwebel (in his personal capacity), 'Chambers of the International Court of Justice Formed for Particular Cases', *International Law at a Time of Perplexity*, p. 739, esp. at p. 754.

[34] ICJ Reports, 1987, p. 3; ICJ Reports, 1988, p. 158.

[35] ICJ Reports, 1987, p. 10; ICJ Reports, 1989, p. 162; and for the revised order of precedence of the members of the Chamber, ICJ Reports, 1992, pp. 351, 353.

category of case, on 19 July 1993. It established a seven-member Chamber for Environmental Matters. Neither the President nor the Vice-President of the Court was a member of that Chamber. This was changed after the election of members of the Court in 1993.[36]

When a Chamber is to decide a case, article 91 of the Rules requires the President of the Court to convene the Chamber at the earliest date compatible with the procedure. It is customary for the President of the Court to be present at the first meeting of an *ad hoc* Chamber, when the proceedings are formally opened and the judges *ad hoc* (if any) make their solemn declaration.

For the interpretation of a judgment, the President, if the Court is not sitting, may fix the time-limit within which the adverse party may submit its observations (article 98, paragraph 3). The same rule applies to a request for the revision of a judgment (article 99, paragraph 2).

In the advisory proceedings, the President, if the Court is not sitting, has comparable powers to make interlocutory orders and decisions. This includes an exceptional power to decide whether oral proceedings shall take place (article 105, paragraph 2(*b*)). In contentious cases before the full Court, an oral phase is obligatory (Statute, article 43, paragraph 1).

The President is frequently requested by the parties to treaties or commercial and similar contracts, not necessarily states entitled to appear before the Court, to appoint an arbitrator or an umpire. In 1923 the Permanent Court was asked to appoint an arbitrator in a commercial dispute. It decided that it could not undertake this task, but that the President, if approached, might be willing to act. This has now developed considerably. The President normally performs such a function, subject to the same disqualifications as are applicable to his acting as President of a Bench. The parties negotiating such a transaction should consult with the President before concluding their contract.[37]

Although many interlocutory powers of the President may appear as matters of routine, they nevertheless call for great qualities of leadership and frequently of diplomatic skill. The presidency of a small cohesive body of highly competent individuals, each with his own personality, cannot be compared to the presidency of a large international gathering, relatively impersonal and highly political in its approach to its business.

During the drafting of the Statute the view was expressed that it would be dangerous to make the presidency of the Court 'too important'. The President

---

[36] *ICJ Yearbook 1992–1993*, 47, p. 17; *ICJ Yearbook 1993–1994*, 48, p. 18.
[37] PCIJ, Series E, No. 3, p. 228 (1927); *ICJ Yearbook 1991–1992*, 46, p. 146.

should be 'only' *primus inter pares*.[38] Developments since 1920 have shown that this might be appropriate for the administrative functions of the President. However, it is not an adequate or proper description of the President's role or functions in the conduct of judicial proceedings. Here he has a dominant and leading role. He faces a major challenge in forging the largest possible majority for any decision the Court may take, be it interlocutory or dispositive. In instances of high political tension, this is no easy matter. It is through this that the office of President has attained its great prestige.

---

[38] Lord Phillimore, at the 20th meeting of the Advisory Committee of Jurists, *Procès-verbaux of the Proceedings of the Committee* (1920), p. 456.

23

Nationality of claims: some relevant concepts

Sir Arthur Watts

ৎৎ

I

The 'nationality of claims' rule is, on the face of it, beguilingly clear and simple. It requires that a state instituting international legal proceedings against another state in respect of damage which that other state has caused to a private person must show that that person possesses its nationality.

The rule is well established in customary international law, and is of pivotal importance for the whole process whereby states may be held responsible for acts causing damage to private persons. Its underlying rationale was set out by the PCIJ in the *Panevezys–Saldutiskis Railway* case, where it said that 'in taking up the case of one of its nationals . . . a State is in reality asserting its own right . . . This right is necessarily limited to intervention on behalf of its own nationals because, in the absence of a special agreement, it is the bond of nationality between the State and the individual which alone confers upon the State the right of diplomatic protection.'[1]

The rule underlies every case in which a state institutes proceedings in the ICJ in respect of damage done to a private person at the hands of the respondent state. In most cases its requirements cause no real difficulty. In three, however, its application has been particularly significant – the Advisory Opinion on *Reparations for Injuries Suffered in the Service of the United Nations*,[2] and the judgments in the *Nottebohm* case,[3] and the case concerning the *Barcelona Traction, Light and Power Company Limited*.[4] This chapter focuses in particular on the development of the 'nationality of claims' rule by the Court in those cases through its consideration of concepts relevant to the operation of the rule.

[1] PCIJ, Series A/B, No. 76, at p. 16.
[2] ICJ Reports, 1949, p. 174.
[3] ICJ Reports, 1953, p. 111 (*Preliminary Objection*); ICJ Reports, 1955, p. 4 (*Second Phase*).
[4] ICJ Reports, 1964, p. 6 (*Preliminary Objections*); ICJ Reports, 1970, p. 3 (*Second Phase*).

II

That rule is a rule of customary international law. Although, accordingly, its precise formulation may be arguable, it is apparent that any formulation of it, such as that given at the beginning of this chapter, embodies a number of concepts – such as 'state', 'international legal proceedings', 'damage', 'private person' and 'nationality'. To apply the 'nationality of claims' rule necessarily requires giving meaning to these concepts, only one of which – 'international legal proceedings' – is scarcely a matter of controversy where proceedings are brought before the ICJ.

A rule is only as clear as the concepts it embodies. Some of the concepts used in rules of international law are themselves concepts of international law; even if they have their roots in municipal law, international law has by now adopted them for its own – 'treaty', 'reservation' and 'continental shelf', for example. But, particularly with rules such as the 'nationality of claims' rule which operate at the interface between international and municipal law, for many other concepts international law has to turn to available analogues in municipal law – it has, in effect, to 'borrow' from municipal law.

'Nationality' is, for example, such a 'borrowed' concept. The possession of a state's nationality is determined by its municipal law, and it alone is qualified to say who are its nationals[5] and who are not. Nationality nevertheless has international consequences; for example, the operation of treaties is frequently dependent on the possession of nationality, and it is relevant to the treatment of aliens (whose very definition is that they are non-nationals), to jurisdiction, and – as in the present context – to the presentation of international claims.

The question that arises is whether the 'nationality' referred to in the rule of international law is identical with 'nationality' as understood in municipal law and, if so, is it the municipal law of the state whose nationality is in question, or some generalized version of relevant municipal laws which give meaning to the concept at the international level? Alternatively, does international law have its own concept of nationality and, if so, of what does it consist? And does it, for purposes of international law, replace the nationality conferred by municipal law, or does it, while acknowledging that the nationality conferred by municipal law is as such relevant on the international plane, render it effective there only if certain additional requirements

---

[5] There are, however, some exceptional cases where international law regards the conferment of nationality as invalid: see the instances given by Judge *ad hoc* Guggenheim in the *Nottebohm* case, ICJ Reports, 1955, at p. 54.

are satisfied – in effect, is an international rule referring to 'nationality' in reality an oversimplification, since it should, to be complete, refer not only to 'nationality' as determined by the relevant municipal law but also to those other, internationally imposed, requirements?

Similar questions can be posed in relation to other relevant concepts, such as 'private person' (particularly in regard to entities that may – or may not – have legal personality attributed to them in municipal law, such as companies and partnerships) and 'damage' (particularly where the incidence of damage is directly related to the possession of legal rights whose violation is in question). The concept of 'state', however, raises different issues, since it is already a concept of international law, and its application is generally unlikely to have to rely on characteristics drawn from municipal law (although even so, that law may be relevant, for example, to the legal standing of various statal entities which are not fully independent sovereign states).

III

It was this concept of 'state' that was in a sense raised in the *Reparations* case.[6] A strict application of the 'nationality of claims' rule to the bringing of an international claim in respect of damage suffered by a private person would require that an international organization, which is not a 'state', could not bring a claim in respect of damage suffered by one of its agents.[7] If an organization was to be allowed to bring such a claim, the ICJ was faced with essentially two choices: either the concepts embodied in the 'nationality of claims' rule would have to be significantly broadened so as to cover the relatively new phenomena of international organizations and their agents, or the Court would have to find some other basis for allowing such an international claim than the traditional rule.

The Court declined to treat the novelty of the situation as reason enough to distort the traditional rule. Although finding that the United Nations was an international person, the Court was emphatic that it was not a state, and that its legal personality and rights and duties were not the same as those of a state.[8]

It was also a self-evident fact that there was no UN 'nationality' which its agents could possess. There was, however, a suggestion that the 'nationality of

---

[6] ICJ Reports, 1949, p. 174.

[7] There was some discussion in the Majority Opinion and the Dissenting Opinions about the different categories of persons affected – 'agents', 'officials', 'servants' and 'experts'. For present purposes nothing turns on these distinctions, and it will usually be convenient to refer to 'agents'.

[8] *Ibid.*, p. 179.

claims' rule might be applied on the basis of allegiance: the argument was that the legal bond existing between the UN and its staff by virtue of article 100 of the Charter established a kind of allegiance which should be assimilated to the legal bond of nationality existing between a state and its nationals. The Court did not agree: such assimilation involved 'a strained use of the concept of allegiance'[9] – by which it appears to have been meant that it was the treatment of the relationship between the UN and its staff as equivalent to 'allegiance' that strained the meaning of that concept.

The Court faced up to the new situation arising from the creation of international organizations by side-stepping the 'nationality of claims' rule, finding that it neither precluded the bringing of a claim by the UN, nor itself justified a claim by the UN. It held instead that the UN's capacity to protect its agents arose on the quite separate basis that its capacity to exercise a measure of functional protection of its agents was necessarily implied in the Charter.[10]

The Court's acknowledgement of the significance of the role now played by international organizations, and its preference for side-stepping the traditional 'nationality of claims' rule rather than being constrained by the rigidities of its formulation, may be contrasted with the stricter and more formal attitude of the dissenting judges.[11] Eschewing any hint of judicial innovation, they took the somewhat static view that, in relation to damage suffered by private persons, existing international law as reflected in the traditional rule provided for international claims to be presented only by states in respect of persons having their nationality, that international organizations were not states and did not have any nationality of their own, and that there was no necessary implication in the Charter that the UN had the capacity to present claims in respect of damage suffered by its agents.

Although the Court did not apply the traditional 'nationality of claims' rule, it established a certain parallel between the bond of nationality (in the traditional rule) and the bond of service (in the functional protection exercised by the UN in respect of its agents). They constituted separate and equally valid bases of protection, coexisting and giving rise to parallel rights of protection.[12] In respect of neither notion, however, did the Court have to draw on

---

[9] *Ibid.*, at p. 182. See also pp. 200–1 and 209–10 for the observations of Judges Hackworth and Badawi Pasha in their Dissenting Opinions (although on this point both in substance agreeing with the Court).

[10] *Ibid.*, p. 184.

[11] *Ibid.*, principally at pp. 197–204 (Judge Hackworth), 206–16 (Judge Badawi Pasha) and 217–19 (Judge Krylov). Judge Winiarski also dissented on this point, in general sharing the views expressed by Judge Hackworth (p. 189).

[12] See also comments by the Court in the *Barcelona Traction* case, ICJ Reports, 1970, pp. 38 and 50.

considerations of municipal law: it limited its consideration of the traditional rule to its operation at the international level, while the bond of service between an organization and its agents is one derived directly from international law.

The Court, by not attributing to the UN either statehood or its own nationality, made the traditional rule in terms inapplicable to the circumstances before it. Nevertheless, it was at pains to show that its response to the new situation was consistent with the underlying philosophy of the traditional rule. Having regard to its substance rather than to its formal expression, the Court identified two bases on which it rested – that the defendant state had broken an obligation towards the national state in respect of its nationals, and that only the party to whom an international obligation was due could bring a claim in respect of its breach.[13] The Court found that this was precisely what happened when the United Nations, in bringing a claim for damage suffered by its agent, did so by invoking the breach of an obligation towards itself. Accordingly, not only did the traditional rule not exclude the bringing of a claim by the UN, but on the contrary, the principle underlying it led to a recognition of the UN's capacity to bring a claim when it did so by invoking, as the ground of its claim, a breach of an obligation to itself.[14]

Both innovation and conservation were thus the hallmarks of the Court's approach to the 'nationality of claims' issues raised by the new situation confronting it in this case.

IV

In the *Nottebohm* case[15] the Court was faced, in relation to the concept of nationality, with no such novel situation. In the normal context of an inter-state claim the Court had to consider whether an individual (Mr Nottebohm) who, as a matter of the law of Liechtenstein, possessed that state's nationality through naturalization[16] should be regarded as a national of Liechtenstein for

---

[13] ICJ Reports, 1949, at pp. 181-2. The Court also invoked these two bases for the rule in the *Barcelona Traction* case (*Second Phase*), ICJ Reports, 1970, at p. 32.

[14] *Ibid.*, at p. 182. Here, and also at p. 184, the Court's language contains strong echoes of the rationale of the traditional rule in the *Panevezys–Saldutiskis Railway* case, cited at p. 424 above.

[15] ICJ Reports, 1955, p. 4.

[16] The Court dealt with the question before it without considering the validity of Nottebohm's naturalization according to the law of Liechtenstein (*ibid.*, p. 20): i.e. it assumed, for its immediate purpose, that the naturalization was valid. Possible questions arising in this respect were referred to in the Dissenting Opinions of Judges Klaestad (at pp. 28–9, 31–2) and Read (at pp. 35–8) and Judge *ad hoc* Guggenheim (at pp. 52–3). The facts as to Nottebohm's naturalization were set out by the Court at pp. 13–16.

the purposes of the 'nationality of claims' rule. The limited question before the Court was, in effect, whether that rule allowed Liechtenstein (as, taken at face value, it did) to rely on the nationality it had conferred upon Nottebohm in order to present a claim against Guatemala in respect of damage suffered by him – this against the background of facts that led the Court to find that Nottebohm's links with Liechtenstein were 'extremely tenuous'[17] while his links with Guatemala were 'long-standing and close'.[18]

The Court acknowledged that the conferment of nationality by a state was a matter for it to settle by its own laws. That was not, however, the end of the matter, since the issue before the Court was not one arising within the legal system of Liechtenstein but was rather one of international law. The Court affirmed that on that international plane 'nationality' did not necessarily mean the same as it did in municipal law. Given that international law left the conferment of nationality to be regulated by each state for itself as a matter within its domestic jurisdiction, it would be wrong, said the Court, to allow the exercise of that freedom of action in municipal law necessarily to have effects at the international level: a state could not as against other states rely on the nationality conferred under its municipal law unless it also reflected the individual's 'genuine connection' with the state. 'The character . . . recognised *on the international level* as pertaining to nationality'[19] required that the formal nationality it had conferred under its nationality law had to represent a substantive link between the state and the individual. Practice in related fields[20] led the Court[21] to establish a definition of 'nationality', as understood in international law. It was, said the Court,

> a legal bond having as its basis a social fact of attachment, a genuine connection of existence, interests and sentiments, together with the existence of reciprocal rights and duties. It may be said to constitute the juridical expression of the fact that the individual upon whom it is conferred, either directly by the law or as a result of an act of the authorities, is in fact more closely connected with the population of the State conferring nationality than with that of any other State.

The Liechtenstein nationality conferred upon Nottebohm was not real and effective in this sense, and had been 'granted without regard to the concept of

---

17 *Ibid.*, p. 25.
18 *Ibid.*, p. 26.
19 *Ibid.*, at p. 23 (emphasis added).
20 *Ibid.*, at pp. 21–3. While the fields from which the Court drew the practice on which it relied in support of its view might have been related to that with which the Court was faced, they were, as Judge Read forcefully pointed out in his Dissenting Opinion (at pp. 40–2), readily distinguishable; see also the Dissenting Opinion of Judge *ad hoc* Guggenheim, at pp. 59–60.
21 *Ibid.*, at p. 23.

nationality adopted in international relations'[22] – again affirming the separate international concept of 'nationality'.

The Court's reluctance to allow a state's unilateral act in conferring nationality to be decisive for purposes of the 'nationality of claims' rule, while in many ways welcome, nevertheless gave rise to certain difficulties. Nottebohm's Liechtenstein nationality, not challenged by the Court, was measured against a distinct, international, concept of nationality and then disregarded: such a clear acceptance of there being two separate concepts of nationality[23] left unclear the role on the international plane of the concept of nationality known to municipal law. It would appear that the possession of nationality under the relevant state's municipal law is a precondition for the operation, at the international level, of its international law analogue: the latter works in conjunction with, and not to the exclusion of, the former. The Court did not question (at least for the purposes of argument)[24] that Nottebohm possessed Liechtenstein nationality as a matter of the law of Liechtenstein: although that nationality was by itself not sufficient to allow Liechtenstein to benefit, as against Guatemala, from the 'nationality of claims' rule, the Court did not hold that the international concept of nationality rendered invalid a nationality inconsistent with it which had been conferred by municipal law. Similarly the Court did not hold that nationality conferred in accordance with municipal law was replaced by the international concept so as to permit the bringing of an international claim on the basis solely of the internationally required 'social fact of attachment' and in the absence of a nationality conferred by municipal law.

The Court can be seen to have given weight at the international level to a nationality of substance ('real and effective', 'genuine connection') rather than to a municipally valid nationality of merely formal or nominal content. The three dissenting judges (Judges Klaestad and Read, and Judge *ad hoc* Guggenheim) favoured the stricter and more formal alternative. For them *lex lata* did not require a validly conferred nationality to reflect some 'genuine link' before it could be allowed its customary role as a necessary and sufficient condition for the exercise of diplomatic protection (particularly since, as they noted, the point had not been argued by the parties). Underpinning their approach by their insistence on the imperviousness, in general, of municipal

---

[22] *Ibid.*, at p. 26.

[23] See also Judge Tanaka's observations in his Separate Opinion in the *Barcelona Traction* case (*Second Phase*), ICJ Reports, 1970, p. 3, at p. 122.

[24] See above, note 16.

legal acts to international legal scrutiny (as Judge Read[25] expressed it, there was 'a long series of decisions,[26] which applied the principle that "municipal laws are merely facts which express the will and constitute the activities of States" and that the Court does not interpret the national law as such'),[27] they considered that the 'nationality of claims' rule involved a straight reference back to nationality as conferred by a state's municipal law, which was of itself a sufficient basis for the application of the rule. In effect, therefore, they considered the concept of nationality employed in the rule of international law to be, by virtue of a *renvoi*, that adopted in the relevant municipal law.

Although the Court's judgment disposed of the particular case before it, it left a number of questions unanswered: were its conclusions as applicable to nationality acquired by birth or descent as to nationality acquired by naturalization? Were they applicable as against a state other than that with which the *de cujus* had a long-standing and close connection? Were they applicable in contexts other than the nationality of claims? And what were the implications for the 'nationality-by-analogy' commonly attributed to other than natural persons, such as ships, aircraft and certain forms of commercial enterprise?

V

Although that last question was not central to the *Barcelona Traction* case,[28] the Court gave it some consideration. That case involved alleged loss caused by Spain to the Barcelona Traction Company (which was neither Spanish nor Belgian), most of whose shareholders were claimed to be Belgian nationals. Proceedings were instituted by Belgium against Spain in respect of the damage suffered by the Belgian shareholders. The Court denied Belgium the right to protect the Belgian shareholders. It did so in part because that company continued in law to exist;[29] and because Canada had the capacity to take action on the company's behalf, so that the exception to the prohibition against 'piercing the corporate veil', which was commonly said to arise where a company's national state lacked capacity to take action on its behalf, did not apply.[30] The Court treated the company as having Canadian nationality.

[25] See also Judge Klaestad, ICJ Reports, 1955, at pp. 28–9. Judge *ad hoc* Guggenheim, at pp. 51–2, also invoked the principle that municipal law was, for an international tribunal, only a fact to be treated as such, but expressed this in a more qualified way.

[26] Judge Read cited the following decisions of the PCIJ: *Polish Upper Silesia*, Series A, No. 7, p. 19; *Serbian Loans*, Series A, Nos. 20/21, p. 46; *Brazilian Loans*, ibid., p. 124; *Lighthouses* case (*France/Greece*), Series A/B, No. 62, p. 22; *Panevezys–Saldutiskis Railway* case, Series A/B, No. 76, p. 19.

[27] ICJ Reports, 1955, p. 36.

[28] ICJ Reports, 1970, p. 3 (*Second Phase*). For the Preliminary Objections see ICJ Reports, 1964, p. 6.

[29] ICJ Reports, 1970, pp. 40–1.   [30] *Ibid.*, at pp. 41–5.

Whatever 'nationality' might mean in this context in relation to natural persons, either in international law or municipal law, it must mean something different again in relation to companies. And as the Court itself noted: 'In allocating corporate entities to States for purposes of diplomatic protection, international law is based, but only to a limited extent, on an analogy with the rules governing the nationality of individuals'.[31]

The Court's attribution of Canadian nationality to the Barcelona Traction Company (accepted by both parties) was based on 'the traditional rule [that] attributes the right of diplomatic protection of a corporate entity to the State under the laws of which it is incorporated and in whose territory it has its registered office'.[32] While noting that further and different links between company and state were sometimes said to be required for a right of diplomatic protection to exist, so as to establish 'between the corporation and the State in question a genuine connection of the kind familiar from other branches of international law',[33] at least in connection with the diplomatic protection of corporations 'no absolute test of the "genuine connection" has found general acceptance'.[34] As to the *Nottebohm* case, 'given both the legal and factual aspects of protection in the present case the Court is of the opinion that there can be no analogy with the issues raised or the decision given in that case'.[35]

It is surprising that the Court was so dismissive, in this context, of the relevance of the kind of 'genuine link' it had earlier asserted in relation to natural persons. If, at the international level, the concept of 'nationality' comprises considerations of effectiveness in the one context, it would seem appropriate for it also to do so in the other. This is especially so given that in this particular case the company's continuing existence was somewhat tenuous, and that the Court acknowledged that in contemporary circumstances companies were essentially a facade for the shareholders who constituted the reality behind them[36] and that in having regard to institutions of municipal law it was motivated by a concern not to 'lose touch with reality'.[37]

The Court's strict regard for the traditional rule and its reluctance to accept additional qualifications establishing an effective link sit uneasily beside its readiness in the *Nottebohm* case to prefer considerations of substance to those of form, and to invoke precedents from 'related' fields.[38] The Court had,

---

[31] *Ibid.*, at p. 42. [32] *Ibid.*
[33] *Ibid.* [34] *Ibid.*
[35] *Ibid.* [36] *Ibid.*, at p. 35.
[37] *Ibid.*, at p. 37. [38] See above, note 20.

however, to some extent paved the way for not adopting the principles of its earlier decision, by noting at the outset that only to a limited extent was there in relation to companies any analogy with the nationality of individuals. Further, there were obvious difficulties in the way of getting drawn too closely into the relationship between the Company and its presumed national state when that state was not a party to the proceedings before the Court.[39]

Nevertheless, the relevance of that earlier decision concerned several of the judges delivering Individual Opinions. For Judge Sir Gerald Fitzmaurice the *Nottebohm* decision 'unquestionably *does*' have a bearing on Canada's entitlement to sustain a claim on behalf of the Company;[40] and if Canada were disentitled from claiming because of the absence of a genuine link, those same circumstances might equally suggest that a different test of nationality from the traditional rule relied on by the Court should be applied.[41] Judge Jessup's view, after a thorough analysis,[42] was clear: 'The existence of a link between a corporation holding a "charter of convenience" and the State granting the charter, is the key to the diplomatic protection of multinational corporate interests.'[43] Indeed, 'the link concept represents a general principle of law and not merely an *ad hoc* rule for the decision of a particular case'.[44] Judges Padilla Nervo and Gros similarly considered[45] that if the 'nationality' of companies was to serve at the international level, it had to be accompanied by a 'real' link with the state in question. Of those delivering Individual Opinions who addressed this point, it seems that only Judge Amoun[46] was content for the *Nottebohm* principle of effectiveness to be disregarded in determining a company's nationality, and the consequential right to protect it.[47]

Closer to the heart of the case than the nationality of the Barcelona Traction Company was the Court's enquiry into the nature of the private interests in relation to which the 'nationality of claims' rule had to be applied, involving the position of shareholders in a company. Spain objected that Belgium had no right in international law to protect its national shareholders in a non-Belgian company. The Court upheld the objection.[48]

A notable feature of the *Barcelona Traction* case was that even though the Court's Decision was arrived at by fifteen votes to one (twelve votes in the

---

[39] See also Judge Jessup's comments, ICJ Reports, 1970, at p. 185.
[40] *Ibid.*, at p. 80.   [41] *Ibid.*, at p. 83.
[42] *Ibid.*, at pp. 182–91.   [43] *Ibid.*, at p. 185.
[44] *Ibid.*, at p. 186.   [45] *Ibid.*, at pp. 254, 281.
[46] Judge Tanaka's conclusion that the Court's Judgment in the *Nottebohm* case was 'not germane to the present case' (*ibid.*, p. 141) flowed from his view that a separate right of diplomatic protection of shareholders existed in international law.
[47] *Ibid.*, at pp. 295, 300.
[48] *Ibid.*, at p. 51.

majority being for the reasons set out in the judgment), there were no fewer than eight Separate Opinions, to which must be added the Dissenting Opinion of Judge *ad hoc* Riphagen. It was common ground between the Court and those judges delivering Individual Opinions that international law and municipal law operated on different legal planes, and that, in municipal law generally, the distinguishing characteristics of a corporate entity were its separate legal personality and the distinction between the company's position and that of the shareholders. Essentially, the question was how those concepts were to be transposed onto the international plane.

The relevant 'private person' in respect of whose losses a claim might have been presented was either the Barcelona Traction Company itself or the shareholders in that company; similarly, the 'damage' forming the basis for the claim was either that suffered by the company or that suffered by the shareholders, depending on whose legal rights had been affected. Since the corporate entity is an institution created by municipal law and not by international law, and the Court expressly recognized that 'there are no corresponding institutions of international law to which the Court could resort',[49] it had to consider the issues on the basis of the characteristics of corporate structures in municipal law.

The Court could not, however, simply take the municipal law institutions of 'company' and 'shareholders' (together with their respective rights) and apply them at the international level,[50] for the presentation of a claim before an international tribunal necessarily involved rights which were conferred by the rules of international law concerning the treatment of foreigners,[51] and Belgium's right (if any) to protect its national shareholders was 'merely a reflection . . . of the antecedent question of what is the juridical situation in respect of shareholding interests, *as recognised by international law*'.[52]

Such a 'borrowing' of municipal law concepts involves their 'recognition' by international law, a process which 'requires that, whenever legal issues arise concerning the rights of States with regard to the treatment of companies and shareholders, as to which rights international law has not established its own rules, it has to refer to the relevant rules of municipal law'.[53] Although the

---

[49] *Ibid.*, at p. 37.

[50] The fundamental differences between international law and municipal law as regards their objectives, planes of operation and requirements were central to the denial by Judges Tanaka and Jessup, and Judge *ad hoc* Riphagen, of any automatic adoption internationally of municipal law notions (*ibid.*, at pp. 121–2, 168 and 341). Cf. Lord McNair's injunction in the *International Status of South West Africa* case, ICJ Reports, 1950, at p. 148, against importing private law institutions 'lock, stock and barrel' into the international field.

[51] ICJ Reports, 1964, at p. 45.

[52] *Ibid.* (emphasis added).   [53] ICJ Reports, 1970, pp. 33–4.

Court's approach was specific in that it limited its observations to the form of corporate entity exemplified by the Barcelona Traction Company (i.e. a limited company whose capital was represented by shares), the Court made clear[54] that it 'is to rules generally accepted by municipal legal systems which recognize the limited company whose capital is represented by shares, and not to the municipal law of a particular State, that international law refers'. Inevitably this means that the relevant concepts – 'company' or 'corporate entity', and the corresponding concept of 'shareholders', along with their respective rights – have meanings in international law that are distinct from, although related to (indeed, generalized and abstracted from), their more specific meanings in municipal law.

Such a generalized *renvoi* to municipal law led the Court to conclude that the

> concept and structure of the company are founded on and determined by a firm distinction between the separate entity of the company and that of the shareholder, each with a distinct set of rights. The separation of property rights as between company and shareholder is an important manifestation of this distinction . . . It is a basic characteristic of the corporate structure that the company alone . . . can take action in respect of matters that are of a corporate character.[55]

Although shareholders had an independent right of action where their direct rights were affected,[56] this was not the case here.[57] Nor[58] did the present case come within the circumstances in which in municipal law it was acknowledged, exceptionally, that shareholders could go behind the separate corporate legal personality.[59]

By looking to the characteristics of corporate structures apparent in municipal laws generally for the meaning to be attributed to the equivalent institutions at the international level, the Court touched on, without really

---

[54] *Ibid.*, at p. 37. See also Judge Amoun's reference, in his Separate Opinion (p. 323) to 'the common fund of the generality of municipal legal systems'. But note also Judge *ad hoc* Riphagen's view, in his Dissenting Opinion, that customary international law 'does not tend in any way to unify the different legal orders, even partially or indirectly, into a common legal order applicable to cases of diversity of citizenship . . . The international responsibility of a State is not based upon rules of any such common legal order' (pp. 336–7).

[55] *Ibid.*, at p. 34.

[56] The Court proceeded on this basis in *Elettronica Sicula SpA (ELSI)*, ICJ Reports, 1989, p. 15: the USA claimed against Italy for loss and damage allegedly suffered by two US companies as a result of action taken by the Italian authorities against an Italian company the shares of which were wholly owned by the US companies, whose direct rights as shareholders were thereby affected. But cf. Judge Oda's Separate Opinion (pp. 83–93).

[57] ICJ Reports, 1970, p. 36.

[58] *Ibid.*, at pp. 40–5.   [59] See p. 431 above.

exploring, an issue to which several of the judges delivering individual opinions attached importance. Such a *renvoi* (which in the *Nottebohm* case had appealed more to the dissenting judges than to the Court) attracted considerable criticism. For Judge Gros rules of national law were, for a court applying international law, just facts, to be taken account of as such and not as the legal basis for reaching decisions as to the conformity of a given situation with rules of international law. *Renvoi* to municipal law did not mean that because a municipal law created a certain legal relationship, an international tribunal had to accept it as possessing the same legal cogency: it was wrong to 'erect definitions taken from certain municipal systems of law into a rule of international law'.[60] Judge *ad hoc* Riphagen was similarly dismissive of any such *renvoi* by international (particularly customary international) law, to rules and concepts of municipal law. The rights of states under customary international law could not be dependent on rules of municipal law concerning the rights and obligations of private persons *inter se*: customary international law and the rules and principles of municipal law were completely separate.

Judge Morelli, on the other hand, considered the rules of international law in issue in the case as having regard solely to specific rights which had already been created or recognized in municipal law; since international law thus presupposed the existence of municipal law rights which were the object of protection, it was the municipal law concept itself that was relevant for international law. Judge Padilla Nervo's approach[61] and that of Judge Amoun[62] were similar.

Associated with the differences of view as to the way in which, for purposes of rules of international law, reference needed to be made to concepts of municipal law was a wider concern about the consequences this might have for the supremacy of international law. Did a need to refer to municipal law concepts make international law dependent upon municipal law and undermine the supremacy of international law? Judge Gros clearly thought so;[63] the Court thought not, but it did no more than assert flatly that the fact that international law had to recognize certain institutions of municipal law did not 'amount to making rules of international law dependent upon categories of municipal law'.[64] Judge Morelli[65] emphasized that, although (in his view) the relevant rule of international law required a specific pre-existing right created in municipal law, since this resulted not from municipal law but, on the contrary, from international law itself, it was consistent with the role of

---

[60] *Ibid.*, at p. 277. [61] *Ibid.*, at p. 254.
[62] *Ibid.*, at pp. 322–8. [63] *Ibid.*, at p. 272.
[64] *Ibid.*, at p. 33. [65] *Ibid.*, at p. 234.

international law; nor was it contrary to the supremacy of international law, a principle of the existence of which he was in any event sceptical.

Despite these considerations, the Court's decision to use, at the international level, a generalized view of the relevant municipal law concepts raised a further problem. Even if that approach is in principle appropriate (and it is less effective as a basis for identifying specific rights than for establishing broad principles), the validity of its application in practice depends on the accuracy with which the process of abstracting those essential principles is carried out. If a concept is to be 'borrowed' for use on the international plane, the 'borrowing' must preserve the integrity of the concept; the Court accepted this, in principle anyway, in saying that in referring to rules generally accepted by municipal legal systems, 'the Court cannot modify them, still less deform them'.[66] But opinions may legitimately differ as to what amounts to deformation. And what if the state of international law does not allow the integrity of a municipal law concept to be preserved – must the concept be abandoned at the international level, or can it be used notwithstanding its (international) imperfections?

Judge Sir Gerald Fitzmaurice, in his Separate Opinion, explored this problem. It was, he noted, essential 'to insist on the principle that when private law institutions are dealt with in the international legal field, they should not there be distorted or handled in a manner not in conformity with their true character, as it exists under the system or systems of their creation'.[67] Fundamental to the basic structure of companies as it existed according to municipal law concepts was not only their separate legal personality, but also the resulting carefully drawn distinctions between the functions and rights of the company and those of the shareholder. Not to maintain these distinctions at the international level 'would be completely to travesty the notion of a company as a corporate entity'.[68] But here lay the problem: 'Certain qualifications or modifications . . . which, in the domestic field, affect and as it were alleviate the situation [of shareholders], are not, in the present state of the law, reflected, or not adequately so, in the international domain.'[69] International law was in this respect deficient and underdeveloped, and did not allow equivalent possibilities whereby the balance between the company and its shareholders, as established at the municipal law level from which international law took its inspiration in this field, was maintained at the international level. Unsatisfactory though this might be, Judge Sir Gerald Fitzmaurice acknowledged that the conclusions to which the Court had come

[66] *Ibid.*, at p. 37.   [67] *Ibid.*, at p. 66.
[68] *Ibid.*, at p. 67.   [69] *Ibid.*, at p. 68.

were enjoined by international law, and that its judgment 'inevitably endorses' the view that so long as a company technically existed there was no room for independent international action on behalf of its shareholders. In effect, therefore, the internationally imperfect concept of corporate structures had nevertheless to be adopted.

The Court itself was not unaware of these deficiencies in the law it was having to apply. It noted[70] that given the significant and substantial developments in recent times of corporate activities and structures, particularly the growth of often multinational holding companies, 'it may at first sight appear surprising that the evolution of law has not gone further and that no generally accepted rules in the matter [of protecting shareholders' interests] have crystallized on the international plane'.[71] But the Court was disappointingly hesitant to do anything about it: it said, in effect, that it was all too difficult, and the 'difficulties encountered have been reflected in the evolution of the law on the subject'.[72]

VI

Such a summary review of the way in which the Court has applied just one rule of international law, and in doing so has considered some of the relevant concepts, does not readily lend itself to the formulation of general conclusions. Nevertheless, some elements of the Court's approach are noteworthy.

In all three cases the Court maintained the 'nationality of claims' rule in substantially its traditional form – either by side-stepping it and so avoiding any need to distort it (*Reparations*), or by applying it (*Nottebohm*; *Barcelona Traction*); even when side-stepping the rule and developing a parallel alternative the Court was at pains to ensure that its approach remained consistent with the underlying principles. In relation to the concepts it was called upon to apply the Court acknowledged the separate existence at the international level of concepts equivalent to, but with meanings different from, their counterparts in municipal law: where international law had to lean on municipal law for some particular concept its meaning at the international level was to be derived not from its meaning in any one system of municipal law, but either from international practice in related fields (*Nottebohm*) or from generalized characteristics evident in a range of relevant systems of municipal law (*Barcelona Traction*). But beyond that the Court's approach was uneven. Although in the *Reparations* case and the *Nottebohm* case the Court did not

---

[70] *Ibid.*, at pp. 46–7.
[71] *Ibid.*, at p. 47.   [72] *Ibid.*

allow itself to be unduly constrained by considerations of form, either in the rule's expression or in the application of relevant concepts, and in the latter clearly demonstrated that international law was more concerned with substance than with form in relation to the nationality of individuals, in the *Barcelona Traction* case its approach was somewhat more formal and conservative.

The Court's innovative approach to new institutional developments and its avoidance of formal constraints in the first two cases were not followed through in the third in the context of contemporary economic developments, in relation to which the Court remarked upon, but left unremedied, the inadequacies of international law.

24

The plea of domestic jurisdiction before the International Court of Justice: substance or procedure?

Gaetano Arangio-Ruiz

ॐ

INTRODUCTION

The Cases in which the issue of domestic jurisdiction has arisen before the ICJ have been, so far, *Anglo-Iranian Oil Co.*, *Interpretation of Peace Treaties with Bulgaria, Hungary and Romania*, *Norwegian Loans*, *Rights of Passage over Indian Territory*, *Interhandel* and *Aerial Incident*. The Court has pronounced itself conclusively on the plea in *Interpretation of Peace Treaties*, *Right of Passage* and *Interhandel*. Of the other cases, *Norwegian Loans* is interesting for the subject of the present chapter in view of opinions expressed by five dissenting judges. Although they are not devoid of interest we must leave out, for the sake of brevity, *Anglo-Iranian Oil Co.* and *Aerial Incident*.

A study of the said jurisprudence indicates with clarity, in our view, that although the Court, the parties, the single judges and commentators continue to refer, explicitly or implicitly, to the traditional concept of domestic jurisdiction, that concept does not seem to have played any effective role in determining the acceptance or the rejection of the objections based on domestic jurisdiction.

By the 'traditional concept' I understand that 'international law criterion' which was resorted to by the practice and doctrine of international adjudication as soon as it became clear to almost all that one could not find any matters belonging *per se* – namely, by their nature – to the domestic jurisdiction of states. As everybody knows, domestic jurisdiction was thus deemed to be, in conformity with this 'international law criterion', the sphere of relationships with regard to which a state is not bound by international obligations. By virtue of that criterion the appurtenance of a matter to domestic jurisdiction would not depend – or would not depend directly – upon the nature of the matter or question *per se*, but upon the attitude currently held with regard to it by treaty or customary international law. Hence the equation – in French – 'domaine réservé/matières non-liées', and the equally well-known relativity of the reserved sphere in time and space. It is also well known that this concept has always been, to say the least, of difficult application:[1] particularly so in that phase of the Hague Court's proceedings in which a state (defendant or, less frequently, applicant) puts forward a plea of domestic jurisdiction in order to challenge the Court's jurisdiction. Once matters of domestic jurisdiction are identified with matters not covered by an international obligation it is inevitable that the question whether the plea should be dismissed or accepted coincides with the question whether the objecting state was actually bound or not by the international obligation invoked by the other party. A way had therefore to be sought in order to avoid prejudging the merits by a positive or negative decision on the preliminary question of jurisdiction. Hence the device known as the 'provisional conclusion'. According to this device it would not be necessary, in dealing with a plea of domestic jurisdiction, for the Court to pronounce itself 'upon the merits of the legal grounds (*titres*) invoked by the Parties'. According to the 1923 Opinion, such a course would admittedly prejudge the merits of the case.[2] The Court should confine itself to 'considering the arguments and legal grounds (*titres*) advanced by the interested Governments in so far as is necessary in order to form an opinion upon the nature of the dispute', namely, in order to see whether the 'legal grounds (*titres*) relied on are such as to justify the *provisional conclusion* that they are of juridical importance for the dispute'.[3]

---

[1] Except, of course, when the domestic jurisdiction reservation is an automatic ('self-judging') one.

[2] *Nationality Decrees in Tunis and Morocco*, PCIJ, Series A/B, No. 4, p. 26.

[3] The sentences in quotation-marks are taken from PCIJ, Series A/B, No. 4, p. 26 – a page which, together with the preceding pages 23–5, is characterized, in my opinion, by a high degree of obscurity. The obscurity is considerably higher than that of the comparatively clear language by which the essence of the 1923 dictum on the point is condensed by the ICJ in the relevant passage of the *Interhandel* judgment (see p. 442 below). It should be noted in particular that the order in which I quote some of the phrases is different from the original in an attempt to make the discourse a bit less obscure.

Confronted once more with a text so frequently referred to in the literature on domestic jurisdiction I am unable to resist the temptation to recall again – for the delight of the eminent judge to whom these modest pages are wholeheartedly dedicated – the 'private information' reported in the 1923 volume of the *American Journal*, according to which one of the oral pleadings in the *Nationality Decrees* case had been so soporific as to give the members of the Court a chance to show 'their aptness for judicial function by falling fast asleep' (M. Ch. Noble Gregory, 'An Important Decision by the Permanent Court of International Justice', *AJIL*, 17 (1923), pp. 298ff at 306). Indeed, the reading of the Advisory Opinion does give the impression that the drafting of some of the passages of pp. 23–6 (perhaps too infrequently read directly by commentators) had been complicated here and there by interruptions. Some of the sentences look as if they had been cobbled together with little regard for that logical sequence that usually characterizes the prose of the Hague Court. An example is indicated in note 9 below.

It is our submission that despite the lip-service (not infrequently tacit) to the concept of domestic jurisdiction which is reflected in the 'international law criterion' – namely the equation 'domaine réservé/matières non-liées' – that concept has not really been applied. The concept of domestic jurisdiction on which both Hague Courts have actually relied in order to reject the objections of domestic jurisdiction seems to be – as will be shown – quite different.

THE MAIN ICJ CASES

To begin with *Interhandel* – the case in which the plea of domestic jurisdiction has been dealt with most significantly – the defendant United States submitted, *inter alia*, the objection that the seizure and retention of the vested shares of *Interhandel* were 'according to international law, matters within the domestic jurisdiction of the United States'.[4] In order to decide on that objection the Court 'based itself on the course followed' by the Permanent Court in the *Nationality Decrees* case:

> Accordingly the Court does not, at the present stage of the proceedings, intend to assess the validity of the grounds invoked by the Swiss Government or to give an opinion on their interpretation, since that would be to enter into the merits of the dispute. The Court will confine itself to considering whether the grounds invoked by the Swiss Government are such as to justify the provisional conclusion that they may be of relevance in this Case and, if so, whether questions relating to the validity and interpretation of those grounds are questions of international law.[5]

In conformity with this plan, the Court proceeded to take note of three points. Point one was that the parties disagreed over the relevance and the interpretation of a Washington Accord; point two that the parties disagreed over the concepts of enemy assets and neutral assets; point three that the parties disagreed over the interpretation of the compromissory clause contained in article VI of the Washington Accord and in a conciliation and arbitration treaty. Considering that the three points involved were related to questions of international law, the Court concluded that the plea of domestic jurisdiction raised by the United States 'must be . . . rejected'.[6]

---

[4] This was the Fourth Preliminary Objection (b), ICJ, 1959, p. 11. Fourth Preliminary Objection (a) was based instead on the well-known US automatic ('self-judging') domestic jurisdiction reservation (*ibid.*).

[5] ICJ Reports, 1959, p. 24.

[6] *Ibid.*, p. 25.

Despite the evocation of the 'international law criterion' which was obviously implied in the reference to the Permanent Court's dicta in *Nationality Decrees*, the ICJ failed, in our view completely – on the Permanent Court's example – to proceed to any serious verification of the existence of an international obligation of the United States. As planned, the Court abstained from any appreciation – to repeat the Court's own words – of the 'validity of the grounds invoked by the Swiss Government or to give an opinion on their interpretation'. The Court added: 'That would be to enter upon the merits of the dispute.'[7] If, however, the Court did not touch in any measure upon the validity and interpretation of the (legal) 'grounds' one does not see in what sense the Court examined whether, in the subject matter of the dispute, there existed that legal obligation (the 'lien') of the US, only the presence of which could justify, according to the concept of domestic jurisdiction to which the Court adhered, the rejection of the US plea of domestic jurisdiction. The Court did not even attempt that superficial appreciation of the claimant state's allegations that could have allowed it to form a provisional view – however summary – of the degree of foundation of the Swiss claim. The Court does not seem to have gone beyond a finding that there was an international (legal) dispute between Switzerland and the US. This was similar to the Permanent Court's approach in the 1923 Opinion.[8] As it was put by Waldock, the Permanent Court had confined itself, in that Opinion, 'to a superficial examination – but we would say "enumeration" – of the four principal points in controversy between the parties', in order to conclude that: 'In deciding the question of domestic jurisdiction arising under Article 15(8) of the Covenant, the relevant issue was not the *actual legal rights* of the parties in the case but the *prima facie* status of the matters in dispute as being governed or not being governed by international law.'[9]

---

[7] *Ibid.*, p. 24.

[8] That the Court has done no more is also manifest in President Klaestad's Dissenting Opinion: 'I concur in the view of the Court that the dispute relating to these questions involves matters of international law, and that this Preliminary Objection should therefore be rejected' (ICJ Reports, 1959, p. 79).

[9] H. Waldock, 'The Plea of Domestic Jurisdiction before International Legal Tribunals', 31 *BYbIL* (1954), pp. 108–10. The Permanent Court's enumeration is at pp. 27–31 of PCIJ, Series A/B, No. 4.

It seems, indeed, strange to us that the Permanent Court could have satisfied itself with such a superficial examination of the parties' positions (as compared with what it should have done in order to maintain the logic of its own 'international law criterion') while the same crucial pages (23–6) of the Advisory Opinion contained the two following considerations: (a) 'It is certain – and this has been

The ICJ's enumeration of the *titres juridiques* in dispute in the *Interhandel* case was shorter and, if possible, even more superficial. It is difficult to avoid the impression that in so doing the Court really applied, on the example of its predecessor, neither the 'international law criterion' nor any theory of a 'provisional conclusion' worthy of the name.

Moving backwards, in *Norwegian Loans* the Court decided not to pronounce itself on the distinct (and main) Norwegian non-automatic reservation of domestic jurisdiction, the majority having applied in favour of Norway – as requested by the latter – the US automatic ('self-judging') domestic jurisdiction reservation. The case is interesting nonetheless, thanks to the opinions expressed by five of the judges, and particularly by Lauterpacht, Basdevant and Read. In his discussion of the nature of the Franco-Norwegian dispute Judge Lauterpacht rejected 'the view that the subject matter of the . . . dispute is not related to international law but exclusively to the national law of Norway'.[10] Despite the fact that the settlement of the matter would have implied the examination of many questions of Norwegian municipal law – a point he readily admitted – he believed that 'in principle, the . . . dispute is *also* one of international law and . . . it comes within the orbit of controversies enumerated in Article 36(2) of the Statute of the Court'.[11]

According to Judge Basdevant, although the main effort of Norway had been to show the non-international nature of the question, it had not succeeded in demonstrating that the question was solely one of national law.[12] Despite the ambiguities of the French conclusions, he believed that 'the discussion before the Court eliminated all assimilation between' the submissions 'of a bondholder proceeding against his Norwegian debtor before

recognized by the [League of Nations] in the case of the Aland Islands – that the *mere fact that a State brings a dispute before the League of Nations does not suffice* to give this dispute an *international legal character* calculated to except it from the application of paragraph 8 [of article 15 of the Covenant of the League of Nations]' (p. 25 at the bottom); (b) 'It is equally true that *the mere fact* that one of the parties *appeals to engagements of an international character* in order to contest the exclusive jurisdiction of the other is *not enough* to render paragraph 8 [of article 15 of the League of Nations Covenant] inapplicable' (p. 26 at the top) (emphasis added). It is difficult not to be impressed by the lack of consistency between these paragraphs (especially the second) and the fact that the Court did not do anything more than verify, by the so-called provisional conclusion, that there was, between the UK and France, an international (legal) dispute. Did it ascertain anything more than the fact that the UK 'appeal[ed] to engagements of an international character'?

[10] ICJ Reports, 1957, pp. 36–7.

[11] *Ibid.*, p. 38.

[12] ICJ Reports, 1957, pp. 72ff esp. 77–8.

a Norwegian tribunal' and the French Submissions.[13] An analogous position was taken by Judge Read. While acknowledging the presence in the case of aspects of municipal law, he also recognized that the French application 'properly construed, was broad enough in its terms to raise those aspects of the problem which consist solely of questions of international law',[14] a state of affairs which emerged even more clearly from the French final submissions.[15]

None of the three judges, however, seems to pay serious attention to the theories on the basis of which the domestic jurisdiction *exceptio* had been allegedly rejected in previous cases. None of them really pays attention either to the equation 'domaine réservé/matières non-liées' or to the provisional conclusion theory.[16] They confined themselves to noting that France and Norway were divided by questions partly covered by international law.[17]

The current equation and the summary conclusion theory do not seem to have had any explicit weight either in the opposing opinions of Judges Badawi and Moreno Quintana. The latter confined himself to the view that state loans, as acts of sovereignty, are governed by national law. The former relied mainly on what he considered a failure by France to demonstrate the international nature of the dispute.

13 *Ibid.*, p. 77.

14 *Ibid.*, p. 87.

15 These submissions, the judge explained, clearly raised 'the questions of discrimination' and 'the question whether Norway could, in conformity with the principles of international law . . . unilaterally modify the substance of the contracts between Norwegian borrowers and French bondholders' (*ibid.*, p. 88).

16 The three judges seem to have thought of the current equation when they asked themselves, and answered in the affirmative, the question whether international legal issues had really emerged, and which ones, and at what 'stage'. The current equation, however, should require that one determine whether the defendant state is or is not bound, in the case, by international obligations *vis-à-vis* the claimant state: and to such a task neither Lauterpacht nor Read nor Basdevant applied himself. They did not even apply themselves to the more limited task of seeking a summary conclusion on the existence of Norwegian international obligations and the degree of legal foundation of the French claim.

17 The essence of the three judges' opinions with regard to the matter was, in conclusion, as follows:

  (i) unnecessary to establish whether the French claim was legally founded in any measure: Judges Lauterpacht, Basdevant and Read confined themselves to finding that there was an international (legal) dispute;

  (ii) it was equally unnecessary to reach a provisional conclusion in that sense: the dispute was obviously there, for any lawyer to see *ictu oculi*;

  (iii) for the Norwegian objection to be rejected (had the automatic reservation not been sufficient) the existence of a dispute of the kind susceptible to adjudication before the Court was quite sufficient.

There is no trace of relevance, to that effect, either of an 'international law criterion' or of a 'conclusion', whether provisional or definitive with regard to the international obligations of Norway alleged by France.

The current equation and its ancillary 'provisional conclusion' theory were not applied any more rigorously in the ICJ's Advisory Opinion on *Interpretation of Peace Treaties*. History repeated itself here by an even more obvious (albeit tacit) acceptance by the Court of a British viewpoint not very dissimilar from the 1923 United Kingdom position in *Nationality Decrees*.[18]

Of course, the Court was right, as in all the other cases, in rejecting the three resisting states' pleas of domestic jurisdiction. The Court was also right as a matter of law – much as one may regret that it had not any reason to touch upon the underlying human rights issue – when it declared that it was not

> called upon to deal with the charges brought before the General Assembly since the Questions put to the Court relate neither to the alleged violations of the provisions of the Treaties concerning human rights and fundamental freedoms nor to the interpretation of the articles relating to these matters. The object of the Request is much more limited. It is directed solely to obtaining from the Court certain clarifications of a legal nature regarding the applicability of the procedure for the settlement of disputes by the Commissions provided for [in the Treaties in question].[19]

As regards the grounds on which the Court rejected the domestic jurisdiction *exceptio* raised by the 'respondent' states, once more one finds no explicit trace of an application, either of the current equation or of the summary conclusion theory. One only finds an implied application of the latter theory. After defining the scope of its task as above, the Court concluded: 'The interpretation of the terms of a treaty [for the above-mentioned purpose] could not be considered as a question essentially within the domestic jurisdiction of a State. It is a question of international law which, by its very nature, lies within the competence of the Court.'[20]

In 1923 the Permanent Court had not gone beyond the *constat* of the international legal nature of the four sets of issues that divided France and the UK over the *Nationality Decrees*. In 1950 the ICJ was even more laconic.

---

[18] As everybody knows, the British viewpoint was that in order to pronounce on the French plea it would suffice for the Court to note that an international legal dispute was before the League of Nations Council; (PCIJ, Series A/B, No. 4, pp. 15–16). France maintained that the plea could not be decided upon without a thorough examination of the Merits (*ibid.*, pp. 11–12).

[19] ICJ Reports, 1950, p. 70.

[20] *Ibid.*, pp. 70–1.

It again did very little indeed if one compares such a simple conclusion with what should have been done – in 1950 as in 1923 and in all the other cases – by way of a proper, rigorous application of the maxim 'domaine réservé/matières non-liées'. The course followed in 1950 was even less of a middle one between the British and French positions of 1923. It was even more purely the *constat* that there was an international (legal) dispute.

The Court seems to revert instead to a rigorous application of the equation – as the PCIJ had done in *Losinger* and *Electricity Co. of Sofia and Bulgaria* – in the *Right of Passage over Indian Territory* case (1960). The parties were as much at odds about the way to handle the Indian plea of domestic jurisdiction as France and the UK had been in 1923, except that respondent and applicant reversed their roles. In 1923, the defendant France had maintained that the plea could not be properly treated without examining the whole merits, while the UK claimed that the plea should be rejected on the mere basis of the fact that the League Council had been seised of an international legal dispute. In *Right of Passage* the respondent India wanted the plea to be accepted *in limine*, on the almost equally simple (although reversed) basis that Portugal did not invoke plausible legal grounds. For claimant Portugal a decision on the plea presupposed an examination of the merits. After identifying the complex issues raised by the two sides, the Court decided that it would not be possible to decide on the *exceptio* of domestic jurisdiction at the preliminary stage without prejudging the merits. Consequently, it joined the plea to the merits. Following consideration of the merits, it rejected the Indian plea in that it acknowledged that 'Portugal had in 1954 a . . . right of passage over intervening Indian territory'.[21]

The Court's decision to join the plea to the merits was dissented from by Judge Klaestad, who believed that the plea should have been rejected *in limine*, and by the Indian *ad hoc* Judge Chagla, who maintained that the objection should have been upheld *in limine*. Both judges referred to the *Nationality Decrees* Opinion, namely to the current equation 'domaine réservé/matières non-liées' and the 'provisional conclusion' theory.[22]

In this case one thus finds both extremes in the application of the 'international law criterion'.

The Court applied that criterion as rigorously as logic suggests it should be applied. By joining the plea to the merits it practically admitted, in our view,

---

[21] ICJ Reports, 1960, pp. 43–4.
[22] ICJ Reports, 1957, pp. 164–5 (Klaestad) and 173–8 (Chagla).

that the plea of domestic jurisdiction, as understood by the 'international law criterion', is a plea to the merits.

The two dissenting judges, for their part, applied the international law criterion as watered down by the provisional conclusion theory, namely by examining so superficially the parties' opposing legal arguments as to contradict, in our view, the international law criterion and taint with arbitrariness their respective conclusions.

This reminds one of the opposite results to which the provisional conclusion theory had led Lauterpacht, Basdevant and Read, on the one hand, and Badawi and Moreno Quintana, on the other hand, in *Norwegian Loans*.

THE PERMANENT COURT'S PRECEDENTS

It should not take long to show that the ICJ's jurisprudence has conformed essentially, with regard to the treatment of domestic jurisdiction objections, to the precedents set by the Permanent Court since 1923. Any difference seems to be to make it even clearer that the Hague Court does not pay any more than a cursory attention to the 'international law criterion' and to the provisional conclusion theory, and that it decides on the issue on the basis of much simpler elements.

Following the *Nationality Decrees* Opinion – reference to which has already been made[23] – the Permanent Court had dealt with domestic jurisdiction in *Treatment of Polish Nationals, Losinger* and *Electricity Co. of Sofia and Bulgaria*.

In the first case, the Court was called upon by the League of Nations Council to advise on the competence of the League's High Commissioner with regard to a dispute between Poland and Danzig arising from the alleged non-compliance by Danzig with provisions of the Danzig Constitution and legislation relating to the treatment of Polish nationals, the Commissioner's competence being subject to the dual condition that the dispute arose between Poland and the Free City and concerned a question pertaining to the relations between them. While not contesting that the interpretation of a constitution was in general a matter of national law, Poland contended that in view of the *sui generis* status of Danzig, the 'ordinary legal distinction between matters of a domestic and of an international character does not hold good in the present

---

[23] At pp. 440–2.

case'.[24] Poland referred in particular to the obligations and the League controls imposed upon Danzig by international rules in force at the time. Consequently, the Polish government claimed that despite the distinction Poland was entitled to put before the High Commissioner the alleged violations by Danzig of the provisions of its constitution and legislation relating to the treatment of Polish nationals.[25] The Court decided that Danzig's special international status did not authorize a departure from the principles that govern the relations between states and establish new rules for the relations between Poland and Danzig. According to the Court, notwithstanding its peculiarities, the constitution of Danzig was and remained, *vis-à-vis* Poland, the constitution of a foreign state. Therefore, the claims of Poland against the Free City based upon the application by Danzig of its constitution *as such* could not give rise, as between Poland and Danzig, to disputes falling within the scope of the High Commissioner's competence. At the international level the question of the treatment of Polish nationals could only be resolved on the basis of the applicable provisions of international law and not on the basis of Danzig's constitution.[26] Poland, therefore, was entitled to seise the High Commissioner with regard to the treatment of given persons in application of the Danzig constitution only 'in the case of disputes concerning the violation, *as a result* of such application, of an international obligation of Danzig towards Poland arising either from treaty provisions in force between them or from ordinary international law'.[27] It seems clear, therefore, that the Court did not really apply any 'international law criterion' in the sense of the current equation. The question was one of relations: and the Court found that the High Commissioner was competent to deal with disputes pertaining to Poland–Danzig relations and not to the relations of Danzig with the people under its jurisdiction and law.[28]

---

[24] *Treatment of Polish Nationals and Other Persons of Polish Origin or Speech in the Danzig Territory*, Advisory Opinion, PCIJ Series, A/B, No. 44, 4 February 1932, p. 23.

[25] *Ibid.*, pp. 23–5.   [26] *Ibid.*, p. 24.

[27] *Ibid.*, at p. 42. The Court had also observed (at p. 24): 'The application of the Constitution of the Free City may, however, result in the violation of an international obligation incumbent on Danzig towards Poland, whether under treaty stipulations, or under general international law; as for instance in the case of denial of justice in the generally accepted sense of that term in international law.' The Court further stated (*ibid.*) that in such an eventuality it would be not the Constitution of Danzig as such that gave rise to the responsibility of the Free City, but the international obligation. In such a case, Poland would undoubtedly be right to seise the organs of the League by virtue of the relevant international rules in force.

[28] The Court gave an essentially correct opinion concerning: (a) the lack of any title for Poland to discuss the conformity of Danzig's conduct with the constitution of Danzig on the international level; and (b) the right of Poland, on the contrary, to file an international complaint with respect to the conformity of Danzig's conduct with international law. We shall see that this case is particularly significant for a proper understanding of the concept of domestic jurisdiction (see pp. 457–8 below).

In *Losinger*, the first contentious case in which a plea of domestic jurisdiction was raised before the Hague Court, Switzerland alleged the violation by Yugoslavia of a compromissory clause contained in a contract between the Yugoslav government and the Losinger company. Yugoslavia contended that the matter was one of 'national' law, the dispute thus not being of an international nature. The Court found that the objection was closely linked to the merits of the case and so joined it to the principal issue.[29] By joining the preliminary exception to the merits – namely, to the examination of the question whether Yugoslavia was or was not in breach of international law – the Court implicitly but unambiguously admitted that, if and in the degree to which the reserved domain was the sphere of 'matières non-liées', the reserved domain did not play any really restrictive role with respect to the jurisdiction of an international organ of a judicial nature. At the same time, by retaining jurisdiction, the Court did not apply the provisional conclusion doctrine. It based itself merely upon the international (legal) nature of the Swiss claim.

In *Electricity Co. of Sofia and Bulgaria*, where Belgium considered the treatment of a Belgian company by Bulgarian authorities to be in breach of the international obligations of Bulgaria, the respondent state invoked domestic jurisdiction, alleging that the object of the Belgian claim was a question of municipal law. It also invoked the non-exhaustion of local remedies in that the acts of Bulgarian authorities which were complained of by Belgium had not reached a definitive stage, the two objections appearing intertwined. The plea of domestic jurisdiction – envisaged by the Court as a *ratione materiae* objection – was examined by it distinctly with regard to the two different titles of jurisdiction invoked by Belgium.[30] From both viewpoints – despite not very relevant *nuances* – the Bulgarian reasoning was considered to be of such a nature as to concern the merits of the dispute. From the viewpoint of one of the titles of jurisdiction the objection was thus considered not to present the character of a preliminary *exceptio* in the sense of article 62 of the Rules, and was joined to the merits. From the viewpoint of the second title of jurisdiction it was declared inadmissible, the parties remaining at liberty to develop the matter as a defence on the merits.

It is difficult to see in what sense the Court could think that the Bulgarian objection raised a question *ratione materiae*. It was not a question of subject matter in *Electricity Company* any more than it was such a question in

---

[29] The Court did the same with the non-exhaustion of local remedies objection raised by Yugoslavia.

[30] One was a Belgo-Bulgarian arbitration treaty; the other was the parties' acceptance of the Optional Clause.

Nationality Decrees or *Losinger*. Even less was it a question of how the subject matter stood under international law, namely 'matière liée' or 'non-liée'. What Bulgaria contested was, essentially, the international nature of the Belgian claim and of the dispute. The only issue to be considered was whether the Court was seised of the international dispute between Belgium and Bulgaria or of the national law dispute between the Belgian company and the Bulgarian state. The Bulgarian exception of domestic jurisdiction was no different, from that essential viewpoint, from the Yugoslav objection in *Losinger*.[31] The doubts raised by Bulgaria over the international nature of the dispute were obviously strengthened (within the framework of one of the titles of jurisdiction) by the absence of that final decision (within Bulgarian law) on the relationship between the company and the Bulgarian state, which was at the basis of the objection relating to the non-exhaustion of local remedies.

Despite its imperfections, the *Electricity Company* decision teaches a good lesson, both positive and negative. From the negative side it tells us once more that the Hague judges did not really believe in the 'international law criterion' of domestic jurisdiction or, for that matter, in the provisional conclusion theory. From the positive viewpoint it tells us, despite language ambiguities, that the really decisive point, in the face of a plea of domestic jurisdiction, was the international (or national) nature of the dispute.[32]

Essentially the same was later to be the issue before the IJC in *Anglo-Iranian Oil Co.*, except for the fact that the plea of domestic jurisdiction was considered in that case only for the purpose of the IJC's competence to indicate provisional measures. Two main points of interest are discernible for us in this case. One is that the Court observed that the dispute submitted by the UK was between that state and Persia, not between the Anglo-Iranian Oil Co. and Persia. The second point related to the object of the dispute. The dispute related to an alleged infringement of international law consisting of a breach of contract and denial of justice. Once more, the Court did not pay any real attention to the 'international law criterion' or the provisional conclusion theory. It could be contended, though, that the lack of regard for the 'international law criterion' was, in this particular case, only a consequence of the fact that the Court considered the problem of its jurisdiction for the purposes not of a decision on the merits but only of an indication of interim measures.

---

[31] Just as Yugoslavia contended that Switzerland raised a question of (Yugoslav) national law, Bulgaria contended that Belgium raised a question of (Bulgarian) national law.

[32] The preliminary objection of Bulgaria concerning the non-exhaustion of the local remedies added, of course, to the doubts about the international nature of the dispute (see p. 458 below).

SUBSTANCE OR PROCEDURE

The difficulties arising from the concept of domestic jurisdiction are so widely perceived by commentators that it would be futile to encumber this chapter with citations from the voluminous literature.[33] Suffice it to mention, first of all, the reports and debates devoted to the subject by the International Law Institute – and not for the first time – between 1950 and 1954. Although the 1954 Session's resulting resolution endorsed the 'international law criterion' which for international legal tribunals had prevailed constantly since 1923,[34] the debates revealed an extremely high degree of ambiguity on the concept of the exclusive domain of states.[35] Furthermore, one must register a high degree of scepticism professed by commentators about the effectiveness of domestic jurisdiction reservations in the area of legal disputes. The prevailing view has been for some time now that those reservations serve either no restrictive purpose at all, or a very small one.

As Waldock put it in 1954: 'If the matter is within the reserved domain, the tribunal is incompetent to investigate the merits at all. Yet it cannot determine whether or not the matter is within the reserved domain without an investigation of the merits.'[36] We would specify, however, the whole of the merits. According to an Italian scholar:

> It is easy to see that the domestic jurisdiction reservation is inapt to achieve the purpose that is typical of any reservation appended to instruments conferring jurisdiction upon the Court, namely, to prevent a decision on the merits of the dispute of which the Court has been seised. Indeed, a finding of lack of jurisdiction based upon the fact that the subject matter of the dispute lies within the exclusive

---

[33] As explained further on, we leave out the even more difficult problems relating to the role that the reservation has played before political bodies, such as the Assembly and the Councils of the League and of the United Nations. The problem and the solution are *mutatis mutandis*, the same (see pp. 461–2 below).

[34] 'The "reserved domain" is the domain of state activities where the jurisdiction of the state is not bound [*liée* in the French text] by International Law.' 'The extent of this domain depends on International Law and varies according to its development' (*Annuaire* of the ILI, 54, 5 (1954), pp. 150 and 299).

[35] The underlying, mostly unexpressed, *leitmotif* of the debate was the confrontation between two different concepts of the essence of domestic jurisdiction. One was the notion of domestic jurisdiction as a *ratione materiae* delimitation protecting the freedom or liberty (our sovereignty–freedom) of states. The other was the notion of an ill-defined delimitation protecting the independence (for us sovereignty–independence) of states. The first concept prevailed. The second concept seemed at times to approach the notion of a demarcation line (see pp. 460–1 below) between areas of relations rather than areas of subject matters. A similar *leitmotif* can be traced between the lines of the Institute's earlier efforts on the matter. It can also be seen that much of the contrast was due to the different (but frequently implied) view of the participants about the relationship between international law and municipal law (see pp. 462–4 below).

[36] Waldock, 'The Plea of Domestic Jurisdiction', pp. 140–2.

domestic jurisdiction of the [objecting] state presupposes a determination of absence of international obligations of that state with regard to the said subject matter; but it is precisely in such determination that the consideration of the merits of the dispute consists.[37]

Other commentators are perhaps equally severe, although less drastic. Sir Hersch Lauterpacht has expressed himself on the point at least three times to the effect that (unless of course the reservation were an automatic one) the reservation *per se* was highly problematic.[38] As for the provisional conclusion theory, it was 'of a more theoretical than practical value'. In a penetrating study on the subject Waldock concluded, for his part, that the domestic jurisdiction reservation 'creates an entirely artificial position in international legal tribunals'.[39]

We fully share the serious perplexities of the cited scholars and many others. We are puzzled, however, by the fact that commentators so conscious of the total or partial futility of domestic jurisdiction reservations to international jurisdiction do not wonder whether the fault lies perhaps not so much with the reservations and the concept originally formulated in articles 15(8) of the Covenant and 2(7) of the Charter as with the manner in which both reservations and the concept have been understood by all concerned since 1923. While rightly perceiving the 'artificiality' of the position created by the reservation before international tribunals, Waldock himself, for example, surrenders to the generally accepted interpretation of the Permanent Court's *Nationality Decrees* Opinion and the consequent ineluctability of the provisional conclusion theory.[40] After noting the perplexities expressed particularly by Lauterpacht, Sir Humphrey wrote in 1954:

---

[37] V. Starace, *La competenza della Corte internazionale di giustizia in materia contenziosa* (Naples, 1970), at pp. 193ff, esp. 196–7 (my translation).

[38] H. Lauterpacht, *International Law and Human Rights* (London, 1950), pp. 166ff; 'The British Reservation to the Optional Clause', *Economica*, 10 (nos. 28–30) (1930), pp. 153–4; and Dissenting Opinion in *Interhandel*, ICJ Reports, 1959, pp. 121–2. I leave out, of course, Sir Hersch's well-known discussion of automatic domestic jurisdiction reservations.

[39] Waldock, 'The Plea of Domestic Jurisdiction', pp. 96ff, at p. 140f.

It is also significant that the state endowed with one of the most knowledgeable foreign office legal departments abandoned, at one stage, the domestic jurisdiction reservation to the Hague Court's competence (Starace, *La competenza*, p. 200).

[40] Waldock's cited article contains actually the best possible (however vain) defence of the provisional conclusion theory.

A certain inconsistency is also present in Lauterpacht's position as expressed in his opinion in the *Interhandel* case. Clearly, while approving the Court's reliance on the 1923 precedent he does not entertain any illusions with regard to the value of the current equation with its corollary, the provisional conclusion theory. After noting that the Court had rejected the plea 'by reference to the principle

It may be that, as Professor Lauterpacht suggested in 1930, though for somewhat different reasons, the 'provisional view' theory will prove to be of 'more theoretical than practical' importance in contentious cases. *But no one has suggested any other practical method of separating the question of jurisdiction from the question of the substantive rights and obligations of the parties* when a tribunal is confronted with a preliminary objection to jurisdiction on the plea that the case concerns matters within a reserved domain of domestic jurisdiction.[41]

We regret not being able to learn whether Sir Humphrey Waldock would have found our 'method of separating' to be a 'practical' one. We do believe, though, that a better method does exist for a tribunal, in considering a plea of domestic jurisdiction, to separate the question of jurisdiction from the question of merits. Our method consists in setting aside, as in our view it deserves, not domestic jurisdiction but that concept of domestic jurisdiction

enunciated' by the PCIJ in *Nationality Decrees*, Judge Lauterpacht stated: 'I concur in that result although it is clear that the test adopted by reference to that Opinion reduces to the bare minimum the practical effect envisaged by the reservation in question. For it is not often that a case may arise in which the grounds of international law relied upon by the applicant State are not, upon provisional examination, relevant to the issue' (ICJ Reports, 1959, p. 121). But this is, in our opinion, an understatement. The possibility envisaged by the judge is not just rare; it is merely a scholastic hypothesis. Judge Lauterpacht also remarked, in the same Opinion (*ibid.*,pp. 121–2), that 'a reservation of that kind [namely, of domestic jurisdiction] is inherent in every declaration of Acceptance and . . . there is no need to spell it out expressly' and that 'States are in any case fully protected from any interference whatsoever by the Court in matters which are according to international law essentially within their jurisdiction. They are so protected not by virtue of any reservation but in consequence of the fact that if a matter is exclusively within the domestic jurisdiction of a State, not circumscribed by any obligation stemming from a source of international law as formulated in Article 38 of its Statute, the Court must inevitably reject the claim as being without foundation in international law.' We are surprised that such considerations did not induce Judge Lauterpacht to wonder whether the traditional, current interpretation of the domestic jurisdiction reservations and of the 1923 definition given by the Permanent Court should not be thoroughly reconsidered. It is indeed difficult to believe that states appended a domestic jurisdiction reservation to their declarations of acceptance of the Court's jurisdiction for no other purpose than that of excluding from that jurisdiction disputes in which the claim would be rejected for lack of valid international legal grounds. A reservation intended to restrict the competence of the Court is not conceivable unless it is of a nature to exclude, in some hypotheses at least, the possibility that the Court's jurisdiction be exercised with regard to the merits of a case. A reservation intended to protect a defendant state from the peril that the Court attribute to it non-existing obligations is not a reservation affecting the Court's competence. It is simply a reminder to the Court that it is a court of law and should not step out of the law.

    This does not affect, of course, the value of Judge Lauterpacht's remarks. And it is not insignificant that those remarks were expressed with regard to a case such as *Interhandel*. Unlike the 1923 *Nationality Decrees* case, where the PCIJ was called to evaluate the impact of the plea of domestic jurisdiction on the competence of another international body (namely, the League Council), in *Interhandel* the Court was deciding on its own jurisdiction. This explains perhaps why reflections such as those of Judge Lauterpacht in 1959 about the relationship between summary view and merits had not occurred to anybody in 1923. It remains for us difficult to explain how Lauterpacht nevertheless accepted, in *Interhandel*, the Court's reference to the *Nationality Decrees* Opinion.

41 Waldock, 'The Plea of Domestic Jurisdiction', p. 114 (emphasis added).

that has afflicted practice and literature since about 1923. I refer to the idea that domestic jurisdiction is the sphere of matters not covered by international obligations (namely to the 'international law criterion') together with the ancillary provisional conclusion theory.

Indeed, the study of the Hague jurisprudence considered in the preceding sections proves beyond any reasonable doubt that the Hague Court does not really apply the 'international law criterion'. The only way to apply that criterion would be to examine the whole merits of the case in order to find out whether the objecting state is or is not bound by the international obligation in question. Only a positive or negative finding on such a point – namely, on the whole of the merits – could justify the rejection or the acceptance of a plea of domestic jurisdiction as currently understood. No provisional conclusion, assuming that the 'international law criterion' were correct, could be an acceptable substitute for a complete consideration of the merits. Such a full consideration would be the only way for the 'international law criterion' to be brought to bear. The provisional conclusion theory cannot be viewed, as a matter of logic, as an answer to the insuperable difficulty of distinguishing jurisdiction from merits which arises from a plea of domestic jurisdiction as currently understood.

As everybody knows, only a few kinds of preliminary objections to jurisdiction or admissibility are such as not to require some incursion into the merits. Beside preliminary objections that seem to be of a purely formal or procedural nature (such as the validity of the application or its presentation, the indication of a plausible jurisdictional link, or the fact that the applicant is a state), everybody recognizes the existence of preliminary objections involving more or less substantial issues pertaining to the merits.[42] Such objections include existence of a dispute, dating of the dispute, legal or political nature of the dispute, exhaustion of local remedies, discontinuance, nationality of the claim. For the Court to decide on objections of this second kind it is indispensable for the Court to take a look at one or more aspects of the merits and reach a summary view in that regard. Considering that only certain elements of the merits are involved (frequently requiring no more than a cursory consideration) such a summary view will normally not be such as really to prejudge the merits. But almost everybody admits that this is not the case with a plea of domestic jurisdiction as currently understood. As has been

---

[42] H. W. A. Thirlway, 'Preliminary Objections', in R. Bernhardt (ed.), *Encyclopedia of Public International Law* (Amsterdam, 1981), pp. 179ff, esp. 179–80.

noted, a provisional conclusion on a plea of domestic jurisdiction (as currently understood) is either meaningless as an application of the 'international law criterion', in the sense that it does not answer in any measure the question whether the matter is or is not the object of an obligation of the objecting state; or it prejudges that question. A plea of domestic jurisdiction is inevitably, under the current concept, a plea to the merits – and the whole of the merits – of the case. It follows that while the rejection of the plea on the basis of a summary view may lead to a manifest contradiction,[43] the acceptance of the plea on the same basis may lead to a legally unjustified practical rejection of the claim on the merits. Although this would be bizarre even in the case where the tribunal is called to decide on the plea against the jurisdiction of another international body,[44] it becomes simply absurd when, as in most cases, the tribunal must pronounce itself *in limine* on its own jurisdiction.

Were logical reasons insufficient to prove the untenability of the current concept, the practice of both Hague Courts is there to prove it. As shown in the preceding sections (pp. 442ff. and 448ff.):

(1) Neither Court has rejected *in limine* the plea of domestic jurisdiction on any basis other than the mere finding that there was an international (legal) dispute: which is far too little for a provisional conclusion on the question whether the matter is one of domestic jurisdiction in the current sense.
(2) In more than one case the Court found it necessary to join the plea to the merits (as in *Norwegian Loans* and *Right of Passage*) or simply to suggest that the parties feel at liberty to address the issue of domestic jurisdiction in the merits phase (as in *Electricity Company of Sofia and Bulgaria*), clearly nullifying, either way, the restrictive role of the reservation as currently understood.

Fortunately, in addition to proving the untenability of the current concept, the Hague jurisprudence also indicates – to anyone willing to see it – in which direction the real and only possible significance of the reservations of domestic jurisdiction should be sought.

Both Courts reject the objection under two conditions relating both to procedure and leaving the merits unprejudged. We discern a positive condition and a negative condition. The positive condition is the presence of

---

[43] As it occurred in the *Åland Islands* case between the three jurists who advised on the preliminary issue and the League Council which dealt with the merits on the basis of a report of three rapporteurs.

[44] As was the case, for example, in the Hague Court's Advisory Opinions in *Nationality Decrees*, *Treatment of Polish Nationals*, *Interpretation of Peace Treaties*; and in the Opinion of the three jurists on the preliminary issue in the *Åland Islands* case.

an international (legal) dispute. The negative condition is that the object of the dispute be such that the Court would not pronounce itself directly on a relationship of national law of the objecting state.[45]

The positive condition is manifestly at the basis of the Court's decision in all the cases in which the domestic jurisdiction objection has been rejected in the preliminary phase: by the Court in *Nationality Decrees, Interhandel, Interpretation of Peace Treaties*; and by Judges Lauterpacht, Basdevant and Read in *Norwegian Loans.*

The presence of the negative condition clearly emerges, in a number of cases, from the express or implied – early or belated – finding by the Court or by dissenting judges that the Court would not be called to pronounce directly on a national law dispute or relationship. Such was the case in *Anglo-Iranian Oil Co.*, where the Court found that it was not called upon to deal with a dispute between the company and Persia; in *Interhandel*, where it found it was not called to deal with a dispute between Interhandel itself and the US; and in *Norwegian Loans*, where three of the dissenting judges believed that the case was not one between the French bondholders and the Norwegian state. It was actually the same negative condition that operated implicitly in the retention of jurisdiction in the cases where the objection was joined to the merits. In *Losinger* the dispute to be determined was between Switzerland and Yugoslavia and not between Losinger and Yugoslavia; and in *Electricity Co.* it was between Belgium and Bulgaria, and not between the company and the Bulgarian state[46]

The negative condition was found instead to be absent in the Advisory Opinion in *Treatment of Polish Nationals*. While obviously facing a dispute between Poland and Danzig – namely an international dispute – the Court expressed itself against the jurisdiction of the League's High Commissioner. The reason given was that Poland was claiming not a breach by Danzig of

---

[45] Of course this does not mean that an international tribunal – and the Hague Court in particular – does not take account (and in that sense apply) national law for the purpose of deciding the international dispute. It actually does so frequently and with no difficulty. What an international tribunal or the Hague Court does not do is apply municipal (national) law in order to decide a national law dispute in the place of national courts. In *Norwegian Loans* for example, it would have been one thing for the ICJ incidentally to consider issues of Norwegian law in order to decide the claim of France against Norway (where the state of Norwegian law would be relevant as part of the conduct of Norway *vis-à-vis* France through the latter's nationals); and another thing for the Court to apply Norwegian law – getting into the shoes of the courts of Norway – to the underlying relationship between the French bondholders and the Norwegian state.

[46] Although less manifest, the negative condition was as present in those cases as in those where the plea was rejected in the preliminary phase.

international obligations *vis-à-vis* Poland itself but a breach by Danzig of the rights of Polish nationals, deriving from the constitution or the legislation of Danzig: clearly a dispute with a non-interstate object.

The role of the negative condition – the essence, in our view, of the domestic jurisdiction reservation – explains the well-known fact that the objection of domestic jurisdiction frequently accompanies or is accompanied by a plea of non-exhaustion of local remedies.

Such has been the case, for example, in *Losinger, Norwegian Loans, Aerial Incident* and *Interhandel.*

As related by Cançado Trindade in his interesting study, Shabtai Rosenne's oral argumentation for Israel in *Aerial Incident* included the observation that '*the exhaustion of local remedies rule appears as a particularization of the exception of domestic jurisdiction,* although it differs from it in that it implies the possibility of subsequent international proceedings of some sort or other' and in certain circumstances it may be treated in the same way as the objection of domestic jurisdiction.[47]

Setting aside the issue of whether the exhaustion requirement is mainly a matter of substance or procedure (our belief being that it is predominantly, although not exclusively, a matter of substance), Rosenne's interesting observation (obviously formulated within the framework of the current concept of domestic jurisdiction) could usefully be tested against the different notion that we defend. Within the framework of our concept, the exhaustion of local remedies would seem to pertain to what we call (see pp. 457–8 above) the negative condition for the rejection of a plea of domestic jurisdiction. In that sense, the plea of non-exhaustion would be 'a particularization of the exception of domestic jurisdiction'. The matter is worthy of further exploration.

A FEW CONCLUDING REMARKS

The study of the Hague Court's jurisprudence on the plea of domestic jurisdiction leads us to believe, more broadly, that the reservations on the basis of which that plea is raised do not really mean what they have generally been considered to mean since 1923. From the very outset, the literature of international law has overlooked, in our opinion, the real significance of, first,

---

[47] Thus, A. A. Cançado Trindade, 'Domestic Jurisdiction and Exhaustion of Local Remedies: A Comparative Analysis', *Indian Journal of International Law*, 16 (1976), quoting from ICJ Reports, 1959; Pleadings, Oral Arguments, Documents; Oral arguments of 25 March 1959, p. 523.

article 15(8) of the League of Nations Covenant and then article 2(7) of the United Nations Charter. This is revealed in particular by a textual analysis of those two provisions and by the *travaux préparatoires* of article 2(7) of the Charter. It is confirmed by the study of the practice of the political organs of the League and the UN.

To confine ourselves to the two cited texts, it seems difficult to avoid the impression that their literal wording does not justify the generally accepted reading, originally put forward, not without ambiguity, in the *Nationality Decrees* Opinion of 1923. According to this reading the sphere of domestic jurisdiction is the sphere where a state is free from international obligations, namely a sphere of freedom or liberty. However, articles 15(8) of the Covenant and 2(7) of the Charter use the English term *jurisdiction* (and the French term 'compétence'), terms the meaning of which should be clear enough, in international as well as municipal law, not to give rise to controversy.

While clearly indicating spheres of functions, powers or attributions, jurisdiction (or 'compétence') is normally not used to mean sphere of liberty, freedom or exemption from obligation. In fact, there is nothing in the concept that would justify the understanding that it means freedom, liberty or exemption from obligation. On the contrary, spheres of jurisdiction are perfectly compatible with spheres of obligation, duty or restriction. National and local legislators are bound by constitutional and legislative rules; administrators and judges are bound by the laws they implement.

Under international law, states are endowed with original or, according to certain theories, delegated jurisdiction (legislative, administrative and judicial). It is perfectly normal that in any such areas they should be subject to international rules the effect of which may be not only to oblige them to restrict their jurisdiction but also to exercise a given jurisdiction in a given manner and in pursuance of given purposes. To take the example of nationality (the matter with regard to which the 1923 Opinion was given) it seems unquestionable that the attribution of nationality is a matter within the exclusive competence of a state. It is simply inconceivable that French nationality could be attributed – or revoked – by any entity other than the French state. Nevertheless, in attributing nationality a state is not *iure solutus* from the viewpoint of international law. Apart from the obvious prohibition on extending arbitrarily its nationality to whole peoples of other states, a state's jurisdiction in that area is restricted in many ways by rules of general and conventional international law. Any such restrictions, however, are perfectly compatible with the exclusiveness of the power of granting or refusing nationality. A nationality that was granted by a state in disregard of international requirements or prescriptions would be not valid for certain international purposes but, even where the state in question had been in breach of its obligations, it would still be the nationality of that state, granted by that state in the exercise of an exclusive power.[48]

Although they are generally viewed as an indistinct group, the restrictive clauses appended by states to dispute-settlement instruments are of two different kinds. One kind is that of the restrictive clauses that are meant to draw – *ratione materiae, personae, loci* or *temporis* – distinctions among the inter-state disputes that may occur among the contracting states. To these kinds of restrictive clauses belong the old reservations of honour or vital interests and the newer reservations excluding disputes concerning given matters or areas (such as territorial questions, fishing zones, maritime boundaries, air spaces), given states (unrecognized states, members of a Commonwealth, non-sovereign entities); or the disputes arising prior to a certain date or from facts prior to a date. Considering that such clauses are all concerned with distinctions between categories of state-to-state disputes – namely, always between disputes arising at the level of international relations – they could be called 'horizontal' reservations.

Of a different kind seem to be the restrictive clauses that are intended to exclude disputes pertaining to the jurisdiction or competence of national authorities. Such clauses as those excluding constitutional questions, questions of domestic legislation, questions reserved to national tribunals or, more generally, questions affecting the independence of states or their sovereignty in the sense of independence seem to us to belong to this class. An obvious instance is the exhaustion of local remedies requirement where it appears (in a settlement instrument) in such terms as to be a procedural condition, giving rise to pleas against jurisdiction.

Restrictive clauses of this kind are obviously not meant to operate distinctions between different species of inter-state disputes. They are intended to exclude, from direct international consideration or decision matters, disputes or issues pertaining not to inter-state relations but to relationships of national law between private parties or between private parties and governmental institutions of the 'reserving' state. It would seem appropriate to classify them as 'vertical' reservations of a state's jurisdiction (in

---

[48] It is possible that this elementary truth was not sufficiently considered by the Permanent Court in 1923 because of the special feature represented by the fact that the nationality decrees that originated the Anglo-French dispute concerned people from Tunisia and Morocco, under French protectorate. This consideration does not justify, however, the obvious confusion, in the Opinion, between the exclusivity of a state's power to grant its nationality, on the one hand, and the freedom (or not) of the state to do so, on the other.

a broad sense) and 'vertical' restrictions of the jurisdiction of international organs.[49]

Now, if domestic jurisdiction reservations were read, as in our view they should be, in the light of the jurisprudence considered in the preceding sections (see pp. 442ff. and 448ff.) and in the light of the interpretation of that jurisprudence briefly set forth on pp. 455–8, they would fall precisely within the class of 'vertical' reservations.

Moreover, domestic jurisdiction reservations embrace, within a broader scope of delimitation, all the traditional 'vertical' restrictive clauses, whether they pertain to the legislative, the administrative or the judicial functions of the state. We have noted, for example, the close relationship revealed by the practice of international adjudication between the plea of domestic jurisdiction and the plea of non-exhaustion of local remedies.[50]

On the present occasion it is, of course, not appropriate to extend the analysis of the nature and function of domestic jurisdiction reservations from the area of international tribunals to that of international political bodies. Considering, however, the obvious unity of the concept of domestic jurisdiction we feel it necessary to stress our belief that the data one collects from the practice of the political organs of the League of Nations and the UN contradicts the current concept of domestic jurisdiction even more clearly than the Hague jurisprudence.[51]

Indeed, the practice of (international) political bodies also indicates that the plea of domestic jurisdiction fails in the presence of two conditions. These are the same, *mutatis mutandis*, as the positive and negative conditions of the rejection of domestic jurisdiction pleas to the jurisdiction of an international tribunal. The positive condition is that the question or dispute to be dealt with by the political body is an inter-state one (whatever the subject matter). The negative condition is that the treatment of the question or dispute does not

---

[49] Of course, the exclusion of such disputes from the scope of third-party settlement obligations (of international disputes) should go without saying. The reservations are appended just the same, *ex abundanti cautela*. The same is true, in our view, judging also from the Hague jurisprudence, of the domestic jurisdiction reservation.

[50] Rosenne's idea (put forward in connection with the *Aerial Incident* case: see p. 458 above) that the plea of non-exhaustion is a 'particularization of the exception of domestic jurisdiction' is significant in this regard: especially if one abandons the fallacious concept of domestic jurisdiction as an area in which the state is not bound by international obligations.

[51] Not in the sense, however, of a simple substitution of 'international concern' or simply arbitrary criteria for the 'international law criterion' (Gaetano Arangio-Ruiz, 'Le domaine réservé: cours général, de droit international public', *Recueil des cours*, 225, 6 (1990), pp. 9–484, esp. 345ff, 378–90).

bring about a direct, interpository intrusion, by the international body, into the governmental structures and social fabric of the target state or states. Considering that the competence of international political bodies is intended mainly to cover questions or disputes of a political nature, namely, non-juridical issues, the 'international law criterion' would be utterly inappropriate as a restrictive factor on the international body's role. This is amply shown by the practice.[52]

The occasion is not appropriate either for an exploration into the causes of what we rightly or wrongly consider to be a gravely fallacious concept of domestic jurisdiction. We confine ourselves, in that respect, to indicating that the prevalence of that concept since the early 1920s has been the consequence of a series of interrelated factors the ultimate roots of which may be traced back to the federal analogy in international law, namely, to the notion of international law as the decentralized order of a legal community of mankind as opposed to the rudimentary law of the inter-state system.[53]

It was the federal analogy, and the notion of national legal orders as legal systems delegated by international law, that led, in the first place, to the distorted interpretations of articles 15(8) of the Covenant and 2(7) of the UN Charter. I refer to the reading of those provisions in the false light of an

---

[52] The activities of international bodies fall, in our view, into one or the other of two classes: 'international activities in a strict sense' and 'vicarious state activities'. 'International activities' of international bodies consist of enactments (binding or non-binding resolutions, decisions or judgments) addressed to states and other international persons. This is the case of most resolutions and decisions of UN bodies, of the Hague Court judgments, of arbitral decisions. These acts remain at interstate level unless incorporated into national law. 'Vicarious state activities' are those actions (usually classified as 'operational' or 'supranational') that are carried out by international organs directly *vis-à-vis* individuals and other persons of national law (River Commissions, mixed arbitral tribunals, EC institutions, operational activities of UN and other international organs). In performing vicarious state activities international organs qualify, from the legal viewpoint, as common organs of the participating states: a more realistic description, in our view, than that of 'supranational' institutions ('The Normative Role of the General Assembly of the UN and the Declaration of Principles of Friendly Relations', *Recueil des cours*, 137, 3 (1972), pp. 419–742, esp. pp. 668ff of the Appendix).

The practice of the Hague Court and that of political bodies (as well as a proper reading of the relevant texts) indicate that the function of the reservations of domestic jurisdiction is to condemn as *ultra vires* the trespassing, by international organs, from the area of interstate activity to the area of vicarious state activity.

A regime of vicarious state activity should be envisaged, in our opinion, for the Code of Crimes against the Peace and Security of Mankind (if adopted) and to any international criminal tribunal(s) eventually called to implement that Code or other provisions relating to international crimes of individuals. The Code should be conceived as a piece of common criminal law and the tribunal as a common organ of the states participating in the constituent treaty. The European Human Rights system seems not to have fully reached that stage yet.

[53] 'Le domaine réservé', pp. 151ff. and Chapter XII.

unwarranted analogy with the clauses of federal constitutions that directly or indirectly reserve given matters to the jurisdiction of the member states of the federation.[54] It was indeed from the utter impossibility of finding any rules of international law specifying matters characterized as domestic from the viewpoint of international law that scholars, counsels and judges had to revert to the impossible notion that the reserved 'matters' were those not covered by international obligations.

It was because of the federal analogy that one was unable to perceive with the necessary clarity the obvious fact that international law and municipal law govern different relations but not different matters.[55] The difference between the relations that they respectively govern is sufficient to permit national and international law to deal with the same matters, as they do in fact all the time, without directly conflicting with each other. In other words, national and international law are not homogeneous. They constantly interact with each other while remaining in their separate and different domains.

Within such a dual context, the function of domestic jurisdiction reservations was, and is, simply to exclude in principle from the direct action of international judicial or political organs – *ex abundanti cautela*, and subject, of course, to any agreed exceptions – those inter-individual relations, the direct regulation, administration and adjudication of which is considered by states to be their exclusive sovereign (in the sense of independent) prerogative.[56] It is precisely that sovereign prerogative that states forfeit when they dissolve into the federal structure of an integrated nation. And it is that same sovereign prerogative that states restrict in compliance with international agreements establishing so-called supra-national institutions or, more simply, common organs.

Now, federal and, more generally, public law analogies are in our view

---

[54] That error was combined with the arbitrary reading of the term 'jurisdiction' (*compétence, giurisdizione, Zuständigkeit*) as meaning freedom from obligation, overlooking the obvious fact that jurisdiction is perfectly compatible with obligation (see pp. 458–60 above).

[55] Fitzmaurice described the difference as one of 'fields' and of 'classes' or 'sets of relations' ('General Principles of International Law', *Recueil des cours*, 92 (1957, II), p. 70f). If he failed, in our view, to see the real nature of domestic jurisdiction it was because of an inadequate perception of the nature of the 'state in the sense of international law', of sovereignty–independence and of the consequent essential difference between international law and municipal law, Arangio-Ruiz, 'Le domaine réservé', p. 435ff.

[56] In 1925 Brierly described domestic jurisdiction (envisaged as a *ratione materiae* reservation) as a 'formidable newcomer' at the side of vital interests and honour (J. L. Brierly, 'Matters of Domestic Jurisdiction', *BYbIL*, 6 (1935), pp. 8–19, at p. 8). On the novelty we would not have been able to agree because domestic jurisdiction was only a consolidation of older 'vertical' restrictive clauses (see p. 460 above). We would have agreed on the 'formidable' because domestic jurisdiction was and is nothing but a reservation of the state's sovereignty–independence: a formidable reservation indeed in the 1920s, only a very little bit more formidable than today.

surely useful in the theory and practice of European integration as well as, perhaps, in the theory and practice of institutionalized systems of protection of human rights and other special areas.[57] Nevertheless, even in those exceptionally advanced areas, the analogies should be used with caution and parsimony.

However, in that area of purely interstate relations whose regulation is still, by far, the predominant *raison d'être* of international law – namely, the realm of Hersch Lauterpacht's 'private [and not public!] law analogies' – federal analogies are more likely to bring confusion than light. The vicissitudes of the concept of domestic jurisdiction since about 1923 are perhaps the best illustration.

[57] See note 52 above.

25

'Partial' judgments and the inherent jurisdiction of the International Court of Justice

E. Lauterpacht

❧

In traditional terms the basis of the jurisdiction of the International Court of Justice has always been presented as resting on the consent of the parties. This consent may be given by various means. At one end of the spectrum we find the clearest and most specific of submissions in an express agreement between the parties accepting the jurisdiction of the Court, setting out the question and indicating precisely the manner in which the dispute may be brought before the Court. At the other end lies the implied acceptance of the Court's jurisdiction arising from the operation of the concept of *forum prorogatum* – by which the plaintiff party opens the door to the Court's jurisdiction by instituting proceedings which, at the moment of inception, have either no basis, or only an uncertain basis, in terms of evidence of the consent of the respondent. The door having thus been opened, the respondent thereupon, so to speak, walks through it by performing some act that is treated by the Court as evidence of consent. Between these two extremes lie other means of expressing consent, such as the use of the Optional Clause or of separate, successive and ultimately concordant acts of the parties.[1] The Court has emphasized that the identification of consent is not governed by questions of form. What matters is that there should be real evidence of consent.

One should, however, recall that in addition to consent given in these various ways which are themselves foreshadowed in article 36 of the Statute of the Court, parties have already given a significant degree of consent to

---

[1] See, for example, the simultaneous unilateral, but virtually identical, applications filed by Denmark and Norway in the *South-Eastern Territory of Greenland*. The Permanent Court of International Justice described the situation as closely approximating, 'so far as concerns procedure, to that which would arise if a special agreement had been submitted to it by the two Governments'. The Court joined the two cases: PCIJ, Series A/B, No. 48, p. 268. However, in that situation there was no jurisdictional problem since both parties had acceded to the Optional Clause and invoked that as the basis of the Court's jurisdiction.

the jurisdiction of the Court independently of any particular case by their adherence to the Statute of the Court, achieved either upon becoming a member of the United Nations or, if a state is not a member, then by adherence to the Statute with the permission of the General Assembly and the Security Council. By this means states give their consent to the jurisdiction of the Court to determine its own jurisdiction, to indicate interim measures of protection and to permit the intervention of third parties not otherwise jurisdictionally connected with the principal parties.

The purpose of mentioning these elementary aspects of the operation of consent in relation to the exercise of jurisdiction by the International Court is to set the scene for consideration of an episode that touches on both these sources of the Court's competence – the immediately consensual and the more remotely consensual – and occasions examination, albeit in a very preliminary manner, of the Court's 'inherent' jurisdiction.

But before embarking on this consideration, one procedural aspect of the Court's treatment of jurisdictional matters must also be recalled. Such matters are normally raised by a respondent state either by way of a preliminary objection filed within the time-limit set for the delivery of the counter-memorial or by way of an objection raised at an earlier stage of the case in a manner that leads the Court to order at the outset that any question of jurisdiction should be dealt with separately from the merits and before the latter are pleaded. But regardless of the stage at which the question of jurisdiction is taken up, it is eventually considered by the Court on the basis of the pleadings, written and oral, of the parties. These must conclude with submissions – succinct statements of what each of the parties wishes the Court to decide, namely, either that the Court has jurisdiction or that it has not. With, so it appears, only limited exceptions,[2] it has been the practice of the Court to respond to the submissions of the parties and to decide, yes or no, whether it has jurisdiction – that is, until its Judgment of 1 July 1994.

In that Judgment, in a case between Qatar and Bahrain,[3] the Court departed in a striking way from the general pattern of its previous jurisprudence in matters of jurisdiction. It is far from clear exactly what this decision implies as to the Court's position on the central question of the basis of its own

---

[2] See the *Chorzow Factory* case, the *Corfu Channel* case and the *Nuclear Tests* case, referred to below at ns. 10–11, 26 and 12 respectively.

In addressing this Judgment at length, it is necessary for the author to declare an interest in the case by reason of his having acted as one of the counsel for Bahrain. However, the subject matter of this essay is not in contention between the Parties.

[3] *Case Concerning Maritime Delimitation and Territorial Questions between Qatar and Bahrain (Qatar v. Bahrain), Jurisdiction and Admissibility*, Judgment of 1 July 1994, ICJ Reports, 1994, p. 112.

jurisdiction. In some respects, the judgment of the Court is, as its Vice-President, Judge Schwebel, said in his Separate Opinion, 'novel and disquieting', in that the Court appears to have accepted the idea that it can impose obligations upon the parties in the face of an objection from the respondent and in the absence of a finding of jurisdiction. In other respects, the judgment, though still undeniably novel, may well be seen as a further step along the path of the gradual erosion of specific consent as the basis of the Court's jurisdiction. If the Court did not wish it to be so seen, then some fuller explanation was needed of the considerations underlying its decision.

Some description of the procedural evolution of the case is essential to an appreciation of the issues involved.

On 8 July 1991 Qatar filed an application with the Court unilaterally instituting proceedings against Bahrain in respect of certain territorial and maritime issues in dispute between the two states. For purposes of the analysis of the jurisdictional questions involved it would have been convenient to have been able to say that the jurisdictional issues are entirely severable from the substantive ones and that the latter could for the moment be disregarded. Unfortunately that is not possible and some brief reference to the underlying facts must be made.

Qatar and Bahrain are neighbouring states lying on the southern side of the Arabian Gulf. Qatar is a substantial peninsula, pointing northwards into the Gulf from a base contiguous to the territory of Saudi Arabia. Bahrain is an archipelago lying to the west of Qatar and consists of the main island of Bahrain, some smaller islands adjacent to its north-western coast, some small islands, reefs and shoals lying to the east and south-east of the main island, and a further group of islands, known as the Hawar Islands, lying approximately 18 miles south-east of the main island close to the western shore of Qatar. Bahrain also claims sovereignty over Zubarah, a locality on the Qatar peninsula near its west coast.

In its application to the Court, Qatar described the proceedings as being 'in respect of certain existing disputes [between the two states] relating to sovereignty over the Hawar Islands, sovereign rights over the shoals of Dibal and Qit'at Jaradah and the delimitation of the maritime areas of the two States'. For some years previously, Qatar and Bahrain had sought to resolve these disputes (as well as that relating to Zubarah) by negotiation, initially with the assistance of Britain and, after British withdrawal from the Gulf in 1971, with the assistance of the King of Saudi Arabia acting as mediator. In the course of that mediation, the King of Saudi Arabia proposed, and the parties accepted, a set of 'Principles for the Framework for reaching a Settlement'. The First Principle provided: 'All issues of dispute between the two countries, relating to sovereignty over the islands, maritime boundaries and territorial waters, are to be considered as complementary, indivisible issues, to be solved comprehensively together.' These Principles were adopted afresh in 1983, including one providing for the formation of a committee with the aim of reaching substantive solutions acceptable to the two parties.

In December 1987, Saudi Arabia proposed four points to the parties which they also accepted. The first was that 'All the disputed matters shall be referred to the International Court of Justice, at The Hague, for a final rule binding upon both parties, who shall have to execute its terms.' The third provided for the formation of a committee composed of representatives of Bahrain, Qatar and Saudi Arabia 'for the purpose of approaching the International Court of Justice, and satisfying the necessary requirements to have the dispute submitted to the Court in accordance with its regulations and instructions so that a final ruling, binding upon both parties, be issued'. This document came to be known as 'the 1987 Agreement'.

There then followed a series of meetings of this Tripartite Committee at which discussions focused on the preparation of a special agreement to submit the dispute to the Court. One of the principal items in these discussions was the formulation of the question. Bahrain insisted that it be sufficiently widely expressed to cover its claim to sovereignty over Zubarah. This town had been the seat of Bahrain's ruling family, the Al-Khalifah, prior to its settlement in Bahrain in 1783, and that family had continued to exercise there a degree of authority and rights until well into the fifth decade of the present century.

In October 1988 Bahrain submitted to the Committee, in the context of its consideration of the formulation of a joint submission to the Court, the following proposal for the question: 'The Parties request the Court to decide any matter of territorial right or other title or interest which may be a matter of difference between them; and to draw a single maritime boundary between their respective maritime areas of seabed, subsoil and superjacent waters.' This proposal came to be called 'the Bahraini Formula'. It was intended and understood to cover the claim to Zubarah as well as the matters eventually referred to by Qatar in its application to the Court.

In December 1988 the Tripartite Committee again discussed the matters to be submitted and, as the Court found in its Judgment of 1 July 1994, 'the two Parties agreed in principle upon the points thus mentioned',[4] namely:

1. The Hawar Islands, including the island of Janan
2. Fasht al Dibal and Qit'at Jaradah

---

[4] *Ibid.*, Judgment, para. 18.

3. The archipelagic baselines
4. Zubarah
5. The areas for fishing for pearls and for fishing for swimming fish and any other matters connected with maritime boundaries.

The Court noted that Qatar made it clear that it could only accept the inclusion of the question of Zubarah in that list 'if the content relates to private rights', not to sovereignty over Zubarah. Bahrain replied that it intended to submit its claims in that regard 'without any limitation'.[5]

On the occasion of the annual Summit Meeting of the Gulf Co-operation Council in December 1990 Qatar raised the question of the special agreement and indicated that it was ready to accept the Bahraini Formula. The outcome of the ensuing discussions was reflected in Minutes (in Arabic) signed on 25 December 1990 by the Foreign Ministers of Bahrain, Qatar and Saudi Arabia. As these Minutes, which came to be known as 'the 1990 Minutes' or 'the Doha Minutes', are a central item in this stage of the case, they must be quoted in full. The translation prepared by Qatar reads as follows:

The following was agreed:

(1) to reaffirm what was agreed previously between the two parties;
(2) to continue the good offices of the Custodian of the Two Holy Mosques, King Fahd Ben Abdul Aziz, between the two countries till the month of Shawwal, 1411H, corresponding to May of the next year, 1991. After the end of this period, the parties may submit the matter to the International Court of Justice in accordance with the Bahraini Formula, which has been accepted by Qatar, and the proceedings arising therefrom. Saudi Arabia's good offices will continue during the submission of the matter to arbitration.
(3) should a brotherly solution acceptable to the two parties be reached, the case will be withdrawn from arbitration.

The translation of these Minutes by Bahrain differed in some details, of which the most important was the use of the words 'the two parties' rather than 'the parties' in the second sentence of paragraph 2, which indicates what might be done following the expiry of the period of six months.

During that period, no further steps were taken in the negotiations. On 8 July 1991 Qatar filed an application unilaterally instituting proceedings in the Court. Qatar asked the Court to declare that it had sovereignty over the Hawar Islands and sovereign rights over Dibal and Qit'at Jaradeh shoals, as well as to draw a single maritime boundary between the two states. The basis of jurisdiction invoked by Qatar was the 1987 Agreement and the 1990

---

[5] *Ibid.*

Minutes, to both of which documents Qatar attributed the status of binding international agreements. Qatar interpreted the 1990 Minutes as according it the right unilaterally to submit the case to the Court once the six-month period had expired.

Bahrain immediately contested the validity of the Qatari application, contending that the 1987 Agreement foresaw the conclusion of a special agreement to submit the case to the Court; that the 1990 Minutes did not amount to an internationally binding agreement; that, in any event, in using the words 'the two parties' in paragraph 2 of the 1990 Minutes the parties continued to foresee the need for a joint submission; and that by reason of the omission of any reference to the claim of Bahrain to Zubarah, Qatar had failed to submit to the Court all the matters in disp..e between the two sides. Accordingly, so Bahrain argued, there was no consent by Bahrain to the exercise of jurisdiction by the Court.

The Court then ordered that, as the first stage of the case, the Parties should address the questions of the jurisdiction of the Court and the admissibility of the Application. There followed two rounds of written pleadings on these matters. After oral hearings had also taken place, the Court, on 1 July 1991, delivered its judgment.

In the *dispositif* of this judgment the Court:

(a) found that the 1987 Agreement and the 1990 Minutes are international agreements creating rights and obligations for the Parties;

(b) found that 'by the terms of those agreements the Parties have undertaken to submit to the Court the whole of the dispute between them, as circumscribed by . . . "Bahraini Formula"';

(c) decided 'to afford the Parties the opportunity to submit to the Court the whole of the dispute';

(d) fixed '30 November 1994 as the time-limit within which the Parties are, jointly or separately, to take action to this end'; and

(e) reserved 'any other matters for subsequent decision'.

As can immediately be seen, the Court did not pass any judgment on the questions of jurisdiction or admissibility foreshadowed in either the title of the case, the terms of the Court's Order of 11 October 1991 or the submissions of the parties. The better to appreciate this feature of the case, it is helpful to recall the terms of the parties' brief formal submissions in their written and oral pleadings. Qatar submitted that 'The Court has jurisdiction to entertain the dispute referred to in the Application . . . and that Qatar's Application is admissible'; Bahrain submitted 'that the Court is without jurisdiction over the dispute brought before it by the Application filed by

Qatar on 8 July 1991'. Thus, although both parties had, in accordance with the Court's Order of 11 October 1991, squarely raised the issue of jurisdiction, the *dispositif* of the judgment did not in any way pass upon that question. Instead it limited itself to two findings of law. The first – that the 1987 Agreement was a binding agreement – was not really contested by Bahrain. Only the second – that the 1990 Minutes also constituted a binding agreement – was seriously in issue, as to both its status and its meaning. Having reached these conclusions, the Court did not then proceed to find either in favour of, or against, its own jurisdiction – a process that would have required it to enter into a detailed consideration of the December 1990 Minutes. Instead, it decided 'to afford the Parties the opportunity to submit to the Court the whole of the dispute', that is to say, to add to the issues presented to the Court by Qatar the one relating to the Bahraini claim to sovereignty over Zubarah.

It is now necessary to refer to the basis on which the Court reached these conclusions.

The Court began, as already stated, by holding that the 1987 Agreement and 1990 Minutes constituted international agreements creating rights and obligations for the Parties.[6] It then proceeded to identify the content of these agreements. It found that the 1987 Agreement contained an undertaking by the parties to refer all the disputed matters to the Court and to determine, with the assistance of Saudi Arabia, the way in which the Court was to be seised in accordance with the undertaking thus given. As to the 1990 Minutes, these were found to have left open the possibility for each of the parties to present its own claims to the Court. However, the Court also observed that the Bahraini Formula presupposed that the whole of the dispute would be submitted to the Court.[7] The 'whole' of the dispute – as the Court had earlier found – would have to include Bahrain's claim to sovereignty over Zubarah.

The next item in the Court's consideration was the scope of the dispute

---

[6] In this connection the Court made certain observations which are of general interest but do not affect the issue upon which the present essay focuses. The Court first stated (*ibid.*, para. 23) that international agreements may take diverse forms – a view which is not likely to be regarded as controversial. The Court also observed that it was not necessary to consider what might have been the intentions of the signatories of the 1990 Minutes: 'The two Ministers [of Foreign Affairs] signed a text recording commitments accepted by their Governments' (para. 22). This statement, however, is likely to be significantly more controversial than the first since it appears to proceed on the basis that it is possible to identify the content of the controverted texts as 'commitments', and to conclude that they were 'accepted by their Governments', without reference to what might hitherto have been regarded as an essential ingredient of the treaty-making process, namely, the intention (or lack of it) of those directly concerned.

[7] *Ibid.*, para. 33.

actually submitted to it by Qatar. Here the Court found that, by reason of the omission of any reference to Zubarah in Qatar's application, 'only part of the dispute contemplated by the Bahrain Formula' had been submitted to the Court.

At this point in the Judgment, and on the basis of what had gone before, namely, that the Court had found that the parties were agreed that the whole dispute had to be submitted to the Court and that, by reason of the omission of the Zubarah claim, the whole dispute had not been submitted to it, it might have been expected that the Court would have concluded that the Application did not fall within the scope of the agreement between the parties contained in the 1987 Agreement and the 1990 Minutes, and that the Court was, therefore, without jurisdiction. A decision by the Court on the question of jurisdiction was, after all, precisely what the parties had sought in their respective submissions.

But instead, the Court, without any statement of reasons, adopted an unusual approach. In paragraph 37 of the Judgment the Court concluded that the Bahraini Formula contemplated the Court being seised of the whole of the questions in dispute. In the next paragraph the Court went straight on to say: 'The Court has consequently decided to afford the Parties the opportunity to ensure the submission to the Court of the entire dispute as it is comprehended within the 1990 Minutes and the Bahraini Formula, to which they have both agreed.' There was no bridge passage between paragraph 37 and paragraph 38 to explain how the Court moved from the Bahraini Formula in the first of these paragraphs to the step of remitting the case to the parties in the second. There then followed a statement of the ways in which the entire dispute could be submitted to the Court: by joint act or by separate acts. But, said the Court, whichever method might be chosen, the Court should have before it the entire dispute as foreseen in the Bahraini Formula. The Court concluded this paragraph by indicating that 'this process must be completed within five months of the date of this Judgment'. Once the reference of the whole dispute to the Court was thus completed, the Court would fix time–limits for the simultaneous filing of pleadings. At this point, the discussion of the elements underlying the *dispositif* of the judgment ended.

We thus have a situation characterized by the following features:

(1) The document issued by the Court is a judgment, not some interlocutory order. It must be so classified because it carries the description 'judgment' and adheres to the standard form of International Court judgments.[8]

---

[8] A question could, of course, be asked as to whether the final *dispositif* of the text – 'reserves any other matters for subsequent decision' – suggests that it is merely an elaborate form of procedural order. A

(2) The *dispositif*, or operative part of the Judgment, did not respond to the submissions of either side. Qatar called for an affirmation of the Court's jurisdiction over the disputes referred to in its application. Bahrain called for a denial of the same. The Court did not produce a finding one way or the other, but instead produced two relevant but not dispositive rulings of law, relating to the force of the 1987 Agreement and the 1990 Minutes, and decided to afford the parties an opportunity to submit to the Court the whole of the dispute by a date approximately five months after the Judgment.

(3) While the conclusions on the two points of law were legally reasoned, the third element in the *dispositif*, the decision to afford the parties the opportunity to submit to the Court the whole of the case, was unsupported by discussion. Yet this was in truth the most important 'decision' in the Judgment because it contained the operative conclusion of the Court – albeit a conclusion neither of the parties had requested either expressly or by implication. The reader, however, is left without any guidance as to the basis on which the Court thus forbore to respond to the submissions of the parties.

(4) It is not possible to point to any clear provision in the Statute or the Rules of the Court which, in the absence of any explanation in the Judgment itself, can serve to cover this unusual step. Yet the decision is now part of the Court's jurisprudence. The fact that it was reached by a majority of fifteen to one[9] excludes any suggestion that it was anything other than a deliberate and carefully considered step, even if it may have been conceived of as an act of constructive diplomacy.

So some effort must be made to explain it. How is this development – this assertion of a power to remit a case to the parties to enable them jointly to perfect the Court's jurisdiction – to be explained in terms of the Court's

---

similar, but not identical, formula often appears in procedural orders fixing the sequence and time-limits of written pleadings: 'reserves the subsequent procedure for further decision'. An affirmative answer seems unlikely for the reasons set out in the text above. Moreover, the Judgment of 1 July 1994 speaks of 'other matters' not 'subsequent procedure', thus avoiding any pre-emption of the question whether there will be any 'subsequent procedure'.

[9] The dissentient vote was that of Judge Oda, who developed a powerful argument that if the Court was unable to find that the 1987 Agreement and the 1990 Minutes authorized the unilateral filing of an application 'it should have declared that it lacked jurisdiction to entertain the present Application' (*ibid.*, para. 2). He expressed the view that the Court was attempting to render an interlocutory judgment, something that it could not do without having disposed of the jurisdictional issue (para. 3). 'It seems to me', he said, 'that actually the Court is simply making a gesture of issuing an invitation, in the guise of a Judgment . . . By avoiding the essential point, the Court seems to be playing a role of conciliator rather than acting as a judicial institution' (paras. 4–5).

established procedures and precedents, and what are its implications for the future?

There are various elements that must be borne in mind in discussing the situation, not all consistent with one another.

The first element is that in the past the Permanent Court and the International Court have both regarded the submissions of the parties as establishing the limits of the dispute in respect of which the Court must render its decision. This approach is reflected, for instance, in the *Chorzow Factory* case. There the Court said: 'For though it can construe the submissions of the Parties, it cannot substitute itself for them and formulate new submissions simply on the basis of arguments and facts advanced'.[10] Even though the Court has recognized the freedom of a party to modify its submissions, it has recognized the significance of such submissions by insisting that 'the other party must always have an opportunity to comment on amended submissions'.[11]

The sensitivity of the Court to the requirement that a judgment should fall within the scope of the submissions of the parties is further demonstrated by its insistence in the *Nuclear Tests* case on interpreting the Australian submissions with a view to determining the object of the Applicant's claim before examining the effect of the unilateral declarations made by France which were ultimately found to dispose of the case.[12] In short, the range of the Court's judgment is controlled by the submissions of the parties.

A second element in the situation is that the Court has on at least one occasion in the past proceeded in a manner not contemplated by the form of action or the submissions before it – and it has done so without giving the parties any opportunity to present their views on the proposed course of action. In these proceedings, brought by Australia against France, the Court ordered the questions of its jurisdiction and of the admissibility of the application to be treated separately and first. In its submissions Australia concluded that 'the Court has jurisdiction to entertain the dispute . . . and that the Application is admissible'. France, though it did not file a formal pleading, indicated to the Court by letter 'that the Court is manifestly not

---

[10] PCIJ, Series A, No. 7, at p. 35.

[11] PCIJ, Series A, No. 17, at p. 7.

[12] The Court must ascertain the true object and purpose of the claim and in doing so it cannot confine itself to the ordinary meaning of the words used; it must take into account the Application as a whole, the arguments of the Applicant before the Court, the diplomatic exchanges brought to the Court's attention, and public statements made on behalf of the applicant Government. If these clearly circumscribe the object of the claim, the interpretation of the submissions must necessarily be affected' (*Nuclear Tests* case, ICJ Reports, 1974, p. 253, at p. 263).

competent in this case and that it [France] cannot accept its jurisdiction'.[13] Yet, even though the written and oral proceedings were conducted on the basis that the issue was about jurisdiction and admissibility, the Court concluded, by reason of unilateral declarations made on behalf of the French Government that it would discontinue atmospheric nuclear testing (the prohibition of which had been the purpose of the Australian claim), that circumstances had arisen which 'render any adjudication devoid of purpose'.[14] In the *dispositif* of the Judgment the Court found 'that the claim of Australia no longer has any object and that the Court is therefore not called upon to give a decision thereon'.[15] This conclusion was reached, however, after a close consideration by the Court of the object of the Australian application[16] and a determination 'that the *fons et origo* of the case was the atmospheric nuclear tests conducted by France . . . and that the . . . objective of the Applicant was . . . to obtain a termination of those tests'.[17] Thus, the Court gave some explanation of its action which, though not in accord with the submissions filed by Australia, was not out of accord with the objective Australia had sought to achieve in the litigation.

A third element in the situation is that the Court is the master of its own procedure – in the sense that it is for the Court to decide, within the constraints set by its Statute and subject to its Rules (which it is, of course, free to amend), in what procedural manner a case should be dealt with. For this proposition it is unnecessary to cite specific authority since this aspect of the Court's competence is reflected constantly in a variety of orders which, for example, establish time-limits, separate issues of jurisdiction or admissibility from the merits, join issues of admissibility to the merits, or separate the consideration of questions of damages from those relating to merits.

A recent and striking example of the exercise of this power of the Court is to be found in the Court's Order of 16 June 1994 in the case concerning the *Land and Maritime Boundary between Cameroon and Nigeria*.[18] The operative part of the Order fixed the time-limits for the filing of the Memorial of Cameroon and the Counter-Memorial of Nigeria. Its recitals, however, recalled that two and a half months after the Cameroon had filed its original application it filed an additional application for the purpose of extending the subject of the dispute to a further dispute; that the Cameroon had requested the Court to join the two Applications and 'to examine the whole in a single case'; that, in further explanation of the additional Application, the Cameroon had stated

---

[13] *Ibid.*, pp. 256–7. [14] *Ibid.*, at p. 271.
[15] *Ibid.*, at p. 272. [16] As referred to above, n. 12.
[17] *Ibid.*, at p. 262. [18] ICJ Reports, 1994, p. 105.

that this application had not been intended as a separate application but rather as an amendment to the initial application; and that Nigeria had indicated that it had no objection to the additional application being treated in this way. The Court indicated that it saw no objection to this procedure and therefore fixed a time-limit for the pleadings on the basis that the two applications would be dealt with together.

The interest of this episode lies in at least two features. One is that the Statute and the Rules of the Court contain no provision at all for the amendment of applications, though article 47 of the Rules provides for the possibility of the Court joining two or more cases. The Court has, therefore, in this instance developed its procedure in a wholly novel way. But at the same time – and this is the second interesting feature of the episode – it seems likely, from the fact that mention is made in the recitals of the indication of non-objection by Nigeria, that the consent of the latter to this new procedure, which significantly altered the dimensions of the case against it, was regarded by the Court as being at least important, if not essential.

The fourth element pertinent to the analysis of the present situation is that the Court undoubtedly possesses a reserve of power under the title of 'inherent jurisdiction'. Thus, in the *Nuclear Tests* case the Court observed that

> it should be emphasized that [it] possesses an inherent jurisdiction enabling it to take such action as may be required, on the one hand to ensure that the exercise of its jurisdiction over the merits, if and when established, shall not be frustrated, and, on the other, to provide for the orderly settlement of all matters in dispute, to ensure the observance of the 'inherent limitations on the exercise of the judicial function' of the Court, and to 'maintain its judicial character'.[19]

Three comments may be made in connection with this inherent power.

The first is that the jurisdiction thus asserted by the Court should be distinguished from the jurisdiction exercised by the Court under the heading, to be found in section D of part III of its Rules, of 'Incidental Proceedings'. Such proceedings comprise 'Interim Protection' (sub-section 1), 'Preliminary Objections' (sub-section 2), 'Counter-Claims' (sub-section 3), 'Intervention' (sub-section 4), 'Special Reference to the Court' (sub-section 5) and 'Discontinuance' (sub-section 6). Of the above-listed matters, interim protection, preliminary objections and intervention are expressly covered by provisions

---

[19] *Nuclear Tests* case, ICJ Reports, 1974, p. 259. The quotations within the Court's statement were taken from *Northern Cameroons*, judgment, ICJ Reports, 1963, at p. 29.

in the Statute which provide specific authority for the Court to deal with them.[20] Although it would no doubt be the case that, even in the absence of statutory provision, the Court would be entitled to deal with these matters in the exercise of its 'inherent' jurisdiction, the fact that they are specifically covered in the Statute means that it is unnecessary to treat them under this heading.

The position with regard to counterclaims is different. No reference is made to the subject in the Statute, and the authority of the Court, first, to prescribe Rules for them and, second, actually to deal with them can only be seen to arise by necessary intendment from the general power accorded to the Court in article 30 of the Statute to 'frame rules for carrying out its functions'. The same appears to be true of the treatment of special references to the Court and of discontinuance. The fact that the Court has regarded itself as competent to regulate these matters has a material bearing on the existence and scope of its inherent jurisdiction.

The second point to be made in connection with the Court's inherent power is that the Court does not appear publicly to have discussed the source, character or limits of the exercise of this power.[21] Its existence seems simply to have been assumed. It must, however, have some source. In the absence of any other that is identifiable, this must presumably lie in the powers of the Court necessarily to be implied from the grant of power to frame rules given in article 30 of the Statute or, possibly, even more widely, from the overall power of the Court to operate, as established generally by the Statute.[22] In this respect, the implication of powers for the International Court is comparable in legal justification and method to the implication of powers for any other international organ operating on the basis of a constitutive instrument. The Court's own jurisprudence has been the most significant authority on the subject of implied powers. As the Court said in the *Reparations for Injuries* Advisory Opinion: 'Under international law, the Organization must be

---

[20] For interim protection, see Statute, article 41; for preliminary objections, see Statute, article 36(6); and for intervention, see Statute, articles 62 and 63.

[21] The question was raised in the 1920 Committee of Jurists as to the power of the Court to supply by its rules omissions in its Statute and was answered affirmatively. The discussion did not refer to the question of the Court's inherent powers (Minutes of the 1920 Committee of Jurists, p. 647, as referred to in M. O. Hudson, *The Permanent Court of International Justice 1920–1942* (New York, 1943), p. 180. See also G. G. Fitzmaurice, *Law and Procedure of the International Court of Justice* (Cambridge, 1986), vol. II, pp. 533–8 and 769–71.

[22] It is useful to recall in this connection the statement by Hudson, *The Permanent Court of International Justice*, p. 270, that 'the Court has recognized that it is entirely free to suspend the application of these rules of judicial practice in a given case, if it finds that the circumstances of the case justify that course'. See PCIJ, Series E, No. 14, p. 158.

deemed to have those powers which, though not expressly provided in the Charter, are conferred upon it by necessary implication as being essential to the performance of its duties'.[23]

The third point is that in the judgment of 1 July 1994 in the case of *Qatar v. Bahrain* the Court appears to have regarded this inherent jurisdiction as empowering it even to give a partial judgment, that is, one that does not dispose of the whole issues presented to it by the submissions of the parties. As explained above, though the Court had itself ordered that the questions of jurisdiction and admissibility should be treated first and separately, and though the parties had directed their written and oral arguments to dealing with those matters in their entirety and in the expectation that the Court would decide whether or not it possessed jurisdiction, the Court did not decide this question. It limited itself to deciding that two relevant texts (the 1987 Agreement and the 1990 Minutes) constituted internationally binding legal instruments.[24] Having decided these points, the Court then in effect remitted the case to the parties by deciding to afford them the opportunity to submit to the Court the whole of the dispute. It thus refrained from deciding whether it had jurisdiction over the dispute as unilaterally submitted to it by Qatar.

It is now necessary to consider on what basis the Court could have determined that it possessed this inherent power to restrict the scope of its judgment.

The power thus exercised by the Court must be distinguished from those situations in which it has limited the exercise of its jurisdiction by reason of the insufficiency of the evidence or arguments before it. Professor Rosenne, in his magisterial study of the Court, has included in a section on 'Derivative Proceedings' a paragraph on two cases in which the Court, though requested in the principal case to assess damages, refrained from doing so. In the *Chorzow Factory* case (*Merits*), the Permanent Court refrained from determining the amount of compensation payable because of the insufficiency of the data presented by the parties.[25] Again, in the *Corfu Channel* case, the Court reserved for further consideration the assessment of compensation because neither of

---

[23] ICJ Reports, 1949, at p. 182. See also the general consideration of implied powers in E. Lauterpacht, 'The Development of the Law of International Organization by Decisions of the International Tribunals', *Recueil des Cours*, 4 (1976), pp. 423–32.

[24] Arguably, the whole of the problem discussed in the present chapter could have been avoided if the Court had, prior to the pleadings, ordered the Parties to limit their arguments to the legal status and effect of the 1987 Agreement and the 1990 Minutes. But see n. 36 below.

[25] S. Rosenne, *The Law and Practice of the International Court* (Leyden, 1965), vol. II, p. 533, and PCIJ, Series A, p. 71.

the parties had provided the Court with all the information required for the eventual determination of the sum payable.[26]

It is the lack of material on which the Court could have based its judgments in these two cases that differentiates them from the *Qatar v. Bahrain* case. In this last case, there was nothing to prevent the Court from reaching a conclusion on the question of jurisdiction on the basis of the elements presented to it. It just decided not to do so.

What material is there that can support in specific terms the power of the Court to give a partial judgment?[27] A comparative examination of the practice of national courts is, regrettably, beyond the scope of the present chapter. In any case the question of the consent of the parties is not pertinent in domestic courts.[28] However, it seems unlikely that such courts would find themselves in a situation where consideration would have to be given to their power to decide *proprio motu* whether to give a partial judgment. For example, in the practice of the British courts, should a judge consider that a decision restricted to an initial point might dispose of the case without the need to canvass a wider range of issues, he would raise the matter with the parties and make appropriate orders for the conduct of the case, after having heard their views and having limited the arguments accordingly.

Recourse to arbitral practice is more helpful since the jurisdiction and powers of all arbitral tribunals, whether operating on the plane of national or international law, is dependent upon consent. Here the material falls into two groups.

One group consists of the practice of tribunals operating on the basis of texts that, more or less directly, give them the power to render partial awards. Thus the Arbitration Rules established by the United Nations Commission on International Trade Law (UNCITRAL) provide in article 32(1) that 'in addition to making a final award, the arbitral tribunal shall be entitled to make interim, interlocutory or partial awards'. These Rules were adopted, subject to the possibility of modification, in the Claims Settlement Declaration accepted by Iran and the United States in January 1981.[29] Article 32(1) was

---

[26] ICJ Reports, 1949, p. 36.

[27] The unilateral assertion by the Court of a power to give a partial judgment in any particular case should be clearly distinguished from the case in which the Court, at the request of the parties, renders a judgment on a point of law on the basis of which the parties then negotiate the substantive settlement of the dispute between them. In effect this is what took place in the *North Sea Continental Shelf* case, ICJ Reports, 1969, p. 3. See also the remarks by Professor Jaenicke in Max Planck Institute for Comparative Public Law and International Law, *Judicial Settlement of International Disputes* (Berlin/Heidelberg/New York, 1974), p. 69.

[28] See also the remarks of Judge Oda in his Dissenting Opinion, para. 3 (ICJ Reports, 1994).

[29] Article III(1). For the text of the Declaration, see 1 *Iran–US Claims Tribunal Reports* 10.

adopted by the Tribunal without change and has been applied from the Tribunal's earliest days.[30]

The Arbitration Rules of the International Chamber of Commerce refer less directly to partial awards. Although no express power is given to arbitrators to issue a partial award, article 21 of the Rules, dealing with the scrutiny of awards by the ICC Court of Arbitration, refers to 'an award, whether partial or definitive' and thus implies that partial awards may be made.[31]

The exercise of this power within the ICC arbitration framework was helpfully considered in an award rendered in 1983:

> Whether a partial award may be rendered or not, lies in the discretion of the arbitrators . . . The rendering of a partial award is usually conditional upon the fulfilment of the following requirements:
>
> - The issue to be dealt with is clearly separable from other parts of the litigation;
> - The question to be decided is liquid, fully exposed by the parties and proved;
> - A partial award will help to decide the remaining questions;
> - There is urgency in clearing this special question
>
> The issue of jurisdiction over a party to an Arbitration is a classical setting for a partial award. It can be clearly separated from the other issues in the actual case and easily be disposed of by the Tribunal without going into the merits of the case. It is clear that a decision of the question of jurisdiction is helpful for all parties involved in the Arbitration. At last [sic] it is obvious that the economic advantages call for an early decision on the question who is a proper party to the case.
>
> It is therefore appropriate to render a partial award on the question of jurisdiction.[32]

The fact that those who prepared the UNCITRAL and ICC Rules made express provision for partial awards does not mean that, in the absence of such provision, partial awards are not permitted. Rather it serves to show that the discharge of the arbitral role carries with it the need to be able to make partial awards. It thus provides the functional justification for the implication of such a power for tribunals to which it is not expressly granted.

As regards *ad hoc* arbitral tribunals which are not expressly given jurisdiction to render partial awards, the following view has been expressed in

---

[30] For example, in *Granite State Maritime Co. Inc. v. Iran et al*, 1982: 1 *Iran–US Claims Tribunal Reports* 185, the Tribunal ordered the payment of the principal amounts of indebtedness admitted by the respondent banks, while retaining jurisdiction to resolve the issues of interest and costs.

[31] See Sigvard Jarvin and Yves Derains, *Collection of ICC Arbitral Awards, 1974–1985* (Paris, 1990). See also W. Craig, W. Park and J. Paulsson, *International Chamber of Commerce Arbitration* (New York, 1984), para. 19.03.

[32] Jarvin and Derains, *Collection of ICC Arbitral Awards*, pp. 153–5.

a leading British treatise on commercial arbitration: 'There is no doubt that an arbitrator generally has power to order a preliminary issue to be tried and to give effect to his decision by publishing either an interim award or, if the decision disposes of the whole dispute, a final award'.[33] While it is no doubt possible to point to differences between interim and partial awards, if one recognizes the inherent power of a tribunal to order the former, there seems to be no reason to deny it a similar power in respect of the latter.[34]

The practice of the European Court of Justice deserves mention if only for the purpose of explaining that there is little in it that sheds light on the question. Neither the Statute nor the Rules of the Court make any provision for partial awards. But in assessing the position one must bear in mind that the Court has jurisdiction in three types of case: (a) original jurisdiction in certain limited cases of direct actions brought against Community institutions; (b) appellate jurisdiction in respect of cases initially commenced before the European Court of First Instance; and (c) jurisdiction to give rulings in cases referred to the Court by courts of member states under article 177 of the European Community Treaty.

The question of partial judgments does not appear to have arisen in respect of categories (a) and (b). So far as category (c) is concerned (cases arising under article 177), although the European Court of Justice not infrequently reformulates the questions put to it by national courts and, in so doing, may give the impression that it is not answering the whole of the question as originally posed, this reformulation is generally an expression of the Court's wish to ensure that it does not exceed its competence which is limited to ruling on the interpretation and validity of Community acts only. It is not competent to consider the effects of national law on the compatibility of such law with Community law. So, while the jurisprudence of the European Court of Justice discloses numerous instances in which the Court has, for one reason or another, refrained from answering a question addressed to it, this practice appears neither to be controversial nor to have occasioned much discussion. It can be of assistance in the present context only in the most general terms.

The position of tribunals operating under the International Convention for the Settlement of Investment Disputes (ICSID) is somewhat different. Article 41 of the Convention expressly accords the Tribunal the power to deal if it thinks fit, as a preliminary question, with an objection to the jurisdiction of the Centre for the Settlement of Investment Disputes. On the other hand,

---

[33] M. Mustill and S. Boyd, *Commercial Arbitration* (2nd edn, London, 1989), p. 331.
[34] There is a helpful discussion in A. Redfern and M. Hunter, *Law and Practice of International Commercial Arbitration* (2nd edn, London, 1991), pp. 379–81.

in other respects the Convention, in article 48(3), expressly provides that 'the award shall deal with every question submitted to the Tribunal, and shall state the reasons upon which it is based'.[35]

There is, of course, a great deal more that could and should be said about this subject, but certain tentative conclusions or questions may be mentioned.

First, it would be difficult to deny that the International Court possesses in general terms an inherent competence to render a partial judgment, that is to say, a judgment deliberately limited to some only of the questions generated by the submissions of the parties.

Second, the *circumstances* in which the Court may do this are by no means clear. Evidently, the Court is free to refrain from answering questions that have been rendered moot or irrelevant by the Court's conclusions on earlier issues in the logical sequence of the totality of questions raised by the parties. But if the case is one where the unanswered questions are not moot or irrelevant, how is the Court to justify stopping short of responding to all the questions submitted to it? One possible answer, as suggested by the decisions in the *Chorzow Factory* case and the *Corfu Channel* case, is where the parties have placed before the Court sufficient material to deal with part of the case, but insufficient to dispose of it all. Another possibility is that the Court may refrain from dealing with a question if it considers that an answer on one question in the series raised by the submissions of the parties would realistically enable the parties to reach a negotiated solution to the remainder. This may be the explanation of what happened in the *Qatar v. Bahrain* case. But there must remain some doubt about the adequacy of such an explanation if its result is to deprive the parties (or either of them) of a definitive decision on a point in respect of which they feel that their submissions entitle them to a conclusive answer.

Third, what has just been said raises a question as to the *conditions* under which the Court should render a partial decision. If the request for a partial judgment is made by both parties, then there is no problem. If no such request has been made, the question is whether the Court should adopt this approach without having first informed the parties of what it has in mind and giving them an opportunity to make fresh submissions in relation to the possible outcome that might follow from the Court's partial treatment of the case.[36]

---

[35] For the text of the ICSID Convention, see 1 *ICSID Reports* 3.

[36] It is this factor of first informing the parties that is to say, of giving them an opportunity to produce pertinent argument, that appears to be a principal point of distinction between the exercise of the power to give a partial judgment and the exercise by the Court of its right, in advance of written or oral Pleadings, to make an order identifying issues to which it wishes to limit the initial stage of the case.

Fourth, it would be to the general advantage – for the Court as well as for litigating parties – if the Court were openly to identify and discuss in any relevant case its resort to a partial judgment or, indeed, to the exercise of any other inherent powers. They are an important source of judicial competence and it is difficult to see how litigating parties can properly prepare themselves or give the Court appropriate assistance if they are not informed of what the Court has in mind. The balance between the right of the Court to decide cases in the manner that it thinks best, even by reference to arguments not canvassed by the parties or to procedures not brought to their attention, and the entitlement of the litigant to an opportunity to argue any point material to the decision of his case is a delicate one. Its maintenance requires full judicial consideration.

Last, the manner in which the Court has acted in the *Qatar v. Bahrain* case may also be placed in a wider context – that of the role of the consent of the parties in determining the extent of the competence of the Court.[37] Thus viewed, the Court's decision may be seen as a further indication of the Court's disinclination – recently shown, for example, in the approach of the Chamber of the Court to the intervention of Nicaragua in the *El Salvador/Honduras* case[38] – to insist on strict standards in the application of the general requirement of consent. This time it takes the form of a decision that the general consent which the parties have given to the jurisdiction of the Court to determine its own jurisdiction extends even to a consent that the Court may send them back to the negotiating table, in the hope that they may perfect that jurisdiction.

Postscript

There is a sequel to the Court's judgment of 1 July 1994. It is, however, one that is likely to disappoint those devotees of the Court's procedures who might have been looking forward to a logical and internally consistent development of the Court's recourse to the concept of an 'interim' judgment.

It will be recalled that in its first judgment the Court decided (*inter alia*) that the parties should have an 'opportunity to ensure the submission to the Court

---

The possibility exists, of course, that at that relatively early stage in the proceedings, the Court may be unable to identify the need for the partial judgment – wherein lies the value of its power to decide later to render a partial judgment.

[37] The Court has, in effect, acted without the consent of the parties in deciding to follow a course neither party has requested – the more so when that decision is itself taken before the Court has determined the threshold question of its own jurisdiction in the case.

[38] ICJ Reports, 1990, p. 92, at pp. 131–5.

of the entire dispute as it is comprehended within the 1990 Minutes and the Bahraini formula'. Discussions thereupon took place between the parties but led to no further agreement before the deadline set by the Court, 30 November 1994. Qatar thereupon filed with the Court a document entitled 'Act to comply with paragraphs (3) and (4) of operative paragraph 41 of the Judgment of the Court dated 1 July 1994' and Bahrain filed a 'Report . . . on the attempt by the Parties to implement the Court's Judgment . . . '.

The Qatari 'Act' purported to submit to the Court 'the whole of the dispute between Qatar and Bahrain, as circumscribed by the text . . . referred to in the 1990 Doha Minutes as the "Bahraini formula"'. The 'Act' then listed the subjects falling within the jurisdiction of the Court by virtue of 'the 1987 Agreement, the 1990 Minutes, Qatar's Application and the present Act'. The items listed corresponded with those appearing in the Minutes of the Tripartite Committee meeting of December 1988 (p. 468 above). Qatar also stated that it understood that Bahrain defined its claim concerning Zubarah as a claim of sovereignty. Qatar requested the Court to declare (*inter alia*) 'that Bahrain has no sovereignty or other right over . . . Zubarah'.

On 5 December 1994 Bahrain submitted 'Comments' on the Qatari 'Act', pointing out that

> the Court did not declare in its Judgment of 1 July 1994 that it had jurisdiction in the case brought before it by virtue of Qatar's unilateral application of 1991. Consequently, if the Court did not have jurisdiction at that time, then the Qatari separate Act of 30 November, even when considered in the light of the Judgment, cannot create that jurisdiction or effect a valid submission in the absence of Bahrain's consent.

In December 1994 the Court resumed its consideration of the case, but did not invite any additional argument, either written or oral, by the parties. On 15 February 1995, the Court delivered its second judgment. This decision did little expressly to explain the relationship between it and the earlier judgment beyond observing that in the first judgment the Court 'reserved for subsequent decision all such matters as had not been decided in that Judgment'. The Court also noted that 'Bahrain maintains the objections that it raised with respect to the Application of Qatar. Accordingly, it falls to the Court to rule on those objections in the decision it must now give on the one hand, on its jurisdiction to adjudicate upon the dispute submitted to it and, on the other, on the admissibility of the Application.'

The Court then proceeded to examine 'the terms of the Agreements of 1989 and 1990, in order to determine whether it has jurisdiction to adjudicate upon the dispute'. The Court concluded that 'it has jurisdiction to adjudicate upon the dispute'. At no point in this examination did the Court refer to the Qatari 'Act' of 30 November 1994. The Court's conclusion appears to have been reached solely on the basis of the arguments before it at the time of its original judgment. Yet the Court had, in that earlier judgment, refrained from reaching a conclusion upon the matter because it took the view that at the time Qatar was under an obligation to submit 'the whole of the dispute' to the Court and that, by reason of the omission of any reference to Zubarah in Qatar's application, 'only part of the dispute contemplated by the Bahraini Formula' had been submitted to the Court.

The Court's conclusion upon jurisdiction is followed by a relatively brief consideration of admissibility. Only here is any reference made to the Qatari 'Act' of 30 November 1994. The Court quoted the list of 'matters referred to the Court' by Qatar in that 'Act' and noted that they coincided with the list proposed by Bahrain in the Tripartite Committee meeting of December 1988 and with the proposals made by Bahrain in October and November 1994, but subsequently withdrawn 'except in so far as these latter related to *sovereignty* over the Hawar Islands and *sovereignty* over Zubarah'. The Court then explained that from the moment that 'the matters' of the Hawar Islands and of Zubarah were referred to the Court 'the claims of sovereignty over the Hawar Islands and over Zubarah may be presented by either of the Parties'. It concluded: 'As a consequence, it appears that the form of words used by Qatar accurately described the subject of the dispute . . . The Court . . . concludes that it is now seised of the whole of the dispute, and that the Application of Qatar is admissible.'

The operative parts of the judgment indicate that by ten votes to five the Court found (a) that it has jurisdiction to adjudicate 'upon the dispute submitted to it'; and (b) 'that the Application of the State of Qatar as formulated on 30 November 1994 is admissible'.

The Judgment of 15 February 1995, narrow as its scope may be, is likely to rank as one of the more controversial of the Court's history though the controversy will centre principally on the unexpected approach of the Court to the use of the *travaux préparatoires* of the 1990 Minutes. That aspect of the matter, however, lies beyond the scope of this chapter. For present purposes – in relation to the consideration of the use of interim judgments and their relationship to subsequent consideration of a case – the Judgment of 15 February 1995 must be regarded as at best tantalizing. The Court reaches a conclusion that it has jurisdiction to adjudicate 'upon the dispute', but does not say what the dispute is. Is it the dispute as defined in the application of 8 July 1991 or as defined at some later date? If it is the dispute as originally defined, then, as the Court had already said in its Judgment of 1 July 1994, that did not comprehend the whole dispute and, therefore, it would have appeared that that submission did not provide the Court with a sufficient jurisdictional basis on which to proceed. If, on the other hand, it is the dispute as subsequently defined by Qatar on 30 November 1994, the Court has, in effect, permitted Qatar to amend its Application and expand the scope of the case as originally submitted to the Court – and the Court has done this against the express objection of Bahrain. The Court thus introduces a significant degree of uncertainty into the existing law and practice relating to the scope and effect of applications, the function of submissions and the permissibility (if any) of amendments.

Nor is this obscurity in any way diminished by the fact that in the Judgment's brief section on admissibility the Court refers to the Qatari 'Act' of 30 November 1994 and, for that purpose (but seemingly not for the purpose of jurisdiction) takes it into account as sufficiently describing the subject of the dispute. Even so, it is not clear whether the 'dispute' thus mentioned is the dispute submitted to the Court in July 1991, or some subsequently described and expanded dispute.

The idea of 'interim' or 'partial' judgments is, if properly used, a valuable one. Used in conjunction with the identification by the Court of appropriate issues, it could do much to eliminate the need for arguments related to or based upon contingencies that may never materialize if the Court decides one or more points in a particular way. This could lead to a simplification and abbreviation of pleadings, coupled with a possibly significant reduction in the costs of the parties and in the use of judicial time. It is, therefore, a matter for regret that the Court has not in its latest decision grappled more precisely with the connection between it and the judgment of 1 July 1994 and has thereby failed to provide litigants with a better understanding of this potentially valuable device.

26

Intervention before the
International Court of Justice

The late J. M. Ruda

ॐ

INTRODUCTION

The jurisdiction of the International Court of Justice to entertain interventions is part of the Court's incidental jurisdiction. This form of the Court's jurisdiction is termed 'incidental' because 'it is a jurisdiction which the Court may be called upon to exercise as an incident of proceedings already before it'.[1]

The Statute of the ICJ envisions two types of intervention: discretionary intervention, which is covered by article 62 of the Statute; and intervention as of right, which is provided for by article 63 of the Statute.[2] In the following, these two types of intervention will be discussed separately.

DISCRETIONARY INTERVENTION

The provisions of the Statute and the Rules of the Court

Discretionary intervention is covered by article 62 of the Statute of the Court, which reads as follows:

(1) Should a state consider that it has an interest of a legal nature which may be affected by the decision in the case, it may submit a request to the Court to be permitted to intervene.

(2) It shall be for the Court to decide upon this request.

---

[1] Gerald Fitzmaurice, *The Law and Procedure of the International Court of Justice* (Cambridge, 1986), pp. 533–4. Other forms of incidental jurisdiction include interim measures of protection, procedural orders, and decisions concerning interpretation and revision of judgments.

See also *Haya de la Torre* case (*Colombia v. Peru*), ICJ Reports, 1951, pp. 71, 76, judgment of 13 June (observing that 'every intervention is incidental to the proceedings in case; it follows that a declaration filed as an intervention only acquires that character, in law, if it actually relates to the subject matter of the pending proceedings').

[2] The terms 'discretionary intervention' and 'intervention as of right' seem established, although it has been noted that 'both labels [are] of doubtful accuracy' (C. M. Chinkin, 'Third-party Intervention before the International Court of Justice', *AJIL*, 80 (1986), pp. 495, 496.

Although under paragraph 2 of article 62 it is 'for the Court to decide upon' a request for permission to intervene, this provision does not supply the Court with unlimited powers to accept or reject a request for permission to intervene. As the Court stated in the *Continental Shelf* case between Tunisia and Libya:

> The Court observes that under paragraph 2 of Article 62 it is for the Court itself to decide upon any request for permission to intervene. The Court, at the same, emphasizes that it does not consider paragraph 2 to confer upon it any general discretion to accept or reject a request for permission to intervene for reasons simply of policy. On the contrary, in the view of the Court the task entrusted to it by that paragraph is to determine the admissibility or otherwise of the request by reference to the relevant provisions of the Statute.[3]

The procedure governing intervention under article 62 is regulated by article 81 of the Rules of the Court. This article reads as follows:

1. An application for permission to intervene under the terms of Article 62 of the Statute, signed in the manner provided for in Article 38, paragraph 3, of these Rules, shall be filed as soon as possible, and not later than the closure of the written proceedings. In exceptional circumstances, an application submitted at a later stage may however be admitted.
2. The application shall state the name of an agent. It shall specify the case to which it relates, and shall set out:
   (a) the interest of a legal nature which the State applying to intervene considers may be affected by the decision in that case;
   (b) the precise object of the intervention;
   (c) any basis of jurisdiction which is claimed to exist as between the State applying to intervene and the parties to the case.
3. The application shall contain a list of the documents in support, which documents shall be attached.

It can be noted that article 81 of the Rules of the Court is more specific than article 62 of the Statute. Of particular interest is paragraph 2 of article 81 of the Rules, which specifies the contents of an application for permission to intervene, and requires that the application must not only specify 'the interest of a legal nature which the State applying to intervene considers may be affected by the decision in th[e] case', which requirement is also embodied in

---

[3] *Case Concerning the Continental Shelf (Tunisia/Libya), Application to Intervene*, ICJ Reports, 1981, pp. 3, 12, Judgment of 14 April (hereafter *Tunisia/Libya Continental Shelf* case (*Intervention*). See also *Case Concerning the Continental Shelf (Libya/Malta), Application to Intervene*, ICJ Reports, 1984, pp. 3, 8–9, Judgment of 21 March (hereafter *Libya/Malta Continental Shelf* case (*Intervention*) (citing *Tunisia/Libya Continental Shelf* case (*Intervention*).

article 62 of the Statute, but also 'the precise object of the intervention', and 'any basis of jurisdiction which is claimed to exist as between the State applying to intervene and the parties to the case'.

The inclusion of the last-mentioned requirement in the Rules of the Court, i.e., that a state seeking intervention shall set out any jurisdictional link that is claimed to exist between that state and the parties in the case, reflects a long-standing controversy within the Court concerning the institution of intervention; namely, whether or not there must exist a jurisdictional link between the state seeking to intervene and the parties to the case. This controversy dates from 1922 when the predecessor of the present Court, the Permanent Court of International Justice, began to consider its rules of procedure for applying article 62 of the Statute.[4] This controversy has been described by the present Court as follows:

> When the Permanent Court began, in 1922, to consider its rules of procedure for applying Article 62 of the Statute, it became apparent that different views were held as to the object and form of the intervention allowed under that Article, and also as to the need for a basis of jurisdiction vis-à-vis the parties to the case. Some Members of the Permanent Court took the view that only an interest of a legal nature in the actual subject of the dispute itself would justify the intervention under Article 62; others considered that it would be enough for the State seeking to intervene to show that its interests might be affected by the position adopted by the Court in the particular case. Similarly, while some Members of the Court regarded the existence of a link of jurisdiction with the parties to the case as a further necessary condition for intervention under Article 62, others thought that it would be enough simply to establish the existence of an interest of a legal nature which might be affected by the Court's decision in the case. The outcome of the discussion was that it was agreed not to try to resolve in the Rules of the Court the various questions which had been raised, but to leave them to be decided as

---

[4] When the present Statute was drafted, article 63 of the Statute of the Permanent Court was included as such as article 63 of the present Statute. As to article 62, a change was made in the English text of the article: the words 'as a third party' at the end of para. 1, which had no corresponding expression in the French text, were omitted. See *Tunisia/Libya Continental Shelf* case (*Intervention*), at p. 15.

For the preparatory work of article 62 of the Statute see *Procès-Verbaux of the Proceedings of the Advisory Committee of Jurists, July 16th–July 24th 1920* (1920). In its report (at pp. 745–6), the Committee explained the proposed article 62 as follows:

> The Committee replies in the affirmative [to the question of whether intervention should be allowed], but on the condition that an interest of a legal nature is involved. The Court is to decide whether the interest is legitimate and consequently whether the intervention is admissible. To refuse all right of intervention, might have unfortunate results. The essential point is to limit it to cases in which an interest of a legal nature can be shown, so that political intervention will be excluded, and to give the Court the right of decision.

and when they occurred in practice and in the light of the circumstances of each particular case.[5]

Subsequently, when the present Rules of the Court, which date from 1978, were drafted, a new subparagraph (c) was included, requiring an application for permission to intervene under article 62 of the Statute to specify 'any basis of jurisdiction which is claimed to exist as between the State applying to intervene and the parties to the case'. The Court has explained that this was done 'in order to ensure that, when the question did arise in a concrete case, [the Court] would be in possession of all the elements which might be necessary for its decision. At the same time the Court left any question with which it might in future be confronted in regard to intervention to be decided on the basis of the Statute and in the light of the particular circumstances of each case.'[6]

The practice of the Court

Article 62 of the Statute has been invoked as a basis of intervention in three relatively recent cases before the Court.[7] In the case concerning the *Continental Shelf between Tunisia and Libya*, Malta sought intervention,[8] and in the case concerning the *Continental Shelf between Libya and Malta*, Italy requested permission to intervene.[9] Most recently, Nicaragua sought intervention in the

---

[5] *Tunisia/Libya Continental Shelf* case (*Intervention*), ICJ Reports, 1981, at p. 14. See also *Libya/Malta Continental Shelf* case (*Intervention*), ICJ Reports, 1984, at p. 2, where the Court noted that 'from the 1922 discussions up to and including the hearings in the present proceedings the arguments on this point [i.e., the need to establish a jurisdictional link as between the state seeking to intervene and the parties to the case] have not advanced beyond the stage they had reached 62 years ago'.

[6] *Tunisia/Libya Continental Shelf* case (*Intervention*), ICJ Reports, 1981, at p. 16.

[7] In *SS Wimbledon* (*UK, France, Italy and Japan v. Germany*), PCIJ, Series A, No. 1 (judgment of 28 June 1923), Poland invoked article 62 in seeking permission to intervene on the side of the applicants. Subsequently, Poland changed its position and indicated that it intended to rely on article 63 of the Statute; the Court accepted the intervention under this article.

Also, in the *Nuclear Tests* case (*Australia v. France/New Zealand v. France*), ICJ Reports, 1973, pp. 320, 324 (Orders of 12 July), Fiji filed an application for permission to intervene. The Court decided to defer the consideration of the application until its decision on the jurisdiction of the Court and the admissibility of the applications. Subsequently, having determined by its judgment of 20 December 1974 that the claims no longer had any object and that the Court therefore was not called upon to give any decision thereon, the Court found that Fiji's application for permission to intervene had lapsed and that no further action thereon was called for on the part of the Court. See *Nuclear Tests* cases (*Australia v. France/New Zealand v. France*), ICJ Reports, 1974, pp. 530, 535 (Orders of 20 December).

It should be noted, however, that although the Court unanimously found Fiji's application to have lapsed, the fundamental issue concerning the requirement of a jurisdictional link again re-emerged within the Court and was discussed by a number of judges in their Separate Opinions.

[8] *Tunisia/Libya Continental Shelf* case (*Intervention*), ICJ Reports, 1981.

[9] *Libya/Malta Continental Shelf* case (*Intervention*), ICJ Reports, 1984.

case concerning the *Land, Island and Maritime Frontier Dispute* between El Salvador and Honduras.[10]

In the *Tunisia/Libya Continental Shelf* case, the Court unanimously denied Malta's application on the grounds that Malta had failed to demonstrate an interest of a legal nature that might be affected by the decision of the Court within the meaning of article 62 of the Statute.[11] Having reached that conclusion, the Court found 'it unnecessary to decide in the present case the question whether the existence of a valid link of jurisdiction with the parties to the case is an essential condition for the granting of permission to intervene under Article 62 of the Statute'.[12]

The *Libya/Malta Continental Shelf* case was more controversial, and Italy's application for permission to intervene was denied only after a vote, by eleven votes to five. In this case, Italy argued that article 62 of the Statute created 'direct jurisdiction' for the Court to entertain Italy's intervention, and that article 81, paragraph 2(c) of the Rules was not intended to impose the existence of a basis of jurisdiction as a condition for intervention, but was included in the Rules merely to ensure that the Court would be provided with all relevant information of the circumstances of the case.[13] Like the *Tunisia/ Libya Continental Shelf* case, the Court did not reach this issue. It concluded that Italy's request could not be granted because, in the Court's view, Italy was requesting the Court to decide on the rights Italy had claimed and not merely to ensure that these rights were not affected. Consequently, according to the Court, 'to permit the intervention would involve the introduction of a fresh dispute' to the Court; and in the absence of consent of the parties, the Court could not entertain any such dispute.[14] The Court held that these consequences of the Court's finding '[could] be defined by reference to either of the two approaches to the interpretation of Article 62 of the Statute'.[15] The Court explained:

> The first way of expressing this reality [i.e., 'the basic principle that the jurisdiction of the Court to deal with and judge a dispute depends on the consent of the parties thereto'] would be to find that, having . . . reached the conclusion that Italy is requesting it to decide on the rights which it has claimed and not merely to

[10] *Case Concerning the Land, Island and Maritime Frontier Dispute (El Salvador v. Honduras), Application by Nicaragua for Permission to Intervene*, ICJ Reports, 1990, p. 92 (judgment of 13 September) (hereinafter *Land, Island and Maritime Frontier Dispute* case (*Intervention*)).

[11] *Tunisia/Libya Continental Shelf* case (*Intervention*), ICJ Reports, 1981, at p. 20.

[12] *Ibid.*, at p. 21.

[13] *Libya/Malta Continental Shelf* case (*Intervention*), ICJ Reports, 1984, at p. 13.

[14] *Ibid.*, at p. 22.

[15] *Ibid.*

ensure that these rights be not affected, the Court must state whether it is competent to give, by way of intervention procedure, the decision requested by Italy . . . The view could be taken that Article 62 does not permit an intervention of the kind referred to except when the third State desiring to intervene can rely on a basis of jurisdiction making it possible for the Court to take a decision on the dispute or disputes submitted to it by the third State . . . A second method of expressing the Court's conviction that Article 62 of its Statute is not an exception to the principle of consent to its jurisdiction to deal with a dispute would be to find that, in a case where the State requesting the intervention asked the Court to give a judgment on the rights which it was claiming, this would not be a genuine intervention within the meaning of Article 62. In such a situation, the State requesting the intervention ought to have instituted mainline proceedings in application of Article 36, and possibly to have asked for the two proceedings to be joined . . . Thus, according to this second approach, Article 62 would not derogate from the consensualism which underlies the jurisdiction of the Court, since the only cases of intervention afforded by that Article would be those in which the intervener was only seeking the preservation of its rights, without attempting to have them recognized, the latter objective appertaining rather to a direct action. Article 62 of the Statute envisages that the object of the intervening State is to ensure the protection or safeguarding of its 'interest of a legal nature' by preventing it from being 'affected' by the decision. There is nothing in Article 62 to suggest that it was intended as an alternative means of bringing an additional dispute as a case before the Court . . . or as a method of asserting the individual rights of a State not party to the case.[16]

The Court concluded that, 'in order to arrive at its decision on the Application of Italy to intervene in the present case, [the Court] does not have to rule on the question whether, in general, any intervention based on Article 62 must, as a condition for its admission, show the existence of a valid jurisdictional link'.[17]

The first case in the history of the present Court and its predecessor in which a state was accorded permission to intervene under article 62 of the Statute was the *Case Concerning the Land, Island and Maritime Frontier Dispute* between El Salvador and Honduras.[18] The Chamber that was formed to deal with the case[19] found that the intervening state, Nicaragua, had shown that it

---

[16] *Ibid.*, at pp. 22-3.

[17] *Ibid.*, at p. 24.

[18] *Land, Island and Maritime Frontier Dispute* case (*Intervention*), ICJ Reports, 1990.

[19] The Court issued an Order forming the Chamber on 8 May 1987. See *Case Concerning the Land, Island and Maritime Frontier Dispute (El Salvador/Honduras)*, Constitution of Chamber, ICJ Reports, 1987, p. 10 (Order of 8 May). On 28 February 1990 the Court issued an Order finding that 'it is for the Chamber formed to deal with the present case to decide whether the Application for permission to intervene under Article 62 of the Statute filed by Nicaragua on 17 November 1989 should be granted': *Case Concerning the Land, Island and Maritime Frontier Dispute (El Salvador/Honduras), Application by*

had 'an interest of a legal nature which may be affected by part of the Judgment of the Chamber in the present case, namely its decision on the legal régime of the waters of the Gulf of Fonseca'.[20] Consequently, the Chamber permitted Nicaragua to intervene in the case 'to the extent, in the manner and for the purposes set out in the Judgment'.[21]

Pursuant to article 2 of the Special Agreement concluded between the parties, El Salvador and Honduras, by which Agreement they submitted the dispute to the Chamber, the function of the Chamber was: '1. To delimit the frontier line in the areas or sections not described in Article 16 of the General Peace Treaty of 30 October 1980; [and] 2. To determine the legal situation of the islands and maritime spaces.'[22] Nicaragua's application for permission to intervene was not related to the first aspect of the proceedings, i.e., the delimitation of the land frontier line, but only to the determination by the Chamber of the legal situation of the islands, the waters of the Gulf of Fonseca, and the waters outside the Gulf.[23]

Referring to article 81, paragraph 2 of the Rules of the Court, the Chamber examined in detail Nicaragua's arguments in support of its application. Dismissing El Salvador's objection that Nicaragua's request was out of time,[24] the Court focused on whether Nicaragua had been able to show an interest of a legal nature which might be affected by the Chamber's decision in the case, the criterion stated in article 62 of the Statute and article 81, paragraph 2(a) of the Rules of the Court. Noting that the Chamber was not required, by the Special Agreement, to give a decision on a single circum-scribed issue, but several decisions on various aspects of the overall dispute between the parties, the Chamber considered 'the possible effect on legal interests asserted by Nicaragua of its eventual decision on each of the different issues which might fall to be determined, in order to define the scope of any intervention which may be found to be justified under Article 62 of the Statute'.[25]

Nicaragua for Permission to Intervene, ICJ Reports, 1990, pp. 3, 6 (Order of 28 February). Nicaragua had argued in its application that its request for permission to intervene was a matter exclusively within the procedural mandate of the full Court.

[20] *Land, Island and Maritime Boundary Dispute* case (*Intervention*), ICJ Reports, 1990, at p. 137.

[21] *Ibid.*   [22] *Ibid.*, at p. 100.

[23] *Ibid.*, at p. 109.

[24] *Ibid.*, at p. 112. The Chamber also dismissed El Salvador's objections that Nicaragua's application should be denied *in limine litis* because of: (1) lack of jurisdictional link between Nicaragua and the parties to the case; (2) failure to state the precise object of the intervention; (3) Nicaragua's stated intention to seek a reformation of the composition of the Chamber (a request which the Chamber noted Nicaragua no longer put before the Chamber); and (4) lack of prior negotiations between Nicaragua and the parties to the case concerning the Gulf of Fonseca: *ibid.*, at pp. 111–14.

[25] *Ibid.*, at p. 116.

Regarding the extent of the burden of proof on a state seeking to intervene, the Chamber noted the differences between the parties and the state seeking to intervene, and concluded:

> In the Chamber's opinion, however, it is clear, first, that it is for a State seeking to intervene to demonstrate convincingly what it asserts, and thus to bear the burden of proof; and, second, that it has only to show that its interest 'may' be affected, not that it will or must be affected. What needs to be shown by a State seeking permission to intervene can only be judged *in concreto* and in relation to all the circumstances of a particular case. It is for the State seeking to intervene to identify the interest of a legal nature which it considers may be affected by the decision in the case, and to show in what way that interest may be affected; it is not for the Court itself – or in the present case the Chamber – to substitute itself for the State in that respect.[26]

Having examined the question whether the decision of the Chamber regarding the legal situation of the islands may affect the legal interest of Nicaragua, the Chamber concluded that:

> Insofar as the dispute relates to sovereignty over the islands, [the Chamber] should not grant permission for intervention by Nicaragua, in the absence of any Nicaraguan interest liable to be directly affected by a decision on that issue. Any possible effects of the islands as relevant circumstances for delimitation of maritime spaces fall to be considered in the context of the question whether Nicaragua should be permitted to intervene on the basis of a legal interest which may be affected by a decision on the legal situation of the waters of the Gulf.[27]

The Chamber then examined the parties' and Nicaragua's arguments regarding the existence of 'an objective legal régime' of a condominium in the waters of the Gulf of Fonseca. The Chamber noted, in particular, Nicaragua's argument to the effect that 'the condominium, if it is declared to be applicable, would by its very nature involve three riparians, and not only the parties to the Special Agreement'.[28] The Chamber concluded that this was 'a sufficient demonstration by Nicaragua that it has an interest of a legal nature in the determination whether or not this is the régime governing the waters of the Gulf: the very definition of a condominium points to this conclusion'.[29] The Chamber likewise held that, on the basis of the Honduran theory to the effect that there was a 'community of interest' in the waters of the Gulf, the result was the same: Nicaragua, as one of the three riparian states, was also interested in that question.[30] However, the Chamber was not satisfied that,

---

[26] *Ibid.*, at pp. 117–18.
[27] *Ibid.*, at p. 119. [28] *Ibid.*, at p. 121.
[29] *Ibid.* [30] *Ibid.*

were it to hold that there was no such condominium or community of interests in the Gulf, Nicaragua had also a legal interest that may be affected by the Chamber's decision in the delimitation within the Gulf.[31] The Chamber reached the same conclusion as to the possible effect on Nicaragua's legal interests of its future decision on the waters outside the Gulf.[32]

As to the two remaining conditions of intervention embodied in article 81, paragraph 2 of the Rules of the Court, the Chamber was satisfied that the two 'objects' of intervention put forward by Nicaragua – to protect its legal rights in the Gulf of Fonseca and the adjacent maritime areas, and to inform the Chamber of the nature of its legal rights in issue in the dispute – were proper ones.[33] The remaining – and controversial – issue was the requirement of article 81, paragraph 2(c) of the Rules, or the question of the existence of a valid jurisdictional link between Nicaragua and the parties to the case. The Chamber noted that in its application Nicaragua had not invoked any jurisdictional basis for its intervention other than the Statute itself. Referring to the Court's past practice, the Chamber stated:

> Although that Judgment [i.e., *Libya/Malta Continental Shelf* case (*Intervention*)] contains a number of valuable observations on the subject, the question remains unresolved. Since in the present case the Chamber has reached the conclusion that Nicaragua has shown the existence of an interest of a legal nature which may be affected by the decision, and that the intervention of Nicaragua has a proper object, the only remaining question is whether a jurisdictional link is required; and since it is conceded that no such link exists, the Chamber is obliged to decide the point.[34]

The Chamber then proceeded to consider 'the general principle of consensual jurisdiction in its relation with the institution of intervention'.[35] Recalling that, as between the parties, consent is the source of the Court's jurisdiction, the Chamber continued:

> Nevertheless, procedures for a 'third' State to intervene in a case are provided in Articles 62 and 63 of the Court's Statute. The competence of the Court in this matter of intervention is not, like its competence to hear and determine the dispute referred to it, derived from the consent of the parties to the case, but from the consent given by them, in becoming parties to the Court's Statute, to the Court's exercise of its powers conferred by the Statute. There is no need to interpret the reference in Article 36, paragraph 1, of the Statute to 'treaties in force' to include the Statute itself; acceptance of the Statute entails acceptance of the competence conferred on the Court by Article 62. Thus the Court has competence to permit

---

[31] *Ibid.*, at p. 125.
[32] *Ibid.*, at pp. 126–8.   [33] *Ibid.*, at pp. 128–31.
[34] *Ibid.*, at pp. 132–3.   [35] *Ibid.*

an intervention even though it be opposed by one or both of the parties to the case; as the Court stated in 1984, 'the opposition [to an intervention] of the parties to a case is, though very important, no more than one element to be taken into account by the Court' (*ICJ Reports 1984*, p. 28, para. 46). The nature of the competence thus created by Article 62 of the Statute is definable by reference to the object and purpose of intervention, as this appears from Article 62 of the Statute.[36]

The Chamber added that intervention was 'not intended to enable a third State to tack on a new case, to become a new party, and so have its own claims adjudicated by the Court'.[37] The difference between intervention and the joining of a new party to the case was not, in the Chamber's view, merely a difference in degree, but a difference in kind. Observing that intervention appears in section D of the Rules of the Court, headed 'Incidental Proceedings', the Chamber emphasized that 'incidental proceedings by definition must be those which are incidental to a case which is already before the Court or Chamber'.[38] Accordingly, 'an incidental proceeding cannot be one which transforms a case into a different case with different parties'.[39] In other words, according to the Chamber, intervention could not have been intended to be employed as a substitute for contentious proceedings.

> Acceptance of the Statute by a State does not of itself create jurisdiction to entertain a particular case: the specific consent of the parties is necessary for that. If an intervener were held to become a party to a case merely as a consequence of being permitted to intervene in it, this would be a very considerable departure from this principle of consensual jurisdiction.[40]

Referring to the *Libya/Malta Continental Shelf* case, the Chamber concluded:

> It is therefore clear that a State which is allowed to intervene in a case, does not, by reason only of being an intervener, become also a party to the case. It is true, conversely, that provided that there be the necessary consent by the parties to the case, the intervener is not prevented by reason of that status from itself becoming a party to the case . . . It thus follows from the juridical nature and from the purposes of intervention that the existence of a valid link of jurisdiction between the would-be intervener and the parties is not a requirement for the success of the application. On the contrary, the procedure for intervention is to ensure that a State with possibly affected interests may be permitted to intervene even though there is no jurisdictional link and it therefore cannot become a party. Article 81, paragraph 2(c), of the Rules of the Court states that an application under Article 62 of the Statute shall set out 'any basis of jurisdiction which is claimed to exist as

---

[36] *Ibid.*, at p. 133.
[37] *Ibid.*, at pp. 133–4.   [38] *Ibid.*, at p. 134.
[39] *Ibid.*   [40] *Ibid.*

between the State applying to intervene and the parties to the case'; the use of the words 'any basis' (and in French the formula 'toute base de compétence qui . . . existerait') shows that a valid link of jurisdiction is not treated as a *sine qua non* for intervention . . . The Chamber therefore concludes that the absence of a jurisdictional link between Nicaragua and the Parties to the case is no bar to permission being given for intervention.[41]

Noting that this was the first case in the history of the two Courts in which a state had been permitted to intervene under article 62 of the Statute, the Chamber found it 'appropriate to give some indication of the extent of the procedural rights acquired by the intervening State as a result of that permission'.[42] The rights were, first, that 'the intervening State does not become party to the proceedings, and does not acquire the rights, or become subject to the obligations, which attach to the status of a party, under the Statute and the Rules of the Court, or the general principles of procedural law'.[43] Second, the intervening state has a right to be heard, which right is regulated by article 85 of the Rules of the Court.[44] Third, the intervening state is permitted to address only such issues with respect to which it has demonstrated an interest of a legal nature in accordance with article 62 of the Statute, i.e., in this case the intervening state, Nicaragua, was permitted to address only such issues as relate to the legal regime of the waters of the Gulf of Fonseca.[45]

The Chamber delivered its judgment on the merits of the *Land, Island and Maritime Frontier Dispute* on 11 September 1992.[46] Recalling that this was the first time in the history of the Court and its predecessor in which a third state had been permitted to intervene under article 62 of the Statute, the Chamber considered it appropriate 'to make some observations on the effect of the present Judgment for the intervening State'.[47]

The Chamber first noted that pursuant to its judgment on the application by Nicaragua for permission to intervene of 13 September 1990, the intervening state, Nicaragua, had not become a party to the proceedings. Based on this, the Chamber held that 'the binding force of the present Judgment for the Parties, as contemplated by Article 59 of the Statute of the Court, does not

---

[41] *Ibid.*, at pp. 134–5.

[42] *Ibid.*, at p. 135. The Chamber found such indication 'particularly desirable since the intervention permitted relate[d] only to certain issues of the many submitted to the Chamber' (*ibid.*).

[43] *Ibid.*, at pp. 135–6.

[44] *Ibid.*, at p. 136.

[45] *Ibid.*

[46] *Case Concerning the Land, Island and Maritime Frontier Dispute (El Salvador/Honduras; Nicaragua intervening)*, ICJ Reports, 1992, p. 351 (judgment of 11 September).

[47] *Ibid.*, at p. 609. According to article 59 of the Statute, 'the decision of the Court has no binding force except between the parties and in respect of that particular case'.

therefore extend also to Nicaragua as intervener'.[48] The Chamber then took note of the fresh attitude of Nicaragua to the effect that Nicaragua no longer regarded itself as being obligated to treat the judgment as binding upon it, and went on to consider 'the effect, if any, to be given to the statement made in Nicaragua's Application for permission to intervene that it "intends to submit itself to the binding effect of the decision to be given"'.[49] The Chamber opined:

> In the Chamber's Judgment of 13 September 1990, emphasis was laid on the need, if an intervener is to become a party, for the consent of the existing parties to the case, either consent *ad hoc* or in the form of a pre-existing link of jurisdiction. This is essential because the force of *res judicata* does not operate in one direction only: if an intervener becomes a party, and is thus bound by the judgment, it becomes entitled equally to assert the binding force of the judgment against the other parties. A non-party to a case before the Court, whether or not admitted to intervene, cannot by its own unilateral act place itself in the position of a party, and claim to be entitled to rely on the judgment against the original parties. In the present case, El Salvador requested the Chamber to deny the permission to intervene sought by Nicaragua; and neither Party has given any indication of consent to Nicaragua's being recognized to have any status which would enable it to rely on the Judgment. The Chamber therefore concludes that in the circumstances of the present case, this Judgment is not *res judicata* for Nicaragua.[50]

INTERVENTION AS OF RIGHT

Another type of intervention, often termed intervention as of right, is provided for in article 63 of the Statute of the Court.[51] This provision states:

---

[48] *Ibid.*

[49] *Ibid.*, at p. 610.

[50] *Ibid.*

[51] See also article 82 of the Rules of the Court, which specifies the procedure to be followed in cases of declarations of intervention under article 63 of the Statute. Article 82 reads as follows:

> 1. A State which desires to avail itself of the right of intervention conferred upon it by Article 63 of the Statute shall file a declaration to that effect, signed in the manner provided for in Article 38, paragraph 3, of the Rules. Such a declaration shall be filed as soon as possible, and not later than the date fixed for the opening of the oral proceedings. In exceptional circumstances a declaration submitted at a later stage may however be admitted.
> 2. The declaration shall state the name of an agent. It shall specify the case and the convention to which it relates and shall contain:
>   (a) particulars of the basis on which the declarant State considers itself a party to the convention;
>   (b) identification of the particular provisions of the convention the construction of which it considers to be in question;
>   (c) statement of the construction of those provisions for which it contends;
>   (d) a list of the documents in support, which documents shall be attached;

1. Whenever the construction of a convention to which states other than those concerned in the case are parties is in question, the Registrar shall notify all such states forthwith.
2. Every state so notified has the right to intervene in the proceedings; but if it uses this right, the construction given by the judgment will be equally binding upon it.

This provision was applied by the Permanent Court of International Justice only once, in the case concerning the *SS Wimbledon*.[52] There, the Court admitted the intervention sought by Poland under article 63 of the Statute, although the application was initially filed under article 62. Taking note of the change of attitude by Poland in the course of the proceedings, abandoning article 62 as the basis of its intervention and instead relying on article 63, the Court found it unnecessary 'to consider and satisfy itself whether Poland's intervention in the suit before it is justified by an interest of a legal nature, within the meaning of Article 62 of the Statute'.[53] The Court then noted that the interpretation of certain clauses of the Treaty of Versailles was involved in the case and that Poland was one of the states parties to the Treaty. Based on this, the Court merely 'recorded' that 'the Polish Government intend[ed] to avail itself of the right to intervene conferred upon it by Article 63 of the Statute', and accepted Poland's intervention.[54]

In the *Haya de la Torre* case, Cuba filed a Declaration of Intervention with the Court, invoking article 63 of the Statute, together with a Memorandum stating its views concerning the interpretation of the Havana Convention of 1928.[55] One of the parties to the case, Peru, having objected to Cuba's Declaration of Intervention on grounds, *inter alia*, that the intervention sought by Cuba did not constitute a proper intervention but rather 'an attempt by a third State to appeal against the Judgment delivered by the Court on November 20th, 1950',[56] the Court stated in that regard:

> The Court observes that every intervention is incidental to the proceedings in a case; it follows that a declaration filed as an intervention only acquires that character, in law, if it actually relates to the subject-matter of the pending

---

3. Such a declaration may be filed by a State that considers itself a party to the convention the construction of which is in question but has not received the notification referred to in Article 63 of the Statute.

[52] PCIJ, Series A, No. 1 (1923); see note 7 above.
[53] PCIJ, Series A, No. 1 (Judgment of 28 June 1923).
[54] *Ibid.*
[55] *Haya de la Torre* case, ICJ Reports, 1951, pp. 76–7.
[56] *Ibid.*, at p. 76. Peru was referring to the *Asylum* case (*Colombia v. Peru*), ICJ Reports, 1950, p. 266 (Judgment of 20 November).

proceedings. The subject-matter of the present case differs from that of the case which was terminated by the Judgment of November 20th, 1950: it concerns a question – the surrender of Haya de la Torre to the Peruvian authorities – which in the previous case was completely outside the Submissions of the Parties, and which was in consequence in no way decided by the above-mentioned Judgment.[57]

The Court then examined whether the object of Cuba's intervention was in fact the interpretation of the Havana Convention. Observing that Cuba's Memorandum was 'almost entirely [devoted] to a discussion of the questions which the Judgment of November 20th, 1950, had already decided with the authority of *res judicata*', the Court found that, to that extent, Cuba's Declaration of Intervention did not satisfy the conditions of a genuine intervention.[58] The Court also held, however, that the statement of the Agent of Cuba at the hearing to the effect that Cuba's intervention was based on the fact that the Court was required to interpret a new aspect of the Havana Convention not subject to the Court's determination in the *Asylum* case conformed to the conditions of article 63 of the Statute. Consequently, 'reduced in this way, and operating within these limits', the Court admitted Cuba's intervention.[59]

The most recent case in which a Declaration of Intervention was submitted to the Court by invoking article 63 of the Statute was the *Case Concerning Military and Paramilitary Activities in and against Nicaragua* between Nicaragua and the US, in which El Salvador sought intervention.[60] The Court summarily disposed of El Salvador's Declaration of Intervention, deciding not to hold a hearing on it and declaring it inadmissible 'inasmuch as it relate[d] to the current phase of the proceedings'; i.e., a phase of the proceedings in which the proceedings on the merits of the case were suspended pending the Court's determination of whether it had jurisdiction to entertain Nicaragua's application and whether the application was admissible. The Court found that El Salvador's Declaration of Intervention 'addresse[d] itself to matters, including the construction of conventions, which presuppose that the Court has jurisdiction to entertain the dispute . . . and that Nicaragua's Application . . . [was] admissible'.[61]

---

[57] ICJ Reports, 1951, at pp. 76–7.

[58] *Ibid.*, at p. 77.   [59] *Ibid.*

[60] *Case Concerning Military and Paramilitary Activities in and against Nicaragua (Nicaragua v. US), Declaration of Intervention*, ICJ Reports, 1984, p. 215 (Order of 4 October).

[61] *Ibid.*, at p. 216. Subsequently, in its judgment on the jurisdiction of the Court and the admissibility of the application, the Court stated that El Salvador, Honduras and Costa Rica, which the US had argued would be affected by the judgment of the Court, 'are free to resort to the incidental procedures of

CONCLUSION

The two forms of intervention contemplated in the Statute of the Court – discretionary intervention under article 62 and intervention as of right under article 63 – are quite distinct and the juridical issues relating to the former appear to be more complicated than those relating to the latter. While the language of article 62 of the Statute is reasonably clear, the differences between the Statute and the Rules of the Court have created some confusion for the Court as well as for the states appearing before it. However, some of the issues have been clarified by the practice of the two Courts, in particular by the recent practice of the present Court. As regards article 62 of the Statute, the following conclusions can be drawn based on that practice:

(1) A state seeking intervention may be granted a permission to intervene in a case even in the absence of a jurisdictional link between that state and the parties to the case; however, in the absence of a consent by the parties to the case, the state seeking intervention does not become a party to the case and therefore will not be bound by the judgment on the Merits nor can it oppose the judgment as against the parties; i.e., the judgment is not *res judicata* as regards the state permitted to intervene.

(2) If a state seeking intervention is able to establish a jurisdictional link as between itself and the parties to the case, or if the parties do not object to the intervention, the state seeking intervention may be granted permission to intervene and it may become a party to the case; in such circumstances, it will also be bound by the decision and will be able to oppose the decision *vis-à-vis* the original parties.

As regards article 63 of the Statute, there appear to be no 'grand' jurisprudential issues and for the states seeking intervention under this article such intervention appears to be, indeed, one 'as of right'. The following limitations, however, can be drawn from the practice of the two Courts:

(1) The state seeking intervention under article 63 must satisfy the Court that its intervention relates to the subject matter of the dispute between the parties, or that the convention it invokes, or the interpretation thereof, is 'in question' in the case.

---

intervention under Articles 62 and 63 of the Statute, to the second of which El Salvador has already unsuccessfully resorted in the jurisdictional phase of the proceedings, but to which it may revert in the merits phase of the case': *ibid.*, pp. 392, 425 (Judgment on Jurisdiction and Admissibility of 26 November). For discussion see Jerzy Sztucki, 'Intervention under Article 63 of the ICJ Statute in the Phase of Preliminary Proceedings: The "Salvadoran Incident"', *AJIL*, 79 (1985), p. 1005.

(2) The state seeking intervention is required to submit its declaration at an appropriate stage of the proceedings; i.e., if the proceedings on the merits of the case have been suspended due to a preliminary objection to the jurisdiction of the Court to entertain the application, and the convention relied on as a basis of intervention is at issue in the merits phase of the case but not in the jurisdictional phase, the state seeking intervention may intervene only in the merits phase (assuming, of course, that jurisdiction is found and the eventual merits of the application reached), but not in the jurisdictional phase. If the convention the intervening state is invoking is also, or solely, at issue in the jurisdictional phase, it is unclear, in light of the practice of the Court, whether such intervention would be permissible, or whether any jurisdictional disputes would be considered strictly bilateral in nature and therefore out of bounds for third parties for purposes of intervention.

27

The use of Chambers of the International Court of Justice

Eduardo Valencia-Ospina

❧

INTRODUCTION

Many jurists, including Sir Robert Jennings and other members and former members of the Court, have extensively examined the history and use of Chambers of the Court and this chapter will avoid, where possible, the temptation to dress up in different language observations and arguments already made on the subject.[1] Rather, it will focus on more recent developments in relation to Chambers. Additionally, the author will make personal observations on aspects of the subject which may or may not have attracted prior commentary.

This part of the chapter will briefly review the types of Chamber that the Court may form under its Statute. The second part will examine whether the advantages that its architects foresaw for the Chamber system have been realized in practice. The third part will address some of the criticisms that have been levelled against the institution of Chambers. Finally, the fourth part will analyse the nature and role of the standing Chamber that the Court has

---

The views the author expresses in this article are his own and do not engage the responsibility of the International Court of Justice, of which he is the Registrar. The assistance of Conor McAuliffe, an official in the Registry of the Court, is gratefully acknowledged.

[1] Sir Robert Jennings, 'Chambers of the International Court of Justice and Courts of Arbitration', in *Humanité et droit international. Mélanges René-Jean Dupuy* (Paris, 1991, p. 197). The writings on the subject by members and former members of the Court are too numerous to cite in this short work. The following are just some examples. Manfred Lachs, 'Some Comments on *Ad Hoc* Chambers of the International Court of Justice', in *ibid.* at p. 203; Nagendra Singh, *The Role and Record of the International Court of Justice* (Dordrecht, 1989); Shigeru Oda, 'Further Thoughts on the Chambers Procedure of the International Court of Justice, *AJIL*, 82 (1988), p. 556; Stephen Schwebel, '*Ad Hoc* Chambers of the International Court of Justice', *AJIL*, 81 (1987), p. 831; Mohammed Bedjaoui, 'Remarques sur la création de chambres "*ad hoc*" au sein de la Cour internationale de Justice', in *La jurisdiction internationale permanente. Colloque de Lyon de la Société française pour le droit internationale*, vol. LXXIII (Paris, 1987); Eduardo Jiménez de Aréchaga, 'The Amendments to the Rules of Procedure of the International Court of Justice', *AJIL*, 67 (1973), p. 1.

recently formed to deal with disputes concerning international environmental law.

The Statute provides for the creation of three different types of Chamber. First, under article 29, the Court is required annually to form a Chamber composed of five judges which may hear and determine a case, at the request of the parties, by summary procedure. A materially identical provision appeared in the same article of the Statute of the Court's predecessor. The Chamber was created to encourage the speedy despatch of disputes that did not involve particularly difficult issues of international law.[2]

The Chamber of Summary Procedure has proved to be a dead letter; in the history of the Court and its predecessor, it has settled only one dispute – *The Treaty of Neuilly* – delivering a judgment on the merits in 1924 and a judgment on interpretation a year later.[3] Subsequent efforts, for example in the case concerning the *Payment of Various Serbian Loans*, to transfer the dispute to the Chamber were rejected.[4] The lack of use of the Chamber is probably due to the understandable reluctance of states to admit that a dispute involving national interests is of minor significance or does not involve important and difficult questions of international law.

Despite its unpopularity, proposals that it should be abolished were rejected during the drafting of the present Statute. Its supporters believed, among other things, that states might be persuaded to use the Chamber because of its ability to conduct hearings of the dispute on location.[5] Although duly formed each year, the Chamber of Summary Procedure has failed in the lifetime of the Court to attract any converts.

The second type of Chamber provided for in the Statute – commonly known as the 'special Chamber' – has never been used. The PCIJ Statute provided for two special Chambers: for labour cases (article 26) and for transit and communications cases (article 27). Article 26 of the present Statute leaves the establishment of special Chambers to the discretion of the Court and does not prescribe any categories, although it mentions 'labour cases and cases relating to transit and communication' as explicit examples of the type of Chamber that the framers of the article envisaged. On 19 July 1993, the Court announced its decision to constitute a special Chamber to deal with cases involving issues of international environmental law. This is the first special Chamber that the Court has formed in its history.

---

[2] Rudolph Ostrihansky, 'Chambers of the International Court of Justice', *ICLQ*, 37 (1988), pp. 30, 32.

[3] *Treaty of Neuilly, Article 179, Annexe para. 4*, PCIJ Series A, No. 3, and 'Interpretation of Judgment No. 3', PCIJ, Series A, No. 4.

[4] Ostrihansky, 'Chambers of the International Court of Justice', p. 32, n. 13.

[5] *Ibid.*, at p. 32.

The third type of Chamber, provided for in article 26 of the Statute, is Chambers formed *ad hoc*, at the request of the parties, to deal with a particular dispute. *Ad hoc* Chambers have their origin in the 1945 Statute of the Court.

The following provisions are common to the formation of *ad hoc* Chambers both before and after the 1972 and 1978 revisions to the Rules of Court.[6] Article 26, paragraph 2 enables the Court 'at any time [to] form a Chamber for dealing with a particular case'. The same paragraph stipulates that it is for the Court to determine the number of judges who will sit on such a Chamber but the number must meet with the approval of the parties. Under paragraph 3 the Chambers thus provided for shall hear and determine a case 'if the parties so request'.

The Court elects the members of the Chamber by secret ballot (Article 18, paragraph 1 of the Rules). Under article 31, paragraph 4 of the Statute, a party is entitled to select an *ad hoc* judge if no member of the Court who is a national of that party forms the Chamber or if he is unable to be present.

The revisions of 1972 and 1978 made two principal additions to the Rules governing *ad hoc* Chambers. First, they provide for consultation by the Court's President with the parties in order to ascertain their views regarding the 'composition' of the Chamber (article 17, paragraph 2 of the Rules). As noted, the Statute requires only that the parties be consulted on the 'number' of judges who would sit on the Chamber. Second, they provide that, once a member of the Court has been elected to a Chamber, he shall continue to sit on that Chamber until final judgment is delivered in the case even if his term on the Court expires in the meantime (article 17, paragraph 4 of the Rules). This last provision is an exception to the general rule that a judge who has been replaced on the Court only continues to sit in a phase of the case if oral argument in that phase took place before his term expired; once that phase is complete, the former judge will no longer sit on the case even if the Court has not yet delivered its final judgment on the merits (article 33 of the Rules).

Although the first was not formed until 1982, the *ad hoc* Chamber has enjoyed considerably greater success than its counterparts, the Chamber of Summary Procedure and the special Chamber. Four *ad hoc* Chambers have been formed to date, in the following cases and order: the *Delimitation of the*

---

[6] The 1972 and 1978 revisions did not materially alter the provisions described in this paragraph. The old Rules did, however, undergo substantial renumbering and for convenience reference in this chapter to the Rules are to the Rules presently in force, unless otherwise stated. The Statute itself has not been amended since it entered into force in 1945.

Maritime Boundary in the Gulf of Maine Area (Canada/United States of America); *Frontier Dispute (Burkina Faso/Mali)*; *Elettronica Sicula SpA (ELSI) (United States of America v. Italy)*; and the *Land, Island and Maritime Frontier Dispute (El Salvador/Honduras: Nicaragua Intervening)*.

THE ARGUMENTS OF THE SYSTEM'S PROPONENTS

To place the discussion in context, a brief review of the developments that prompted the 1972 and 1978 revisions is necessary.

The revisions to the Rules concerning Chambers came at a time when the Court's docket was impoverished.[7] Academics and practitioners of international law alike were concerned that the Court would lose its prime position unless changes were introduced that would make it a more attractive forum for potential litigants.[8]

One of the major reasons identified for the failure of states to entrust their legal disputes to the Court was the inability of parties to influence the composition of the Court. In *ad hoc* arbitration, the parties are free to select judges favourable to each. In adjudications by the full Court, the parties have no choice but to accept the identity of the judges who would sit to hear their dispute. Judge Pétren explained what in his view was the reason why this lack of choice made states reluctant to submit their disputes to the Court:

> The actual presence on the bench of judges from States which do not themselves recognize the jurisdiction of the Court is bound to have a negative effect on the readiness of States which do recognize its jurisdiction to submit cases to the Court. Although these States, in recognizing the Court's jurisdiction, have shown their positive attitude towards the judicial settlement of international disputes, their governments would certainly hesitate before having questions of national interest decided by Judges from States who cannot be relied upon to allow international adjudication of disputes in which they themselves are involved.[9]

The reluctance of states towards a judicial forum whose members they could not select was highlighted by the composition of the arbitral panel in the *Beagle Channel* case.[10] This case involved one of a series of frontier

---

[7] Stephen Schwebel, 'Chambers of the International Court of Justice', in Y. Dinstein and M. Tabory (eds.), *International Law at a Time of Perplexity: Essays in Honour of Shabtai Rosenne* (Dordrecht, 1989), pp. 739, 744.

[8] *Ibid.*, at pp. 744–7.

[9] B. A. S. Pétren, 'Some Thoughts on the Future of the International Court of Justice", *NYbIL*, 6 (1975), pp. 59, 61–2.

[10] The award in this case is reported in 52 *ILR* 93 (1979).

disputes between Argentina and Chile and was therefore the type of case the Court had wide experience in determining. However, instead of submitting the dispute to the Court, the parties selected five members of the Court to sit as an *ad hoc* arbitral panel. The judges received an arbitral fee in addition to their regular salary as members of the Court and the parties were obliged to incur the expense of secretarial assistance, housing and archives, etc., which would have been offered to them by the United Nations had they gone to the Court. The case starkly illustrated that international disputes that properly belonged to the principal judicial organ of the UN were being diverted to other forums where the parties had a voice in the selection of judges.

Thus, when the Court asked former judges of the Court, former judges *ad hoc* and international lawyers who had pleaded before the Court on at least three occasions to give an opinion on those aspects of the Rules that urgently required amendment, it came as little surprise that a majority of those canvassed advocated an amendment to facilitate recourse to the Court by granting the parties a voice in the personal composition of *ad hoc* Chambers formed under article 26, paragraph 2 of the Statute. At about the same time, the Secretary-General of the UN, at the request of the General Assembly, published a report entitled 'Review of the Role of the International Court of Justice', in which a number of states advocated a similar amendment.[11] Influenced by these developments, the Court adopted, on 10 May 1972, the revisions to its Rules already described to give parties a greater influence in the composition of *ad hoc* Chambers, thus encouraging them to bring their disputes to the Court.

The revisions to the Rules respecting Chambers were designed to give the Court a new lease of life. Whether the revisions revitalized the Court, or rather whether they were necessary to build up the international confidence in the Court that was undoubtedly lacking at the time they took effect, is open to question, as can be seen from a review of the Court's docket in the two decades subsequent to the revisions.

In the period between 10 May 1972 and 25 November 1981, the date Canada and the United States notified to the Court the Special Agreement to submit their dispute in the *Gulf of Maine* case to an *ad hoc* Chamber, seven contentious cases were submitted to the full Court. However, to present the real picture of the state of the Court's docket in the same period, it should be pointed out that in only three of these cases did the Court deliver judgment

---

[11] UN Doc. A/8382 (1971), at p. 6.

on the Merits.[12] Moreover, in four of the cases, the respondent failed to appear before the Court.[13]

The Court's docket after the filing of the *Gulf of Maine* case paints a healthier picture. A total of eighteen contentious cases were submitted to the full Court during this period; at the time of writing, the Court has ten contentious cases on its docket, none of which has been referred to *ad hoc* Chambers.

The point of the above review since the revisions to the Rules is to illustrate that whatever the pros and cons of the Chamber system, the increasing confidence that the international community has placed in the Court in recent years cannot be attributed in any great measure to the introduction of more flexible rules governing *ad hoc* Chambers. The vast majority of the cases submitted to the Court in the wake of the revisions were submitted to the plenary Court, indicating that a large number of states did not share or no longer share the reservations that had prompted the Court to allow parties a voice in the composition of *ad hoc* Chambers.

The proponents of Chambers, whether *ad hoc* or otherwise, predicted that Chambers would be an attractive judicial forum, particularly for less wealthy states, because the proceedings would be conducted more swiftly than proceedings before the full Court and would therefore be less expensive.[14] This prediction has not been borne out in practice mainly because in no case have the parties applied the principle in article 92, paragraph 1 of the Rules, that the written proceedings before a Chamber should consist of only one pleading by each side.

In the *Gulf of Maine* case, thirty-two months elapsed from the time the Court first fixed time-limits for the submission of written pleadings until final

[12] *Fisheries Jurisdiction (Federal Republic of Germany v. Iceland)*, ICJ Reports, 1974, at p. 175; *United States Diplomatic and Consular Staff in Tehran*, ICJ Reports, 1980, at p. 3; *Continental Shelf (Tunisia/Libyan Arab Jamahiriya)*, ICJ Reports, 1982, at p. 18. In *Nuclear Tests (Australia v. France)*, ICJ Reports, 1974, at p. 253 and *Nuclear Tests (New Zealand v. France)*, ICJ Reports, 1974, at p. 457, the Court found that because France had assumed an obligation to discontinue the nuclear tests complained of, the claims of Australia and New Zealand, respectively, no longer had any object and therefore no pronouncement on the merits was required. In *Aegean Sea Continental Shelf (Greece v. Turkey)*, ICJ Reports, 1978, at p. 3, the Court decided that it lacked jurisdiction to entertain the application. Finally, in *Trial of Pakistani Prisoners of War*, ICJ Reports, 1973, at p. 347, the Court discontinued the proceedings at the request of the applicant.

[13] *Fisheries Jurisdiction (Federal Republic of Germany v. Iceland)*; *Nuclear Tests (Australia v. France)*; *Nuclear Tests (New Zealand v. France)*; and *Aegean Sea Continental Shelf (Greece v. Turkey)*. The respondent also did not appear in *Fisheries Jurisdiction (United Kingdom v. Iceland)*, a case pending before the Court at the time of the revisions, but the application in this case was filed prior to 10 May 1972, and is thus excluded from the time frame of the present analysis.

[14] See, for example, Eduardo Jiménez de Aréchaga, 'The Amendments to the Rules of Procedure of the International Court of Justice', *AJIL*, 67 (1973), pp. 1, 2.

judgment. The corresponding figure in the *Frontier Dispute* was twenty months, for *Elettronica Sicula* twenty-seven months and for the case concerning the *Land, Island and Maritime Frontier Dispute* more than five years. Representative corresponding figures for disputes submitted to the full Court in the same period include the case concerning the *Continental Shelf (Libyan Arab Jamahiriya/Malta)* (thirty-four months), the case concerning *Military and Paramilitary Activities In and against Nicaragua (Nicaragua v. United States)* (twenty-five months) and the case concerning *Maritime Delimitation in the Area Between Greenland and Jan Mayen (Denmark v. Norway)* (almost five years).[15]

These figures reveal the fallacy of the argument that, because the Court consists of fifteen members, its procedure is necessarily complex and, conversely, that because an *ad hoc* Chamber consists of a smaller number of judges, its procedure is quicker and simpler. If the case is difficult, then as much time is required to take it before a Chamber as before the Court as a whole, a point underscored by Sir Robert's observation in a statement to the General Assembly following its consideration of the 1992 Report of the International Court of Justice, that *El Salvador v. Honduras (Nicaragua intervening)* was the 'largest' case ever submitted to the Court in terms of 'the extent and variety of the questions to be resolved'.[16] The failure to apply article 92, paragraph 1 also inevitably means that the reduction in costs that it was hoped would come about from its application has failed to materialize.[17]

In favour of the revisions, it is undoubtedly true that the flexibility that they introduced into the Chamber system has attracted litigants who, absent the changes, might have sought another forum to resolve their international legal disputes. In the *Gulf of Maine* case, it is clear from the provisions of their Special Agreement that the Parties would not have submitted their dispute to the Court if they had not been allowed in effect to dictate the physical

---

[15] It is true that two of the Chamber cases did involve incidental proceedings (a request for the indication of provisional measures in the case between Burkina Faso and Mali and an application for permission to intervene in the case between El Salvador and Honduras). By the same token, however, the Court in the case between Nicaragua and the US had to address not only a request for the indication of provisional measures but also issues of jurisdiction and admissibility before turning to the merits.

[16] UN Doc. A/47/PV.43 (1992).

[17] The author has no relative figures upon which to base this conclusion. However, the number of pleadings in each of the Chamber cases, the length of time it took to resolve each and the impressive lists of Agents, Counsel, Advisers and Assistants appearing for the parties in all four cases, suggest that there has been little or no difference between the size of the bill for a case before a Chamber and a case before the full Court. The costs before either forum are inevitably related to the complexity of the particular dispute. It should be noted, as a matter of historical interest, that in the only case to be considered by a Chamber of the Permanent Court, the case concerning the *Treaty of Neuilly, Article 179, Annexe, paragraph 4 (Interpretation)*, the parties obtained the Court's consent, by way of exception to the provisions of article 69 of the Rules then in force, to present replies which they duly filed.

composition of the Chamber.[18] There is also evidence in the other three Chamber cases that the parties were instrumental in the choice of the judges who sat on the Chamber and might not have submitted their dispute to the Court if the revised Rules did not allow them to wield a decisive influence over the composition of a Chamber.[19] Moreover, four of the seven states involved in the four cases, Burkina Faso, Canada, El Salvador and Mali, appeared as parties before the Court for the first time. The facility of recourse to an *ad hoc* Chamber may well have encouraged these states which would otherwise have been shy to submit a case to the full Court. Finally, three of the four cases concerned the territorial domain of the parties concerned. 'This is always a delicate matter, and it is likely that the Parties' ability to influence the composition of the Bench may well have been a factor leading them to adopt this course in preference to other available procedures.'[20]

While Chambers have much to commend them, their role and importance should not be exaggerated. Quite independently of the 1972 and 1978 revisions to the Rules of Court, states began to display a growing confidence in the Court and in most cases have sought a judgment of the full Court rather than a judgment of a Chamber. However, the revisions pragmatically recognize that some states do not share the same confidence in the Court and attempt to soothe fears and suspicions by allowing parties a greater say in the selection of the judges who will sit to hear their disputes. By doing so, the revisions have attracted disputes to the Court that the parties, absent the revisions, would in all probability have brought elsewhere.

THE ARGUMENTS OF THE SYSTEM'S ANTAGONISTS

This part will focus on three principal criticisms that have been levelled against the modern institution of *ad hoc* Chambers. First, it has been argued that the Rule allowing the parties a voice in the composition of the *ad hoc* Chamber is incompatible with the Statute of the Court. Second, all three dissenting judges to the Court's Order of 28 February 1990 in the *Land, Island and Maritime*

---

[18] A detailed examination of the provisions of the Special Agreement filed in the Registry of the Court by Canada and the United States is found in Robert Brauer, 'International Conflict Resolution: The ICJ Chambers and the Gulf of Maine Dispute', *VJIL*, 23 (1983), p. 463.

[19] See Schwebel, 'Ad Hoc Chambers of the International Court of Justice', pp. 843–8. Judge Schwebel explicitly concludes, from his review of materials available to the public, that the personal composition of the first three Chambers was in accordance with the wishes of the parties. He would appear implicitly to reach the same conclusion in the *El Salvador/Honduras* case from his analysis of Judge Oda's declaration to the Order of the Court forming the Chamber in that case: *ibid.*, at p. 848.

[20] Shabtai Rosenne, *The World Court: What It Is and How It Works* (4th edn, Dordrecht/London, 1989), p. 236.

Frontier Dispute (El Salvador/Honduras)[21] have questioned the propriety of the Court's decision that the Chamber formed to hear the case, and not the full Court, should determine whether to grant Nicaragua's application for permission to intervene in that case. This criticism calls into question the precise relationship between the plenary Court and the Chambers that it creates. Finally, although other commentators have explored the issue, the author will add his own response to the critics who have argued that according the parties a voice in the composition of Chambers will lead to the establishment of regionalized Chambers, fragmentation of the Court's jurisprudence and a consequent decline in the respect that states have traditionally displayed for the Court.

A voice in the composition of *ad hoc* Chambers

Article 17, paragraph 2 of the Rules requires the President to consult with the parties with respect to the composition of the Chamber. As the Statute contains no provision that either explicitly requires or prohibits this practice, the question is whether the Statute by its silence implicitly outlaws it. If it does, the Statute prevails and the Rules of Court are, to borrow an analogous notion from municipal law which applies with equal force in this instance 'unconstitutional'.

The most cogent criticism to date of Rule 17, paragraph 2 was penned by Judge Shahabuddeen in his Dissenting Opinion to the 28 February 1990 Order of the Court. There, Judge Shahabuddeen expressed the view that allowing the parties a decisive or substantial voice in the selection of members of the Court who will sit on a Chamber violates the Statute of the Court and is at odds with the Court's role as a 'court of justice'.

In support of his position that the Statute implicitly outlaws consultation with the parties concerning the personal composition of a Chamber, Judge Shahabuddeen engages in an extensive review of the *travaux préparatoires* of the Statute of the Permanent Court of International Justice, in particular the proceedings before the Advisory Committee of Jurists. The following passage from the report of the Advisory Committee underlines the distinction between the Permanent Court and the Court of Arbitration organized by the Conventions of The Hague of 1889 and 1907: 'In the Court of Arbitration, it falls to the Parties to choose their judges after the commencement of the dispute whereas in the case of the Permanent Court of International Justice, the contesting Parties no longer have the choice of Judges.'[22] Indeed,

---

[21] ICJ Reports, 1990, at pp. 3, 18.

[22] Permanent Court of International Justice, Advisory Committee of Jurists, *Procès-Verbaux of the Proceedings of the Committee 16–24 June 1920* (1920), Annexe No. 1, p. 695.

the 1920 Committee of Jurists emphatically rejected a written proposal that parties to a dispute before the Court should be allowed to choose its composition.[23]

Judge Shahabuddeen also draws support for his position from municipal law. Citing both English and Sri Lankan case law, he notes that domestic courts have uniformly and consistently rejected attempts by parties interested in the litigation to select the judges who will sit to hear their dispute. While stressing that principles of municipal law cannot be transposed wholesale to the international legal plane, Judge Shahabuddeen maintains that the meaning of a 'court of justice' found in municipal law is one of 'general jurisprudence'.[24]

Judge Shahabuddeen's conclusions, from a review of these authorities, are summarized in the following passage of his Opinion:

> The whole nature of the Court, as a court of justice, constitutes a prohibition, no less clear for being implied, against giving the parties any say in the selection of judges to hear a case, whether through the Rules of Court or otherwise, and whether in whole or in part, except in the case of *ad hoc* judges. So fundamental was that prohibition to the character of the Court as a court of justice, as distinguished from an arbitral body, that it was no more necessary to express it in its Statute than it would have been to do so in the constitution of any other 'court of justice' within the normal acceptation of the meaning of this expression.[25]

Judge Shahabuddeen's concerns merit serious consideration because they suggest that the present rules governing Chambers violate the Statute of the Court, and therefore the validity of the judgment of the Chambers formed to date might be open to question. They also suggest that the present system is at variance with the ethos and role that its creators sought to craft for the Court as a 'court of justice' as distinct from an arbitral tribunal.

Several responses can be made to Judge Shahabuddeen's concern that article 17, paragraph 2 of the Rules is unconstitutional. First, it is not certain what bearing, if any, the *travaux préparatoires* to the Statute of the Permanent Court can have on the institution of *ad hoc* Chambers. The *ad hoc* Chamber has its origin in the Statute of the present Court and has no counterpart in the Statute of the Permanent Court. Therefore, whatever vision the framers of the old Statute had for the Permanent Court as a 'court of justice', their statements on the subject were not made with reference to the institution of *ad hoc* Chambers introduced for the first time twenty-six years later. In this connection, the *travaux préparatoires* to the present Statute are curiously silent

---

[23] ICJ Reports, 1990, at pp. 31–2.
[24] *Ibid.*, at p. 42.   [25] *Ibid.*, at pp. 40–1.

on whether the parties would have a voice in the composition of *ad hoc* Chambers, as Judge Shahabuddeen confirms in his Opinion.[26] The discussion of article 26 of the Statute before the Washington Committee of Jurists and in the subsequent proceedings in San Francisco focused on the role of the parties in agreeing the number of judges to sit on a Chamber and made only oblique and inconclusive references to the role of the parties in the personal composition of the Chamber.

Second, it is open to question whether the definition in municipal law of a 'court of justice' is one of 'general jurisprudence' applicable to the International Court of Justice. The jurisdiction of the Court, by contrast to the jurisdiction of a municipal court, is based on the consent of the parties, 'qu'on le déplore ou qu'on s'en réjouisse'.[27] Efforts to equip the Court with compulsory jurisdiction have invariably failed. They were scuttled at the discussions that led to the creation of both the Statute of the Court and its predecessor. They were abandoned in the face of fierce opposition on the four occasions since 1946 that the General Assembly considered the issue.[28] Also, as Rosenne observes, the dispute over the Court's jurisdiction is 'a factor that has dominated the work of the United Nations in the field of the codification of international law, and it nearly wrecked the most important of the codification conferences, that held in 1968–1969 on the codification of the law of treaties'.[29]

The Court therefore lacks the essential element of the jurisdiction of a municipal court – that it is compulsory for defendant or respondent. In reality the Court shares some of the characteristics of both a domestic court and an arbitral tribunal. As with an arbitral tribunal, and in contradistinction to a domestic court, the Court's jurisdiction to hear a dispute is dependent on the agreement of the parties, whether the agreement is *ad hoc* for the purposes of a particular dispute or by means of a jurisdictional clause inserted in a treaty or of the 'Optional Clause' declaration embodied in article 36, paragraph 2 of the Statute. On the other hand, the Court, like a domestic court, is under an obligation to reach a judicial solution to the dispute submitted to it, based upon the sources of law enumerated in article 38 of the Statute which may be compared to the 'law of the land' that national courts are obliged to apply in determining domestic disputes. In the case of an arbitral tribunal, the parties

---

[26] *Ibid.*, at pp. 34–5.

[27] Mohammed Bedjaoui, 'Universalisme et Regionalisme au Sein de la Cour internationale de Justice; La Constitution de Chambres "Ad Hoc"', in *Colección de Estudios Juridicos en Homenaje al Profesor José Perez Montero* (Oviedo, 1988), vol. CLXV.

[28] Rosenne, *The World Court*, pp. 30–1.

[29] *Ibid.*, at p. 29.

have greater flexibility to dictate the sources that the Tribunal will rely on in reaching its decision.[30]

Thus, in laying down its own rules of procedure as required by article 30 of the Statute, the Court has to chart a course that preserves its judicial character while at the same time recognizing that its jurisdiction to act is based on the consent of the parties. Arguably, the provisions governing the formation of *ad hoc* Chambers strike the proper balance. Both the Court and the parties must agree the number of judges who will sit in the Chamber. Although the parties may present their views with regard to the composition of the Chamber, the Court elects its members by secret ballot. Finally, the parties have the power to withdraw their case under articles 88 and 89 of the Rules if they are dissatisfied with the outcome of the Court's selection, and the Court has previously held that it will not enquire into the motives of such a withdrawal.[31] Thus both the Court and the parties retain a measure of control. As Rosenne observes, having reviewed the provisions governing the formation of *ad hoc* Chambers: 'If, as it is sometimes put, these Chambers are a bridge between the full Court and arbitration, they are at the Court end of the bridge.'[32]

Most significantly, the Court's ultimate power of election makes it clear that article 17, paragraph 2 of the Rules does not transfer to the parties a power that the Statute clearly vests in the Court. In particular, the power will operate to safeguard the judicial integrity of the Court should the parties' selection of judges threaten to encroach upon it. If the Court considers that the choice made by the parties would produce a Chamber that is too parochial or regional in nature, it can decline to comply with the wishes of the parties and elect other members to serve on the Chamber. The Court can take the same action if it considers that the choice of judges would have a divisive internal effect among members of the Court. Indeed, it is at least arguable that according substantial or decisive influence to the parties would have precisely the

---

[30] The mandatory language of article 38 embodies the maxim *jura novit curia*, which implies that the Court knows and will apply the law. See Sir Gerald Fitzmaurice, *The Law and the Procedure of the International Court of Justice* (Cambridge, 1986), vol. II, p. 531. This may be contrasted with provisions of arbitration conventions, which invariably permit the parties to choose the applicable law. For example, article 42, paragraph 1 of the Convention of the International Centre for the Settlement of Investment Disputes provides in part that 'the tribunal shall decide a dispute in accordance with such rules of law as may be agreed by the Parties'. It should also be noted that if the parties agree that the Court should decide the dispute *ex aequo et bono*, pursuant to article 38, paragraph 2 of the Statute, it is for the Court, and not the parties, to decide which equitable principles are best suited for resolution of the dispute.

[31] *Barcelona Traction, Light and Power Company, Limited (Belgium v. Spain)*, ICJ Reports, 1964, at pp. 19–20 ('these provisions [on discontinuance] are concerned solely with the "how" and not the "why" of the matter. They impose no conditions as to the basis on which a discontinuance may be effected').

[32] Rosenne, *The World Court*, p. 236.

opposite effect and avoid internal dissention because it is the parties, and not the Court, who decide the composition of the Chamber.

A review of the provisions of the Statute relating to the formation of *ad hoc* Chambers reveals that it contemplates a substantial role for the parties in the selection of the judges who sit in a Chamber. Even in the absence of the consultation provisions of article 17, paragraph 2 of the Rules the combined effect of these provisions would, under the right conditions, give the parties effective control over the number of the judges that would constitute a majority.

If the parties request the Court, under article 26, paragraph 2 of the Statute to constitute a Chamber consisting of three judges, and the Court accedes to this request, then if no member of the Court who is a national of either party forms the Chamber or if such a member is unable to be present, the parties will have control over the identity of a majority of the members of the Chamber through the appointment of *ad hoc* judges.[33]

The possibility that parties could agree to a Chamber of three judges, and the Court accede to the request, is increased by the non-applicability to Chambers of article 9 of the Statute. Article 9, which is materially identical to the same article of the 1920 Statute of the Permanent Court, visualizes that in the Court 'as a whole the representation of the main forms of civilization and the principal legal systems of the world should be assured'. Articles 26 and 27 of the Statute of the Permanent Court, dealing with special Chambers formed to deal with labour and transit and communications disputes, respectively, specifically refer to article 9, unlike paragraph 1 of article 26 of the Statute of the present Court. The *travaux préparatoires* do not cast light on the reason for the non-applicability of article 9 of the present Statute to Chambers. While adherence to the principle of article 9 is a worthwhile objective, its omission in relation to Chambers removes a potential obstacle to the Court's agreement to form a Chamber with a small number of judges aimed at maximising the parties' influence over its composition. It is of course always open to the Court to decline to form a Chamber of three judges. But it is equally open to the Court under the Rules in force to decline to accede to the wishes of the

---

[33] The 1920 Committee of Jurists considered that although the selection of *ad hoc* judges by parties was a practice more suited to an arbitral tribunal than a court of justice, the variation was necessary because 'States attach much importance to having one of their subjects on the Bench when they appear before a Court of Justice' (Report of the Advisory Committee of Jurists, *Procès-Verbaux*, at p. 722). Using this reasoning, which experience has shown not to be the case as explained later in this chapter, if the Chamber were to include a member of the Court who is a national of a party, thus making inapplicable that party's right to select an *ad hoc* judge, the parties' choice of judge could be said to have been implicitly satisfied.

parties as to the Chamber's composition. And, in both instances, the parties may decide to bring their disputes to another forum.

The use of three-judge Chambers would have the unfortunate consequence that, if *ad hoc* judges were selected, judgments might be delivered by Chambers composed of a majority of judges who are not members of the Court, thus arguably undermining the jurisprudential value that traditionally attaches to judgments of the full Court. Yet these judgments would stand on an equal footing with judgments of the Court because under article 27 of the Statute, a 'judgment given by any of the chambers provided for in Article 26 and 29 shall be considered as rendered by the Court'. The jurisprudential value of the judgment would more seriously suffer should the member of the Court elected to sit on the Chamber dissent from the majority judgment of the two *ad hoc* judges.

A three-person Chamber could be formed under the present regime. However, in each *ad hoc* Chamber formed to date, the parties have opted for a five-judge Chamber and members of the Court have always outnumbered non-members, at least at the time the Court formed the Chambers.[34] True, there is no empirical evidence to suggest that parties would opt for a three-person Chamber if they were not consulted regarding the personal composition of the Chamber (because the *ad hoc* Chamber was a dormant institution prior to the taking effect of article 17, paragraph 2 of the present Rules). But it might not be too far-fetched to suggest, bearing in mind the greater influence advocated by states in the composition of Chambers that prompted the revisions to the Rules, that parties would agree to a three-person Chamber to ensure the maximum influence in its personal composition.

---

[34] In *Land, Island and Maritime Frontier Dispute (El Salvador/Honduras, Nicaragua intervening)*, of the five judges composing the Chamber at the date of judgment, two were members of the Court. The President of the Chamber, Judge Sette-Camara, whose term of office at the Court had expired, continued to sit in the Chamber in accordance with article 17, paragraph 4 of the Rules which, as we have seen, provides that members of the Chamber, once elected, shall continue to sit until the Chamber has delivered final judgment even if their terms of office on the Court have expired. The other two judges were judges *ad hoc* chosen by El Salvador and Honduras, respectively. The lack of a majority of the members of the Court on the Chamber may have been offset by the fact that the two members of the Court who remained on the Chamber, Sir Robert Jennings and Judge Oda, were elected President and Vice-President of the Court, respectively, at the time of Judge Sette-Camara's retirement from the bench, thus arguably wedding the Chamber closer to the Court. Besides, it should be noted that in the *Gulf of Maine* case the member of the Court having the nationality of one of the parties was elected member of the Chamber, as also were the two such members in the case concerning *Elettronica Sicula SpA*. In the two other cases brought before a Chamber article 31, paragraph 4 of the Statute was not applied, presumably because each of the parties had in advance chosen an *ad hoc* judge.

Intervention before Chambers

In its Order of 28 February 1990 in the *Land, Island and Maritime Frontier Dispute (El Salvador/Honduras)* case, the Court, by a majority of twelve votes to three, decided that the Chamber formed to hear the case was the proper forum to rule upon Nicaragua's application for permission to intervene under article 62 of the Statute.[35] The majority considered that the request for permission to intervene should be dealt with by the organ that is to decide the merits of the case because '"every intervention is incidental to the proceedings in a case"'.[36] Moreover, the majority was of the view that, while intervention presupposes a legal interest on the part of the intervening state to be affected by the decision, such an interest can only be dealt with by the Chamber that deals with the case.[37] Finally, the Court considered that a state that is about to ask permission to intervene must take the procedural position in the case as it finds it.[38]

The wisdom of leaving to the Chamber the decision whether to grant the application for permission to intervene was challenged in the three Dissenting Opinions to the Order, delivered by Judges Elias, Tarassov and Shahabuddeen. Judge Elias considered, *inter alia*, that the Order was 'too narrow' in that it was preoccupied with the concept of intervention as an incidental proceeding and failed to anticipate the broader problems 'such as the appointment of an *ad hoc* Judge or other issues of the composition of the Chamber itself'.[39] Judge Tarassov noted that the Court did not relinquish control over the proceedings when it formed the Chamber; it was the full Court that made changes in the composition of the Chamber, electing new judges or approving new judges *ad hoc* to fill any vacancies that may arise.[40] He also noted that the original parties have a voice in both the numerical and personal composition of the Chamber but that the intervening party did not enjoy the same right even though it has an interest in the dispute.[41] Finally, Judge Shahabuddeen noted that by leaving Nicaragua with no recourse except to the Chamber, the Court effectively denied Nicaragua its right to have its application decided under article 62 of the Statute which provides that the Court 'shall' decide upon a request to intervene.[42]

In the aftermath to the Court's Order, the Chamber permitted Nicaragua to intervene with respect to some of its claims, but the level of representation

---

[35] ICJ Reports, 1990, at p. 3.
[36] *Ibid.*, at p. 4, quoting *Haya de la Torre*, ICJ Reports, 1951, at p. 76.
[37] *Ibid.*, at p. 5.   [38] *Ibid.*
[39] *Ibid.*, at p. 10.   [40] *Ibid.*, at p. 13.
[41] *Ibid.*, at p. 15.   [42] *Ibid.*, at p. 18.

it accorded to Nicaragua would not have assuaged any of the concerns expressed in the Dissenting Opinions to the Court's Order. In its judgment, the Chamber stated that the extent of Nicaragua's representation is governed by article 85 of the Rules, which provides for the submission of written pleadings and participation in the hearings.[43] Nicaragua was not permitted an *ad hoc* judge, nor allowed a voice in the numerical or physical composition of the Chamber.

The division in the Court clearly reveals that the development of the *ad hoc* Chamber system is not without its teething problems, which can be resolved only as the circumstances arise. In particular, the division reveals sharp differences of opinion over the relationship between the Court and its Chambers, which is in need of thorough examination, particularly in the light of the apparent inconsistencies between the Order of the Court and the judgment of the Chamber. In its Order, the Court noted that the Chamber had the power to determine incidental proceedings but that the full Court had the power to form a Chamber to deal with a particular case and to determine its composition. The Chamber permitted Nicaragua to intervene but denied that an intervening state has the rights to appoint an *ad hoc* judge and to have any voice in the numerical and personal composition of the Chamber. Although it did not say so expressly, the Chamber presumably reached its conclusion that intervening states are excluded from those rights because the provisions under which they are conferred expressly reserve them for 'parties', and article 62 of the Statute does not classify an intervening state as a party. Whether or not this reasoning is correct, under the terms of the Court's Order, in which it stated that the full Court has the power to form and determine the composition of Chambers, the argument could be made that the intervening state's right to have a say in the composition of the Chamber should have been referred back to the Court.

The subsequent judgment of the Chamber on the merits on the effect of the judgment for the intervening state, although more apposite to a discussion on intervention *simpliciter*, merits a brief discussion. Nicaragua in its application for permission to intervene stated that it 'intends to submit itself to the binding effect of the decision to be given'. The Chamber, however, concluded that the binding force of the judgment under article 59 of the statute did not apply to Nicaragua as intervener.[44] While this conclusion removes the spectre of judges hand-picked by a 'third' state influencing the determination of the conflicting legal interests of the state parties, it reduces the effectiveness of the judgments of Chambers, and of the Court, with respect

---

[43] ICJ Reports, 1990, at p. 92.   [44] ICJ Reports, 1992, at p. 609.

to the legal interests of non-party interveners. Rosenne was unbridled in his criticism of this part of the Chamber's judgment:

> As a matter of principle it is difficult to accept the categoric assertion by the Chamber regarding the effect of the judgment on the non-party intervener. Regardless of the tenor of Article 59 of the Statute . . . surely a judgment stating what the law is as regards a – any – territorial dispute is valid *erga omnes*.[45]

Regionalization of Chambers

Critics have charged that allowing the parties a substantial or decisive voice in the composition of Chambers would lead to the creation of regionalized or 'Eurocentric' Chambers that would alienate from the Court states whose regional area is not represented in the hallowed circle.[46] This criticism has not been borne out in practice. The composition of all four *ad hoc* Chambers reveals that judges drawn from three continents have delivered the judgments in the four Chamber cases to date, thus belieing any argument that the Chambers will become the domain of judges of any one 'civilization' or legal system.[47] And it should be pointed out that the *Gulf of Maine* Chamber, which consisted exclusively of judges of European and North American extraction and which attracted the original charge of Eurocentrism, did not wholly consist of judges from the North Atlantic when originally formed, and would not therefore have been labelled 'Eurocentric'.[48]

Two features common to all four cases further weaken the argument that allowing parties a say in the composition of Chambers will lead to regionalized Chambers. First, the parties have displayed a marked tendency to select non-nationals as their *ad hoc* judges. Of the six *ad hoc* judges chosen to serve on the four Chambers (Judges *ad hoc* Cohen, Luchaire, Abi-Saab, Valticos and Virally (deceased – replaced by Torres Bernárdez)), only one, Judge *ad hoc* Cohen, was a national of the selecting state, Canada. Rosenne observes that this practice of selecting non-nationals as Judges *ad hoc* has grown in popularity in recent years and 'certainly enhances the general standing of the international judicial system'.[49]

---

[45] Shabtai Rosenne, *Intervention in the International Court of Justice* (Dordrecht, 1993), p. 155.

[46] See, for example, Edward McWhinney, 'Special Chambers within the International Court of Justice: The Preliminary, Procedural Aspect of the Gulf of Maine Case', *Syr J Int'l L & Com*, 12 (1985), pp. 1, 7–11.

[47] For a breakdown of the nationality of the judges who have served on the Chambers to date, see Lukas Meyer, 'The *Ad Hoc* Chambers: Perspectives of the Parties and the Court', *Archiv des Völkerrechts*, 27 (1989), pp. 413, 435.

[48] Schwebel, 'Ad Hoc Chambers of the International Court of Justice', pp. 831, 844.

[49] Rosenne, *The World Court*, p. 237.

Second, the voting patterns of judges in Chambers reveal that those whom cynics might believe are chosen to 'represent' diametrically opposite interests have invariably joined on the same side of the judgment. In the *Gulf of Maine* case, Judge Schwebel and Judge *ad hoc* Cohen both voted for the majority judgment; in *Burkina Faso/Mali*, Judges *ad hoc* Luchaire and Abi-Saab joined in the unanimous judgment of the Chamber; in *Elettronica Sicula SpA*, Judges Ago and Schwebel were on the same side in a unanimous judgment of the Chamber; finally, in *El Salvador/Honduras: Nicaragua intervening*, Judges *ad hoc* Valticos and Torres Bernárdez voted with the majority. These voting patterns reveal that rather than 'representing' the states of which they are nationals or which select them to serve as judges *ad hoc*, the judges serving in Chambers have sought a solution to the dispute by reference to international law and not by reference to the individual interests of the states they are perceived to represent.

Critics of the revised Rules have also argued that the dignity of the Court as an institution is compromised by the sight of parties dictating to it precisely who should sit to hear a case. The point was made forcibly by Judge Morozov in his Dissenting Opinion to the Order by which the Court agreed to compose an *ad hoc* Chamber to hear the *Gulf of Maine* case, where he referred to 'some kind of ultimatum' that the parties had handed to the Court as to the choice of judges who would sit on the Chamber.[50]

It is clear from the increasing number of contentious cases on the Court's docket in the last two decades that the supposed affront to the Court's dignity by revisions to the Rules governing Chambers has not deterred states from resorting to the Court to resolve their legal differences. Indeed, as noted earlier, many states endorsed the revisions. When the Secretary-General circulated a questionnaire to the member states of the UN in 1970 to elicit suggestions on the role of the Court, a large number of states expressed the view that the Court would be more attractive to litigants if the Rules governing *ad hoc* Chambers were revised to allow parties a greater say in their composition.[51] No state expressed a view to the contrary. Moreover, the General Assembly lent its support to the modern institution of *ad hoc* Chambers in resolution 3232 (XXIX) ('Review of the Role of the International Court of Justice'), where it welcomed the 1972 revisions of the Rules of Court, noting that their purpose was to facilitate recourse to the

---

[50] ICJ Reports, 1982, at p. 11.

[51] 'Review of the Role of the International Court of Justice', Report of the Secretary-General, UN Doc. A/8382 (1971), at p. 6. See also 'Review of the Role of the International Court of Justice', Report of the Sixth Committee, UN Doc. A/8568 (1971), at p. 6.

Court for the judicial settlement of disputes by 'allowing for greater influence of parties on the composition of *ad hoc* chambers'. Additionally, the ringing endorsement that the revisions received in the report of the Asian–African Legal Consultative Committee on 'The Role of the International Court of Justice' reveals that the legal advisers of Asian and African countries considered them a positive development and free from the trappings of a European or Atlantic outlook.[52] As Judge Singh noted: 'There can be no doubt that [the *ad hoc* Chamber] does represent a popular procedural access to the Court, helping to divert to it the cases that otherwise may quite easily go to the arbitral domain.'[53]

Critics have pointed to the danger that the jurisprudence of the Court may become fragmented if its judgments are composed and delivered by different groups of judges sitting in different Chambers. Because of the special political factors in the Chamber's composition and organization, their judgments 'will become to be classified, jurisprudentially, as a decision *inter partes* – like that of the arbitral tribunal it was supposed to avoid – and thus not be ranked as general International Law or part of the "progressive development of International Law"'.[54]

It is perhaps too early to bring in a verdict on the jurisprudential impact that the judgments delivered by Chambers will have. But the treatment of the judgment in the *Gulf of Maine* case is encouraging. In subsequent cases submitted to the full Court concerning the delimitation of maritime areas, both the Court in its judgments and the parties in their written and oral submissions have cited the judgment as an authoritative interpretation of the law of the sea. This reliance on the judgment supports Judge Schwebel's observation that 'it could as easily have been a Judgment of the full Court as it was a Judgment of a Chamber'.[55]

THE ENVIRONMENTAL CHAMBER

On 19 July 1993, the Court announced its decision to establish a Chamber under article 26, paragraph 1, to deal with disputes concerning international environmental law. This is the first special Chamber that the Court has created since its inauguration in 1946. The precise ambit of the Chamber's jurisdiction is to deal with any environmental case that falls within the

---

[52] UN Doc. A/40/682 (1985).
[53] Singh, *The Role and Record of the International Court of Justice*, p. 113.
[54] McWhinney, 'Special Chambers Within the International Court of Justice', pp. 1, 9.
[55] Schwebel, '*Ad Hoc* Chambers of the International Court of Justice', pp. 831, 846.

jurisdiction of the Court.[56] The Chamber consists of seven members of the Court.[57]

Prior to its establishment, some members of the Court had advocated the creation of such a Chamber.[58] Writing in 1989, Judge Singh attributed the Court's decision not to establish an environmental Chamber to a perception that the alternative course, consisting of the creation of a Chamber to deal *ad hoc* with each particular environmental dispute, would be a more attractive and flexible solution.[59] It is evident that the establishment of the Chamber does not remove the parties' right to submit a dispute to an *ad hoc* Chamber or indeed to the plenary Court but simply provides an alternative forum composed of members of the Court who are experienced in environmental matters.

A special Chamber dealing with environmental issues may have greater appeal today in light of the recognition at the United Nations Conference on Environment and Development (UNCED) held in Rio de Janeiro in June 1992 that the Court has a role to play in the settlement of disputes relating to sustainable development. In particular, on 14 June 1992, UNCED adopted chapter 39.9 of its Agenda 21 which encourages states to resolve their disputes relating to sustainable development by, *inter alia*, 'recourse to the International Court of Justice'.

Judge Singh considered that the major problems facing a coherent international response to environmental problems were that '(a) there was no properly codified law of the environment and (b) there was no proper machinery for settlement of environmental disputes'.[60] The same stumbling blocks were identified during the discussions at UNCED. The environmental Chamber would seem in a unique position to assist in overcoming these problems.

---

[56] ICJ Communiqué No. 93/20 of 19 July 1993.

[57] The original members of the Chamber, elected by the Court in July 1993, were Judges Schwebel, Bedjaoui, Evensen, Shahabuddeen, Weeramantry, Ranjeva and Herczegh (*ibid.*). The Chamber entered office on 6 August 1993 and had an original mandate of six months (*ibid.*). Upon the expiration of its original term of office, the Court extended the Chamber's mandate until 5 February 1995 and Judge Fleischhauer was elected to replace Judge Evensen, who did not seek re-election to the Court upon the expiration of his term of office (ICJ Communiqué No. 94/10 of 14 March 1994). The experience of the environmental field of the members of the Court elected to serve on the Chamber reveals that the Court was faithful to article 16, paragraph 2 of its Rules, which provides that the Court should have regard to 'any special knowledge, expertise or previous experience which any of the Members of the Court may have in relation to the category of case the Chamber is being formed to deal with'.

[58] Manfred Lachs, 'The Revised Procedure of the International Court of Justice', in F. Kalshoven, P. J. Kuypers and J. G. Lammers (eds.), *Essays in the Development of the International Legal Order* (Aalphen aan den Rijn/Rockville, 1980), p. 21; President Singh in his speech on the commemoration of the fortieth anniversary of the Court, *ICJ Yearbook 1985–1986*, 40, at p. 179.

[59] Singh, *The Role and Record of the International Court of Justice*, p. 165.

[60] *Ibid.*, at pp. 164–5 n. 4.

With respect to the first problem, the Chamber could assist both in the interpretation of treaties and conventions relating to the environment and in the identification of general principles that will assist states in their future codification efforts to regulate increasing environmental pollution and exploitation of natural resources. The Court is well versed in the interpretation of treaty law and in particular has in the past identified treaty provisions that have developed into general law. Attention should be drawn to the role of the Court in the progressive development of international law which, as Sir Robert has observed, has assumed a far greater significance than might appear from article 38 of the Statute which envisaged the Court as a 'subsidiary means for the ascertainment of the law'.[61]

Much of the reluctance of states to submit their environmental disputes to judicial bodies for resolution has been attributed to the novelty of the subject matter and the consequent unpredictability of the results of judicial determination. It should be pointed out, however, that international environmental law is not a virgin field but is impregnated by many general principles of international law which the Court has already had occasion to consider. In particular, the Court's statement in the *Corfu Channel* case that it is 'every State's obligation not to allow knowingly its territory to be used for acts contrary to the rights of other States', which bears many of the characteristics of the 'neighbour principle' under domestic tort law, is a solid foundation upon which to build a structure of environmental norms.[62] Indeed, prior to this pronouncement, the arbitration panel in the *Trail Smelter* case had already applied this general principle to environmental law when it held that a state has an obligation to prevent domestic activities from harming the environment in other countries to a significant degree.[63] International environmental law also involves complicated questions of state responsibility that the Court has tackled in the past.[64]

Moreover, issues of environmental law have directly arisen in cases pending before the Court both in the past and at present.[65] In the *North Sea Continental Shelf* cases, the Court considered that the conservation of the natural resources of the continental shelf was an important consideration in the area of maritime delimitation.[66] Again in the *Nuclear Tests* cases, the Court indicated provisional

[61] Jennings, 'Chambers of the International Court of Justice', p. 200.

[62] ICJ Reports, 1949, at pp. 4, 22.

[63] *RIAA*, 3 (1938/1941), p. 1905.

[64] See, for example, *United States Diplomatic and Consular Staff in Tehran*, ICJ Reports, 1980, at p. 3.

[65] Owing to the sensitivity of his position, the author will not comment upon cases that are presently pending before the Court.

[66] ICJ Reports, 1969, at pp. 51–2.

measures based on the 'possibility that damage to Australia might be shown to be caused by the deposit of radio-active fall-out' resulting from nuclear tests conducted by France in the region.[67] In the *Gulf of Maine* case, although the Chamber did not address the issue, preferring instead to resolve the dispute along traditional lines of maritime delimitation, both Canada and the United States explored in considerable depth the environmental risks of hydrocarbon development in the disputed maritime area. Further, the case entitled *Certain Phosphate Lands in Nauru (Nauru v. Australia)* involved questions of Australia's responsibility to compensate Nauru for the exploitation of its phosphate resources that took place when Australia, together with New Zealand and the United Kingdom, administered Nauru first under a mandate from the League of Nations and later a trusteeship from the UN.[68] Most recently, on 3 September 1993, the Director-General of the World Health Organization (WHO) transmitted to the Registry of the Court resolution WHA 46.40 of the Assembly of WHO, which requested an Advisory Opinion on the following question: 'In view of the health and environmental effects, would the use of nuclear weapons by a State in war or other armed conflict be a breach of its obligations under international law including the WHO Constitution?'

With respect to the need for a machinery for the settlement of environmental disputes, the environmental Chamber is a forum well suited to fill this lacuna. By article 90 of the Rules of Court, procedures before Chambers are, subject to the Statute and the Rules relating specifically to Chambers, governed by the provisions of the Rules applicable in contentious cases before the Court. Several features of the Court's procedure are of practical significance in relation to the resolution of international environmental disputes. These features, which the Chamber also enjoys and which other Chambers have already availed of, are numbered for convenience.

(1) The judgments of Chambers are binding on the parties and the parties have a right under article 94 of the Charter of the United Nations to request the Security Council to take measures to enforce the judgment in the event of non-compliance. Given the marked tendency of the Security Council to act with one voice in recent years, the judgment of

---

[67] ICJ Reports, 1973, at pp. 105 and 141.

[68] By a joint letter, filed in the Registry of the Court on 9 September 1993, the Agents of Nauru and Australia notified the Court that, having reached a settlement, the two parties had agreed to discontinue the proceedings. In consequence, the Court, on 13 September, made an Order recording the discontinuance of the proceedings and directing the removal of the case from the Court's List (ICJ Reports, 1993, at p. 322).

a Chamber will be a powerful weapon in the hands of a prevailing litigant.

(2) Should resolution of the dispute require extensive factual or scientific determinations, as it sometimes inevitably would, the Chamber could make these determinations in consultation with assessors appointed under article 30, paragraph 2 of the Statute. Moreover, the Court has the power, under article 50 of its Statute to request an individual, body, bureau, commission or other organization to carry out an inquiry or give an expert opinion. The Chamber in the *Gulf of Maine* case appointed an expert to assist the Chamber in respect of technical matters, in particular the preparation of a map of the maritime area in dispute.[69]

(3) The Chamber has the power, under article 41 of the Statute, to indicate interim measures of protection to preserve the rights of parties pending the Court's judgment, if circumstances require it. The Chamber, in the case concerning the *Frontier Dispute (Burkina Faso/Mali)*, indicated provisional measures ordering the parties, *inter alia*, to withdraw their armed forces from the disputed territory within twenty days of the delivery of the Order.[70]

(4) Under article 62 of the Statute, the Chamber may allow a state to intervene if it has 'an interest of a legal nature which may be affected by the decision in the case'. As noted earlier, the Chamber in the case concerning the *Land, Island and Maritime Frontier Dispute (El Salvador/ Honduras)* granted Nicaragua's application to intervene with respect to certain aspects of the case.[71] The right to intervene has obvious advantages in the light of the ubiquitous and trans-boundary nature of pollution. Also important with respect to the interpretation of treaties is the right of a state to intervene under article 63 of the Statute, when a convention to which it is a party is subject to construction by the Chamber.

(5) Unlike the vast majority of adjudicative fora, the Court not only has jurisdiction in contentious cases but also an advisory jurisdiction the very purpose of which, as Sir Robert stressed in a speech which the author had the honour to deliver on his behalf at UNCED, 'is not the settlement of a particular dispute but an authoritative statement of the law in answer to the requests from certain qualified bodies'.[72] While the Security Council and General Assembly may request an Advisory Opinion 'on any legal question' (article 96, paragraph 1 of the Charter), other organs of the UN and Specialized Agencies may request an Advisory Opinion on 'legal

[69] ICJ Reports, 1984, at p. 165.   [70] ICJ Reports, 1986, at pp. 3, 12.
[71] ICJ Reports, 1990, at p. 92.   [72] *ICJ Yearbook 1991–1992*, 46, at pp. 212, 215.

questions arising within the scope of their activities' when the General Assembly authorizes them to do so (article 96, paragraph 2).[73]

Judge Jessup suggested that Chambers should be used for consideration of Advisory Opinions. He noted that a Chamber could, for example, perform advisory functions by providing its services to international conferences.[74] Although Judge Jessup was speaking specifically in the context of the Chamber of Summary Procedure, his suggestion applies with equal force to the newly created special environmental Chamber. It is not inconceivable that other international organizations with an environmental portfolio will apply for and be granted the power to seek Advisory Opinions of the Court, making Judge Jessup's suggestion all the more attractive. Indeed, the British government has suggested that the United Nations Environmental Programme might eventually be converted into a Specialized Agency of the UN, in which case it would presumably be granted competence to ask for the Court's Advisory Opinions on legal questions concerning environmental protection.[75]

Delivery of Advisory Opinions by a Chamber, however, may be difficult to reconcile with the provisions governing their disposition. The disappearance from the present Rules of the provisions in article 84, paragraph 1 of the 1936 Rules of the Permanent Court, according to which Advisory Opinions must be delivered by the full Court, would appear to facilitate delivery of Advisory Opinions by the environmental Chamber. Article 26, paragraph 3 of the Statute, however, provides that cases shall be heard and determined by the Chambers provided for in this article 'if the parties so request' and appears to contemplate that the Chamber may be formed only for contentious cases where two parties square off against one another. Nevertheless, the jurisdiction of a Chamber to deliver Advisory Opinions has the support of an eminent scholar of the Court's procedure, Shabtai Rosenne, who is of the view that, under a liberal interpretation of the Court's Statute, the Court may convey the request for Opinion to the Chamber, although he does concede that in principle the full Court should deal with Advisory Opinions.[76]

---

[73] See *ibid.*, at pp. 65–6, which lists the other organs and Specialized Agencies the General Assembly has authorized to request Advisory Opinions. To date the General Assembly has requested thirteen Advisory Opinions of the Court (*ibid.*, at p. 65 n. 3). Prior to its most recent request concerning the legality of the use of nuclear weapons in time of war, the WHO, an authorized Specialized Agency, requested one Advisory Opinion of the Court (*ibid.*, at p. 66 n. 4).

[74] Philip Jessup, 'To Form a More Perfect United Nations', *Recueil des cours*, 129 (1970), pp. 5, 17.

[75] Statement of Sir Crispin Tickell before ECOSOC, 9 May 1989, at p. 2.

[76] Shabtai Rosenne, 'The 1972 revisions of the Rules of the International Court of Justice', *Israel Law Review*, 8 (1973), pp. 197, 215.

Moreover, at least two other jurists have argued that the Court has the authority under the broad provisions of article 68 of the Statute to apply provisions governing contentious proceedings to its advisory function and therefore to transfer an Advisory Opinion to a Chamber.[77]

The establishment of a special Chamber to deal with international environmental issues will, it is hoped, provide the catalyst for states to turn to the Court to reach a settlement of their environmental disputes. Standing on an equal footing with judgments of the plenary Court, judgments of the Chamber enjoy the prestige of being delivered by the principal judicial organ of the UN. The Chamber could provide a permanent body not only for the resolution of particular disputes but also for the coherent development of general legal principles and norms that will guide states in their future codification efforts to combat a growing global problem.

---

[77] C. Wilfred Jenks, *The Prospects of International Adjudication* (London, 1964), p. 160; Leo Gross, 'The International Court of Justice: Consideration of Requirements for Enhancing the Role of the International Legal Order', *AJIL*, 65 (1977), pp. 253, 277.

28

The use of experts
by the International Court

Gillian White

☙

INTRODUCTION

In the context of the aims of this volume, the present chapter must be seen as an evaluation of a quite minor and relatively little-used procedural aid to the due administration of international justice. The present Court has appointed experts under article 50 of its Statute on only two occasions, early in its history,[1] and has appointed experts pursuant to a provision in a special agreement on two other occasions. It has twice rejected a party's request that experts be appointed, and has decided *proprio motu* in other cases that such appointment was not necessary to assist it in determining the issues. In other cases the aspect on which an expert inquiry might have been ordered was not reached, as the Court held that it lacked jurisdiction, or that the claim was inadmissible. Whether the Court may order an expert inquiry or opinion in advisory proceedings remains an open question. To date, no such order has been made.

International arbitral tribunals have used independent experts on technical questions, in maritime boundary cases in the 1980s; and the Iran–United States Claims Tribunal has resorted to such aid on several occasions. The Court of Justice of the European Communities has used its power to obtain expert opinions, and such a power has recently been conferred upon the conciliation and arbitration bodies created under the 1993 Convention of the Conference on Security and Co-operation in Europe (CSCE) and upon the Permanent Court of Arbitration in the 1992 Optional Rules

---

[1] The PCIJ appointed experts in the *Chorzow Factory (Claim for Indemnity)* case, Series A, No. 17 (1928), at p. 99.

for Arbitrating Disputes between Two States.[2] Resort to independent experts in addition to, or in the absence of, experts called by litigating states is well established as an acceptable and helpful procedure in appropriate cases.

THE *CORFU CHANNEL* CASE

The writer's previous work on this subject identified the *Corfu Channel (Merits)* case as 'the outstanding example of the use of experts by the ICJ'.[3] Subsequent instances have not displaced this case from its position as the leading illustration. The experts' report on the visibility of any mine-laying operation in the Channel from the Albanian coast was of crucial importance in aiding the Court to determine the issue of Albania's responsibility. It will be recalled that the evidence on this issue was largely circumstantial and was disputed on vital points. The Court said: 'As regards the possibility of observing minelaying from the Albanian coast, the Court regards the following facts, relating to the technical conditions of a secret minelaying and to the Albanian surveillance, as particularly important.'[4] The Court then quoted from the experts' report, which considered it 'indisputable' that if a normal look-out was kept at specified points on the Albanian coast, and if the look-out personnel were equipped with binoculars (as had been stated), under normal weather conditions the mine-laying operation must have been noticed. The Court properly concluded that it could not fail 'to give great weight to the opinion of the experts who examined the locality in a manner giving every guarantee of correct and impartial information'.[5]

When the experts' reports were made available to the parties[6] Albania objected that the experts had exceeded the limits of their mandate by interpreting the findings of fact. In other words, the experts had usurped to an extent the judicial function of the Court.[7] However, the criticism was not well founded. The information in the experts' reports and in their replies to questions from judges was weighed and evaluated by the Court together with other evidence. The Court's method of approach, as well as the wording of this passage of the judgment, demonstrate 'that the Court itself discharged

---

[2] See p. 537 below.
[3] G. White, *The Use of Experts by International Tribunals* (Syracuse, NY, 1965), p. 107.
[4] ICJ Reports, 1949, at p. 20.
[5] *Ibid.*, at p. 21.
[6] Required by article 57(2) of the then Rules of the ICJ; see now article 67(2) of the 1978 Rules.
[7] For discussion of the issue of principle involved and relevant case law see White, *Use of Experts*, pp. 163–82.

the judicial duty of interpreting the evidence and drawing the resulting inferences'.[8]

In view of the differing opinions expressed with regard to the non-use of experts by the Court in the *Nicaragua* case,[9] it is worth recalling the co-operation given to the experts in *Corfu Channel*, not only by the respondent, Albania, but also by Yugoslavia, a non-party. The Court asked its experts to proceed to Sibenik, in Yugoslavia, and to Saranda, in Albania, to make certain inquiries and investigations.[10] This decision had been preceded by a letter to the Court from the Yugoslav government declaring that government's disposition 'not to prevent, but to give the necessary facilities so that the Experts of the Court might make enquiries on the spot at Sibenik as to the material facts concerning the visibility . . . and so that, if necessary, the Experts could carry out a demonstration on the spot with object of verifying their conclusion on that question'.[11]

In the final phase of *Corfu Channel*, dealing with the reparation to be awarded to the United Kingdom, the Court envisaged the appointment of experts pursuant to agreement between the parties as to their identity and terms of reference. But after Albania declined to appear to present observations on the amount of compensation, the Court held that article 53 of the Statute applied and itself designated experts to examine the estimates submitted by the UK. Presumably, article 53 could apply equally to a situation in which parties had agreed that experts should be appointed to carry out a task in regard to some aspect of the litigation, but one party had then failed to nominate its expert, or in some other respect defaulted on implementing the agreement. Such default could be regarded as failure by that party 'to defend its case', in terms of article 53(1).

USE OF EXPERTS BY THE COURT IN MORE RECENT CASES

Maritime boundary cases

The Chamber of the Court in the *Gulf of Maine* case appointed an expert, Commander P. B. Beazley, RN (retired), to assist it in technical matters, in

---

[8] *Ibid.*, p. 180.

[9] See p. 536 below.

[10] ICJ Reports, 1949, p. 21.

[11] *Ibid.*, Pleadings, vol. V, p. 253 (writer's translation from the French). On the part played by the Yugoslav government in bringing evidence before the Court in *Corfu Channel* see S. Rosenne, *The International Court of Justice* (Leyden, 1957), pp. 407–8.

particular preparing the description of the maritime boundary and illustrative charts depicting its course. This appointment was made pursuant to the Special Agreement between Canada and the United States submitting the case to the Chamber.[12] The parties undertook to request the Chamber to appoint an expert, nominated jointly by them, to carry out these functions. Strictly, the Chamber was not bound to accede to this request, but in reality it had no choice but to comply and to appoint the parties' nominee.[13]

The parties did not leave the Court of Arbitration any such residual discretion in the *Case Concerning Delimitation of Maritime Areas between Canada and the French Republic*. Article 2(2) of the compromis required the Court of Arbitration to describe the course of this delimitation in a technically precise manner. The geometric nature of the elements of the delimitation were to be indicated, and the positions of all points mentioned were to be given by reference to their co-ordinates on a specified North American Datum geodesic system. Article 2(3) then provided: 'After consultation with the Parties, the Court shall designate a technical expert to assist it in carrying out the duties specified in paragraph 2 above.'[14] At the first meeting of members of the court with the parties' agents, the Court in consultation with the agents decided to appoint Cdr Beazley as expert. His technical report is annexed to the Court's decision of 10 June 1992.[15]

A comparable provision was included in the compromis between Guinea and Guinea-Bissau submitting the delimitation of their maritime frontier to arbitration. Article 9(2) provided: 'This decision must include the drawing of a boundary line on a map. In this regard, the tribunal will designate one or more technical experts to assist in the preparation of the map.'[16] Cdr Beazley was appointed the technical expert.

The Arbitration Agreement between Guinea-Bissau and Senegal submitting the delimitation of their maritime boundary is similar. The Tribunal was required to inform the parties of its decision on two questions, formulated in the Agreement. If the answer to the first, whether a 1960 agreement had

---

[12] ICJ Reports, 1984, pp. 252–3.

[13] Cf. the PCIJ's rejection of France's request in the *Free Zones* case that it should order an expert inquiry and arrange for an investigation on the spot by a delegation of judges: Series A/B, No. 46 (1932). The Special Agreement between France and Switzerland provided that either party might request the Court 'to delegate one or three members for the purposes of conducting investigations on the spot'. The Court held that its judgment must be limited to questions of law, so that the request had ceased to have object, and it could not regard that provision of the Agreement as binding upon the Court 'in any event' (at p. 162).

[14] 31 *ILM* 1145 (1992).

[15] *Ibid.*, 1178.

[16] 77 *ILR* 635, at p. 644; 25 *ILM* 255 (1986).

the force of law between the two states, was in the negative, the Tribunal had to state the course of the delimitation line. Article 9(2) of the Agreement provided: 'That decision shall include the drawing of the boundary line on a map. To that end, the Tribunal shall be empowered to appoint one or more technical experts to assist it in the preparation of such a map.' The Tribunal held the 1960 Agreement to be valid and to have effected the delimitation as between the two states. It was not called upon to answer the second question or to prepare a map showing the boundary line. Bedjaoui dissented and proceeded to delimit the maritime boundary *de novo*, utilizing the work of the Tribunal's expert, Cdr Beazley.[17]

In *Gulf of Maine* the Chamber's Order appointing Cdr Beazley as the technical expert[18] instructed the Registrar to place the pleadings and documents in the case at the expert's disposal, on a basis of confidentiality so long as they had not been made public under article 53(2) of the Rules. The expert was to be present at the oral proceedings, and available for consultations with the Chamber as it might deem necessary. The judgment declares that 'the conditions laid down for his participation in the work of the Chamber have duly been complied with'.[19]

The expert's technical report is annexed to the judgment.[20] Cdr Beazley is an expert hydrographer who served on the UK delegation to UNCLOS III.[21] His report relates to the corrective exercise the Chamber judged necessary in determining the second segment of the boundary. The Chamber observed that 'though it may be the shortest, [it] will certainly be the central and most decisive segment for the whole of the delimitation line'.[22] A median line approximately parallel to the coasts of Nova Scotia and Massachusetts was judged inappropriate, as the boundary between the states at its landward end did not terminate in the centre of the coastline at the back of the Gulf, but further north-east of the central point. In making the correction the Chamber used the proportionality of the lengths of relevant US and Canadian coastlines on the Gulf as a criterion, with a further correction to give only half effect to Seal Island (Canadian) off the south-west coast of Nova Scotia. Cdr Beazley's report shows how the ratio between the lengths of coastline was calculated, and how relevant points were located.[23]

---

[17] 83 *ILR* 1, at pp. 47, 85, 106 and 119.   [18] ICJ Reports, 1984, p. 165.

[19] *Ibid.*, p. 265, para. 18.   [20] *Ibid.*, pp. 347–52.

[21] See his contribution 'Maritime Boundaries: A Geographical and Technical Perspective', in E. D. Brown and R. R. Churchill (eds.), *The UN Convention on the Law of the Sea: Impact and Implementation* (Honolulu, 1987), p. 319 (Law of the Sea Institute Proceedings, vol. XIX).

[22] ICJ Reports, 1984, p. 333, para. 214.

[23] See paras. 221 and 222 of the judgment: *ibid.*, pp. 335–7.

In the case concerning *Maritime Delimitation in the Area between Greenland and Jan Mayen* the Court was asked by Denmark to decide where a single line of delimitation should be drawn between Denmark and Norway's fishing zones and continental shelf in the waters between Greenland and Jan Mayen. This case was not brought to the Court by Special Agreement: proceedings were instituted by Denmark relying on declarations under article 36(2) of the Statute. In its judgment the Court stated that it was satisfied that it should so define the delimitation line that any remaining questions would be matters strictly relating to hydrographic technicalities which the parties, with the help of their experts, could resolve. The Court did not itself appoint experts, nor was it asked to do so by Denmark or Norway.[24]

Case concerning the *Frontier Dispute (Burkina Faso/Mali)*

The Special Agreement of 1983 by which these states agreed to submit the frontier dispute to a Chamber of the Court asked the Chamber to state the frontier line in the disputed area. The parties undertook to accept the judgment as final and binding, and to effect the demarcation of the frontier within one year from delivery of the judgment. Article IV(3) of the Agreement provided: 'The Parties request the Chamber to nominate, in its Judgment, three experts to assist them in the demarcation operation.'[25] In its judgment of 22 December 1986 the Chamber indicated its readiness to accept this task, but felt it inappropriate to make the nomination immediately. It wished first to ascertain the parties' views 'particularly as regards the practical aspects of the exercise by the experts of their functions'.[26] The Chamber's Order of 9 April 1987, Nomination of Experts, cited article 48 of the Statute, pointing out that the parties were not requesting the Chamber to order an expert opinion in the sense of article 50. The purpose of such an opinion would be to assist the Court in giving judgment on the issues for decision[27] and any costs would be borne by the Court.[28] The parties here were asking the Chamber to exercise the power conferred by the Special Agreement 'of nominating three persons whom the Parties have themselves decided to entrust with the task of giving an expert opinion for the purpose of implementing the Judgment of the Chamber'. The Order declared that there

---

[24] ICJ Reports, 1993, p. 38.
[25] ICJ Reports, 1986, p. 558.
[26] *Ibid.*, p. 648.
[27] Quoting from the *Application for Revision and Interpretation* case, ICJ Reports, 1985, p. 228, para. 65. See p. 534 below.
[28] Rules, article 68.

was nothing in the Statute or 'in the settled jurisprudence' to prevent the Chamber from exercising this power, whose very object was to enable the parties to achieve a final settlement of their dispute in implementation of the judgment. The Chamber nominated two technical experts: an Algerian geographer and cartographer and a Dutch geodetic consultant; and a legal expert, a French *conseiller* at the Cour de Cassation of France.[29]

NON-USE OF EXPERTS BY THE COURT

Rejection of a party's request

Following the Court's 1982 judgment in the *Tunisia/Libya Continental Shelf* case[30] Tunisia requested its revision and interpretation.[31] Tunisia's fifth request for relief, made during oral argument, related to the possible appointment of experts. By its 1982 judgment the Court had determined the course of the boundary in the Gulf of Gabes in two sectors, in the second of which the line veered to give effect to the change in direction of the Tunisian coastline. Tunisia sought interpretation of the starting-point on the coast for this change in direction. In the Court's phrase, the change should begin at the point of intersection with a parallel passing through 'the most westerly point on the shoreline (low-water mark) of the Gulf of Gabes',[32] indicating approximate co-ordinates for this point. Fixing of the exact point was for the parties' experts to determine.[33] Under article 2 of the Special Agreement submitting the case to the Court, the parties were to meet immediately after delivery of the judgment, to determine the line of delimitation in accordance with the principles and rules laid down in it. In view of the dispute that had emerged over the fixing of co-ordinates for this point, Tunisia submitted that the Court should order an expert survey to resolve the issue under article 60, the interpretation provision of the Statute.

It is important to note that this was a unilateral request. Libya argued that the entire application for interpretation was unjustified, and did not comment specifically on the request. But the Court was careful to observe that Libya had not expressly objected to it.[34]

---

[29] ICJ Reports, 1987, p. 7.

[30] ICJ Reports, 1982, p. 18.

[31] *Application for Revision and Interpretation of the Judgment of 24 February 1982 in the Case Concerning the Continental Shelf (Tunisia/Libyan Arab Jamahiriya)*, ICJ Reports, 1985, p. 191.

[32] ICJ Reports, 1982, p. 87, para. 124.

[33] See article 1 of the Special Agreement of 1978, ICJ Reports, 1982, pp. 21 and 23.

[34] ICJ Reports, 1985, p. 227, para. 64.

The Court rejected Tunisia's request, holding that the purpose of an expert opinion must be to assist it in giving judgment on issues submitted for decision, and that it would be appropriate to accede to the request 'only if the determination of the exact co-ordinates of the most westerly point of the Gulf of Gabes were required to enable the Court to give judgment on matters submitted to it'.[35] Interpretation could add nothing to a judgment, which was *res judicata*. Determination of the precise co-ordinates had been left by the Court to the parties' experts.[36]

However, the Court did not leave the matter there. Observing that in 1982 it could have appointed an expert to fix the co-ordinates but had preferred to leave the task to the parties' experts, so that the decision in this respect was *res judicata*, the Court said that the force of *res judicata* was not 'such as to prevent the Parties returning to the Court to present a *joint request* that it should order an expert survey'.[37] The general issue of whether, and in what circumstances, the Court might accede to a unilateral request to appoint an expert was raised, but left open.[38] The obligation undertaken in the Special Agreement, to conclude a delimitation treaty, remained in force and had to be fully implemented. The parties must ensure that their experts and representatives 'engage in a sincere exercise involving a genuine effort to determine the precise co-ordinates . . . with a view to the conclusion of the delimitation treaty'.[39]

No further request was made to the Court by either party. One must assume that their experts were able to agree on co-ordinates and that a delimitation treaty has been concluded.

The Chamber of the Court in the *Land, Island and Maritime Frontier Dispute*[40] turned down a request by El Salvador that it should consider obtaining evidence *in situ*,[41] in view of difficulty in collecting evidence in certain areas relevant to the disputed frontier with Honduras, due to acts of violence. The Chamber did not consider it necessary to exercise its power to obtain evidence, nor to accede to El Salvador's request that it should arrange for an inquiry or expert opinion under article 50 of the Statute.

---

[35] *Ibid.*, p. 228, para. 65.
[36] The Court now made it clear that it was to the parties' experts that it had referred in 1982, not to an expert appointed by the Court (*ibid.*).
[37] *Ibid.*, para. 66 (emphasis added).
[38] *Ibid.*, p, 229, para. 67.
[39] *Ibid.*, para. 68.
[40] *El Salvador and Honduras, Nicaragua intervening*, ICJ Reports, 1992, p. 351.
[41] Under article 66 of the Rules.

Decision *proprio motu* that expert opinion or inquiry not necessary

No aspect of the judgments in the *Nicaragua* case is entirely free from controversy. This applies to evidential matters as well as to the Court's pronouncements on jurisdiction, admissibility and substantive law. In its judgment on the *Merits*[42] the Court referred to the power under article 50 to entrust any person or body with the task of carrying out an enquiry or giving an expert opinion. Such a body could be a group of judges chosen from those sitting in the case. But the Court declined to exercise this power.

> In the present case, however, the Court felt it was unlikely that an enquiry of this kind would be practical or desirable, particul*· ﾟ* since such a body, if it was properly to perform its task, might have found it necessary to go not only to the applicant State, but also to several other neighbouring countries, and even to the respondent State, which had refused to appear before the Court.[43]

Judge Schwebel in his Dissenting Opinion identified several states as the suggested *locus* for the fact-finding mission he considered appropriate and, indeed, necessary 'given the controversy that surrounded charges by the United States of Nicaragua's support of foreign insurrection and Nicaragua's adamant denial of those charges'. He said that the Court, acting under article 50, could have entrusted a commission of judges or another organization with the task of carrying out a fact-finding enquiry in Nicaragua, the US, El Salvador, Honduras, Costa Rica, Guatemala and Cuba.[44]

It is clear from these passages, as well as from the careful comments of Judge Oda in his Dissenting Opinion[45] that what had been under consideration was a fact-finding enquiry, whether by independent outside experts or by a group of judges, rather than the seeking of expert aid or opinion on technical matters. Nevertheless, the issue of practicality, in the sense of co-operation or lack of it from the state or states in whose territory an inquiry needs to be carried out, arises equally for any expert investigation 'on the ground', such as was ordered in *Corfu Channel* and undertaken by Court-appointed experts with the co-operation of both Albania and Yugoslavia.[46] As Judge Jennings put it: 'There are limits to what the Court can do, in accordance with Article 53 of the Statute, to satisfy itself about a non-appearing party's case; and that is especially so where the facts are crucial.'[47]

---

[42] ICJ Reports, 1986, p. 14.

[43] *Ibid.*, p. 40, para. 61.   [44] *Ibid.*, p. 322, para. 132.

[45] *Ibid.*, p. 245, para. 69.   [46] See p. 529 above.

[47] *Nicaragua* case (*Merits*), at p. 544. See Oscar Schachter, 'Disputes Involving the Use of Force', in L. F. Damrosch (ed.), *The International Court of Justice at a Crossroads* (Dobbs Ferry, NY, 1987), p. 223, at

The Court's lack of the right to insist on the co-operation of litigating parties, or other states, with a fact-finding mission or expert inquiry[48] could be remedied only by amendment of the Statute. The new Optional Rules of the Permanent Court of Arbitration for Arbitrating Disputes between Two States[49] contains a full article on experts to be approved by the Tribunal, including the following provision:

> Rule 27(2): The parties shall give the expert any relevant information or produce for his/her inspection any relevant documents or goods that he/she may request of them. Any dispute between a party and such expert as to the relevance and appropriateness of the required information or production shall be referred to the arbitral tribunal for decision.

A briefer but possibly even more effective provision is found in the Convention on Conciliation and Arbitration within the CSCE[50] which establishes a Court of Conciliation and Arbitration from which an arbitral tribunal may be drawn for a particular dispute. The Court is to adopt its Rules, subject to approval by the states parties to the Convention, but article 29(2) already provides: 'The Arbitral Tribunal shall have, in relation to the parties to the dispute, the necessary fact-finding and investigative powers to carry out its tasks.'[51]

More than twenty years before the *Nicaragua* case the Court in the *Temple* case determined the issues on which a decision was required in order for it to give judgment and, having eliminated certain questions as irrelevant, saw no reason for ordering its own expert enquiry.[52] Judge Wellington Koo dissented, and was critical of the Court's failure to use its powers under articles 44 and 50 of the Statute to send experts to investigate the disputed locations and make a report and recommendations.[53]

---

p. 236: 'A non-cooperating respondent (especially a state that has denied jurisdiction) will be unlikely to assist in such fact-finding in its territory or through its nationals.'

[48] Articles 44(2) and 49 of the Statute do not extend to the imposition of such an obligation on parties or on other states.

[49] Effective from October 1992: 32 *ILM* 572 (1993).

[50] Not yet in force. Opened for signature December 1992: 32 *ILM* 557 (1993).

[51] Cf. Articles 5 and 6 of the Treaty of Peace and Friendship of 1984 between Argentina and Chile, creating conciliation and arbitration procedures for any future disputes concerning the Beagle Channel and navigation rights therein. The conciliation commission or Arbitral Tribunal may call upon expert advice, and in an arbitration the Tribunal is empowered 'to summon and hear witnesses or experts in their respective territories as well as to carry out inspections at first hand': Annexe, article 30; text in 82 *ILR* 684 and UN, *Law of the Sea Bulletin*, No. 4 (February 1985), p. 50.

[52] ICJ Reports, 1962, p. 6, at p. 35.

[53] Dissenting Opinion, *ibid.*, p. 100, para. 55. Cf. Judge Fitzmaurice, Separate Opinion, *ibid.*, p. 66.

Aspect not reached on which expert inquiry possible

Three examples can be mentioned briefly. In the *Anglo-Iranian Oil Company* case the UK suggested in its observations responding to Iran's preliminary objection that there was a complicated issue of fact between the parties, namely, the confiscatory nature of the Iranian Oil Nationalization Act which set a totally inadequate ceiling on the compensation payable for the nationalized concession rights. This issue possibly required an inquiry or expert opinion under article 50.[54] In the event, the Court held that it lacked jurisdiction.

In the *Nottebohm* case (*Second Phase*) Liechtenstein requested the Court to order under article 50 'such enquiry as may be necessary into the account of profits and quantification of damages'.[55] The Court's decision on the inadmissibility of Liechtenstein's claim against Guatemala meant that no enquiry was needed.

Finally, in the *Aegean Sea Continental Shelf* case the Court was given the Greek text of draft legislation approving Greece's accession to the 1928 General Act for the Pacific Settlement of Disputes. Judge *ad hoc* Stassinopoulos referred in his Dissenting Opinion to the Greek expression translated by 'et, notamment' in the French official text of the Greek instrument of accession. He observed that the Greek word strengthened the argument made by Greece for the interpretation of 'et, notamment', but rejected by the Court. Thirlway has commented that probably none of the other judges knew modern Greek, but that it was interesting 'to speculate whether, if necessary, the Court could rely on expert evidence to inform it of the "natural and ordinary meaning" of the words of a treaty or other relevant text written in a language unfamiliar to most or all of the judges'.[56] Article 51(3) of the Rules requires any document annexed to a pleading which is not in English or French to be accompanied by a translation into one of these languages certified by the party submitting it as accurate. The rule also empowers the Court to 'require a more extensive or more complete translation to be furnished'. If problems of comprehension remain after translation, article 50 of the Statute is sufficiently broadly phrased to allow the Court to seek expert linguistic help.

---

[54] *Anglo-Iranian Oil Company* case, Pleadings, p. 360; and see UK Memorial, paras. 26, 30A–34A, *ibid.*, at pp. 101, 106–9.

[55] ICJ Reports, 1955, p. 9 and Pleadings, vol. 1, p. 70, Liechtenstein Memorial, Final Conclusions.

[56] H. W. A. Thirlway, 'The Law and Procedure of the International Court of Justice, 1960–1989, Part Three', BYbIL, 61 (1991), at pp. 71–2. He suggested that such a problem may arise in the case concerning *Maritime Delimitation and Territorial Questions between Qatar and Bahrain*.

Advisory proceedings

Does the Court possess its powers under article 50 in advisory as well as in contentious proceedings? The question has not been directly answered. In the *Namibia* case the Court was asked by South Africa to receive 'further factual material' concerning the situation in Namibia, but decided that 'it does not find itself in need of further arguments or information'.[57] However, there was no suggestion that an expert inquiry or opinion be sought.

In *Western Sahara* one of the grounds for Spain's opposition to the Court pronouncing on the questions posed in the General Assembly's request for an Opinion was the alleged inability of the Court in advisory proceedings to 'fulfil the requirements of good administration of justice as regards the determination of the facts'.[58] The Court held that the test was whether it had before it 'sufficient information and evidence to enable it to arrive at a judicial conclusion upon any disputed questions of fact the determination of which is necessary for it to give an opinion in conditions compatible with its judicial character'. This test was satisfied by the 'very extensive documentary evidence of the facts' considered relevant by Mauritania, Morocco and Spain with which they had furnished the Court.[59] Judge De Castro canvassed the threshold issue of whether, in advisory proceedings, the Court has the means of conducting investigations, if such would be appropriate or necessary to enable it to carry out its responsibility 'for verifying the factual data on which it bases its reply'. His view was, simply, that the Court's procedure does not permit it, in such proceedings, either to make arrangements for the taking of evidence under article 48 of the Statute, or to order an inquiry or expert opinion under article 50.[60] The judge had found difficulties in evaluating the historical data presented, and with the geographical, ethnic and linguistic material.[61]

Judge De Castro's negative answer rested on a bare assertion that 'even if Article 68 of the Statute is interpreted in the broadest manner, it would not seem that in advisory proceedings the Court is entitled'.[62] But the Court has a wide discretion under article 68 to apply any of the provisions relating to contentious cases 'to the extent to which it recognizes them to be applicable' in the exercise of its advisory functions. The PCIJ expressed its belief that it

---

[57] ICJ Reports, 1971, p. 17, at p. 21, paras. 17 and 18. See also Judge De Castro, Separate Opinion, at pp. 177–8.

[58] ICJ Reports, 1975, p. 13, at p. 28, para. 44.

[59] *Ibid.*, paras. 46, 47.   [60] Separate Opinion, *ibid.*, p. 138.

[61] *Ibid.*, p. 141.   [62] *Ibid.*, p. 138.

could order its own inquiry, if necessary, in advisory proceedings.[63] It may be that some future request for an Advisory Opinion will involve the Court in appraising non-legal information to such a degree that it will consider it necessary to use its powers under article 50.

A PROPOSAL FOR ASSESSORS AND EXPERTS

An experienced practitioner before the Court and before courts in the United States of America, Keith Highet, has suggested that the Court might consider modifying the Rules to provide for special masters for findings of fact, similar to the practice of the US Supreme Court in exercising its original juris-diction.[64] He considered that such an innovation would not be inconsistent with the Statute, and could be based on the unused provisions for assessors – article 30(2), and articles 9 and 21(2) of the Rules. Assessors could be combined with the use of experts.

It does not lie with one who lacks forensic experience before national or international courts to evaluate the desirability and implications of this suggestion. But it would seem to be worthy of serious consideration when the Court next reviews its Rules. As Jenks wrote over thirty years ago, referring to the interrelationship of substantive and procedural law in every legal system: 'So it is with international law; if we wish so to develop the law as to respond to the challenges of our times our procedures and remedies must be sufficiently varied and flexible for the purpose.'[65]

---

[63] See *Jurisdiction of the European Commission of the Danube*, Series B, No. 14 (1927), at p. 46; *Competence of the ILO to Regulate Incidentally the Personal Work of the Employer*, Series B, No. 13 and Series C, No. 12 (1926), at pp. 12, 287–88; M. O. Hudson, *The Permanent Court of International Justice* (New York, 1943), p. 378; White, *Use of Experts*, pp. 43–5.

[64] K. Highet, 'Evidence and Proof of Facts', in Damrosch (ed.), *The International Court of Justice at a Crossroads*, p. 355, at p. 372, referring to R. L. Stern and E. Gressman, *Supreme Court Practice* (5th edn, Washington, 1978), pp. 601–26.

[65] C. Wilfred Jenks, *Prospects of International Adjudication* (London, 1964), p. 184.

29

Provisional measures

The practice of the International Court of Justice

Shigeru Oda

೮ೂ

Provisional measures – so called in the Statute and the Rules of Court, but placed under the heading of 'interim protection' in the latter (part III, Section D, sub-section 1) – are called in French 'mesures conservatoires', which more properly reflects the nature of this institution. The indication of provisional measures – which is deemed to be an almost essential instrument in the panoply of any judicial process – is intended to preserve, pending the final decision, the respective rights of the parties before the Court. The provision constituting article 41 of the PCIJ's 1920 Statute, which relates to this institution, was inherited by the Statute of the ICJ which provides in article 41 that 'the Court shall have the power to indicate, if it considers that circumstances so require, any provisional measures which ought to be taken to preserve the respective rights of either party'. The practice of both the predecessor and present Courts, in relation to this proceeding, is indicated in table 1.

PRACTICE

During the period of the PCIJ, there were six cases in which the Court received requests for the indication of provisional measures. In only two of them were provisional measures indicated by the Court. In the case concerning *Denunciation by China of the 1865 Treaty* (No. 1 in table 1), the Court's Order granting the request of an applicant, Belgium, was, however, withdrawn some weeks later. In the other case, the *Electricity Company of Sofia* case (No. 6), the outbreak of the Second World War disrupted the proceedings and the case itself was discontinued by the applicant, Belgium, after the end of the

This article is taken from a series of lectures given by the author at the Hague Academy of International Law in July 1993.

Table 1. *Requests for provisional measures*

I. Permanent Court of International Justice

No. 1   *Denunciation of the Treaty of 2 November 1865, between China and Belgium*

Belgium v. China

26 November 1926	Application
26 November 1926	Request for provisional measures
8 January 1927	Order (A8), request admitted
15 February 1927	Order (A8), the previous Order ceased to be operative
25 May 1929	Order (A18), removed from the list (withdrawal by the applicant)

No. 2   *Factory at Chorzów*

Germany v. Poland

8 February 1927	Application
26 July 1927	Judgment (A8), preliminary objections dismissed
15 October 1927	Request for provisional measures
21 November 1927	Order, request rejected
13 September 1928	Judgment (A17)

No. 3   *Prince von Pless Administration*

Germany v. Poland

18 May 1932	Application
4 February 1933	Order (A/B52), preliminary objections joined to the merits
3 May 1933	Request for provisional measures
11 May 1933	Order (A/B54), request ceased to have object
2 December 1933	Order (A/B59), removed from the list (withdrawal by the applicant)

No. 4   *Legal Status of the South-eastern Territory of Greenland*

Norway v. Denmark

18 July 1932	Application
18 July 1932	Request for provisional measures
2 August 1932	Order (A/B48), cases joined
3 August 1932	Order (A/B48), request rejected
11 May 1933	Order (A/B55), removed from the list (withdrawal by both parties)

No. 5   *Polish Agrarian Reform and the German Minority*

Germany v. Poland

3 July 1933	Application (1 July 1933)
3 July 1933	Request for provisions measures
29 July 1933	Order (A/B58), request rejected
2 December 1933	Order (A/B60), removed from the list (withdrawal by the applicant)

Table 1 (*cont.*)

No. 6.	*Electricity Company of Sofia and Bulgaria*

Belgium v. Bulgaria

26 January 1938	Application
4 April 1939	Judgment (A/B77), preliminary objections upheld in part
15 October 1939	Request for provisional measures
5 December 1939	Order (A/B79), request admitted
1 December 1945	Discontinuance

II. International Court of Justice

No. 7	*Anglo-Iranian Oil Co.*

United Kingdom v. Iran

26 May 1951	Application
26 May 1951	Request for provisional measures
5 July 1951	Order (ICJ Reports, 1951, p. 89), request admitted
22 July 1952	Judgment, preliminary objections upheld

No. 8	*Interhandel* case

Switzerland v. United States

2 October 1957	Application
3 October 1957	Request for provisional measures
24 October 1957	Order (ICJ Reports, 1957, p. 105), request rejected
21 March 1959	Judgment, preliminary objections upheld

No. 9A/B	*Fisheries Jurisdiction*

United Kingdom v. Iceland/Germany v. Iceland

14 April 1972	Application
19 July 1972 (UK); 21 July 1972 (Germany) requests for provisional measures	
17 August 1972	Order (ICJ Reports, 1972, pp. 12, 30), requests admitted
25 July 1974	Judgment

No. 10A/B	*Nuclear Tests*

Australia v. France/New Zealand v. France

9 May 1973	Application
9 May 1973	Requests for provisional measures
22 June 1973	Orders (ICJ Reports, 1973, pp. 99, 135), requests admitted
20 December 1974	Judgment (discontinuance)

No. 11	*Trial of Pakistani Prisoners of War*

Pakistan v. India

11 May 1973	Application
11 May 1973	Request for provisional measures
13 July 1973	Order (ICJ Reports, 1973, p. 328), request lapsed
15 December 1973	Order, removed from the list (discontinuance by the applicant)

Table 1 (*cont.*)

No. 12   *Aegean Sea Continental Shelf*

Greece v. Turkey

10 August 1976	Application
10 August 1976	Request for provisional measures
11 September 1976	Order (ICJ Reports, 1976, p. 3), request rejected
19 December 1978	Judgment, preliminary objections upheld

No. 13   *United States Diplomatic and Consular Staff in Tehran*

United States v. Islamic Republic of Iran

29 November 1979	Application
29 November 1979	Request for provisional measures
15 December 1979	Order (ICJ Reports, 1979, p. 7), request admitted
24 May 1980	Judgment

No. 14   *Frontier Dispute*

Burkina Faso/Republic of Mali (ad hoc Chamber case)

20 October 1983	Filing of joint letter of 14 October 1983
2 January 1986	Request for provisional measures
10 January 1986	Order (ICJ Reports, 1986, p. 3), request admitted
22 December 1986	Judgment

No. 15   *Military and Paramilitary Activities in and against Nicaragua*
                 (Nicaragua v. United States of America)

Nicaragua v. United States

9 April 1984	Application
9 April 1984	Request for provisional measures
10 May 1984	Order (ICJ Reports, 1984, p. 169), request admitted
27 June 1986	Judgment
26 September 1991	Order, removed from the list

No. 16   *Border and Transborder Armed Actions (Nicaragua v. Honduras)*

Nicaragua v. Honduras

28 July 1986	Application
21 March 1988	Request for provisional measures
31 March 1988	Order (ICJ Reports, 1988, p. 9), request withdrawn
27 May 1992	Order, removed from the list (discontinuance by the applicant)

No. 17   *Arbitral Award of 31 July 1989*

Guinea-Bissau v. Senegal

3 August 1989	Application
18 January 1990	Request for provisional measures
2 March 1990	Order (ICJ Reports, 1990, p. 64), request rejected
12 November 1991	Judgment

Table 1 (*cont.*)

No. 18	*Passage through the Great Belt*
	Finland v. Denmark
17 May 1991	Application
23 May 1991	Request for provisional measures
29 July 1991	Order (ICJ Reports, 1991, p. 12), request rejected
10 September 1992	Order, removed from the list (discontinuance by the parties)
No. 19A/B	*Questions of Interpretation and Application of the 1971 Montreal Convention arising from the Aerial Incident at Lockerbie*
	Libyan Arab Jamahiriya v. United Kingdom/Libyan Arab Jamahiriya v. United States
3 March 1992	Application
3 March 1992	Requests for provisional measures
14 April 1992	Order (ICJ Reports, 1992, pp. 3, 114), requests rejected
	pending
No. 20	*Application of the Convention on the Prevention and Punishment of the Crime of Genocide (Bosnia and Herzegovina v. Yugoslavia (Serbia and Montenegro)*
	Bosnia and Herzegovina v. Yugoslavia (Serbia and Montenegro)
20 March 1993	Application
20 March 1993	Request for provisional measures
8 April 1993	Order (ICJ Reports, 1993, p. 3), request admitted
27 July 1993	Further request for provisional measures
13 September 1993	Order (ICJ Reports, 1993, p. 325), further request admitted
	pending

war. Thus, in the period of the PCIJ, there was no case in which provisional measures indicated by the Court had any real effect.

There have been twelve cases in which the ICJ has had occasion to respond to requests for provisional measures. Requests were rejected in five of these twelve cases; in another seven cases provisional measures were ordered. Let me briefly review this past practice.

The 1950s

In the 1950s there were two occasions on which provisional measures were requested. In the *Anglo-Iranian Oil Co.* case (No. 7), which related to the confiscation of the British-owned company under the 1951 Laws of Iran, the Court indicated some provisional measures in 1951 – in the absence of the respondent state – which would apply on the basis of reciprocal observance. One year later, however, in 1952, the Court found that it lacked jurisdiction to deal with this case, thus depriving those provisional measures of further legal effect. It is significant that among the cases eventually terminated by the ICJ for lack of jurisdiction (see pp. 548–51 below), the only one in which the Court had indicated provisional measures is this early example. Another case in the 1950s, the *Interhandel* case (No. 8), related to a dispute that had arisen with respect to the claim by Switzerland to the restitution by the United States of the assets of the Interhandel Company entered in the Commercial Register of Basle. As the US had declared that it would not take action for the time being to fix a time schedule for the sale of the shares in question, the Court, in 1959, dismissed the request on account of the lack of urgency of the relevant matters.

The 1970s

In the early part of the 1970s, apart from a request in 1973 by Pakistan in the case of *Trial of Pakistani Prisoners of War* (No. 11) (which lapsed owing to successful negotiations between the applicant and respondent states), the Court received two requests for the indication of provisional measures, both of which were granted. In the *Fisheries Jurisdiction* cases (No. 9A/B), the Court indicated in 1972 some provisional measures to the effect, among others, that Iceland should refrain from taking any measures to enforce the relevant regulations against British and German vessels within the unilaterally estab-lished 50-mile fishery zone. Iceland did not comply with the Court's Order indicating provisional measures. In the *Nuclear Tests* case (No. 10A/B), the Court indicated, in 1973, some provisional measures to the effect, in particular, that the French government should avoid (atmospheric) nuclear tests causing the deposit of radioactive fall-out on Australian and New Zealand territories. Since France announced its intention to cease the conduct of such tests, the Court found that, the objective of the applicants having been accomplished, the claims no longer had any object and that the dispute had thus disappeared.

A few years later, in 1976, a request for provisional measures was made by Greece in the *Aegean Sea Continental Shelf* case (No. 12). The Court on this occasion rejected the request to order abstention from all exploration activity or any scientific research in the disputed areas, for the reason that the effects of the alleged breach by Turkey would be reparable by appropriate means in the event that judgment were rendered in Greece's favour. These three cases of provisional measures in the 1970s were different in nature and context but there was one common element in all three, in that the respondent state had declined to appear in the case at all and the Orders of the Court were made *in absentia*.

The 1980s

Around 1980, the Court indicated provisional measures in two cases of a highly political nature in which the Court's Orders were not complied with by the respective respondent states. In the *Tehran Hostages* case (No. 13), the Court stated in 1980, in the absence of the respondent state, Iran, that Iran should immediately ensure the restoration of the premises of the US Embassy to the possession of the US authorities and the immediate release of all persons of US nationality who had been held as hostages in the Embassy and elsewhere. The Court's Order was not, however, observed by Iran. In the *Nicaragua/US* case (No. 15), the Court indicated provisional measures in 1984 which stated, *inter alia*, that the US should immediately cease and refrain from any action blocking access to or from Nicaraguan ports and the laying of mines, and that the right of Nicaragua to sovereignty and to political independence should be fully respected and should not in any way be jeopardized by any military and paramilitary activities which were prohibited by the principles of international law. In fact, the situation in Nicaragua remained unchanged even after the indication of these provisional measures. In the *Burkina Faso/Mali Frontier Dispute* case (No. 14), presented to a Chamber by a special agreement of the parties in dispute on boundary issues, the Chamber responded, in 1986, in favour of the requests for provisional measures submitted separately by both states and ordered that no action that might affect the delimitation of boundaries and cease-fire agreements should be taken. The Court's Order is believed in this case of joint submission to have been observed by both parties. In the case concerning *Border and Transborder Armed Actions* between Nicaragua and Honduras (No. 16) a request by Nicaragua, in 1988, for provisional measures was withdrawn by the applicant state for some political reasons only ten days after it was filed in the Registry of the Court.

The 1990s

In three cases around 1990, requests for provisional measures were all rejected for one reason or another. In the *Arbitral Award* case (No. 17), the request of Guinea-Bissau for provisional measures requiring the parties, Guinea-Bissau and Senegal, to abstain in the disputed areas from any action of any kind during the whole duration of the main proceedings concerning the existence and validity of the 1989 Arbitral Award was rejected in 1990 for the reason that the alleged rights sought to be made the subject of provisional measures were not the subject of the proceedings before the Court on the merits of the case. In the case concerning *Passage through the Great Belt* (No. 18), which was brought unilaterally by Finland against Denmark, the Court declined, in 1991, to indicate the provisional measures requested by Finland whereby Denmark would have been required to refrain from continuing construction work on a bridge, so that the right to navigate through the Great Belt would not be infringed by that construction work during the pendency of the proceedings, as it took the view that pending a decision of the Court on the merits any negotiation between the parties with a view to achieving direct and friendly settlement was to be welcomed and that the circumstances were not such as to require provisional measures. In the *Lockerbie* case (No. 19A/B), Libya's request for provisional measures to the effect that the US and the UK should be enjoined from taking any action to compel Libya to surrender the accused individuals to any jurisdiction outside Libya was rejected by the Court in 1992 for the reason that, in accordance with article 103 of the UN Charter, the obligation of the parties to accept and carry out a decision of the Security Council should prevail over their obligations under the Montreal Convention, on which Libya attempted to base its own claim.

After these three successive cases during 1990–2 in which requests for provisional measures were dismissed, the Court, in a recent case concerning the *Application of the Genocide Convention*, brought in March 1993 by Bosnia–Herzegovina against Yugoslavia (Serbia and Montenegro) (No. 20), responded in April 1993 to a request for the indication of provisional measures by making an Order requiring the respondent state to take all measures to prevent commission of the crime of genocide. No real effect has been observed with respect to the Court's Order. With respect to a further request for provisional measures made by Bosnia and Herzegovina in July 1993, the Court reaffirmed in its Order of September 1993 the provisional measures indicated in its previous Order as mentioned above.

IS THE COURT'S JURISDICTION A PREREQUISITE OF THE INDICATION OF PROVISIONAL MEASURES?

A request for provisional measures serves to institute proceedings incidental to the main proceedings on the merits. One may therefore be led to wonder whether the jurisdiction of the Court is a prerequisite of the indication of provisional measures. This question did not arise to any particular extent during the period of the PCIJ since, in most of the cases before that Court, no objections concerning jurisdiction were raised by the respondent state, but the present Court has been confronted with this question on many occasions. The issue of a jurisdictional link in this context was first dealt with in the *Anglo-*

548

Iranian Oil Co. case (No. 7), in which the Court took the position, in 1951, that provisional measures could be indicated unless the Court obviously lacked jurisdiction, stating that 'it cannot be accepted *a priori* that a claim based on such a complaint falls completely outside the scope of international jurisdiction'.[1] In fact the Court found at the later jurisdictional stage, in 1952, that it lacked the requisite jurisdiction and the UK's application was accordingly dismissed.

Probably because of this precedent, the ICJ was inclined to adopt subsequently a somewhat more severe position in this respect, stating that the basis of the Court's jurisdiction would, *prima facie*, have to be founded. In the *Fisheries Jurisdiction* cases (No. 9A/B), the Court, finding that the 1971 exchange of letters between the UK and Germany, on the one side, and Iceland, on the other, appeared, *prima facie*, to afford a possible basis on which the jurisdiction of the Court might be founded, stated, in 1972, that it 'need not, before indicating [provisional measures], finally satisfy itself that it has jurisdiction on the merits of the case, yet it ought not to [indicate provisional measures] if the absence of jurisdiction on the merits is manifest'.[2] This approach was adopted by the Court in the *Nuclear Tests* case (No. 10A/B), in which it was stated, in 1973, that 'the Court need not, before indicating [provisional measures], finally satisfy itself that it has jurisdiction on the merits of the case, and yet ought not to indicate such measures unless the provisions invoked by the Applicant appeared, prima facie, to afford a basis on which the jurisdiction of the Court might be founded'.[3] It was also adopted in the *Aegean Sea Continental Shelf* case (No. 12) in which the Court observed, in 1974, that it 'is not called upon to decide any question of its jurisdiction to deal with the merits of the case . . . [and that] the decision given in these proceedings in no way prejudges any such question or any questions relating to the merits'.[4]

Since the end of the 1970s, the Court seems to have taken the position that a *prima facie* basis of jurisdiction is required. In the *Tehran Hostages* case (No. 13), the Court stated, in 1979, that it 'ought to indicate [provisional measures] only if the provisions invoked by the Applicant appear, prima facie, to afford a basis on which the jurisdiction of the Court might be founded'.[5] In the *Nicaragua/US* case (No. 15), the Court, in 1984, employed the same form of words as had previously been used in the *Nuclear Tests* cases, saying that 'it ought not to indicate such measures unless the provisions invoked by the Applicant appear, prima facie, to afford a basis on which the jurisdiction of

---

[1] ICJ Reports, 1951, p. 93.
[2] ICJ Reports, 1972, p. 15. [3] ICJ Reports, 1973, pp. 101, 137.
[4] ICJ Reports, 1974, p. 13. [5] ICJ Reports, 1979, p. 13.

the Court might be founded'.[6] A practically identical form of words was employed in 1993 in the *Application of the Genocide Convention* case (No. 20).[7] In those three cases, the Court granted the requests for provisional measures made by the applicant states, the US (against Iran), Nicaragua (against the US) and Bosnia–Herzegovina (against Yugoslavia (Serbia and Montenegro)), respectively. In a few other recent cases such as the Guinea Bissau/Senegal *Arbitral Award* case (No. 17) and the *Lockerbie* cases (No. 19A/B), in which the requests for provisional measures were dismissed, in 1990 and 1992 respectively, for reasons unrelated to the matter of the Court's jurisdiction, the Court seemed to require that the basis of jurisdiction should be, *prima facie*, afforded by the relevant provisions.

The statutory purpose of provisional measures is to protect the respective rights of the parties (see pp. 551–4 below). However, once indicated, they will result in constraints being placed upon the respondent state's possibilities of further action and tend therefore to protect the political interest of the applicant state at the expense of that of the respondent state. If provisional measures are granted on a weak basis of jurisdiction, this will lead to an abuse of the right of the applicant state not to have its interest endangered without due authority.[8] On the other hand, considering that the institution of provisional measures is almost essential to any judicial process and is required because of the imminent necessity of preventive action, and having regard to its interim nature, one cannot expect a request for such measures to be made only if or when the jurisdiction for proceeding on the merits of the dispute is firmly established.

Much subtlety has been deployed in the reasoning of judges concerning this requirement of *prima facie* jurisdiction. The matter came to a head in the *Nuclear Tests* case (No. 10A/B), when the Court was apparently divided among those members who viewed *prima facie* jurisdiction as manifestly

---

[6] ICJ Reports, 1984, p. 179.

[7] ICJ Reports, 1993, p. 11.

[8] It should be added that the terms 'applicant' and 'respondent' states are here used to refer respectively to the party applying for provisional measures and its opponent, which are not necessarily the respective applicant and respondent in the main proceedings. Indeed, in the case brought by special agreement between Burkina Faso and Mali, both states were applicants in the main proceedings, as well as both applicants and respondents to their overlapping requests for interim measures. It is noteworthy that requests for such measures tend to provoke counter-requests (ICJ Reports, 1986, p. 3), hence it cannot be presumed that only the state taking the initiative of instituting proceedings will feel the need of interim protection. This appears to be reflected in the Court's power to indicate measures *sua sponte*. It may further be noted that in the *Lockerbie* cases (No. 19A/B), Libya was in effect a respondent before the Security Council when it became an applicant before the Court; in fact, irrespective of its formal request for interim measures, its entire application can be construed as such a request directed against the Council.

present, those who considered it not manifestly absent, and those who believed (or also believed) that to grant that it existed with sufficient certainty to justify the indication of provisional measures would prejudice the expected discussion at the jurisdiction stage (which was never resolved) of the continuing validity and efficacy of the 1928 General Act cited by the applicants as the basis of jurisdiction. This is not the place to discuss this dilemma further. It may, however, be remarked that the great importance of the political issues at stake in this case undoubtedly weakened the position of those who argue that, since the possession of jurisdiction is not required by the Statute, it is not a condition which the Court may impose upon itself.

THE PURPOSE OF PROVISIONAL MEASURES

Preservation of rights exposed to imminent breach which is irreparable

The purpose of provisional measures is to preserve the rights of either party, and it is established in the jurisprudence (most clearly in the *Arbitral Award* case (No. 17)) that the rights in question are those to be confronted at the merits stage of the case, and which constitute or are directly engaged by the subject of the application. The urgency of the relevant action or inhibition is a prerequisite. The anticipated or actual breach of the rights to be preserved ought to be one that could not be erased by the payment of reparation or compensation to be ordered in a later judgment on the merits, and this irreparable prejudice must be imminent. These conditions have been regarded by the Court as the criteria by which it has determined its position in indicating or refusing to indicate provisional measures as requested by the applicant in each case.

In the following cases the requests were dismissed for the lack of these conditions. The request by Switzerland in the *Interhandel* case (No. 8) was dismissed on account of a lack of urgency of the relevant matters, as 'the sale of [the shares in the Swiss company that were possessed by the US government] can only be effected after the termination of a judicial proceeding which is at present pending in [the US]', while the US government was 'not taking action at the present time to fix a time schedule for the sale of such shares'.[9] The request by Greece for provisional measures in the *Aegean Sea Continental Shelf* case (No. 12) was rejected by the Court for the reason that the alleged breach by Turkey of the exclusivity of the right claimed by Greece to acquire information concerning the natural resources of areas of continental shelf was

---

[9] ICJ Reports, 1957, p. 112.

one that might be capable of reparation by appropriate means. In the *Passage through the Great Belt* case (No. 18), the Court dismissed the request of Finland for the reason that the right of Finland to navigate through the Great Belt would not be infringed by construction work to be undertaken by Denmark, which might not be completed during the pendency of the proceedings.

In contrast with these examples of dismissal of the request, the Court indicated provisional measures in the following cases which appeared to it to satisfy the required conditions as mentioned above. In the *Anglo-Iranian Oil Co.* case (No. 7), the Court accepted the contention of the UK that the confiscation of the company by the Iranian government could not be indemnified by the payment of reparation or compensation which might be indicated in the judgment to be delivered in the merits phase. The Court held, in the *Fisheries Jurisdiction* cases (No. 9A/B), that the immediate implementation by Iceland of its regulations concerning its 50-mile fishing jurisdiction would affect the possibility of their full restoration were a judgment eventually to be rendered in favour of the UK and Germany. In the *Nuclear Tests* case (No. 10A/B), the Court also found that the possibility could not be excluded that damage to Australia and New Zealand might be caused by the deposit on Australian and New Zealand territories of radioactive fall-out resulting from atmospheric tests and be irreparable, and indicated provisional measures to the effect, *inter alia*, that, pending judgment, France should avoid such tests.

Prevention of aggravation and extension of disputes

The question may be raised as to whether a request for provisional measures can be made even in order to avoid the aggravation and extension of a dispute. In the *Aegean Sea Continental Shelf* case (No. 12), while being requested to indicate provisional measures to the effect that the governments of both Greece and Turkey should 'refrain from taking further military measures or actions which may endanger their peaceful relations', the Court found, in 1976, that there was no need for it 'to decide the question of whether Article 41 of the Statute confers upon it the power to indicate provisional measures for the sole purpose of preventing the aggravation or extension of a dispute'.[10]

It seems, however, that the Court has become inclined to interpret article 41 of the Statute much more widely so as to cover cases in which the prevention of an aggravation or extension of the dispute is required or even

---

[10] ICJ Reports, 1976, p. 13.

where the status quo needs to be maintained, although it has not indicated provisional measures solely to that end. In fact, whenever provisional measures have been indicated, the Court has not failed to mention this element as one of the measures specified in the operative parts of each of the Orders. In the *Anglo-Iranian Oil Co.* case (No. 7), the *Fisheries Jurisdiction* cases (No. 9A/B) and the *Nuclear Tests* cases (No. 10A/B), the Court stated, in 1951, 1972 and 1973 respectively, that the parties in dispute should each 'ensure that no action of any kind is taken which might aggravate or extend the dispute submitted to the Court'.[11] In the *Tehran Hostages* case (No. 13), the Court stated, in 1979, that both the US and Iran 'should ensure that no action is taken which may aggravate the tension between the two countries or render the existing dispute more difficult of solution'.[12] Likewise, the Court stated in April 1993 in the *Application of the Genocide Convention* case (No. 20) that both governments 'should ensure that no action is taken which may aggravate or extend the existing dispute over the prevention or punishment of the crime of genocide, or render it more difficult of solution'.[13]

Requests for interim judgments

I must point out that the institution of provisional measures has greatly changed in nature over the past twenty years. Originally provisional measures were to be indicated as incidental proceedings in cases that themselves might not necessarily have to be dealt with as a matter of great urgency, in order to preserve the rights of parties exposed to an imminent breach which would not be reparable by the later judgment on the merits.

In fact, however, in recent cases, the actual matters to be considered during the merits phase have been made the object of the requested provisional measures. If we look at certain cases brought in the 1980s which were of a highly political nature, the applicant states appear to have aimed at obtaining interim judgments that would have affirmed their own rights and preshaped the main case. In the *Tehran Hostages* case (No. 13) the restoration of the premises of the US Embassy and the release of the American diplomats – the subject of the request for provisional measures – corresponded precisely to the object of the application made by the applicant state, the US. Also, in the *Nicaragua/US* case (No. 15), what Nicaragua asked the Court to indicate as provisional measures, i.e., the suspension of the blockade and cessation of

[11] ICJ Reports, 1951, p. 93; ICJ Reports, 1973, pp. 106, 142; ICJ Reports, 1974, pp. 17, 31.
[12] ICJ Reports, 1979, p. 21.
[13] ICJ Reports, 1993, p. 25.

military or paramilitary activities interfering with the sovereignty or political independence of Nicaragua, was the very object of the application instituting proceedings before the Court.

The requests for provisional measures in those cases appear to have tried to pre-empt the Court's judgment under some extraordinary circumstances, and the Court's Orders appear to have been close to a decision to pre-empt the eventual judgment on the merits. The Court, without waiting for the proceedings on the merits, appears to have taken the position that the case blatantly involved violations of international law on the part of the defendant state. As a member of the Court, I should refrain from making any comment on the provisional measures indicated in 1993 in the *Application of the Genocide Convention* case (No. 20). I would simply like to say that what was at issue in that case might not have been the preservation of the rights of Bosnia–Herzegovina under the Genocide Convention pending the judgment to be delivered, but that the Court had to dispose of the case unilaterally brought by Bosnia–Herzegovina as a matter of urgency, given that it concerned purported violations of that Convention.

There has been a recent trend for the Court to be tempted to deliver an interim judgment under the name of provisional measures and for such measures not to be observed in any effective manner. If the tendency is to be for the Court to arrive at a quick decision on matters relating to the merits, while reserving for the future other much more judicious considerations on the question of jurisdiction as well as the merits and avoiding any measure of responsibility in the event of a reverse judgment in the future, then the whole matter requires very careful consideration. If the dispute in question really requires an urgent solution, then that solution had better be found not via an incidental proceeding but by an expeditious deliberation on the merits. It is my view that proceedings on provisional measures must essentially constitute a type of proceeding *incidental to, not coincidental with*, the proceedings on the merits of such contentious disputes as fall within the jurisdiction of the Court. I personally have some doubt about whether the recent requests for provisional measures can really be regarded as falling within the scope of the institution as originally planned at the outset of the PCIJ and reintroduced in the Statute of the present Court.

THE EFFECTS OF PROVISIONAL MEASURES

Whether the provisional measures indicated by the Court are binding on the parties in dispute has been argued ever since the tentative word 'indicate' was introduced into the Statute of the PCIJ. The affirmative position has been argued from the standpoint that provisional measures are given in the form of an 'Order' of the Court. Conversely, it has been asserted that such measures are simply 'indicated' by the Court,[14] i.e., that there is no iron fist inside the velvet glove. The Court has never taken an overt position in this respect but, as a matter of principle, the Court's 'Order' ought to be properly observed. In this connection, I should mention that notice of measures has to be given to the Security Council (Statute, Article 41(2)).

It seems to me, however, that this question may be argued from a different angle. If the later judgment on the merits is rendered in favour of the applicant state, the respondent state may be made responsible for any action taken in defiance of the provisional measures. On the other hand, the question arises whether an applicant state, which has been granted provisional measures but subsequently loses the proceedings on jurisdiction so that the application is dismissed (as in the *Anglo-Iranian Oil Co.* case (No. 7)) or loses the case on the merits (for which there is no precedent), should be considered liable for such losses as the respondent state or states may have borne through having complied with the provisional measures. It may be interesting as a hypothetical exercise to consider these problems on the assumption that, in the *Passage through the Great Belt* case (No. 18), the Court had ordered the suspension of the construction of the bridge in response to the request made by Finland.

In fact there has not been any precedent in which the Court gave a judgment against an applicant state in favour of the respondent state after having made an Order indicating provisional measures at the request of that same applicant state. The fact is that the provisional measures indicated by the Court in the past have usually not been implemented by the respondent state. Apart from the *Nuclear Tests* cases (No. 10A/B) which became moot, in the *Anglo-Iranian Oil Co.* case (No. 7), the *Fisheries Jurisdiction* cases (No. 9A/B) and the *Tehran Hostages* case (No. 13), the respondents did not participate in the proceedings and did not observe the provisional measures indicated by the Court. In the *Nicaragua/US* case (No. 15) in which the respondent state was represented in the proceedings for provisional measures, it did not seem to comply fully with the Court's Order, although there was no open act of defiance on its part. In the *Application of the Genocide Convention* case (No. 20), the respondent state was represented in the proceedings but is not noted to have made any explicit attempt to comply with the Court's Order indicating the provisional measures, though it must be realized that to have done so

---

[14] See Mr Anzilotti's observation at the 34th meeting of PCIJ (10 February 1931): PCIJ, Series D, second addendum to No. 2, pp. 182–3.

would have been inconsistent with its claim of lack of responsibility for the acts complained of.

The issues in each case in which the request was granted were not actually brought to a final settlement – even by the judgments on the merits which followed the Court's indication of provisional measures. The dispute in the *Fisheries Jurisdiction* case (No. 9A/B) disappeared with the emergence of the 200-mile fisheries zone as a new law of the sea. The *Nuclear Tests* case ceased to exist as France announced that it would not be continuing with nuclear testing. The *Tehran Hostages* case (No. 20) came to an end (being withdrawn) only through some means other than the judicial settlement of the Court, in other words through the mediation of Algeria (involving *inter alia* the establishment of the Iran–US Claims Tribunal). I do not need to repeat the outcome of the Court's Order in the *Application of the Genocide Convention* case referred to in the above paragraph. It is not going too far to state that the provisional measures indicated by the Court have had hardly any practical effect in most cases of a highly charged political nature.

30

Remedies in the
International Court of Justice

Ian Brownlie

ৎৡ

THE TOPIC

The remedies available in the International Court are a subject generally neglected in the literature of the law.[1] The textbooks include a section of 'modes of reparation' but, of course, this is a related but different area of inquiry. This general neglect is difficult to explain. It cannot be laid at the door of civil law training because writers with a common law background show the same trait.

The principal purpose of this chapter in honour of my friend Sir Robert Jennings[2] is to review the forms of judicial relief available. Familiar keywords will be employed in spite of the fact that such keywords may prove to be question-begging and freighted with unreliable implications. The familiar headings of declaratory judgments, actions for damages, and *restitutio in integrum* will therefore be used.

THE REMEDIAL COMPETENCE OF THE COURT

The competence of the Court to indicate remedies is based on article 36 of the Statute which indicates 'the jurisdiction of the Court in all legal disputes concerning: . . . (d) the nature and extent of the reparation to be made for the breach of an international obligation', in cases of compulsory jurisdiction by virtue of paragraph 2.[3] No doubt the Court was expected to follow the

---

[1] For an exception, see Christine Gray, *Judicial Remedies in International Law* (Oxford, 1987), pp. 59–119.

[2] In the academic year 1955–6, the writer held a Humanitarian Trust Studentship in Cambridge. Professor Jennings, the newly elected holder of the Whewell Chair, acted as my supervisor. During his tenure of the Senior Editorship of the *British Year Book*, 1974 to 1981, the writer was co-editor.

[3] See further Gray, *Judicial Remedies*, pp. 59–69.

practice of courts of arbitration in presuming a power to award damages and, apart from special agreement cases, the power of the Court to award damages has gone unquestioned.

In other respects the Court has had to make its own way because the formulation in article 36 provides no express guidance in respect of declaratory judgments, specific performance and injunctive relief. It is precisely in the remedial sphere that the Court has applied general principles of procedural law. The creative process has been pragmatic, unselfconscious, and somewhat unreflective. The results have been practically useful but rather cryptic in terms of formulation. In practice the parties have avoided raising issues of competence in relation to forms of judicial relief, except in certain proceedings based on compromissory clauses. When issues of competence have been the subject of argument, both the Permanent Court and its successor have tended to take a robust line. Thus the Permanent Court rejected an argument that a jurisdictional clause referring to 'differences of opinion resulting from the interpretation and the application of' certain treaty provisions did not include claims for reparation.[4]

CONNECTED QUESTIONS

The question of remedies extends beyond the topic of the forms of judicial relief available to include matters that are, practically speaking, cognate. Such matters include the question of *res judicata*,[5] the limits of the judicial function in face of a request to the Court to indicate how a judgment should be carried out,[6] and the process by which the Court should determine the object of the claim.[7]

The 'incidental proceedings' provided for in the Rules of Court also have a remedial role. This is particularly true of intervention, where advantages may be obtained both as a consequence of the grant of permission to intervene,[8] and also as a consequence of the pleadings pertaining to a request for permission to intervene which is refused, when the Court is nonetheless informed of the form and geographical extent of the requesting state's legal

---

[4] *Chorzow Factory (Jurisdiction)* case, PCIJ, Series A, No. 9, p. 21. See further Gray, *Judicial Remedies*, pp. 59–64.

[5] See Gerald Fitzmaurice, *The Law and Procedure of the International Court of Justice* (Cambridge, 1986), vol. II, pp. 584–6.

[6] *Ibid.*, pp. 555–8.

[7] *Nuclear Tests (Australia v. France)*, ICJ Reports, 1974, p. 253.

[8] *Case Concerning the Land, Island and Maritime Dispute (El Salvador/Honduras, Nicaragua intervening)*, ICJ Reports, 1992, p. 351.

interest and acts upon such data during the merits phase.[9] It is also true of interim measures. In formal terms, a request for the indication of interim measures of protection may appear to have a peripheral and highly contingent role. In practical terms the requesting state can present cogent documentary evidence, and especially if the oral proceedings receive substantial media attention, very useful affirmations of wrongs endured and impending may be made and a wrongdoer effectively exposed. By the same token requests should not be raised without careful consideration, and an unsuccessful request may produce adverse effects.

DECLARATORY JUDGMENTS

This category is in general use and, though convenient, is unreliable. A useful starting-point is the relevant part of the Court's judgment in the *Northern Cameroons* case:[10]

> Throughout these proceedings the contention of the Republic of Cameroon has been that all it seeks is a declaratory judgment of the Court that prior to the termination of the Trusteeship Agreement with respect to the Northern Cameroons, the United Kingdom had breached the provisions of the Agreement, and that, if its Application were admissible and the Court had jurisdiction to proceed to the merits, such a declaratory judgment is not only one the Court could make but one that it should make.
>
> That the Court may, in an appropriate case, make a declaratory judgment is indisputable. The Court has, however, already indicated that even if, when seised of an Application, the Court finds that it has jurisdiction, it is not obliged to exercise it in all cases. If the Court is satisfied, whatever the nature of the relief claimed, that to adjudicate on the merits of an Application would be inconsistent with its judicial function, it should refuse to do so.
>
> Moreover the Court observes that if in a declaratory judgment it expounds a rule of customary law or interprets a treaty which remains in force, its judgment has a continuing applicability. But in this case there is a dispute about the interpretation and application of a treaty – the Trusteeship Agreement – which has now been terminated, is no longer in force, and there can be no opportunity for a future act of interpretation or application of that treaty in accordance with any judgment the Court might render.
>
> In its *Interpretation of Judgments Nos. 7 and 8 (the Chorzow Factory)* (P.C.I.J., Series A, No. 13, p. 20), the Court said:

---

[9] *Case Concerning the Continental Shelf* (Request for Permission to Intervene), ICJ Reports, 1985, p. 25, para. 41; ICJ Reports, 1985, pp. 24–8, paras. 20–3.

[10] ICJ Reports, 1963, pp. 36–7.

> The Court's Judgment No. 7 is in the nature of a declaratory judgment, the intention of which is to ensure recognition of a situation at law, once and for all and with binding force as between the Parties; so that the legal position thus established cannot again be called in question in so far as the legal effects ensuing therefrom are concerned.

The Court here affirms its competence to make a declaratory judgment and the main point of the decision otherwise is to indicate certain limits to the judicial function, which limits are described by Fitzmaurice as 'the question of judicial propriety'.[11]

The distinguishing characteristic upon which the Court appears to rely is that a declaration should have a 'forward reach'.

The difficulty is that the writers prefer to segregate the 'declaratory judgment' from other remedial forms and are tempted to rely on the difference between a request for a declaration and a claim for damages, or a claim for specific performance. It may be doubted whether this segregation and the distinction it implies can be justified.

There are no problems of form and, as will be shown in due course, the category of declaratory judgments is very diverse in content. Even when an award of damages, or an order for restitution, is made, this is premissed upon a finding of legal entitlement. The provisions of article 36 involve a broad mandate for the Court to resolve 'legal disputes' and all judgments are declaratory of the existence of international obligations or of other forms of legal entitlements or of the absence of legal justification (state responsibility).

It follows that there is no useful purpose in seeking to separate out a category of 'declaratory judgments'. The essential question is to determine the limits to the judicial function. This view is reinforced when consideration is given to the variety of remedial forms sheltering under the umbrella of the declaratory judgment.

The declaratory judgment as a first stage in proceedings

In the *Case Concerning Certain Phosphate Lands in Nauru*,[12] Nauru requested the Court 'to adjudge and declare that the Respondent State bears responsibility for breaches of the following obligations', and, finally, 'to adjudge and declare that the Respondent State is under a legal duty to make appropriate reparation in respect of the loss caused to the Republic of Nauru as a result of the breaches of its legal obligations detailed above'. The application did not

<hr>

[11] *Ibid.*, pp. 100–8 (Separate Opinion).
[12] *Nauru v. Australia (Preliminary Objections)*, ICJ Reports, 1992, p. 240.

request the Court to proceed to an assessment of damages. Thus the finding on liability, assuming it were favourable, would provide a juncture at which negotiations would provide an appropriate option. A similar two-stage proceeding resulted from the judgment on the merits in the *Corfu Channel* case, in which the Court, having made a declaration as to Albania's responsibility, reserved the question of the amount of compensation.[13] The Albanian contention that the Court lacked jurisdiction with respect to the assessment of compensation was rejected in subsequent proceedings.[14] The *Corfu Channel* case was, it may be recalled, founded upon a Special Agreement.

A declaration of some form of legal entitlement

An important mode of declaration relates to the legal entitlement of the parties in their mutual relations. In the *Anglo-Norwegian Fisheries* case the Court found 'that the method employed for the delimitation of the fisheries zone by the Norwegian Decree of July 12th, 1935, is not contrary to international law'.[15] In the *Temple* case (*Merits*) the Court found 'that the Temple of Preah Vihear is situated in territory under the sovereignty of Cambodia'.[16] In such cases the primary objective is the issue of entitlement, and determinations as to the legality of the conduct of the parties are either not requested or are otherwise marginalized. In the *Fisheries* case the application included a claim for damages for illegal interferences with fishing vessels, but this was laid aside during the oral proceedings.

A declaration that certain conduct is contrary to international law

The Court has on several important occasions been asked to give a declaration of the illegality of specific conduct of the respondent state, not simply as a basis for an *ex post* finding of state responsibility, but as a categorical issue, that is, the legality or not of a particular type of activity. At least in the view of the joint Dissenting Opinion in the *Nuclear Tests* cases, the Australian application and submissions involved a request for a declaration of the illegality of France's atmospheric nuclear weapons tests.[17] In the case of *Nicaragua v. United States* (*Merits*), the Court made a series of decisions to the effect that certain actions

---

[13] ICJ Reports, 1949, p. 36.

[14] *Ibid.*, p. 248. The Court relied upon article 60.

[15] ICJ Reports, 1951, p. 143.

[16] ICJ Reports, 1962, p. 36. See also the case concerning the *Land, Island and Maritime Frontier Dispute*, ICJ Reports, 1992, p. 351, at pp. 610–17.

[17] ICJ Reports, 1974, p. 63, at p. 319 (*Australia v. France*); *ibid.*, p. 494, at p. 501 (*New Zealand v. France*).

of the United States constituted breaches of various obligations under customary international law, or in some cases breaches of the Treaty of Friendship, Commerce and Navigation.[18] The Court also decided that the US was under an obligation to make reparation for all injury caused to Nicaragua by the breaches of the obligations previously elaborated. An additional finding of particular interest was the following paragraph in the *dispositif*: 'The Court . . . *rejects* the justification of collective self-defence maintained by the United States of America in connection with the military and paramilitary activities in and against Nicaragua the subject of this case.'

There is no reason to see any qualitative distinction between this type of declaratory judgment and the previous group relating to legal entitlements. Both types satisfy the criterion indicated by the Permanent Court[19] according to which a declaratory judgment was designed 'to ensure recognition of a situation at law, once and for all, and with binding force as between the Parties; so that the legal position thus established cannot again be called in question in so far as the legal effects ensuing therefrom are concerned'.

A declaration that specific acts of implementation of a decision are required

In three cases the Court has responded to requests in applications by requiring the respondent state to perform specific acts or refrain from specific conduct as a consequence of the findings as to the legal entitlements of the applicant. Thus in the *Temple* case (*Merits*)[20] the *dispositif* is as follows:

> The Court, by nine votes to three, finds that the Temple of Preah Vihear is situated in territory under the sovereignty of Cambodia;
> finds in consequence, by nine votes to three,
> that Thailand is under an obligation to withdraw any military or police forces, or other guards or keepers, stationed by her at the Temple, or in its vicinity on Cambodian territory;
> by seven votes to five,
> that Thailand is under an obligation to restore to Cambodia any objects of the kind specified in Cambodia's fifth submission which may, since the date of the occupation of the Temple by Thailand in 1954, have been removed from the Temple or the Temple area by the Thai authorities.

---

[18] ICJ Reports, 1986, pp. 146–8.

[19] *Chorzow Factory* case (*Merits*), PCIJ, Series A, No. 13, p. 20; quoted in the joint Dissenting Opinion, *Nuclear Tests* cases, ICJ Reports, 1974, p. 139 (*Australia v. France*); ibid., p. 501 (*New Zealand v. France*).

[20] ICJ Reports, 1962, pp. 36–7.

Similar orders were made by the Court in the *Tehran Hostages*[21] and *Nicaragua*[22] cases. In the latter, the Court decided 'that the United States of America is under a duty immediately to cease and to refrain from all such acts as may constitute breaches of the foregoing legal obligations' (by twelve votes to three).

This 'preventive' role is sometimes seen as the specific function of declaratory judgments.[23] Gray is of the opinion that declarations of this type are radical in some way, at least in the context of the competence of the Court.[24] The present writer is unable to discern any significant difference between this mode of declaration and the other types examined above. The form depends on the requests of the parties in the application. The substance of the matter is that a judgment is binding and the performance required is the consequence of the decision on entitlement.

The declaration as a form of satisfaction

In the *Corfu Channel* case (*Merits*) the Court found that the action of the British Navy on 12/13 November 1946, the mine-collecting operation, 'constituted a violation of Albanian sovereignty'. As a consequence the Court stated:[25] 'This declaration is in accordance with the request made by Albania through her Counsel, and is in itself appropriate satisfaction.'

This finding has been criticized on not very substantial grounds by Charles De Visscher.[26] However, it appears to qualify as a declaratory judgment and the Court, as is its custom, was responding to the request of the party concerned in the matter of remedies.

The declaration of the applicable principles and rules of international law

In the *North Sea Continental Shelf* cases the Special Agreements requested the Court to decide the question:[27] 'What principles and rules of international law are applicable to the delimitation as between the Parties of the areas of the

[21] ICJ Reports, 1980, pp. 44–5.

[22] ICJ Reports, 1986, p. 149.

[23] Charles De Visscher, *Aspects récents du droit procédural de la Cour Internationale de Justice* (Paris, 1966), p. 187.

[24] Gray, *Judicial Remedies*, pp. 64–8.

[25] ICJ Reports, 1949, p. 35. The issue is not referred to in the *dispositif*.

[26] De Visscher, *Aspects récents*, pp. 190–1.

[27] ICJ Reports, 1969, p. 6.

continental shelf in the North Sea which appertain to each of them beyond the partial boundary determined by the above-mentioned Convention of 1 December 1964?'

The Court had no difficulty in dealing with this case. Although fears have at times been expressed that a readiness to give relatively abstract declaratory judgments might lead to the contentious jurisdiction being used by states to obtain Advisory Opinions,[28] the judicial function in the *North Sea* cases was related in several practical ways to the resolution of specific disputes. This is evident from the terms of article 1(2) of the two Special Agreements: 'The Governments [the respective parties] shall delimit the continental shelf in the North Sea as between their countries by agreement in pursuance of the decision requested from the International Court of Justice.'

Declaratory judgments in such cases are closely related to the ascertainment of the legal entitlements of the parties and involve a legitimate and constructive exercise of the judicial function.

CLAIMS FOR DAMAGES

The question that presents itself at this stage is: to what extent, if at all, is the declaratory judgment distinct from judgments involving the award of damages?[29] In all essentials, the answer must be in the negative. The element of compensation, whether this itself is in the form of a declaration that there is an obligation to make reparation, or in the form of a separate phase of the proceedings for the assessment of compensation, is contingent upon a declaration of a legal entitlement of some kind.

It may be recalled that in *Nicaragua v. United States*[30] the applicant state had included in its submissions a request that the Court make an interim award of damages. The Court did not accede to this request, but did not deny the existence of a competence to give such awards.

RESTITUTIO IN INTEGRUM

It is doubtful whether this is a separate category any more than claims for damages. In appropriate cases the applicant state will request restitution in kind, and if the Court has jurisdiction over the subject matter, and the

---

[28] Hersch Lauterpacht, *The Development of International Law by the International Court* (London, 1958), pp. 250–1.

[29] Cf. Gray, *Judicial Remedies*, pp. 96–7.

[30] ICJ Reports, 1986, p. 143, para. 285.

relevant legal principles point to restitution or specific performance, then such orders will be consequential upon the finding of a legal entitlement. Such orders were made in the *Temple*,[31] *Tehran Hostages*[32] and *Nicaragua*[33] cases. Whether such orders are made depends closely on the nature of the requests of the parties. If *restitutio in integrum* is not a separate remedy but the natural result of certain forms of request for a declaratory judgment, the question of the competence of the Court to give specific performance does not arise, apart from cases based on compromissory clauses.[34]

CAUSES OF ACTION: MULTIPLE COMPLAINTS

In his General Course at the Hague Academy in 1967,[35] Jennings pointed to the significance of the selection of causes of action. This significance can be seen in the case of *Nicaragua v. United States*.[36] An early version of Nicaragua's application based exclusively on multilateral treaties as to the merits would have been sunk by the multilateral treaty reservation in the US Declaration under the Optional Clause, and indeed the causes of action based on multilateral treaties were ruled out.[37] The application as presented to the Registry contained a useful and effective array of causes of action based on customary international law which escaped the reservation and which provided multiple characterizations of the activities of which Nicaragua complained.

The definition of 'the precise nature of the claim' is required by the Rules of Court (article 38(2)), and the use of multiple causes of action may be warranted by the circumstances. However, there may be issues of judicial policy if causes of action appear to overlap. Thus, in the *Nicaragua* case in a Dissenting Opinion Jennings adopted the position that the Charter prohibition on the use of force was identical with the relevant principle of customary law.[38] In the context this was a question going to jurisdiction, but it is possible that similar questions might arise in relation to the award of damages in relation to similar or overlapping causes of action.

---

[31] ICJ Reports, 1962, pp. 36–7.
[32] ICJ Reports, 1980, pp. 44–5.
[33] ICJ Reports, 1986, p. 149.
[34] Cf. Gray, *Judicial Remedies*, pp. 64–6, 95–6, where the issue of competence is considered to be problematical.
[35] *Recueil des cours*, 127 (1967), p. 507. See also the present writer, *System of the Law of Nations: State Responsibility*, part I (Oxford, 1983), pp. 53–88.
[36] ICJ Reports, 1986, p. 14.
[37] *Ibid.*, pp. 29–38, paras. 37–56.
[38] *Ibid.*, pp. 529–34; and see also his views on the principle of non-intervention, *ibid.*, pp. 534–6. The Court's view appears at p. 38, para. 56.

FINALE

By way of conclusion, it may be observed that there is no great profit in seeking to erect internal partitions within the sphere of judicial remedies. The distinctions between declaratory judgments, actions for damages, and *restitutio in integrum* involve operational variations stemming from the requests of applicant states and the circumstances of each case. The more profitable and difficult areas involve the outer boundaries of justiciability and judicial propriety. Another area, still little explored, concerns the nature of the links between causes of action and the assessment of compensation. This question may emerge when a proceeding is based on an acceptance of liability and is therefore devoted exclusively to the assessment of damages. The difficulty that then arises is this. In the case of intentional wrongs the heads of loss and the approach to causation should in principle be different from ordinary cases of objective responsibility or *culpa*. If the wrongs themselves have not been identified, the Court will have to construct the liability picture in its own way.[39]

---

[39] Problems of this kind arose during the arguments in the Arbitration between *Stichting Greenpeace Council v. The French State* (1987). The Award, dated 30 September 1987, has not been published.

31

A comment on the current health of Advisory Opinions

Rosalyn Higgins

෮

It is appropriate, in a book of essays to mark Judge Sir Robert Jennings's eightieth birthday and the fiftieth anniversary of the Court, to take stock of the state of health of the Advisory Opinion. As this volume goes to press there are several matters relating to Advisory Opinions under consideration in the United Nations. There is debate as to whether the Secretary-General should be given authorization under article 96(2) of the Charter to request an Advisory Opinion. And there is discussion of the Court's future role in reviewing judgments of international Administrative Tribunals. The Court itself has been asked to give two new Advisory Opinions. And this will place under scrutiny the meaning of 'legal questions arising within the scope of their activities' in article 96(2) and 'any legal question' under article 96(1). But these interesting current matters should properly be seen against a background of the status of Advisory Opinions in the work of the Court.

The Advisory Opinion has from the outset been associated with a recurrent range of problems – certain technical and political problems concerning the request for, and the giving of, the Opinion. These difficulties have, over the years, attracted as much attention as the content of the Opinion itself. There has been different emphasis on different elements during the life of the Permanent Court[1] and the International Court; but the constancy of troublesome themes is undeniable. We may single out the following:[2] the

---

[1] From 1922 to 1940 the Permanent Court of International Justice gave twenty-seven Advisory Opinions. For discussion, see D. Negulesco, 'L'evolution de la procedure des avis consultatifs de la Cour Permanente de Justice Internationale', *Recueil des cours*, 57, 3 (1936), pp. 1–96; C. De Visscher, 'Les avis consultatifs de la Cour Permanente de Justice International', *Hague Recueil*, 26 (1929), pp. 23ff; M. Pomerance, *The Advisory Function of the International Court in the League and United Nations Eras* (Baltimore, 1973); S. Schwebel, 'Was the Capacity to Request an Advisory Opinion Wider in the Permanent Court of International Justice than it is in the International Court of Justice?', *BYbIL*, 62 (1991), 77.

[2] Each of these themes, and more, is addressed in the leading books on Advisory Opinions. See K. Keith, *The extent of the Advisory Jurisdiction of the International Court of Justice* (Leyden, 1971); M. Pomerance, *The*

discretionary nature of the advisory jurisdiction; the distinction between legal and political questions[3] (especially against the background of a discretion to refuse to give an Opinion); the uncertain legal effect of Advisory Opinions;[4] the difficult relationship between advice sought by a UN organ and a dispute existing between states, or between the Organization and a state;[5] the implications of the assimilation of the advisory procedure to that for contentious cases, including questions concerning the equality of parties and *ad hoc* judges;[6] the implications of the different wording of article 96(1) and article 96(2) on the question to be asked; the question of whether there is any limit to article 96(1); the desirability or otherwise of expanding the list of those bodies or organs so far authorized under article 96(2);[7] and the desirability or otherwise of the Advisory Opinion as review of the judgments of international Administrative Tribunals.[8]

It has to be said that, while the Court's jurisprudence has necessarily begun to develop answers to many of these problems, few of them (save perhaps for the legal–political debate) are finally resolved. Some of them are beyond the reach of the Court to resolve. Certain issues continue to absorb the UN at present: the desirability or otherwise of extending to the Secretary-General the authority to seek an Advisory Opinion; the question of Advisory Opinions on Administrative Tribunal decisions; and the question of whether article 96(1) permits the asking of any legal question whatever. This short chapter will make some comments on these matters. But its underlying theme is that they cannot be answered in isolation, but only by locating them in the

---

Advisory Function of the International Court; D. Pratap, *The Advisory Jurisdiction of the International Court* (Oxford, 1972); S. Rosenne, *The Law and Practice of the International Court* (2nd edn, Dordrecht, 1985).

[3] T. Elias, 'How the International Court deals with Requests for Advisory Opinions', in Jerzy Makarczyk (ed.), *Essays in International Law in Honour of Judge Manfred Lachs* (The Hague, 1984), at p. 355; B. Sloan, 'Advisory Jurisdiction of the International Court of Justice', *Calif. Law Rev.*, 38 (1950), p. 830.

[4] S. Rosenne, *The World Court: What It Is And How It Works* (4th edn, Dordrecht, 1989); R. Ago, '"Binding" Advisory Opinions of the International Court of Justice', *AJIL*, 85 (1971), p. 439; E. Hambro, 'The Authority of the Advisory Opinions of the International Court of Justice', *ICLQ*, 3 (1954), p. 2.

[5] D. Grieg, 'The Advisory Jurisdiction of the International Court and the Settlement of Disputes between States', *ICLQ*, 15 (1966), p. 325.

[6] T. Sugihara, 'The Advisory Function of the International Court of Justice', *Japanese Annual of International Law*, 18 (1974), p. 23.

[7] J. de Arechaga, 'The Participation of International Organisations in Advisory Proceedings before the International Court of Justice', *Comunicazioni e Studi*, 14 (1975), p. 411; S. Schwebel, 'Authorizing the Secretary-General of the United Nations to Request Advisory Opinions of the International Court of Justice', *AJIL*, 78 (1984), p. 869.

[8] R. Ostrihansky, 'Advisory Opinions of the International Court of Justice as Reviews of Judgments of International Administrative Tribunals', *Polish Yearbook of International Law*, 17 (1988), p. 101.

much wider list of problems associated with Advisory Opinions, for every answer that one gives to one question has implications for another.

The recent suggestion by the Secretary-General that he be authorized to request Advisory Opinions is not new. That request has been intermittently made since the early years of the UN. It is well known that in 1950 the Secretary-General prepared a report on the Human Rights Committee to be established under the International Covenant for Civil and Political Rights, and addressed the possibility that it might be authorized to request an Advisory Opinion. He concluded, correctly, that as the Human Rights Committee would be a treaty body, and not an organ of the UN or a Specialized Agency, it could not be so authorized by the General Assembly under article 96. He proposed rather that the Secretary-General be so authorized – and that he be entrusted by the General Assembly 'with the function of considering suggestions of the Human Rights Committee in regard to requests for Advisory Opinions arising out of that Committee's work. Pursuant to this, the General Assembly could then extend an authorisation to the Secretary General under article 96(2).'[9]

The issue had already arisen as to whether the Commission on Human Rights should become an authorized organ under article 96(2) – this body, unlike the Committee on Human Rights, is undoubtedly a subsidiary organ of the UN. Here, too, the Secretary-General suggested that he should be substituted, as principal organ, to deal with all requests from the Commission.[10] Judge Schwebel recalls in his article supporting the extension of authorization to the Secretary-General[11] that in 1955 the Secretary-General again took the opportunity to remind the General Assembly that it could 'authorise the Secretary-General who is the head of a principal organ of the United Nations, to request Advisory Opinions on legal questions concerning Administrative Tribunal Judgments'.[12] These suggestions were not accepted.

The idea has since been kept alive by occasional references in various Annual Reports of the Secretary-General,[13] and was specifically referred to in paragraph 38 of the celebrated Agenda for Peace.[14]

Accordingly – and especially in the light of the impact of Agenda for Peace

---

[9] UN Doc. E/1732 (26 June 1950), at p. 7.

[10] See G. Elian, *The International Court of Justice* (Leyden, 1971), at pp. 75–6; Schwebel, 'Authorizing the Secretary-General of the United Nations to Request Advisory Opinions', p. 860.

[11] 'Authorizing the Secretary-General of the United Nations to Request Advisory Opinions', at p. 871.

[12] Judicial Review of United Nations Administrative Tribunal Judgments, working paper submitted by the Secretary-General, UN Doc. A/AC.78/L.1 and Corr.1 (1955).

[13] E.g. UN Doc. A/45/1, part III (16 September 1990), p. 7; A/46/1 (16 September 1991).

[14] A/47/277; S/24111 (17 June 1992).

and the acknowledged need to review existing practices and structures at the end of the cold war – the matter has again been receiving serious attention. The topic has fallen for special consideration by the Special Committee on the Charter of the United Nations and on the Strengthening of the Role of the Organization ('the Charter Committee'). There is an interesting detailed examination in the 1992 report of the Charter Committee. The Secretary-General's proposal, in its revised formulation, had moved away from the early idea of a 'facilitator' for more lowly organs to ask for Advisory Opinions. The new focus was on peace and security considerations, and the role of both the International Court and the Secretary-General in relation thereto. Agenda for Peace had made various suggestions about the better use of the International Court and the contribution that that could make to international peace. In that context, attention was again drawn to the possibilities afforded by Advisory Opinions. And the Secretary-General, in turn, proposed that he be authorized to request Advisory Opinions from the International Court. His statements have, since 1991, focused on the peace and security purposes of such a proposal. In so doing, he was building on and expanding a request from the General Assembly in 1988 that the Security Council use its powers under article 96(1) 'for promoting the prevention and removal of disputes' through requesting Advisory Opinions.[15]

The proposals relating to the Secretary-General's proposed powers under article 96(2) have thus become inextricably tied with the question of the use of Advisory Opinions to 'settle disputes'. We are here speaking of dispute settlement in an immediate rather than long-term sense, i.e. recourse to Advisory Opinions to assist in the resolution of specific disputes existing between identified parties – and not just the general contribution to peace of all legal views that emanate from the Court. The reaction of states to the proposal has been somewhat mixed. It has had a surprisingly good reception from the Court itself, notwithstanding that the relationship between Advisory Opinions and existing disputes has been one of the most problematic areas for the Court over the years. Sir Robert Jennings, then President of the Court, addressed this topic in his comments to the Sixth Committee in 1992. He observed that the advisory procedure could be usefully employed to clarify the legal aspects of a dispute. But he envisaged that the states concerned would have to agree.[16] The topic has been addressed in scholarly detail by the current President of the Court, Judge Mohammed Bedjaoui, in his contribution, 'Les Ressources Offerts par la Fonction Consultative de la Cour Internationale de

---

15 General Assembly resolution 43/51, para. 15 (15 December 1988).
16 See *ICJ Yearbook 1991–1992*, 46, pp. 204–10.

Justice: bilan et perspectives', to the UN Congress on Public International Law in March 1995.

The Court has had in several of its Advisory Opinions to see whether it is precluded, as a matter of law or discretion, from answering a question from an authorized organ on a matter claimed to be the subject matter of an existing dispute between states or between states and the UN. The early *South-West Africa* case (1950), the *Expenses* case (1962), the *Western Sahara* case (1975), the case concerning the *Interpretation of the Agreement of 25 March 1951 between the WHO and Egypt* (1980) and the *Mazilu* case (1989) afford well-known examples. In each of these cases states claimed that the Advisory Opinion would be used to pronounce upon their rights when they were not parties to contentious litigation before the Court. They insisted that the request for an Opinion should be declined.

The Court has not taken this view, and has not accepted that, by giving an Opinion in such circumstances, it would be violating the principle in the *Eastern Carelia* case, whereby Opinions may not be used 'for circumventing the principle that a state is not obliged to allow its disputes to be submitted to judicial settlement without its consent'.[17] The Court has done this, essentially, by emphasizing in each case that a UN organ[18] needed legal advice in order to know how to conduct its business. The Court did not deny the parallel existence of an interstate dispute, or a dispute between the state(s) and the UN, but said that it was not asked to determine that dispute. From the early years, the implication has been that a state member of the UN must be prepared to bear the risk of the Court fulfilling its advisory function in these circumstances, and that this was a differentiating factor from the *Eastern Carelia* case.[19] The Court seemed to have attempted a further gloss of this doctrine in the *Mazilu* case, where it sought to make a distinction between the abstract applicability of the UN Convention on Privileges and Immunities of 1946 and its actual application in the specific case, asserting that it was only engaged in the former task.[20] This seems both unnecessary and unpersuasive – but the Court's perceived need to go this extra step illustrates the underlying difficulties of the Advisory Opinion–dispute relationship.

---

[17] PCIJ, Series B, No. 5 (1923).

[18] Whether the requesting organ or not: thus in the *Mazilu* case the advice was needed by the sub-commission of the Commission on Human Rights – not itself an authorized body under article 96(2). The request was made by the General Assembly.

[19] A further complex issue is the parallel – and not always very consistent – jurisprudence that the Court has developed on the position of third parties in international litigation. This in turn has had implications for the provisions for third-party intervention under the Rules of Procedure.

[20] *Applicability of Article VI, Section 22 of the Convention on the Privileges and Immunities of the United Nations*, ICJ Reports, 1989, p. 177, at p. 191.

We must now ask how the reformulated proposal for authorizing a request from the Secretary-General, to assist in the resolution of disputes, fits into this picture. The General Assembly and Security Council can already request Opinions even where states are engaged in disputes, provided that there are legal questions for the Court to answer concerning the functioning of a UN organ. What would an authorization by the Secretary-General add? The implication must be that considerations of peace and security require that the Secretary-General be allowed to request an Opinion even when there is no question arising for the Court about the functioning of the Secretariat (or other organ). In other words, exactly contrary to the distinction made by the Court in the *Mazilu* case, the Court would overtly deal with the very substance of the dispute. And that is what is apparently envisaged by Sir Robert Jennings in his statements to the Sixth Committee in 1991.

If that is so – that is to say, the Secretary-General would request an Advisory Opinion having previously received the consent of the states concerned – then this is tantamount to states being able to ask for Advisory Opinions. The role of the Secretary-General is merely to encourage this possibility, and to act as a 'facilitator' through authorization powers to be given under article 96(2). There has, of course, been a long history of debate about whether states should be allowed to ask for Advisory Opinions and different views have been offered.[21] But it is hard to see that, if it is now decided that it is useful for Advisory Opinions to be given on the legal aspects of interstate disputes, this should be done through the back door of a new authorization to the Secretary-General under article 96(2). The idea is either a good one or not.[22]

Nor is it easy to see why a 'peace and security' factor should entail an authorization linkage between disputing states and the Secretary-General rather than between disputing states and the Security Council. The latter body is directly concerned with the maintenance of peace. It is true that the mediation and good offices functions of the Secretary-General probably make him better placed to carry out preventive diplomacy. But the proposal would appear directed to securing a reference to the Court for an Advisory Opinion

---

[21] For a helpful brief review of this issue under the League, and at San Francisco, and before the International Court, see Rosenne, *The World Court*, chap. 4. See further, in the specific context of possible references by national courts, the debate between S. Schwebel, 'Preliminary Rulings by the International Court of Justice at the Instance of National Courts', *VJIL*, 28 (1988), p. 495; and S. Rosenne, 'Preliminary Rulings by the International Court of Justice at the Instance of National Courts: A Reply', *VJIL*, 29 (1989), p. 40.

[22] The present writer for the moment remains sceptical. States that are unwilling to resolve their disputes by resort to the contentious jurisdiction of the Court are also likely to see great political risks in advisory pronouncements on their legal claims. And there might be a danger that states would less use the contentious jurisdiction if a 'softer option' was available.

when the Security Council or the General Assembly (which could also make such a request, if a category of consent-based, interstate dispute Opinions is to be envisaged) would not themselves agree to make the request. It is understandable that the proposal seems either alarming or, if consent really is the key, unnecessary. The UN Legal Counsel has assured the Charter Committee that 'if the Secretary General himself has the competence to request Advisory Opinions, he would be able to do so in a quiet and discreet manner and without having to involve states not parties to the dispute' – i.e. states who are members of the Security Council or General Assembly, the traditional authorizing organs under article 96(1).[23]

The Secretary-General affirms in his own proposals that the consent of states would be a precondition for a request being made pursuant to a future authorization under article 96(2). During the forty-sixth Session of the General Assembly, the Secretary-General 'clarified that he would request an Advisory Opinion from the International Court of Justice when exercising his good offices and with the consent of the parties to the dispute'.[24] When the Legal Counsel of the UN was asked by the Charter Committee to provide further clarification of the issues involved in the proposal, this aspect was repeated.[25] The suggestion is made that an authorization would allow the Secretary-General 'to receive authoritative legal advice as to questions of international law arising within the scope of his activities, particularly in respect of disputes in which the Secretary-General has been asked to play a role (such as the exercise of his good offices or mediation)'.[26] Legal Counsel gives no examples of occasions when the good offices or mediation function of the Secretary-General have ever in fact been hampered by lack of authoritative legal advice. In truth, the Secretary-General seems not really to be seeking legal advice as to questions of international law, to facilitate the carrying out of his functions, but rather recourse to Advisory Opinions as a further diplomatic option to offer the parties.

The proposal for authorization of the Secretary-General under article 96(2) is tied not so much to any articulated need for matters relating generally to the work of the Secretariat, but to a perception that states are nervous of contentious procedure but would be more willing to allow advisory procedure. The proposal does not address the implications for the burgeoning recourse to the Court in contentious cases; nor provide any persuasive evidence that states would wish to use this procedure; nor does it explain why,

---

[23] A/47/33, p. 10, para. 31.
[24] A/47/33, GAOR 47th session, Suppl. No. 33, Report of the Special Committee on the Charter (1992), para. 31.
[25] *Ibid.*, p. 11. [26] *Ibid.*, p. 9.

if the proposal is essentially for a consent-based recourse by states to the Court's advisory procedure, the intercession of the Secretary-General is needed.[27]

After the explanations of the Legal Counsel, opinions by states remain divided. Some reservations seem not very weighty.[28] But some serious concerns remain to be addressed:

> The meaning of the phrase 'within the scope of their activities' in Article 96 and whether the authorisation of the Secretary General to seek an Advisory Opinion from the International Court of Justice would encompass the entire range of his activities or only those activities related to the settlement of disputes between states; whether the consent of the parties to the request for an Advisory Opinion extended to the actual formulation of the question addressed to the [Court];[29] how the advisory role of the Court would relate to the role of the Legal Counsel.

In resolution 47/120B of 8 October 1993, the General Assembly signalled its reluctance to move forward on this proposal, merely deciding to keep it (and all the other recommendations relating to the use of the Court) 'under examination'. And the Secretary-General has not returned to the fray in the forty-ninth Session of the Assembly by providing any further answers to the concerns expressed.

The matter thus lies dormant for the moment. The advisory competence of the Court is not to be forced. Nor is its recent relatively limited use necessarily to be deplored. It may rather be instructive to speculate about the (natural) circumstances in which there is recourse to the advisory procedure.

Since 1948 the Court has rendered ninety-three decisions, at either the preliminary phase or on the merits, or with regard to preliminary measures. Of these, twenty-one have been Advisory Opinions. Seven out of the first twelve cases were Advisory Opinions; as were eleven out of the first twenty-six. From 1957 to 1980 Advisory Opinions were rather evenly spread across the Court's caseload – roughly about one in every seven, turning up at strikingly regular intervals. Out of the next fourteen cases, only one was an Advisory Opinion – but the rate of contentious cases had greatly increased. From 1981 to 1986 the Court had fourteen cases. Then from 1987 to 1989

---

27 On this last point the only answer can be that authorization of the Secretary-General, as the representative of a principal organ, would be perfectly possible under article 96; whereas direct recourse by states would require amendment of the Charter and of the Rules.

28 Among these the present author would list the query as to whether the General Assembly and the Security Council 'would be bound by the Advisory Opinion' if the matter eventually came before them; whether it was appropriate to grant such authorization 'to an individual'; and whether due weight would be given to an Advisory Opinion emanating from a request of the Secretary-General rather than the Security Council or General Assembly.

29 A/47/33 actually refers at p. 11 to 'the actual formulation of the question addressed to the Counsel', but this is obviously a typographical error.

the Court had three Advisory Opinions among the five matters it dealt with. The request for an Advisory Opinion, if taken in 1994, will come after seven contentious matters that have preoccupied the Court since 1990.

These data are hardly the stuff of scientific statistics. Yet, when an international lawyer looks both at the distribution and clusters of Advisory Opinions, and at their subject matter – and at the subject matter of the contentious cases surrounding them – it is tempting to make the following observations: the greatest role for Advisory Opinions is when there are uncertainties about the institutional arrangements within the UN, and particularly about the distribution of power between different organs or between the UN and its member states. In the early years of the UN that body was, for example, still resolving issues relating to membership conditions,[30] to its own legal personality and the international protection of its staff,[31] to the scope of its powers regarding the supervision of mandates and trusteeships,[32] and to internal administrative matters.[33] All of these matters required the advice of the Court in the first ten years. Comparable advice was sought only a handful of times in the next thirty years.[34] The UN had settled into the realities of a Security Council dominated by the cold war, and a General Assembly dominated by a third-world majority.

In recent years the ending of the cold war has had profound implications for the UN. The Security Council has the possibility to operate in areas previously precluded by the veto – but it is doing so often beyond the limits of a strict textual reading of the Charter, and by means other than those envisaged under the Charter. The changes in the distribution of power among the permanent members have implications for the relationship between the Security Council and the General Assembly.

---

[30] See *Conditions of Admission of a State to Membership in the United Nations (Article 4 of the Charter)*, Advisory Opinion of 28 May 1948; *Competence of the General Assembly for the Admission of a State to the United Nations*, Advisory Opinion of 3 March 1950.

[31] *Reparation for Injuries Suffered in the Service of the United Nations*, Advisory Opinion of 11 April 1949.

[32] *International Status of South West Africa*, Advisory Opinion of 11 July 1950; *Voting Procedure on Questions Relating to Reports and Petitions Concerning the Territory of South West Africa*, Advisory Opinion of 1 July 1956; *Admissibility of Hearings of Petitioners by the Committee on South West Africa*, Advisory Opinion of 1 June 1956.

[33] *Effects of Awards of Compensation Made by the United Nations Administrative Tribunal*, Advisory Opinion of 13 July 1954; *Judgments of the Administrative Tribunal of the ILO upon Complaints Made against UNESCO*, Advisory Opinion of 23 October 1956.

[34] *Constitution of the Maritime Safety Committee of the Intergovernmental Maritime Consultative Organisation*, Advisory Opinion of 8 June 1960; *Certain Expenses of the United Nations (Article 17, para. 2 of the Charter)*, Advisory Opinion of 20 July 1962; *Legal Consequences for States of the Continued Presence of South Africa in Namibia (South West Africa) Notwithstanding Security Council Resolution 276 (1970)*, Advisory Opinion of 21 July 1971; *Western Sahara*, Advisory Opinion of 16 October 1975; *Interpretation of the Agreement of 25 March 1951 between the WHO and Egypt*, Advisory Opinion of 20 December 1989.

It might be thought that the situation has returned to the underlying conditions of the first ten years of the UN, in the sense that new distributions of competences among UN organs, or between the UN and its membership, would once again need to be tested through Advisory Opinions. But there is a further reality to be borne in mind – there has to be a majority in the organs or agencies authorized to ask for Advisory Opinions, so to ask. All organs and subsidiary bodies develop their own practices. All institutional structures like to be masters of their own procedures. The longer they are in existence the less they are likely to want advice on their practices from the Court. No request can be made to the Court for an Advisory Opinion unless a decision for such a request is made by the necessary majority in the organ concerned; but the practices that might be the subject of Advisory Opinion are often exactly the practices that have been fashioned by the requisite majorities in the body concerned.[35]

How then does it ever come about that an Advisory Opinion is sought by a UN organ, which without the constraint of such advice as is rendered would be free to take such actions as it chose? The answer seems to be that in some matters, the opposition to the majority of a key state is a factor that cannot be ignored. Its opposition to the majority view will have profound financial or political consequences. Although the requesting organ could still pass resolutions based on its own political instincts, they will be operationally ineffective in the face of such opposition: and the need is felt to draw in a judicial dimension. Thus Soviet opposition to the prevailing view on peace-keeping finance led to the request for the Advisory Opinion on *Certain Expenses* in 1962; South African non-co-operation over South West Africa led to the request for three Advisory Opinions of 1950, 1955 and 1956. The same phenomenon lay behind the requests for the Advisory Opinion on the IMCO constitution of 1960 and for the Advisory Opinion on Western Sahara in 1975.

The circumstances that led to the more recent requests for Advisory Opinions to the *Headquarters Agreement* case[36] and the *Mazilu* case[37] share some of these characteristics. But in the post-cold war world we may expect fewer, rather than more, requests for Advisory Opinions of this sort.

If organs are reluctant to seek advice on the development of their own competencies, except when forced to do so by the behaviour of occasional

---

[35] The reluctance of the financial agencies of the UN to make use of their powers of recourse to the Court is well known.

[36] Advisory Opinion of 26 April 1988.

[37] Advisory Opinion of 15 December 1989.

recalcitrant states, the Court's role as the supreme 'in-house counsel' to the UN will remain limited. In theory, one organ could in fact ask for an Advisory Opinion on a legal matter concerning the work and decisions of another organ. Although the bodies referred to in article 96(2) of the Charter may only request Advisory Opinions 'on legal questions arising within the scope of their activities', article 96(1) provides that the General Assembly may request the Court to give an Advisory Opinion 'on any legal question'. That question could refer to the work or activities of another body. It is interesting to speculate whether the General Assembly, if aggrieved at certain decisions of the Security Council, could ask for an Advisory Opinion on whether they were lawful. To answer this question it is first necessary to determine whether article 96(1) is indeed to be read as allowing the General Assembly and Security Council to ask for Advisory Opinions on legal questions beyond the scope of their own jurisdiction. Legal opinions on this point are divided.[38]

Kelsen takes the view that:

> The determination of any organ's jurisdiction implies the norm not to act beyond the scope of its activity as determined by the legal instrument instituting the organ. It is not very likely that it was intended to enlarge, by Article 96, paragraph 1, the scope of the activity of the General Assembly and the Security Council determined by other Articles of the Charter. Hence the words 'arising out of the scope of their activities' in paragraph 2 of Article 26 are redundant.[39]

Judge Schwebel appears to find this argument persuasive.[40] But we would note that such a request entails no substantive enlargement of the scope of activity of the requesting organ – merely the seeking of advice.

If the Court were to find in such a case that article 96(1) does authorize the General Assembly to ask for an Advisory Opinion on action of the Security Council (or vice versa), the Court would nonetheless have to take the second step of deciding whether, in its discretion in the particular case, it wished to exercise that discretion. The Advisory Opinions given during Sir Robert Jennings's time on the Bench provide striking evidence of this two-step approach.[41] In the *Application for Review of Judgment No. 273 of the United Nations Administrative Tribunal*, the Court first addressed its competence in the

---

[38] See L. Gross, *Essay on International Law and Organization* (Dobbs Ferry, NY, 1984), vol. II; Sloan, 'Advisory Jurisdiction of the International Court of Justice', p. 830.

[39] H. Kelsen, *The Law of the United Nations* (London, 1950), at p. 546.

[40] Schwebel, 'Authorizing the Secretary General of the United Nations to Request Advisory Opinions', at p. 875.

[41] Where the scope of the Court's competence is at all in issue. In the *Headquarters Agreement* case, there being no issue at all as to whether the Court should answer the question formulated (but only as to what its answer should be), the Court did not go through these preliminary elements in its Opinion.

particular case by reference to article 11(1) and (2) of the Statute of the Administrative Tribunal. The Court affirmed that the Committee on Application for Review of Administrative Tribunal Judgments was indeed an organ of the UN duly authorized under article 96, paragraph 2 of the Charter to request Advisory Opinions for the purpose of article 11 of the Statute of UNAT, and that the Court's advisory competence was not altered by virtue of the fact that the request to the Committee in fact originated with an individual state.[42] But the second step still remained. Referring to its 1973 Opinion on the *Application for Review of Judgment No. 158 of the United Nations Administrative Tribunal*, the Court affirmed that it must first find whether it was competent to give the Advisory Opinion, and then turn to 'the discretionary nature of the power it might thus exercise', to see whether certain aspects of the procedure of article 11 of UNAT 'should not lead it to give an Advisory Opinion'.[43] The Court voted by nine votes to six to give the Opinion.[44]

In the *Application for Review of Judgment No. 333 of the United Nations Administrative Tribunal* of 1987, too, the Court dealt first with its competence and then proceeded to look at certain matters which went to the discretionary exercise of its advisory jurisdiction. The Court unanimously decided to give the Opinion, and proceeded to answer the two questions asked.[45]

Thus, if ever faced by a request from the General Assembly to advise on certain matters relating to the Security Council, or vice versa, the Court would first assess its own competence by reference to article 96, and then deal with any points that remained in relation to the exercise of its discretion.

The written statements and oral arguments under the pending request from the WHO are not likely to address this precise point (because it does not arise) but rather the issue that arises under article 96(2) – namely, whether the question put by the WHO, a duly authorized body, is one arising within the scope of its activities. The Court is asked:[46] 'In view of the health and environmental effects, would the use of nuclear weapons by a state in war or other armed conflict be a breach of its obligations under international law including the WHO Constitution?' The Court will have to decide whether the issue is, in a general sense, one within the remit of the WHO as well as of

---

[42] Advisory Opinion, ICJ Reports, 1982, p. 325, at p. 333.

[43] *Ibid.*, at p. 334.

[44] Sir Robert voting with the majority.

[45] *Ibid.*, pp. 29-31. Sir Robert formed part of the unanimous majority on question 1; but on question 2 he uncharacteristically found himself in a twelve to three minority, and appended a long Dissenting Opinion.

[46] The request for this Advisory Opinion from the 46th World Health Assembly of the WHO was received, and Orders issued, during Sir Robert's Presidency.

the political and disarmament bodies of the UN; and, presumably, whether the fact that action predicated would have health and environmental effects necessarily brings the question at the current time within the scope of the WHO's activities for purposes of article 96(2). Attempts to get the General Assembly itself to adopt the request (whether because of its broader competence under article 96(1), or because of its remit of the First Committee on nuclear issues) were abortive.[47] However, the Assembly has made its own request to the Court for an Advisory Opinion on the question: 'is the threat or use of nuclear weapons in any circumstance permitted under international law?'

What is certain is that there has already been, over the years, a somewhat collegial use by UN bodies and organs of the possibilities under article 96. The request of the General Assembly for an Advisory Opinion in the *Peace Treaties* case[48] made it clear that what was sought was authoritative advice for the Secretary-General in the fulfilment of his functions under the Treaties of Peace.[49] Again, the request in the *Reparations for Injuries* case[50] was made by the General Assembly to determine whether the Secretary-General could bring an international claim against a member state. The need for the *Genocide Convention* Advisory Opinion, requested by the Assembly, was in significant part directed to the Secretary-General's practice under that treaty. The *Application for Review of Judgment 273 of the United Nations Administrative Tribunal*[51] came from an application by a member state to the Committee on Applications for Review of Administrative Tribunal Judgments – a provenance that the Court found presented no legal obstacle. The approach of the General Assembly to the Court over the *Mazilu* affair reflected the concern of a different organ of the UN.

In November 1992 the General Assembly was presented with a request to seek an Advisory Opinion from the International Court.[52] This came from virtually all of the Latin American members, supplemented by Spain, Portugal and, later, Iran. The demand arose out of the findings of the Supreme Court of the US that the abduction of Mr Alvarez-Machain (who was suspected of kidnapping, torture and murder of a US drug enforcement agent) from Mexico, and his transfer to the US to stand trial, did not violate the extradition treaty between Mexico and the US and render the US courts without

---

[47] See the draft resolution proposed by Indonesia, A/C.1/48/L.25 (4 November 1993).
[48] *Interpretation of Peace Treaties with Bulgaria, Hungary and Romania (First Phase)*, 1950.
[49] See General Assembly resolution 294 of 22 October 1949.
[50] ICJ Reports, 1949.
[51] ICJ Reports, 1982.
[52] A/47/249/Add.1/Corr.1 (24 December 1992).

jurisdiction. The draft resolution proposed for the Court was in somewhat abstract terms, carefully avoiding mention of Mr Alvarez-Machain and the ensuing dispute between Mexico and the US, no doubt in order to mitigate the 'existing dispute' problem so familiar in requests for Advisory Opinions. The sponsors hoped that the breadth of the General Assembly's competence under article 96(1), to request an Opinion 'on any legal question', would have been sufficient. On the recommendation of the Sixth Committee this proposal has essentially been stood down.[53] The clear implication is that although the phrase 'any legal question' may be wider than the formula in article 96(2), it must at least refer to a legal question under consideration within the UN. And the matter had only been brought to the UN for the purpose of seeking an Advisory Opinion. The abstract formulation would not disguise the dispute: and as the matter was not otherwise on the UN's agenda, the absence of consent of one of the parties to the dispute would seem to have been determinative.

Finally, we briefly note the rather detailed consideration being given in the UN to review of the procedure provided for under article 11 of the Statute of the Administrative Tribunal. It has long been suggested that the article 11 procedures engage the International Court in relatively minor matters; and that as the Court had become busier and busier this had become inappropriate. The debates in the General Assembly have been well informed, and the problems for the Court have been matched by expressions of dissatisfaction by members of the Committee on Applications for Review by the procedures there operating. The resources and efforts expended on the Committee seemed disproportionate to results achieved.[54] The mood seems to be for abolition of article 11 and its replacement by a different review procedure. The Sixth Committee has recommended a thorough review of the matter by the Secretary-General[55] and this has been approved by the General Assembly,[56] which will come back to the matter at its forty-ninth session. The useful life of the Advisory Opinion in relation to staff disputes is drawing to a close.

The Advisory Opinion will surely continue to serve a useful judicial function.

---

[53] Through a resolution of the General Assembly to 'continue its consideration of the item': General Assembly resolution 48/414 (9 December 1993).

[54] The UK representative observed that only three out of eighty applications to the Committee had led to requests for Advisory Opinions, and that in those three cases the Court had upheld the judgment of the Administrative Tribunal: A/C.6/48/SR 36, p. 6.

[55] A/48/619 (3 December 1993).

[56] General Assembly resolution 48/415 (9 December 1993).

The relatively infrequent contemporary recourse to Advisory Opinions is not necessarily a matter to be regretted. Its use most naturally occurs at certain moments in the institutional life of an international organization (in the early years), and from time to time when unforeseeable problems arise for the working of UN organs or agencies. Little purpose is served by artificially inventing new business for the Advisory Opinion, whether in the context of interstate dispute settlement or through new powers to be afforded to the Secretary-General. Recourse to the Court must work with the seams of political and institutional realities and not against the grain.

PART V

The International Court of Justice and the United Nations

❧

32

The General Assembly, the International Court and self-determination

James Crawford

❧

INTRODUCTION

It is a paradox that among controversial and uncertain fields of modern international law, few seem more controversial or less certain than self-determination; that the problem of self-determination has been central to the history – and to a lesser but still significant extent the jurisprudence – of the International Court; yet that so little has been written directly about the contribution of the Court to this field.[1]

The distinction between the history and the jurisprudence of the Court is apposite. Important pronouncements of the Court on a wide variety of issues occurred in cases that directly or indirectly involved the processes of colonization and decolonization. This is true of decisions in the procedural field – for example, the impact of the dissolution of the League of Nations on substantive obligations[2] and on jurisdictional clauses,[3] mootness,[4] the procedural issues arising from third party status.[5] But it is also true in many areas of substantive law, as witness decisions on the competence of

---

[1] Self-determination in general has attracted a vast literature. For recent work see, e.g. C. Tomuschat (ed.), *Modern Law of Self-determination* (Dordrecht, 1993); H. Hannum. 'Rethinking Self-determination', *VJIL*, 34 (1993), p. 1; M. Koskenniemi, 'National Self-determination Today: Problems of Theory and Practice', *ICLQ*, 43 (1994), p. 241; J. Salo, 'Self-determination: An Overview of History and Present State with Emphasis on the CSCE Process', *Finnish YbIL*, 2 (1991), p. 268; R. McCorquodale, 'Self-determination: A Human Rights Approach', *ICLQ*, 43 (1994), p. 857. For earlier work see the bibliography in J. Crawford (ed.), *The Rights of Peoples* (Oxford, 1988), pp. 230–2. Among writers on the role of the Court, see esp. R. Falk, *Reviving the World Court* (Charlottesville, VA, 1986), and see the review by L. Gross in *AJIL*, 82 (1988), p. 166.

[2] *Status of South West Africa*, Advisory Opinion, ICJ Reports, 1950, p. 128.

[3] *South West Africa* cases (*Preliminary Objections*), ICJ Reports, 1962, p. 319.

[4] *Northern Cameroons* case, ICJ Reports, 1963, p. 15.

[5] *Certain Phosphate Lands in Nauru*, ICJ Reports, 1992, p. 240.

United Nations bodies,[6] on the binding effect of decisions of the Security Council,[7] on the status of African territories and peoples in the nineteenth century,[8] to give only some examples.

Other, perhaps even more important, principles derive from cases occasioned by decolonization or its immediate aftermath – for example, the 'objective' legal personality of the UN,[9] and its implied powers in the field of peacekeeping.[10]

But the work of the Court in the field of self-determination and decolonization has not been merely the occasion for international law on other topics. It has been a positive source of that law itself. One can trace with fair completeness the lineaments of the modern law of external self-determination through decisions and dicta of the Court. And it is interesting to do so, if only as a corrective to the programmatic treatments that characterize much of the literature. Whether one likes the image of the law so presented is another question. But it is worthwhile to suspend belief in one or another set of formulae and to observe what the Court has said and done.

This is not made easier in that there appears to be a series of divides in the Court's work – temporally, between its case law before and after 1966; thematically, between its strong affirmative approach (at least in the post-1966 period) to decolonization and its comparative silence on general problems of self-determination outside the colonial context; substantively, in that the Court has combined insistence on colonial self-determination as a basic norm with insistence on the doctrine of *uti possidetis*, which might almost be considered the antidote to self-determination.

These three dichotomies – temporal, thematic and substantive – provide a useful framework within which to assess the Court's contribution. In doing so I will argue that the dichotomies are more apparent than real, and that the Court has shown subtlety, no doubt, but (within the limits of its role and of the cases it has actually had to decide) also a degree of coherence.

---

6 *South West Africa (Voting Procedure)*, Advisory Opinion, ICJ Reports, 1955, p. 67; *South West Africa (Hearing of Petitioners)*, Advisory Opinion, ICJ Reports, 1956, p. 23; *Namibia (South West Africa)*, Advisory Opinion, ICJ Reports, 1971, p. 17.

7 *Namibia (South West Africa)*, Advisory Opinion, ICJ Reports, 1971, p. 17.

8 *Western Sahara*, Advisory Opinion, ICJ Reports, 1975, p. 12.

9 *Reparations for Injuries Suffered in the Service of the United Nations*, ICJ Reports, 1949, p. 149. The decolonization of Palestine under mandate was of a special character, and is still incomplete.

10 *Certain Expenses of the United Nations*, ICJ Reports, 1962, p. 151. The immediate occasion for the Opinion was the dispute over involvement of UN forces in the Congo immediately after its decolonization.

SOUTHWEST AFRICA CASES (SECOND PHASE): DECOLONIZING THE COURT?

If legal issues arising in the course of decolonization have been among the most prominent categories of matters coming before the Court, they have also been a key element in forming opinion about the Court. In particular, decolonization provided a defining moment in the history of the modern Court, the moment of the *South West Africa* cases (*Second Phase*), in 1966.[11]

That case presented the Court with a key strategic decision about the character of modern international law and about the nature of its role in the law-making process *vis-à-vis* the political organs of the UN. On the one hand, there were proponents of the strict separation of international law and politics, of the virtual non–justiciability of obligations of a 'political' character, of strict construction of treaties as originally drafted.[12] On the other hand, there were those who thought that the strict separation of law and politics was unsustainable, that the Court could decide controversial issues arising under legal instruments notwithstanding that those issues had strong political overtones or were the subject of major controversy, and that treaty commitments should be interpreted in certain cases in the light of the progressive development of international law, where this was necessary to give full effect to their purpose.[13]

Such themes underlay the actual decisions in 1962 and 1966 on the technical issues of the survival of the jurisdictional clause in the Mandate for South-West Africa, the standing of the applicant states (which had been members of the League of Nations) to invoke the jurisdictional clause, and the admissibility of their claims based on the 'conduct' provisions of the Mandate, as distinct from its 'special interest' provisions. But the minority judges who had taken the strict constructionist position on these issues in 1962 became, as it happened, a chance 'statutory' majority in 1966, with one of their number, President Spender, exercising a casting vote in favour of the spirit of his dissenting views of 1962, on an issue only barely distinguishable in form from the issue decided by the majority in 1962.

---

[11] ICJ Reports, 1966, p. 6.

[12] A key figure here was Sir Gerald Fitzmaurice: see his joint Dissenting Opinion (with Judge Spender) in ICJ Reports, 1962, at pp. 465ff and his monumental dissent in the *Namibia* Opinion, ICJ Reports, 1971, at pp. 220ff.

[13] See esp. the Dissenting Opinions of Judges Tanaka and Jessup in ICJ Reports, 1966, at pp. 248ff, 323ff.

The judgment raised 'a storm of indignation' in the General Assembly,[14] and there was little tendency to defend it in the literature. It is widely credited with having discredited the Court in the eyes of the General Assembly majority (since 1960 increasingly a third-world majority), and even with being a cause of the long fallow period of the Court in the years after 1966.

The Court itself, it may be surmised, sensed this too, since it seized the few opportunities it had in the following years to distance itself from the 'majority' of 1966. In 1970, in its next but one judgment – where, as in 1966, it dismissed the claim on a technical ground left over from an earlier jurisdictional phase – the Court nonetheless said:

> When a State admits into its territory foreign investments or foreign nationals, whether natural or juristic persons, it is bound to extend to them the protection of the law and assumes obligations concerning the treatment to be afforded them. These obligations, however, are neither absolute nor unqualified. In particular, an essential distinction should be drawn between the obligations of a State towards the international community as a whole, and those arising vis-à-vis another State in the field of diplomatic protection. By their very nature the former are the concern of all States. In view of the importance of the rights involved, all States can be held to have a legal interest in their protection; they are obligations *erga omnes*. Such obligations derive, for example, in contemporary international law, from the outlawing of acts of aggression, and of genocide, as also from the principles and rules concerning the basic rights of the human person, including protection from slavery and racial discrimination. Some of the corresponding rights of protection have entered into the body of general international law . . . others are conferred by international instruments of a universal or quasi-universal character. Obligations the performance of which is the subject of diplomatic protection are not of the same category. It cannot be held, when one such obligation in particular is in question, in a specific case, that all States have a legal interest in its observance.[15]

This is one of the best-known and most often-quoted statements of the Court on any subject, and it was entirely unnecessary for the purposes of that case. It is true that the Court did not specifically mention self-determination in its catalogue of obligations *erga omnes*. But its dictum is entirely inconsistent with the idea that states can have no legal interest in the performance of obligations

---

14 E. Klein, 'South West Africa/Namibia (Advisory Opinions and Judgments)', in R. Bernhardt (ed.), *Encyclopedia of Public International Law* (Amsterdam, 1981), vol. II, p. 260, at p. 266. Incidentally, this made politically impossible the election of Sir Kenneth Bailey, who was nominated by Australia as a candidate for Sir Percy Spender's seat at the 1967 elections. In 1958 Spender had taken at the last minute the opportunity to be nominated for election to the Court, a nomination initially intended to go to Bailey. Further on the 1966 decision see W. Friedmann, 'Jurisprudential Implications of the South West Africa Cases', *Columbia Journal of Transnational Law*, 6 (1967), p. 1; J. Stone, 'Reflections on the South West Africa Cases', in J. Stone, *Of Law and Nations* (Buffalo, 1974), p. 331.

15 *Barcelona Traction* case (*Second Phase*), ICJ Reports, 1970, p. 3, at p. 32, paras. 33–5.

conferred by international instruments such as the Mandate for South West Africa, which gave effect to the idea of a 'sacred trust' embodied in the Covenant, an international instrument of a 'quasi-universal character'. The point of the dictum, it seems, was not just to contrast with the distant law of diplomatic protection but to contrast with the Court's recent approach to putative obligations *erga omnes* in *South West Africa (Second Phase)*.

The recantation was taken further, this time in the specific context of self-determination, in the *Namibia* Opinion in 1971, when the Court said:

> Mindful as it is of the primary necessity of interpreting an instrument in accordance with the intentions of the parties at the time of its conclusion, the Court is bound to take into account the fact that the concepts embodied in Article 22 of the Covenant – 'the strenuous conditions of the modern world' and 'the well-being and development' of the peoples concerned – were not static, but were by definition evolutionary, as also, therefore, was the concept of the 'sacred trust'. The parties to the Covenant must consequently be deemed to have accepted them as such. That is why, viewing the institutions of 1919, the Court must take into consideration the changes which have occurred in the supervening half-century, and its interpretation cannot remain unaffected by the subsequent development of law, through the Charter of the United Nations and by way of customary law. Moreover, an international instrument has to be interpreted and applied with the framework of the entire legal system prevailing at the time of the interpretation. In the domain to which the present proceedings relate, the last fifty years, as indicated above, have brought important developments. These developments leave little doubt that the ultimate objective of the sacred trust was the self-determination and independence of the peoples concerned. In this domain, as elsewhere, the *corpus iuris gentium* has been considerably enriched, and this the Court, if it is faithfully to discharge its functions, may not ignore.[16]

The words 'if it is faithfully to discharge its functions' here are eloquent. 'Mindful' of its 1966 decision, the Court took the next two opportunities substantially to contradict it.

At the political level the 1966 decision had even more immediate impacts, both in terms of the composition of the Court itself, and of the handling of the South West Africa dispute at the international level. In particular the General Assembly took the Court at its word; if the 'conduct' provisions of the Mandate were matters for political rather than legal judgement, then political judgement there would be. By resolution 2145(XXI) of 27 October 1966 the General Assembly declared that South Africa was in breach of the terms of the Mandate and purported to terminate its authority to administer the territory. The Security Council subsequently passed a series of resolutions in support of

---

[16] *Namibia (South West Africa)*, Advisory Opinion, ICJ Reports, 1971, p. 17, at pp. 31–2, para. 53.

that decision, and the Court was eventually asked to determine the legal consequences for states of the continued presence of South Africa in South West Africa (Namibia) despite those resolutions.

The Court did not miss this second chance. By a substantial majority it upheld the validity and spelt out in a rather extensive way the legal effects of the action of the political organs in relation to Namibia, including their legal effect for third parties.[17] Its reliance on article 25 of the Charter to bolster the authority of the Security Council resolutions not expressed to be passed under Chapter VII made new law, and has potentially far-reaching effects. On the other hand, the Court declined to treat at face value the General Assembly's request for an Advisory Opinion. The request focused on the legal effects of the relevant resolutions rather than on the validity of the termination of the Mandate as such. But the Court pointed out that the one presupposed the other, and went on to deal with the underlying issues.[18] It is sometimes said that the Court has no power of 'judicial review' of resolutions of political organs,[19] and in the sense of 'judicial review' as a separate or special institution this is of course true. But it provides no ground for thinking that the legal basis of resolutions of the Security Council or the General Assembly is somehow privileged and immune from scrutiny, or that the 'presumption' of validity is more than a presumption.[20]

The most significant aspects of the decision for present purposes were twofold. First, as we have seen, the Court affirmed the principle of self-determination as a generating principle of a legal character. It stressed that

the subsequent development of international law in regard to non-self-governing territories, as enshrined in the Charter of the United Nations, made the principle of self-determination applicable to all of them. The concept of the sacred trust was confirmed and expanded to all 'territories whose peoples have not yet attained a full measure of self-government' (Art 73). Thus it clearly embraced territories under a colonial régime. Obviously the sacred trust continued to apply to League of Nations mandated territories on which an international status had been conferred earlier. A further important stage in this development was the Granting of Independence to Colonial Countries and Peoples (General Assembly resolution 1514 (XV) of 14 December 1960), which embraces all peoples and territories

---

[17] Ibid., p. 17.

[18] Ibid., at pp. 45–7, paras. 88–95. See further J. Crawford, The Creation of States in International Law (Oxford, 1979), pp. 350–5.

[19] Indeed the Court said as much itself: ICJ Reports, 1971, p. 17, at p. 46, para. 89 (no power of 'judicial review or appeal').

[20] See the case concerning Questions of Interpretation and Application of the 1971 Montreal Convention arising from the Aerial Incident at Lockerbie (Libya v. United Kingdom), ICJ Reports, 1992, p. 3, at p. 15 ('prima facie [article 25] extends to the decision contained in resolution 748 (1992)').

which 'have not yet attained independence'. Nor is it possible to leave out of account the political history of mandated territories in general. All those which did not acquire independence, excluding Namibia, were placed under trusteeship. Today, only two out of fifteen, excluding Namibia, remain under United Nations tutelage. This is but a manifestation of the general development which has led to the birth of so many new States. All these considerations are germane to the Court's evaluation of the present case.[21]

Second, it adopted a mode of co-operation with the political organs, and in particular with the General Assembly, that has characterized its work in this field since. As the just-cited passage from the *Namibia* Opinion shows, the Court has treated the 'subsequent development of international law in regard to non-self-governing territories' as in large part resulting from the application of Charter norms by the political organs, and in particular the General Assembly. It has not treated the decisions of these organs as unreviewable in principle, except in the special context of concluded transactions resulting in the absorption of a territory in a third state (as in *Northern Cameroons*).[22] But it has sought wherever possible to align 'the *corpus iuris gentium*' with the policies and practice of the Assembly.

This is very clear from its Opinion – at once nuanced and affirmative – in *Western Sahara* in 1975.[23] There the Court was able to resolve disputed legal issues arising in relation to the people of the Western Sahara in the late nineteenth century in such a way as to give firm support to the General Assembly's policy towards that territory.

At one level, the right itself is taken to flow from the Charter, with the General Assembly's role essentially one of deciding on the modalities of its expression. As the Court put it: 'The right of self-determination leaves the General Assembly a measure of discretion with respect to the *forms and procedures* by which that right is to be realised.'[24] Yet at the same time the evidence that the right of self-determination applies in any case is largely drawn from the practice of the General Assembly. The recitation of 'the basic principles governing the decolonization policy of the General Assembly'[25] leads to the affirmation of the 'validity of the principle of self-determination', that is to say, of its legal validity. According to the Court:

> The validity of the principle of self-determination, defined as the need to pay regard to the freely expressed will of peoples, is not affected by the fact that in certain cases the General Assembly has dispensed with the requirement of

[21] *Namibia (South West Africa)*, Advisory Opinion, ICJ Reports, 1971, p. 13, at p. 31, paras. 52–3.
[22] ICJ Reports, 1963, p. 15.   [23] ICJ Reports, 1975, p. 12.
[24] *Ibid.*, at p. 53, para. 71 (emphasis added).   [25] *Ibid.*, at p. 34 (para. 60).

consulting the inhabitants of a given territory. Those instances were based either on the consideration that a certain population did not constitute a 'people' entitled to self-determination or on the conviction that a consultation was totally unnecessary, in view of special circumstances.[26]

In relation to any given territory, the specific content of that principle is to be sought, as far as possible, in 'those resolutions which bear specifically on the decolonization of' the relevant territory, and in 'the different ways in which the General Assembly resolutions . . . dealt with' that territory as compared with others.[27] Consideration of those resolutions leads to the conclusion that

> the decolonization process to be accelerated which is envisaged by the General Assembly . . . is one which will respect the right of the population of Western Sahara to determine their future political status by their own freely expressed will . . . The right of that population to self-determination constitutes therefore a basic assumption of the questions put to the Court.[28]

In such circumstances the right of the people could be unequivocally affirmed.[29]

Thus 'in the whole context of the decolonization process'[30] the Court's role has been to an extent secondary, with 'the *corpus iuris gentium*' taking the form, more or less, of an administrative law, a body of rules relating to and supportive of the application of Chapters XI and XII of the Charter by the political organs, and in particular the General Assembly. The Court has not – as it has so markedly in the field of maritime delimitation – played the role of 'lead agency'. But its role has not been merely adjectival. It has consistently supported the principle of self-determination, as implemented by the General Assembly, unless special considerations embodied in the resolutions of the Assembly or to be clearly drawn from its conduct have otherwise dictated.

This can be seen, for example, from the Court's decision in the case concerning *Certain Phosphate Lands in Nauru (Preliminary Objections)*.[31] One of the more important Australian preliminary objections in that case related to the legal effects of termination of the trusteeship for Nauru by General Assembly resolution 2347(XXII). That resolution did not expressly reserve any rights of the people of Nauru against the administering authority as to the rehabilitation of the mined-out phosphate lands, although the rehabilitation of those lands had been an issue in the pre-independence period, and had been brought to the attention of the General Assembly. It was argued that the

---

[26] *Ibid.*, at p. 33, para. 59. [27] *Ibid.*, at p. 34, para. 60.
[28] *Ibid.*, at p. 36, para. 70. [29] *Ibid.*, at p. 68, para. 162.
[30] *Ibid.*, at p. 36, para. 71. [31] ICJ Reports, 1992, p. 240.

silence of the resolution, which at the same time recorded that the independence of Nauru was an expression of the self-determination of its people, had the effect of terminating any pre-independence right that may have existed in respect of the conduct of the administering authority.[32] Australia relied in particular on the Court's decision in *Northern Cameroons*: there the General Assembly's action in terminating the British trusteeship over the Cameroons was held to have 'definitive legal effect'.[33]

In rejecting the preliminary objection, the Court noted that

> when, on the recommendation of the Trusteeship Council, the General Assembly terminated the Trusteeship over Nauru in agreement with the Administering Authority, everyone was aware of subsisting differences of opinion between the Nauru Local Government Council and the Administering Authority with regard to rehabilitation of the phosphate lands worked out before 1 July 1967. Accordingly, though General Assembly resolution 2347 (XXII) did not expressly reserve any rights which Nauru might have had in that regard, the Court cannot view that resolution as giving a discharge to the Administering Authority with respect to such rights. In the opinion of the Court, the rights Nauru might have had in connection with rehabilitation of the lands remained unaffected. Regard being had to the particular circumstances of the case, Australia's third objection must in consequence be rejected.[34]

This passage is remarkable in a number of ways. First, the Court did not suggest (nor had it been argued) that the General Assembly could not have given a discharge to the administering authority in respect of its administration of Nauru. If this had been a legal impossibility,[35] it would not have been necessary to have regard 'to the particular circumstances of the case'.

Second, and crucially, the Court seems to have proceeded on the basis that the rights of the people of Nauru were to be presumed to continue, unless clearly discharged by the competent political organ. The circumstances surrounding Nauruan independence were equivocal, and different delegations at the Assembly had different views. As so often in the practice of the political organs a compromise was reached: there was no express reference to the rehabilitation issue in resolution 2347(XXII), but the preamble recalled earlier resolutions in which that issue had been referred to, and the

---

[32] See *Preliminary Objections of the Government of Australia* (December 1990), vol. I, pp. 95–114.

[33] ICJ Reports, 1963, p. 15, cited with approval in *Certain Phosphate Lands in Nauru*, ICJ Reports, 1992, p. 240, at p. 251, para. 23.

[34] *Certain Phosphate Lands in Nauru*, ICJ Reports, 1992, p. 240, at p. 253, para. 30. Of the dissentients, only Judge Oda disagreed on this point: at pp. 321–2.

[35] As Judge Fitzmaurice thought, from his very different perspective, in *Northern Cameroons*: ICJ Reports, 1963, at p. 120.

administering authority called on to rehabilitate the mined-out lands.[36] In these circumstances it was open to Australia to argue that independence was being granted on the basis that the Nauruan people would take responsibility for their lands, including the rehabilitation of lands already mined. But this was not the only possible interpretation of the resolution, and in these circumstances the asserted rights of the people of Nauru must be presumed to have survived the termination of trusteeship.

Third, the strength of this presumption – and the role of the Court – needs to be assessed in the light of the following fact. Although the General Assembly had, in the Court's words 'requested' that the lands be restored,[37] there had been no definitive finding that restoration or rehabilitation was legally required under the Trusteeship Agreement. In other words the rights on which Nauru relied had never been found by any competent organ to exist,[38] unlike the position with the rights of the Namibian people to permanent sovereignty over the uranium resources, which had been the subject of active measures by UN organs.[39] The Court quite properly treated the Nauruan claim as unproved, and expressly left open the issue of liability on the merits.[40] Any such right would have derived from the Trusteeship Agreement and the UN Charter, and would not have depended on the finding of political organs. The Court's role was ancillary in that it had to interpret the relevant transactions, and in particular the relevant resolutions. It was nonetheless an independent legal role.

But perhaps the most interesting aspect of the case in terms of the underlying law of self-determination was a point assumed but not explored either in the arguments of the parties or by the Court.[41] After independence, the legal claims of the Nauruan people could be asserted by the government of Nauru acting as the representative of the state, and thus of the people in whom the right was vested. Thus the effect of the exercise of self-determination by the people of Nauru was, if not to vest substantive rights in the newly independent state, at least to allow that state as a legal person to claim rights

---

36 See ICJ Reports, 1992, p. 240, at pp. 251–3, paras. 24–9.

37 See *ibid.*, at p. 252, para. 26, referring to General Assembly resolution 2111(XX) (21 December 1965).

38 But see C. Weeramantry, *Environmental Damage under International Trusteeship* (Melbourne, 1992), which summarizes the results of a Nauruan Commission of Inquiry over which Professor Weeramantry (as he then was) presided.

39 See the report of the UN Commissioner for Namibia, *AJIL*, 80 (1986), p. 442 for UN action pursuant to the UN Council for Namibia's Decree No. 1 for the Protection of the Natural Resources of Namibia.

40 ICJ Reports, 1992, p. 240, at p. 262, para. 56.

41 It may have been this point to which the Court referred in an otherwise mysterious passage: *ibid.*, p. 251, para. 23.

on behalf of its people. This raised for the first time in the practice of the Court the spectre of post-independence claims in respect of pre-independence violations of legal rights (such as self-determination or permanent sovereignty over natural resources), rights which were at the time vested in the people of the territory. To be sure, the extent of that potentially unsettling precedent was left open: it could have been limited to trust and mandated territories, and/or to claims articulated by or on behalf of the people prior to independence.[42] But however limited, the acknowledgement of the possibility stands in stark contrast to the majority judgment in the *South West Africa* cases (*Second Phase*).

To summarize, there is a clear link, legally and politically, between the decisions in the *South West Africa* cases (*Second Phase*) and *Namibia*. In the latter the Court did what it could to undo the damaging effects of the former. One illustration may be given of the long-term impact of this reversal, the most important reversal of position in the history of the Court.[43] This is provided, again, by the *Nauru* case, which raised issues of the justiciability of mandate and trusteeship obligations in a way rather reminiscent of the *South West Africa* cases, although in a very different factual and procedural context. The point is that the justiciability of those obligations – specifically of the obligation to administer the territory in the interests of the inhabitants – was never in issue in the case. Non-justiciability of the 'conduct' obligations of the Mandate was a *leitmotif* of the majority in 1966. In the *Nauru* case, by contrast, the principle of justiciability was expressly conceded in the Australian pleadings,[44] and the Court's judgment on the preliminary objections cast no shadow of doubt on that issue either.[45]

It is thus understandable that the years 1966–71 are seen by many as marking a watershed in the history of the Court, and in particular of its transition from a 'first-world' to a 'third-world' court – in terms not only

---

[42] The General Assembly has so far only entertained rights of this kind in relation to the former mandated territories of Namibia and Palestine; in both cases the claims were articulated before independence.

[43] The Court has never expressly reversed or overturned a previous decision. But in other cases it has been able to rely on institutional changes to justify departures from earlier authority (see *Eastern Carelia*, Advisory Opinion, PCIJ, Series B, No. 5 (1923) as interpreted in *Status of Peace Treaties (First Phase)*, ICJ Reports, 1950, p. 65) or else on changes in the law (*Continental Shelf (Libya/Malta)*, ICJ Reports, 1983, p. 13, departing in this respect from the *North Sea Continental Shelf Cases*, ICJ Reports, 1969, p. 6). No such change had occurred in relation to self-determination or decolonization between 1966 and 1971.

[44] *Australian Preliminary Objections*, paras. 217–18.

[45] The Court referred only to issues of the 'determination of the content of the applicable law': ICJ Reports, 1992, p. 240, at p. 255, para. 36. It was not suggested that the applicable law had no content. In fact the issue was never tested: the case was withdrawn after a friendly settlement, based on a 'without prejudice' payment by Australia of A$107 million. See 32 *ILM* 1471 (1993).

of composition but also of orientation. But this shift, real enough no doubt, should not be exaggerated. Leaving aside issues of composition and of 'the representation . . . of the principal legal systems of the world', the *South West Africa* cases (*Second Phase*) might rather be seen as an aberration in a Court otherwise consistently attentive to the rights and interests protected by Chapters XI and XII of the Charter.

In the three Advisory Opinions concerning South West Africa in the 1950s this was certainly the case, although the Court was careful to avoid general pronouncements on the principle of self-determination that characterize both the *Namibia* and *Western Sahara* Opinions.

In particular in the *Status of South West Africa* Opinion in 1950 the Court emphatically upheld the principle of the sacred trust embodied in the Mandate, and did so explicitly in terms of the right of the peoples of that territory. South Africa had argued that the termination of the Mandate *qua* treaty with the dissolution of the League of Nations had dissolved the legal obligations embodied in the Mandate. Referring to the obligations 'to promote to the utmost the material and moral well-being and the social progress of the inhabitants', the Court said:

> These obligations represent the very essence of the sacred trust of civilization. Their *raison d'être* and original object remain. Since their fulfilment did not depend on the existence of the League of Nations, they could not be brought to an end merely because this supervisory organ ceased to exist. Nor could *the right of the population to have the Territory administered in accordance with these rules* depend thereon.[46]

This view was merely 'confirmed' by article 80 of the Charter, and by the practice of the competent organs of the League and the UN.[47]

Moreover, although the General Assembly was not a successor *stricto sensu* of the League of Nations in respect of its supervisory functions over mandated territories, and although there was no legal obligation on a mandatory to bring a territory under the trusteeship system, nonetheless the General Assembly was competent to perform these supervisory functions, and there was no other body that could now do so. Thus, the Court held:

> The necessity for supervision continues despite the disappearance of the supervisory organ under the Mandates System. It cannot be admitted that the obligation to submit to supervision has disappeared merely because the supervisory organ has ceased to exist, when the United Nations has another international organ performing similar, though not identical, supervisory functions.[48]

---

[46] ICJ Reports, 1950, p. 128, at p. 133.
[47] *Ibid.*, at pp. 134–6.   [48] *Ibid.*, at p. 136.

Again, this conclusion was 'confirmed' by article 80 of the Charter, and by the recognition by South Africa of the General Assembly's competence in the matter.[49]

In subsequent Opinions the Court continued this general approach, affirming the General Assembly's right to apply its own voting procedure in the exercise of supervisory functions[50] and to hear petitioners from a mandated territory.[51] Evidently the pattern of teleological interpretation in the interests of the peoples of a dependent territory, and of judicial support for UN supervisory competence, long pre-dated the *South West Africa* cases (*Second Phase*).[52]

DECOLONIZATION AND SELF-DETERMINATION: CONTINUITY OR DICHOTOMY?

Enough has been said to illustrate the Court's affirmative attitude to issues of self-determination arising in the context of decolonization. This may be said to have found its apogee in the *Western Sahara* Opinion, where the Court concluded that

> the materials and information presented to it do not establish any tie of territorial sovereignty between the territory of Western Sahara and the Kingdom of Morocco or the Mauritanian entity. Thus the Court has not found legal ties of such a nature as might affect the application of resolution 1514 (XV) in the decolonization of Western Sahara and, in particular, of the principle of self-determination through the free and genuine expression of the will of the peoples of the Territory.[53]

But it has been continued since, in decisions and dicta. For example in the *Nicaragua* case (*Merits*), the Court said: 'There have been in recent years a number of instances of foreign intervention for the benefit of forces opposed to the government of another State. The Court is not here concerned with

---

[49] *Ibid.*, at pp. 136–8.

[50] *South West Africa (Voting Procedure)*, Advisory Opinion, ICJ Reports, 1955, p. 67.

[51] *South West Africa (Hearing of Petitioners)*, Advisory Opinion, ICJ Reports, 1956, p. 23.

[52] In a more minor key the Court has been consistent in upholding the legal personality or, where relevant, the statehood of entities outside Europe in the eighteenth and nineteenth centuries, and thus indirectly the idea of the universality of international law: see e.g. *United States Nationals in Morocco*, ICJ Reports, 1952, p. 176, at pp. 185, 188; *Rights of Passage Case (Second Phase)*, ICJ Reports, 1962, p. 6, at p. 38; *Western Sahara*, Advisory Opinion, ICJ Reports, 1975, p. 12, at pp. 39, 44–5.

[53] ICJ Reports, 1975, p. 12, at p. 68, para. 162. Unfortunately this affirmation has yet to be realized in practice: cf. T. Franck, 'The Stealing of the Sahara', *AJIL*, 70 (1976), p. 694. For Namibian independence see R. Goy, 'L'indépendence de la Namibie', *Annuaire de droit international française*, 37 (1991), p. 387.

the process of decolonization; this question is not in issue in the present case.'[54]

This approach may be contrasted with the considerable reserve shown by the Court to the principle of self-determination in non-colonial cases, in which category the Court seems to include the relations of territory and people to an independent state which does not claim to be an 'administering authority' under Chapters XI or XII of the Charter. The case law in this context may be briefly reviewed.

The *Northern Cameroons* case[55] has already been referred to in the context of the finality of a determination by the General Assembly of the exercise of self-determination. The Court did not suggest that the Republic of Cameroon's complaint as to the administrative union between the Northern Cameroons and Nigeria did not raise a justiciable legal issue under the Trusteeship Agreement. It was rather that the General Assembly's resolution rejecting that complaint had definitive legal effect, notwithstanding that it was a decision of a political and not a legal body. According to the Court:

> Whatever the motivation of the General Assembly in reaching the conclusions contained in [resolution 1608 XV], whether or not it was acting wholly on the political plane and without the Court finding it necessary to consider here whether or not the General Assembly based its decision on a correct interpretation of the Trusteeship Agreement, there is no doubt . . . that the resolution had definitive legal effect.[56]

In its context of the termination of a Trusteeship Agreement under Chapter XII, there can be no doubt as to the correctness of this. The people of the Northern Cameroons having elected to join Nigeria, that decision, approved by the Assembly, could not be reopened by raising legal issues relating to the earlier form of administration of the territory under trusteeship.

But it might be possible to construe the Court as at least tacitly favouring the idea that self-determination is a once and for all right, and moreover a right specifically associated with decolonization, rather than a general and continuing right having specific but not exhaustive application to colonial territories.

Some support for this view of self-determination as nothing more than 'the

---

[54] ICJ Reports, 1986, p. 14, at p. 108, para. 206. For criticism see Judge Schwebel (dissenting), *ibid.*, at pp. 350–2, paras. 178–81.

[55] ICJ Reports, 1963, p. 15.

[56] *Ibid.*, p. 14, at p. 32.

right to decolonization'[57] can also be gleaned from the majority decision in the *Nicaragua* case. There the Court placed considerable emphasis on the customary international law duty of non-intervention as a basis for condemning the United States for support for insurgents fighting the Nicaraguan government.[58] By the same token, it had difficulty in discovering any legal commitment on the part of Nicaragua with respect to its internal democratic processes.[59] It was as if the principle of non-intervention stood in the way of acceptance of Nicaraguan statements to that effect as legal commitments. Thus the Court said:

> The assertion of the commitment raises the question of the possibility of the State binding itself by agreement in relation to a question of domestic policy, such as that relating to the holding of free elections on its territory. The Court cannot discover, within the range of subjects open to international agreement, any obstacle . . . to hinder a State from making a commitment of this kind. A State, which is free to decide upon the principle and methods of popular consultation within its domestic order, is sovereign for the purposes of accepting a limitation of its sovereignty in this field.[60]

It went on to point out that the OAS Charter referred to 'the effective exercise of representative democracy' only as an aspect of 'solidarity' and as a 'high aim'. Given this unspecific language it rejected the view 'that Nicaragua actually undertook a commitment to organise free elections, and that this commitment was of a legal nature . . . The Court cannot find an instrument with legal force . . . whereby Nicaragua has committed itself in respect of the principle or methods of holding elections.'[61]

In fact, Nicaragua was a party to the International Covenant on Civil and Political Rights and to the American Convention on Human Rights, both of which contain explicit commitments with respect to 'the principle or methods of holding elections'.[62] It is true that at the time the US was party to

---

[57] This is the title of the relevant chapter in M. Bedjaoui (ed.), *International Law: Achievements and Prospects* (Paris/Dordrecht, 1991). See F. Abdullah, 'The Right to decolonization', at pp. 1206–18. In other respects 'the rights of peoples' bulk large in the volume: see esp. M. Bedjaoui, 'The Right to Development', *ibid.*, p. 1177.

[58] ICJ Reports, 1986, p. 14, at pp. 106–10, paras. 202–9.

[59] The specific commitments on which the US relied are set out in the Dissenting Opinion of Judge Schwebel: *ibid.*, at pp. 398–401. The Majority Opinion referred to them only in general terms at p. 130, para. 257 ('questions such as the composition of the government, its political ideology and alignment, totalitarianism, human rights, militarization and aggression').

[60] *Ibid.*, at p. 131.

[61] *Ibid.*, at pp. 131–2. See the Separate Opinion of Judge Ago (at pp. 186–7) for justified doubts on this point.

[62] See ICCPR, article 25; American Convention, article 23. For criticism of the dictum see J. Crawford, 'Democracy and International Law', *BYbIL*, 64 (1963), p. 113, at pp. 120–1.

neither instrument, so that the dictum quoted above may be accurate if it is read as relating only to commitments specifically made to the US. But the dictum nonetheless lends credence, if again only indirectly, to the limited view of self-determination as a once-and-for-all right to decolonization, dissociated from broader issues of representative government.

In this context it is also perhaps legitimate to refer to the rather embarrassed silence observed by the Court in the *Right of Passage* case (*Second Phase*)[63] as to the status of the enclaves there after Indian occupation. The extreme reserve shown by the Court can be seen, for example, from the following passage:

> With reference to what date must the Court ascertain whether the right invoked by Portugal exists or does not exist? If the date is the eve of the events of 1954 which brought about a new situation which has since prevented the exercise by Portugal of its authority in the enclaves without, however, having substituted therefor that of India, the factors relevant for the guidance of the Court in its decision will be those existing on the eve of those events. If, on the other hand, the issue is viewed as it stands at the date of the present Judgment, it will be necessary to take into account – whatever may be their weight – the arguments of India designed to establish that the right of passage, assuming it to have existed previously, came to an end as a result of the events of 1954 and has lapsed in the present circumstances.[64]

Portugal had remained silent as to the 'critical date', and the Court, relying on this and on the complex and indirect way in which Portugal had seemed to raise the issue of events subsequent to 1954, decided to limit itself to the situation in 1954.[65]

The Portuguese enclaves in India raised issues of decolonization, but in the special context of 'enclaves' which were claimed by the surrounding state irrespective of any right of the local people to decide on their future status.[66] Plainly these were issues the Court preferred to avoid.[67]

Outside the framework of the Court's jurisprudence there is much practice in support of the view that the principle of self-determination is not to be limited to colonial territories. In the Charter itself that term appears in article

---

[63] ICJ Reports, 1960, p. 6.

[64] *Ibid.*, at pp. 28–9.

[65] *Ibid.*, at pp. 29-32, 36. See the criticism of President Klaestad on this point: at p. 47.

[66] For the problem of 'colonial enclaves' see e.g. Crawford, *The Creation of States in International Law*, pp. 377–85, and for criticism see D. W. Greig, 'Reflections on the Role of Consent', *Australian YbIL*, 12 (1992), p. 125, at pp. 155–7.

[67] Rather similar issues are raised in the *East Timor* case, pending before the Court. Unlike India in *Right of Passage*, Indonesia is not a party to those proceedings.

1 but not in either Chapter XI or XII. The Friendly Relations Declaration plainly treats self-determination as going beyond issues of decolonisation; so does common article 1 of the International Covenants of 1966. The same is true of the practice of the CSCE.[68] But this practice so far finds little or no echo in the jurisprudence of the Court.

On balance it would be wrong to draw any firm conclusions from these indications. Each of the three cases referred to above can be accounted for on its own terms. The fact is that — leaving unsolicited dicta such as that in *Barcelona Traction*[69] to one side — courts can only develop the law in cases they are asked to decide.

DECOLONIZATION AND *UTI POSSSIDETIS*: A PROBLEM OF CONSISTENCY?

A connected issue arises in relation to the *uti possidetis* doctrine, which purports to allocate territory to one state or another by reference to the pre-independence status quo. That principle has been strongly supported by the Court, echoing the strong support it has had in state practice and in the resolutions of regional organizations such as the OAU. It has been applied as a determinant of boundaries in both Africa[70] and Central America.[71]

It is not only a criterion for the location of boundaries, but at a legal level appears to induce a presumption of the interpretation of transactions affecting boundaries. Thus in the *Libya/Chad* case, the Court was called on to interpret the provisions of a treaty that 'recognized' certain frontiers. It was argued for Libya that the treaty did not convert lines which were not territorial boundaries into such boundaries, and this was a possible interpretation of the relevant words. But the Court preferred an interpretation that would settle the boundary. It said:

> The fixing of a frontier depends on the will of the sovereign States directly concerned. There is nothing to prevent the parties from deciding by mutual agreement to consider a certain line as a frontier, *whatever the previous status of that line* . . . If it was not previously a territorial boundary, the agreement of the parties to 'recognize' it as such invests it with a legal force which it had previously lacked.

---

[68] For a review of the sources and arguments see e.g. J. Crawford, 'Self-Determination outside the Colonial Context', in W. J. A. Macartney (ed.), *Self-Determination in the Commonwealth* (Aberdeen, 1988), p. 1.

[69] ICJ Reports, 1970, p. 3, at p. 32, paras. 33–5.

[70] *Frontier Dispute* case (*Burkina Faso/Mali*), ICJ Reports, 1986, p. 554.

[71] *Case Concerning the Land, Island and Maritime Frontier Dispute (El Salvador/Honduras: Nicaragua intervening)*, ICJ Reports, 1992, p. 351; see esp. at pp. 386–8.

International conventions and case-law evidence a variety of ways in which such recognition can be expressed.[72]

And the Court referred here to the implied recognition of a boundary line by Thailand in the *Temple* case.[73]

Thus even where the boundary in question is the product of transactions with a colonial power, the outcome of the transaction is not merely recognized; the transaction itself is construed as far as possible so as to produce a settled outcome. Any disparity in the power relationship between the parties at the time – a matter to which the Court might otherwise be sensitive – will be ignored.[74]

This is not the place for a detailed account of the *uti possidetis* doctrine, which in most contexts does not directly implicate issues of self-determination or decolonization.[75] Indeed in one aspect, the doctrine reinforces a principle of the law of decolonization, the idea of the territorial integrity of non-self-governing trust and mandated territories. But in particular cases, where the territory in question contains distinct peoples with different views as to their future, the potential for conflict does exist.

The Court has so far been rather categorical in preferring the stability of boundaries against any potential disruption that the principle of self-determination might produce, although the only direct discussion of the problem was by the Chamber which dealt with the *Frontier Dispute* case (*Burkina Faso/Mali*) in 1986. The Chamber asked

how the time-hallowed principle has been able to withstand the new approaches to international law as expressed in Africa, where the successive attainment of independence and the emergence of new States have been accompanied by a certain questioning of traditional international law. At first sight this principle conflicts outright with another one, the right of peoples to self-determination. In fact, however, the maintenance of the territorial status quo in Africa is often seen as the wisest course . . . The essential requirement of stability in order to survive, to develop and gradually to consolidate their independence in all fields, has induced

---

[72] *Case Concerning the Territorial Dispute (Libyan Arab Jamahiriya/Chad)*, ICJ Reports, 1994, p. 6, at p. 23, para. 45. It was thus unnecessary for the Court to consider the complex political history of the disputed area, which had been much discussed in the pleadings: see *ibid.*, at pp. 38–40, paras. 75–6 for a catalogue of issues the Court did not need to consider. And cf. Judge Ago, Separate Opinion, *ibid.*, at p. 43.

[73] *Temple of Preah Vihear (Merits)*, ICJ Reports, 1962, at p. 33.

[74] See in this context the striking dissent of Judge Spender in the *Temple* case, *ibid.*, at p. 101, esp. pp. 128–9. See also the reservations of Judge Shahabuddeen in *Libya/Chad*, ICJ Reports, 1994, p. 6, at pp. 49–50.

[75] In *Libya/Chad*, for example, neither party treated the principle of self-determination as relevant to its claim to the disputed territory.

African States judiciously to consent to the respecting of colonial frontiers, and to take account of it in the interpretation of the principle of self-determination of peoples. Thus the principle of *uti possidetis* has kept its place among the most important legal principles, despite the apparent contradiction which explained its coexistence alongside the new norms. Indeed it was by deliberate choice that African States selected, among all the classic principles, that of *uti possidetis*. This remains an undeniable fact. In the light of the foregoing remarks, it is clear that the applicability of *uti possidetis* in the present case cannot be challenged merely because in 1960, the year when Mali and Burkina Faso achieved independence, the Organization of African Unity which was to proclaim this principle did not yet exist, and the above-mentioned resolution calling for respect for the pre-existing frontiers dates only from 1964.[76]

It should be noted that the Chamber describes the conflict between the two principles as merely 'apparent', and treats the *uti possidetis* rule as a means of 'the *interpretation* of the principle of self-determination of peoples'. In this it is surely correct. Human communities, as presently conceived and structured, operate as territorial communities, and there is no way back to any 'original condition' prior to the world of (mostly arbitrary, often colonial) boundary-drawing of past centuries. No tenable general theory of self-determination proposes otherwise. If there is a difficulty with the Chamber's dictum – again not necessary to the decision since no issue of self-determination was raised there and the parties did not dispute that the criterion of *uti possidetis* applied – it lies in the apparent assumption that self-determination would require a redrawing of boundaries along ethnic lines.

CONCLUSIONS

It seems likely that the relatively large place taken by decolonization cases in the Court's docket will decline. Unless the *Nauru* case generates a large following (and there is no sign of this), the gradual mopping-up of residual cases of colonial territories will be enough to produce this effect. Only one case on the Court's list at present involves a classical 'blue-water colony', the *East Timor* case, and that case is special in a number of ways.

Of course, each of the situations dealt with by the Court in the field of decolonization and self-determination has had its own special features. But this review of the cases suggests a number of conclusions.

On the one hand, the Court has been instrumental in reinforcing the changing conviction of jurists that the principle of external self-determination

---

[76] ICJ Reports, 1986, p. 554, at pp. 566–7, paras. 25–6.

is part of international law.[77] It has applied a broad and flexible category of statehood and legal personality, including of the indigenous inhabitants of territories before colonization, rejecting theories of personality based on a western 'standard of civilization' as a criterion for legal personality.[78] It has supported the work of the General Assembly and other UN agencies in the field of decolonization, without abandoning its legitimate judicial role or treating political determinations as inherently unreviewable. It has, overall, played a useful role in relation to specific territorial controversies, and in particular to Namibia (South West Africa), both before and after 1966. On the other hand, it has as far as possible emphasized that political change including change through the exercise of self-determination should not unsettle agreed or established boundaries.

What it has not done, in relation to issues of internal self-determination (or for that matter internal colonization), has largely been a function of its case-

---

[77] It cannot be said that issues of decolonization or self-determination have occupied a large place in the work or writings of Sir Robert Jennings himself. But his work does reflect rather faithfully the change in attitude that has occurred. Thus in his *The Acquisition of Territory in International Law* (Manchester, 1963), he stated that the right of self-determination enunciated in resolution 1514(XV) was not a legal right 'of the kind that could be vindicated before a court' (at p. 83), while at the same time posing the question whether political action by the General Assembly under the rubric of self-determination 'might be, or become, relevant to questions of legal title to territorial sovereignty; more particularly perhaps in the case where a specific recommendation is addressed to a particular party' (*ibid*.). His conclusion was cautious, but essentially negative: self-determination was but one of a number of 'guiding principles for the determination of the proper destiny of territories' (at p. 78), but it was not more than a guiding principle: 'Only when we can see the beginnings of a constitutional machinery for the deprivation of title of territory in possession we can begin to think in terms of legislation in the matter of title' (at p. 87). In the meantime General Assembly resolutions such as resolution 1514 merely related to 'a political claim to a change of sovereignty . . . a *political* claim to territory' (at p. 86, emphasis in original).

This may be compared with the discussion, not dissimilar in structure or theme but very different in its conclusions, in the 9th edn of *Oppenheim* (edited by Sir Robert Jennings and Sir Arthur Watts). There it is said that 'international law has come to embody general considerations different from modalities of acquisition or loss', and in particular the principle of self-determination, which is unequivocally described as a legal principle:

> The principle has often appeared in practice to be an adjunct of the decolonization process rather than an autonomous principle, and this perhaps saved it at least during the decolonisation period from being a solvent of the unity of existing independent states . . . Whatever the difficulties of determining what is a 'people' for this purpose, there can be no doubt that so lively a legal principle has a part to play in the determination of territorial sovereignty . . . The principle of self-determination, both as an autonomous legal principle, and as a vehicle of United Nations policies, insofar as the United Nations properly has functions and discretions in the matter, must clearly affect and modify the law governing territorial sovereignty.

R. Y. Jennings and A. D. Watts (eds.) *Oppenheim's International Law* (9th edn, Harlow, 1992), vol. I, at pp. 712, 713, 715.

But its actual effect is left entirely open: it is stated to 'vary with particular cases' (*ibid.*, p. 717).

[78] In this respect it has contributed indirectly to the reassessment of the rights of indigenous peoples within a number of states: see, e.g., *Mabo v. Queensland (No. 2)* (1992) 175 CLR 1.

load. The few cases that did raise these issues have been affected by the procedural posture of the parties (*Right of Passage* case) or the issues have been submerged in a wider dispute (*Nicaragua* case). But overall the Court has made a real contribution to 'the legal ordering of territorial stability and territorial change' which Sir Robert Jennings identified in 1963 as lying 'at the heart of the whole problem of the legal ordering of international society'.[79]

POSTSCRIPT

The Court's decision in the *East Timor* case

Since this chapter was written the Court gave judgment in the *Case Concerning East Timor (Portugal v Australia)*. By a large majority (fourteen to two, Judge Weeramantry and Judge *ad hoc* Skubiszewski dissenting) the Court held that Portugal's application was inadmissible under the principle in the *Monetary Gold* case (IJC Reports, 1954, p. 19). The reason was that it would 'necessarily have to rule upon the lawfulness of Indonesia's conduct as a prerequisite for deciding on Portugal's contention that Australia violated its obligation to respect Portugal's status as administering power, East Timor's status as a non-self-governing territory and the right of the people of the Territory to self-determination and to permanent sovereignty over its wealth and natural resourses' (judgment of 30 June 1995, para. 33). The Court took the opportunity to affirm the status of the right of self-determination as having an *erga omnes* character; it is 'one of the essential principles of contemporary international law' (para. 29). But *adjudication* on that right, or on its consequences in a given case, was only possible if the conditions for the exercise of the Court's jurisdiction were otherwise met: 'the *erga omnes* character of a norm and the rule of consent to jurisdiction are two different things' (*ibid.*). Moreover the Court interpreted the relevant Security Council and General Assembly resolutions as not 'intended to establish an obligation on third States to treat exclusively with Portugal as regards the continental shelf of East Timor' (para. 32). It also emphasized the failure of those organs to respond to a Portugese protest at the conclusion of the 1989 treaty between Australia and Indonesia which was the cause of Portugal's application (para. 32).

This is a further example of the Court's role (described at p. 592 above) as secondary to that of the political organs in the field of self-determination. Although this is only hinted at in the judgment, Portugal expressly disavowed any reliance on the obligation of non-recognition based on the unlawful use of force, an obligation generally held to be automatic and not contingent on action by the political organs of the United Nations.

[79] Jennings, *The Acquisition of Territory in International Law*, p. 87.

33

The International Court of Justice and the Security Council

Krzysztof Skubiszewski

࿇

What the International Court and the Security Council have in common is their status as principal organs of the United Nations and their participation in the settlement of disputes. These factors influence the various relationships between the two bodies.

This chapter begins by an analysis of the parallelism in the functioning of the Court and the Council (first section). One specific point of that topic is negotiations by parties to a dispute which is simultaneously subject to judicial proceedings (second section). Another problem pertaining to parallelism is co-ordination resulting from a Council recommendation under article 36, paragraph 3 of the Charter (third section). Recently, there arose the question whether the Security Council has changed its hitherto adopted stance of correlating its competences with those of the Court and, consequently, whether it would no longer hesitate to restrain the Court. Is this the lesson of *Lockerbie*? The matter is dealt with in the fourth section, while the fifth takes up the discussion on the related though more general issue of the existence or non-existence of an exclusive competence of the Security Council. Some attention has also been devoted to the hypothesis of a judicial review of the Council decisions (sixth section).

This writer does not comment on the Council measures to give effect to the Court's judgments (article 94, paragraph 2 of the Charter). This is mainly due to the necessity of keeping the size of this chapter within certain limits. But one can also point to a reason of substance: it is a separate subject in the sense that the writer concentrates on the relations between the two organs in the adjudicative phase, not beyond it.

PARALLEL FUNCTIONS

There is no obstacle to the simultaneous submission of a dispute to the Security Council and the Court provided the delimitation of functions is respected.

A party to the dispute, any other state (article 35, paragraphs 1 and 2 of the Charter) or the Secretary-General (article 99) may bring the dispute to the attention of the Council, and at the same time the party or parties may institute proceedings before the Court. This parallelism of settlement[1] of the dispute is possible; it has its basis in the law of the UN.

In the Court itself the relief sought is always legal.[2] But the Council will not necessarily be restricted to what constitutes the political part or ingredient of the dispute and the political (or non-legal) means of settlement. As far as the Council is concerned that division is not definite in the sense that the Council can occupy itself with those legal matters that have not been submitted to the Court and decided by it in a judgment. If the judgment has dealt with only some legal aspects of the dispute, the Council is competent to take up the remaining legal matters beside other (i.e. non-legal) parts of the conflict. In such an instance the remedy may or may not be legal, depending on what criterion prevails. The Security Council is a political authority and if turning to it gives the action a predominantly political colour, then the relief obtained has to be termed 'political'. On the other hand, the Council is not released from the respect of law, and if legal remedies are those 'obtainable in accordance with rules of law',[3] the decision by the Council may satisfy that requirement and be regarded as a 'legal relief'. Needless to say even then the Council does not exercise any judicial function.[4] For 'it may take legal considerations into account but, unlike a court, it is not bound to apply them'.[5]

Whether the parallelism of action results in any restriction for the Court *ratione materiae* depends on the merits of each case. In the armed incident that

---

[1] Not of remedies. According to Judge Tarazi the *Aegean Sea* dispute was not an 'example of the simultaneous use of two parallel remedies, inasmuch as the Security Council, unlike the Court, is a political organ. The rule *electa una via* did not have to be applied: *Aegean Sea Continental Shelf, Interim Protection*, Separate Opinion, ICJ Reports, 1976, p. 31, at p. 33. Judge Tarazi said that the 'Court, if the circumstances so require, ought to *collaborate* in the accomplishment' by the Security Council of its task of maintaining peace and security (*ibid.*).

[2] In their Separate Opinions in *Aegean Sea Continental Shelf, Interim Protection*, Judges Lachs and Elias referred to 'legal and political relief': *ibid.*, p. 19, and 'legal and political remedies or reliefs', p. 28, respectively. On the other hand, Judge *ad hoc* Stassinopoulos spoke of the reference of the different 'aspects' of 'the same question' to the Security Council and the Court: Dissenting Opinion, *ibid.*, p. 35, at p. 38, and not of 'reliefs' or 'remedies'.

[3] David M. Walker, *The Oxford Companion to Law* (Oxford, 1980), p. 1056.

[4] This was explicitly denied by Brazil during the discussion of the Corfu incident in the Security Council: 'The Security Council is not and cannot be a tribunal . . . Ours is not a judicial function, nor do we meet here as international judges': SCOR, Second Year, No. 32, 125th Meeting, 3 April 1947, p. 686.

[5] Judge Schwebel, Dissenting Opinion, *Case Concerning Military and Paramilitary Activities in and against Nicaragua (Merits)*, ICJ Reports, 1986, p. 259, at p. 290, para. 60.

occurred in the Corfu Channel on 22 October 1946 the Security Council recommended by its resolution of 9 April 1947 that the United Kingdom and Albania should refer their whole dispute to the Court.

In the conflict on the continental shelf in the Aegean Sea the Council laid emphasis on negotiations and called upon Greece and Turkey 'to resume direct negotiations over their differences' (resolution 395 (1976), paragraph 3). It is 'in this respect' that the two parties were invited by the Council 'to continue to take into account the contribution that appropriate judicial means, in particular the International Court of Justice, [were] qualified to make to the settlement of any remaining legal differences which they [might] identify in connection with their present dispute' (paragraph 4). Here the Security Council has placed the Court in the broader framework of negotiations; the possible decision by the Court would relate to some or all 'remaining legal differences', i.e. those that have not been resolved by negotiation. Judge Lachs spoke of 'the compatibility and complementarity of all means of peaceful settlement'; he referred to a dictum of the Permanent Court of International Justice according to which the judicial resolution was 'simply an alternative to the direct and friendly settlement' by the parties.[6] He stressed the link between the Statute of the Court and the Charter. Consequently, in his view, the Court 'should the more readily seize the opportunity of reminding the member States concerned in a dispute referred to it of certain obligations deriving from general international law or flowing from the Charter'.[7] It seems that this is what the Court did; in the Order of 11 September 1976 various citations to, and quotations from, the Security Council resolution figure prominently.[8] In particular, the Court reminded the parties that the Council called on them 'to resume direct negotiations over their differences.[9]

In the *Case Concerning United States Diplomatic and Consular Staff in Tehran* the Court put questions to satisfy itself that what was done by the Security Council and, consequently, the Secretary-General, did not constitute a bar to the pursuit of the case before the Court. At the very outset of the oral proceedings the President of the Court asked 'what significance should be attached by the Court, for the purpose of the present proceedings, to resolution 457 adopted by the Security Council on 4 December 1979'.[10] Later

---

[6] *Free Zones of Upper Savoy and the District of Gex*, PCIJ, Series A, No. 22, p. 13; *Aegean Sea Continental Shelf* case, Separate Opinion, ICJ Reports, 1978, p. 50, at p. 52. The word 'alternative' should not, in this context, be understood as excluding the parallelism of settlement.

[7] *Aegean Sea Continental Shelf* case, *Interim Protection*, Separate Opinion, ICJ Reports, 1976, at p. 20.

[8] ICJ Reports, 1976, p. 3, at pp. 12–13, paras. 37–41.

[9] *Ibid.*, p. 12, para. 38.

[10] *Pleadings*, p. 19. For the US answer, see *ibid.*, pp. 28–9.

the Secretary-General established 'a commission of enquiry to undertake a fact-finding mission to Iran to hear Iran's grievances [towards the US] and to allow an early solution of the crisis between Iran and the United States'.[11] While Iran's grievances were not the object of adjudication, that part of the crisis concerning hostages was. Again the President of the Court asked a question, this time explicitly raising the issue of competence; the Court wanted to know 'whether the establishment or work of the commission of inquiry . . . [affected] in any way the jurisdiction of the Court to continue the present proceedings or the admissibility or propriety of these proceedings'.[12] It was rather obvious that in answering these questions the applicant state would be in favour of the exercise by the Court of its jurisdiction.[13] Nonetheless the questions revealed certain doubts on the part of the Court or at any rate its interest in clarifying the problem of concurrent competence.

In the judgment itself there is no trace of any doubts:

> It is for the Court, the principal judicial organ of the United Nations, to resolve any legal questions that may be in issue between parties to a dispute; and the resolution of such legal questions by the Court may be an important, and some-times decisive, factor in promoting the peaceful settlement of the dispute. This is indeed recognized by Article 36 of the Charter.

The Court also recalled Security Council resolution 461 (1979). That resolution

> expressly took into account the Court's Order of 15 December 1979 indicating provisional measures; and it does not seem to have occurred to any member of the Council that there was or could be anything irregular in the simultaneous exercise of their respective functions by the Court and the Security Council. Nor is there in this any cause for surprise.[14]

In *Nicaragua v. United States (Judgment on Jurisdiction and Admissibility)* the Court recalled that position and added that 'the fact that a matter [was] before the Security Council should not prevent it being dealt with by the Court and that both proceedings could be pursued *pari passu*'.[15]

---

[11] *Ibid.*, p. 455.   [12] *Ibid.*, p. 254.

[13] *Ibid.*, pp. 28–9, 270–2 and 288. Cf. the strong emphasis on the independence of the Court action on the part of the US Agent: *ibid.*, p. 29. In answer to a question by Judge Morozov, *ibid.*, p. 298, he explained that 'it was not part of the commission's function to hear the United States grievances with respect to the seizure of the United States Embassy. On the other hand it was the hope of the Secretary-General and the United States Government that, once Iran had been given an opportunity to air its grievances before the commission, this would in fact lead the Government of Iran to release the hostages': *ibid.*, p. 315.

[14] ICJ Reports, 1980, at pp. 21 and 22, para. 40.

[15] *Ibid.*, 1984, p. 392, at p. 433, para. 93.

It may be concluded that until the beginning of the 1990s there arose no jurisdictional conflict between the two organs. While the Court considered the foregoing cases, the Council did not take any action that would create an obstacle to the treatment of these disputes by the Court, though the Council remained seised of them. There was no infringement of the *sub judice* principle. One may say that there was more than that: there was a measure of coordination, including 'complementarity'.[16] This was important in view of the possibility of inconsistency between the decisions of the two organs. In view of the division within the Court that possibility was particularly probable in the *South West Africa* cases.

One may add by way of comparison that another principal (and political) organ of the UN, the General Assembly, continued to act on the question of South West Africa after the Court proceedings had been instituted by Ethiopia and Liberia against the Union of South Africa (as it then was). The activity of the Assembly, simultaneous to that of the Court, could be compared to the position of the Security Council in the instances discussed above.[17] In the *South West Africa* cases (*Preliminary Objections*), the Court said that the dispute in the UN and the one before the Court might be regarded as being different. However, it also recognized that the questions at issue were identical.[18] Let us observe, again, that there was identity of facts and claims, but the remedy was different in each of the organs concerned. As to the parties – there was of course a difference, but it was of a rather formal nature.

NEGOTIATIONS SPONSORED BY THE SECURITY COUNCIL AND ADJUDICATION

The fact that the Security Council deals with a dispute and calls on the parties to resume or continue negotiations is not a bar to the Court's jurisdiction. As

---

[16] Lachs, in the *Aegean Sea Continental Shelf* case, Separate Opinion, ICJ Reports, 1978, p. 50; Ni in his Declaration in the *Lockerbie* cases, ICJ Reports, 1992, p. 20, at p. 22, and p. 132, at p. 134. At the same meeting of the Security Council at which the request for an Advisory Opinion on the issue of Namibia was made, the Council indicated some other steps to be taken. The Court drew attention to this simultaneity: *Legal Consequences for States of the Continued Presence of South Africa in Namibia*, ICJ Reports, 1971, p. 16, at p. 55, para. 120. In this phase of the dispute the initiative belonged exclusively to the Council and it was that organ that 'divided the labour'.

[17] The practice of the Permanent Court and the *South West Africa* cases have led Shabtai Rosenne to speak, with regard to the General Assembly and the Court, of 'the functional parallelism of two principal organs of the United Nations, each of which has a competence, under the combined Charter and Statute, to deal with the same "dispute"': *The Law and Practice of the International Court* (2nd rev. edn, Dordrecht/Boston/Lancaster, 1985), p. 87.

[18] ICJ Reports, 1962, p. 319, at p. 345.

long as the dispute is not settled the Court may consider it provided the Statute's requirements are met.

The point is illustrated by the dispute between Greece and Turkey relating to the *Continental Shelf in the Aegean Sea*. After Greece applied to the Court the Security Council dealt with the dispute and called upon the parties to resume negotiations. The Council also invited the two governments 'in this respect to continue to take into account the contribution that appropriate judicial means, in particular the International Court of Justice, [were] qualified to make to the settlement of any remaining legal differences that they [might] identify in connection with their present dispute' (resolution 395 (1976), paragraph 4).

Turkey refused to appear before the Court. In her view the negotiations were irreconcilable with the continuation of international judicial proceedings. The Court rejected this view:

> Negotiation and judicial settlement are enumerated together in Article 33 of the Charter of the United Nations as means for the peaceful settlement of disputes. The jurisprudence of the Court provides various examples of cases in which negotiations and recourse to judicial settlement have been pursued *pari passu*. Several cases, the most recent being that concerning the *Trials of Pakistani Prisoners of War (I.C.J. Reports 1973*, p. 347), show that judicial proceedings may be discontinued when such negotiations result in the settlement of dispute. Consequently, the fact that negotiations are being actively pursued during the present proceedings is not, legally, any obstacle to the exercise by the Court of its judicial function.[19]

The Court explicitly maintained that position in *Nicaragua v. United States*.[20]

The rule that there is no incompatibility between negotiations and judicial settlement applies also when the former are recommended or commanded by the Security Council without any mention of adjudication. Such a recommendation or command does not exclude action in the Court. This applies also to a negotiating 'process' in the framework of a regional arrangement (Chapter VIII of the Charter). In the judgment in the *Case Concerning Military and Paramilitary Activities in and against Nicaragua (Jurisdiction of the Court and Admissibility of the Application)* we find the following statement:

> The Court is unable to accept either that there is any requirement of prior exhaustion of regional negotiating processes as a precondition to seising the Court;

---

[19] ICJ Reports, 1978, p. 3, at p. 12, para. 29, quoted by S. M. Schwebel, Deputy Agent and Counsel for the USA Government, in the *Hostages* case, Pleadings, p. 288.

[20] ICJ Reports, 1984, at p. 440.

THE ICJ AND THE UN

or that the existence of the Contadora process[21] constitutes in this case an obstacle to the examination by the Court of the Nicaraguan Application and judicial determination in due course by the submissions of the Parties in the Case.[22]

CO-ORDINATION: RECOMMENDATIONS UNDER ARTICLE 36, PARAGRAPH 3 OF THE CHARTER

Though there is separation of competences and independence of action[23] of the two organs (and this is one side of the parallelism of their functions), both the law and the practice of the UN leave room for, and in some circumstances require, correlation. Indeed, correlation seems to be part of the system which includes an explicit rule on the possibility of dividing the task of settling a dispute between the Council and the Court.

That rule is article 36, paragraph 3 of the Charter.[24] Under that provision the Security Council may recommend that 'legal disputes should as a general rule be referred by the parties to the International Court of Justice in accordance with the provisions of the Statute of the Court'.[25] In deciding whether to make such a recommendation the Council enjoys a wide latitude or discretion.[26] In particular, it can single out only one or some legal aspects for the settlement by the Court, while putting other legal points aside.

By itself, a Security Council recommendation does not confer jurisdiction

---

[21] This is the name of a diplomatic initiative, preceding the case and contemporaneous with it, which aimed at solving various security and political problems of Central America, including Nicaragua.

[22] *Ibid.*, at p. 444, para. 108.

[23] In the *Hostages* case the US Agent spoke of the 'duty' of the Court to indicate provisional measures 'quite without regard to any parallel action' by the Security Council: Pleadings, at p. 29.

[24] One dictum seems to suggest that the Court regards article 36, para. 3 of the Charter as evidence of separation rather than co-ordination. In the *Diplomatic and Consular Staff* case the Court said:

> Whereas Article 12 of the Charter expressly forbids the General Assembly to make any recommendation with regard to a dispute or situation while the Security Council is exercising its functions in respect of that dispute or situation, no such restriction is placed on the functioning of the Court by any provision of either the Charter or the Statute of the Court. The reasons are clear. It is for the Court, the principal judicial organ of the United Nations, to resolve any legal questions that may be in issue between parties to a dispute; and the resolution of such legal questions by the Court may be an important, and sometimes decisive, factor in promoting the peaceful settlement of the dispute. This is indeed recognized by Article 36 of the Charter
> ICJ Reports, 1980, p. 3, at p. 22, para. 40.

[25] For recent comments on article 36, para. 3, see in particular Brigitte Stern in Jean-Pierre Cot and Alain Pellet (eds.), *La Charte des Nations Unies: Commentaire article par article* (2nd edn, Paris, 1991), pp. 621–7; Torsten Stein and Stefan Richter in Bruno Simma (ed.), *Charta der Vereinten Nationen. Kommentar* (Munich, 1991), pp. 512–15.

[26] Stein and Richter, in *Charta der Vereinten Nationen*, p. 514.

on the Court.[27] Article 25 of the Charter is not applicable here. There must be acceptance of the recommendation by the parties resulting in the acceptance of the jurisdiction. That acceptance is a 'voluntary' act.[28] The Security Council is in no position to impose it on the addressees of the recommendation.

If subsequently to the act or acts of their acceptance the parties sign a Special Agreement (*compromis*) on the resolution of their dispute by the Court, that agreement does not create the Court's jurisdiction but confirms it by dealing with other issues of the proceedings, e.g. the description of questions to be resolved by the Court.[29]

If the parties have earlier recognized the compulsory jurisdiction of the Court under article 36, paragraph 2 of its Statute, and the dispute falls under their declarations made according to that provision, the Court is competent to adjudicate once the case has been brought before it by one party through its application addressed to the Court. But in that instance the road to judicial settlement already existed. Consequently, here the role of the recommendation is more limited than in the situation where the parties have not yet agreed to the Court's jurisdiction and the Security Council resolution prompts them to arrive at such an agreement.

In the *Corfu Channel* case, prior to the acceptance by Albania of the recommendation contained in resolution 22 (1947) and prior to the expression of her readiness to appear before the Court,[30] it was premature for the UK to contend that the Court already had jurisdiction.[31] The Court attached constitutive effect to the Albanian acceptance of the Security Council

---

[27] The nature and effect of the recommendation made under article 36, para. 3 have been extensively discussed by the parties during the oral proceedings in the *Corfu Channel* case (*Preliminary Objection*), Pleadings, vol. III, pp. 15–156.

[28] *Corfu Channel* case (*Preliminary Objection*), ICJ Reports, 1947–8, p. 15, at p. 26; Judge *ad hoc* Daxner, Dissenting Opinion, p. 33, at p. 35.

[29] In the *Corfu Channel* case the Court has already resolved, in the positive, the problem of jurisdiction and admissibility when Albania and the UK concluded their Special Agreement defining the questions to be submitted to the Court for decision: Pleadings, vol. II, pp. 28–9. For the explanations of the parties on their Agreement, see *ibid.*, vol. III, pp. 162–3. The Agreement was signed on the day on which the delivery of the judgment relating to the preliminary objection took place (25 March 1948) but prior to that delivery; it was notified to the Court on the day after that delivery. The Agreement stated that it '[had] been drawn up as a result of' Security Council resolution 22 (1947). Nonetheless that Agreement was not creative of the Court's jurisdiction because the jurisdiction followed from earlier acts of the two states, i.e. the UK application of 13 May 1947 and the Albanian letter of 2 July 1947. The UK has pointed out that '[a] special agreement is not necessary': Pleadings, vol. II, p. 14, at p. 18. See also the Court's view: ICJ Reports, 1947–8, at p. 28. The Order of 26 March 1948 states that 'this Special Agreement now forms the basis of further proceedings before the Court in this case' (*ibid.*, p. 53, at p. 55).

[30] Letter of 2 August 1947, *Pleadings*, vol. II, p. 25, at p. 26, para. 4.

[31] Letter of 13 May 1947, *Pleadings*, vol. I, p. 8, para. 2.

recommendation and the Court's jurisdiction. Such acceptance removed 'all difficulties concerning the question of the admissibility of the [British] Application and the question of the jurisdiction of the Court'.[32]

Article 36, paragraph 3 is not an instance of creating compulsory jurisdiction. The Statute 'founds the jurisdiction of the Court on the consent of States' and the word 'recommendation' does not here lose its 'normal meaning', i.e. it is not binding.[33]

Once consent is present the parties are not subordinated to the observance of any particular method of bringing the case before the Court.[34]

A recommendation under article 36, paragraph 3, while not creating an obligation, can carry with it some (permissible) pressure on the parties to the dispute or an element of persuasion. The degree of pressure or the strength of persuasion will vary. In resolution 22 (1947), the language of the recommendation conveyed a certain insistence and a feeling of urgency on the part of the Security Council: 'the United Kingdom and Albanian Government should immediately refer the dispute' to the Court. In resolution 395 (1976) the Council was less emphatic. It only[35] invited the governments of Greece and Turkey 'to take into account the contribution that appropriate judicial means, in particular the International Court of Justice, [were] qualified to make to the settlement of any remaining legal differences which they [identified] in connexion with their present dispute' i.e. the conflict concerning the Aegean Sea continental shelf. This formula left a lot of discretion to the parties.[36]

There is nothing in the Charter or the Statute to make proceedings in certain matters before the Council a condition precedent to proceedings before the Court.[37] The Council may recommend a certain sequence of

---

[32] ICJ Reports, 1947–8, pp. 26–7.

[33] *Corfu Channel* case (*Preliminary Objection*), Separate Opinion by Judges Basdevant, Alvarez, Winiarski, Zoricic, De Visscher, Badawi Pasha and Krylov, *Ibid.*, p. 31, at p. 32.

[34] Cf. the Court in the same case, *ibid.*, p. 28.

[35] Stein and Richter, in *Charta der Vereinten Nationen*, p. 514.

[36] Cf. Stern, in *La Charte des Nations Unies*, pp. 626–7. As to the disputes or situations in which an attempt to secure a recommendation under article 36, paragraph 3 failed (validity of the 1936 Treaty between Egypt and Great Britain; Indian–Pakistani dispute of 1957; the RB-47 incident in 1960), see *ibid.*, 625 and Stein and Richter, *Charta der Vereinten Nationen*, p. 514.

[37] This type of link between the two proceedings was considered by the Permanent Court with regard to the Council of the League of Nations in connection with the interpretation of article 17 of the Convention concerning the Territory of Memel signed on 8 May 1924 in Paris: *Interpretation of the Statute of the Memel Territory (Preliminary Objection)*, PCIJ, Series A/B, No. 47, p. 243, at pp. 248 and 243. Cf. the US Counter-Memorial in the *Nicaragua* case, para. 499 (at the moment this contribution goes to the press the Pleadings in that case have not yet been published). For the text of the Convention, see *League of Nations Treaty Series*, vol. XXIX, p. 85.

action. The decision on when to institute proceedings in the Court rests with the parties or party to the dispute, but in the hypothesis considered here the Court would certainly make an effort to give attention to the Security Council recommendation on timing.

In its turn the Security Council will occasionally include the Court action into the framework of settlement. In resolution 461 (1979) the Council took 'into account' the Court's Order of 15 December 1979 indicating provisional measures in the dispute between the UN and Iran resulting from the seizure and detention by the latter of American personnel in Tehran. This shows that the Council goes further than mere parallelism.

RESTRICTION OF PARALLELISM: THE *LOCKERBIE* CASES

It is convenient now to discuss the question whether in dealing with the dispute (or disputes) resulting from the aeroplane crash that occurred on 21 December 1988 over Lockerbie in Scotland (destruction of PanAm Flight 103 through a bomb placed aboard), the Security Council adopted a stance different from that which emerges from cases examined in the first three sections.

The conflict, which at the moment of this writing remains unresolved, involves the UK and the US on the one hand, and Libya on the other. The Council also dealt with requests by France.[38]

The UK and the US seek, in particular, through the submission of the matter to the Security Council, the extradition of the two Libyan nationals whom they charged with the said placing of the bomb; they also presented other demands. The Security Council first acted under Chapter VI of the Charter (resolution 731 (1992)) and subsequently under Chapter VII (resolution 748 (1992)). In the latter resolution the Council decided that the Libyan government had to comply with paragraph 3 of the former resolution, i.e., 'to provide a full and effective response' to the requests addressed to that government by France, the UK and the US, and also to take some steps (indicated in the second resolution) with regard to international terrorism. Pending the compliance by Libya with these decisions the Council ordered the application of certain sanctions against that country.

In the time between the adoption of each of the two resolutions Libya instituted proceedings against the UK and the US invoking the Montreal

---

[38] On account of the earlier destruction of Union de transports aériens flight 772. Libya did not institute proceedings before the Court against France.

Convention.[39] She asked the Court to adjudge and declare that she 'fully complied' with all her obligations under that Convention, that the UK and the US were in breach of the Convention, and that they were obliged, *inter alia*, 'to cease and desist' from threat or use of force against Libya. The Libyan government also applied for the indication of provisional measures, in particular to prevent the taking against it 'measures calculated to exert coercion on it or compel it to surrender the accused individuals'.[40] The Court decided not to indicate any provisional measures.[41]

In discussing the American and British requests resulting from the Lockerbie tragedy[42] the Security Council did not accept the view of those of its members who suggested that it should rather act according to its previous pattern, i.e., co-ordinate its measures with judicial proceedings, including postponement of action until the Court took its decision.[43] The Council created a situation in which the Court was left with no choice.[44] The Court was in fact excluded. Some judges forming the majority seem to have been uneasy on this account. Speaking of the relations between the two organs they remind us of the requirement of 'coordination and cooperation, not competition or mutual exclusion';[45] not 'a blinkered parallelism of functions, but a fruitful interaction'.[46] Yet that was not the Council's stance.

The dates speak for themselves: the closing of the Court hearings on provisional measures took place on 28 March; resolution 748 was adopted on 31 March; and the Court issued its Order on 14 April 1992. These dates show that the Council, as Judge Oda observed, 'must . . . have acted in full

---

[39] Convention for the Suppression of Unlawful Acts against the Safety of Civil Aviation done at Montreal on 23 September 1971, 10 *ILM* 1151 (1971).

[40] *Case Concerning Questions of Interpretation and Application of the 1971 Montreal Convention Arising from the Aerial Incident at Lockerbie (Libyan Arab Jamahiriya v. United Kingdom) (Request for the Indication of Provisional Measures)*, ICJ Reports, 1992, p. 3 and under the same name *Libyan Arab Jamahiriya v. United States of America, ibid.*, p. 114. The quoted words are on pp. 6–7, para. 7, and p. 9, para. 19, and pp. 117–18, para. 7, and p. 120, para. 20, of the respective Orders.

[41] *Ibid.*, pp. 15 and 127. For writings on the various issues raised by the *Lockerbie* cases, see n. 82 below.

[42] As already noted, the request by France (UTS crash) had no counterpart in any ICJ proceedings.

[43] Cape Verde, India and Zimbabwe; the latter country presided over the Council. Their position is reported by Judge El-Kosheri, Dissenting Opinions, *ibid.*, p. 94, at pp. 105–6, paras. 37–9, and p. 199, at pp. 210–11, paras. 37–9. As to the changing US position see n. 23 above.

[44] Judge Oda points out that the Court 'has at present no choice but to acknowledge the pre-eminence of that resolution': Declarations: *ibid.*, pp. 17 and 129. In his Separate Opinions Judge Lachs expressed the view that the Orders should not be seen 'as an abdication of the Court's powers': *ibid.*, p. 26, at p. 27, and p. 138, at p. 139. Abdication implies earlier possession of the powers to be abdicated. Did they still exist after resolution 748 (1992)? The action by the Council aimed at the Court's jurisdiction.

[45] Judge Ni, Declarations, *ibid.*, p. 20, at p. 22, and p. 132, at p. 134.

[46] *Ibid.*, pp. 26 and 138.

cognizance of the impact of its own decision on that which still fell to be taken by the Court as well as of the possible consequences of the latter'.[47] One may say more: the Council and in particular the initiators of resolution 748 aimed at frustrating the Libyan action in the Court. They were, in that phase of the dispute, successful: the Court refused to indicate provisional measures.

During its deliberations the Court was aware of the implications of resolution 748 for its decision,[48] though characteristically it avoided any elaboration. But the Court realized that had it acted otherwise, had it indicated any measures (whether those requested by Libya or those of its own choice), it would have contradicted the Council.[49]

The Court referred to the obligation of the parties under article 25 of the UN Charter: 'This obligation extends to the decision contained in resolution 748 (1992).'[50] The Court also stressed that 'an indication of the measures requested by Libya would be likely to impair the rights which appear[ed] prima facie to be enjoyed' by the UK and by the US by virtue of resolution 748 (1992).[51]

The Court found, in the Operative Clauses of the Orders, that 'the circumstances of [the cases were] not such as to require the exercise of its power under Article 41 of the Statute to indicate provisional measures'.[52] Now, the 'circumstances' were created unilaterally and peremptorily by the Council, and what they 'required' was abstention by the Court. Otherwise there would be conflict.

The Court applied article 103 of the Charter, thus recognizing the primacy of obligations resulting from resolution 748 (1992).[53] But in this and in other cases the matter cannot be reduced to that Charter provision as the governing rule.

In the *Lockerbie* case litispendence was no obstacle to the treatment of the

---

[47] *Ibid.*, pp. 18 and 130.

[48] Cf. *ibid.*, p. 14, para. 34, and p. 125, para. 37.

[49] Judge Bedjaoui speaks of the 'risk' of 'contradictory solutions' and of 'inconsistency': Dissenting Opinions, *ibid.*, p. 33, at p. 35, para. 6, and p. 143, at p. 145, para. 6.

[50] *Ibid.*, p. 15, para. 39, and p. 126, para. 42. The Court said that the obligations of the parties under article 25 and resolution 748 (1992) prevailed, in accordance with article 103 of the Charter, 'over their obligations under any other international agreement, including the Montreal Convention' (*ibid.*). Though the Court did not regard itself 'at this stage' to be 'called upon to determine definitively the legal effect' of resolution 748, it nonetheless determined one such effect: 'Whatever the situation previous to the adoption of that resolution, the rights claimed by Libya under the Montreal Convention cannot now be regarded as appropriate for protection by the indication of provisional measures': *ibid.*, p. 15, para. 40, and p. 126, para. 43.

[51] *Ibid.*, p. 15, para. 41, and p. 127, para. 44.

[52] *Ibid.*, pp. 15 and 127.

[53] *Ibid.*, p. 15, para. 39, and p. 126, para. 42.

dispute (or disputes)[54] by the Security Council. The question was not limited to 'political' treatment alone.[55] Resolution 748 (1992) dealt with, and had an impact on, the issue of extradition which by definition is one of application of law.

Resolution 748 (1992) deprived Libya of the right not to extradite her citizens which she would have under the Montreal Convention provided she acted in conformity with the Convention's provisions on criminal proceedings. This resolution, as some judges emphasized, changed 'the legal situation' the Court was considering.[56] But there was more than that. The Council has brought about a change that had a direct effect on the Court's jurisdiction. The Council modified the scope of that jurisdiction.[57] In the collision between the duty under the resolution and the right under the Montreal Convention the former has primacy. There was concurrent competence of the two organs and the action of the Security Council cut down the Court's competence.[58] The Court could not exercise its function.[59] The effect of resolution 748 was to prevent the Court from indicating the provisional measures as requested by Libya. To avoid collision with the Council[60] the Court refrained from indicating these

[54] The disputes submitted to the Security Council and the Court might be regarded as separate disputes, and not only different parts or aspects of the same dispute. Be that as it may, in the hypothesis of more than one dispute, they certainly coincided, thus leading to the overlap of jurisdiction.

 The presentation of the same conflict in the Security Council as a 'situation' and in the Court as a 'dispute' is not a criterion for resolving the latter's jurisdiction. On this distinction, in connection with the ICJ, cf. Domingo E. Acevedo, 'Disputes under Consideration by the UN Security Council or Regional Bodies', in Lori Fisler Damrosh (ed.), *The International Court of Justice at a Crossroads* (Dobbs Ferry, NY, 1987), p. 242, at pp. 252–4 and 256.

 On litispendence, see J. H. Elsen, *Litispendence between the International Court of Justice and the Security Council* (The Hague, 1986).

[55] Cf. the conclusions by Rosenne, *The Law and Practice of the International Court*, p. 87, with regard to the simultaneous consideration of a dispute (in particular that involving the territory of South West Africa) by the UN General Assembly and the Court.

[56] Joint Declarations of Judges Evensen, Tarassov, Guillaume and Aguilar Mawdsley, ICJ Reports, 1992, p. 24, at p. 25, para. 4, and p. 136 at p. 137, para. 4. Judge Lachs spoke of 'a new situation': *Ibid.*, pp. 27 and 139.

[57] On the other hand, Judge *ad hoc* El-Kosheri expressed the opinion that 'paragraph 1 of Security Council resolution 748 (1992) should not be considered to have any legal effect on the jurisdiction of the Court': *ibid.*, at p. 107, para. 47, and at p. 212, para. 47.

[58] Judge Bedjaoui speaks of 'a [Court's] power "constrained" by a decision of the Security Council': p. 40, para. 16, and p. 150, para. 16.

[59] Cf. *ibid.*, p. 46, para. 27, n. 1, and p. 156, para. 27, n. 1.

[60] Judge Shahabuddeen denies that there was 'any collision between the *competence* of the Security Council and that of the Court' (emphasis added), Separate Opinions, *ibid.*, p. 28, at p. 29, and p. 140, at p. 141. With respect, the present writer disagrees with that view. He rather follows Judge Bedjaoui in para. 7 of his Dissenting Opinions, *ibid.*, at pp. 35 and 145.

measures.[61] The resolution 'concerned the very object of the legal dispute submitted to the Court', and the Court's power has been 'constrained'.[62] Each of the respondent states made no bones about it: the UK contended that the provisional measures 'were designed to fetter the Security Council of the United Nations in the exercise of its proper powers',[63] while the US also asked the Court to refrain from exercising its judicial function[64] and assumed that if the Court did not do it, there would be a conflict with the Council.[65]

EXCLUSIVE COMPETENCE OF THE SECURITY COUNCIL?

This question was not absent from the thinking of some in regard to the problem treated in the previous section, though it then arose implicitly rather than expressly. It should now be considered.

The dictum of the Permanent Court of International Justice in the *Minority Schools* cases retains its relevance: the provision of article 36, paragraph 1 of the Statute becomes inoperative only 'in those exceptional cases in which the dispute which States might desire to refer to the Court would fall within the exclusive jurisdiction reserved to some other authority'.[66] Needless to say, if there is a matter which belongs to the exclusive competence of the Security Council, the Court has no jurisdiction, and an application to the Court is inadmissible.[67]

The difficulty with this obvious truth is that it is inconclusive for the purposes of our analysis: one may wonder whether the practice of the two organs does supply any clue. Referring to article 12 of the Charter the Court

---

[61] Judge Weeramantry saw room for the indication of provisional measures 'while preserving full respect for resolution 748 (1992) in all its integrity', but it seems that in this hypothesis they would be different from those requested by Libya; they would be indicated *proprio motu*: Dissenting Opinions, *ibid.*, p. 50, at pp. 67 and 70–1, and p. 160, at pp. 177 and 180–1. See also Judge Ranjeva, Dissenting Opinions, *ibid.*, p. 72, at pp. 74ff, and p. 182; Judge Ajibola, Dissenting Opinions, *ibid.*, p. 78, esp. at pp. 92–3, and p. 183, at pp. 197–8; and Judge *ad hoc* El-Kosheri, *ibid.*, pp. 107–12 and pp. 212–17.

[62] Judge Bedjaoui, *ibid.*, p. 40, para. 16, and p. 150, p. 16.

[63] The UK view as summarized by the Court, *ibid.*, p. 11, para. 27. The pleadings in the *Lockerbie* cases have not yet been published.

[64] This position was taken by the two states in reference to Security Council resolution 731 (1992) alone. For an appraisal of the significance of that resolution, cf. Judge Weeramantry, *ibid.*, at pp. 66 and 176. The position of the US in the *Hostages* case was different: Pleadings, p. 29; and see n. 13 above.

[65] See quotations from the pleadings in ICJ Reports, 1992, p. 3, at p. 44, para. 23, and p. 154, para. 23.

[66] *Rights of Minorities in Upper Silesia (Minority Schools)*, PCIJ, Series A, No. 15, at p. 23. The *Minorities* case concerned the interpretation and application of the Polish–German Convention on Upper Silesia signed on 15 May 1922 in Geneva: *League of Nations Treaty Series*, vol. IX, p. 466; quoted by US Counter-Memorial in the *Nicaragua* case, Pleadings, para. 500.

[67] As to the relative significance of the distinction between jurisdiction and admissibility in this respect, see the Court's dictum in *Military and Paramilitary Activities in and against Nicaragua (Jurisdiction and Admissibility)*, ICJ Reports, 1984, at p. 429, para. 84.

itself reminds us that 'no such restriction is placed on the functioning of the Court by any provision of either the Charter or the Statute of the Court'.[68] Nor is there any exclusiveness[69] in the conferment on the Council of 'primary responsibility for the maintenance of international peace and security' (article 24, paragraph 1 of the Charter).

The Court will not arrogate to itself, as actually it never did, any executive functions which are those of the Security Council, in particular under Chapter VII of the Charter. The Court always remained in the framework of its adjudicative function. Under Chapter VI the Court can deal with legal elements or aspects of a dispute which otherwise has a political content or may even be predominantly political – in its outlook, role, implications or consequences. Such nature of the dispute does not eliminate the Court. The judicial organ of the UN makes a legal determination and gives a remedy. In this abstract sense a legal dispute constitutes a separate category, though often a legal dispute actually constitutes a fragment of a broader conflict.

It is only in the foregoing meaning that one can divide the competences of the two organs. The task of splitting these competences *ratione materiae* is difficult. The American attempt to prevent the Court from making determinations falling under the head of Chapter VII of the Charter has failed. In *Nicaragua v. United States* the latter country contended that 'all allegations of ongoing threats to the peace, breaches of the peace, and acts of aggression [were] confided to the political organs for consideration and determination', primarily to the Security Council. Adjudication is therefore excluded. Judicial settlement is not a means of resolving 'ongoing armed conflict', including 'the evaluation of claims' concerning the exercise of the right of self-defence.[70]

It may be added that in the light of its specific facts the *Nicaragua* case was not one of choice between the Council and the Court. While questioning the Court's jurisdiction and the admissibility of the application in regard to conflicts involving 'the ongoing use of force' the US was also reluctant to have

---

[68] *United States Diplomatic and Consular Staff in Tehran*, ICJ Reports, 1980, p. 3, at p. 22, para. 40. The Court quoted its position in the *Nicaragua* case, ICJ Reports, 1984, p. 433, para. 93. See also Pleadings in the *Diplomatic and Consular Staff* case, pp. 29 and 34.

[69] *Military and Paramilitary Activities (Jurisdiction and Admissibility)*, ICJ Reports, 1984, p. 432, para. 90, and p. 434, para. 95. See also the rejection by the Court of the Yugoslav argument based on article 25 and Chapter VII of the Charter in the *Case Concerning Application of the Genocide Convention (Request for the Indication of Provisional Measures)*, ICJ Reports, 1993, p. 3, at pp. 18–19, para. 33.

[70] US Counter-Memorial, paras. 450ff, quotations taken from paras. 450, 454 and 455. Judge Schwebel says that despite the force of the US arguments and of the San Francisco documentation in support of them he finds himself 'unable to agree that it was the design of the drafters of the Charter and the Statute to exclude the Court from adjudicating disputes falling within the scope of Chapter VII of the United Nations Charter, and unable to agree that the practice of States in interpreting the Charter, and the Statute confirms such a design': ICJ Reports, 1986, p. 289, para. 56.

the matter dealt with in the Security Council.[71] Be that as it may, the Court rejected the American arguments and did not take the stance that the law did not entrust it with any authority in the subject matter of Chapters VII and VIII of the Charter.[72]

Where the law, the decision of the parties or the unilateral declaration under the Optional Clause confers exclusive competence on the Security Council[73] or excludes the Court's jurisdiction[74] the position is clear.

But even in the face of silence by law or the parties there is still room for discussing the problem. The area, of course, remains difficult to delimit. The issue is one of judicial propriety: are there disputes that, while they contain legal elements, should, in their entirety, be settled through a political process and in the framework of political arrangements? The category of disputes not suitable for adjudication is hard to define and can easily become highly controversial. The point is well illustrated by the pleadings in *Nicaragua v. United States.*

In the *Northern Cameroons* case the Court spoke of the 'inherent limitations on the exercise of the judicial function which the Court, as a court of justice, can never ignore'.[75] Though this dictum belongs to the context of a particular case, it is general enough to be taken into consideration in discussing the division of competences between the Court and the Security Council. One such limitation may flow from the 'overwhelmingly political nature'[76] of the dispute notwithstanding its legal aspects. Theoretically, and depending on

---

[71] Acevedo, 'Disputes under Consideration', p. 262.

[72] ICJ Reports, 1984, pp. 431–41, paras. 89–108; in particular, the Court observed (*ibid.*, p. 435, para. 96): 'It must also be remembered that, as the *Corfu Channel* case (*I.C.J. Reports 1949*, p. 4) shows, the Court has never shied away from a case brought before it merely because it had political implications or because it involved serious elements of the use of force . . . What is also significant is that the Security Council itself in that case had "undoubtedly intended that the whole dispute should be decided by the Court" (p. 26)'.

[73] Under article 298(1)(c) of the United Nations Convention on the Law of the Sea (21 *ILM* 1261 (1982)), a state may declare that it does not accept the compulsory procedures provided for in the Convention in the case of disputes 'in respect of which the Security Council of the United Nations is exercising the functions assigned to it by the Charter of the United Nations, unless the Security Council decides to remove the matter from its agenda or calls upon the parties to settle it by the means provided for in this Convention'. This provision is briefly discussed by Acevedo, 'Disputes under Consideration', p. 259.

[74] Acevedo, 'Disputes under Consideration', p. 263, refers to reservations of this nature in the declaration of acceptance of the Optional Clause.

[75] ICJ Reports, 1963, p. 15, at p. 29. The US Counter-Memorial in the Nicaraguan case contended that the framers of the Charter assigned 'functional responsibility' for 'dealing with situations of ongoing armed conflict' to 'the political organs, and in particular to the Security Council. They did so at least in part in recognition of the inherent limitations of the judicial function in settling such situations' (para. 521).

[76] *Military and Paramilitary Activities in and against Nicaragua (Merits)*, Dissenting Opinion of Judge Oda, ICJ Reports, 1986, p. 212, at p. 238, para. 55, and p. 239, para. 57.

THE ICJ AND THE UN

circumstances, there could be room for the view that under the Charter and the Statute such a dispute is non-justiciable,[77] though this is not said in any explicit provision.

Nor did the Court adopt, up to now, such a stance. In the *Nicaragua* case it rejected it. In the *Lockerbie* cases, in view of Security Council resolution 748 (1992), the Court was practically left with no choice other than inaction: the Council actually excluded the exercise by the Court of its competence to indicate provisional measures. But in its Orders the Court did not elaborate on the issue.[78] One may, therefore, debate whether this was a situation of judicial restraint actually imposed by the Council or a situation where jurisdiction was at stake. This writer favours the latter interpretation. In the *Lockerbie* cases the Council came rather close to Judge Alvarez's view:[79]

> If a case submitted to the Court should constitute a threat to world peace, the Security Council may seise itself of the case and put an end to the Court's jurisdiction. The competence of the Council results from the nature of the international organization established by the Charter, and from the powers of the Council.

It has also been argued that 'the judicial process is unsuited to dealing with situations that are by their nature exceptionally fluid'. For the Court to adjudicate, 'a sufficiently coherent and legally static pattern of facts must be found to exist'.[80] But the criterion of 'non-fluidity' is so general that it is not helpful.

To pursue the question any further in an abstract way does not seem useful. The decisions of the Court show that in dealing with the category discussed here it protected 'the interests of the integrity of the judicial function'.[81] One could not say that in the *Lockerbie* cases the Security Council necessarily and intentionally ignored these high interests. Yet it pursued its own course of action which unavoidably had its effect on what the Court would do and indeed did. Is this a pattern for the future?

---

[77] Judge Oda, *ibid.*

[78] ICJ Reports, 1992, at pp. 14–15 and 125–7.

[79] Dissenting Opinion in *Anglo-Iranian Oil Co.* case, ICJ Reports, 1952, p. 124, at p. 134. According to Rosenne, *The Law and Practice of the International Court*, p. 73, there is 'no express authority in the Charter or in the Statute for the proposition advanced by Judge Alvarez'. In the *Lockerbie* cases Judge Weeramantry quoted Rosenne: ICJ Reports, 1992, pp. 57 and 167.

[80] US Counter-Memorial in the *Nicaragua* case, para. 524. In the American view an allegedly existing armed conflict did not fulfil that test.

[81] *Ibid.*, para. 435, referred to that factor; quoted (without reference) by the Court in its judgment on jurisdiction and admissibility, ICJ Reports, 1984, p. 429, para. 84.

JUDICIAL REVIEW OF COUNCIL DECISIONS?

The Advisory Opinion in the *Namibia* case contains a clear and explicit answer: 'Undoubtedly the Court does not possess powers of judicial review or appeal in respect of the decisions taken by the United Nations organs concerned.'[82] Indeed, in analogy to municipal law, for such powers to exist there must be an express norm authorizing judicial review. These powers cannot be implied. No appeal, review or similar procedure has been provided for either in the Charter or in the Statute. Consequently, the proceedings in the Court do not and cannot constitute an appeal from a decision of the Security Council to the principal judicial organ of the Organization.[83] In other

---

[82] ICJ Reports, 1971, at p. 45, para. 89. The problem has been amply discussed in connection with the decision of the Court on provisional measures in the *Lockerbie* case, ICJ Reports, 1992, pp. 3 and 114. See, in particular, M. P. Andrés Saénz de Santa María, 'De maximis non curat praetor . . . ? El Consejo de Seguridad y el TIJ en el asunto Lockerbie', *Revista española de derecho internacional*, 44 (1992), pp. 327–50; Mohammed Bedjaoui, 'Du Contrôle de légalité des actes du Conseil de Sécurité', in *Nouveau itinéraires en droit, Hommage à François Rigaux* (Bibliothèque de la Faculté de Droit de l'Université Catholique de Louvain, vol. XXII, Brussels, 1993), pp. 69–110; Fiona Beveridge, 'The Lockerbie Affair', *ICLQ*, 41 (1992), pp. 907–20; Derek Bowett, 'The Impact of Security Council Decisions on Dispute Settlement Procedures', *European Journal of International Law*, 5 (1994), pp. 89–101; Bernhard Graefrath, 'Leave to the Court what Belongs to the Court: The Libyan Case', *European Journal of International Law*, 4 (1993), pp. 184–205; Gerald P. McGinley, 'The ICJ's Decision in the Lockerbie Cases', *Georgia Journal of International and Comparative Law*, 22 (1992), pp. 577–607; Edward McWhinney, 'The International Court as Emerging Constitutional Court and the Co-ordinate UN Institutions (Especially the Security Council): Implications of the Aerial Incident at Lockerbie', *Canadian Yearbook of International Law/Annuaire canadien de droit international*, 30 (1992), pp. 261–72; E. Sciso, 'Può la Corte internazionale di giustizia rilevare l'invalidità di una decisione del Consiglio di sicurezza?', *Rivista di diritto internazionale*, 75 (1992), pp. 369–74; Jean-Marc Sorel, 'Les ordonnances de la Cour internationale de Justice du 14 avril 1992 dans l'affaire relative à des questions d'interprétation et d'application de la convention de Montréal de 1971 résultant de l'incident aérien de Lockerbie (Libye c. Royaume Uni et Libye c. Etats-Unis)', *Revue générale de droit international public*, 97 (1993), pp. 689–726; Christian Tomuschat, 'The Lockerbie Case before the International Court of Justice', *International Commission of Jurists, The Review*, 48 (1992), pp. 38–48; Geoffrey R. Watson, 'Constitutionalism, Judicial Review, and the World Court', *Harvard International Law Journal*, 34 (1993), pp. 1–45.

[83] In the *Lockerbie* cases Judge Bedjaoui said that it was 'as a rule not the Court's role to exercise appellate jurisdiction in respect of decisions taken by the Security Council': ICJ Reports, 1992, p. 35, para. 7, and p. 145, para. 7. Is the formula 'as a rule' a qualification allowing for exceptions? For a denial of the existence of 'the review or appellate jurisdiction', see also Judge Weeramantry, *ibid.*, pp. 55 and 165. The learned judge also refers to the Court as 'guardian of the Charter and of international law': *ibid.*, pp. 56 and 166. Obviously, that role means something other than the said jurisdiction.

According to Judge Lachs 'a number of mentions' which the Court receives 'outside its own Chapter' in the UN Charter 'tend to confirm its role as a general guardian of legality within the system' of the UN, and also beyond that system: *ibid.*, pp. 26 and 138. That statement does not seem to admit of any review competence *sensu stricto*.

In his Separate Opinion in the *Case Concerning Application of the Convention on the Prevention and Punishment of the Crime of Genocide (Further Requests for Indication of Provisional Measures)*, Judge ad hoc E. Lauterpacht, while denying any unlimited power of the Court to review the acts of the Council,

words, the Court cannot place itself, or be placed by the claimant state, in the position of controlling the act or acts of the Security Council with the effect normally entailed by such judicial supervision (invalidity of the act, the duty to correct it, or other consequences). The fact that the two organs deal with an identical subject matter does not mean that one of them is passing a judgment on the other.[84] Occasionally the Court would emphasize that the actions of the two organs existed side by side: 'The Council has functions of a political nature assigned to it, whereas the Court exercises purely judicial functions. Both organs can therefore perform their separate but complementary functions with respect to the same events.'[85] That approach does not favour any control.

The failure of a claim or claims in the Security Council and the likelihood that such a claim or claims will fail again when resubmitted to the Council does not vest the Court with jurisdiction.[86] In the Court's practice the issue of lawfulness of the acts of UN political organs is not a novel one.

In the *Expenses*[87] and *Namibia*[88] cases the Court considered the objection that certain actions of the General Assembly were *ultra vires*. In both instances

---

said that 'some power of this kind [could] hardly be doubted': ICJ Reports, 1993, p. 407, at p. 439, para. 99. Judge *ad hoc* Lauterpacht explained this in the following way: 'The Court, as the principal judicial organ of the United Nations, is entitled, indeed bound, to ensure the rule of law within the United Nations system and, in cases properly brought before it, to insist on adherence by all United Nations organs to the rules governing their operation' (*ibid.*). This is what the Court did: in several cases it examined the legality of acts of the UN political organs. But insistence on 'adherence' is a far cry from judicial review. Judge *ad hoc* Lauterpacht was right when on another occasion he wrote: 'The Security Council is not subject to any judicial control that can be invoked at the instance of a party against which it directs its political reaction': Elihu Lauterpacht, *Aspects of the Administration of International Justice* (Cambridge, 1991), p. 39.

[84] The Court rejected the US contention in the *Nicaragua v. United States* case, Counter-Memorial, paras. 511–14, that it would act in such a capacity had it found that the Nicaraguan application was admissible: ICJ Reports, 1984, p. 436, para. 98. At the moment this book goes to press the ICJ Pleadings in the case have not yet been published.

[85] *Ibid.*, p. 435, para. 96.

[86] US position as reported by the Court, *ibid.*, p. 432, para. 91. Prior to the submission of her case to the Court Nicaragua was not successful in pursuing her claims in the Security Council: UN Doc. S/PV.2529 (4 April 1984). Nor was Bosnia and Herzegovina in her efforts to have the arms embargo lifted in her favour. The embargo was imposed on all parties to the Yugoslavian conflict by Security Council Resolution 713 (1991) and maintained in subsequent decisions of that organ. She then sought the lifting of the embargo by way of action in the ICJ: see n. 90 below.

[87] ICJ Reports, 1962, p. 151, in particular at p. 168.

[88] ICJ Reports, 1971, at p. 45, para. 87 and throughout. See also Judge Ammoun, Separate Opinion, *ibid.*, p. 67, at p. 72, para. 3; Judge Petrén, Separate Opinion, *ibid.*, p. 127, at p. 131; Judge Onyeama, Separate Opinion, *ibid.*, p. 138, at pp. 143–4; Judge de Castro, Separate Opinion, *ibid.*, p. 170, at p. 180; Judge Sir Gerald Fitzmaurice, Dissenting Opinion, *ibid.*, p. 220, at pp. 279–95, paras. 90–116. These Opinions are referred to and discussed by Judge *ad hoc* El-Kosheri in the *Lockerbie* cases, ICJ Reports, 1992, pp. 103–4, paras. 27–32, and pp. 208–9, paras. 27–32. As to the *Namibia* case, cf. the position of France, Pleadings, vol. I, p. 362.

these actions resulted in obligations for member states. Hence the fact that the Court examined the General Assembly resolutions is not an obstacle to drawing an analogy. In *Nicaragua v. United States* the whole domain of Chapter VII (and VIII) of the Charter was discussed extensively by the parties and the Court in regard to the Council–Court relationship[89] (see pp. 620–1 above). In the *Lockerbie* cases Libya regarded Security Council resolution 748 (1992) 'as contrary to international law'.[90] In its Orders of 14 April 1992 the Court rejected the Libyan demand for provisional measures and took full account of resolution 748 (1992): the parties had the duty to implement it (see pp. 617 and 622 above). The Court did not put the lawfulness of the resolution in doubt; nor did it engage in any analysis of the issue of legality.[91] It is true that the Court said that it was 'not at this stage called upon to determine definitively the legal effect of Security Council resolution 748 (1992)'.[92] But the reference to 'legal effect' need not necessarily imply an examination of lawfulness; other legal questions may be involved. The expression is general enough to have various meanings.[93]

In a number of its pronouncements the Court had the occasion to refer to Security Council decisions as being adopted in accordance with the Charter. Depending on the context this could mean that the Court satisfied itself that

---

[89] Judge Sir G. Fitzmaurice examined also the powers of the Security Council: ICJ Reports, 1971, pp. 291–5, paras. 108–16.

[90] ICJ Reports, 1992, p. 14, para. 36, and p. 126, para. 39.

This is different to the position Bosnia and Herzegovina took before the Court (*Application of the Genocide Convention*). In addressing her requests to the Court she did not contend that resolution 713 (1991) and subsequent decisions of the Council, as far as they imposed a weapons embargo on her, were contrary to the Charter and/or general international law. Bosnia and Herzegovina requested the Court to adopt an interpretation of the resolution which would exclude the embargo in regard to herself. In one of the specific requests relating to this interpretation she referred to Charter articles 24(1) and 51 and to 'the customary doctrine of *ultra vires*': ICJ Reports, 1993, pp. 3 and 325, at pp. 6 and 328, subparas. (o). She requested the indication of provisional measures which, among other things, would free her from the weapons embargo. That specific request (which was repeated) was not granted, see Orders of 8 April and 13 September 1993, ICJ Reports, 1993, in particular at pp. 18–19, para. 33 and pp. 344–5, para. 41. In the first Order the Court implicitly regarded that request as not falling 'within the scope of the Genocide Convention'; in the second Order the Court pointed out that the said request lay 'outside the scope of Article 41 of the Statute': *ibid.*, p. 19, para. 35 and p. 345, para. 41, respectively. At the moment of this writing the dispute is *sub judice*.

[91] At the stage of making Orders on provisional measures, this would have been premature: see Judge Bedjaoui, ICJ Reports, 1992, p. 41, para. 18, and p. 151, para. 18.

[92] *Ibid.*, p. 15, para. 40, and p. 126, para. 43.

[93] In the *Lockerbie* cases some see a potential for clarifying or even developing the issue of judicial review in the UN: see, in particular, Thomas M. Franck, 'The "Powers of Appreciation": Who is the Ultimate Guardian of UN Legality?', *AJIL*, 86 (1992), p. 519. On the other hand, Bedjaoui, ICJ Reports, 1992, at pp. 41–2, paras. 18–19 and pp. 151–2, paras. 18–19, sees some possibilities in the advisory function alone, in contradistinction to contentious procedures.

At the moment of this writing the *Lockerbie* cases are still *sub judice*.

the act conformed to law or that it regarded such conformity as a requirement of the validity of the act.

When the Court interprets the Charter provisions relating to the functions and powers of the Security Council, it cannot avoid the issue of legality of the Council's action, be it implicitly. Advisory jurisdiction opens up a road here.[94] It need not be a direct question raising the problem of lawfulness with regard to the Council.

The latter point is illustrated by the *Admission to Membership* case.[95] Here the Court said what a UN member state could not do when pronouncing itself by its vote under article 4, paragraph 1 of the Charter. As individual votes that are being cast in the Security Council lead to the creation of the act of that organ,[96] in this instance a recommendation to admit a candidate country to the Organization, the Court's Advisory Opinion, by explaining the limits of action under that provision, equally and actually concerned the conformity of the conduct of the Security Council with the Charter. This is a method whereby the Court reaches the Council by elucidating what is lawful for the Council members when they vote on the Council's act. In fact, the Soviet veto and the resulting practice of the Council of non-recommending the admission of several candidates in 1946–7 caused the General Assembly to turn to the Court. Notwithstanding the Court's explanations (which are true) on the meaning of the question put to it, and notwithstanding the abstract terms in which the question was couched, the Court – by interpreting the Charter – resolved the issue of whether the Council acted within the bounds of the powers conferred upon it.

On the other hand, when the Court refers to article 103,[97] it avoids the issue or at any rate deals with a different problem. For under that provision nothing can be said on the lawfulness of the Council decision in the light of the Charter, not to speak of general international law. But a reference to article 103 is not evidence of any tendency on the part of the Court to refrain from an examination of the lawfulness of Council decisions. If the Court relies on article 103, it does so for reasons inherent in the case under consideration.

In the problem discussed here two of its components should be distinguished. One is the Council's duty to respect law (within the latitude of article 103), another is the mechanism for judicial control of the Council's acts.

---

[94] Bedjaoui, ICJ Reports, 1992, pp. 41–2, paras. 18–19 and pp. 151–2, paras. 18–19.

[95] ICJ Reports, 1947–8, p. 57.

[96] Or to the absence of the act, which also amounts to taking a position.

[97] As it did in the *Lockerbie* cases, ICJ Reports, 1992, at p. 15, para. 39, and p. 126, para. 42.

As to the first, the Council operates under limitations resulting from the rule of law which is an essential element of the constitution of the international community. The Council must abide by the UN Charter and general international law, in particular by peremptory norms of the latter. That duty is capable of judicial determination and is part of the function of the Court. The Court's jurisprudence confirms this.

The existence of a review procedure is another matter. Such procedure is not the only means of guaranteeing that the Council will respect law. Up till now a mechanism of judicial review of Council decisions has not been created, and in no case did the Court assume the role of an appeal or reviewing instance in the strict sense of judicial control of constitutionality. Would the Court be inclined to build up, by its practice, a procedure similar to that control? In the judgment on jurisdiction and admissibility in *Nicaragua v. United States* there is a passage that might give some food for thought on the Court's caution.[98] Nonetheless, the *Lockerbie* cases have led to some hopes for a development of the Court's role in this respect.[99]

CONCLUSIONS

To recapitulate the foregoing survey[100] attention can be drawn to the following points.

(1) There is no complete separation of powers between the Court and the Security Council in regard to the settlement of disputes.

(2) In that field their functions are both parallel, and complementary. The latter feature should facilitate the avoidance of inconsistency between the decisions of the two organs in the same matter.

(3) Action undertaken in the Security Council, including action initiated by

---

[98] ICJ Reports, 1984, at p. 436, para. 98:

> Nor can the Court accept that the present proceedings are objectionable as being in effect an appeal to the Court from an adverse decision of the Security Council. The Court is not asked to say that the Security Council was wrong in its decision, nor that there was anything inconsistent with law in the way in which the members of the Council employed their right to vote. The Court is asked to pass judgment on certain legal aspects of a situation which has also been considered by the Security Council, a procedure which is entirely consonant with its position as the principal judicial organ of the United Nations.

Does this statement mean that the Court would adopt a different stance, i.e. admit that it would be 'objectionable' to proceed, had it indeed been asked to pronounce an opinion along the lines indicated?

[99] See note 93 above.

[100] The author recognizes his obligation to the writings on the ICJ and the UN. The limited size of the contribution made more extensive references to, and the discussion of, the literature impossible.

a party to a dispute, does not impede that party's action before the Court in seeking legal relief in the same dispute or in a component part of it.

(4) The Court may take cognizance of one aspect of the dispute irrespective of the fact that another aspect of it is being dealt with by the Security Council. In that sense there is separation of competences and independence of action of the two organs.

(5) There is room for co-ordination between the two organs without infringing upon the integrity of the judicial function and its freedom from any influence on its exercise. Use should be made of article 36, paragraph 3 of the UN Charter.

(6) In its action the Security Council must take account of the fact that a dispute it considers, or a matter that constitutes part of such a dispute, is *sub judice*. In its practice the Court has recognised the limitations inherent in the exercise of its function or which follow from judicial propriety. This stance of the Court has permitted it to avoid any difficulties in the relations between the two organs.

(7) Such a stance by the Court is particularly important in view of the fact that there is no general division of powers between the two organs *ratione materiae*. In particular, the Court is not excluded from dealing with matters pertaining to the existence of a threat to the peace, breach of the peace or act of aggression (Chapter VII of the Charter). On the other hand, such a division of powers may result, specifically, from treaties, the decision of the parties to the dispute or an act of the Security Council.

(8) The Court is not, and it is submitted *de lege ferenda* that it should not become, a tribunal of judicial review with power to declare null and void those acts of the Security Council that it finds contrary to law. But the Court, in view of its function, cannot and in fact did not shy away from pronouncing on the conformity of Security Council acts with law in both contentious and advisory procedures. No competence of any international organ is legally unlimited and the Court, provided it possesses jurisdiction in the matter submitted to it, is the proper authority to make a statement on whether an action by the Security Council remains within the bounds of law. Such decision or expression of opinion does not amount to judicial review in its proper sense, i.e. as emerging from, and comparable to, various systems of municipal law or the system of law of the European Union.

(9) What is, then, the contemporary perspective of our problem? As Sir Robert Jennings observes, 'the wise "management", rather than settlement, of disputes may often be far better'. The learned judge envisages a configuration where management is superior and settlement should not

even be tried.[101] This is one hypothesis that is relevant to our study. Another is that of disputes or situations where 'management' proves the only way of proceeding as no 'settlement' is in sight, though it is sought. While political circumstances may leave no choice for the Security Council but to 'only' manage a dispute or a situation for a long or even indefinite time, the Court can be in a position to resolve a component of the dispute or to clarify a question through an Advisory Opinion and thus to contribute to the more effective management by the Security Council.

(10) However, to achieve this we need a more coherent system of dispute management and settlement. One element of building such a system would be a better definition of the place the Court would have in it, a place of less isolation and more links and co-ordination with other modes and institutions. The Court would here be conceived as constituting part of a process of settlement without detracting from, and complementing, the traditional adjudication as an autonomous means where one party wins and the other loses. The relationship between the Court and the Security Council is part of the broader issue of the relationship of adjudication with other methods of conflict control and conflict resolution in the changed international society of the post-cold war era.

---

[101] Sir Robert Jennings, Note préliminaire, 'Comité restreint sur le règlement pacifique des différends', *Institute of International Law Yearbook*, 65, Part II, Session of Milan (1993), p. 279, at pp. 279–80. Judge Jennings gives the example of the Antarctica Treaty of 1959, article IV.

INDEX

❦

states (*cont.*)
    notification of danger, 330, 339, 383
    relations
      ICJ, 212–15
      international organizations, 227–8
    unification, 598
    see also nationality of claims; sovereignty; state
        jurisdiction; state practice
Stockholm Declaration on Environment, 293,
    298, 299
submissions, 205–6, 474–5, 482–3
summary procedure chamber, 306, 420, 504

teachings of publicists
    municipal law analogies, 91–2
    source of international law, 64, 83–4, 88
territorial acquisition
    methods, 237–8
      judicial adjudication, 237–9, 243–8
      quasi-judicial adjudication, 239–43, 263
    see also adjudication of territory; boundary
        delimitation; maritime delimitation
territorial boundaries
    effects of self-determination, 361–2
    see also boundary delimitation
territorial jurisdiction *see* state jurisdiction
terrorism
    aircraft destruction, 322–6
    enforcement proceedings, 233
    see also human rights
treaties
    acquiescence in breach, 151–2
    conclusion, 147–8, 151–3
      by force, 373–4
      provisional application, 150
    consent, 147–9, 151–3, 157
    construction, 158–60, 415–16
    formal requirements, 152–3, 157–8, 162–5
    ICJ's role, 65–6
    intentions of parties, 152–3, 163–5
    limits of state jurisdiction, 229–32
    parties, 148–50, 151
      international experience, 163
    ranking, 150–1, 191, 229–32
    ratification, 148–9, 151, 157
    reservations, 66, 73, 96, 146–9, 330–1
    source of international law, 64, 65–6
      relation with custom, 72–9, 151
    termination, 156–7, 311–13

acquiescence in breach, 151–2

UN *see* United Nations
UN Administrative Tribunal
    Advisory Opinions, 580
    judicial review, 400–4
    see also international organizations
UN Committee of Jurists, 56–8
UN Conference on Human Environment, 293,
    298
UN Secretary-General
    international employment disputes, 194
    requests for Advisory Opinions, 187–8,
      269–74
unilateral acts, 85, 216, 475
United Nations
    formation of IATs, 195–6
    judicial review, 190–2
    legal personality, 331–2, 426–7
    nationality of claims, 426–8
    relation with ICJ, 16
    use of Advisory Opinions, 181–3, 185–6,
      571–2
    see also General Assembly; international
      employment; Security Council
universal jurisdiction, 212, 232–3
use of force
    air law, 317–18, 321–2
    counter-measures, 381–2
    effect on treaties, 373–4
    hostage-taking, 374–5
    humanitarian law, 339–41, 383–4, 385
    ICJ's role, 373, 376–8, 384–5
    jus in bello, 382–3
    justiciability, 373, 374–7
    prohibition, 172, 224, 378–9
    self-defence, 341, 378, 379–82
uti possidetis juris
    application, 71, 221, 247–8, 586
    effect of acquiescence, 117–18
    self-determination, 361–2, 601–3

Vice-President of ICJ, 406–7, 409–10
violations of sovereignty *see* sovereignty

war *See* use of force
witnesses
    examination, 415
    see also evidence; expert evidence; hearings